T0329232

Corporate Sustainability

Second Edition

This introductory textbook explores key issues and recent discussions within the field of corporate sustainability and social responsibility, through theoretical and practical perspectives. Written by an international team of experts, the chapters introduce the actors and corporate processes that shape firms' management of environmental, social and governance (ESG) issues. Spanning strategy, communication, changing regulation and governance, the book grapples with critical issues such as anti-corruption, labour rights and climate change, balancing incisive critique with suggestions for meaningful change. This analysis, supported by study questions and further learning resources in each chapter, equips students to tackle sustainability challenges effectively in their future work. A regularly updated companion website provides adaptable lecture slides and case studies with discussion questions for instructors. This is an essential text for undergraduate and postgraduate courses on corporate sustainability, CSR and business ethics, and is also relevant to political science, international relations and communications.

Andreas Rasche is Professor of Business in Society at Copenhagen Business School's Sustainability Centre, and Associate Dean for the Full-Time MBA Programme. He has taught courses in the MBA and doctoral programmes, chaired Executive Education programmes, authored more than sixty academic articles and cases, and published six books. He has collaborated with the United Nations on several projects and served on the UN Global Compact LEAD Steering Committee. Professor Rasche is an award-winning teacher and case author. He is Associate Editor of *Business Ethics Quarterly*.

Mette Morsing is Head of PRME, Principles of Responsible Management Education, UN Global Compact (New York). Morsing was Professor and Mistra Chair of Sustainable Markets at Stockholm School of Economics (Sweden) and Professor of Corporate Social

Responsibility and Organization Theory at Copenhagen Business School (Denmark). Morsing has served on boards and held honorary and advisory positions on committees and councils locally and internationally. She has taught at Bachelor, Master and MBA Executive as well as PhD programmes. Morsing has published in *Journal of Management Studies*, *Human Relations*, *Business Ethics Quarterly*, *Organization Studies* and *Organization, Business & Society*, among other places.

Jeremy Moon is Professor of Sustainability Governance, Copenhagen Business School. He was Founding Director of the International Centre for Corporate Social Responsibility, University of Nottingham, and was Director of the CBS Sustainability Centre. He is author of *Corporations and Citizenship* (2008, with Andrew Crane and Dirk Matten); *Corporate Social Responsibility: A Very Short Introduction* (2014); and 'The Meaning and Dynamics of Corporate Social Responsibility', *Academy of Management Review* (2020, with Dirk Matten).

Arno Kourula is Professor of Business & Sustainability at the University of Amsterdam Business School, and Docent (honorary title) at Aalto University. He has published widely in international management, business ethics, and policy and environmental studies. Kourula has won multiple awards for his research and teaching and collaborates extensively with business, public sector and civil society actors. He has served in editorial roles and on boards for several journals, including as Section Editor of *Journal of Business Ethics*.

Corporate Sustainability

Managing Responsible Business in a Globalised World

SECOND EDITION

Edited by

Andreas Rasche
Copenhagen Business School

Mette Morsing
Principles for Responsible Management Education (PRME), UN
Global Compact, United Nations

Jeremy Moon
Copenhagen Business School

Arno Kourula
Amsterdam Business School, University of Amsterdam

Shaftesbury Road, Cambridge CB2 8EA, United Kingdom

One Liberty Plaza, 20th Floor, New York, NY 10006, USA

477 Williamstown Road, Port Melbourne, VIC 3207, Australia

314–321, 3rd Floor, Plot 3, Splendor Forum, Jasola District Centre, New Delhi – 110025, India

103 Penang Road, #05–06/07, Visioncrest Commercial, Singapore 238467

Cambridge University Press is part of Cambridge University Press & Assessment,
a department of the University of Cambridge.

We share the University's mission to contribute to society through the pursuit of
education, learning and research at the highest international levels of excellence.

www.cambridge.org
Information on this title: www.cambridge.org/9781009114929

DOI:10.1017/9781009118644

First edition © Cambridge University Press 2017
Second edition © Cambridge University Press & Assessment 2023

First published 2017
4th printing 2019
Second edition 2023

A catalogue record for this publication is available from the British Library

ISBN   978-1-009-10040-3   Hardback
ISBN   978-1-009-11492-9   Paperback

Additional resources for this publication at www.cambridge.org/rasche2.

Contents

Figures

Tables

Boxes

Contributors

Kristin Apffelstaedt is an advisor for human rights due diligence in global supply chains at the German development agency Deutsche Gesellschaft für Internationale Zusammenarbeit (GIZ) GmbH. She holds a PhD in Business Ethics from the University of Hamburg. Her research focuses on multi-stakeholder governance and labour rights in global supply chains.

Karin Buhmann is Professor and Director of the Centre for Law, Sustainability & Justice at the University of Southern Denmark, and Professor (Chair) in Business & Human Rights at Copenhagen Business School. Since 2012, Buhmann has served on the Danish National Contact Point under the OECD's Guidelines for Multinational Enterprises.

Joep Cornelissen is a Professor in Management at Rotterdam School of Management, Erasmus University and Chair in Strategy and Organisation (part-time) at the University of Liverpool Management School. He is the Editor-in-Chief of *Organization Theory*, a former Associate Editor for the *Academy of Management Review*, a former General Editor of the *Journal of Management Studies* (2006–12) and serves on the editorial boards of the *Academy of Management Journal, Academy of Management Review*, the *Journal of Management Studies* and *Organization Studies*.

Frank G. A. de Bakker, PhD, is full Professor of Corporate Social Responsibility at the Department of Management & Society at IÉSEG School of Management, Lille, France, where he also coordinates the IÉSEG Centre for Organizational Responsibility (ICOR). He is co-editor of *Business & Society* and his research focuses on the interactions between activist organisations and firms on issues of sustainability and firms' responses to these interactions.

Frank den Hond, PhD, is the Ehrnrooth Professor in Management and Organisation at Hanken School of Economics (Helsinki, Finland) and affiliated with Vrije Universiteit (Amsterdam, the Netherlands). He is currently Editor of the Springer book series on 'Issues in Business Ethics' and Co-Editor-in-Chief of *Business Ethics Quarterly*.

Sergiy Dmytriyev is Assistant Professor of Management at James Madison University. He teaches and researches in fields including strategic management, management consulting, corporate social responsibility and stakeholder theory. Prior to his academic career, Dr Dmytriyev worked as a management consultant as well as in managerial positions in the fast-moving consumer goods sector.

R. Edward Freeman is University Professor and Olsson Professor of Business Administration, and an academic director of the Institute for Business in Society at the University of Virginia Darden School of Business. He is also Adjunct Professor of Stakeholder Management at the Copenhagen Business School in Denmark, Visiting Professor at Nyenrode Business School (Netherlands) and Adjunct Professor of Management at Monash University (Melbourne). In 1984, he originally detailed the Stakeholder Theory of organisational management and business ethics that addresses morals and values in managing an organisation. His award-winning book *Strategic Management: A Stakeholder Approach* identifies and models the groups which are stakeholders of a corporation, and both describes and recommends methods by which management can give due regard to the interests of those groups.

Dirk Ulrich Gilbert is Professor of Business Ethics and Management at the University of Hamburg, Germany. He received his PhD from the University of Frankfurt (Germany) and held positions at the University of New South Wales (Sydney, Australia) and the University of Nuremberg (Germany). His most recent research focuses on accountability standards, labour rights in global supply chains, political CSR and strategy.

Jean-Pascal Gond is Professor of Corporate Social Responsibility at the Bayes Business School of City, University of London, where he heads ETHOS – The Centre for Responsible Enterprise. His research mobilises organisation theory, economic sociology and psychology to investigate CSR and sustainable finance. He has published extensively in the fields of CSR, organisational behaviour and organisation theory in leading academic journals such as *Academy of Management Review, Business Ethics Quarterly, Journal of Management,* and *Organization Studies.* He is currently Associate Editor at *Human Relations.*

Minna Halme is Professor of Sustainability Management at Aalto University School of Business. Her research focuses on co-creation of sustainability innovations, sustainable business models and corporate responsibility topics. She is co-founder of Aalto University's cross-disciplinary Creative Sustainability Master programme, and has received a number of scientific and societal impact awards.

Hans Krause Hansen is Professor of Governance and Culture Studies at Copenhagen Business School. His current research focuses on public and private governance, corruption and anti-corruption, transparency and surveillance regimes. He publishes widely in the fields of international studies and organisation studies.

Christian Herzig is professor at Justus Liebig University Giessen, Germany. His research and teaching revolves around the role of food business in society, with a particular focus on sustainability accounting, reporting and accountability.

He is Programme Director of the MSc in Sustainable Food Business and a founding member of the University's Centre for Sustainable Food Systems.

Andrew Hoffman is the Holcim (US) Professor of Sustainable Enterprise at the University of Michigan; a position that holds joint appointments in the Stephen M. Ross School of Business and the School for Environment and Sustainability.

Sarah L. Jack is the Jacob and Marcus Wallenberg Professor of Innovative and Sustainable Business Development at the House of Innovation, Stockholm School of Economics and Professor of Entrepreneurship at Lancaster University Management School. Her research interests relate to the social structure of entrepreneurship.

Jette Steen Knudsen is Professor at the Fletcher School of Law and Diplomacy at Tufts University. Her research centres on the interface between government regulation and business actions. Knudsen is also a Visiting Professor at Copenhagen Business School. Knudsen holds a PhD in Political Science from MIT (2001).

Arno Kourula is Professor of Business & Sustainability at the University of Amsterdam Business School and Docent (honorary title) at Aalto University. He has published widely in international management, business ethics, policy and environmental studies. Kourula has won multiple awards for his research and teaching and collaborates extensively with business, public sector and civil society actors. He has served in editorial roles and boards for several journals, including as Section Editor of *Journal of Business Ethics*.

Evgenia I. Lysova is Associate Professor in Organizational Behavior at Vrije Universiteit Amsterdam. Her research focuses on meaning in work and careers as well as on CSR, exploring how individuals themselves and with the help of their organisations can create and sustain meaningful work. Her publications appeared in diverse academic journals.

Florian Lüdeke-Freund is Professor for Corporate Sustainability and Director of the MSc Sustainability Entrepreneurship & Innovation, at ESCP Business School, Berlin. He serves on the editorial boards of different journals and has authored or edited four books, including *Sustainable Business Model Design*. Lüdeke-Freund founded the research blog www.SustainableBusinessModel.org.

Jeremy Moon is Professor of Sustainability Governance, Copenhagen Business School. He was founding director of the International Centre for Corporate Social Responsibility, University of Nottingham. He is author of *Corporate Social Responsibility: A Very Short Introduction* (2014) and 'The Meaning and Dynamics of Corporate Social Responsibility', Academy of Management Review (2020, with Dirk Matten).

Mette Morsing, PhD, Head of PRME Principles of Responsible Management Education, UN Global Compact (New York). Morsing was Professor at Stockholm School of Economics and Copenhagen Business School. Morsing has published in *Journal of Management Studies*, *Human Relations*, *Business Ethics Quarterly*, *Organization Studies*, *Organization* and *Business & Society*, among others.

Christine Moser is Associate Professor of Organization Theory at Vrije Universiteit Amsterdam. Her research is on CSR, knowledge flows in social networks and the role of technology in social interaction. Her work has been published in different academic journals and books.

Luisa Murphy holds a PhD in Global Governance from Copenhagen Business School and an MSc in Latin American Studies from the University of Oxford. She is currently Senior Manager, Global Impact at the Principles for Responsible Management Education, UN Global Compact.

Afua Owusu-Kwarteng is a PhD researcher at the Department of Entrepreneurship and Strategy, Lancaster University Management School, UK. She is also an affiliate of the Mistra Centre for Sustainable Markets (Misum) at the Stockholm School of Economics, Sweden. Her research interests relate to gender issues in the knowledge-based economy, including university–industry collaboration.

Andreas Rasche is Professor of Business in Society at the Centre for Sustainability at Copenhagen Business School (CBS) and the Associate Dean for the CBS Full-Time MBA programme. He has taught courses in the MBA and doctoral programmes, chaired Executive Education programmes, authored more than fifty academic articles and cases, and published five books. He has collaborated with the United Nations on a number of projects, and served on the UN Global Compact LEAD Steering Committee. More information can be found at www.arasche.com.

Sukanya Roy is a doctoral student in Management and Organizations at the University of Michigan's Stephen M. Ross School of Business.

Stefan Schaltegger, Prof. Dr Dr h.c., is the founder and head of the Centre for Sustainability Management and worldwide first sustainability management MBA at Leuphana University Lüneburg, Germany. With his more than 500 publications, he is ranked among the top 2 per cent of researchers in the Stanford world scientist ranking 2020. His research deals with sustainability and strategic management, sustainability accounting, sustainable entrepreneurship and stakeholder theory.

Sankar Sen is the Lawrence and Carol Zicklin Chair in Corporate Integrity and Governance, and Professor of Marketing at Baruch College/City University of New York. Sen's research is at the intersection of sustainability and consumer behaviour. He is also interested in prosocial behaviours, social marketing and moral perspectives on consumption behaviour.

Laura Spence, PhD, Professor of Business Ethics at Royal Holloway, University of London, UK. Spence specialises in research on ethics, corporate social responsibility and sustainability in small and medium-sized enterprises. She has published in *Accounting, Organizations and Society, Human Relations, Journal of Management Studies* and *Journal of Business Ethics*, among others.

Lea Stadtler is Associate Professor at the Grenoble Ecole de Management, France. In her research, Lea explores questions related to the design and management of sustainability partnerships, especially cross-sector partnerships, to address complex societal challenges. She has received three international research awards and works as Associate Editor for *Business & Society.*

Robert G. Strand is Executive Director of the Center for Responsible Business and Lecturer at the Berkeley Haas School of Business, University of California Berkeley, and Associate Professor of Leadership & Sustainability at the Copenhagen Business School. His research and teaching compares US and Nordic approaches to sustainable and socially responsible business. He has more recently turned attention to contrast varieties of capitalism in the United States and Nordic contexts and is currently working on a new book, *Sustainable Vikings.*

Laurence Wainwright is Course Director of the MSc in Sustainability, Enterprise and the Environment and a Departmental Lecturer at the University of Oxford. A teaching- and learning-oriented academic, Laurence has a decade of experience in lecturing, facilitation and supervision across universities in Australia, Sweden, the United States and the United Kingdom.

Carolin Waldner is an Assistant Professor for Sustainability Management at ESCP Business School in Berlin, Germany. Her research focuses on social businesses, particularly the management of organisational reputation, investment decisions and tensions of hybrid organisations, as well as social entrepreneurship and sustainable development in the Global South.

Glen Whelan is Professor at ESG UQÀM, Montréal. His research focuses on how corporations, and corporate developed technologies, shape the moral, political and social environment.

Christopher Wickert is Associate Professor in Ethics & Sustainability at Vrije Universiteit Amsterdam, Netherlands and Director of the VU Business & Society Knowledge Hub (www.business-society.org). His research examines corporate social responsibility by mobilising various strands of organisation and management theory. Christopher's research has appeared, amongst others, in *Academy of Management Discoveries, Business & Society, Human Relations, Journal of Business Ethics, Journal of International Business Studies, Journal of Management Studies, International Journal of*

Management Reviews, and *Organization Studies*, as well as in several book chapters. He is currently an associate editor at the *Journal of Management Studies*.

Dieter Zinnbauer is a Marie-Skłodowska-Curie Research Fellow at Copenhagen Business School. He holds a PhD in Development Studies from the London School of Economics. His research and work as policy advisor for various international organisations focuses on business, governance and technology issues.

Preface

Why This Text?

In 2014, Andreas was looking for a textbook for his course, The Corporation in Society: Managing Beyond Markets, but he couldn't find a suitable one. In conversation, Andreas, Mette and Jeremy found they all agreed: a different kind of textbook on corporate social responsibility (CSR) was needed. Existing textbooks focused on CSR as a concept, but they did not discuss specific environmental, social and governance (ESG) issues such as human rights or corruption. They often gave limited attention to some specific actor groups and institutions, like investors and standard setters, that influence what companies do in practice.

To produce a textbook with a more comprehensive scope, we decided to do something unusual. Rather than write it from our own vantage points, we invited thought leaders in the field to introduce students to their area of expertise. We then carefully integrated the different contributions, standardising the style and features of each chapter, so that a coherent textbook emerged that represents the best thinking in the field.

This 'Let the experts speak' approach works very well in the field of corporate responsibility and sustainability. The field is massive, covering many topics, debates and theories. Moreover, unlike other business courses, there is no standard curriculum. This makes it very challenging for a single author (or even an author team) to develop in-depth knowledge on all the important aspects of corporate sustainability that students should learn about.

What's New in This Edition?

The most obvious change is the title: from *Corporate Social Responsibility* to *Corporate Sustainability – Managing Responsible Business in a Globalized World*. Changing a textbook title is unusual, but we wanted to highlight that the move from CSR to corporate sustainability does *not* just reflect a change in language, but also a change in the nature and scope of business responsibility and engagement in society.

Since 2016, when we delivered the first edition of this textbook to Cambridge University Press, the academic field has evolved significantly. Consider just three developments: (1) social and environmental issues are now much more intertwined; (2) sustainability management has become mainstream; and (3) academics and practitioners are increasingly discussing the social and ecological systems in which sustainability activities are embedded. Framing the overall debate in terms of corporate sustainability better captures these (and other) developments. Our textbook has not lost its CSR content to make room for this new emphasis; we do not view corporate sustainability and CSR as fully separated concepts or practices (see Chapter 1). Instead, as the subtitle of the book suggests, we understand responsible business as part and parcel of making corporations more sustainable.

Moving towards corporate sustainability significantly broadened the scope of the book. We added eight new chapters on topics such as sustainable finance, sustainable corporate governance, climate change and firms' contributions to international development. We believe that this gives instructors more choice to align this textbook with the needs of their particular course. We are aware that few instructors will be able to assign all twenty-six chapters as core reading, but we hope that instructors will choose those chapters that best suit their course design and recommend the remaining chapters as further reading.

The final significant change is the addition of a fourth editor: Arno Kourula. He is an award-winning scholar and teacher from the University of Amsterdam who brings a wealth of experience in researching and teaching corporate sustainability, and a knowledge of interdisciplinary approaches to the associated issues.

Our Approach to the Contents of This Book

Our general approach to this textbook is to be accessible without oversimplifying the debate. While the book can be used for introductory courses without any problem, it asks students to critically question prevailing assumptions, to reflect on newly developed regulation, and to understand explicit and implicit connections between topics and debates.

We ensure coherence and accessibility by structuring the book as four parts:

1. Approaches: Discussion of different conceptual and theoretical underpinnings of the corporate sustainability developments and debate. For example, in Chapter 5, we look at how corporate sustainability can be approached from a strategic perspective.
2. Actors: An introduction to different kinds of actors that shape corporate sustainability. For example, we discuss in Chapter 11 how investors have shaped the corporate sustainability debate in recent years.

3. Processes: A presentation of different mechanisms that shape how firms enact corporate sustainability, such as business model innovation, reporting and forming partnerships.
4. Issues: Discussion of different topics that firms must address through their corporate sustainability activities and the challenges that arise. For example, we look at the latest management approaches to secure human and labour rights, fight corruption and respond to climate change.

Special Features

We are pleased to offer extra pedagogical features that will help students take ownership of their learning journey. Instructors also benefit from additional online teaching resources.

- Each chapter starts with a well-defined list of learning objectives, which not only outlines the topic, but also enables students to check whether they have fully grasped it.
- All chapters have a Further Resources section containing links to videos (such as Ted Talks), websites and other articles. Students can use these resources to dig deeper.
- Each chapter concludes with a chapter summary and a list of study questions that students can use to recap the relevant content. These questions also invite students to further reflect on some of the puzzles and conundrums introduced in the chapter.
- The textbook is accompanied by online materials available from Cambridge University Press (www.cambridge.org/rasche2). The website contains thirteen short case studies, accompanied by discussion questions, that can be used to further explore certain chapter themes; as well as PowerPoint slides for instructors.
- The editors and contributors to this textbook also regularly share their opinion on recent developments through *The Business of Society* (BOS) blog (https://bos.cbs.dk).

Acknowledgements

We thank our editors at Cambridge University Press, Valerie Appleby and Tineke Bryson, for developing this second edition with us. They provided excellent feedback on our ideas, and also introduced a number of ideas that improved the readability and accessibility of this book. We also thank Amaya Debal (Copenhagen Business School) who assisted us in compiling the final manuscript. A book with twenty-six chapters reflects a huge project with a high degree of complexity. Amaya always saw the bigger picture and helped us and the contributors to navigate the journey of turning the single chapters into a coherent final product.

Andreas and Jeremy also thank their academic home: CBS Sustainability at Copenhagen Business School. We both profited from many discussions with colleagues along the way, and we couldn't think of a better academic home than CBS Sustainability. Mette would like to thank her colleagues from the global PRME community where she has benefitted from stimulating ideas and discussion. Arno would like to thank the incredibly supportive Amsterdam Business School community at the University of Amsterdam.

Finally, we want to sincerely thank all the contributors to the book for working with us so patiently and for investing the time to write/update their contributions. Doing an edited textbook brings special challenges. Often, we approached contributors with unusual requests (e.g., to change their chapter title so that it aligns with the others), and they always responded favourably and kindly. Thank you!

Abbreviations

AA1000AS	AA1000 Assurance Standard
AAC	Anglo-American Corporation
AC-DC	alternating current-direct current
ACFTU	All-China Federation of Trade Unions
ACTA	Alien Tort Claims Act
ADX	Abu Dhabi Stock Exchange
AFWA	Asia Floor Wage Alliance
AGM	Annual General Meeting
AI	artificial intelligence
AIDFI	Alternative Indigenous Development Foundation Incorporated
ALEC	American Legislative Exchange Council
ANC	African National Congress
API	American Petroleum Institute
ASEAN	Association of Southeast Asian Nations
BAT	British American Tobacco
BHR	business and human rights
BII	Biodiversity Intactness Index
BOP	bottom-of-the-pyramid
BSR	Business for Social Responsibility
C2B	consumer-to-business
CBM	Consultative Business Movement
CCC	Clean Clothes Campaign
CDM	Clean Development Mechanism
CDP	Carbon Disclosure Project
CDSB	Climate Disclosure Standards Board
CEO	Chief Executive Officer
CH_4	methane
CO_2	carbon dioxide
COP	Communication on Progress
CPI	Corruption Perception Index
CS	corporate sustainability
CSEAR	Centre for Social and Environmental Accounting Research
CSO	civil society organisation
CSP	cross-sector partnership
CSR	corporate social responsibility

CSRD	Corporate Sustainability Reporting Directive
CSRep	corporate sustainability reporting
CSV	creating shared value
DJSI	Dow Jones Sustainability Index
E/MSY	extinctions per million species per year
EITI	Extractive Industries Transparency Initiative
EMAS	European Union Eco-Management and Audit Scheme
EMS	environmental management systems
ESG	environmental, social and governance
ESGT	environmental, social, governance and technology
ETI	Ethical Trading Initiative
EU	European Union
FCCC	Framework Convention on Climate Change
FCPA	US Foreign Corrupt Practices Act
FDI	foreign direct investment
FIFA	Fédération Internationale de Football Association
FLA	Fair Labor Association
FMCG	fast-moving consumer goods
FNB	First National Bank
FRC	Financial Reporting Council
FSC	Forest Stewardship Council
GCC	Global Climate Coalition
GDP	gross domestic product
GMO	genetically modified organism
GP	Guiding Principle
GRI	Global Reporting Initiative
GSP	Generalized System of Preferences
HFCs	hydrofluorocarbons
HRM	human resources management
IBHR	International Bill of Human Rights
IBLF	International Business Leaders Forum
ICCPR	International Covenant on Civil and Political Rights
ICESCR	International Covenant on Economic, Social and Cultural Rights
ICN	India Committee of the Netherlands
ICTI	International Council of Toy Industries
IIRC	International Integrated Reporting Council
ILO	International Labour Organization
IMF	International Monetary Fund
INGO	international non-governmental organisation
IO	international organisation

IPO	initial public offering
ISAE	International Standard on Assurance Engagement
ISSP	International Society of Sustainability Professionals
ITTO	International Tropical Timber Organization
JO-IN	Joint Initiative on Accountability and Workers' Rights
KPI	key performance indicator
LEED	Leadership in Energy and Environmental Design
LET	Logistics Emergency Team
LETS	local exchange trading systems and networks
LOHAS	Lifestyles of Health and Sustainability
MACN	Maritime Anti-Corruption Network
MAS	Monetary Authority of Singapore
MDGs	Millennium Development Goals
MNC	multinational corporation
MSC	Marine Stewardship Council
MSCI	Morgan Stanley Capital International
MSI	multi-stakeholder initiative
N_2O	nitrous oxide
NAPs	national action plans
NCPs	National Contact Points
NFI	non-financial information
NFRD	Non-Financial Reporting Directive
NGO	non-governmental organisation
NHRI	National Human Rights Institution
N	Nitrogens
NP	Afrikaner National Party
NPO	non-profit organisation
NVC	National Value Commission
NYSE	New York Stock Exchange
OECD Convention	OECD Convention on Combating Bribery of Foreign Public Officials in International Business Transactions
OECD	Organisation for Economic Co-operation and Development
OPT	Occupied Palestinian Territory
OSH	occupational safety and health
PACI	Partnering Against Corruption Initiative
PAC	Pan Africanist Congress of Azania
PBC	public benefit corporation
PFCs	perfluorocarbons
P	phosphorous
PIE	public interest entity

PRA	Prudential Regulation Authority
PRI	Principles for Responsible Investment
RBA	Responsible Business Alliance
R&R	repeatability and reproducibility
REDD+	Reducing Emissions from Deforestation and Forest Degradation
RSPO	Roundtable on Sustainable Palm Oil
SAN	Sustainable Agriculture Network
SASB	Sustainability Accounting Standards Board
SBSR	Small Business Social Responsibility
SCDL	Supreme Committee for Delivery and Legacy
SCG	Sustainable Corporate Governance
SDGs	Sustainable Development Goals
SEBI	Securities and Exchange Board of India
SEC	Securities and Exchange Commission
SF_6	sulphur hexafluoride
SFDR	Sustainable Finance Disclosure Regulation
SME	small and medium-sized enterprise
SMO	social movement organisation
SOI	sustainability-oriented innovation
SOX	Sarbanes-Oxley Act 2002
SRI	socially responsible investing
SRI	socially responsible investment
SSE	Sustainable Stock Exchanges
TBL	triple bottom line
TCFD	Task Force on Climate-related Financial Disclosures
TI	Transparency International
UAE	United Arab Emirates
UDHR	Universal Declaration of Human Rights
UN	United Nations
UNCAC	UN Convention against Corruption
UNCED	UN Conference on Environment and Development
UNDP	UN Development Programme
UNGC	UN Global Compact
UNGPs	UN Guiding Principles
UNICEF	UN Children's Fund
UNODC	UN Office for Drugs and Crime
UN SDGs	UN Sustainable Development Goals
WEF	World Economic Forum
WWF	World Wide Fund for Nature

1 Corporate Sustainability – What It Is and Why It Matters

ANDREAS RASCHE, METTE MORSING, JEREMY MOON AND

ARNO KOURULA

LEARNING OBJECTIVES

- Reflect on how the relationship between businesses, nature and society has been reshaped and how this has affected corporate sustainability.
- Define corporate sustainability, responsibility and ethics.
- Learn about ways to categorise corporate sustainability issues.
- Understand different motivations for firms to adopt corporate sustainability.
- Recognise key tensions that surround the debate of corporate sustainability.

1.1 Introduction

Imagine for a moment you are in the year 2050. As you look around you, you see that the world has changed dramatically. Although the entire world economy is two and half times bigger than in 2019 (from around 94 trillion USD in 2019 to 251 trillion), the gains of this economic growth are distributed very unevenly among and within countries. The rising inequality sparks social frictions and armed conflicts. Even though extreme poverty and hunger are mostly eradicated, accelerated urbanisation and economic growth have caused significant natural degradation, which in turn negatively affected the well-being of people around the globe. Global warming is severe and has produced many irreversible effects, such as increased pressure on the availability of arable land and freshwater. Biodiversity loss has hit many of the Earth's ecosystems and made the world's poor and marginalised more vulnerable (e.g., smallholders in developing countries).

The scenario that we just described is not unrealistic. It was identified by a group of well-known researchers as likely to happen if economic and political actors around the world continue with 'business-as-usual' (Randers et al., 2018). This scenario rests on the assumption that although countries and businesses officially commit to fulfilling the Sustainable Development Goals (SDGs), which define the

UN's agenda for sustainable development until 2030, no extraordinary policy efforts or regulatory measures are applied. Many politicians and business leaders make a sincere effort to make the world a more sustainable place, but in doing so they apply well-established thinking that focuses primarily on economic growth as a means to finance sustainable development. But, as we all know, more of the same is usually not enough to make big and lasting changes.

This book takes you on a journey to study how corporations can move beyond business-as-usual when it comes to corporate sustainability. We do not claim to have all the answers. Rather, we aim to make you aware of what sustainability challenges firms (and the society they are embedded in) are facing, which ways to tackle these challenges exist to date and what remains to be done. The contributors to this book will not always have positive messages to share, as many environmental and social problems continue to grow in terms of scope and impact.

Section 1.2 of this chapter will discuss the changing context in which business, nature and society at large operate. It is important to understand this context, because it shapes the problems that corporate sustainability aims to address, and it influences how firms can cope with these problems. Section 1.3 will look at three interrelated, yet distinct, concepts: corporate sustainability, Corporate Social Responsibility (CSR) and business ethics. We define each of the concepts and discuss differences and similarities among them. Section 1.4 introduces frameworks that help companies structure the many sustainability issues that they are facing. Next, in section 1.5, we introduce you to four key motivations that may drive firms' engagement in corporate sustainability. Although these motivations are presented as separate, they overlap in practice. Finally, in section 1.6, we look at key tensions that surround the debate of corporate sustainability. Understanding these tensions will help you to better grasp the problems and opportunities that are associated with corporate sustainability.

1.2   A Changing Context for Business, Nature and Society

To understand why discussions around corporate sustainability have gained so much momentum, it is useful to look into the broader context in which business, nature and society are embedded these days. We believe there are four central developments that have reshaped the relationship between business actors, the natural environment and society in recent years.

1.2.1   Increasing Relevance of ESG Challenges

Through their operations and strategies, corporations impact many *environmental, social* and *governance* (ESG) challenges. Of course, the reverse is true as well: these challenges also impact how firms do business, as they shape relevant risks and opportunities. Although we cannot provide a full review of all possible ESG challenges here, we can zoom into some important facts within all three dimensions.

The 'E' dimension within ESG refers to a wide variety of environmental issues (e.g., greenhouse gas emissions, freshwater supply, pollution; see also Chapter 23). One relevant framework to organise some of these issues relates to research showing that those environmental processes that regulate the stability of the Earth system are increasingly crossing irreversible thresholds. In 2009, a group of international researchers defined nine so-called 'Planetary Boundaries' (Rockström et al., 2009). These boundaries define specific thresholds at global or regional levels. The boundaries characterise the conditions that are necessary for planet Earth to remain in a stable state. According to further research (Steffen et al., 2015b), four out of the nine boundaries have already been transgressed (see Figure 7.2; see also Chapters 7 and 23). These four boundaries that have already been crossed relate to climate, biodiversity, biogeochemical cycles (regarding phosphorous and nitrogen in fertilisers) and land-system change (regarding deforestation). In other words, planet Earth has entered a danger zone. We have left the 'safe operating space' that the planet originally provided us with, and crossing these boundaries is likely to trigger nonlinear, abrupt environmental changes. It is vital to recognise that these nine boundaries also define the safe space within which the global economy operates. Likewise, our societies depend on Earth system processes to work sustainably for habitats, communities and societies to thrive. If these processes come out of balance, businesses will operate under increasingly unstable conditions (e.g., exposing firms to higher levels of risk).

To return to ESG, the 'S' dimension within ESG refers to the human and labour rights agendas (see Chapters 21 and 22), with labour rights usually being framed as a subset of broader human rights. Protecting and respecting human and labour rights remains a challenge in many countries around the globe, and the COVID-19 pandemic has worsened some problems (e.g., due to austerity policies that weakened public infrastructure). Due to the comprehensive nature of human rights, it is difficult to find one common measure. Nonetheless, one good point of orientation is the so-called *Fragile States Index*, which contains as one of its dimensions the *Human Rights and Rule of Law Index*. The index looks at whether there is widespread abuse of different types of rights (e.g., civil and political rights) and ranges from 0 (high protection) to 10 (low protection). The 2021 edition shows that out of 173 assessed countries, 60 had a score of at least 7 (The Fund for Peace, 2021). In other words, governments often do not do their job to protect citizens' basic human rights, which shows the need for non-state actors (e.g., businesses, NGOs) to become more engaged in respecting and protecting such rights. However, we also know that business actors are often the source for human rights abuses – for instance, when operating global supply chains in which labour rights are violated.

Finally, the 'G' dimension within ESG refers to issues that relate to the proper governance of corporations, such as the structure and composition of the Board of Directors, shareholder rights, transparency, corporate lobbying and anti-corruption measures. In particular, corporate lobbying and corruption very much shape the societies we are living in. One widely accepted measure of corruption around the world is the annual *Corruption Perception Index* (CPI) by Transparency International (see also Chapter 24). This index measures the perception of public sector corruption in 180 countries and ranges from 0 (highly corrupt) to 100 (very clean). The 2020 CPI shows how widespread corruption is around the world: two-thirds of all countries score below 50, indicating that public sector corruption (e.g., bribery of government officials) remains a significant problem throughout the world. Even countries in Western Europe and the European Union only achieve an average score of 66 out of 100 (Transparency International, 2021a). It is therefore safe to assume that most countries still fail to address corruption effectively. Hence, business actors are central in the fight against corruption, as they can take precautionary measures directly at the individual and organisational levels.

1.2.2   Rising Scale and Scope of Corporate Activities

In many cases, businesses contribute directly or indirectly to the outlined ESG challenges. Think, for instance, about climate change, deforestation, labour rights and corruption. At first, this seems like bad news, as it shows that businesses are key contributors to many of the problems faced by societies around the globe. However, we can also flip this argument around. If businesses contribute to the very existence of many of these challenges, they can also help to address them. In fact, corporations are considered critical actors when addressing ESG issues because of their size and reach. Multinational corporations (MNCs) often dominate industries because of their disproportionate size. Consider the following example. In the global fishery industry, only thirteen businesses control 11 to 16 per cent of the global marine catch (Österblom et al., 2015). These corporations have significant power, as they operate an extensive global network of subsidiaries. Prior research has referred to such corporations as keystone actors – that is, corporations that (1) dominate the volume of production within a sector, (2) connect different ecosystems across the globe through a network of subsidiaries and (3) have an impact on global governance processes (Hileman et al., 2020).

Many argue that with this increasing scale of corporate activities also come enlarged corporate responsibilities. Corporations are increasingly seen as potentially reliable partners that can mobilise resources, provide innovations and comply with emerging standards. But the hope that corporations can help to solve some of today's biggest problems also creates risks. For instance, it furthers our dependence on corporations as the dominant institution in modern life, and it also blurs the relationship between public and private authority. Globalisation together with an emerging privatisation of public goods/services has given rise to a situation where the state has withdrawn from many areas where it traditionally exercised a regulatory monopoly or even a controlling and directing hand. Nowadays, the scope of corporate operations has increased significantly. Corporations provide goods like water, transport, education and healthcare. Private firms even run prisons and provide security, and have become important actors in the conduct of war. In short, corporations are critical to an increasing number of aspects of society, many of which are fundamental to security and welfare. As a result, firms have turned not only into more powerful actors, but also political ones.

Despite the dominance of MNCs, we should not forget that there is a plurality of corporate actors. Corporations are not a homogenous category of organisations, especially not when thinking about sustainability and responsibility. In fact, most firms in the economy are not large MNCs, but rather small and medium-sized enterprises (SMEs). These SMEs are the backbone of any economy; they offer essential services and are often part of larger value chains. We have also witnessed the emergence of several alternative types of organisations that address ESG-related challenges. Social businesses, for instance, often have a specific social or environmental mission as their main purpose. Such social businesses are for-profit organisations; they depend on making a profit and thus are financially self-sustaining (see also Chapter 9).

1.2.3   Digitalisation and Datafication

The relationship between corporations and (global) society has also shifted because of the rise of the digital economy. We are increasingly living in a 'datafied' society and this has significant consequences for the responsibilities of corporations. To datafy something implies to put it into a quantified format so that it can be analysed through digital means (Mayer-Schönberger and Cukier, 2013). Google datafies an enormous number of books through its Google Books project, while Facebook datafies friendships through 'like' buttons, and LinkedIn datafies Human Resources through online CVs. This datafication impacts corporations' responsibilities in numerous ways, and it also leads to a concentration of power in the hands of just a few companies (Whelan, 2021).

On the one hand, the rise of the digital economy has increased public scrutiny and has made responsible as well as irresponsible corporate conduct more transparent. Datafication has increased the connectivity of people who share more content in faster ways (e.g., stories about corporate misconduct). Some apps even give consumers direct access to a product's sustainability assessment, while other apps measure air pollution and allow for tracking deforestation. On the other hand, datafication has created new powerful corporations with a new set of responsibilities. Tech giants like Apple, Google, Microsoft and Facebook belong to the most valuable corporations in the world (when comparing the market capitalisation of all publicly traded companies). These firms impact peoples' rights in new and often unforeseen ways. In early 2006, Google announced that it would censor the Chinese version of its search engine upon request by the Chinese government. Similarly, Yahoo was asked to disclose information on at least two email customers to the Chinese government. Both customers, who were known to be government critics, were later jailed for revealing state secrets.

Digitalisation and artificial intelligence (AI) also offer new ways to strengthen ESG-related assessments. Consider the following example. Investors, like the fund manager Arabesque, use AI to analyse ESG data to better understand firms' sustainability performance. Technologies like machine learning and AI can help to analyse not only vast amounts of data, but also data that is not pre-structured (e.g., that is not neatly available in an Excel spreadsheet). News data, for instance, is not structured in any way. Investors increasingly analyse such data to learn more about firms' sustainability performance, also because firms' own sustainability reports usually underreport on negative ESG incidents (Selim, 2021). However, there is also a flipside to the rise of the digital economy. Digital applications and processes require significant levels of electricity. The Internet alone uses about 10 per cent of world electricity, while Bitcoin mining uses 0.5 per cent of world electricity (which is more than the amount used by the entire country of Finland; Kim, 2021).

1.2.4   Globalisation and (the Lack of) Global Governance

Economic, political and cultural globalisation are no longer news. They have been around for decades. Yet, their effects on corporations' sustainability and responsibility are still very visible because the regulation of *global* business activity remains a challenge. There is an imbalance between the flexibility of MNCs to spread their value chain activities across different countries and the still limited capacity of nation states and international governmental organisations to adequately regulate corporate conduct across borders. Scherer and Palazzo (2008) call this the 'regulatory vacuum effect'. Such a vacuum exists because the sovereignty of political authorities is greatest within their national borders and more tenuous outside them, while businesses have become transnational actors. This makes it difficult for individual countries' governments to address social and environmental problems that reach beyond single state boundaries. The failure to address global warming is a case in point. MNCs also have the chance to arbitrate among alternative regulations, that is, they escape strict regulations by moving their operations or supply activities to countries with rather low standards (e.g., to lower their tax burden or cost of production). All of this has led to a globalisation of sustainability and responsibility and calls for alternative ways to regulate global business activity.

Existing international governmental organisations, which reach beyond individual nation states (e.g., the UN system or the World Bank), lack the formal powers or political support to develop and enforce any binding rules or even sanction corporate misconduct. The UN system was mostly designed for state actors and falls short of regulating its Member States, but also when it comes to regulating non-state actors. Even when international law and UN-based treaties/conventions have been designed as a legal framework to direct the behaviour of nation states, it is rarely possible to apply these legal frameworks *directly* to corporations, especially when it comes to regulating their impact on social and environmental issues. In principle, it is technically possible to craft legally binding international frameworks applying to corporations, but political interests and corporate lobbying have curtailed such efforts until now.

Some have argued that the missing direct applicability of international law to corporations can partly be compensated by stronger extraterritorial regulation. Extraterritorial jurisdiction refers to 'the ability of a state, via various legal, regulatory and judicial institutions, to exercise its authority over actors and activities outside its own territory' (Zerk, 2010: 13). Put differently, states can apply certain domestic legal instruments beyond their own territory and hence can regulate the activities of corporate actors 'abroad'. Although the application of extraterritorial law has given rise to tensions between nation states, which see their sovereignty endangered, the use of such legal instruments is commonplace in a few areas relevant to the sustainability debate. For instance, the US Foreign Corrupt Practices Act allows the US government to sue corporations (even non-US ones) for offering or accepting bribes in another country (see Chapter 24). Even though the extraterritorial nature of certain domestic laws has helped to better regulate anti-corruption, it has not much affected other areas of the ESG spectrum. In 2013, the US Supreme Court rolled back the impact of the Alien Tort Claims Act (ATCA), which allowed the prosecution of human rights violations by corporate actors in other countries. Many proceedings under ACTA were objected to be based on the argument that the cases raise 'political questions' and that judicial action by a US court in this area would interfere with 'foreign policy interests' (Zerk, 2010: 152). Overall, we can state that extraterritorial law has improved the regulation of global business activity in some selected areas, but it has not sufficiently closed the general regulatory vacuum that surrounds the conduct of MNCs.

1.3 Sustainability, Responsibility and Ethics: What Are They?

Often, there is confusion around the terminology used when talking about businesses' roles in and relationships to society. Part of this confusion comes from academic work using concepts/terms in different ways, as well as differences in the language used by practitioners and academics. Some of the confusion is also due to concepts overlapping with one another. While we cannot ultimately resolve these problems, we hope to provide some clear definitions of the main concepts used throughout this book. We want to highlight three key terms, which we believe are at the heart of debates around businesses changing role in global society: *corporate sustainability*, *corporate (social) responsibility* and *business ethics*.

1.3.1 Defining Corporate Sustainability and Corporate (Social) Responsibility

Discussions around corporate sustainability are usually based on and relate to the popular notion of sustainable development. The World Commission on Environment and Development defined such development in a much-cited report as being about meeting 'the needs of the present without compromising the ability of future generations to meet their own needs.' (World Commission on Environment and Development, 1987: 54) This definition is *not* centred on the role of organisations or even corporations. Rather, it understands sustainable development as being concerned with the development of entire societies.

The idea of being sustainable can, of course, also be applied to the corporate context. Corporations can, for better and for worse, impact how sustainable the development of a society is and can therefore align their activities more or less with wider sustainability imperatives. We therefore define corporate sustainability in the following way:

> Corporate sustainability focuses on managing and balancing an enterprise's embeddedness in interrelated ecological, social and economic systems so that positive impact is created in the form of long-term ecological balance, societal welfare and stakeholder value.

This definition offers some important implications.

1. Corporate sustainability views an enterprise's activities in the *context of larger systems*. In the 1990s, several researchers used the term corporate sustainability exclusively in an ecological sense. The focus was predominantly on discussing businesses' impact on the natural environment and opportunities resulting from innovation and eco-efficient production (Shrivastava, 1995). We use the term corporate sustainability to emphasise that economic, social and environmental issues are part of larger systems, and that these systems interact with one another. Corporations, for instance, impact and are impacted by various natural systems, like the Earth's climate system. These systems, in turn, influence the risks and opportunities that firms face (e.g., climate transition risks) and hence companies' long-term economic bottom line. Whether and how firms address these risks and opportunities affects living conditions within societies (e.g., not taking action on climate change will undermine the living conditions of many people around the world).

2. Corporate sustainability aims at *balancing* social, environmental and economic interests while doing business. It therefore aims to avoid situations where taking action in support of one sphere comes at the expense of another sphere. Finally, the definition also highlights that corporate sustainability is concerned with outcome measures such as ecological balance, societal welfare and the creation of stakeholder value. Creating value therefore reaches beyond a rather narrow focus on a firm's monetary bottom line, but includes generating value for the company's stakeholders and the society it operates in, as well as the natural environment that surrounds its operations.

While the corporate sustainability debate emphasises the need for systems-level change, discussions around CSR are often more focused on relevant management practices within corporations. CSR does not neglect the connected nature of social, environmental and economic aspects, but its main focus is on how to manage these aspects in a corporate context and regarding the impact of corporations on the social, environmental and economic circumstances of their stakeholders. Corporate sustainability, on the other hand, puts more emphasis on how changes made by an individual corporation connect and contribute to larger systems-level change (Montiel, 2008). We therefore define CSR as follows:

> CSR refers to the integration of an enterprise's social, environmental, ethical and philanthropic responsibilities towards society into its operations, processes and core business strategy in cooperation with relevant stakeholders in a context-specific way.

This definition, which builds on the definitions by the European Commission (2001, 2011), stresses that CSR is not entirely about philanthropy (e.g., companies' charitable donations). While a firm's CSR strategy can include philanthropic activities, and may have been built on these, it is much more than that. Well-designed CSR goes into the very core of a corporation; it influences its everyday practices and business processes and is aligned with its overall business strategy. Corporate philanthropy is sometimes detached from a firm's core activities, while CSR is about reflecting on the social, environmental and ethical impact of these activities. This is not to say that CSR always must be 'strategic' (a term that is often used as a synonym for 'being profitable'; Porter and Kramer, 2006). Rather, it means that CSR should be embedded into a firm's purpose and what it does on a day-to-day basis, and it should also be reflected upon when deciding upon a firm's strategic direction (e.g., which markets or regions it wants to enter).

The CSR debate is often confronted with one essential question: What are firms responsible for? One good way to discuss possible answers to this question is to look at Carroll's (1979, 1991) pyramid of corporate responsibilities (Figure 1.1). At a fundamental level, firms have to make sure that they meet economic responsibilities (i.e., making a profit). Without being profitable in the long run, corporations will

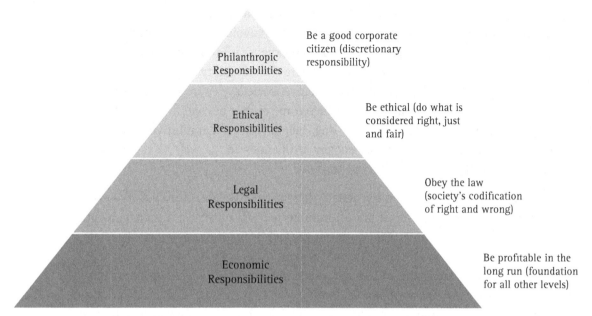

Figure 1.1 The pyramid of corporate responsibilities.
Adapted and modified from Carroll (1991).

cease to exist and hence cannot address other types of responsibilities. The next two levels of Carroll's pyramid consist of legal responsibilities (compliance with the rule of law) and ethical responsibilities (acknowledging what is regarded as right and just within a society). The final level consists of philanthropic responsibilities that are discretionary and therefore only desired, but not expected, by society.

Let's reflect for a moment on the definitions of corporate sustainability and CSR. At first, it is important to note what both definitions do *not* mention. Neither definition indicates that corporate sustainability or CSR are voluntary concepts. We believe it would be misleading to conceptualise both constructs in this way. Addressing social and environmental issues is a de facto requirement in some industries and countries. For instance, it is hard to find firms in the automotive or extractive industries without any relevant sustainability activities, because their sectors have developed industry-wide norms and standards. In many countries, companies observe 'implicit' obligations to undertake certain responsibilities simply by virtue of being members of those societies, as Matten and Moon (2008) revealed in their comparison of US and European CSR. Also, some governments have started to incentivise or even regulate social and environmental activities (e.g., the disclosure of relevant non-financial information; see Chapters 12 and 17). This has pushed the debate beyond talking about purely voluntary actions.

We explicitly use the term 'enterprise' in both definitions. With this we want to highlight that corporate sustainability and CSR are not only concepts that are relevant for larger (multinational) corporations, but also for SMEs. SMEs are defined as firms with fewer than 250 employees. They make up the vast majority of businesses in an economy and provide the most jobs. The social and environmental activities of SMEs differ in several ways from those of larger firms (Baumann-Pauly et al., 2013). Often, the main motivation to integrate sustainability and CSR into an SME is influenced by the personal beliefs and values of the founder (who in many cases is also the owner and manager of the firm). By contrast, corporate sustainability and CSR in larger firms are more often driven by the hope that responsible business practices will yield some positive financial return and hence satisfy shareholder interests. SMEs' activities are also more connected to the specific needs of the local communities in which they are embedded, while larger firms usually operate a portfolio of social and environmental practices that cut across different geographic contexts. Chapter 8 provides a more in-depth discussion of differences between larger firms and SMEs in the context of sustainability and responsibility.

Our definitions also emphasise that corporate sustainability and CSR are multidimensional constructs. Despite the English term 'corporate *social* responsibility', CSR also includes discussions about firms' environmental footprints. The discussions throughout this book therefore follow the internationally agreed upon view that both constructs encompass social issues, environmental issues and economic issues. Recently, the issues underlying corporate sustainability have been labelled as referring to ESG. Here, the 'G' dimension brings new, and important, issues to the table, such as anti-corruption and diversity among executives and directors (see Chapters 15 and 24). This is on the assumption that these 'G' issues should support and enable the social and environmental objectives of the enterprise. Regardless of how we cut the pie and organise relevant problem areas, it is important to see corporate sustainability and CSR as giving firms a 'moral compass' outlining minimum standards about what should be expected from corporations.

It is important not to draw a too sharp distinction between corporate sustainability and CSR. As Bansal and Song (2017) have shown, although both concepts have different historical origins, they are increasingly converging and sometimes even used as synonyms. For instance, both concepts share a common concern for moving business thinking beyond a purely egocentric perspective that only considers shareholders as a relevant interest group. Throughout this book, we will mostly use the corporate sustainability terminology, also because it is increasingly used in the world of practice as a concept that discusses the relationship between business, nature and society. Yet, we must bear in mind that corporate sustainability and CSR share a number of key concerns and focus areas.

1.3.2 Corporate Unsustainability and Irresponsibility

Many of the discussions on corporate sustainability and CSR are focused on how firms can become more sustainable and responsible. However, there is also another side to this debate. Corporations can also act unsustainably, irresponsibly and unethically. The occurrence of such 'negative' behaviour is often a trigger for firms to implement more 'positive' sustainability and responsibility practices. Yet, firms' unsustainability and irresponsibility are more than just their failure to design and implement proper sustainability and responsibility practices. While corporations can deliberately decide to become engaged in irresponsible behaviour (e.g., when paying bribes) or unsustainable business practices (e.g., when polluting a river), they can also stumble into such behaviour without any direct intention (e.g., when underestimating business risks). We therefore characterise unsustainable and irresponsible behaviour as being based on a corporate activity that 'negatively affects an identifiable social stakeholder's legitimate claims (in the long run)' (Strike et al., 2006: 852).

We should not think of sustainable and unsustainable as well as responsible and irresponsible corporate behaviour as being mutually exclusive. In most cases, positive as well as negative behaviour exists simultaneously in a corporation. Kotchen and Moon (2012) find in a study of 3,000 publicly traded companies that firms that do more harm also do more good. Firms often invest in corporate sustainability to compensate for past, present or anticipated unsustainable acts. For instance, the US supermarket chain Whole Foods, which was acquired by Amazon in 2017, is often praised for its responsible behaviour and active stakeholder management, while it also neglects unions and the right to collective bargaining.

In other cases, firms' public talk around sustainability and responsibility can become misaligned with their lobbying efforts. For instance, BP and Shell's engagement in the Global Climate Coalition (GCC) is a case in point (den Hond et al., 2014). Created in 1989, the GCC was set up to represent the interests of energy companies vis-à-vis US policy-makers, mostly trying to prevent regulatory measures. As both BP and Shell started to develop their corporate sustainability policies and practices, their sustainability-related public talk became increasingly misaligned with the position of the GCC. Hence, both firms had to leave the GCC, which was then deactivated in 2002.

1.3.3 Defining Business Ethics

Finally, there is a need to clarify the role of ethics in discussions around corporate sustainability and CSR. We view business ethics as a foundation for all discussions about sustainable and responsible corporate conduct (see Chapters 2 and 3). While corporate sustainability stresses how changes made by firms connect and contribute to larger systems-level change and CSR focuses on relevant management practices, business ethics is more concerned with questions of right and wrong in the context of business situations. We therefore follow Crane, Matten, Glozer and Spence (2019: 3) and define business ethics as:

The study of business situations, activities, and decisions where issues of right and wrong are addressed.

Right and wrong can be assessed from several different perspectives (e.g., something can be financially right but morally wrong). Business ethics focuses exclusively on moral judgments. Such judgments are usually informed by a certain moral point of view, such as different philosophical, social or religious perspectives. Ethical reflection goes beyond the law (see Chapter 3). In fact, it is particularly concerned with those areas that are not clearly covered by the law. Although the law embodies ethical norms, it cannot regulate all possible business situations. There are always loopholes and managers have a certain degree of interpretive flexibility, that is, they need to reflect on how to best comply with the law (e.g., when paying taxes). Business ethics is also concerned with those situations where values are unclear, in conflict or in tension and ethical dilemmas occur as a result. For instance, managers may wonder whether to blow the whistle when suspecting misconduct by one of their peers. We view business ethics as an analytical lens to reflect on the values that should guide corporate conduct.

Defining corporate sustainability, CSR and business ethics is not a simple task. There are at least three reasons for this (Matten and Moon, 2008: 405). First, all three concepts are contested and hence they are defined (and applied) differently by different groups of people. We could even argue that this ambiguity is part of the reason why the three concepts have been so successful. However, this ambiguity has also caused critique. If the meaning of the three concepts cannot be agreed upon and specified, corporations can easily exploit the concepts by selectively applying them to those issue areas they can conveniently address.

Hence, there is no one-size-fits-all approach towards corporate sustainability, CSR and business ethics. Discussing a firm's sustainable, responsible and ethical conduct is contextually dependent and multidimensional by nature. It depends, among other things, on what kind of firm is being analysed (e.g., its size and ownership structure), what sector the firm operates in, and the location of relevant business activities. *Contexts and events matter* when it comes to sustainability, responsibility and ethics, and that is why general recipes need to be treated with care. Table 1.1 provides a summary of the main pillars of the three concepts. The examplary sources for all three concepts can be found in the final reference list at the end.

1.3.4 Related Concepts: Corporate Accountability and Corporate Citizenship

Corporate accountability is another concept that has attracted much attention in recent years, especially from civil society organisations and activists. Generally speaking, accountability implies the exchange of reasons for behaviour; 'to account'

Table 1.1 Corporate sustainability, corporate social responsibility and business ethics summarised

	Corporate sustainability	Corporate (social) responsibility	Business ethics
Level of Analysis	Firm embedded in larger social, environmental and economic systems (macro)	Processes within firms to meet social and environmental responsibilities (meso)	Doing what is morally right in business-related situations (micro)
Focus	Balancing different sustainability-related interests (avoid trade-offs)	Managerial processes to enable responsible corporate action	Morally justified action
Main foundations	Sustainability science, complexity science, political science, economics	Management and leadership thinking	Moral philosophy, psychology, leadership thinking
Exemplary contributions	Bansal (2005)	Carroll (1979), Matten and Moon (2008)	Crane et al. (2019)

for something means that actions and omissions are explained and justified (Messner, 2009). Corporate accountability is about a firm's ability to be answerable for what it did or did not do. Many argue that corporate accountability is a stronger concept than CSR and corporate sustainability (Utting, 2008). While a firm can assume responsibility for several things, being accountable means informing relevant stakeholders about specific practices that enact this responsibility. In practice, firms can work towards increased accountability through various means, including the provision of mechanisms that allow external stakeholders to raise complaints against a firm's actions. Corporate accountability can also be strengthened through rigorous corporate sustainability reporting. A major criticism here, however, is that some corporations appear to prioritise their reporting methods over the conduct of their responsibilities. While some reports remain superficial, other firms have succeeded in creating reports that inform stakeholders about relevant actions and omissions (see Chapter 17).

Corporate citizenship is a concept that shares many insights with a political perspective on CSR. Most obviously, it denotes the forms of corporate political involvement related to discussions of responsibility and sustainability (Moon et al., 2005). Matten and Crane (2005) have distinguished three different views of corporate citizenship. In the limited view, corporate citizenship is used to describe firms' philanthropic activities (e.g., charitable donations and other types of community action). This view reflects the early usage of the term and comes close to a philanthropic understanding of CSR. In the equivalent view, corporate citizenship becomes another way to describe firms' CSR activities, however without defining any new relationship between business and society. The extended view of corporate citizenship assumes that corporations start to protect, facilitate and enable citizens' rights whenever governments are not willing or not able to do this. This makes corporate citizenship a concept that is concerned with how businesses affect and are affected by social, civil and political rights. Many discussions throughout this book focus on the political nature of corporate sustainability and CSR and their relationship with government and hence include discussions of corporate citizenship.

1.4 Which Issues to Address? Organising Sustainability Discussions

Corporate sustainability can be difficult to grasp as a concept because it has many dimensions. Over time, numerous frameworks were developed to better organise the issues that corporations can potentially address. These frameworks offer an overview of the issues that corporations can address as part of their sustainability activities. Here, we discuss two well-known frameworks that help us to organise the debate.

1.4.1 Environmental, Social, Governance (and Technology)

One widely used framework is the distinction between environmental, social and governance (ESG) issues for corporate sustainability (see also above). Although this distinction does not belong to any official framework, it is a categorisation scheme that is commonly used by corporations. Table 1.2 gives an overview of possible sustainability issues that fall within each of the three categories. It is important to note that there is no definitive list of ESG issues that firms need to address. Table 1.2 just provides an overview of those issues that are commonly addressed. Practically speaking, firms usually do not have problems identifying environmental indicators

Table 1.2 Examples of ESGT (environmental, social, governance and technology) issues

Environmental	Social	Governance	Technology
Carbon emissions	Health and safety	Corruption	Cybersecurity
Waste & recycling	Community relations	Executive pay	Fake news
Water management	Diversity and inclusion	Board diversity	Dark web
Biodiversity	Employee pay	Stakeholder rights	Data mining
Land use	Union relations	CEO duality	Robotic processing
Deforestation	Poverty	Voting procedures	Bioengineering
Raw material sourcing	Training and education	Lobbying	Surveillance

(as the underlying problems are easier to quantify), while social indicators are often more difficult to define and hence proxy measures are used. However, in recent years, some issues in the social domain (e.g., modern slavery) have received significant public attention, which has also given rise to new discussions about relevant indicators.

In some cases, firms look at reporting standards like the Global Reporting Initiative (GRI) (see www.globalreporting.org/) to get an overview of the universe of possible ESG issues that could potentially apply to them. In other cases, they look at more generic frameworks like the Sustainability Accounting Standards Board's (SASB) (see www.sasb.org/standards/materiality-map/) materiality maps to get a first idea about which issues might matter. Whatever approach firms choose, they must narrow down the universe of *potential* ESG issues to those issues that specifically apply to *their own* corporate context. This 'narrowing down' is often approached through so-called materiality analyses – that is, analyses that filter out those ESG issues that matter most for a specific corporation (see Chapters 5 and 17 for a detailed discussion).

Some have argued that the ESG agenda needs to be extended to better account for technological issues that cannot be easily assigned to either E, S or G. The extended framework is referred to as ESGT, where T stands for technology (Bonime-Blanc, 2020). One good example of an emerging T issue is cybersecurity, which increasingly reflects a risk for corporations. Consider, for instance, the Colonial gas pipeline ransomware attack in 2021. This cyber-attack caused the pipeline, which supplies about 50 per cent of the gas for the US East Coast, to be out of operation for several days, resulting in price spikes and gas shortages.

1.4.2   The Sustainable Development Goals

Another widely used framework are the UN-backed Sustainable Development Goals (SDGs). The SDGs focus on sustainable development as a whole and not corporate sustainability specifically. The SDGs were developed to establish goals for national governments and address a much broader audience than just corporations. Nevertheless, many corporations around the world have embraced the SDGs and use them as a yardstick to organise their own sustainability discussions.

Launched in 2015, the SDGs reflect the UN's development agenda until the year 2030. The SDGs build on the so-called Millennium Development Goals (MDGs), which reflected the UN's development agenda from 2000 until 2015. The SDGs encompass 17 goals to which 169 specific targets are attached (see Table 1.3). While the MDGs were more focused on traditional development objectives (e.g., eradicating poverty), the SDGs are based on the concept of sustainability and thus the interplay of environmental, social and economic issues (Rasche, 2020). Table 1.3 lays out these SDGs. Many of these topics are explicitly discussed throughout this book – for instance, the role of human rights (SDGs 1–5; Chapter 21), decent work conditions and labour rights (SDG 8; Chapters 22 and 25), innovation for

Table 1.3 The UN-backed Sustainable Development Goals.

SDG	Short Description of the Goal	Exemplary Targets Covered by the Goal
1	No poverty	Eradicate extreme poverty for all people everywhere
2	Zero hunger	Ensure that all people have access to safe and nutrious food all year around
3	Good health and well-being	Reduce global maternal mortality / end AIDS, tubercolosis, and malaria
4	Quality education	Ensure that all girls and boys complete free primary and secondary education
5	Gender equality	End all forms of discrimination against women and girls
6	Clean water and sanitation	Ensure universal and equitable access to safe and affordable drinking water
7	Affordable and clean energy	Ensure reliable access to modern energy / increase share of renewable energy
8	Decent work and economic growth	Sustain per capita economic growth / achieve higher levels of economic productivity
9	Industry, innovation and infrastructure	Promote inclusive and sustainable industrialization / develop sustainable infrastructure
10	Reduced inqualities	Achieve and sustain income growth for bottom 40% of population
11	Sustainable cities and communities	Ensure access to safe and affordable housing and transport systems
12	Responsible consumption and production	Achieve sustainable management and efficient use of natural resources
13	Climate action	Strengthen resilience and adaptive capacity to climate-related hazards
14	Life below water	Prevent and reduce marine pollution / protect marine coastal ecosystems
15	Life on land	Conserve inland freshwate ecosystems / implement sustainable management of forests
16	Peace, justice and strong institutions	Reduce corruption / end trafficking of all kinds / develop transparent institutions
17	Partnerships for the goals	Enhance global multi-stakeholder partnerships for sustainability

Source: https://sdgs.un.org/goals

sustainability (SDG 9; Chapter 19), responsible consumption (SDG 12; Chapter 14), climate action (SDG 13; Chapter 23), anti-corruption (SDG 16; Chapter 24) and cross-sector partnerships (SDG 17; Chapter 18).

The SDGs need to be viewed as a 'system' – that is, as a list of issues that interact with one another. Naturally, this implies that there are also trade-offs and synergies among the different goals. For instance, the UN Resolution on which the SDGs are based views economic growth as a foundation for sustainable development, but it does not acknowledge that such growth can also undermine some of the ecological and social goals (Spaiser et al., 2017). On the other hand, there are also numerous synergistic effects – for instance, when considering that addressing deforestation (SDG 15) has positive effects on climate change (SDG 13). Countries' progress vis-à-vis these 17 goals is monitored through the SDG Index (see www.sdgindex.org).

Due to the UN acting as the sponsoring institution, most firms view the SDGs as a legitimate framework to organise sustainability-related discussions. Many firms even structure their corporate sustainability activities around a selection of the 17 goals. In these cases, businesses perform a so-called SDG Screening in which they assess (1) how far they contribute to the 17 goals (positively and negatively) and (2) how the 17 Goals impact their own operations and strategies (positively and negatively).

1.5   Why Do Corporations Engage in Sustainability?

Firms engage in corporate sustainability for a variety of reasons. In practice, there is usually not *the one* reason. Rather, different motivations interact with one another when companies make decisions on how they manage responsibility and sustainability. Of course, the context that a firm operates in (e.g., its size, its history and its ownership structure) also shapes how motivations are being seen by a particular company. Figure 1.2 provides an overview of four key motivations that we will discuss in the following sections.

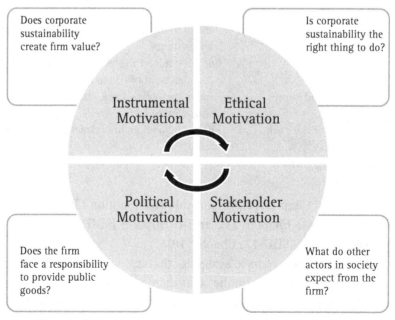

Figure 1.2 Four key motivations to engage in corporate sustainability.

1.5.1   Instrumental Motivation – 'It Pays to Be Sustainable'

The most widely mentioned (and also most debated) reason for engaging in corporate sustainability is the so-called *business case*. Some corporations create corporate sustainability policies and practices because they believe that they positively influence their financial bottom line. Corporate sustainability becomes a means to an end; a strategic tool to achieve competitive advantage. Although corporate sustainability and also CSR are rarely defined in a purely economic fashion, many scholars have emphasised their instrumental character. McWilliams and Siegel (2001: 119), for example, state that 'CSR can be viewed as a form of investment' and that managers need to 'determine the appropriate level of CSR investment' (118).

We need to be careful about assuming a general and definite link between firms' financial performance and their ESG performance; much depends on the context in which the business operates (e.g., its exposure to certain risks) and also on how and which ESG issues are being addressed. There are several practical difficulties when trying to measure the impact of sustainable and responsible firm conduct on financial performance. Some ESG activities are so embedded in a firm's overall operations that it is difficult to isolate their effects on financial performance. Although there is no universal link between firms' ESG performance and their financial results, a meta-study which aggregated evidence from more than 2,000 empirical studies on this subject matter (Friede et al., 2015) found that approximately 90 per cent of studies report a non-negative relation between both types of performance. In other words, while it may not always 'pay to be good', it also does not hurt firms' financial bottom lines. Usually, this strategic and financial motivation is thought to reflect the *business case* for corporate sustainability.

The UN Global Compact and the Principles for Responsible Investment (2013) have identified three categories of value drivers that influence how firms' ESG performance and their financial performance are linked: revenue growth, productivity improvement and risk minimisation (see Table 1.4).

1. Revenue growth: Some firms profit from sustainability financially because their ESG activities result in innovative products and services, which in turn improve revenue growth. In some cases, firms can expand their market share and customer base for existing products based on enhancing these with social and environmental features (e.g., when offering Fairtrade coffee). Revenue growth can also come from entering new geographic markets with sustainability-minded products, particularly if social and environmental product attributes act as differentiators.
2. Productivity improvement: Well-managed ESG practices can also lead to productivity improvements. For instance, environmental management practices can lead to operational efficiencies and result in cost savings (e.g., through reduced waste and better use of natural resources). Productivity gains can also result from

Table 1.4 How corporate sustainability influences firm value

Growth	New Markets & Geographies	Gain access to new markets and geographies through sustainability strategies (e.g., BOP markets).
	New Customers & Market Share	Use sustainability to engage customers and build knowledge and expectations.
	Product & Service Innovation	Develop innovative products and services addressing unmet social or environmental needs.
Return on Capital	Operational Efficiency	Enable bottom-line cost savings through environmental operations and practices (e.g., energy, water, waste).
	Human Capital Management	Attract and retain better and highly motivated employees by positioning company as sustainability leader.
	Reputation Pricing Power	Develop brand loyalty and reputation through ESG efforts that garner customers' willingness to pay price premium.
Risk Management	Operational and Regulatory Risk	Mitigate risks by complying with regulatory requirements and industry standards, ensuring uninterrupted operations.
	Reputational Risk	Facilitate operations and entry in new markets through community dialogue and engaging citizens.
	Supply Chain Risk	Secure consistent and long-term access to high-quality raw materials.

Source: UN Global Compact and the Principles for Responsible Investment (2013).

better human resources management, such as when firms are able to attract and retain talent because of their sustainability commitment or when workers become more productive due to improved health and safety policies.

3. Risk minimisation: Sustainability can enable companies to minimise business risks and hence better connect with investors. *Risk minimisation* can occur in different areas, such as regulatory risks (e.g., when emerging regulations could constrain resource use), supply chain risks (e.g., when non-compliant suppliers could lead to business interruptions) and reputational risks (e.g., when activists initiate boycotts or public shaming campaigns).

1.5.2   Ethical Motivation – 'It Is the Right Thing to Do'

Of course, corporate sustainability commitments do not always pay off in financial terms, and it is important to understand that sustainability and responsibility are often most needed when there are no financial gains to be realised. Some firms engage in corporate sustainability because it is quite simply the right thing to do. We call this motivation the *moral case* for corporate sustainability. The moral case is prevalent in business settings where, for example, a family or a manager owns the firm. Research has pointed at how this is most often the case in SMEs. They are often managed by an owner-manager with strong personal values and integrity to do the right thing vis-á-vis his or her stakeholders – sometimes irrespectively of the right thing being less profitable in a short-term economic calculation (Spence and Rutherford, 2003).

Theoretically speaking, the ethical motivation to engage in sustainability and responsibility has mostly been framed in the context of normative discussions. Scholars working in this tradition have argued that firms need to accept their social and environmental responsibilities, because it is their ethical obligation to align their activities with the values of society. Early on, Bowen (1953: 6) defined business responsibility as referring to:

> the obligations of businessmen to pursue those policies, to make those decisions, or to follow those lines of actions which are desirable in terms of the objectives and values of our society.

Of course, one can use different ethical principles to evaluate how managers ought to act and how they are supposed to reflect on the 'objectives and values of our society'. Some have emphasised the universal nature of rights (reflecting a Kantian perspective), while others have suggested that businesses, like other societal actors, must contribute to 'the common good' of society (reflecting an Aristotelian perspective). Chapter 3 provides an overview of relevant ethical theories.

1.5.3   Stakeholder Motivation – 'Others Ask Us to Do It'

Institutional and stakeholder theorists have also identified reasons why firms become engaged in sustainability. Explanations reaching in this direction focus on the institutional environment facing corporations. Firms often adopt corporate sustainability policies and practices because other firms have done the same. Such imitative, or mimetic, behaviour is particularly relevant if corporations are faced with a high degree of uncertainty (e.g., when there is uncertainty around future regulations). Faced with uncertainty, companies often look at their competitors and their national business systems (Matten and Moon, 2008) when deciding whether to adopt new management practices, especially as these practices are usually diffused either intentionally through industry associations or unintentionally through employee transfer or turnover.

Such 'copy-paste behaviour' among corporations was particularly visible in the early days of corporate sustainability and CSR. Back then, progressive companies started to implement social and environmental practices, which were then copied by competitors. Consider these two examples. (1) The Danish pharmaceutical company Novo Nordisk incorporated the triple-bottom line (i.e., environmental, social and economic) management approach into its company bylaws as early as in 2004 (Girschik et al., 2021). Later, Novo Nordisk's competitors in the pharmaceutical industry moved in similar directions. (2) Royal Dutch Shell was one of the first companies in the extractive industry to publish a sustainability report in 1997. Other major actors in the industry followed, with BP publishing its first report in 2004 and

Chevron in 2002. Shell's early commitment to sustainability and responsibility was significantly shaped by several high-level corporate scandals in the mid-1990s, ranging from a public clash with Greenpeace related to the disposal of one of its oil rigs (the Brent Spar) to alleged human rights violations in Nigeria.

The stakeholder motivation is not limited to just competitive, copy-paste behaviour. Often, firms face pressure to adopt corporate sustainability practices from other stakeholder groups as well (e.g., NGOs, unions, investors, governments, media). In many cases, these stakeholders ask the company to address ESG issues in more proactive ways, and they see such proactive behaviour as an important step in securing and maintaining the firm's societal 'licence to operate' (sometimes also referred to as the 'social licence to operate'). Such a licence to operate is different from enterprises' legal licence to do business, which in most countries is given based on the assumption that firms meet certain minimum legal standards. A societal licence to operate refers to whether a company is seen as a legitimate part of society by its stakeholders, or, as Gunningham, Kagan and Thornton (2017: 313) put it: 'the degree to which a corporation and its activities meet the expectations of local communities, the wider society, and various constituent groups'.

1.5.4   Political Motivation – 'There Is a Public Responsibility for Us'

Some firms become engaged in corporate sustainability because they start to administer the rights that affect citizens. As indicated above, the extended version of the corporate citizenship concept has captured this situation very well (Matten and Crane, 2005). In many cases, corporations need to think about sustainability and responsibility because their actions directly affect how different rights (e.g., human and labour rights) are governed. In situations where national governments are either unwilling or unable to secure such rights for their citizens, it is often corporations that must act. Consider, for instance, how some companies in the textile industry try to enforce labour rights throughout their supply chains through social audits (see Chapter 21). In such contexts, companies fill a void because governmental regulations are either non-existent, too weak or not properly enforced.

A more recent version of this discussion has been labelled 'political CSR'. It 'entails those responsible business activities that turn corporations into providers of public goods in cases where public authorities are unable or unwilling to fulfil this role.' (Scherer et al., 2016: 3) This definition emphasises that corporations are often entering the political sphere, as they directly or indirectly become involved in the regulation of social and environmental problems (e.g., by joining voluntary multi-stakeholder initiatives). Such a view presupposes a new understanding of global politics and the role of business in society. Rather than only focusing on the interaction of governmental actors, business firms and civil society actors become active participants in the regulation of market transactions.

The political motivation for engaging in corporate sustainability also has another side. Often, firms engage in corporate sustainability because they show a certain level of political responsiveness and alignment with governmental actions. For instance, some governments have started to mandate selected aspects of corporate sustainability (e.g., the disclosure of information), which makes addressing sustainability a legal obligation for certain companies. Some governments also incentivise firms to address ESG issues – for instance, by tying public procurement decisions to ESG criteria (Gond et al., 2011b). In the United Kingdom, for instance, corporations' participation in some public tender processes is dependent on them having a well-developed corporate sustainability strategy (see Chapter 12).

In practice, companies rarely base their corporate sustainability actions on just one of the four motivational pillars. We should therefore not think of these four motivations as being mutually exclusive, but rather as working together. For instance, firms that start to provide public goods because they have operations in countries with no or only weak regulation (political motivation) will usually also look at what the provision of these goods will do to their financial bottom line (instrumental motivation).

1.6 Key Tensions around Corporate Sustainability

Corporate sustainability is full of tensions that organisational actors must address. Not all of these tensions are necessarily logical contradictions in the sense that both poles of the tension mutually exclude each other. However, these tensions usually reflect organisational situations in which actors are likely to experience discomfort or even stress when making sustainability-related decisions (Putnam et al., 2016). We list some of the most prominent tensions in the sustainability field below:

1. Shareholder versus stakeholder: This tension is at the heart of many debates within corporate sustainability. Should corporations just serve their shareholders (and thus follow mostly financial objectives) or should they also serve broader stakeholder interests (and thus address social and environmental objectives)? Sometimes, this tension is reframed as a dilemma between corporate short-termism versus a longer-term orientation. In some situations, this tension will be less visible or even disappear because corporations have a 'business case' for addressing ESG issues and hence they can smoothly align shareholder and stakeholder interests. However, such win-win situations do not always exist, and corporate sustainability is also about doing the right thing regardless of whether it pays off in financial terms (Taylor, 2017).

2. Economic versus social/environmental: There are not always synergies between different sustainability issues. Our discussion of the SDGs above showed that in

some cases economic growth cannot be easily aligned with progress on social and environmental issues. As with the shareholder–stakeholder tension above, the ideal scenario is that economic objectives can be achieved through addressing social and environmental objectives. For instance, when economic growth is achieved because countries adopt a different type of energy policy that favours renewable sources. Yet, such win-win scenarios do not always exist, and economic objectives can turn out to be incompatible with social or environmental aims.

3. Internalisation versus externalities: Historically, corporate sustainability has had important links to the concept of negative externalities – that is, indirect costs of corporate activity to uninvolved parties. A typical example would be that a company's production causes pollution or emissions that it does not pay for but which are borne by society as a whole. More recently, companies have been (made) responsible for internalising their negative impacts through improving supply chain working conditions, instituting fair wages, paying for emissions, estimating climate risks and anticipating stranded assets. Thus, companies have been increasingly called to internalise into their operations the costs of their negative externalities.

4. Mandatory versus voluntary: Corporate sustainability is both mandatory and voluntary. On the one hand, many actions in support of ESG issues are not legally regulated and hence depend on corporations' voluntary commitment. On the other hand, regulators increasingly tighten legal frameworks so that some aspects of corporate sustainability (e.g., anti-corruption measures) have turned into legal obligations for some types of firms. It remains the case that corporations retain discretion in how they respond to mandates, and some mandates are designed to enable such discretion (e.g., the use of reporting frameworks). Especially for regulators, the mandatory/voluntary distinction can be a dilemma. While they reach more firms with legal measures, they also know that regulating through legal means can undercut flexibility and innovation. Some have therefore suggested keeping selected aspects of corporate sustainability outside of the legal domain, as innovation cannot be regulated and usually emerges out of trial-and-error processes.

5. Global versus local: MNCs often face a dilemma while developing their corporate sustainability strategy. On the one hand, they want a universal sustainability policy that applies to operations in all countries. Usually, such high-level policies rest on universal agreements that are supposed to apply everywhere and for everyone, such as the Universal Declaration of Human Rights (see Chapter 21). However, sustainability problems and practices 'on the ground' are highly contextual. For instance, they are influenced by the national context in which they appear. Hence, many firms must balance and align generic global policies with precise local implementation practices.

You will come across these (and other) tensions while reading this book. Whenever you recognise a tension, ask yourself: What would you do to address it? Unfortunately, there is no silver bullet for coping with corporate sustainability tensions. It is, however, a first important step to acknowledge them in the first place.

1.7   Chapter Summary

This opening chapter introduced you to the basic elements of the debate around corporate sustainability. We discussed several factors that influence the changing relationship between business, nature and society. We focused on the increased severity of ESG challenges, the rising scale and scope of corporate activities, the swift increase in digitalisation and datafication, and the rapid globalisation of markets and the associated gaps in global governance. Together, these four factors help you to understand why corporate action in support of sustainability is (1) needed and (2) possible.

We then turned to a discussion of what corporate sustainability, CSR and business ethics are all about. We defined all three terms, and we discussed similarities and differences between the three concepts. Although we will use primarily the sustainability language throughout this book, it is important to remember that concepts like CSR and business ethics are closely associated with the debates covered in this book. We then looked at two frameworks that help us to organise the multidimensional debate around corporate sustainability: ESG and the SDGs.

Next, we discussed what motivates firms to become engaged in corporate sustainability. We highlighted four different motivations – instrumental, ethical, stakeholder and political – and we showed that in corporate practice these motivations will overlap. Finally, we discussed key tensions that surround corporate sustainability. These tensions should make you aware that some aspects of corporate sustainability remain contested, also depending on who is evaluating a particular aspect. Therefore, studying corporate sustainability is best understood as a task that involves individual reflection (by reading the chapters of this book), but also, and perhaps most of all, discussion with your peers.

CHAPTER QUESTIONS

1. In what ways, if any, have changes in the relationship between business, nature and society impacted the emergence of corporate sustainability?
2. Outline differences and similarities between corporate sustainability, CSR and business ethics.
3. What motivates firms to engage in corporate sustainability? How do you think these motivations overlap in practice?

4. Identify two tensions that surround the corporate sustainability debate. Give practical examples that make these tensions visible. How would you address these tensions?

Case Study: *Volkswagen: Engineering the Truth*
Available from Cambridge University Press at www.cambridge.org/rasche2.

FURTHER RESOURCES

• Moon, J. (2015). *Corporate Social Responsibility: A Very Short Introduction.* Oxford: Oxford University Press.

A concise introduction to CSR, reviewing arguments for and against CSR and also discussing how CSR is exercised in different national contexts.

• The UN Sustainable Development Goals (SDGs), https://sustainabledevelopment.un.org

Launched in 2015, the SDGs consist of seventeen key goals that represent the 2030 agenda of the United Nations (and its partners) with regard to sustainable development. The goals include vital aspects like poverty reduction, gender equality and action on climate change.

• *Ethical Corporation*, www.ethicalcorp.com

Ethical Corporation is the leading monthly magazine on issues related to CSR and sustainability.

• The Business of Society (BOS) Blog, https://bos.cbs.dk

The Business of Society (BOS) Blog is a blog devoted to corporate sustainability and related debates; check BOS for the latest updates on responsible and sustainable business practices.

PART I
Corporate Sustainability: Approaches

2 Historical Perspectives on Corporate Sustainability

JEREMY MOON, LUISA MURPHY AND JEAN-PASCAL GOND[*]

LEARNING OBJECTIVES

- Understand corporate sustainability history in relation to the older concepts of business ethics and corporate social responsibility (CSR).
- Understand three historical perspectives on corporate sustainability:
  1. the issues, modes and rationales;
  2. the actors: society, business, government and the natural environment;
  3. three historical phases: industrialisation; the modern corporation; internationalisation.
- Understand the dynamics of corporate sustainability.

2.1 Introduction

Corporate sustainability is a relatively recent term. Its uses are contextual and dynamic, reflecting its status as an 'essentially contestable concept', meaning that there are always disagreements about its meaning and application (Gallie, 1956; Crane et al., 2008; Okoye, 2009; Moon, 2014). We use the term corporate sustainability to refer in general terms to business contributions to sustainability (Moon, 2007). We introduce the related concepts of business ethics and CSR in their respective historical contexts, but we also retrospectively describe developments as corporate sustainability that might, in their time, have been described as ethics or CSR.

Business ethics emerged from wider ethical foundations of ancient and premodern times, often related to religious concepts. These concepts were originally applied to business organisations very different from modern corporations, specifically to owner-managed enterprises, or simply to individuals with great wealth. CSR was grounded in business ethics drawing particularly upon the notions of

---

[*] We thank Christian Stutz for his helpful comments on a draft.

philanthropy ('love of humanity' – e.g., charitable giving) and paternalism ('taking fatherly' or 'parental' (Etchanchu and Djelic, 2019) care of others – e.g., employees and communities). In the last 100 years or so, it emerged as a corporate practice, rather than as a leadership characteristic, and an established management term after World War II, particularly in the United States (Heald, 1970). It spread to Europe in the latter part of the twentieth century, and more or less worldwide thereafter. In the present century, CSR has become internationalised and extended to issues beyond the corporation's workforce and immediate community, throughout its value chains.

Also in the present century many corporations, civil society organisations and analysts have adopted the term corporate sustainability usually to refer to an extension and particular application of CSR. We see business ethics as providing a normative underpinning for CSR, which we see as a corporate contribution to the wider concept of sustainability. The concept of corporate sustainability gives greater stress to intended outcomes than do CSR and business ethics, particularly for the natural environment, society and the corporation itself. While CSR originally brought a narrower lens onto the societal agendas (including environmental), delineating issues for which respective corporations are particularly responsible, CSR agendas have also widened, over the last twenty years, to include planetary- and society-wide concerns, thus overlapping with corporate sustainability. However, corporate sustainability also reflects a greater focus on scientific assessments of human impacts and dependencies on the natural environment (Bansal and Song, 2017), as well as reviving some quasi-religious themes (Acquier et al., 2011).

As concerns with corporate sustainability are very present, you might ask 'why look backwards?' As Henry Ford reputedly said, 'History is more or less bunk'. Others contend that history enables lessons which can be applied today, warning that: 'those who cannot remember the past are condemned to repeat it' (Santayana, 1905: 284). History also gives insights into 'path dependencies' whereby corporate sustainability is informed not just by today's agendas, but also by inherited assumptions about and approaches to ethics, CSR and sustainable development more generally. History is a powerful tool to reflexively analyse the long-term underlying social transformation which may account for the contemporary acceleration of corporate shifts towards sustainability (Rowlinson et al., 2014). Moreover, an understanding of corporate sustainability's genealogy enables students to better distinguish what is recurrent and what is novel, and to understand the significance of its different contexts.

We offer three *perspectives* on how to conceptualise historical and comparative corporate sustainability. The first addresses 'what?', 'how?' and 'why?' questions, focusing respectively on corporate sustainability 'issues', 'modes of practice' and 'underlying rationales'. Second, we discuss the 'who?' question of corporate sustainability, focusing on key actors: society, business, government and the natural environment. Third, we investigate the 'when?' question, focusing on three key phases of corporate sustainability: (1) *industrialisation*, in Western systems in the late eighteenth and nineteenth centuries; (2) *the rise of the modern corporation* and 'managerial capitalism' in the late nineteenth and early twentieth centuries; and (3) rapid *internationalisation* in the late twentieth and early twenty-first centuries, bringing wider impacts of corporate power and the greater awareness of the Anthropocene and human interdependency illustrated by COVID-19.

2.2 Corporate Sustainability Issues, Modes and Rationales

When asked to describe corporate sustainability, experts, supporters and critics often refer to issues, modes and rationales. Focus on these enables us to identify how corporate sustainability has changed:

1. *issues* addressed by corporate sustainability (e.g., community development, ecological diversity, social inequality, planetary limits);
2. *modes* used to address the issues (e.g., foundations, corporate codes, cause-related marketing, partnerships, regulation); and
3. *rationales* offered for addressing these issues and adopting these modes, whether based on principles (e.g., customary ethics), strategies (e.g., the business case) or business dependencies (e.g., legitimacy, environmental conditions), for example.

2.2.1 Corporate Sustainability Issues

Corporate sustainability *issues* are the problems or opportunities to which corporate sustainability is invoked or addressed, such as education, employee welfare and environmental security, usually reflecting societal and governmental agendas. They include underlying *trends* which are beyond single issues, such as climate change or loss of ecological diversity. They can include *events* which trigger new sustainability agendas that companies face, such as industrial disasters (e.g., the 1984 Bhopal gas leak at the Union Carbide India Limited pesticide plant and the 2013 Bangladesh Rana Plaza disaster).

Corporate sustainability issues have shifted in several main ways. First, there have been changes from corporate welfare policies associated with support for communities and other forms of charitable action; to responsibilities for the welfare of their own workers and families; and subsequently to responsibility for the welfare of workers in corporations' supply chains. Second, it has been noted that whereas corporate sustainability was once about what companies did with their profits, it is now as much about how they make their profits, illustrating a greater concern for the social, economic and environmental impacts of their production and commercial processes. Third, whereas corporate environmental policies were often focused on ameliorating the negative impacts of their operations, there is now greater attention on corporations' wider, positive, contributions to averting environmental degradation and climate change, and in restoring levels of biodiversity. Fourth, corporate sustainability issues now reflect specific consumer or investor preferences as represented, for example, by the fair trade movement or the frameworks of new sustainable finance initiatives. Fifth, corporations are expected to engage their corporate sustainability in relation to relatively core governmental issues, including the provision of physical infrastructure, education, security and taxation. Finally, corporate sustainability has recently attached itself to wider societal agendas (e.g., the Black Lives Matter, #MeToo and LGBTQ+ movements).

2.2.2   Corporate Sustainability Modes

Change in corporate sustainability has also been reflected in its *modes* or organisational and regulatory forms. The modes of corporate sustainability have developed from discretion on the part of individual business owners and leaders, to the creation of in-house CSR departments, to the corporation-wide organisation of sustainability from its corporate governance to its wider business functions.

There has been a general historical development of corporate sustainability modes, specifically with the shift *from* corporate sustainability being organised entirely in and by the corporations themselves *to* being organised with other actors. This is a shift from 'complete organisation' of CSR (Rasche et al., 2013), where all its organisational 'elements' (i.e., 'membership, hierarchy, rules, monitoring, sanctioning') are provided by the corporation itself. Instead, corporate sustainability reflects 'partial' organisation by the corporation in conjunction with other actors (Rasche et al., 2013) whether in business associations (Grayson and Nelson, 2013), cross-sector partnerships (Seitanidi and Crane, 2009) or multi-stakeholder initiatives (MSIs) (Chapter 18). While corporations thus open their sustainability policies to outside influences, they also learn to deal with complexity as a result of the confluence of expertise, interest and value brought by these new organisational approaches, and gain legitimacy thereby.

2.2.3   Rationales for Corporate Sustainability

The changes in corporate sustainability have been reflected in the *rationales* offered by businesses for their policies, or which are attributed to them. Six recurring rationales of corporate sustainability are presented (see Table 2.1), but note that more negative rationales are also attributed to corporate sustainability, such as managers' exploitation of company resources for their personal interest and greenwashing of less responsible business practices, suggesting that corporate sustainability deflects from issues of wider corporate reform.

2.2.3.1   The Social Responsibility of Business Is to Create Wealth

This rationale in some ways sits oddly in this context as it could be regarded as a legitimisation of corporate social *irresponsibility* and *un*sustainability. Yet, it not

Table 2.1 Six recurring rationales of corporate sustainability

Rationale	Illustration
1. The social responsibility of business is to create wealth	'To say then, that a man is entitled to a living wage is absurd ... if you take from the strong and give to the weak you encourage weakness; let men reap what they and their progenitors sow' (Charles Elliot Perkins)
2. To use wealth created by business for social ends	'great wealth should be administered for the common good ... the man of wealth thus becoming a mere agent and trustee for his poorer brethren' (Andrew Carnegie)
3. Business as a vehicle for social responsibility and sustainability	'the help that nourishes civilization is ... the investment of effort or time or money ... to the power of employing people at a remunerative wage, to expand and develop the resources at hand, and to give opportunity for progress and healthful labor' (John D. Rockefeller)
4. Corporate sustainability legitimises business to society and government	'the continuing socio-institutional influences were, if anything, more important than those influencing the businessmen's earlier lives' (Jonathan Boswell)
5. Corporate sustainability as a vehicle for wealth creation	'(Robert Owen) argued that fair treatment of workers could result in a return equal to 50 percent to 100 percent on money invested' (Husted, 2015)
6. Corporate sustainability as a contribution to societal welfare	'The purpose of a company is to engage all its stakeholders in shared and sustained value creation. In creating such value, a company serves not only its shareholders, but all its stakeholders – employees, customers, suppliers, local communities and *society at large*' (Schwab, 2019; emphasis added)

only represents a manifesto for greed and social negligence, but this view can also reflect a more developmental appreciation of a laissez-faire approach towards wealth creation (Smith, 1776/1982) illustrated in the context of corporate responsibility by railway entrepreneur, Charles Elliot Perkins (Table 2.1, quoted in Husted, 2015: 130). A century later, Milton Friedman (1970) argued that societal benefits arise when business leaders focus on building profitable companies which pay taxes, employ workers and provide goods and services that customers and societies desire.

2.2.3.2 To Use Wealth Created by Business for Social Ends

This more familiar rationale for CSR and corporate sustainability is rooted in expectations of philanthropy on the part of wealthy citizens and business leaders and, latterly, by corporations (Heald, 1970; Tables 2.1, 2.2). This idea is shared in Eastern and Western societies. It has been associated with the expectation of stewardship of wealth, whether on behalf of a deity or humanity. It has been criticised for focusing on what is done with the profits of a company (which could be made irresponsibly or unsustainably) rather than on creating wealth in a sustainable way. In other words, it is about the distribution of wealth as advocated by Andrew Carnegie, a poor Scottish immigrant who became one of the richest men in the United States, only to preach the 'Gospel of Wealth' (Table 2.1, quoted in Husted, 2015: 129).

2.2.3.3　Business as a Vehicle for Social Responsibility and Sustainability

Whereas the second rationale is predicated on the use of corporations' surplus wealth, this rationale for corporate sustainability presumes that the very activity of business is itself an opportunity for responsibility. An early version is captured by John D. Rockefeller (Table 2.1, quoted in Husted, 2015: 129) whereby the provision of employment inside the company is regarded as a social investment. It is illustrated latterly by companies like Ben & Jerry's and the Body Shop, whose founding owners saw creating companies as an opportunity to address their chosen social agendas as well as to create wealth. It is also reflected in the many social enterprises, including cooperatives and B corporations (Chapter 9).

2.2.3.4　Corporate Sustainability Legitimises Business to Society and Government

Many long-standing accounts of CSR point to the rationale of legitimacy and this prevails for corporate sustainability. Accordingly, corporate sustainability is as much a reflection of expectations of society, stakeholders and governments as it is of the inspiration of business leaders and innovative companies. Businesses, individually and collectively, thereby acquire a social licence to operate. The details of what is legitimised reflect the variation of expectations of business across sector and country as well as era (Boswell, 1983 in Table 2.1, Rationale 4).

2.2.3.5　Corporate Sustainability Is a Vehicle for Wealth Creation

This rationale, also known as the 'business case for CSR' (Carroll and Shabana, 2010), was illustrated by Robert Owen, known for his blending of business with social innovation in the early 1800s through model communities (New Lanark Mill, New Harmony), who introduced rules against hiring young children and on maximum working hours, and built schools for workers' children. Nevertheless, he described this approach as combining social and business benefits (Table 2.1, quoted in Husted, 2015:127). This rationale is also evident in the stakeholder approach to corporate sustainability (Chapter 4), as well as 'bottom of the pyramid' strategies by which means companies can serve the poor through enlightened business models (Prahalad and Hart, 2002) and in Porter and Kramer's concept of Creating Shared Value (2011).

2.2.3.6   Corporate Sustainability as a Contribution to Societal Welfare

Corporate sustainability has also been understood as business contributions to societal welfare. These contributions are normally in the form of services and infrastructure, and in the administration of rights. These contributions to societal welfare can emerge in the absence of government provision (e.g., pre-welfare state Europe, developing country contexts, cross-border contexts – Matten and Crane, 2005; Scherer and Palazzo, 2011). They are also increasingly illustrated in partnerships where companies operate *with* rather than *in place of* governments. These are often instigated by governmental encouragement for business to help in addressing problems such as mass unemployment, reflecting the distinctive resources and capabilities they can bring to such tasks (Moon, 2002). This rationale points to the common societal roots of corporate governance and corporate sustainability concepts in early scholarly debates about the roles and responsibilities of corporations (Clark, 1916; Berle and Means, 1932; Bowen, 1953), and is now closely associated with corporate citizenship (Moon et al., 2005). It is also illustrated in recent corporate accounts of the purpose of the company (Table 2.1), including their approaches to questions about planetary survival as illustrated by former Unilever CEO, Paul Polman (Skapinker and Daneshkhu, 2016).

So, change in corporate sustainability history can be understood in terms of its issues, modes and rationales. However, there is little sense of linear development here. Rather, the picture is one of recurrence of issues, modes and rationales, but always in different contexts reflecting changing relationships among society, business, government and the natural environment, to which we now turn.

2.3   Corporate Sustainability Actors: Society, Business, Government and the Natural Environment

We investigate how corporate sustainability actors reflect and shape its issue agendas, choices and effects of its modes, and the articulation of rationales.

2.3.1   Society

Society is ostensibly the core context of corporate sustainability. Societies have expectations of business and certain powers over business, particularly concerning legitimacy (Davis, 1960; Carroll, 1979; Matten and Moon, 2020). These expectations are conveyed through everyday social interactions and institutions (e.g., in churches, political parties, clubs) and processes of socialisation of business leaders. They are also conveyed more directly to corporations by, for example, new social movements and the media.

Societies are made up of people who, notwithstanding differences in, for example, status and wealth, nonetheless share cultural expectations and norms. Societies develop as institutionalised systems, with regular habits of interaction and norms of acceptable and appropriate behaviour, including of business organisations (Boswell, 1983). They develop organisational forms that enable the development of social identities and points of solidarity. These include organisations collectively known as 'civil society' (e.g., media, non-governmental organisations) that convey expectations based on particular interests and values to corporations.

From ancient times, societies have developed ethics, based on religion or other forms of cultural organisation and belief, and these have been applied to business activities and the uses of wealth. About half of the Code of Hammurabi (1700 BC) is devoted to Babylonian labour and consumer contracts and corresponding responsibilities. Subsequent civilisations also recorded norms and codes to give guidance to wealthy people and those engaged in commerce (Table 2.2). Many of these have been adapted to contemporary corporate sustainability.

A number of key themes emerge. First, many norms that were assumed to apply principally to people, in modern times have been extended to business organisations, and corporations in particular (Heald, 1970). Historically, these ethics simply accompanied daily life, and in many societies, particularly in Asia, they are reflected in everyday religiosity and are therefore part of the conduct and legitimisation of business life. In medieval Europe, distinctive forms of organising and regulating responsible business emerged, ranging from the obligations that attended corporate status, to the collective social duties that were concomitants of guild of trade membership (Caulfield, 2013: 223–226). Second, the concepts of charity and stewardship have retained an everyday meaning, and are invoked in CSR (Bowen, 1953). Third, corporate sustainability systems not only reflect national institutions, but also diverse cultural mores within a single country (e.g., Malaysia's Malay, Indian and Chinese business cultures). Fourth, modernity has seen the emergence of more secular ethical expectations of business reflecting changing social structures and political identities, and informing expectations around diversity and equality, for example. Environmental expectations of business responsibility and sustainability were historically defined around the use of natural resources, particularly water, and the effects of industry on air pollution (Berrier-Lucas, 2014), and more recently around global warming and ecological diversity.

The media for communicating social expectations of business have increasingly pluralised following successive inventions, from the printing press, the telegraph, radio and television, to contemporary information and communication technology (Castells, 2000). The nineteenth century saw mass campaigns on social issues such as slavery, working conditions, employee rights and remuneration often involving the culpability of business. But some businesses also aligned themselves with these causes (e.g., the Wedgwood pottery company opposed slavery). The early twentieth-century print media were used by 'muckraker' journalists to reveal and shame business irresponsibility, particularly in the new oil, gas and railway corporations.

Table 2.2 Ethical foundations of business responsibility and sustainability

Religion/ Society	Keyword	Definition	Corporate Sustainability Concept
Ancient Greece/Rome			
	Paternalism	as if by a father to children	care of employees
	Philanthropy	love of humanity	giving (wealth/profits) to the needy
Buddhism			
	Dāna	giving	charity/justice
	Dharma	duty	righteousness
	Karuṇā	compassion	compassion for others
	Mettā	benevolence	goodwill
	Sila	ethics	ethical conduct
Christianity			
	Charity	benevolence	community/public service
	Stewardship	responsibility for the world	care of resources in trust
Confucianism			
	Li	good manners	ethical conduct
	Ren	benevolence	altruism
	Shu	reciprocity	reciprocity
	Xiao / Zhong	obedience/loyalty	responsibility/duty
	Xin	sincerity	integrity
	Yi	righteousness	justice
Hinduism			
	Dāna	giving as a duty	charity/justice
	Dharma	righteousness	duty
	Sanatana dharma	eternal order	unity
	Sarva loka hitam	well-being of others	philanthropy
Islam			
	Adalah	justice	justice
	Amanah	trust	integrity
	Khalifah	trusteeship	stewardship
	Riba	fair commerce	fairness
	Sadaqah / Waqf / Zakat	charity	charity/philanthropy
	Tawhid	unity of profit & morality action	unity
	Ummah	communal use of wealth	unity/justice

Table 2.2 (*cont.*)

Religion/ Society	Keyword	Definition	Corporate Sustainability Concept
Japanese (Shinto/ Bukkyo)			
	Keiei	governing for the well-being of the people	management
	Keiretsu geisha	affiliates	ethics towards suppliers
	Kigyo jokamachi	company-town	community
	Shogai koyo	life-time employment	employee welfare
	Asha	truth	righteousness
	Bushido	relationship between master and vassal	ethical relationship between company and employee
	Sanpo-yoshi	three-way satisfaction	good for the seller (yourself), the buyer (customer), and the world (society)
Judaism			
	Bal tashchit	do not destroy	environmental responsibility
	Chesed	kindness, love	charity
	Tikkun olam	repairing the world	philanthropy
	Tzedakah	justice	Charity/stewardship
Taoism			
	Chi'i	natural energy	unity
	De	virtue	integrity
	Yin yang	harmony	balance

Source: Adapted from Kim and Moon (2015); see Kim and Moon's Appendix 1 for Asian Sources; and Ray et al. (2014).

Consumer leagues emerged such as the *Ligue Sociale d'Acheteurs* in France whose, mainly female, members promoted more ethical consumption by publicising shops whose supply chains featured acceptable working conditions (Chessel, 2012). The twenty-first century saw the extensive use of social media both by NGOs and other civil society organisations to: mobilise support for campaigns against corporations' roles in such issues as deforestation (e.g., Greenpeace attacks on Nestlé's sourcing of palm oil) (Whelan et al., 2013; Castelló et al., 2016); internationalise the Occupy Wall Street movement; and encourage activism against the oil and gas industry.

As Carroll et al. (2012) observe of CSR in America, business 'has sought and secured public acceptance, endorsement, and support – in other words, social legitimacy' (2012: 1). At various points in history, the significance of societal expectations has reshaped corporate and business regulators' practices because of perceived unethical, irresponsible or unsustainable business behaviour (e.g., Enron, the Global Financial Crisis, the Panama Papers).

2.3.2 Business

In these societal contexts, it is the choices of business actors that give corporate sustainability substance and shape. Businesses are, of course, in society, and their members and stakeholders reflect social affinities, values and interests. However, businesses are also apart from society, reflecting their distinctive organisational designs and purposes.

Although our principal focus is corporations, it is important to note the social relations of the range of business forms that vary from the sole trader, through partnerships, small and medium-sized companies (Chapter 8), corporations and multinational corporations (MNCs). The balance of these has varied historically. Corporations have long existed for special licensed purposes (Avi-Yonah, 2005) and some have had huge historical impacts (e.g., the British East India Company). Their significance has never been greater than in the period from the second half of the nineteenth century (Chandler, 1984), and particularly in the multinational manifestation from the late twentieth century. While historically, most businesses have been privately owned and managed, many modern corporations saw the separation of ownership (whether shareholders or private owners) and management (section 2.4.2) (Berle and Means, 1932). Other important variants include cooperatives, whether owned by consumers or employees, and corporations owned/part-owned by governments notably in socialist systems (e.g., China), but also in European mixed economies. Although corporations' purposes have varied historically, most involve the selling of goods and services with some surplus. The use of the surplus has also varied, from rewarding owners and investors, to reinvesting in the corporation and funding foundations. But many businesses have combined these purposes with intrinsic social objectives, including doing business in a particular way (e.g., with acceptable working conditions and remuneration), sourcing products with socially valued attributes (e.g., organic), or serving particular social groups (e.g., ethnically defined) or meeting the needs of the vulnerable (e.g., the poor). In many US states, and now internationally, a new form of business incorporation 'B Corps' recognises companies with mixed profit and social objectives (Rawhouser et al., 2015), while the corporate law in France has been amended recently to enable the creation of 'profit-with-purpose' corporations (Levillain and Segrestin, 2019), but the model of multiple purposes itself is as old as business (Chapter 9).

While most corporate sustainability has reflected individual company policies and activity, businesses have also developed collective approaches. Historically this was through business guilds (often trade- or sector-based) and associations (e.g., chambers of commerce). There has been a recent growth of business associations for corporate sustainability, whether: national (e.g., the United Kingdom's Business in the Community); international (e.g., ASEAN CSR, World Business Council for Sustainable Development); issue-based (e.g., the Global Business Coalition on HIV/AIDS); or sectoral (e.g., Responsible Business Alliance of electronics corporations). Most recently, a variety of cross-sector partnerships and MSIs have emerged in which corporations collaborate with civil society and governmental actors to pursue their sustainability goals (e.g., Forest and Marine Stewardship Councils; UN Global Compact with its 100+ national chapters; Extractive Industries Transparency Initiative; ethical trading initiatives). These new organisations often develop private regulation of their own members and their supply chains, which in turn often interact with public regulation (Cashore et al., 2021; Chapter 12).

In this light, we see that corporate sustainability is not simply a cipher enabling societal values and expectations to be translated into business. Business has also shaped corporate sustainability agendas in order to win legitimacy, innovate, attract new customers, motivate employees and make efficiency savings.

2.3.3 Government

If society is the context for corporate sustainability and businesses the key actors, then governments are its key institutional shapers, ostensibly on behalf of society (Chapter 12; Moon et al., 2010) given their unique authority (Weber, 1968). Moreover, businesses look to governments to ensure functioning markets (e.g., by making and applying rules of competition) and to influence governments regarding these rules.

The role of government in shaping corporate sustainability is partly predicated upon its role in regulating the corporate form, including such issues as membership and the development of legal personality; the ability of corporations to operate for profit; and share ownership and the emergence of the global firm (Avi-Yonah, 2005). Increased government welfare provision has led to the substitution of some corporate services (e.g., schools), and the withdrawal of such government services has often led to renewal of corporate welfare provision.

However, the relationships are not always those of substitution. Governments create tax incentives for philanthropy (e.g., charitable giving) and for paternalism (e.g., for employee health insurance); subsidise corporate sustainability investments (e.g., for clean energy); adopt fair trade or environmental criteria in their own public procurement policies and make 'soft rules' to encourage corporate sustainability (e.g., for non-financial reporting, see Chapter 12). Ironically perhaps, national governments have also contributed to the internationalisation of corporate sustainability. The US and UK governments regulate corporate corruption overseas, and several European governments (e.g., France, Germany, the Netherlands, the United Kingdom) require corporate due diligence in respect of modern slavery in supply chains (Chapter 21). Some governments have used corporate sustainability to stimulate international competitiveness (e.g., the United Kingdom and Denmark) or to win legitimacy for their exports (e.g., China).

International governmental organisations have also emerged which bring the collective authority of their members to bear. The United Nations has supported corporate sustainability through the UN Global Compact and related initiatives (e.g., UN Principles for Responsible Investment, UN Principles for Responsible Management Education, UN Guiding Principles Human Rights Declaration). The Organisation for Economic Co-operation and Development (OECD) has issued considerable corporate sustainability guidance (e.g., Guidelines for Multinational Enterprises), as has the European Union (e.g., European Commission Strategy on CSR, EU Multi Stakeholder Forum on Corporate Social Responsibility, and latterly the Non-financial Reporting Directive 2014/95/EU).

2.3.4 Natural Environment

Early conversations about CSR and business ethics barely mentioned the natural environment beyond its role as a context for the deployment of business activities (Bowen, 1953; Bansal and Song, 2017) and its status as a stakeholder (Driscoll and Starik, 2004). However, it has (re-)emerged as a central factor in government and business policy and strategy. This development was underpinned by the emergence, structuring and development of environmental social movements across the planet since the late 1960s and through the 1970s (Hoffman, 1999), and nurtured by whistle-blowing exercises about the negative impacts of extended industrialisation on the natural environment (Carson, 1962; Meadows et al., 1972). In recent years, the imperative to consider the environment in corporate sustainability analysis became even more central in light of alarming ecological trends, such as increased water scarcity, the loss of biodiversity and climate change (IPCC, 2021).

These transformations led to the awareness of the existence of multiple 'planetary boundaries' weighing on economic activities and the recognition that we now live at the age of the 'Anthropocene' – a period characterised by the drastic influence of human activity on the ecological environment. These changes have multiple implications for business and governmental approaches to corporate sustainability. Radically, they involve moving beyond the human–nature dualism that has informed the Westernised approach to the ecological environment (Descola, 2013) and which still influences contemporary analyses of corporate sustainability, in order to recognise the multiple ways in which different social groups across time and space have engaged with nature in a less destructive way (Banerjee and Arjaliès, 2021). Minimally, these changes require businesses and governments to embrace a more holistic and systemic approach to contemporary 'grand challenges' formed by the multiplication of social and environmental issues (Whiteman et al., 2013), and to recognise the necessarily deeply intertwined interactions of business, government and the environment when considering corporate sustainability.

This section has presented corporate sustainability as reflecting interactions between society, business, government and the natural environment. In the next section, we illustrate these relationships in three historical phases of corporate sustainability.

2.4   Three Phases of Corporate Sustainability

We distinguish three phases of corporate sustainability: industrialisation, the modern corporation and internationalisation. *Industrialisation* emerged in the United Kingdom in the late eighteenth century, spread to much of Western Europe and North America in the nineteenth century, and more widely, particularly in East Asia in the twentieth century. While many countries are yet to experience their own industrialisation, most of the world is now reshaped by its effects as a result of internationalisation. The *modern corporation* has emerged as a distinctive organisational form, albeit in different ways in different places, reflecting national institutions for corporate ownership, control and purpose, and related corporate governance systems. *Internationalisation* has proceeded at a dramatic pace since the late twentieth century (Rosenau, 1990). The international dependencies of society, business and the natural environment have become all too apparent in the light of the clearer understandings of the dominance of global value chains, of how planetary boundaries are being encroached upon by the Anthropocene, and of the global spread of COVID-19 and its attendant health, social and economic effects.

In each phase we distinguish key corporate sustainability issues, modes and rationales, and their respective society – business – government – environment contexts. Each phase is illustrated by snapshots of corporate sustainability in two long-standing companies, Boots (UK) and Tata (India). These both emerged in the nineteenth century as family-run companies with some commitment to responsible business conduct. Boots began as a pharmaceutical retailer (1848) and became the UK market leader in the twentieth century when it developed research and manufacturing capacity, and expanded its products to household goods, photography and electricals. In the twenty-first century, it was acquired by a European private equity fund to form Alliance Boots (2006), which merged with a US pharmaceutical retailer to form Walgreens Boots Alliance (2014). (The three Boots' 'snapshots' draw upon the following references: Blythe, 2011; The Boots Company PLC 2015a, 2015b, 2016.)

Tata commenced as a trading company (1868) and soon expanded into cotton milling, iron and steel, electricity generation and diverse other businesses. During the twentieth century, it became India's largest conglomerate with companies, often part-owned by Indian public authorities, in such sectors as electricity, steel and aviation. In the twenty-first century, it embarked on internationalisation, including through acquisitions in European steel and motor manufacturing, and the spread of its consultancy business. (The three Tata 'snapshots' draw upon the following references: Tata Sons Ltd 2016, 2022.)

2.4.1 Industrialisation

Industrialisation constituted a systemic change in business – society relations, with implications for business responsibility and sustainability agendas. Societies were reshaped by the exodus from agricultural communities to new industrial cities first in the United Kingdom and latterly in China, the first and the most recent 'workshops of the world'. Industrialisation brought new concentrations of wealth and power, and with these, challenges for corporations to secure legitimacy with society and regulators. It brought concentrations of employment raising issues of labour conditions, the working week and remuneration, which also prompted pressure for labour rights and unionisation. Increases in literacy and improvements in communications popularised critical images of industrial exploitation and pollution in, for example, the writings of Charles Dickens and Emile Zola. Government regulation slowly emerged to address these issues often following, or in tandem with, company initiatives.

Responsible business models focused on housing, welfare and education in communities where workers were located, epitomised by Robert Owen's New Lanark Mill, Lever Brothers' Port Sunlight, Cadbury's Bourneville, Pullman's company town outside Chicago, and Godin's *familistère* (Social Palace) in Guise, France. Even where companies did not create whole communities, many nonetheless invested heavily in employee housing, schools, hospitals and even recreation through swimming pools, pubs and casinos. Company-based regulation for working conditions often preceded government legislation, including for working hours and child labour, wages (e.g., Owen's New Lanark), health insurance (e.g., Krupp in Germany), pension schemes (e.g., London and North Western Railway) and profit-sharing (e.g., Lever Brothers). In Japan, this extended to life-long employment in many companies.

Turning to the environment, while many industrialists viewed 'smoke as prosperity' (quoted in Husted, 2015: 130), others used self-restraint and technological investment to moderate their adverse environmental impact. In Germany, the Hamburg Chamber of Commerce led a collective initiative to lower smoke pollution and this was complemented by relaxation of taxes – an early example of governmental rewards for self-regulation.

Rationales for responsible business varied across the range. Many business leaders believed that business should be a vehicle for wealth creation (Table 2.1, rationale 1) and a vehicle for social responsibility (rationale 3), and that business can contribute to societal governance (rationale 6). Boots provided low-cost drugs to the poor, combining mass production techniques and a network of retail outlets, and marketed with the slogan 'health for a shilling'. This strategy was complemented by

SNAPSHOTS | BOX 2.1 Boots: corporate sustainability in industrialisation

Motto: 'We declare – For Pure Drugs For Qualified Assistants For First-class Shops For Reasonable Prices For your Good Health For our Moderate Profits We minister to the comfort of the community in a hundred ways.' (Jesse Boot, son, founder of Boots, 1897)

Issues: health, poverty, community, employee welfare and accountability

Modes: paternalism (e.g., schools around factory, lending library, athletic and social clubs); philanthropy; transparency (e.g., minutes at first meeting of the Directors of Boots, 1888, twenty years before legal requirement); pricing (e.g., subsidised pharmaceuticals for the poor, 1894, over a decade prior to the UK National Insurance Act tax).

SNAPSHOTS | BOX 2.2 Tata: corporate sustainability in industrialisation

Motto: 'In a free enterprise, the community is not just another stakeholder in business, but is in fact the very purpose of its existence.' (Jamsetji Tata, founder, Tata Group, 1868)

Issue: community in the context of nation building

Modes: philanthropy (e.g., JN Tata Endowment, 1892: education trust for higher education studies); ownership transferred to charitable trusts.

Rationale: stakeholder orientation in the community as a business model

social investments (e.g., library services), employee initiatives (e.g., social clubs) and free education for local communities, all social services that were later assumed by government (Box 2.1).

Likewise, Tata displayed an early dedication to community engagement and employee welfare, coupled with a broader social purpose. Jamsetji Tata's 'main impulse for founding the company ... and setting community engagement as its core goal was to create a company that served India as a country and provided a basis for self-reliance against the British colonial rule' (Tata and Matten, 2016: 3). This commitment was associated with ethical assumptions that Parsees should be especially charitable, also illustrated in the Jamsetji Nusserwanji Tata Endowment (1892) to encourage young Indians to study. Thus, Tata's approach reflected rationales 2, 3 and 6 (Table 2.1; Box 2.2).

2.4.2 The Modern Corporation

The distinctive resources that business can mobilise for private and societal ends became yet more apparent in the late nineteenth and early twentieth centuries with the emergence of modern corporations first in the United States, prompting anxieties about the anti-social purposes lying behind such power, illustrated by journalists and authors known as 'muckrakers' (e.g., Upton Sinclair's *Oil!* (1927), which inspired the film, *There Will Be Blood* (2007)). Some corporations responded by investing in their own image: telephone monopoly AT&T marketed itself as a person 'to make people understand and love the company' (Bakan, 2004: 17).

The modern corporation marked several other departures. Most obviously, they were distinguished by the separation between ownership and control giving rise to a new class of management professionals who were thought better able to respond to social demands than were the increasingly dispersed shareholders. Many managers advocated the 'doctrine of social responsibility' as possible and desirable for corporations to legitimise their own roles and those of the corporations (Bowen, 1953: 84–106). This sparked new debates about the governance and social responsibilities of corporations captured in Clark's (1916) seminal paper, 'The Changing Basis of Economic Responsibility', and in Gantt's contention that 'the business system must accept its social responsibility and devote itself primarily to service, or the community will ultimately make the attempt to take it over in order to operate it in its own interest' (1919; quoted in Husted, 2015: 125).

While the doctrine of social responsibility fell from favour in the United States during the 1930s, it re-emerged after 1945, encouraged by the emerging PR industry's use of such terms as business 'considerations of the public' and 'ethical awakening'. In this context, the modes of corporate–community relations and corporate philanthropy were institutionalised in American business (Kaplan, 2015).

In Europe, as the welfare state emerged in the early twentieth century, many corporations reduced their community level contributions (e.g., schools, housing). However, a century later, new corporate sustainability agendas related to social deprivation and environmental risks have repositioned business as a contributor to mainstream societal welfare (Table 2.1, rationale 6). European corporations also adopted various American modes, such as employee volunteering, and addressed wider sustainability activities to win the loyalty and commitment of employees, combining rationalisations of legitimisation and wealth creation (Table 2.1, rationales 5, 6). By the end of the twentieth century, on both sides of the Atlantic, there was functional specialisation and professionalisation of corporate sustainability, reflected in dedicated units of qualified and experienced staff.

SNAPSHOTS | BOX 2.3 Boots: corporate sustainability and the modern corporation

Motto: 'When we build factories in which it is a joy to work, when we establish pension funds which relieve our workers of fears for their old age, when we reduce the number of working days in the week, or give long holidays with pay to our retail assistant, we are setting a standard which Governments in due time will be able to make universal.' (John Boot, 1938)

Issues: workplace and public community development

Modes: first full-time welfare staff appointed (1911); Boots Day Continuation School for younger employee education (1920); recycling machinery (1930s); five-day work week (1934); bottle recycling (1940s); 24-hour opening times; Boots Charitable Trust (1970); Environment Manager hire (1972); Social Responsibilities booklet (1977).

Rationale: workplace and public community development as a business model

SNAPSHOTS | BOX 2.4 Tata: corporate sustainability and the modern corporation

Motto: 'Be sure to lay wide streets planted with shady trees, every other of a quick-growing variety. Be sure that there is plenty of space for lawns and gardens. Reserve large areas for football, hockey and parks. Earmark areas for Hindu temples, Mohammedan mosques and Christian churches.' (Jamsetji Tata, 1902)

Issues: workplace and public community development in rural and disadvantaged areas

Modes: The Indian Institute of Science for Advanced Studies, Bangalore (1911), eight-hour work days (1912), Tata provident fund (1920) thirty-two years ahead of government regulation, Tata townships for employees.

Rationale: workplace and public community development as a business model

Over the twentieth century, Boots evolved from a family firm with a focus on pharmaceuticals to having a dispersed shareholding ownership and a wider product range. It continued to offer employee and community welfare initiatives, despite some of its nineteenth-century core initiatives having been replaced by government (compare Box 2.3 with Box 2.1). It was an early adopter of electronic vehicles.

Tata also grew prodigiously in the twentieth century. The ownership structures vary among the enterprises, ranging from dispersed shareholding to joint ownership with state and national governments. Tata emphasised employee welfare with the eight-hour working day (1912), an employee insurance scheme (1920) and the development of industrial townships. Reflecting its developing country home and its unusual size and reach, Tata's corporate sustainability reflected a continuing engagement with wider societal welfare, including for rural and disadvantaged communities, whereas this diminished for Boots given the increased UK state roles in this period. (Compare Tata in Box 2.4 with Boxes 2.2 and 2.3.)

2.4.3 Internationalisation

Internationalisation is distinguished by increased: volume of international trade; movement of people across borders; information and communication technologies; international corporate value chains and global financial markets. In some countries and regions, particularly in Asia, industrialisation, the modern corporation and internationalisation have occurred in different sequences and in China, virtually simultaneously.

These trends have immense implications for corporate sustainability issues, modes and rationales. There is a greater emphasis on planetary issues, notably climate change and biodiversity, and natural resource issues such as water. Rather than addressing these through firm-level policies and practices, corporations now do so in more collaborative modes (e.g., in business associations, cross-sector partnerships, MSIs), resulting in shared approaches and practices reflecting coercive isomorphisms, mimetic practices and new global norms (Matten and Moon, 2008).

Although corporations also address local sustainability issues, especially in developing countries, MNC agendas increasingly focus on social and environmental issues that are 'global', either because of their value chain implications or because of the interactions between the new forms of private authority and the sustainability agendas of national governments (Chapter 12). Climate change is the primary issue, as it is planetary by definition, intergovernmental in institutionalisation, of growing material concern to business (Stern et al., 2006) and an issue of widespread social awareness and mobilisation reflecting popularised scientific revelations (e.g., David Attenborough), environmental activism (e.g., Greta Thunberg) and celebrity advocacy (e.g., Arnold Schwarzenegger, Leonardo DiCaprio).

Reflecting corporations' greater connection with societal and governmental sustainability priorities, many have adopted, evaluated and communicated their policies in terms of the UN Sustainable Development Goals. This is encouraged by international financial institutions which increasingly encourage the

SNAPSHOTS | BOX 2.5 Boots: corporate sustainability and internationalisation

Motto: 'Caring for our communities, our customers, patients and colleagues is at the heart of who we are and what we do. For 170 years, we have demonstrated an ongoing commitment to operating as a socially responsible business and we recognize the active role we can play in helping to build happier and healthier communities.' (Corporate Social Responsibility – Boots, our approach, website)

Issues: stakeholder orientation in community, environment, sustainable marketplace and healthy and inclusive workplace

Modes: Fundraising and volunteering in the community: for example, Boots Charitable Trust (1970), BBC Children in Need (2003), Macmillan Cancer Support; Environment initiatives: for example, UK Plastics Pact Waste Resources Action Programme (WRAP) (2018), Logistics Carbon Reduction Scheme (LCRS), Steering committee member of national Circular Economy Task Force; Sustainable marketplace: Boots 'Code of Conduct for Ethical Trading' (2002), member of Roundtable on Sustainable Palm Oil (RSPO) and WWF's Global Forest and Trade Network (GFTN); Inclusive workplace: 'Dignity at Work' diversity policy (2012), Women in IT programme, employment schemes, Big Tick award from Business in the Community for 'Inspiring Young Talent" (2014)

Rationale: corporate sustainability as a business model

integration of environmental, social and governance (ESG) issues into investment decisions.

Boots' international mergers and private equity buy-out certainly led to some criticisms of its claims to responsible and sustainable business, notably regarding the Head Office move to Switzerland reducing Boots' UK corporate tax payments (Chakrabortty, 2013). Nevertheless, it continues to focus on the community and workplace issues, and has expanded its attention to environmental matters. Box 2.5 indicates that corporate governance mechanisms further institutionalise sustainability as a feature of a successful business.

Tata's sustainability reputation has also been tarnished through internationalisation, particularly from downsizing its UK steel industry business (Ruddick and Stewart, 2016). Nevertheless, its sustainability approach retains a focus on the community, workplace, marketplace and environment, complemented by its commitment to a long-term sustainable business model (Box 2.6).

SNAPSHOTS | BOX 2.6 Tata: corporate sustainability and internationalisation

Motto: 'The Tata group believes that the role of business is not just about giving back to society from its profits but also about ensuring that the processes it employs to earn these profits are ethical, socially responsible and environmentally sound.' (Tata, *Tata Releases Report on Contribution to Sustainable Development Goals*, website)

Issues: stakeholder orientation in community, environment, sustainable marketplace and workplace

Modes: Volunteering and engaging the community: for example, 'Tata Engage' (2014); Training: 'Tata Strive' (2014); Disaster management: for example, 'Disaster Response Framework' (2014); Environment: for example, Climate Change Policy (2009), Tata Sustainable Group (2014), Water Footprint Assessment (2012), ReSOLVE framework within India Business Biodiversity Initiative (IBBI); Sustainable marketplace: for example, Tata Sustainability Policy, Tata Group Sustainability Council (TGSC), Safety & Health Policy, adoption of Global Reporting Initiative (GRI), UN Global Compact (UNGC) and Carbon Disclosure Project (CDP) reporting frameworks; Workplace: Equal Opportunity Statement, Diversity & Inclusion Programme.

Rationale: corporate sustainability as a business model

2.5 Wider Reflections

Although we have referred to instances of corporate irresponsibility and unsustainability, these themes have been *sotto voce*. This is not because we do not recognise the negative and/or the way face-value corporate sustainability can mask unsustainability (e.g., Marens, 2012). Indeed, we note that despite centuries of corporate responsibility and sustainability, the planet is hardly in a more sustainable condition than, say, at the outset of industrialisation, and that corporations have been pivotal in this story of depletion of resources for human well-being. Rather, our focus is on different historical actors' practices for, ostensibly, more positive developments in order to understand the 'provenance of corporate (sustainability) thought and practice' (Phillips et al., 2020: 205) which we have traced through changing corporate sustainability issues, modes and rationales; the changing roles of actors; and in different historical contexts and institutional settings. This 'past-of-CSR (/sustainability)' approach has been distinguished from two other historical approaches by Phillips, Schrempf-Stirling and Stutz (2020), and to these we briefly turn to encourage further reflection.

Phillips, Schrempf-Stirling and Stutz (2020) also distinguished the 'Past-in-CSR' and the 'Past-as-CSR' approaches which we adopt for corporate sustainability. We can reflect on the 'Past-*in*-Corporate Sustainability' by seeing how reference to history enables us to problematise and rethink conceptualisations of corporate sustainability that are bound in the present and not therefore as generalisable as we might imagine. Rather, they often reflect contemporary institutional structures, power resources and circumstances. We can also reflect on the 'Past-*as*-Corporate Sustainability' as we consider how companies address the implications of their past for their approaches to sustainability. While a company's past is often regarded as an asset (e.g., by virtue of longevity), various cases have come to light of corporations' predecessors' involvement in historic slavery, the holocaust and other atrocities which have achieved judicial, legislative and social media status. Whether reflecting ethical sincerity or reputational strategy, some companies have offered apologies to affected people, publicly condemned the behaviour of their forefathers, paid compensation to survivors and contributed to the costs of memorials (Schrempf-Stirling et al., 2020; Federman, 2022). This theme now also extends to environmental issues, with the Danish window company VELUX's (2020) commitment to capture its historic carbon footprint in forest conservation projects run by its partner, the World Wide Fund for Nature.

Reflecting on historic corporate sustainability can involve not only attention to our 'past-of-corporate sustainability' perspectives, but also to the insights it brings to understanding contemporary assumptions about corporate sustainability, and to the challenges to and responses of corporations in addressing issues arising from their own histories.

2.6   Chapter Summary

Our corporate sustainability history presented the issues companies have addressed, the modes they have deployed and the rationales they have offered for corporate sustainability. It has focused on how different society – business – government – environment relationships have underpinned the dynamics of corporate sustainability, illustrated in three key historical stages: industrialisation; the modern corporation; and internationalisation, with special reference to the cases of Boots and Tata.

It is hard to identify a dominant corporate sustainability trajectory. There have been patterns of *continuity*, as in the case of the prominence of corporate responsibility for proximate communities, interrupted in Europe by the post-war welfare state. European MNCs have also taken on community concerns abroad as they have acquired international value chains reaching developing countries. There is also evidence of *development* illustrated by the shift from prioritisation of community to the sustainability of the products and processes entailed in business. Moreover, while the environment had been an historic focus, it is now axiomatic in corporate sustainability agendas. There has been development in corporate sustainability from being focused on corporate value chains to collective societal well-being and corporate roles in related societal governance. Second, there has been *development* in the *modes* of corporate sustainability from business leader-based philanthropy and paternalism, to company-level foundations and codes (first evident in the nineteenth century, but multiplying subsequently), and then to the adoption of collective business and multi-stakeholder partnerships and standards (Rasche et al., 2013). Third, there have been corporate sustainability *recursions* whereby once extant themes get forgotten and then reinvented. This is probably most evident in the corporate sustainability rationalisations (Table 2.1), illustrated by Porter and Kramer's concept of Creating Shared Value reflecting Robert Owen's explanation of how social and economic value can be added simultaneously. Contemporary CEO activism is also reminiscent of late industrial business leadership roles.

These continuities, developments and recursions also reflect very different contexts of corporate sustainability with their own dynamic society – business – government – environment relationships. However, some concluding remarks can be made. First, internationalisation notwithstanding, national contexts retain abiding significance (Matten and Moon, 2008), including for how corporations deal with sustainability agendas abroad (Leitheiser, 2021). Second, corporate sustainability increasingly reflects collaboration with other businesses, society and government, and these alliances, partnerships and MSIs are increasingly international.

CHAPTER QUESTIONS

1. What corporate sustainability issues, modes and rationales seem prevalent in your country? Have these changed recently? Do they vary by sector?
2. What are the corporate sustainability relationships between society, business, government and the environment in your country? Have these changed recently? To what extent do you think these relationships will change in the future?
3. What issues, modes and rationales characterised the Boots and Tata approaches to corporate sustainability over the three periods? What are the differences and/ or similarities? What explains these patterns?
4. As you read each chapter in the book, can you identify the nature of the key corporate sustainability issues, modes and rationales?

5. As you read each chapter in the book, can you identify the key corporate sustainability relationships between society, business, government and the environment?

6. Can you identify other corporations that could/should/have accepted their historic responsibility for unsustainable practices? How do they deal with those darker aspects of their corporate histories?

> **Case Study:** *Marks and Spencer's Corporate Sustainability – From Community to Global Responsibility*
> Available from Cambridge University Press at http://www.cambridge.org/rasche2

FURTHER RESOURCES

- Attenborough, D. *A Life on Our Planet,* https://attenboroughfilm.com/

  This provides a summary account of the problems raised by the Anthropocene by a leading broadcaster on nature and the environment – and a call to action.

- Baars, G. and Spicer, A. (Eds.). (2021). *The Corporation: A Critical, Multi-Disciplinary Handbook.* Cambridge: Cambridge University Press.

  A variety of critical perspectives.

- Enron – The Smartest Guys in The Room, www.youtube.com/watch?v=rDyMz1V-GSg

  Documentary about the rise and fall of Enron, the quintessentially irresponsible company, and its criminal leadership. It became a reference point in debates about the need for ethical renewal in American business.

- Kourula, A., Moon, J., Salles-Djelic, M.-L., and Wickert, C. (2019). New Roles of Governments in the Governance of Business Conduct: Implications for Management and Organizational Research. *Organization Studies*, 40(8), 1101–1123.

  This article focuses on the changing role of government in regulating business.

- Husted, B. W. (2015). Corporate Social Responsibility Practice from 1800–1914: Past Initiatives and Current Debates. *Business Ethics Quarterly*, 25(1), 125–141.

  This article presents a comparative history of CSR in the nineteenth century, exploring its relevance for contemporary CSR.

- Moon, J. (2014). *Corporate Social Responsibility: A Very Short Introduction.* Oxford: Oxford University Press.

This short introduction introduces one of the core elements of corporate sustainability, corporate social responsibility.

- *The Corporation* (2003).

  A documentary based on Bakan (2004), and includes interviews with some of CSR's leading advocates (e.g., Ray Anderson, founder of Interface) and long-standing critics (e.g., Milton Friedman, Noam Chomsky). Edited versions of this rather long documentary are available.

- Phillips, R., Schrempf-Stirling, J. and Stutz, C. (2020). The Past, History and Corporate Social Responsibility. *Journal of Business Ethics*, 166(2), 203–213.

  A typology of approaches to the 'past' of corporate social responsibility.

3 Ethical Approaches to Corporate Sustainability

ANDREAS RASCHE

LEARNING OBJECTIVES

- Reflect on different ethical theories and their limitations.
- Discuss how ethical decisions are made and what influences them.
- Learn why ethics is needed in the context of corporate sustainability.
- Explore why firms have a capacity for ethical reflection beyond their individual members.
- Study how business ethics can be managed in a firm.

3.1 Introduction

Consider the following hypothetical example that was first discussed by Thomson (1985). Imagine you are the driver of a trolley car. As your trolley moves down a hill and you leave a bend behind, you suddenly see five workers at the end of the track. Of course, you try to stop the trolley, but you realise that the breaks do not work. You also realise that the workers do not have enough time to get off the track and hence you know that if you hit the five workers all of them will die. Suddenly, you realise that there is a side-track on the right-hand side. However, at the end of this track you also see one worker. Again, the worker does not have enough time to get off the track quickly and hence you can assume that s(he) will die if you hit her/him. Your steering wheel in the trolley car still works. Is it morally justified for you to turn the trolley car?

Most of you will be inclined to turn the trolley to the side-track. After all, you sacrifice one life and this enables you to save five other lives. Now, consider an adjusted version of the trolley car example that was discussed by Michael Sandel (2010). This time you do not drive the trolley, but you are standing on a bridge and you look at the track. You see the trolley coming down the track. Again, there are five workers at the end of the track. You see the trolley driver wildly waving and you realise that the breaks do not work. The trolley car is about to crash into the five workers at the end of the track. You feel rather helpless until you realise that next to you on the bridge there is a very heavy man. You consider pushing the man onto the track so that he blocks the trolley. Of course, the man would die, but the five workers at the end of the track would be saved. Would you push the man from the bridge onto the track?

Most of us would *not* push the heavy man. Pushing a heavy man off a bridge somehow seems not the right thing to do, even if it saves the lives of five others. Why, then, does the moral principle – sacrifice one life so that five other lives can be saved – seem correct in the first example, but incorrect in the second one? Ethics can be puzzling and business ethics even more so.

We will return to the trolley car example later while discussing normative ethical theories. For the moment, let us understand the term business ethics as 'the study of business situations, activities, and decisions where issues of right and wrong are addressed' (Crane et al., 2019: 5). Ethical questions and dilemmas are an integral part of discussing corporate sustainability; however, they are rarely explicitly noticed. For instance, we usually assume that firms have strategic reasons to engage with corporate sustainability (e.g., because there is a business case; Chapter 5). However, what do firms do when such strategic reasons do not exist? Do we always need a business case to do the right thing?

The relevance of ethical reflection for corporate sustainability should therefore not be underestimated. Ethics is at the heart of discussions about how firms can become more sustainable and also why many businesses act in unsustainable ways. This chapter explores the relevance of ethics for discussions on corporate sustainability and responsibility. We start by discussing normative ethical theories, which outline different ways to think about what is right and wrong. Next, we investigate how individuals in firms make ethical decisions and what influences their decision-making. In the following section, we ask two essential questions: Why do we need ethics when discussing corporate sustainability? and Can corporations engage in ethical reflection or is this something that only individuals can do? The final section discusses how firms can manage ethics, and we distinguish two orientations that can guide such management: compliance and integrity.

3.2   Normative Ethics – 'What Is the Right Thing to Do?'

Ethics is a big word. Therefore, we must first reflect on its theoretical foundations before discussing implications for corporate sustainability. To start with, it is important to distinguish morality and ethics. Morality can be understood as a code that steers the conduct of people within a society (Gert and Gert, 2020). This code usually differs between societies and it consists of implicit norms and values. While the law can rest on morality and there is usually overlap between what is legal and what is ethical, they are not the same thing. The law consists of explicitly defined rules and there is an expectation that people comply with these rules. By contrast, morality acts more as a guide to conduct. Ethics, then, is 'concerned with the study of morality and the application of reason to elucidate specific rules and principles that determine morally acceptable courses of action' (Crane et al., 2019: 8). In other words, ethics is a way to reflect on morality and to justify relevant norms and values.

If ethics is a way to reflect on morality, we need to ask which 'tools' exist to guide this reflection. This is where normative ethical theories enter the picture. Such theories reflect the 'rules and principles' that Crane et al. (2019: 8) talked about in the text quoted above. Normative ethical theories search for these rules and principles that guide ethical reflection and thereby enable people to determine what is morally permissible.

The question 'What is the right thing to do?' has been answered in different ways. We start by introducing three of the most widely used normative ethical theories (Sandel, 2010): (1) utilitarianism (based on the idea of maximising welfare); (2) Kantian ethics (based on the idea that individual freedom needs to be respected); and (3) virtue ethics (based on the idea that moral character must be promoted). As these theories assume that we as humans are the centre of moral decisions, we also introduce a posthuman ethical theory that aims to balance human and non-human needs. Table 3.1 provides a summary. Our goal is not to identify the best theory

Table 3.1 Three main normative ethical theories

	Utilitarian Ethics	Duty-based Ethics	Virtue Ethics	Posthuman Ethics
Leading Contributor(s)	Jeremy Bentham; John Stuart Mill	Immanuel Kant	Aristotle, Plato	Arne Næss, Bill Devall, George Sessions
Foundation of Morality	The greatest happiness of the greatest number	Acting autonomously in accordance with categorical imperative	Moral action results from 'good' people who are equipped with virtues	The well-being of all organisms (human and non-human) is of intrinsic value
Image of Man	Driven by instrumental reason; desire to maximise collective welfare	Driven by practical reason; desire to act according to self-imposed principles	Driven by desire to develop intellectual and moral virtues	Driven by acknowledging man's dependence on other species
Focus	Outcomes of actions (consequences)	Motivation for actions (duties)	Character of the decision-maker (virtues)	All organisms are part of one biospherical net

(as there is no such thing). Rather, we aim to outline different alternatives for ethical reasoning in the context of corporate sustainability.

3.2.1   Utilitarianism – Maximising Welfare

Theories that base ethical reflection on welfare start from the assumption that the latter needs to be maximised. The most influential ethical theory dealing with collective welfare is called utilitarianism and it was developed by the English moral philosopher Jeremy Bentham (1748–1832). Utilitarianism's basic principle rests on a simple idea: morality occurs if we seek the greatest happiness for the greatest number. In other words, the right thing to do depends on maximising utility, where utility is defined as achieving happiness (pleasure) and avoiding pain. According to Sandel (2010: 34), Bentham believed that 'we are all governed by the feelings of pain and pleasure. They are our "sovereign masters". They govern us in everything we do and also determine what we ought to do.' Utilitarianism focuses on the consequences of human action. It is based on the assumption that good and bad outcomes are weighed against each other, and that morality is rationalised by trying to maximise collective utility. This type of thinking is reflected by economic reasoning and is therefore widespread within today's business world. Consider, for instance, the extensive use of cost-benefit analyses by corporations in the context of sustainability-related projects.

There are several objections to utilitarian thinking. One key critique is that it is almost impossible to measure happiness on a single scale. Consider the following example. In 2006, Google came under pressure to censor the Chinese version of its search engine. The Chinese government asked Google to block content that it found objectionable. Google defended itself, arguing that even a censored version of its search engine would help to provide the greatest access to information to the greatest number of people (Waddock and Rasche, 2012). Different moral goods are at stake in this case – for instance, freedom of speech, security and access to information. It is difficult to measure the value of these goods on a *single* and common scale for *different* stakeholders. Even if the construction of such a scale was possible, there is still the question of whether the resulting utility value for different stakeholder groups should be weighed equally. This brings us to another objection.

Utilitarianism focuses on *collective* welfare. One key attraction of utilitarian thinking is that it treats all parties as equal when calculating utility. However, this non-judgmental nature of the theory does not always reflect real-life circumstances, where the utility of single stakeholder groups may deserve special recognition (e.g., vulnerable groups like children). Hence, utilitarian thinking does not respect individual rights very well. In extreme cases, utilitarian thinking could even be used to justify torture or murder. Dick Cheney, former US Vice President, defended the use of 'enhanced interrogation techniques' by the CIA on the ground of it providing valuable information in the fight against terrorism (Jackson, 2014). Of course, we should not conclude from this that utilitarian thinkers necessarily favour torture. Rather, it shows that utilitarian thinking, if consistently applied, focuses on collective welfare and therefore considers the preferences of individuals only insofar as they are calculated together with the preferences of all other stakeholders.

3.2.2   Duty-Based Ethics – Respecting Freedom

If we assume that ethics does not rest on collective welfare, we need another basis for judging right and wrong. Connecting ethics to our individual freedom implies focusing on people's capacity to think and reason autonomously. This approach to ethics was shaped significantly by the philosophy of Immanuel Kant (1724–1804). Kant focuses on human beings' capacity to reason, which sets us apart from other species. It is this capacity to reason that acts as the foundation for his ideas about ethical reflection. Freedom, for Kant, does not imply freedom of choice (e.g., when choosing between different alternatives). Freedom in a Kantian sense implies that we as rational beings can act in autonomous ways according to self-chosen laws (imperatives). 'To act freely is not to choose the best means to a given end; it is to choose the end itself, for its own sake' (Sandel, 2010: 109).

Of course, utilitarianism also focused on humans applying some sort of reason. However, the application of reason was focused on being instrumental (maximising utility). Kant emphasises a different kind of reason. His philosophy highlights that it is reason that makes us independent and therefore allows us to give ourselves laws. According to Kant, the law that governs morality is called the categorical imperative. Categorical, here, implies that this law is unconditional and therefore applies irrespective of the circumstances that a human being may be in. Within Kant's philosophy, there are different formulations of the categorical imperative. Two imperatives, however, are known widely and we therefore revisit them in more detail.

1. Universalise your maxim: The most famous formulation of the categorical imperative reads as follows: 'Act only on that maxim whereby you can at the same time will that it should become a universal law' (Kant, 1785/1964: 421). Kant uses the term 'maxim' to refer to the need for rational human beings to create principles that rationalise an action. This first version of the categorical imperative stresses that (a) moral actions should be based on maxims that can be universalised (i.e., that everybody else could follow if acting in a rational way) and (b) such universalisation cannot create any contradiction. Consider the example of firms breaking promises about their sustainability goals. Kant would ask us to construct a maxim first: 'It is morally permissible to break sustainability promises.' We would then need to check whether this maxim can become a universal law without ending up in a contradiction. If all firms can legitimately

break sustainability promises, such promises would be worth nothing. Hence, it would not make sense to give such promises in the first place (Bowie, 1998a). In other words, the universalised maxim becomes self-defeating and hence is morally prohibited.

2. Treat persons as ends: Kant's second formulation of the categorical imperative asks us to value humans as ends in themselves. The important aspect here is that Kant does not suggest considering preferences or interests (as these would always be relative to the person being observed). Rather, he highlights that humans have an intrinsic value and that we should respect this inherent dignity of human life (Sandel, 2010). Kant writes: 'Act in such a way that you always treat humanity, whether in your own person or in the person of any other, never simply as a means, but always at the same time as an end' (Kant, 1785/1964: 429). Consider the example of firms providing misleading information on the sustainability attributes of their products (i.e., 'greenwashing'). In this case, firms manipulate us as consumers and hence they use us as a means only (e.g., to enhance their profitability). Greenwashing therefore would not acknowledge that consumers have an intrinsic value as humans and are therefore worthy of respect.

For Kant, actions are only free if they are carried out in accordance with the categorical imperative. Of course, humans may also base their actions on other motivations – for instance, guided by interests that are determined by other people. In such a case, Kant would argue that one's will is not really free, because it is influenced by other forces.

Kantian ethics faces several objections. Crane et al. (2019: 103) have argued that Kant's assumption of rational actors, who act based on self-imposed laws, 'seems more of an ideal than a reality with regard to fast-paced contemporary lifestyles'. After all, Kant assumes that we do not reason based on our own interests, desires or preferences, as these are not moral principles. This makes moral action very demanding. One may also wonder how moral duty (to obey the categorical imperative) and the assumed individual freedom go hand in hand. They only work together in a special case: when we are the author of the law (Sandel, 2010: 125). Human dignity does not imply that we subordinate ourselves to the categorical imperative without reflection. It implies that we as rational beings are the author of this law and that we follow it precisely because of this reason.

We can now return to the trolley problem outlined at the start of this chapter. As you will have probably noticed, the problem shows a tension between utilitarian thinking and Kantian ethics. In the first version of the problem most people lean towards a utilitarian solution (i.e., turn the trolley car so that you kill one to save five), while in the second case most of us prefer a Kantian solution (i.e., not pushing the heavy man, as this makes him a means to an end). By judging these two cases we usually draw on our *moral intuition*. While conscious moral reasoning involves deliberate application of certain moral principles, moral intuition happens spontaneously and works without conscious awareness of such principles. Prior research shows that our moral intuition is designed in a way that we distrust those who ostensibly use others as a means to an end (Everett et al., 2016). We are therefore more hesitant to push the heavy man. Our moral intuition also tells us that if we cause harm through physical contact with a victim (as in the second case), this is usually perceived worse than harm involving no physical contact (Cushman et al., 2006).

3.2.3   Virtue Ethics – Promoting Moral Character

One critique that is often raised against utilitarian thinking as well as Kantian ethics is that both theories rely on abstract principles and hence remain rather impersonal. Virtue ethics, by contrast, does not depart from abstract principles, but rather emphasises the virtues of those who make decisions. A virtue can be understood as 'an excellent trait of character' (Hursthouse and Pettigrove, 2016). Virtue ethics, therefore, puts the moral character of a person into the centre of analysis and does not focus on the motivation for or consequences of moral action. Moral actions result from persons that are equipped with certain character traits (i.e., virtues). The roots of virtue ethics date back to ancient Greek philosophy, in particular the philosophy of Aristotle and Plato. What these thinkers have in common is that they do not link ethical reflection to the question 'What should I do?' (as Bentham and Kant did), but rather to 'What kind of person should I be?'.

Virtues are more than an ad hoc attitude that we may have. They are deeply embedded into the person possessing the virtues. Virtues define us and they are acquired through a lengthy process of learning and practice. For instance, a person who has developed courage as a virtue would always show courageous behaviour. Aristotle (2000), in particular, highlighted that virtues can be enhanced, developed and trained through practising self-discipline. Of course, this also implies that a lack of self-discipline can degrade the moral character of a person.

There is no definite and universally agreed-upon list of virtues. A good point of departure is provided by Aristotle (2000), who distinguished between intellectual virtues and moral virtues. Intellectual virtues relate to the part of us that engages in reasoning. These virtues refer to our mind and Aristotle emphasised practical wisdom (phronesis) as the highest intellectual virtue. Phronesis highlights the importance of considering the principles that guide our action in the light of context. It is about prudent behaviour and our ability to apply ethical knowledge to the context we are in. Such practical wisdom is needed to fully practise moral virtues. Moral virtues provide us only with ideas about which ends to value, while practical wisdom teaches us how to pursue these ends. There is no conclusive list of moral virtues, but we can exemplarily think of character traits such as courage, loyalty, honesty, patience and, most of all, justice. According to virtue ethics, a person who has developed these virtues will naturally act in ways that can be considered ethically justified. Crane et al. (2019) emphasise that balance is important when it comes to these virtues. Having more is not necessarily better. For instance, having too little courage can be a problem, but having too much of it can be equally problematic.

Virtue ethics is more holistic than utilitarian or Kantian ethics. It does not just focus on single, isolated acts of ethical behaviour, but also on the fully virtuous person that develops its moral character. Consider a manager who plans to give to charity (Koehn, 1995). Virtue ethics brings the moral character of the decision-maker into the analysis. What are her/his desires and options in this case? Is s(he) maybe only giving to charity to attend a fancy gala event? Kantian analysis would ask the decision-maker to do what the categorical imperative 'dictates', irrespective of whether that person would want to perform that act. Virtue ethics, on the other hand, would focus on asking whether the decision-maker is habituated to desire what is just and good for the community.

3.2.4 Posthuman Ethics – Serving All Organisms

So far, we have discussed three ethical theories that share one common characteristic: they all assume that we as humans are at the centre of moral decisions. Yet, when reflecting on nature and ecological systems, such an approach can be misleading. For instance, some have argued that traditional ethical theories tend to view nature as something to be preserved for the sake of humans (Aretoulakis, 2014). Applying traditional ethical theories towards sustainability problems can therefore lead to a human-centric view on ethics; a view that assumes that the human mind is superior to non-human organisms (Merchant, 1992).

While there are several posthuman ethical theories (e.g., focusing on the ethics of robotics), theories concerned with ecological posthumanism are the most relevant in the context of sustainability. One well-known theory within ecological posthumanism is 'deep ecology' (Devall and Sessions, 1985). Deep ecology thinkers challenge the belief that humans and nature are separate entities and that humans are 'in charge of' nature. The ethical view that emerges is centred around the needs of all organisms rather than the specific needs of humans. Human and non-human organisms are all thought to be elements of a larger biospherical net (Schuler et al., 2017). If humans start to understand that they are embedded in and dependent upon this net of relations among organisms, they must agree that all species are inherently valuable and hence have rights that need to be respected. In such a view, no species deserves to receive special attention or recognition, as all species must be valued intrinsically independent of their usefulness to others. One key principle of deep ecology thinkers is therefore that humans have no right to reduce natural diversity in any way (except for those situations where vital human needs must be addressed; Devall and Sessions, 1985: 70).

Deep ecology differs significantly from other ethical theories in terms of how it assesses sustainability-related problems. For instance, while utilitarian thinking usually emphasises the need to conserve nature out of human self-interest (e.g., conserving resources for later use by humans), deep ecology thinking stresses that all living things are equal and that nature has to be preserved because the natural world has an intrinsic value. The deep ecology version of posthuman ethics is very demanding, and some have argued that it promotes a utopian vision that cannot be implemented in practice (Anker and Witoszek, 1998). On the other hand, deep ecologists are convinced that their ethics reaches beyond shallow environmental protection and asks humans to live in a way 'as if nature mattered' (Devall and Sessions, 1985: 1).

3.3   Making Ethical Decisions

If we want to understand the link between ethics and corporate sustainability, it is not just important to ask 'What is the right thing to do?' as normative ethical theories do. It is equally important to look at *how* we make ethical decisions. After all, we see more than enough unethical behaviour around us, so we cannot assume that humans simply follow normative guidelines in everyday business situations. What influences whether, how and why we make ethical decisions? This question is answered by so-called descriptive ethical theories. We can distinguish between individual and situational factors that influence ethical decision-making (Treviño, 1986). While individual factors focus on the characteristics of the decision-maker (e.g., shaped by socialisation processes), situational factors consider the context in which we make ethical decisions (e.g., in terms of location and time).

3.3.1   Individual Factors

One factor which shapes how we make ethical decisions is our own cognitive moral development. Kohlberg (1973) outlined three main levels of humans' moral development. These levels refer to our cognitive development, because they relate to the process of thinking and reasoning that occurs once we need to decide whether a behaviour is right or wrong. The emphasis is therefore on how we react to moral dilemma situations and what kind of reasoning we use to justify something as a moral deed.

1. Pre-conventional Level: At this level, our moral judgment is mostly externally controlled and exclusively concerned with our own self – for instance, when individuals obey certain pre-given rules to avoid punishment or to receive rewards. Morally right action is considered to consist of deeds that primarily satisfy our own needs.

2. Conventional Level: Conventional reasoning implies that our judgment is still influenced by social rules around us – however, with less emphasis on self-interest and more importance given to our social relationships. Individuals may still comply with externally imposed rules, but they do so primarily to gain others' approval and support. Reasoning at this stage therefore judges morality based on what social expectations are put upon us (e.g., by society or organisations).

3. Post-conventional Level: The individual moves beyond socially imposed rules at this level. Morally right action is based on abstract and self-chosen principles that apply to everybody. Post-conventional reasoning therefore implies that humans can universalise the underlying principles so that they consider how others could be affected by their actions (which comes close to Kantian reasoning).

Kohlberg assumed a linear progression through the levels. Someone who progresses to the post-conventional level cannot skip the conventional level. Individuals will move to the next level only if they find their reasoning regarding a moral dilemma situation at the current level to be not satisfactory. According to Kohlberg, most individuals will not move beyond the conventional stage of moral development. Only 10 per cent of individuals (aged 16 or older) progress to the post-conventional level (Baxter and Rarick, 1987).

Another factor that shapes individuals' ethical decision-making is their moral awareness. If people do not perceive a certain situation to have ethical content, they will also not engage in ethical decision-making. Moral awareness is shaped by several factors such as gender, prior ethical experience and people's value orientations (Tenbrunsel and Smith-Crowe, 2008). Awareness is different from importance. It is about whether we are capable of recognising moral issues *at all*. Some people may be unable to identify a moral issue as such and hence are 'ethically blind'. Ethical blindness is a common phenomenon and refers to the 'temporary inability of a decision-maker to see the ethical dimension of a decision at stake' (Palazzo et al., 2012: 325). Such blindness is described as temporary because it is context-bound. We may fail to recognise the ethical dimension of a situation when acting in our professional lives, but we may be perfectly aware of it when acting in our private lives.

The lack of moral awareness by some people already shows that ethical decision-making has many dimensions. Table 3.2 gives an overview of possible decision scenarios based on (1) whether an actor is aware of the ethical dimension of a decision situation and (2) whether the decision outcome is ethical or not. The two scenarios resulting in unethical behaviour deserve special attention, as they help to explain misconduct in and by corporations. *Intended* unethical behaviour implies the deliberate breaking of rules and neglect of compliance systems. Often, such

Table 3.2 Possible decision scenarios in ethical decision-making

Level of Awareness Decision Outcome	Moral Awareness	Lack of Moral Awareness
Ethical	Intended ethical action	Unintended ethical action
Unethical	Intended unethical action	Unintended unethical action

Source: Adapted and modified from Tenbrunsel and Smith-Crowe (2008: 554).

behaviour is based on decision biases. For instance, managers can face social pressure to conform with the beliefs of a peer group in which they are embedded ('groupthink' bias). If the peer group holds strong beliefs about non-compliance, it is likely that such a bias can cause intended unethical action because the individual manager can rationalise misconduct much easier. For instance, the Salmon Brothers treasury auction scandal in the 1990s was attributed to widespread groupthink in the company. Sims (1992: 657) argued that there was an unrealistic belief held by some groups in the organisation 'that everything boils down to a monetary game'.

One problem leading to *unintended* unethical behaviour is information overload. Most people are exposed to enormous amounts of information in their daily lives and at work. We receive countless emails, phone calls and memos each day. Some people struggle with processing all of this and therefore make decisions based on incomplete or even false information. One consequence is that we often use decision heuristics when evaluating moral dilemma situations – that is, rules of thumb that only roughly guide our actions because they do not fit the decision situation very well. Consider these two examples: (1) to reduce complexity we often over-rely on one piece of information only (e.g., the latest sales report); and (2) we often blindly trust the expertise of authority figures (e.g., senior management). Using such heuristics creates decision biases and can lead to a situation where we fail to adequately consider different angles of a decision context. Taken seriously, a focus on such heuristics helps to understand why even 'good' people (people with moral intentions) can make 'bad' (unethical) decisions.

3.3.2 Situational Factors

Just focusing on individual factors cannot fully explain why we act in (un)ethical ways. After all, our decisions are embedded into specific contexts, and the nature of these contexts can influence how we address ethical problems and whether we recognise them at all. Although the list of possible situational influences is long (Crane et al., 2019), we highlight three factors in particular.

First, *corporate culture* can impact how and whether we make ethical decisions. A corporation's culture can be understood as 'a set of norms and values that are widely shared and strongly held throughout the organization' (O'Reilly and Chatman, 1996: 166). Corporate culture is critical when discussing ethics, because it highlights the role of values (Which things matter to the organisation?) and norms (What kind of behaviour is consistent with these values?). For instance, many firms have 'integrity' as one of their core values. A norm that is consistent with this value would be to speak up when we see ethical misconduct. An organisation's norms and values influence how we make ethical decisions. For instance, the norm to not voice any moral concerns during meetings impacts whether ethically challenging situations are discussed at all. As a result, corporate culture can support moral muteness.

Such muteness appears if people fail 'to voice moral concern regarding issues about which they possess moral convictions' (Bird, 2015: 1). Consider the example of Volkswagen's (VW) manipulation of diesel emissions. In September 2015, VW admitted that it had installed illegal manipulation devices to make some of its diesel cars seem cleaner than they were. Some observers argued that VW's polluted corporate culture prevented the scandal from being discovered earlier. Former employees described the culture as consisting of a 'climate of fear, an authoritarianism that went unchecked' (Cremer and Bergin, 2015). This culture also played a role when a VW senior executive disregarded a warning by an engineer over possibly illegal practices in 2011.

Another important situational factor that influences ethical decision-making relates to *reward and incentive schemes*. On the one hand, rewards are an important change agent that managers can use to incentivise ethical behaviour. For instance, stock options are often used to incentivise managers to take forward-looking actions that benefit the company in the long run. A focus on long-term value creation is particularly important in the context of corporate sustainability, where firms are often asked to address problems that may result in short-term costs, but create benefits in the future. On the other hand, poorly designed reward systems can also invite and enable unethical employee behaviour. For instance, in some professions employees are judged based on the number of 'billable hours' they record (e.g., lawyers and consultants). When work is scarce, employees can feel pressure to bill more hours than they worked for a particular client (Parker and Ruschena, 2012).

Finally, *national culture* also shapes ethical decision-making. Countries differ with regard to the norms and values they consider to reflect legitimised behaviour. What is considered right and wrong therefore also depends on the societal context in which a person operates. Take the example of climate change, which is perceived differently by people around the world. While 83 per cent of French people see it as a major threat, only 38 per cent of Israelis agree that a changing climate is a cause of concern (Fagan and Huang, 2019). Such differences in attitudes are influenced by societal norms and broader national institutions (e.g., the role of politics). Differences in attitudes towards climate change depend, for instance, on whether people trust government information on pollution (Tjernström and Tietenberg, 2008). Such differences can explain whether and when sustainability problems are framed as morally charged issues that should be addressed.

3.4   Ethics and Corporate Sustainability

So far, we have explored normative ethical theories and concepts related to ethical decision-making. We now want to discuss how ethics relates to corporate sustainability. As indicated at the beginning of this chapter, 'business ethics' deals with questions of right and wrong in the context of business situations. Inevitably, such questions arise when reflecting on the what, why and how of corporate sustainability. We will first discuss why ethics is needed in the context of corporate sustainability (necessity of ethical reflection) and then examine whether firms as collective actors are actually capable of acting in ethical ways (possibility of ethical reflection).

3.4.1   Necessity of Ethical Reflection for Corporate Sustainability

The 'Moral Case' for Corporate Sustainability. Why do we need ethics when reflecting on corporate sustainability? The most straightforward answer to this question is: because there is also a 'moral case' for sustainable and responsible corporate behaviour. The 'business case' for corporate sustainability (see Chapter 5) tells us that firms should engage in social and environmental activities because it makes good business sense. Corporate sustainability becomes a win-win situation. However, what do we do when there is no business case for corporate sustainability? Do we simply disregard sustainable action whenever it does not pay? The moral case for corporate sustainability is more comprehensive and emphasises that we should not always need to have a business case to do the right thing. As Taylor (2017) writes: 'the problem is that our obsession with making the business case ... makes us sound apologetic and hollow. After all, there is also a business case for tax avoidance, deregulation, and even higher death rates. We do ourselves – and the world – no favours by locking ourselves into this instrumentalist argument.'

Of course, ethical arguments in favour of sustainability efforts are more difficult to defend within a firm – for instance, when such efforts are presented to sceptical senior executives. Consider the example of living wages. Many global brand name firms have come under pressure to pay workers in their global supply chains not just a legal minimum wage, but a living wage. In many countries, minimum wages are not high enough for workers to make a living. However, paying living wages, which are often twice as high as minimum wages, reduces profit margins. It is therefore difficult to make the business case for paying living wages, at least as long as we focus on short-term corporate behaviour. However, there is a strong moral case for it. Advocates of Kantian ethics, for instance, would argue that denying workers a living wage is to not respect their humanity and to use them as a means to an end only (Bowie, 1998b).

Although we hear moral arguments less often than the well-known strategic considerations for corporate sustainability, we should not conclude from this that the moral case is irrelevant. Making the moral case for corporate sustainability efforts is more widespread among small and medium-sized enterprises (SMEs). Often, SMEs do not separate ownership and management (see Chapter 8). The owners of the firm are also managing it (e.g., in family businesses). In such situations, personal values and moral convictions often act as the driving force behind corporate sustainability engagement, especially because SMEs have much closer and more informal ties to their stakeholders (e.g., local communities). Research shows that such moral motives induce stronger and more lasting involvement in corporate sustainability efforts than strategic considerations that are purely based on a business case logic (Graafland and van de Ven, 2014).

Ethics as Complementing Regulation. Ideally, irresponsible and unsustainable corporate behaviour is supposed to be stopped by the law. And yet we see a lot of such behaviour around us despite the existence of legal regulation. Bribery, for instance, is formally forbidden by law in almost all countries. Bribery therefore mostly occurs because people intentionally break the law. In some cases, however, it is a matter of interpretation whether the law covers an ethical challenge. For instance, the US Foreign Corrupt Practices Act (FCPA) forbids bribery, but also contains an exception clause for so-called facilitation payments. Such payments are sometimes offered by firms to speed up the action of foreign government officials (e.g., when trying to process goods through customs). However, this 'exception can be open to interpretation' (Longstreth, 2012) and it is usually the prosecutors who need to decide whether or not an alleged wrongdoing is covered by the exception.

Ethics is needed because no law can account for all possible courses of action. The letter of the law is usually insufficient to fully ensure sustainable and responsible business behaviour. As we all know, each law has loopholes and it is impossible to write a perfect law that could foresee *all* possible contexts of its own application. Ethical reflection is required because responsible and sustainable companies do not just rely on the letter of law. Firms must also acknowledge the spirit underlying the law, so that grey areas are 'filled' through moral judgments.

Some may argue at this point that we just need to work on improving legal means to reduce corporate misconduct. Of course, such improvements are always welcome and necessary, but they still do not reduce the need for ethical reflection. First, improved regulations usually occur *after* legal loopholes are uncovered. For instance, the 2007–08 financial crisis exposed several regulatory gaps related to the behaviour of financial institutions. It took time to close these gaps and improve financial regulations. Second, improving the enforcement of legal regulations usually creates significant costs. One of the reasons why regulators approved the FCPA exception clause (see above) was that it 'would not be practical' (Longstreth, 2012) to target such petty crimes due to the limited availability of resources for law enforcement.

Embedding ethics into corporate sustainability thinking is also necessary because societal expectations in terms of ethical behaviour can differ from companies' legal requirements. Corporate sustainability often deals with cases where the legal and ethical levels of responsibility are not well aligned with each other, especially when considering that legal and ethical requirements are often defined relative to the national context in which a firm operates. Consider the example of Yahoo. In 2005, the company helped Chinese authorities to identify a government dissident, Shi Tao, who sent emails using a Yahoo email account. The dissident was jailed after Yahoo helped to identify and locate the person. The company faced strong critique and boycott calls by human rights activists and journalists after this incident. Yahoo, however, argued that Chinese authorities requested the information through a warrant and that it was obliged to comply with the laws of countries in which it operates (Cheng, 2007). As the example shows, ethical and legal expectations can easily diverge.

3.4.2 Possibility of Ethical Reflection in the Context of Corporate Sustainability

So far, we have discussed why ethical reflection is needed when thinking about corporate sustainability. We now turn to the question: Can corporations be held morally responsible? The economist Milton Friedman once famously argued that '[o]nly people can have responsibilities' (Friedman, 2007: 173). The argument often goes that corporations cannot be morally culpable; only people within corporations can assume moral responsibility and make moral judgments. So, can we attribute moral responsibility to firms? Of course, corporations cannot make moral judgments like humans can, and firms also cannot experience guilt the same way because they do not directly have a capacity for emotion (Sepinwall, 2017). And yet there are still good reasons to argue that corporations can be held morally responsible.

First, corporations are often portrayed as collective actors in their own right. That is to say that they possess agency beyond the accumulation of individual members' agency. Bromley and Sharkey (2017), for instance, find that firms depict themselves increasingly as entities with agency and values. Corporations possess internal structures for making decisions and can therefore also act independent of their individual members (Crane et al., 2019). Firms also have rules that fix authority relationships. These rules specify when and under which conditions an individual action becomes 'official' and should be seen as an action of the organisation

(Goodpaster and Mathews, 1982). Corporations are therefore more than just 'legal fictions' and can show a certain degree of agency. Firms' codes of conduct, for instance, that define morally appropriate behaviour cannot usually be traced back to any particular individual. Rather, such codes are the outcome of internal decision-making processes that involve multiple organisational members within different parts of the organisation.

Second, firms also possess norms and values that reach beyond individual members and define what is considered right and wrong within the context of the organisation. These norms and values define a firm's culture and they set the normative context in which individuals make decisions (see above). Although this context can be shaped by individuals, it also exists regardless of them. If an individual leaves the company, the corporate culture does not change overnight.

Consider the following example. In 2001, US-based energy company Enron filed for bankruptcy after reports uncovered a systematic accounting fraud. At the time, Enron was the seventh largest corporation in the United States, with revenues of $101 billion and around 20,000 employees. Enron's toxic corporate culture was seen as a major cause of the scandal. The culture was characterised by aggressive targets and high levels of competitiveness among employees. Performance standards were continuously being raised and poorly performing employees were publicly punished (Sims and Brinkman, 2003). One important internal structure that shaped this culture was Enron's peer-review committee, which was better known as the 'rank-and-yank' (Fusaro and Miller, 2003) system inside the company. The committee gave formal performance reviews to employees every six months. In each review cycle, the two lowest performing employees were dismissed. Enron's culture was therefore primarily characterised by two motivational forces: fear and greed (Free and Macintosh, 2006). Former employees recalled that the rank-and-yank system created 'an environment where employees were afraid to express their opinions or to question unethical or potentially illegal business practices' (Fusaro and Miller, 2003: 52). Although the performance review system was created by senior management (and hence can be attributed to individual deeds), it affected basic norms and values that defined the normative context that employees faced when making decisions.

Reflecting on whether firms can assume moral responsibility is important to be clear about the reference point for discussing corporate sustainability. Who do we hold accountable in case corporate misconduct is uncovered – the firm as a collective actor, single employees or perhaps even both? In 2010, British Petroleum (BP) caused an oil spill in the Gulf of Mexico which turned out to be the greatest environmental disaster in the history of the United States. The oil spill was generated by a massive explosion on one of BP's offshore drilling rigs, the Deepwater Horizon. Investigations revealed that, technically speaking, the accident was due to minor errors of a few individuals. But does this assessment really tell us the whole story about what caused this disaster? The National Commission on the

BP Deepwater Horizon Oil Spill and Offshore Drilling (2011: ix), which was created to investigate the accident, found that 'the business culture succumbed to a false sense of security. The *Deepwater Horizon* disaster exhibits the costs of a culture of complacency.' This incident shows the need to view BP as a moral agent with a deficient corporate culture that contributed to the misconduct.

This is not to say that corporations simply possess the same level of moral agency as individuals do. However, it shows that we need to see the individual *and* the collective actor when analysing ethical decision-making in the context of corporate sustainability. Palazzo (2007: 113) claimed in this context: 'Organizational integrity goes beyond managerial integrity and is more than the presence of individuals with good characters within the organization. Having "good" managers is certainly a precondition for organizational integrity, but it does not prevent organizations from obtaining bad ethical results.'

3.5   Managing for Ethical Reflection in Corporations

What, then, can corporations do to manage ethical reflection? Of course, it would be naïve to believe that ethical reflection in corporations can simply be enforced. However, what can be done is to set the right framework conditions for ethical reflection to take place, so that employees' awareness of problems is increased and they are provided with tools to address these problems. There are two basic orientations that managers can follow when thinking about how to shape individuals' ethical behaviour: compliance and integrity (Paine, 1994). While the compliance orientation is about formal ethics management that uses explicit tools (e.g., codes of ethics) and primarily aims at preventing ethical misconduct, the integrity orientation is aimed at defining shared values that enable ethical conduct (see Table 3.3).

3.5.1   Compliance – Formal Ethics Programmes

Compliance programmes define explicit rules showing employees what the organisation regards as right and wrong. The aim of compliance is to educate workers about the rules of the game so that misconduct can be prevented and non-compliance punished. The overall purpose is 'standardizing employee behavior within the domains of ethics and legal compliance' (Weaver et al., 1999: 42). Because of their emphasis on conformity with predefined rules, compliance programmes are mostly reactive. They capture those ethical dilemma situations that are (1) known to the company and (2) codified in explicit policies. Paine (1994: 111) therefore suggests that compliance provides a kind of minimalist motivation that is based on a 'don't get caught' attitude.

Table 3.3 A compliance orientation to ethics management contrasted with an integrity orientation

	Compliance	Integrity
Objective	Prevent illegal and unethical conduct	Enable ethical reflection and create and raise moral awareness
Mechanism	Control employees' behaviour and sanction misconduct	Inspire ethical conduct and create shared values
Tools	Formal ethics programme – code of ethics, ethics training, auditing, ethics officers	Strong leadership and creation of an ethics-minded corporate culture
Main Advantage	Simple approach that is (relatively) easy to implement	Can inspire / can better cope with unknown ethical challenges
Main Disadvantage	Reactive – mostly deals with predefined dilemma situations	Slow to change and adapt – need to redefine 'lived' values

Source: Adapted and modified from Paine (1994: 113).

Compliance programmes have a strong legal orientation. They translate legal expectations that are codified in law (e.g., regarding equal opportunities in the workplace) into firm-specific policies. Due to the legal emphasis of such programmes, compliance programmes are often anchored in firms' legal departments. In the United States, companies are even legally incentivised to have such programmes. The US Sentencing Guidelines (USSG) recommend more lenient sentences and fines for companies that can prove the existence of compliance programmes aimed at preventing corporate misconduct (Treviño et al., 1999: 131). Some aspects of compliance programmes also reach beyond the law and codify a firm's ethical aspirations, such as the exercise of due care and honesty (Babri et al., 2021).

Compliance programmes consist of a variety of components – for instance, whistle-blowing hotlines and ethics trainings. Yet, the most widely used component is the creation of a code of ethics. Such codes reflect 'a set [of] prescriptions developed by a company to guide the behaviour of managers and employees' (Kaptein, 2011a: 233). Codes of ethics need to be distinguished from supplier codes of conduct. While codes of ethics are mainly developed to regulate the behaviour of internal employees, supplier codes of conduct are designed to control firms' supply partners (see also Chapter 22). There is no predefined list of requirements that a code must include because the salience of legal/ethical issues is shaped by contextual factors such as firm size, sector and country of operation. Despite this lack of standardisation, research has identified some issues that are frequently addressed. Kaptein (2004), for instance, shows that most codes focus on how to properly use corporate funds and equipment (e.g., no diversion of funds), how to work with corporate information (e.g., no use of insider information), how to treat other employees (e.g., no bullying) and how to avoid corruption (e.g., restrictions on accepting gifts). Prior research has also shown that the effectiveness of codes is particularly shaped by their embeddedness into a corporation's culture and support by senior leaders (Stevens, 2008). Compliance and integrity are therefore *complementary* orientations.

3.5.2   Integrity – Enabling Shared Values

There is no question of the relevance of well-designed compliance programmes for steering ethical behaviour. Compliance, however, also has its limits. Almost by definition, compliance is a reactive strategy. This makes compliance a bad strategy for coping with unknown and novel ethical dilemma situations. Paine (1994: 111) emphasises this point by arguing that 'compliance is unlikely to unleash much moral imagination or commitment'.

Unlike compliance, an integrity orientation is not based on a set of formal measures. Managing for integrity means most of all to shape the collective set of norms and values that make up an organisation's culture. Although it is difficult to directly influence and steer culture, managers can set the right context for an integrity culture to emerge. One important factor is the leadership style that defines the 'tone from the top'. Management's leadership style is often regarded as a key driver of corporate ethics. Often, transformational (i.e., charismatic) leaders are seen as a key ingredient for defining and living the values that are attached to an integrity culture. Such leaders can stimulate ethical behaviour because they are believed to use their own power to serve others, they are open to continuously learn from criticism, they stimulate followers to think independently and they use moral standards to satisfy organisational interests (Palazzo, 2007).

An integrity orientation is based on senior managers' commitment to core ethical values. Paine (1994) argues that such an approach is deeper and broader than compliance: deeper because it can influence decision-making in more powerful ways; and broader because ethical principles cover more ground than any set of predefined compliance rules. Focusing too much on rules and sanctions can even produce unethical behaviour, because it undercuts trust and hence causes an erosion of shared values (Frey, 1997).

Managing for integrity is less straightforward than managing for compliance. And yet there are still some concrete things that managers can do. Three actions seem particularly noteworthy:

1. Address ethics openly: Managers can make sure that values are openly addressed in discussions and meetings. Treviño et al. (1999: 143) give an example of how this is *not* to be approached. In one company, they studied an employee who wanted to raise an ethical issue during a meeting. The response was: 'If he wants to talk ethics, let him talk to a priest or a psychiatrist. The office is no place for it.' Addressing values explicitly, and not only in informal or even hidden conversations, underscores the seriousness of ethics in the workplace.

2. Reward systems: An integrity culture can also be reinforced through an organisation's reward system. Aligning rewards with values can encourage ethical conduct, because it shows what kind of behaviour the organisation finds desirable. It is important to not just think of financial rewards in this context. Rewarding ethical conduct can also happen by making ethics part of promotion decisions, as well as by embedding it into annual performance reviews and recognition programmes.

3. Hiring practices: Another practical way to put an integrity culture into practice is to rethink criteria for hiring new employees and the process of hiring them. As Epley and Kumar (2019: 150) remark: 'For many employees, an organization's values were revealed during the hiring process.' It is therefore important to reflect on the questions that are being asked in job interviews and to consider the intended and unintended signals they send about company values.

Without doubt, no company can easily implement these actions. Nevertheless, they are a reminder that an integrity culture is not just a matter of luck, but the product of managerial decisions.

3.6　Chapter Summary

This chapter explored the ethical foundations of corporate sustainability. There are two key take-aways. First, ethical dilemma situations are deeply embedded into reflections on corporate sustainability. We cannot avoid ethics when thinking about how firms should become more sustainable and responsible. Although strategic thinking and win-win scenarios are important when discussing corporate sustainability, they are by themselves not a sufficient basis for thinking about how we want firms to behave in society. It is therefore important to understand normative and descriptive ethical theories, which we revisited in this chapter. These theories reflect tools that enable you to put an ethical perspective on ESG issues. Such a perspective allows you to explore new angles of well-known corporate sustainability problems, such as when realising that there is not only a business case to lower a firm's emissions, but that, in the end, it may simply be the right thing to do.

Another key take-away is that business ethics is not at all an oxymoron (i.e., a phrase in which contradictory terms occur together). We have demonstrated that managing for high ethical standards in corporations is not only desirable, but also possible. Given that ethical decision-making is impacted by multiple biases, which often push 'good' people towards 'bad' decisions, ethics management with a compliance *and* integrity perspective in mind is an indispensable part of making corporate behaviour more sustainable.

CHAPTER QUESTIONS

1. Why do you think we need an ethical perspective when discussing corporate sustainability?
2. How would you distinguish the four main normative ethical theories: utilitarianism, Kantian ethics, virtue ethics and posthuman ethics?
3. What factors influence the ethical decisions that we make in corporations?
4. Where do you see advantages and disadvantages of managing ethics via (a) compliance and (b) integrity?

FURTHER RESOURCES

- Crane, A., Matten, D., Glozer, S. and Spence, L. (2019). *Business Ethics: Managing Corporate Citizenship and Sustainability in the Age of Globalization.* Oxford: Oxford University Press.

  For those who want to gain a more comprehensive understanding of business ethics in theory and practice. The book introduces ethical theories in detail and discusses in which way different stakeholder groups can address ethical dilemma situations.

- Kaptein, M. (2018). *Ethicisms and their Risks: 150 New Cartoons about Ethics at Work.* Independently published.

  A great collection of cartoons that illustrate business ethics concepts. Each cartoon discusses a perspective on ethics in the workplace and associated risks. A good way to reflect on some key concepts in an entertaining way.

- Sandel, M. J. (2010). *Justice: What's the Right Thing to Do?* London: Penguin.

  A book that takes you on a journey through different normative ethical theories. It is packed with practical examples and real-life dilemma situations.

4 Stakeholder Approaches to Corporate Sustainability

R. EDWARD FREEMAN, LAURENCE WAINWRIGHT,

SERGIY DMYTRIYEV AND ROBERT G. STRAND

LEARNING OBJECTIVES

- Identify the core features of a stakeholder approach to corporate sustainability and responsible business.
- Understand why and how the stakeholder approach was pioneered and developed in the Nordic context.
- Analyse the past, present and possible future of company–stakeholder relationships.

4.1 Introduction

Since the previous edition of this chapter, the task of defining, managing and collaborating with stakeholders has taken on new and unprecedented levels of importance. We could well say that our successful future as a species literally depends on thoughtful and successful engagement with and between organisations and their stakeholders, so that we can address the complex multifaceted wicked problems facing humanity and nature. The groups and individuals who affect – and are affected by – the actions of an organisation are no longer a side show; rather, they are increasingly being understood as integral to an organisation's successful pursuit of its purpose. Societal norms pertaining to expectations of organisations – especially business – have dramatically evolved from 2000 to 2023. There has been a minor-to-moderate shift away from shareholder primacy. Businesses are increasingly expected to create value, not just for their owners, but for all parties with whom they interact. We are in what many consider to be the 'age of sustainability'.

The world today is marked by unprecedented levels of turbulence, unpredictability, uncertainty, novelty and ambiguity. The COVID-19 pandemic has brought massive impacts to almost every aspect of our societies, healthcare systems and economies. US government turmoil has thrown political, environmental and social agreements and exchanges into disarray. Social media activity has become perhaps the most powerful tool globally for exponential interaction and subsequent and immediate social change. It has become a phenomenal force for implementing social justice and addressing pressing problems such as climate change and sustainability. Think of hashtag activism campaigns such as MeToo or Black Lives Matter. Think of Greta Thunberg's lone demonstration outside the Swedish Parliament in August 2018. Her 'school strike for the climate' grew into a global movement that brought more than 10 million people onto streets worldwide to demand action on climate change. Successful navigation of such unusual times requires effective management – and leadership – of stakeholders.

Social activism and stakeholder interactions present a powerful force for change in this age of sustainability as we work to address the need for sustainability to become incorporated in our way of life. The UN Sustainable Development Goals (SDGs) (2015) set 'a blueprint to achieve a better and more sustainable future for all by 2030'. As established in Chapter 1, the SDGs are a collection of seventeen interlinked global goals which address the global challenges we face, including poverty, inequality, climate change, environmental degradation, peace and justice. Building on the principle of 'leaving no one behind', the new Agenda emphasises a holistic approach to achieving sustainable development for all.

Successful implementation of these SDGs relies primarily on the sustainable management of stakeholders. Therefore, in working towards a future which is realistic about the carrying capacity of the planet and the need for social equality, we need to gain clearer insights into how and why organisations change their behaviour, particularly in relation to corporate sustainability and stakeholders.

The history of General Motors (GM) over the past thirty years gives some interesting insights into how the world of corporate sustainability and stakeholder interactions has evolved rapidly, showing how the old order is changing as we move into the age of sustainability. At the beginning of the 1990s, Jack Smith, the then GM CEO, brought José Ignacio López, who had previously served as the successful GM head of purchasing in Europe, to purchasing operations at Detroit. The objective was clear: to stop the automaker's losses by cutting costs. Often described as a fanatically dedicated and hard-working manager, Lopez became a GM hero by ripping-up long-standing contracts with dedicated suppliers and demanding lower prices. Within his first year in Detroit, Lopez achieved an astounding $1.1 billion of savings.

Was López successful in his managerial position with the cost-cutting strategy he was using? For those who consider maximising financial returns to be the primary objective of any business, it is only logical to put a 'yes' as an answer. The rationale behind this train of thoughts runs, generally speaking, in the following way: shareholders own the company and their primary objective is to maximise a company's financial returns within legal boundaries; shareholders hire an executive manager to run the company and serve their interests in the best possible way; the hired executive will be rewarded, both financially and career-wise, based on his/her success in serving shareholders' interests; thus, keeping shareholders happy, within legal boundaries, is the executive's primary responsibility, and the interests of all other parties in the business are secondary.

López was certainly successful in keeping his shareholders happy. However, this phase of the GM story does not end happily: López's deeds significantly undermined the level of trust between GM and its long-term suppliers. Over time, this strategy of constantly squeezing suppliers turned out to be less productive compared to the trusting long-term relationship built by Japanese car producers. The lesson is self-evident. Maximising immediate profits at the expense of ruining relationships with a stakeholder holds the company back. The tension with suppliers, along with other mistakes in managerial practices, contributed to the deterioration of GM's position in the automobile industry over the next decade (Helper and Henderson, 2014). GM's market share in the United States fell considerably. A damning survey in 2014 revealed that GM was considered the worst company to work with (PR Newswire, 2014).

Yet, GM has learned from its mistake of not building sustainable relationships with stakeholders, so it has transformed its operations in more recent years, through successful management of stakeholders. In 2019, Chairman and CEO Mary Barra signed a Business Roundtable statement on the purpose of a corporation and committed to lead GM to a stakeholder-centric, sustainable future:

> It's easier to live your values when things are going well, but it's more difficult when the going gets tough. At General Motors, we are determined to lead the automotive industry in creating a world with zero crashes, zero emissions and zero congestion, and to do it with integrity. This recognition as one of the World's Most Ethical Companies is a testament to the men and women of General Motors who are committed to doing the right thing, even when it's hard.

So, for GM, business is no longer simply a way to increase wealth for shareholders because a company owes its existence to its founders and owners. The corporation is being managed for the benefit of all stakeholders – not just shareholders.

Even before the 1980s, when stakeholder theory was first described (Freeman, 1984b), there had been a groundswell of management scholars and business leaders who intuitively felt that a company should be doing more than just serving the interests of its shareholders, even if the law did not require more; something that felt as important as fiduciary duty for shareholders. These ideas found their way into Freeman's work on an alternative, more sustainable and more ethical view of business, known as stakeholder theory.

The initial ideas about stakeholder theory were further developed by management scholars, so stakeholder theory became more comprehensive and was shown to apply to numerous industries and settings. Yet, the core principles of stakeholder theory have remained the same. This chapter looks at stakeholder theory as follows.

Section 4.2 covers the fundamental ideas of stakeholder theory. It considers the jointness of stakeholder interests and reviews the advent of the phenomenon of 'shaking stakeholders'. Section 4.3 looks at different stakeholder models. It illustrates stakeholder model development in business settings over time, as well as the influence of the cultural context, such as the one found in Scandinavia, to foster a stakeholder mindset in business. Section 4.4 moves on to look at stakeholder theory in the age of sustainability. It considers the world of sustainability and corporate social responsibility, and the urgent need for a stakeholder approach, before delving into the world of secondary stakeholders and the impact of advancing communication technologies. It also looks at the growing role of 'name and shame' in enhancing stakeholder impact.

4.2 Stakeholder Theory Overview

Organisations do not, and cannot, exist in isolation.[1] Whether a for-profit business or otherwise, all organisations exist within a set of relationships, interactions and interdependencies – involving a variety of different groups and individuals. These 'stakeholders' both affect, and are affected by, an organisation and the achievement of its objectives. Stakeholder theory provides a novel, useful and impactful lens through which to view organisations, and opens up many exciting possibilities in terms of reorienting the relationship between business, society and nature.

4.2.1 Business as Relationships among Stakeholders

Stakeholder theory has been developed over the last forty or so years by an interdisciplinary group of scholars from various management disciplines – from strategy and ethics to finance and accounting. The basic idea is that businesses, and the executives who manage them, actually do and should create value for customers, suppliers, employees, communities and financiers (or shareholders). And that we need to pay careful attention to how these relationships are managed and how value gets created for these stakeholders. Stakeholder theory has been developed to solve three main problems (Freeman et al., 2010). First, how is value creation and trade possible in fast-changing environments that have little stability? Second, how do we understand the ethics of capitalism, and how can we put capitalism on firmer ethical ground? And, third, what should we teach in business schools?

Stakeholder theory in part grew out of dissatisfaction with the current ideology of business across the world; namely, that shareholders were the only group who

---

[1] Note: this section draws on Freeman (2008). Passages are reprinted here with permission of the copyright holder.

should have managerial priority. The scholars who developed the idea of corporate social responsibility (CSR) were instrumental in supporting the development of the stakeholder idea, as a more precise and managerially relevant way to talk about the social responsibility of business. Freeman et al. (2010) argue that, in fact, stakeholder theory can replace the idea of CSR by substituting 'stakeholder' for 'social' in the definition of CSR. Furthermore, such a substitution redefines the very nature of business. Let us be a little more specific.

The basic idea of managing for stakeholders is quite simple. Business can be understood as a set of relationships among groups that have a stake in the activities that make up the business. Business is about how customers, suppliers, employees, financiers (stockholders, bondholders, banks, etc.), communities and managers interact and create value. To understand a business is to know how these relationships work. Furthermore, the executive's or entrepreneur's job is to manage and shape these relationships, and keep them working together in some kind of harmony.

Stakeholder theory considers the dynamic relationships between groups and individuals who affect and are affected by an organisation, usually but not always a for-profit business, and its decision-making processes. It considers the question of what characteristics a group/individual must have to be considered to hold a 'stake' in the actions and outcomes of an organisation (Donaldson and Preston, 1995). While a stakeholder approach to the firm focuses on enabling management to adopt a broader perspective of their external environment, which includes considering the interests and demands of interest groups other than just shareholders, stakeholder theory grapples with questions around who or what constitutes a stakeholder, and which are deserving of management attention.

Figure 4.1 depicts the idea of 'managing for stakeholders'. At the centre of the figure is the firm. Four examples of typical 'primary' stakeholders are shown. There is interdependence between these stakeholders and the firm: both affect, and are affected by, one another, just as the survival of each to some extent depends on the others.

The outer circle shows some examples of 'secondary' stakeholders. These individuals, groups, entities and species both affect and are affected by the firm's pursuit of its objectives. However, they are a little further removed than primary stakeholders. Some academics and practitioners believe that nature – such as the biosphere and the species within it – is in fact a primary stakeholder due to the fact that the firm by definition could not exist without it. Depending on the nature of a firm's area of business, it is also possible that a particular species of plant or animal could be constituted as a stakeholder. For example, if a fishing company frequently catches turtles in its trawl nets, it could be fair to say that they are a legitimate stakeholder of the firm. The question of who, or what, counts as a stakeholder is not always a precise process. It depends in part on what problem we are trying to solve.

Figure 4.1 The firm and its primary and secondary stakeholders. The firm (centre) and its primary stakeholders (inner ring) and secondary stakeholders (outer ring) are interdependent.

It is important to note that the stakeholder idea is perfectly general. Corporations are not the centre of the universe, and there are many possible pictures. One might put customers in the centre to signal that a company puts customers as the key priority. Another might put employees in the centre and link them to customers and shareholders. Or even society, without which business could not exist. We prefer the generic diagram because it suggests, pictorially, that 'managing for stakeholders' is a theory about management and business; hence, managers and companies are in the centre. But, there is no larger metaphysical claim here.

Owners or financiers (a better term) clearly have a financial stake in the business in the form of stocks, bonds and so on, and they expect some kind of financial return from them. Economist Milton Friedman (in)famously argued in his 1970 *New*

York Times piece, 'The Social Responsibility of Business is to Increase Its Profits', that financiers are the ones to whom business owes it obligations. Of course, the stakes of financiers will differ by type of owner, preferences for money, moral preferences and so on, as well as by type of firm. The shareholders of Google may well want returns as well as be supportive of Google's mission statement: 'to organize the world's information and make it universally accessible and useful' (Google, 2021). To the extent that it makes sense to talk about the financiers 'owning the firm', they have a concomitant responsibility for the uses of their property (Stout, 2012a).

Employees have their jobs and usually their livelihood at stake; they often have specialised skills for which there is usually no perfectly elastic market. In return for their labour, they expect security, wages, benefits and meaningful work. Often, employees are expected to participate in the decision-making of the organisation, and if the employees are management or senior executives, we see them as shouldering a great deal of responsibility for the conduct of the organisation as a whole. Furthermore, employees are sometimes financiers as well, since many companies have stock ownership plans, and loyal employees who believe in the future of their companies often voluntarily invest. One way to think about the employee relationship is in terms of contracts. Customers and suppliers exchange resources for the products and services of the firm and in return receive the benefits of the products and services. As with financiers and employees, the customer and supplier relationships are enmeshed in ethics. Companies make promises to customers via their advertising, and when products or services don't deliver on these promises, then management has a responsibility to rectify the situation. It is also important to have suppliers who are committed to making a company better. If suppliers find a better, faster and cheaper way of making critical parts or services, then both supplier and company can win. Of course, some suppliers simply compete on price, but even so, there is a moral element of fairness and transparency to the supplier relationship.

Finally, the local community grants the firm the right to build facilities and, in turn, it benefits from the tax base and economic and social contributions of the firm. Companies have a real impact on communities, and being located in a welcoming community helps a company create value for its other stakeholders. In return for the provision of local services, companies are expected to be good citizens, as is any individual person. A company should not expose the community to unreasonable hazards in the form of pollution, toxic waste, etc. It should keep whatever commitments it makes to the community, and operate in a transparent manner as far as possible. Of course, companies do not have perfect knowledge, but when management discovers some danger or runs afoul of new competition, it is expected to inform and work with local communities to mitigate any negative effects, as far as possible.

While any business must consist of financiers, customers, suppliers, employees and communities, it is possible to think about other stakeholders as well. We can define 'stakeholder' in a number of ways. First of all, we could define the term fairly narrowly to capture the idea that any business, large or small, is about creating value for those groups without whose support the business would cease to be viable. The inner circle of Figure 4.1 depicts this view. Almost every business is concerned at some level with relationships among financiers, customers, suppliers, employees and communities. We might call these groups 'primary' or 'definitional'. However, it should be noted that as a business starts up, sometimes one particular stakeholder is more important than another. In a new business start-up, sometimes there are no suppliers, and paying the majority of attention to one or two key customers, as well as to the venture capitalist (financier), is the right approach.

There is also a somewhat broader definition that captures the idea that if a group or individual can affect a business, then the executives must take that group into consideration in thinking about how to create value. Or, a stakeholder is any group or individual that can affect or be affected by the realisation of an organisation's purpose. At a minimum, some groups affect primary stakeholders and we might see these as stakeholders in the outer ring of Figure 4.1 and call them 'secondary' or 'instrumental.'

Recent perspectives on secondary stakeholders and firm relations, such as Sulkowski, Edwards and Freeman (2018), argue that cooperation between secondary stakeholders and firms do not have to be zero-sum games, but can be 'win-win' scenarios where cooperation can create shared, sustainable value that benefits both parties. Sulkowski et al. (2018: 31) describe how a recent trend has seen firms being proactive and actively seeking out and initiating relations with secondary stakeholders, 'possibly even starting, propagating, or leveraging movements – to affect positive change', leading to 'sustainable value'.

Other definitions and terms have emerged during the last forty years, some based on risks and rewards, some based on mutuality of interests.

Some thinkers focus more on asking questions than giving precise definitions. Mitchell et al. (1997: 277) ask 'which groups are ... deserving or requiring of management attention, and which are not?' Who gets this attention, when and how much they get is not fixed. Phillips et al. (2003: 16) note that such a mandate given to these stakeholders by companies is not based on 'objective, predetermined structures, but [is a] processes of ... construction and meaning creation, wherein social order is negotiated'. There is in many cases a continual arrangement in the relations between a company and stakeholders.

Other academics have focused more on definitions. Donaldson and Preston (1995: 67) defines a stakeholder as follows:

> Stakeholders are persons or groups with legitimate interests in procedural and/or substantive aspects of corporate activity. Stakeholders are identified by their interests in the corporation, whether the corporation has any corresponding functional interest in them.

The debate over finding the one 'true definition' of 'stakeholder' is not likely to end. We prefer a more pragmatist approach of being clear on the purpose of using any of the proposed definitions. Business is a fascinating field of study. There are very few principles and definitions that apply to all businesses all over the world. Furthermore, there are many different ways to run a successful business, or if you like, many different flavours of 'managing for stakeholders'. We see limited usefulness in trying to define one model of business, either based on the shareholder or stakeholder view, which works for all businesses everywhere. We see much value to be gained in examining how the stakes work in the value-creation process and the role of the executive.

Executives play a special role in the activity of the business enterprise. On the one hand, they have a stake like every other employee in terms of an actual or implied employment contract. Furthermore, that stake is linked to the stakes of financiers, customers, suppliers, communities and other employees. In addition, executives are expected to look after the health of the overall enterprise, to keep the varied stakes moving in roughly the same direction and to keep them in balance.

4.2.2   The Jointness of Stakeholder Interests

No stakeholder stands alone in the process of value creation. The stakes of each stakeholder group are multifaceted, and inherently connected to one another. How could a bondholder recognise any returns without management paying attention to the stakes of customers or employees? How could customers get the products and services they need without employees and suppliers? How could employees have a decent place to live without communities? Many thinkers and models – for example, Mitchell et al.'s (1997) Theory of Stakeholder Identification and Salience – see the dominant problem of 'managing for stakeholders' as how to solve the priority problem, or 'which stakeholders are more important,' or 'how do we make trade-offs among stakeholders?' We see this as a secondary issue.

First and foremost, we need to see stakeholder interests – especially where these interests intersect with society and the natural world – as joint, as inherently tied together. The overlapping circles in Figure 4.1 hinted at this. Seeing stakeholder interests as 'joint' rather than opposed is difficult. It is not always easy to find a way to accommodate all stakeholder interests. It is easier to trade off one versus another. Why not delay spending on new products for customers in order to keep earnings a bit higher? Why not cut employee medical benefits in order to invest in a new inventory control system? Many companies are facing these problems by managing stakeholders through partnerships and collaborations – for example, a seafood company that utilises its partnership with an environmental NGO as a means of collaborating with other stakeholders.

Managing for stakeholders suggests that executives try to reframe the questions away from all-or-nothing, good or bad, into questions that capture the nuance of interactions with different groups and individuals – and the time spectrums over which these interactions take place. For example, a company may ask questions such as: How can we invest in new products and create higher earnings – in both the immediate term and the long term? How can we be sure our employees are healthy and happy and are able to work creatively so that we can capture the benefits of new information technology such as inventory control systems? Which of our stakeholders may offer opportunities for shared value creation, and how might we best engage with them? In a book reflecting on his experience as CEO of Medtronic, Bill George (2004) summarised the managing for stakeholders mindset:

> Serving all your stakeholders is the best way to produce long term results and create a growing, prosperous company ... Let me be very clear about this: there is no conflict between serving all your stakeholders and providing excellent returns for shareholders. In the long term it is impossible to have one without the other. However, serving all these stakeholder groups requires discipline, vision, and committed leadership.

The primary responsibility of the executive is to create as much value as possible for stakeholders. Where stakeholder interests conflict, the executive must find a way to rethink the problems so that these interests can go together, so that even more value can be created for each. If trade-offs have to be made, as often happens in the real world, then the executive must figure out how to make the trade-offs, and immediately begin improving the trade-offs for all sides. Managing for stakeholders is about creating as much value as possible for stakeholders, without resorting to trade-offs.

Managing for stakeholders also means simultaneously creating value for multiple parties, such as employees, government, suppliers, customers, the environment and even society as a whole, which requires a multiple-criteria decision-making approach (Serrano-Cinca et al., 2021).

4.2.2.1 'Shaking Stakeholders'

The majority of studies on stakeholder interactions have historically focused on how stakeholders can influence the firm to change its practices, whether through activism or characteristics such as power and urgency. Such studies can reinforce the view that the firm's interests are different from, or even opposed to, those of stakeholders, and that firms will only adopt sustainable practices in response to stakeholder action and conducive institutional settings rather than as a result of internal decisions.

Sulkowski, Edwards and Freeman (2018)[2] have proposed extending the framework for interpreting firm–stakeholder interactions, and postulate that firms play a critical role in 'shaking' stakeholders. In their own words:

---

[2] This section draws on Sulkowski et al. (2018). Passages and a table are reprinted here with permission of the copyright holders.

Shaking stakeholders means to proactively initiate cooperation with those affected by a firm to alter awareness, behaviour, and networks so as to catalyse change in society and the marketplace to reward cocreated innovations in core operations of the firm that improve social and environmental impacts.

First, they build on the idea that a firm can be the entity that leads engagement that shakes stakeholders out of complacency. Second, they show how firms can catalyse collaborative relationships to co-create sustainable value that is shared with stakeholders. In Table 4.1, they show the key features of different forms of stakeholder agreement and contrast them with stakeholder shaking.

As portrayed in the last two rows of their table, Sulkowski et al. (2018: 231) state: 'the motivations and desired outcomes of stakeholder shaking is to ultimately change behavior and marketplace norms so as to reward firms that commit to sustainability-related changes'. The authors present various case studies to show that firms can pursue and achieve positive results for themselves, societies and the environment when they agitate for changes – when they shake their stakeholders.

When the firm takes the initiative to shake stakeholders out of complacency and to solicit input on cooperation in encouraging behaviors and consumption patterns that involve less harm to the consumer and possibly reduced negative externalities to society and the environment, they create and shift markets so that society, consumers, the environment, and – ultimately, if it plans well – the firm can thrive in the long term. (Sulkowski et al., 2018: 228)

Stakeholder shaking can have a part to play in any business environment, but in particular when global ecological crises, societal problems and governance failures heighten the need for firms to take action to bring about profound and systemic changes.

4.3 Cultural Context and Historic Development of Stakeholder Models

In no way does stakeholder theory deny the relevance and importance of a firm's economic success. What stakeholder theory rejects is a narrowly economic view which focuses solely on financial returns. Instead, stakeholder theory posits that value creation for a broader range of stakeholders (including shareholders) should be the primary objective of a company.

Managing for stakeholders requires a certain type of managerial mindset. This stakeholder mindset can develop more easily in cultures that go beyond a narrowly economic view of the firm and value a more society-oriented business approach. In this regard, the Nordic context – which includes the countries of Sweden, Norway,

Table 4.1 Stakeholder 'shaking' contrasted with other forms of stakeholder agreement

	Stakeholder response	Stakeholder involvement	Stakeholder shaking
Communication ideal	Two-way asymmetric communication	Two-way symmetric communication	Open communication involving networks
Stakeholders	Must be reassured company is ethical and socially responsible	Coconstruct corporate social responsibility (CSR) efforts	Coconstruct altered environment in which the firm operates
Stakeholder role	Stakeholders respond to corporate actions	Stakeholders are involved, participate and suggest corporate actions	Stakeholders' awareness and actions on issues of urgent global importance are stimulated
Identification of CSR focus	Decided by top management, based on feedback from stakeholders	Negotiated concurrently	Proactive identification of needed systemic changes
Strategic communication task	Demonstrate how the company integrates stakeholder concerns	Invite and establish frequent, systematic, and proactive dialogue with stakeholders	Proactive dialogue, plus advocacy on the part of the firm
Corporate communication task	Identify relevant stakeholders	Build relationships	Build relationships and align networks
Third-party endorsement of CSR initiatives	Integrated element of surveys, rankings, and opinion polls	Stakeholders are themselves involved in corporate CSR messages	Verification and support of the elimination of environmental harms
Motivations	Instrumentalist (ultimately self-serving)	Some goals beyond self interest	Coequal goals of sustained profits and achieving systemic sustainability
Outcome	Company communication adjusted to take into account opinions of stakeholders	Measures of sustainability success possibly agreed on, measured, and reported on	Fundamental changes in market dynamics that allow a business to operate while verifiably eliminating social and environmental harms (creating sustainable value)

Source: Adopted from Sulkowski et al. (2018).

Denmark, Finland and Iceland – can be of great interest. According to Geert Hofstede, the founder of the cultural dimension theory, Nordic culture can be described as the most feminine in the world. In contrast to masculine cultures, such as the United States or Japan, feminine cultures can be characterised as societies driven by care for others rather than competition and achievement. In feminine cultures: 'An effective manager is supportive to his/her people, and decision making is achieved through involvement. Managers strive for consensus and people value equality, solidarity and quality in their working lives' (The Hofstede Centre, 2016). Strand and Freeman (2015) summarised the previous academic works on the Nordic context to show that its dominant cultural norms and institutional structures encourage engagement between companies and their stakeholders (see Strand et al., 2015 for further elaborations on the Nordic context). Norms and structures in Nordic countries include a general tendency to embrace and promote participatory leadership; rejection of self-protective (i.e., 'face-saving') leadership that entails engagement with critical voices; reflection by practitioners; flatter organisational hierarchies and corresponding high degree of employee involvement; egalitarianism, democratic principles, peace, consensus-building and cooperation; embeddedness of economic interests within broader societal interests; strong regulatory bodies and active non-governmental organisations (NGOs); employee representation on boards of directors and a general stakeholder orientation to corporate governance; and concentrated company ownership with comparatively high levels of ownership of public companies by the state, by foundations and by families. In the Nordic context, even 'shareholders are less likely to behave as a disparate assemblage of faceless entities with a lone objective of short-term share price maximization' (Strand and Freeman, 2015: 75).

These cultural norms and institutional structures were reflected in the works of Scandinavian management scholars led by the Swedish academician Eric Rhenman. In particular, he developed many ideas (Rhenman, 1968) akin to stakeholder theory in parallel to the work going on in the United States at that time. All this contributed to Scandinavian companies pioneering stakeholder engagement in business.

The Danish global healthcare company Novo Nordisk is a great illustration of stakeholder engagement dynamics over time. Figure 4.2 shows stakeholder maps developed at Novo Nordisk starting as early as 1970 and finally moving into the twenty-first century. First, we can observe that the sheer number of stakeholders has increased dramatically over time. In the 1970s, the company was primarily concerned with the interests of those groups that had a very direct tangible impact on the company's activities. Satisfying the needs of customers, investors and regulators was vital for the company's existence. To a certain degree, this initial map corresponds to the curtailed inner circle on Freeman's stakeholder map. Twenty years onwards, the initial stakeholder list saw a considerable expansion that among other things reflected Novo Nordisk's strong commitment to corporate social

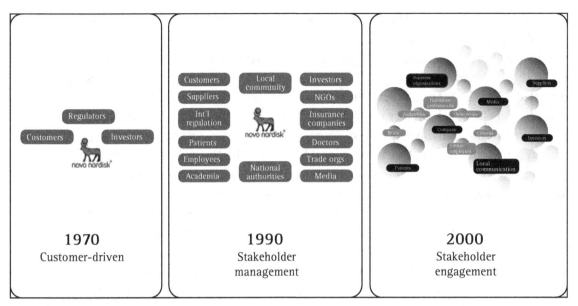

Figure 4.2 Evolution of stakeholder engagement at Novo Nordisk between 1970, 1990 and 2000. Based on Novo Nordisk company materials. Reproduced with permission.

responsibility and sustainability, adding NGOs, academia and community, among others, to their list. The media was also added, especially in the context of Novo Nordisk's focus on transparency. By the end of the 1990s, Novo Nordisk took to the idea that a company itself did not need to be at the very centre of a stakeholder map. Rather, the entire business environment could be treated as a constellation, with multiple stakeholder-players constantly interconnecting and co-influencing one another. In the 2020s, Novo Nordisk is considered a world leader in social and environmental performance, due in part to its early adoption of deliberate and coordinated efforts to map out its stakeholders, understand the interrelationship between their objectives and the objectives of each stakeholder, and take steps to seek out shared value creation. In 2020, the company reached its long-held target of using 100 per cent renewable electricity. By 2030, it plans to get to net zero.

Over time, we are seeing a growing trend of applying the stakeholder approach by many businesses across the globe. Today, for any Nordic company engaged in managing for stakeholders, such as H&M, IKEA, Nudie Jeans, Carlsberg, Novo Nordisk, Novozymes, Norsk Hydro, and Statoil (Strand and Freeman, 2015), there will be numerous US counterparts such as Patagonia, Cisco Systems Inc., Hewlett Packard Enterprise Co. and Whole Foods Markets. These companies, which regularly feature in lists of 'most sustainable companies', for the most part give due respect to all their stakeholders and try to create value for all of them.

Driven by the best practices in managing for stakeholders, many companies have committed to the common trend of writing a stakeholder engagement chapter when it comes to company mission and values. Nowadays, in the oil and gas industry, for example (apart from Statoil), there are many other major players, such as Exxon Mobil, ConocoPhillips, BP and others, who talk about focusing on stakeholder engagement on their website front pages. There may be criticism that it is easier to write about it than to implement 'managing for stakeholders' in practice, but recognising stakeholder engagement as a priority for a company can definitely be viewed as moving in the right direction. The growing pressure for implementing the stakeholder approach in business is also stipulated by significantly changing societal norms regarding how companies should interact with society and the natural environment.

4.4 Stakeholder Theory in the Age of Sustainability

Stakeholder theory has taken on a new level of importance in the age of sustainability. The complex, multifaceted social and environmental challenges that we face require, by definition, a stakeholder approach.

4.4.1 The Urgency of Social and Environmental Challenges Calls for a Stakeholder Approach

We find ourselves at a genuine crossroads point in history. It is not an exaggeration to say that the choices humanity collectively makes in the next ten to twenty years will have significant (and in many cases, irreversible) consequences for the state – and future viability of – planet Earth. All scientific evidence indicates that we are presently overshooting four of the nine planetary boundaries and must reformulate the relationship between economic systems, human society and ecological systems. While we have made a start, there is a very long road ahead of us.

Fundamental to this reformulation is understanding the role of business and markets both as a cause of – but also solution to – many of the interconnected problems we face. These 'wicked problems' we currently face, whether it be climate change, overfishing or significant inequalities in health outcomes between countries, are wicked because they are complex and non-linear, and don't have straightforward 'answers'. They can't be solved per se, but can be 'tamed'. This requires genuine leadership rather than management. Such leadership may need to bring about changes so profound that we may need to, in fact, put society, or the planet, at the centre of our stakeholder models.

There is at last a fairly wide appreciation for the urgency of many of these challenges. The COVID-19 pandemic of 2019–21, Australian bushfires of 2019–20 and several other key events seems to have jolted humanity to face the uncomfortable reality of these wicked problems – and the urgency with which they need to be addressed. Central to acting quickly on these issues is firms engaging not just with those stakeholders in their immediate transactional environment, but with those further afield.

The data is fairly sobering. The period between 2010 and 2019 was the warmest decade since measurements began in 1850. Climate change is estimated to cause over 150,000 human deaths annually. If we take only minimal action on climate, average global GDP will decline by around 15 per cent by 2050. That's comparable to a triple whammy of COVID-19 pandemic economic impacts. Since 1970, we have reduced populations of mammals, birds, reptiles and amphibians across the globe by almost 70 per cent. Nearly 500 vertebrate species – animals with a spine – have become extinct in the last 100 years; extinctions that would typically take around 10,000 years without humans. When it comes to fish stocks, 93 per cent are being fished at or beyond sustainable levels. We can't keep doing this to ourselves – and to nature.

4.4.2   Stakeholders, Sustainability and New Information Communication Technologies

Advancements in information communication technologies between 2000 and 2020 have been so massive, so fast and so impactful on almost every dimension of human life that many are labelling it as the 'fourth industrial revolution'.

Like it or loathe it, one cannot get through a typical day in most countries without interacting in some way, shape or form with a computer, smartphone, website, email provider or social media account. In 2018, Apple became the largest public company in the United States, with a value of $1 trillion. In 2020, seven out of the ten most valuable companies in the world had their core business in ICT. Think Amazon, Alphabet (Google, YouTube), Apple, Facebook, Alibaba Group and even Tesla. Humans have more information available at their fingertips – for example, via a smartphone – than at any other point in human history. Attention is perhaps the most valuable commodity of all, in a world where humans have literally millions of possible things to read, watch and listen to online. Flows of information are rapid and abundant, and individuals and organisations alike are having to become more proactive at pre-empting and responding to situations as they emerge.

These dramatic and unprecedented changes have created a range of opportunities and challenges for how firms interact with their stakeholders.

New communication technologies can help to make stakeholder groups more organised, so their role in a firm's success becomes even more salient. Now stakeholders can act as a coordinated group and their opinions, whether customer feedback or employees sharing experiences, can instantaneously spread across the market, with consequences for the company to benefit from or deal with. Social media, whether Instagram, TikTok, Twitter or LinkedIn, can enable millions of previously disconnected individual stakeholders to unite under common ideas –

and their voices get stronger. With video-conferencing during the COVID-19 pandemic having transformed the way the business world connects, stakeholders too are reaping benefits, with shareholders attending AGMs and business forums remotely.

Stakeholder voices are empowered by these communication developments, and businesses can be too if they formulate a method of using different digital tools to communicate effectively with their target audience. There are still untapped opportunities for investors and suppliers who have not been leveraging social media effectively.

What do the dramatic advancements in technology and communications mean for stakeholder theory? The cornerstone of stakeholder theory lies in 'creating as much value as possible for stakeholders, without resorting to trade-offs' (Freeman et al., 2010: 28). Stakeholder theory also aims at integrating business and ethical components in managerial decision-making (the integration thesis) and 'as such, matters of ethics are routine when one takes a "managing for stakeholders" approach' (Freeman et al., 2010: 29). Rapid technological developments have amplified the role of stakeholders and made it obvious that a stakeholder approach is both a necessary condition for any business to remain successful and an ethical approach of simply doing the right thing. Stakeholder theory has moved to the very front page of the managerial agenda.

Another significant aspect of technological advancement has been the way that stakeholders 'talk' to one another – and the speed at which it can occur. Academics have in the last decade carried out a number of studies on the use of social media by primary and secondary stakeholders as a way to apply pressure to firms on particular social and/or environmental issues. Gomez-Carrasco and Michelon (2017: 855) attempted to quantify this impact in terms of influence on firm stock price, finding that 'Twitter activism of key stakeholders has a significant impact on investors' decisions'. More broadly, the concept of 'hashtag activism' has been explored in the context of recent campaigns. One such campaign, Swedish environmental activist Greta Thunberg's use of social media to pressure governments and firms to act on anthrophonic climate change, illustrated the ability to facilitate large-scale and sudden social movements and amplify the voice of the public in order to apply pressure. While both 'carrots' and 'sticks' are used in such campaigns to pressure firms to change their ways, it is the 'stick' of shaming that has been a key feature of many effective social media campaigns launched by primary and secondary stakeholders against firms.

4.4.3 NGO Activism

Organisations, for example, NGOs with a stated social or environmental purpose, can apply pressure to companies in order to push them to change their ways. This pressure – led by NGOs which can often be considered a stakeholder of a company in their own right – often calls on companies to do a better job of interacting with their stakeholders, especially with society and nature.

One increasingly common specific method of holding firms to account on particular issues – and in some cases even contesting their overall legitimacy and right to exist – is the use of shame-based campaigning. Shaming draws on 'shared social meaning and on norms about permissible and impermissible behaviour' (Skeel, 2001: 1811) in an attempt to alter the behaviour of a firm. Shaming often manifests around one particular issue or event – for example, an NGO posting a photo of a dolphin in a trawl net on social media as a way of publicly shaming the actions of a fishing company – and demanding them to change their practices. Waldron, Navis and Fisher (2013: 397), for example, describe how most research on stakeholder pressure on firms has focused on the phenomena of how these actors 'target firms by using publicity oriented tactics to erode those firms' reputations, consequently damaging key stakeholder relationships and fiscal performance'.

Early studies in the academic literature focusing on shame considered the way in which activist groups such as NGOs use shame-based tactics against large corporations by targeting reputation towards the end of having them change to a more sustainable or responsible supplier. While the language of shaming is used in these early papers, the emphasis seems to be more on the reputational side, rather than looking directly at how and why shaming manifests. Studies looking at shaming specifically seem to have come into the corporation-external actor/stakeholder vernacular more recently, perhaps alongside the rise to prominence in social media, which has allowed shaming to take place at previously unseen speeds and scales (Fine, 2019). Haufler (2015: 199) found that shaming can indeed lead to change in organisational behaviours, but cautioned that '[t]he degree to which shame functions to change behaviour varies widely across firms and sectors'.

Taebi and Safari's (2017) study on the effectiveness and legitimacy of shaming as strategy against anthropogenic-induced climate change found that shaming can be effective (especially when the corporation operates in a business-to-consumer rather than business-to-business or state-to-state domain), but that shaming carries with it several 'ethical pitfalls', which have the possibility of existing at the end of both the shamer and the shamee.

4.5   Chapter Summary

As Freeman et al. (2010: 212) mentioned, stakeholder theory is 'first, and most fundamentally, a moral theory that specifies the obligations that companies have to their stakeholders'. A company should bear responsibility to every stakeholder it has in a manner that does not allow any trade-offs. Customers, employees, financiers, suppliers and communities should all matter. Moreover, as it turns out, treating all stakeholders equally puts everyone in a win-win situation because stakeholder theory is also about 'value creation and trade and how to manage a business effectively' (Freeman et al., 2010: 9). Overall, managers should be guided in their work by the principles of stakeholder theory because it provides 'a better way to live, it allows us to be authentic, and it enables cooperation with other stakeholders such that, over time, everybody wins' (Freeman et al., 2010: 215).

The age of sustainability makes stakeholder mapping, engagement and ongoing dialogue more critical than ever before, due to the scale and urgency of the challenges facing our planet.

Companies do not exist in isolation. Like fish in a coral reef, they are part of an ecosystem. They both affect, and are affected by, this system. Continued relevance, and survival, means they must understand and proactively engage with their stakeholders, and implement effective stakeholder management. While not to understate the seriousness of the current predicament we find ourselves in, there is much to be optimistic about. The shift to net zero and sustainable development presents huge opportunities: new markets and wealth to be created; genuine win-win, shared-value outcomes which reward entrepreneurship and initiative while simultaneously benefiting the planet; and opportunities for businesses to evolve to a higher form of capitalism that integrates meaning and purpose into their identity. Firms and their stakeholders, cooperating hand-in-hand rather than competing, can do this.

CHAPTER QUESTIONS

1. What is a stakeholder?
2. Why is it important to create as much value as possible for stakeholders without resorting to trade-offs?
3. In what ways have rapid advancements in information communication technologies – such as the rise of social media – influenced the ways in which firms interact with their stakeholders (and vice versa)?
4. Select one of following lines of argument and respond to it in relation to the goal of achieving sustainable development and net zero. In your answer of between 200 and 400 words, you will apply the knowledge you have gained from this chapter in order to create a high-quality piece of writing that shows independent, critical thought and an ability to make nuanced, refined points towards a broader argument.
   a. 'While the Nordic countries are not perfect, their model of "conscious capitalism" – and associated ways of interacting with stakeholders – represents a North Star, towards which we should be orienting our efforts.'

b. 'The SARS-CoV-2/COVID-19 pandemic showed us that human society can, when it wants to, act quickly and decisively to bring about rapid change to societal and economic systems and structures.'

c. 'Milton Friedman was right. The social responsibility of business should only be to its shareholders. And this is a good thing.'

d. 'The constant-growth feature of most enactments of capitalism is – by definition – incompatible with planetary boundaries.'

e. 'The UN SDGs are a nice wish list, but in reality, they will fail to achieve any meaningful change because they contradict one another.'

Case Study: *Anti-Scampi – The Shrimp Sustainability Saga in Sweden*
Available from Cambridge University Press at www.cambridge.org/rasche2

FURTHER RESOURCES

- Freeman, R. E., Harrison, J. S. and Wicks, A. C. (2007). *Managing for Stakeholders: Survival, Reputation, and Success.* New Haven, CT: Yale University Press.

  The authors set out to explore the question of how we can develop a 'managing for stakeholders' mindset and create as much value as possible for all stakeholders. They propose ten specific principles and seven techniques for managing stakeholder relationships.

- Freeman, R. E., Parmar, B. L. and Martin, K. (2020). *The Power of And: Responsible Business Without Trade-Offs.* New York, NY: Columbia University Press.

  The idea that business is only about the money doesn't hold true in the twenty-first century, when companies around the world are giving up traditional distinctions in order to succeed. Yet, our expectations for businesses remain under the sway of an outdated worldview that emphasises profits for shareholders above all else. *The Power of And* offers a new narrative about the nature of business, revealing the focus on responsibility and ethics that unites today's most influential ideas and companies. R. Edward Freeman (lead author of this chapter), Kirsten E. Martin and Bidhan L. Parmar detail an emerging business model built on five key concepts: prioritising purpose as well as profits; creating value for stakeholders as well as shareholders; seeing business as embedded in society as well as markets; recognising people's full humanity as well as their economic interests; and integrating business and ethics into a more holistic model.

- Grunewald, E. W. and Henriksson, H. (2020). *Sustainability Leadership: A Swedish Approach to Transforming Your Company, Your Industry and the World.* Cham, Switzerland: Palgrave Macmillan.

As business leaders navigate a world of complex global challenges, sustainability and effective stakeholder engagement is no longer optional, but rather an imperative. In this book, two sustainability leaders with decades of experience – Henrik Henriksson, CEO of Scania and Elaine Weidman Grunewald, Co-founder of the AI Sustainability Centre, and former Chief Sustainability & Public Affairs Officer at Ericsson – offer a simple but powerful three-step model for leading an organisation on a sustainability transformation journey that aims at big, bold, world-changing goals.

- Harrison, J. S., Bosse, D. A. and Phillips, R. A. (2010). Managing for Stakeholders, Stakeholder Utility Functions, and Competitive Advantage. *Strategic Management Journal*, 31(1), 58–74.

The article explains how building trusting relationships with stakeholders, based on principles of justice, leads to increased competitive advantage of a firm.

- Parmar, B. L., Freeman, R. E., Harrison, J. S., Wicks, A. C., Purnell, L. and de Colle, S. (2010). Stakeholder Theory: The State of the Art. *The Academy of Management Annals*, 4(1), 403–445.

A major summary work on stakeholder theory literature, this book looks at what problems it tries to solve and reviews misunderstandings and misuses of stakeholder theory. It also analyses the relationship between stakeholder theory and business ethics and CSR, and examines the implications of stakeholder theory for capitalism, arguing for a new narrative for business.

- Sustainable Vikings: Sustainability & Corporate Social Responsibility in Scandinavia, www.coursera.org/learn/sustainability-csr-scandinavia.

A free online course, set up by Dr Robert Strand. This course gives you immediate access to the world's leading sustainability and CSR practices. Scandinavian firms dominate the major sustainability and CSR performance indicators, including the Dow Jones Sustainability Index (DJSI). This course explores the concepts of sustainability and CSR and focuses attention on how Scandinavian firms, like Novo Nordisk, have achieved superior sustainability and CSR performances. The course considers what lessons can be learned by managers and firms irrespective of where they may be located in the world.

5 | Strategic Approaches to Corporate Sustainability

ANDREAS RASCHE

LEARNING OBJECTIVES

- Reflect on what corporate strategy is and how it relates to corporate sustainability.
- Learn about inside-out and outside-in approaches to link corporate strategy with corporate sustainability, including the benefits and limits of creating shared value.
- Reflect on differences between corporate and business strategy in the context of corporate sustainability.
- Learn how to identify material ESG issues through materiality assessments.
- Identify different stages of alignment between a firm's strategy and its corporate sustainability activities.

5.1 Introduction

Few executives would deny the importance of corporate sustainability these days. In a survey, over 90 per cent of managers agreed that aligning ESG issues with corporate strategy is important; however, only 60 per cent believed such alignment was present in their company (Unruh et al., 2016). In another survey, 64 per cent of board members said that their ESG efforts are linked to corporate strategy, but only 25 per cent of them said that they understood ESG risks very well (PwC, 2021). What do these results tell us? On the one hand, they show that awareness for corporate sustainability is very high among senior executives and company boards. Companies that ignore ESG risks do so at their own peril. On the other hand, the results also show that many companies still have a way to go to integrate and align their strategies with their corporate sustainability activities.

You might have heard a practitioner or even an academic claiming that corporate sustainability and CSR are not 'strategic' enough. Often, it is unclear what exactly is meant by this phrase, as the term strategy is used in different ways by different people. Sometimes the term strategy is simply used to denote that something is important – for instance, when we say that this was a 'strategic decision'. Reflecting on what makes corporate sustainability strategic can become more meaningful if we consider how corporate sustainability and firms' strategies are *interrelated*. The relationship between both constructs has been subject to much discussion emphasising that a strategic approach towards corporate sustainability implies: (1) to better embed ESG activities into the organisation as a whole; (2) to improve these activities' alignment with long-term corporate objectives; and (3) to move them beyond pure philanthropy (see, e.g., Porter and Kramer, 2006; Orlitzky et al., 2011). Many argue that once corporate sustainability and corporate strategy are aligned, companies will find it easier to connect positive financial business results with their sustainability engagement. *Strategic* corporate sustainability therefore supposes an instrumental perspective on corporations' engagement in sustainable business practices (see Chapter 1).

This chapter introduces you to the debate about how a firm's strategy and corporate sustainability are interrelated. Section 5.2 looks at the term 'strategy' and identifies some key characteristics of strategic decisions. Based on this, we discuss which characteristics a strategic approach towards corporate sustainability would entail. Section 5.3 introduces two types of approaches to link business strategy and corporate sustainability: outside-in thinking (based on the assumption that sustainability-strategy alignment starts with reflections on a firm's competitive context); and inside-out thinking (based on the assumption that such alignment starts with reflections on a firm's value chain). Section 5.4 extends this debate and shows how sustainability-strategy alignment can be achieved for companies with multiple business units (corporate strategy) as well as for firms that target only one market (business strategy). Section 5.5 demonstrates how firms can identify 'material' (i.e., strategic) ESG issues through so-called materiality assessments. Finally, section 5.6 distinguishes different stages of alignment between a firm's strategy and its sustainability efforts, ranging from complete detachment and denial to companies that build their entire strategy around sustainability.

5.2 Strategy and Corporate Sustainability

In order to understand how strategy and corporate sustainability are linked, we first need to take a look at what strategy means at all in a corporate context. Based on this, we can explore what potentially makes corporate sustainability strategic.

5.2.1 What Is Strategy in the Corporate Context?
Strategy is a term that we all use a lot in our everyday language. Strategy derives from the ancient concept of strategos which is compounded of stratos (an encamped

army) and agein (to lead). Before the term entered business language, it was (and still is) mostly used in the context of military decision-making. Some of the first writings on strategy date back to Prussian general Carl von Clausewitz (1832/1983) who in his book *On War* distinguished strategy from tactics. While strategy is much about how an army deploys (or positions) its troops, tactics is concerned with how these troops are employed (or organised). Later, this distinction was introduced to the business world in the first organised writings on corporations' strategy. Alfred Chandler (1962: 11) famously wrote: '*Strategic* decisions are concerned with the long-term health of the enterprise. *Tactical* decisions deal more with the day-to-day activities necessary for efficient and smooth operations' (emphasis in the original).

Chandler's emphasis on strategy being about the long-term health of a corporation is also reflected in a widely cited definition:

> Strategy is the direction and scope of an organisation over the long term: which achieves advantage for the organisation through its configuration of resources within a changing environment, to meet the needs of markets and to fulfil stakeholder expectations. (Johnson and Scholes, 1999: 10)

This definition highlights some important elements of corporate decisions that are strategic. First, strategic decisions are usually concerned with the entire firm. For instance, a decision about whether a firm should enter a certain product market concerns the entire organisation, while the decision whether to purchase a certain machine would in most contexts not be a strategic decision. Second, strategic decisions deal with the future which makes them anticipatory reflections and hence risky. Third, strategic decisions aim at achieving a competitive advantage for the corporation and aspire to fulfil stakeholder expectations. The last point is particularly relevant in the context of corporate sustainability. If strategy is defined as fulfilling stakeholder expectations, there is a need to align a firm's sustainability practices with its strategic decisions.

5.2.2   Strategic Corporate Sustainability

We can use Johnson and Scholes's (1999) definition, which we discussed above, as a starting point for thinking about what makes corporate sustainability strategic.

- *Organisational Embeddedness*: Non-strategic corporate sustainability suffers from a lack of embeddedness into the organisation. As discussed above, strategic decisions are those that concern the entire organisation (in the case of corporate strategy) or an entire business unit (in the case of business strategy). Hence, strategic corporate sustainability should be embedded into organisational practices whenever and wherever relevant. You can also flip this argument around: strategic corporate sustainability is *not* about single, isolated sustainability or responsibility projects that exist detached from the operational core of the organisation.

- *Future Orientation*: Corporate strategy deals with the long-term direction of a company. Strategic corporate sustainability therefore tries to identify those ESG issues that support the long-term goals of the corporation in its competitive environment. For instance, an automotive company like Volkswagen, which has announced it will stop producing combustion engine cars by 2035, will need well-developed innovation practices that increase battery storage capacity.

- *Alignment with Key Resources*: Johnson and Scholes's (1999) definition emphasises the need to align corporate strategy with a configuration of resources. The strategic plans that a company makes need to be backed by the resources that the firm has or can develop. Non-strategic corporate sustainability ignores a company's key resources and capabilities, whereas strategic corporate sustainability uses them as a springboard to become more sustainable. Think of a company that uses its corporate sustainability activities to protect resources on which it depends (e.g., human resources).

- *Consideration of Stakeholder Expectations*: Johnson and Scholes's (1999) definition emphasises that a corporate strategy aims to fulfil stakeholder expectations. Hence, non-strategic corporate sustainability would neglect stakeholder expectations, while strategic engagement with corporate sustainability implies looking for early warning signals by stakeholders that enable a proactive management of relevant expectations. Often, companies ignore stakeholders at their own peril. For instance, many companies think of stakeholder engagement as an exercise geared towards external audiences and hence ignore internal stakeholders (e.g., employees). However, employees are increasingly speaking out when they see corporate hypocrisy (Taylor, 2019) and thus are an important group to consider in strategic decision-making. You can also think of Novo Nordisk's strategic stakeholder approach, which was discussed in Chapter 4.

All of the above shows that strategic corporate sustainability would not just address some generic ESG issues. Approaching corporate sustainability from a strategic perspective implies addressing those ESG issues that support the future success of the business and strengthen its competitive positioning and financial performance. In fact, many view value creation for society *and* the company as an outcome of strategic corporate sustainability. As discussed in Chapter 1, such an instrumental perspective assumes that addressing ESG issues reduces risks (e.g., litigation risks or supply chain risks) and enhances opportunities (e.g., developing innovate products).

There is a collaborative element to strategic corporate sustainability. In the sustainability context, competition and collaboration do not always reflect a tension. For instance, many firms engage in so-called 'pre-competitive collaborations' (Grabs, 2020) – that is, partnerships between otherwise competing firms from the same industry, which are focused on solving a jointly experienced problem. In some cases, such collaborations are joined by non-business actors such as NGOs. For instance, in the global coffee industry several large buyers have joined forces in the Global Coffee Platform to initiate projects that secure the supply of sustainably sourced coffee (e.g., by educating farmers about responsible weed management).

5.3 How to Link Business Strategy and Sustainability?

We now look at different ways in which corporations can connect their strategic thinking and sustainability practices. If strategic corporate sustainability is about reaching beyond generic ESG issues (i.e., those that are not linked to a firm's strategy), there is the question of how we identify those issues that really are aligned with a firm's strategy.

To identity points of intersection between strategy and sustainability we can turn towards two different schools of thought. On the one hand, we can follow what some have called *outside-in thinking* (Porter and Kramer, 2006; Rasche, 2008). Such thinking assumes that to classify which ESG issues are of strategic importance we must investigate a firm's competitive environment. The assumption underlying outside-in thinking is that this competitive context enables and restricts how firms can implement their strategies. A firm should choose those ESG issues that shape this competitive context in favourable ways – that is, in ways that the firm can implement its strategic goals. On the other hand, we can follow a more resource-oriented perspective. Such an inside-out view focuses on the firm's routine business activities that are captured by its value chain. Sustainability thinking should ideally help to redesign these activities in ways that they support the firm's strategic goals (Porter and Kramer, 2006).

5.3.1 Outside-In Approaches

Outside-in approaches try to identity which conditions in firms' market and non-market environment influence its competitiveness. One good way to understand these conditions is to look at Porter's (1998) model that discusses the competitive advantage of industries. This model identifies four conditions which influence the competitiveness of firms within a certain industry. Porter and Kramer (2006) used this model as a point of departure to identify which ESG issues help firms become more competitive.

1. *Factor (Input) Conditions*: Each company needs certain natural, financial and human resources to do its business. Some countries have more of these resources than others. Firms that operate in countries and industries which possess, create and upgrade these resources usually enjoy a competitive advantage. You can think, for instance, of German automotive manufacturers that thrived, among other things, because of the strong engineering education in the country.

A strategic approach to corporate sustainability would identify those ESG issues that help to preserve or even strengthen these input conditions. Nestlé, for example, engaged in knowledge transfer to Indian farmers so that they learn how to improve the quality of the milk they delivered to the company. It thereby changed its competitive context in a way that milk farmers produced higher-quality milk (and hence got paid better) while the company enjoyed a stable local supply.

2. *Demand Conditions*: If a company is placed in a market with demanding customers it is pushed towards innovation and improving quality because of the existing rivalry on the market. Customers in these markets can give a company insights into trends and emerging buyer needs. For instance, Scandinavian countries are known for their bicycle culture. It is therefore not surprising that a Swedish company first developed an airbag bike helmet. A firm's ESG activities can be aligned with and even reinforce these demand conditions. Many UK retailers, for example, give preference to Fairtrade products, as the country has the highest retail sales for Fairtrade products in Europe due to strong consumer demand (Statista, 2017).

3. *Supporting Industries*: Firms' competitiveness often depends on the competitiveness of suppliers or firms in closely related industries. Competitive suppliers can deliver innovations that spill over to buyer companies. Again, consider the example of German car manufacturers whose success was supported by clusters of excellent suppliers, such as Bosch and Continental. These suppliers constantly provided innovation for selected car parts and hence pushed industry standards. ESG practices that are aligned with a firm's competitive context can secure the existence and competitiveness of these suppliers. As an example, consider Italian tyre manufacturer Pirelli. One of their suppliers of natural rubber assumed a strong role in supporting the company's development of the first tyre with a Forest Stewardship Council (FSC) certification.

4. *Strategy Context*: The context in which competition occurs and the level of rivalry among firms shapes a company's strategy. Competition does not exist in a vacuum, but it is governed by certain rules and incentives. Governments play an important role in shaping these rules and incentives. For instance, they can promote healthy competition among firms (by shaping anti-trust laws) or they can fight corruption and promote transparency. Firms' ESG practices can shape the rules and incentives that govern competition in an industry or country. For instance, many companies from the extractive industries support the Extractive Industries Transparency Initiative (EITI) which sets standards for anti-corruption in countries where relevant operations exist. Firms participate in the EITI to strengthen and protect their own competitive context, as corruption can be a major impediment when doing business.

By analysing these four conditions a firm can identify possible points of overlap between their ESG activities (existing as well as planned) and the competitive

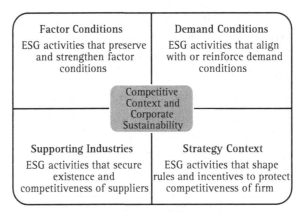

Figure 5.1 Links between competitive context and corporate sustainability.
Source: Adapted and modified from Porter and Kramer (2002, 2006).

context they operate in (see Figure 5.1). A strategic approach to corporate sustainability would imply selecting those ESG activities that help a firm to strengthen its own competitive context.

The four conditions can also be used as a yardstick to reflect on whether a firm's philanthropic projects are aligned with its strategy (Porter and Kramer, 2002). Often, firms' philanthropic donations and charity projects, although well-intended, are not much associated with the strategic direction of the company. While we may argue that philanthropy does not need to be strategic and should rather focus on the needs of the communities that the company interacts with, a practitioner adopting a strategic view on corporate sustainability would try to understand how philanthropy and strategy interact. Strategic philanthropy is usually defined as those practices that align a firm's charitable activities with its business objectives (Carroll, 2018). Porter and Kramer (2002) argue that firms' philanthropic activities can be deemed strategic if they positively influence one or more of the four identified competitive context conditions. Consider the example of Chrysler, which donates money to education as part of its philanthropic activities. The company focused its donations on trainings for people in the automotive industry, which in turn decreased their costs for the training of future employees (Heisler, 2018). It thereby directly influenced its own factor (input) conditions.

5.3.2   Inside-Out Approaches

Inside-out approaches start the alignment of corporate sustainability and strategy from the 'inside' of the corporation. There are different tools to analyse which of a corporation's activities yield a competitive advantage. One well-known tool is the value chain analysis (Porter, 1985). The value chain breaks up a company's activities into those elements that create added value for customers. Each company relies on certain inputs (e.g., natural resources, labour). Through its activities it aims to transform these inputs into outputs. This transformation needs to happen in a way that the customer value, which is yielded, is greater than the original costs of producing these outputs. The difference between the created value and the costs of creating that value is usually referred to as a company's margin.

Porter (1985) identified two types of activities in a value chain. The first are *primary activities* that are directly related to the creation of the product or service:

1. inbound logistics (organising, receiving, storing and distributing inputs);
2. operations (a firm's systems that transform inputs into outputs);
3. outbound logistics (distributing the product/service);
4. marketing and sales (communicating the value of the product/service);
5. service (service activities aimed at value maintenance).

These primary activities are backed up by four types of *support activities*:

1. procurement (identifying suppliers and building supplier relationships);
2. human resource management (recruiting, training and motivating employees);
3. technological development (identifying, integrating and maintaining technologies);
4. infrastructure (management systems that allow a company to operate, e.g., accounting, public affairs and legal).

Each support activity can help to maintain one or more of the primary activities. For instance, human resource management affects all the primary activities because it makes sure that sufficiently trained employees work in relevant organisational functions. Porter's (1985) value chain reflects an *idealised* model. In practice, companies' value chains will differ, for instance, depending on the sector they operate in and the characteristics of the product or service that is being created and sold.

The value chain model can be used as a framework to identify in which ways a firm's primary and support activities influence ESG issues (either positively or negatively). Figure 5.2 outlines an idealised value chain model and gives some examples of how relevant corporate activities can influence ESG issues (Porter and Kramer, 2006). Consider two examples: (1) Inbound logistics often affects a firm's CO_2 footprint, as it makes a difference whether input resources reach the firm by road, rail, air or sea. Although companies cannot easily change the mode of transportation, they can switch to low-carbon solutions within a certain transportation mode (e.g., using ships powered by alternative fuels). (2) A firm's marketing and sales practices can throw up ESG issues related to the handling of consumer information (e.g., affecting peoples' right to privacy) or advertising practices (e.g., targeting vulnerable groups). Some firms in the fast-moving consumer goods (FMCG) sector have designed campaigns in ways that they do not target children under 12 years of age.

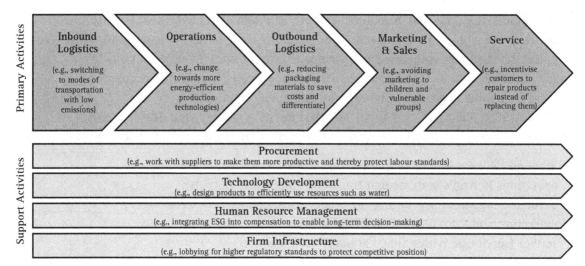

Figure 5.2 Value chain activities aligned with ESG issues.
Source: Adapted and modified from Porter and Kramer (2006).

Aligning value chain activities with ESG issues can be done in two ways (Porter & Kramer, 2006). On the one hand, relevant activities can be redesigned so that potential or real harm is either reduced or eliminated. Although such harm mitigation is necessary and important, its 'strategic' potential is often limited because it requires firms to *respond* to an existing problem (Porter and Kramer, 2006). However, harm mitigation often does not reinforce strategic goals. For instance, a firm that reduces packaging materials as part of outbound logistics mitigates harm caused by its value chain activities. Such reductions, however, lack alignment with strategic objectives unless the firm achieves significant cost savings through such a redesign and/or uses it to differentiate its products.

On the other hand, it is possible to transform value chain activities themselves in a way that they become aligned with a firm's strategic objectives and competitive context. Consider the example of procurement practices. To address bad working conditions in their supply chains global apparel companies did not just mitigate harm (e.g., by auditing factories), they also redesigned procurement practices so that working conditions could be improved. Nike, for instance, adopted supply chain practices that required workers to learn new skills, which in turn allowed factories to pay higher wages (Zadek, 2004). This change in how procurement was organised helped to upgrade working conditions, while it also allowed Nike to design longer-term supply chains and thus secure product supply.

5.3.3 Inside-out and Outside-In: Creating Shared Value

The inside-out and outside-in approaches share one feature: they both aim to unlock what Porter and Kramer (2006, 2011) have called creating shared value

(CSV). Porter and Kramer (2006: 88) believe that 'both inside-out and outside-in dimensions [need to work] in tandem. It is here that the opportunities for shared value truly lie.' The CSV approach restates what the outside-in and inside-out approaches already emphasised: a firm's strategic choices must benefit the firm *and* society. Without such a link, the choices may still be strategic choices, but they would not be aligned with a firm's corporate sustainability. Porter and Kramer (2011: 66) define CSV as 'policies and operating practices that enhance the competitiveness of a company while simultaneously advancing the economic and social conditions in the communities in which it operates'.

The CSV concept is aligned with the instrumental view on corporate sustainability. CSV's basic premise is that firms are supposed to move beyond trade-offs between ESG issues and their financial profitability. Firms should look for a 'business case' that is linked to their ESG activities. Without such a business case, firms' ESG activities would not be strategic enough and hence should not be undertaken at all (unless the firm switches to a different motivation, such as ethical reasoning; see Chapter 1).

Porter and Kramer (2011) define three ways in which shared value can be created.

1. *Reconceiving Products and Markets*: Firms following CSV thinking should design products/services in ways that societal problems are addressed. According to Porter and Kramer (2011), many existing products/services are not sufficiently designed to address societal needs. CSV therefore requires rethinking products/ services or opening entirely new markets to serve needs that are unmet. For instance, poorer people in developing and emerging economies are often overlooked by large companies although redesigned products could serve their needs very well. This, however, requires product innovations. Unilever developed Comfort One Rinse, a detergent that was designed to significantly reduce water usage for hand-washing laundry in water-stressed regions (Lawrence et al., 2015). This combines outside-in thinking (e.g., which customers can be served) with inside-out thinking (e.g., which products can be offered).

2. *Redefining Productivity in the Value Chain*: Many ESG challenges impact firms' value chains in the sense that they create risks and economic costs. Consider, for instance, the negative externalities that are created by excessive waste generation. These are costs for society, but also costs for the firm. CSV rests on innovations related to value chain activities which would help to redefine productivity, while keeping the demands of the competitive context in mind. For instance, redefining procurement practices by sharing technology with suppliers or offering them financing can help companies to upgrade their quality, while it assists buyer firms to maintain access to reliable quality.

3. *Enabling Local Cluster Development*: Many firms are embedded into local clusters, which influence their ability to innovate as well as their productivity.

Clusters can be best described as a geographically restricted rather dense network of businesses (e.g., buyers, suppliers, investors, competitors), as well as supporting institutions (e.g., universities). Silicon Valley, for instance, is a well-known cluster consisting of world-class technology firms, venture capitalists, major universities (e.g., Stanford) and specialised lawyers (e.g., on intellectual property rights). Firms can support such cluster creation through CSV initiatives – for example, by providing infrastructure (to connect different businesses), by educating people (to secure a skilled workforce) and by enabling open and fair competition (to attract reliable suppliers). CSV efforts that contribute to cluster creation often generate multiplier effects because effects 'spill over' to other companies, such as when a firm that grows due to positive cluster effects often also creates jobs in supporting industries.

While CSV has resonated well with practitioners, it has also received considerable scholarly critique. Vallentin and Spence (2017: 73) remind us that Porter and Kramer assume that the CSV mindset should be applied to all corporate decisions, while the examples that are given in support of the concept usually point to rather isolated corporate actions. Hence, it remains unclear how well aligned CSV decisions and corporate strategy really are. We also need to ask: What should firms do if shared value *cannot* be created? Porter and Kramer (2006, 2011) outline a win-win worldview in which tensions between the interests of firms and the interests of society either do not exist or are not considered (Crane et al., 2014: 136). Yet, firms should still do the right thing, even if the resulting actions do not create any shared value. We cannot always wait for shared value opportunities to arise whenever we would like firms to address the ESG challenges that surround all of us.

It is also unclear how exactly shared value should be operationalised (Vallentin and Spence, 2017: 76). While the economic side of shared value is rather easy to measure, it is more difficult to adequately quantify the social or environmental impact of firms' CSV initiatives. For this, companies would need to be able to isolate the impact of their CSV actions, which is difficult in some contexts. For instance, a firm that supports local cluster development by improving roads would need to show how much of the positive social development in and around that cluster really occurred due to the road (and not other effects).

5.4   Corporate and Business Strategy in the Sustainability Context

So far, we have assumed that corporations only have one strategy, and that this strategy should ideally be aligned with its corporate sustainability efforts. However, when we look at companies that operate in more than one business (e.g., think about Siemens producing trains, healthcare devices and other products), we must distinguish between corporate strategy and business strategy. Corporate strategy asks: '*Where should we compete?*', while business strategy asks: '*How should we compete?*'. Business strategy is about how a firm competes in a given market. It concerns decisions regarding choice of product and source of competitive advantage. Corporate strategy is about deciding which markets to enter and which business to be in. For smaller firms, with only one business unit, this distinction is usually less relevant (unless the firm aims to enter a new market). However, for larger firms with multiple business units, it makes sense to distinguish between corporate and business strategy.

5.4.1 Business Strategy and Corporate Sustainability

Business strategy looks at how a company can achieve a competitive advantage within the market that it addresses. Many of the reflections above on outside-in and inside-out thinking are focused on how to achieve a competitive advantage vis-à-vis competitors. A firm's competitive context and its value chain are usually tied towards *one* business unit, and companies with multiple business units will be faced with several value chains and multiple competitive contexts.

We can further sharpen our understanding of how business strategy and sustainability can be aligned by focusing on the source of competitive advantage that a firm uses. Porter (1985) distinguished two sources of competitive advantage: (1) firms can either gain a competitive edge by being a cost leader in their specific market; or (2) they can achieve a competitive advantage by differentiating their product. As an example, you can think of the difference between low-cost airlines and more traditional full-service carriers. Porter (1985) believed that firms can use the cost leadership or differentiation strategy either to serve a broad (mass) market or to focus on a market niche.

When considered from the perspective of corporate sustainability, each generic strategy throws up different questions (see Figure 5.3).

1. *Cost Leadership*: A firm's cost leadership can be based on different sources, such as reduced costs for input factors or economies of scale. However, lower costs usually come at a 'price', and often workers or the natural environment need to pay this price in terms of low wages or increased levels of pollution. In the global apparel industry, for instance, many retailers have been criticised for being able to offer low-cost products because their suppliers exploit workers. In some cases, however, low costs can also be a result of efficiency gains that were reached precisely because ESG issues were addressed (e.g., low-cost airlines often operate fuel-efficient jets).

2. *Differentiation*: Firms that follow a differentiation strategy look for ways to make their product or service stand out. Differentiation can be based on superior levels of service, certain product features or a unique brand image. Firms that are

Figure 5.3 Four generic business strategies and related ESG considerations

differentiators are usually strong when it comes to innovation as well as marketing and sales. However, differentiation can also throw up ESG problems. For instance, some brands strive to offer 'the best' product possible and thereby use highly specialised materials (e.g., crocodile leather) which, at least in some cases, challenge biodiversity. On the other hand, a strong ESG performance can also act as a differentiator, especially if you think about companies that have been built on a unique sustainability-related value proposition (e.g., Patagonia) or companies that use certification schemes with a mass market appeal (e.g., Fairtrade).

3. *Cost or Differentiation Focus*: Focusing on a specific market niche can either be done by being a cost leader serving a narrow market (e.g., Papa Murphy's delivering pizzas that are baked at home) or by offering highly differentiated products to customers (e.g., Rolls Royce luxury cars). Although market niches can be attractive due to their specialised nature, targeting customers in these niches can throw up ESG issues. For instance, targeting people with disabilities is often considered a niche market, while it also creates challenges because firms deal with vulnerable groups whose rights need to be protected. However, market niches can also exist because of ESG issues. For instance, Bird Friendly Coffee is a certification system that aims at targeting customers who prefer coffee that comes from farms which provide forest-like habitat for birds. Moreover, some market niches may develop in the future because of fundamental shifts in demand. Diesel cars, for example, are likely to become a niche market in the future (unless such cars are outlawed altogether).

5.4.2 Corporate Strategy and Corporate Sustainability

Companies with multiple business units usually need to ask themselves whether they should further differentiate (by adding more units) or focus (by selling units). Corporate strategy considers such multi-business firms and asks what businesses a company wants to compete in. This question can be approached from different angles. On the one hand, managers can simply make cost-benefit calculations when deciding which businesses to compete in. The strategy literature recommends that managers should build a portfolio of business units with complementary capabilities so that costs can be shared across units (Zhou, 2011). Moreover, managers also consider the attractiveness of a specific market (e.g., in terms of anticipated profits) and whether elements of the competitive context make market entry attractive (e.g., the costs of overcoming market barriers).

On the other hand, you can also link ESG considerations to such analyses. In general terms, there are two ways to include ESG in corporate strategy reflections:

1. *Business Units' ESG Risks*: If a multi-business company looks for ways to diversify and hence wants to add business units (e.g., through an acquisition), it needs to be aware of the potential ESG risks that exist vis-à-vis the market it plans to target. For instance, firms increasingly factor in climate-related risks when assessing possible targets for a takeover. Failure to address such risks on the side of the target company is often viewed as a future cost driver by buyers (National Law Review, 2021). However, you can also turn this argument around. Multi-business companies can also reduce their overall ESG risk exposure by selling or closing certain business units. In 2019, multi-business giant Unilever warned that it considers selling businesses that it views to be not in alignment with its overall sustainability strategy, such as its Magnum ice-cream business (Wood, 2019).

2. *Business Units' ESG Opportunities*: A multi-business company can equally consider the opportunity side that is attached to ESG. In many cases, venturing into new markets or buying other companies makes sense because of strong ESG opportunities. BP, for example, created a business unit entirely devoted to renewable energy, being aware of the long-term limitations of its other (fossil fuel) business units. In some cases, companies with a strong ESG value proposition become targets for takeover bids. In 2000, Ben & Jerry's – a funky ice cream company with a unique social value proposition – was acquired by Unilever because of its excellent ESG credentials and resulting consumer attractiveness. The challenge resulting from such takeovers is to preserve the unique identity of the acquired companies. In 2021, Ben & Jerry's announced that it will stop selling ice cream in the Occupied Palestinian Territory (OPT), a move the company viewed as being consistent with its core values. Although Unilever did not endorse this move, it emphasised that the company could make independent

decisions related to its social mission (and that this was fixed as part of the acquisition agreement; Unilever, 2021).

These examples show that multi-business companies must factor in corporate sustainability considerations when expanding or scaling down their portfolio of businesses.

5.5   Materiality Analysis: Identifying Strategic ESG Issues

Another approach to identify those ESG issues that are strategic (and not just generic) relates to the concept of 'materiality'. First developed within accounting, materiality refers to 'the status of information where its omission or misstatement could reasonably be expected to influence decisions that users make' (European Parliament, 2013, Article 2(16)). Put differently, an ESG issue would count as material if the omission or misstatement of this issue (e.g., in a corporate report) would influence the decisions of the users of this information (e.g., investors). The level of materiality of an ESG issue therefore shows the *strategic importance* of this issue for a particular company. Materiality analyses can be performed at different levels. Some firms identify material issues for the entire company, while others focus on material issues that are relevant for specific business units or countries of operation. An in-depth discussion of the regulatory frameworks that have shaped materiality analyses as well as the link between materiality and reporting are discussed in Chapter 17.

The materiality of ESG issues can be assessed from two perspectives.

1. *ESG Materiality (External View)*: An ESG issue can be material for a company because the organisation has a significant impact on the issue. For instance, a company with high levels of greenhouse gas emissions has, relatively speaking, a higher impact on climate change than a firm with lower emission levels.
2. *Financial Materiality (Internal View)*: An ESG issue can also be material for a company because the issue has a high financial impact on the company. This internal view emphasises that certain ESG issues can be a risk or an opportunity for a company and hence influence its financial results.

The joint consideration of both perspectives is often called 'double materiality'. Both perspectives are present in the basic materiality assessment model (see the option A scatterplot diagram in Figure 5.4). In this model, the firm categorises ESG issues according to (1) the importance of an issue to relevant stakeholders (external view) and (2) the potential impact of an issue on the business (internal view). There are various ways to modify this model. Option B shows an assessment model that is more externally oriented by contrasting (1) the importance of an issue to relevant

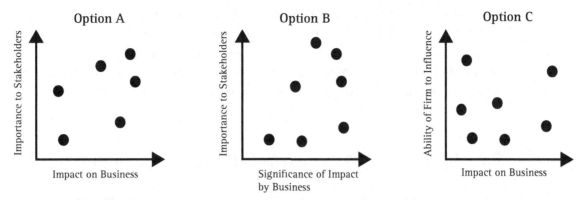

Figure 5.4 Different assessment models to determine the materiality of ESG issues

stakeholders and (2) the significance of a corporation's impact on this issue. Option B assumes that stakeholders do not necessarily need to perceive those ESG issues as important on which the company has the most significant impact (e.g., because stakeholders may be biased in their assessment). Option C shows an assessment model that is more internally oriented by contrasting (1) the ability of a firm to influence a certain ESG issue and (2) the potential impact of this issue on the business. Option C emphasises that firms may not be able to influence certain ESG issues although these issues impact them in business terms.

The sector in which a firm operates has the most significant influence on whether an ESG issue becomes material for a company, although the exact level of materiality will depend on a whole range of factors (e.g., Who are a firm's stakeholders? What is the size of the firm? In which countries is the firm active?). The Sustainability Accounting Standards Board (SASB) has developed so-called materiality maps showing which ESG issues are *likely* to be material for a company operating in a specific industry (see SASB, 2022). For instance, water and waste management is likely to be material in the beverages industry, while it is unlikely to be of importance in the advertising sector. Industry-specific materiality maps reflect that ESG risks and opportunities vary across industries, yet remain rather stable within an industry. This is because businesses within one sector often have comparable business models and hence are similar in the way they create value. Industry-specific materiality maps can be a starting point for discussing which ESG issues are material. They do not replace a full assessment, but they can help to narrow down the universe of potential ESG issues for management and stakeholders to discuss.

Materiality assessments should not just be valued for their output (a list of strategically relevant ESG issues). It is important to also value the process of conducting the materiality assessment as such. This process can throw up many unanswered questions, such as: Who are our stakeholders? What do these stakeholders expect from us? If done correctly, a materiality assessment requires a good deal of discussion within the organisation and can sharpen an organisation's understanding of why it engages with ESG issues and what it hopes to gain from such engagement. It is therefore essential to value materiality assessments for their own sake and to not outsource all work to external consultants.

5.6 Different Stages of Strategy-Sustainability Alignment

Up to this point, we have viewed the link between corporate sustainability and corporate strategy as an either-or choice: either firms align their corporate sustainability activities with their strategic direction or they do not. In practice, however, such alignment is less dichotomous and rather exists on a continuum. This is where stage models come into play (see e.g., Zadek, 2004; Mirvis and Googins, 2006; Valente, 2017). Such models provide a more granular perspective because they outline different stages of alignment between a firm's strategy and its corporate sustainability activities.

Valente's (2017) stage model shows how firms cope in different ways with the strategy-sustainability link. The identified stages are influenced by three criteria which jointly impact how firms make decisions about corporate sustainability:

- Level of inclusiveness: Does the firm acknowledge the existence of multiple systems (e.g., ecological and economic systems) within its decision-making?
- Level of interconnectedness: Does the firm acknowledge that these systems are interconnected with one another?
- Level of equity: Even if firms acknowledge interconnected systems dynamics, do they treat social, environmental and economic objectives as equitable?

Taken together, these three criteria allow the identification of five stages of alignment between a firm's strategy and its corporate sustainability practices (see Figure 5.5).

The *denial stage* shows a complete disconnect between strategy and corporate sustainability. Firms at this stage understand sustainability as isolated philanthropy that has little (or even nothing) to do with the company's operations. Firms at this stage would even deny the relevance of ESG issues for their operations, such as when the tobacco industry denied for a long time that their products cause various forms of cancer (Valente, 2017). At the *defensive stage*, firms start to admit partial responsibility for ESG challenges; however, they do not yet change their operations or strategic direction in any major way. Firms at this stage react to stakeholder pressure and emerging regulations that make it difficult to fully deny responsibility. At the defensive stage, companies address those ESG issues that are obvious to

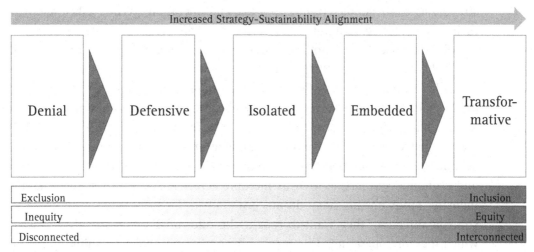

Figure 5.5 Inclusivity, interconnection and equality form the criteria for five stages of strategy-sustainability alignment. *Source:* Valente (2017: 93).

address and where 'quick wins' can be realised through minor adjustments. Both the denial and defensive stages reflect that firms do not relate ESG discussions to their competitive context or value chain in any substantial way.

Firms on the *isolated stage* start to take corporate sustainability seriously. Usually, sustainability is managed within a specific department of the organisation and the company has started to launch one (or more) products that exhibit specific sustainability features. A good example includes BMW releasing its first real electric vehicle (the i3) in 2013, but at the same time not changing its general strategy of selling fossil-fuel-powered cars. Such moves isolate corporate sustainability choices within the firm. The isolated product or service may very well be part of the firm's strategy and even require innovation (e.g., as a special business unit focused on sustainability), but sustainability is not yet part of the company's broader strategic positioning. The isolated stage moves much beyond the defensive stage where firms tried to use minor ESG actions 'to mask the system degradation of their traditional operations' (Valente, 2017: 97).

Companies operating on the *embedded stage* see sustainability as their key differentiator; they move beyond an isolated treatment of ESG issues. Companies like The Body Shop and Ben & Jerry's fall into this category. Sustainability discussions are part of the company's DNA and corporate culture, and there is a high degree of parity between social, environmental and economic objectives. While firms at the isolated stage had committed employees in single departments or units, businesses at the embedded stage have strong sustainability-related values that permeate the entire organisation. Patagonia, for instance, is known for a corporate culture that combines sustainable product innovation with genuine care for employees. Culture is an important mechanism to embed sustainability into a firm's strategy as it affects day-to-day routines and operations. When asked about how their job relates to sustainability, employees will often 'struggle to answer the question because they do not see sustainability as distinct from their daily routines and activities' (Valente, 2017: 100).

Finally, firms on the *transformative stage* share some similarities with companies on the embedded stage. However, while embeddedness aimed at linking strategy and sustainability within the scope of the firm, transformative companies aim to change their industry in ways that more sustainable practices are adopted. This requires acknowledging a high degree of interconnectedness between social, environmental and economic systems, as well as multiple actors in the firm's supply chain and industry. Firms on this stage do not just want to be sustainable in terms of their strategic direction: they want to rewrite the rules of the game for the industry in which they are operating. This reaches beyond traditional CSV thinking as introduced above because it requires a shift in perspective: from a concern with aligning corporate sustainability with strategy to a concern with using an already existing alignment to change industry norms. For instance, Interface Carpets, a US-based carpet company, not only pioneered technologies that lowered (toxic) carpet waste; it also challenged the business model of an entire industry (e.g., by starting to offer carpet-leasing solutions, see Valente, 2017).

It is important to *not* understand this stage model as linear. Companies do not necessarily need to linearly pass through the denial, defensive, isolated and embeddedness stages before reaching the transformative one. Some firms are 'born' with a transformative strategy because they are set up as social businesses, while other firms remain in a defensive mode. The stage model shows the importance of organisational learning (Zadek, 2004). Only if firms are willing and able to continuously learn about how ESG issues relate to their strategic direction will they be able to adopt a strategic approach towards corporate sustainability. Corporate sustainability is not a static topic. Like many other elements in a firm's competitive context, ESG issues change. Some issues increase in importance, while the salience of other issues decreases. For instance, climate change, just a fringe topic two decades ago, is a cause for concern for many these days (Revkin, 2019). Firms respond to changes in society's awareness of ESG issues in different ways, and this inevitably shapes how they align their strategic direction with their corporate sustainability efforts.

5.7   Chapter Summary

This chapter discussed different approaches that allow you to align firms' strategy with their sustainability practices. It is important to view the presented tools and arguments in context. Strategic corporate sustainability is just one possible way to organise a firm's engagement with ESG issues. While most firms will find such a strategic perspective attractive (as it supports the financial bottom line), other firms will base their ESG activities on more ethical (Chapter 3) or political (Chapter 6) considerations. Corporate strategy is often viewed as being amoral due to its instrumental focus. Strategic reasoning may allow us to see whether corporate sustainability makes business sense, but it may also prevent us from assigning a moral status to humans and the natural environment (Crane, 2000). Hence, basing our corporate sustainability engagement *exclusively* on strategic consideration runs the risk of making us 'ethically blind'. As King and Pucker (2021) remark, strategic reasoning about sustainability can reflect a dangerous allure of uncritically following win-win thinking.

You therefore need to view the concepts that were discussed in this chapter as one possible, but not the only, way to think about corporate sustainability. We started by asking what characterises strategic corporate sustainability. We identified several characteristics that distinguish strategic and non-strategic corporate sustainability. Based on this, we outlined inside-out and outside-in thinking. Both approaches represent different ways to align a firm's strategy with its ESG practices. Next, we discussed the difference between business and corporate strategy, and we concluded that both types of strategic reasoning give rise to different sustainability-related questions that managers must find answers to. We then discussed materiality assessments as another way to identify strategic ESG issues that a firm can address. While such assessments are a practical tool to approach corporate sustainability from a strategic angle, we also cautioned that materiality can potentially sideline ethical dilemmas that are attached to ESG issues. Finally, we reviewed different stages of firms' strategy-sustainability alignment. The underlying model demonstrated that firms' strategic corporate sustainability considerations are at different levels of maturity.

The discussed concepts reflect 'general recipes', and like all general recommendations they need to be treated with care. What works for company A in context A may not work for company B in context B. You can therefore think of these concepts as being *necessarily* 'empty' – in the sense that they are devoid of contextualised meaning (Rasche, 2008). Filling them with information that reflects the unique context of a company is the hard work that strategy and sustainability professionals must undertake.

CHAPTER QUESTIONS

1. How would you differentiate strategic from non-strategic corporate sustainability?
2. How can corporate strategy and corporate sustainability be aligned via inside-out and outside-in approaches?
3. What is the difference between corporate strategy and business strategy? How does this distinction influence a strategic approach towards corporate sustainability?

4. How can you identify material ESG issues that are interlinked with a firm's strategic decisions?

5. Differentiate different stages of alignment between a firm's strategy and its corporate sustainability efforts.

Case Study: *Unilever's Sustainable Living Plan*
Available from Cambridge University Press at www.cambridge.org/rasche2

FURTHER RESOURCES

- Ted Talk by Michael Porter, 'The Case for Letting Business Solve Social Problems', www.ted.com/talks/michael_porter_the_case_for_letting_business_solve_social_problems.
- In this Ted Talk, Porter outlines how he thinks about the relationship between businesses and society. Many of his reflections align directly with the topics discussed in this chapter.
- Crane, A., Palazzo, G., Spence, L. J. and Matten, D. (2014). Contesting the Value of 'Creating Shared Value'. *California Management Review*, 56(2), 130–153.
- An important reading to understand the limits of Porter's Creating Shared Value (CSV) concept.
- Polman, P. and Winston, A. (2021). *Net Positive: How Courageous Companies Thrive by Giving More than they Take*. Cambridge, MA: Harvard Business Review Press.
- A book that discusses the strategy-sustainability alignment more indirectly, but with a wealth of good and very practical examples.
- Ted Talk by Ray Andersen, 'The Business Logic of Sustainability', www.youtube.com/watch?v=iP9QF_lBOyA.
- Founder of Interface carpets, Ray Andersen, shares how the company connects the business and sustainability logics in a way that a transformative strategy emerged.

6 Political Approaches to Corporate Sustainability

GLEN WHELAN

LEARNING OBJECTIVES

- Build insight regarding corporate involvement in global governance.
- Discuss corporate political influence at the national and international levels.
- Reflect on the current trend towards CEO activism.
- Learn about the profound and complex influence that corporate products and services can have on sustainability, politics and daily life.

6.1 Introduction

Slowly but surely, people are recognising that corporate influence on political and sustainability concerns is wide-ranging. Thus, and in addition to their (legal) lobbying activities, their (illegal) bribery activities and their (more or less impactful) involvement in multi-stakeholder initiatives such as the UN Global Compact and the Forest Stewardship Council (FSC), it is increasingly acknowledged that corporations shape the politics and sustainability of daily life in other, much more general, ways, too. A corporation like Alphabet, for example – whose most famous asset is Google – does not just have an impact on sustainability concerns through its influencing elected officials or the carbon emissions for which it is directly responsible, but through its technologies enabling, among other things, the recording, analysing and directing of individual and social life.

As these remarks suggest, the purpose of this chapter is to encourage you to recognise, and begin to critically analyse, the diverse ways in which corporations can influence, and be responsible for, political and sustainability concerns. Indeed, the present chapter suggests that, in some instances at least, questions of sustainability, politics and corporate responsibility are inseparable. To get a quick sense of why this might be considered the case, ask yourselves the following: are corporations the problem, the solution or both the problem and the solution, to our climate change concerns? In short, and whatever answer you provide, this chapter proposes that any meaningful response to this sort of question will require that you simultaneously consider such matters as your expectations regarding corporate behaviour, the possibilities and limitations associated with political processes, and humanity's overall demand for carbon-emission-generating goods and services.

While the chapter's ultimate goal is to develop such complex understanding, the section 6.2 starts more simply, with a discussion of 'political' corporate social responsibility (CSR) and the role that corporations play in multi-stakeholder initiatives and global governance. Following this, section 6.3 outlines the influence that corporations can have on inter-national politics. Given the continuing trend for CEOs to speak out on social issues – even those that appear to have little relation to their corporation's core business interests – section 6.4 then provides you with a brief elaboration on (potential) CEO activism. Section 6.5 then returns to consider the ways in which corporate responsibility, politics and sustainability can intertwine. Following the chapter's brief concluding summary in section 6.6, you will find a short list of questions and further resources that can help reinforce and further develop your understanding.

6.2   'Political CSR': Governance Gaps, Multi-stakeholder Initiatives and Democracy

The idea of 'political' CSR (Scherer and Palazzo, 2007), and the associated idea of corporate citizenship (Matten and Crane, 2005), have enjoyed a relatively prominent status within the management and organisation studies literatures. By and large, these concepts emphasise that corporations, and multinational corporations in particular, do, and increasingly should, play a key role in the provision of global public goods given the presupposition that globalisation results in states (national governments) suffering a loss of power. Furthermore, these writings have tended to emphasise that corporations often can, and once again should, participate within multi-stakeholder initiatives or international accountability standards so as to better ensure that their policies and practices are democratically legitimate (Rasche, 2012). While the literature on 'political' CSR has its problems (see Whelan, 2012), it nevertheless possesses some descriptive and explanatory value. Accordingly, the present section outlines three aspects that are central to the 'political' CSR literature, and that can help give you a sense of why 'private' governance initiatives exist worldwide (e.g., the FSC).

6.2.1   Governance Gaps

Embedded liberalism is a term coined by John Ruggie in a 1982 article for *International Organization*. In this article – entitled 'International Regimes,

Transactions, and Change: Embedded Liberalism in the Postwar Economic Order' – Ruggie built upon what he described as Karl Polanyi's 'magisterial' 1944 work, *The Great Transformation*, to characterise the post-World War II order as one in which states agreed (with significant directive advice from the United States) to enable global market forces while simultaneously subjecting them to domestic (national) controls. As financial markets and production chains became increasingly global, however, and as global production chains became increasingly internalised within the institutional form of multinational corporations, Ruggie suggested that the embedded liberal compromise was under threat. In particular, Ruggie (2008: para. 3) proposed that we were living in a world characterised by 'governance gaps ... between the scope and impact of economic forces and actors, and the capacity of societies to manage their adverse consequences'.

The idea of 'governance gaps' has played a key role in the 'political' CSR literature because it suggests the need for multinational corporations to increasingly provide for a variety of (global) public goods that have predominantly been associated with states since World War II (e.g., basic human rights, rules of governance). Although this idea can be overstated – in that powerful states such as China and the United States will often be in a position to close governance gaps within specific regions as and when they desire – it points towards a more general consideration of importance. Specifically, the notion of governance gaps, or 'regulatory vacuums' (e.g., Matten and Crane, 2005: 172), helps quickly reveal that multinational corporation (MNC) policies and practices are not always subject to any sort of meaningful regulation or democratic legitimation.

As the idea of governance gaps has a helpful conceptual role to play in the analysis of global governance matters, it should be distinguished from the 'race to the bottom' thesis it is often related to (e.g., Matten and Crane, 2005: 173). The reason being that the race to the bottom thesis – which amounts to the suggestion that governments are actively competing with one another to attract multinational corporate investment through the (significant) lowering of environmental standards, occupational health and safety standards, and so on – is undermined by evidence throughout the social sciences (e.g., Whelan, 2012: 712–715). Accordingly, and given that the emergence of multi-stakeholder initiatives need not be based on this controversial thesis, it is proposed that the notion of governance gaps be taken as providing the general context within which they have emerged.

6.2.2 Multi-Stakeholder Initiatives

Although 'political' CSR writings are associated with other empirical phenomena – such as the (unilateral) provision of various citizenship rights (Matten and Crane, 2005) – they are most closely associated with multi-stakeholder initiatives. Multi-stakeholder initiatives are generally conceived as voluntary, self-regulatory and cross-sector governance structures that 'address a variety of social and environmental problems by bringing together corporations and civil society organizations as well as, in some cases, governments, labor organizations, and academia' (Rasche, 2012: 679–680). In contrast to states (national governments), whose influence is underpinned by coercive capacities (e.g., the police and military), multi-stakeholder initiatives are generally conceived as governing without the threat of force or violence. Rather, they make use of standards, principles, organisational learning, certification mechanisms, verification mechanisms and so on to regulate and improve the performance of corporations with regard to human rights, sustainability, deforestation and so on.

The UN Global Compact is perhaps the most prominent multi-stakeholder initiative. First proposed at the World Economic Forum in Davos on 31 January 1999, the Global Compact was formally launched on 26 July 2000. The Global Compact's board is comprised of four constituency groups: business, civil society, labour and the United Nations. Nevertheless, it is primarily concerned with improving the performance of just one of these constituents, business. In particular, the Global Compact seeks to promote organisational learning among the business and multinational corporate community with regard to their better discharging responsibilities relating to human rights, labour, the environment and anti-corruption. To this end, the Global Compact requires participant companies to submit an annual 'Communication on Progress' with regard to one or more of its ten principles (e.g., principle 5: the effective abolition of child labour), and encourages businesses to participate in its global and local learning networks (Rasche, 2012).

While the merits of the Global Compact and other multi-stakeholder initiatives are the subject of considerable debate (see below), they are not without their supporters. Indeed, the Global Compact, which aspires to be the world's most inclusive voluntary corporate citizenship initiative, currently has over 13,000 participants. It is thus more than half-way towards achieving the goal of 20,000 participants set by the UN Secretary-General in 2013.

Another multi-stakeholder initiative to have enjoyed some success is the FSC. Following 'the failure of governments at the 1992 United Nations Conference on Environment and Development (UNCED) to develop shared standards and activities for the protection of forests worldwide … a group of NGOs and corporations' decided to address this governance gap by creating the FSC in 1993 (Scherer and Palazzo, 2007: 1110). Regarding structure:

> The General Assembly, as the highest decision-making body of the FSC [Forest Stewardship Council], is organized into three membership chambers – environmental, social, and economic – for balancing the voting power of its diverse members. On the basis of its principles and criteria, the FSC has developed a certification for timber and timber products that is approved by independent bodies. The certification process itself contains rigorous

standards and independent monitoring procedures, which lead to a broad acceptance of the council among critical civil society organizations. (Scherer and Palazzo, 2007: 1110)

With more than 220 million hectares of forest certified worldwide, and with its 'state of the art' organisational structures and certification mechanisms, Scherer and Palazzo's (2007: 1110) suggestion that the FSC is a standout example of 'political' CSR is reasonable. Nevertheless, Scherer and Palazzo (2007) also recognise that the FSC, like multi-stakeholder initiatives more generally, has its critics. In many instances, such critiques are informed by one or more of the following considerations.

First, multi-stakeholder initiatives are often charged with enabling multinational corporations to avoid or escape meaningful responsibility for any social good concerns they are directed towards. This charge relates to the recognition that corporations are profit-focused actors who control significant resources. These resources can enable corporations to co-opt civil society voices by making the smallest of compromises, and to their thus minimising the extent to which such potentially dissenting, corporate-critical, voices can be heard (e.g., Levy, 2008).

The second criticism is that multi-stakeholder initiatives are limited by a neo-liberal (rather than embedded liberal) global order more generally. Representatives of developing countries, for example, have made use of neo-liberal limitations when they argue that multi-stakeholder initiatives, or developments in global governance more generally, should not be used as a trade barrier by the developed world. In reversing this point, both champions (Ruggie, 2008: para. 12) and critics (Moog et al., 2014) of multi-stakeholder initiatives have suggested that existing neo-liberal trade regimes should not be allowed to limit the advance and adoption of progressive, multi-stakeholder-led developments.

The third criticism, by way of contrast, is that multi-stakeholder initiatives enable a neo-liberal global order of trade and finance. Thus, and in mirroring the suggestion that individual corporations can benefit from the ceremonial and co-optation opportunities that multi-stakeholder initiatives provide, critics suggest that global capitalism as a whole can benefit from multi-stakeholder initiatives that reduce the perceived need for more coercive, state-enforced rules and regulations (e.g., Levy, 2008).

Finally, many of the main criticisms of multi-stakeholder initiatives relate to the existence of different theoretical interpretations and orientations. Thus, and in addition to the above-mentioned critical management scholars, who, in being informed by the likes of Gramsci, can be situated within the Marxist tradition (e.g., Levy, 2008; Moog et al., 2014); there are many other commentators influenced by any number of theoretical perspectives, who suggest that the posited merits of multi-stakeholder initiatives and 'political' CSR are often much less obvious than their defenders would have you believe (see, for example, the mention of Habermas, Rawls and Næss below).

6.2.3   Democracy

Many of the most interesting debates that 'political' CSR is subject to revolve around democracy: a fundamental political good within liberal- and social-democratic societies. To immediately constrain a discussion that could easily fill an entire book, it is here simply noted that many of these debates relate to the actuality, possibility and desirability of democratic corporate governance.

As the label itself suggests, a key purpose of multi-stakeholder initiatives is to democratise the governance of multinational corporations. Nevertheless, and as even their most vocal supporters recognise, the democratic possibilities inherent to multi-stakeholder initiatives are limited by the impossibility of all individuals interested in the activities of a large multinational corporation participating (directly) in all of its decision-making processes. Indeed, it is because of this that multi-stakeholder initiatives are generally populated by formal organisational actors – for example, environmental and human rights non-governmental organisations (NGOs) – who indirectly represent a diversity of social voices more generally (Scherer and Palazzo, 2007). But as more critical voices have argued, the fact that multinational corporations commonly possess far more resources (e.g., lawyers and money) than all the other participants (e.g., Moog et al., 2014); and the fact that corporations, NGOs and various other organisations involved in multi-stakeholder initiatives have significant vested interests that act to prevent them seeing eye to eye on many issues, can result in even the 'sub-ideal' of 'deliberative democracy' being un-actualised. Petroleum corporations like Shell and 'deep' green environmental organisations like Greenpeace, for example, have long seemed more interested in opposing, rather than reaching agreement with, each other in democratic fora.

One way by which this 'under-democratised' status of multi-stakeholder initiatives and corporate decision-making could be addressed is through the development of more directly democratic corporate governance structures. In addition to its having been suggested by advocates of 'political' CSR (e.g., Scherer and Palazzo, 2007), the need to democratise corporate governance structures is suggested by scholars in other disciplines such as social and environmental accounting (Cooper and Owen, 2007). The possibility of this occurring 'across the board', however, seems low. The reason why is that private investors generally provide capital in the hope of generating (more or less significant) financial returns. Given that the actualisation of democratic corporate governance structures is proposed to result in managers *not* being instrumentally concerned to generate significant financial returns, but, rather, to provide for the (less profitable) social good (Scherer and Palazzo, 2007), it may be presumed that many private investors would choose to invest their monies elsewhere. Moreover, the fact that powerful non-democratic states like China and Russia are also major financiers of corporations – for example, Sinopec, Gazprom – suggests that the possibility of states providing finances that enable increasingly democratic corporate governance structures should not be overstated either.

While the above concerns regarding the actualisation and possibility of democratic corporate governance structures are very real, they are by no means insurmountable. The next question that must be raised, then, is: *Should* democratic corporate governance structures be developed? While a final answer to this question cannot hope to be provided here, it is possible to quickly identify a number of points that have informed prior considerations of it.

In the first instance, it is noted that the vast bulk of work in 'political' CSR (implicitly) suggests that, in addition to helping 'fill' existing governance gaps, the democratisation of corporate governance structures could have the benefit of positively enabling a cosmopolitan citizenry worldwide. That is, the 'political' CSR literature tends to suggest that the democratisation of multinational corporate governance structures, in particular, can potentially enable 'citizens of the world' to transcend national boundaries and participate, more or less directly, in the democratic determination of the policies and practices of globally influential corporate actors.

In contrast, the work of the influential German philosopher Jürgen Habermas suggests that the democratisation of corporate governance structures would undermine the functional differentiation of contemporary, modern, Western societies, and that any potentially actualised democratisation of corporate governance would pale in comparison to the (cosmopolitan) democracy enabled by existing liberal- and social-democratic state institutions. Much like Habermas, the work of the (just as influential) American philosopher John Rawls suggests that – because markets have efficiency benefits, and given the presumed importance of free association among individuals of diverse 'comprehensive' beliefs (e.g., different religious beliefs) – the broad principles of political justice that apply to democratic state organisations should not be directly applied to all organisations (e.g., business corporations). Where Rawls's work departs from that of Habermas, however, is in its suggesting that a more or less pluralistic global political order is desirable. What Rawls's work appears to suggest, then, is that multi-stakeholder initiatives founded on deliberative democratic principles may not be consistent with, and thus legitimately rejected by, 'decent hierarchical peoples' whose political traditions do not emphasise the importance of (thoroughgoing) democratic participation (see Whelan, 2012, for a fuller discussion of Habermas, Rawls and global governance).

On a much more radical note, various writers from a diverse range of scholarly traditions (e.g., Alberto Melucci's work on social movements; Arne Næss's work on deep ecology) suggest that, rather than asking questions about corporate democracy, what we should really be asking is: Should large-scale multinational corporations even exist? In suggesting that the answer might be no, such authors come into fundamental conflict with other perspectives. For example, they come into conflict with business ethicist Tom Donaldson, who used his 1982 book *Corporations and Morality* to argue that the reason corporations and markets exist is because they help societies solve a whole host of political-economic problems that would otherwise be found in a state of nature characterised by the frightening prospect of a Hobbesian war of all against all.

6.3   Corporations and Inter-National Politics

While corporate involvement in multi-stakeholder initiatives and global governance is interesting, and potentially capable of having an impact on vital sustainability concerns, the importance of such involvement is arguably overshadowed, considerably, by the influence that corporations can have at the level of national and international politics. For this reason, the chapter now provides you with a brief explication of how corporations try to shape political affairs at each of these respective levels.

6.3.1   National Politics

The corporate political activity and strategy literature has long investigated 'corporate attempts to shape government policy in ways favourable to the firm ...' (Lawton et al., 2012: 87). Whereas writings on corporate responsibility are often underpinned by a normative agenda (i.e., the concern to identify what it is that corporations morally should or should not do), writings on corporate political activity have generally sought to 'mirror the natural and formal sciences and [have thus] relegate[d] ethics and (irrational) human behaviour to matters of secondary importance' (Lawton et al., 2012: 87). For this reason, 'political' CSR scholarship appears to have largely ignored the corporate political activity literature, and vice versa (Rasche, 2014).

When one looks to the broader CSR, management and politics literatures, however, the possibility of bridging this existing divide becomes readily apparent. The extensive literature on corporate lobbying, for example (Lawton et al., 2012), raises questions as to whether or not the liberal notions of citizenship that underpin self-interested practices are justified. Indeed, the fact that corporations often promote legislation that clearly benefits themselves more than it does society, and that corporations can 'capture' governmental actors (e.g., regulators) for their own purposes, highlights that powerful corporate lobbying capacities often entail significant moral and political concerns. As a result, corporate political actions need to be considered as part of corporate responsibility more generally (e.g., Lyon et al., 2018).

This last point becomes even more important once you recognise that corporations often seek to develop much less explicit, and sometimes illegal, relations with governments. Writings on corporate-government relations in non-Western countries, for example, highlight the importance of friendly or familial networks. Indeed, scholars speculate that, 'for many emerging economies, CPA [corporate political activity] essentially involves corruption, or ... cronyism' (Lawton et al., 2012: 92). Given the extent to which bribery and corruption varies from country to country, it is generally recognised that such (illegal) practices are shaped by a given country's domestic political structure and culture. Moreover, the comparative analysis of foreign direct investment suggests that the willingness of multinational corporations to engage in corrupt practices abroad increases along with the extent of corruption found within its home country (Cuervo-Cazurra, 2006). As a result, anyone concerned with corporate responsibility and sustainability needs to think about how corporations are shaped by their political, economic and social environments at 'home' and abroad (e.g., Matten and Moon, 2020).

6.3.2 International Politics

National and international political matters often overlap in complicated, international, ways. The Siemens bribery scandal of 2008, for example, involved employees within the German engineering giant reportedly paying in the realms of US $1.4 billion in bribes to win contracts in many countries around the world. Further to raising the ire of people globally, and further to other penalties in other countries having to be paid, these bribes resulted in the German company reaching a settlement with the US Securities and Exchange Commission in which the company agreed to disgorge $350 million, and in which they paid a $450 million fine to the US Department of Justice to settle criminal charges.

Despite what such complicated cases suggest, it is still helpful to analytically differentiate between national and international politics. In the present chapter, then, it is suggested that corporate political relations can be said to occur at the national level when they are focused on shaping political environments within discrete state borders (e.g., Siemen's bribing of Greek officials to win contracts within Greece). By way of contrast, corporate political actions can be said to occur at the international level when they are focused on influencing international organisations, international treaties and so on. Moreover, and as summarised in Table 6.1 below, it is suggested that international politics and global governance, while obviously overlapping, can also be distinguished on the basis of the actors and mechanisms involved.

Levy and Egan (1998) provide a good illustration of corporate political relations at the international level when they document the multitudinous efforts that corporations made to influence climate change negotiations at the 1992 UN Conference on Environment and Development in Rio de Janeiro. In particular, they note that – with 'Maurice Strong, head of the Canadian electric utility Ontario Hydro ... appointed to the position of secretary general of the conference', and with Strong appointing 'as his principal advisor the Swiss industrialist and multimillionaire Stephan Schmidheiny, who organized' the (World) Business Council for Sustainable

Table 6.1 Corporate national, international and global governance relations

	Scope	Governance Actors	Governance Mechanisms
National	Within State Boundaries	Mainly National Governments	National Legislation and Regulation
International	Multi-State through Global	Mainly National Governments and International Organizations (e.g., the United Nations, the European Union)	International Directives and Treaties
Global Governance	Regional through Global	Mainly NGOs (e.g., those affiliated with the FSC)	International Accountability Standards

Development, 'a group of industrialists representing forty-eight of the world's largest multinational corporations' – corporate interests were better able to 'ensure that the Framework Convention on Climate Change (FCCC) agreed to at the conference contained little commitment to concrete action' (Levy and Egan, 1998: 343).

Banerjee (2012) tells a similar story regarding the role of industry at the UN Durban Climate Change Conference in 2011. In particular, he suggests that the 'Platform for Enhanced Action' that emerged from the conference was a non-binding agreement to reach an agreement at some time in the future, and that this flexible arrangement was consistent with corporate interests at the conference, who tended to argue that:

> ... emissions reductions would be too costly and would erode the profitability of firms, lead to increased prices for consumers, slow economic recovery, [and] give polluting competitors in developing countries an unfair advantage resulting in the closing down or relocation of plants. (Banerjee, 2012: 1774)

As many have highlighted the efforts that corporations make to block or 'slow down' the development of international standards, it is important to remember that corporations can also try to speed them up. Thus, if a specific corporation, or group of corporations, expects that the implementation of higher international standards (e.g., those relating to human rights) will result in their enjoying some sort of competitive advantage, then you can safely assume that they will quickly push for their development (Whelan, 2012: 714–715).

6.4   (Potential) CEO Activism

Hitherto, the chapter has been concerned with the actions of corporations. But of course, corporations are comprised of many different people with different ideas and understandings, and some of these people possess relative power in their own right. CEOs in particular, are widely recognised as occupying a privileged position from which to organise affairs and make their voices heard. Indeed, there is at least anecdotal evidence to suggest that CEOs are increasingly inclined to use their post as a sort of lever for political and social change. For better or worse, this has given rise to a new term, the CEO activist.

While it may ultimately be difficult to prove that a specific CEO advocates for a specific social cause that is beyond, or goes against, the interests of the business they direct, it is safe to say that at least some CEOs act in political ways that are not immediately, directly or obviously beneficial to the 'core' business of their corporate employer (Chatterji and Tofel, 2018). If we presume that this is a relatively new or increasingly prominent phenomenon, the obvious question that arises is: Why now? Why are CEOs discounting the 'so-called Michael Jordan dictum that Republicans buy sneakers too', which is meant to remind 'executives that choosing sides on divisive issues can hurt sales' (Chatterji and Tofel, 2018).

Perhaps the best explanation is that, in our present digital age, 'silence is more conspicuous – and more consequential' (Chatterji and Tofel, 2018). In other words, what one might say is that some CEOs concerned about their career prospects, and ultimately their legacy, want to be on the 'right side' of history. CEOs who believe in moral progress, for example (e.g., the idea that there is a general trend towards moral norms being universally applied), could be inclined to act today in accord with what they predict will be the norms of tomorrow (see Figure 6.1). Additionally, when CEOs acknowledge that digital technologies make it infinitely easier to keep a record of what they do (or don't) say, and do (or don't) support, they could be very strongly motivated to make a stand for the 'right thing' right now – even if it does not currently enjoy popular support (Whelan, 2021: 80–81).

Even if you personally are not a CEO, you could still be concerned about being perceived as regressive, as not being 'woke' enough. Think about it for a moment: are there any corporations that you would not want to work for, that you would not want listed on your CV and social media accounts? Would you be personally willing to work for a company that is a major contributor to greenhouse gases? For a company that is in the business of slaughtering animals? For a company whose CEO has publicly advocated against LGBTQ2+ rights? While it was previously relatively simple to hide your work history and career path, at least from those people who didn't work in your occupational or professional sphere, it is becoming much more difficult to do so given digital technologies.

More generally, have you ever thought about not just what your posts on social media and the Internet mean for you today, but what they will mean for you in the future? These sorts of questions relate to the potential need you might already feel to manage your 'personal (future) past' (Whelan, 2021: 89) – especially if you want to occupy some sort of coveted and public position at a future point in time. If, for

Figure 6.1 CEO activism can be motivated by desire to be ahead of moral trends

instance, you want to be a CEO in the future, then you might want to think about your 'activism' today – because what you choose to (not) advocate for right now could significantly shape your employment prospects, and many other things, in the years to come.

6.5   Products, Services and the Corporate Governance of Sustainable Lifestyles

As the section 6.4 suggests, considerations of corporate political and sustainability responsibilities go beyond such matters as corporate involvement in multi-stakeholder initiatives, appropriate lobbying and the environmental improvement of their operational activities. In beginning to flesh this suggestion out, this penulti-mate section of the chapter looks into how corporate products and services can impact, in complex ways, upon political and sustainability concerns that are a part of daily life. Moreover, you will be asked to reflect upon how such impacts could, for better or worse, further extend the breadth and depth of considerations for which corporations are held responsible.

To get things started, it will help for you to think about Alphabet, some of whose assets you are almost certain to already know: for example, Android (the phone operating system); YouTube (the online video platform); Nest (a company that aims at developing the 'helpful' home); and Google (the search engine). What is perhaps less well known is that Alphabet also owns a share of other well-known companies too, such as the ride share giants Uber and Lyft, and the 'meat from plants' manufacturer Impossible Foods. Given this rich network of products and services, a number of which many people use more or less continuously, it is to be expected that Alphabet shapes political and sustainability concerns in complex, and potentially very problematic, ways.

Back in 2016, Alphabet's 'moonshot' factory – which is simply known as X – produced a short film called *The Selfish Ledger* that does a good job of introducing Alphabet's (potential) influence. The film's substantive concern was to demonstrate that the data we all continually generate can be collectively conceived as some sort of general will or common good that possesses a life of its own. According to Alphabet insiders, the film was conceived as a thought experiment. Whatever the case, the film – which is easily found by searching for its title – is both intriguing and problematic.

In terms of the intrigue, the short film (less than 10 minutes long) quickly reveals how *The Selfish Ledger* – the name given to the 'common will' formed through the continuous collection and analysis of our digitally recorded life-stories – can form a considered perspective on our wants and values (Whelan, 2021: 129–130). Additionally, it quickly demonstrates how an integrated network of hardware and software – of physical, material goods (e.g., Uber vehicles, Android phones, Nest smart home equipment) and their more cognitive, informational counterparts (e.g., databases, algorithms) – could come to form its own ideas about what we should want, value and do.

With this in mind, and given current levels of technological development, it is easy to imagine a world where many people have an automated voice assistant that is connected to a mobile or wearable device and that has access to your 'digital dossier' (Whelan, 2021: 72–73). This assistant, once it reaches a given level of sophistication, would not be limited to responding to your questions or demands as and when you make them (e.g., 'what time is it?', 'please book me a haircut for 4.30 tomorrow'), but could also try to convince you to value different things and make different choices. Among other things, then, this assistant could try to help you become a 'better' you: for example, someone who goes to the gym at 5.30 every morning; who actually stops eating meat and dairy; who finally volunteers down at the local soup kitchen (see Figure 6.2).

Which brings us to the problematic aspect. In short – and as those of you who have already seen *The Selfish Ledger*, or who are familiar with Zuboff's work (e.g., 2015), will likely attest – these possibilities are at least a little frightening when it comes to the matter of personal privacy, the seeming loss of individual agency, and the prospect of corpocratic and/or algocratic (Danaher, 2016) rule. Yet, as has just

Figure 6.2 The corporate governance of sustainable lifestyles

been suggested, many of us already live in a world that looks quite a lot like that of *The Selfish Ledger.* social media feeds, search engine suggestions and even plain old legacy media (e.g., television, radio, newspapers) already create a variety of pre-formed, or informed, realities (Flyverbom and Whelan, 2019). As people increasingly inhabit these pre-structured, informed spheres, they may also be increasingly inclined to accept them as the norm. In its turn, this acceptance gives rise to the prospect of people actively desiring increasing levels of paternalistic guidance with regard to such things as the realisation of sustainability.

Hitherto, humanity has proven rather unsuccessful when it comes to ameliorating a whole host of environmental problems. Carbon emissions, for example, continue to increase despite their climate change implications having been recognised for decades. This reality raises the question as to whether or not individual consumers and citizens will freely make the changes that are seemingly needed. Thus, and while those of a liberal and/or democratic sentiment will shy away from top-down measures designed to radically reduce carbon emissions, others might suggest it is our only way out.

In addition to looking to state actors – such as the Chinese Communist Party, who enjoyed huge success in limiting the spread of Corona virus (COVID-19) via digital authoritarian means in 2020 – those with less than liberal inclinations could also look to the current crop of big tech companies as their potential saviours. At the moment – and as those opposed to the existence of monopolies commonly lament – the likes of Alphabet, Amazon and Apple are a key part of the day-to-day lives of many around the world. Consequently, it might be suggested that if various sustainability concerns are to be ameliorated, let alone resolved, any time soon, then these corporate actors will need to play a significant role.

For example, it might be thought that, in addition to improving their corporate operations (e.g., their own labour standards, reducing their environmental footprint), these corporations should play a more active role in the guidance and directing of people's everyday decision-making. Thus – and just as it is often now expected that internet and social media companies should counter, minimise and prevent the spread of fake news – it might be thought that such companies should actively seek to promote a more sustainable ethic among global society. No doubt, this would prove – and has already proven – difficult to do. But as those critical of big tech companies suggest when noting the depth and breadth of their influence, if any organisations can do it, it may well be them.

For obvious reasons, those whose interests align with big tech are not slow to suggest the same thing. Thus, and further to their being presented in a somewhat more creative fashion in Alphabet's short film *The Selfish Ledger*, leading lights at Alphabet, such as current CEO Sundar Pichai (2020), regularly go on the record to emphasise the ways in which Alphabet can empower the billion plus people that use their products worldwide to 'make sustainable choices'. Moreover, once it is noted that these billion plus users continuously reveal their preference for the convenience and utility of the megacorporation's (privacy infringing/transforming) products and services, it is not ridiculous to imagine these same people advocating for Alphabet, or other corporations, to play an increasingly active role in making them live a sustainable life. After all, life's hard when you have to make choices: so why not just let someone or something else make them for you?

6.6   Chapter Summary

This chapter began by introducing you to the idea of 'political' CSR. In particular, it was noted that 'political' CSR has been used to suggest that multi-stakeholder initiatives (like the UN Global Compact) do, and should, play a key role in addressing 'governance gaps' or 'regulatory vacuums', and that multinational corporations should be 'democratised'. Following this, it was noted that – in addition to their being key actors within multi-stakeholder initiatives, and with regard to global governance concerns more generally – corporations are also key actors when it comes to considerations of inter-national politics: for example, corporate lobbying and corruption of nation states, corporate pressure on international organisations and treaties. In moving from a more organisational to a more individual level, it was then suggested that the recent and rapid development of information and communication technologies provides a succinct explanation as to why activism appears to be currently experiencing a surge in popularity among (potential) CEOs. And in section 6.5, you were provided with a brief introduction to the complex ways in which corporate products and services give rise to complex possibilities in terms of the governance of sustainable lifestyles.

The underlying purpose of the present chapter, then, has been to encourage you to recognise that corporations can have a profound impact on political and sustainability concerns. While the more obvious ways in which corporations can exert political and sustainability impacts are undoubtedly important (e.g., corporations who lobby for, or against, national or global carbon emission targets), the importance of such manifest impacts is arguably overshadowed by other, less immediately apparent was, in which corporations can shape daily life. In particular, and as the preceding discussions of (potential) CEO activism and corporate products and services have begun to suggest, corporations are in the process of transforming how we educate and entertain ourselves, how we present ourselves to the world at large and how we socialise with others. They are also transforming the ways by which our lifestyles can be governed and directed. Whether for good or bad, then, it seems necessary that you take questions of corporate responsibility seriously when considering the planet's, complexly intertwined, political and sustainability concerns.

CHAPTER QUESTIONS

1. What are the pros and cons of multi-stakeholder initiatives for enhancing sustainability? On balance, do you think they are a positive or negative development?

2. Imagine that fifteen years from today, you will achieve your career ambition of being the CEO of a globally renowned corporation or organisation (e.g., Adidas, Proctor & Gamble, Tesla). What does this mean in terms of your political activism today? What contemporary social concerns (e.g., Animal Rights, Black Lives Matter, Climate Change, LGBTQ2+ rights) should you be digitally 'on the record' as (not) supporting?

3. Do you think that big tech corporations (e.g., Alphabet, Amazon) need to play a larger or smaller role in the governance of daily life if we are to successfully address climate change concerns?

Case Study: *Google Glass – The Future of Political Transparency?*
Available from Cambridge University Press at www.cambridge.org/rasche2

FURTHER RESOURCES

- Elon Musk

Given the evidence, the CEO of SpaceX and Tesla, and (co)founder of The Boring Company, Neuralink and OpenAI, likes to share his opinions. On any given day, you'll find him talking about his democratic dreams for space exploration, the carbon costs of bitcoin, or a pig with a computer chip in its brain. Whatever the actual value of his various points of view, Musk is good viewing for those interested in how corporations, sustainability and politics intertwine.

- Epstein, E. J. (1996). *Dossier: The Secret History of Armand Hammer.* New York, NY: Carrol & Graf.

For a real-life story of corporations and politics you couldn't make up, Epstein's story of Armand Hammer is hard to beat. Epstein reveals that Hammer – the key player in the emergence of the still-existent Occidental Petroleum Corporation, a significant benefactor to the arts and self-proclaimed champion of world peace – had (covert) links to the Soviet Union throughout much of his career, and played a seemingly key role in changing the nature of oil geopolitics. For a primer on the importance and vanity of corporate political relations and CEO activism, this book is hard to beat.

- *Silicon Valley* (TV Series, 2014–19).

No doubt, there are some very intelligent and well-intentioned people working within Silicon Valley. But as this critical and very funny series suggests, the southern San Francisco Bay Area may not be as merit based, let alone trustworthy, as tech CEOs like to suggest.

7 Ecological Approaches to Corporate Sustainability

ARNO KOURULA AND MINNA HALME

LEARNING OBJECTIVES

- Review key environmental challenges and trends.
- Outline key principles for corporate sustainability.
- Propose a framework to organise ecological lenses within corporate sustainability.
- Call for not merely systems thinking, but also 'systems action'.

7.1 Introduction

The history of sustainability thinking has evolved significantly in the past centuries and especially decades. This chapter reviews some of the key principles typically adopted within ecological approaches to (corporate) sustainability; enumerates the main (environmental) challenges we face; aims to provide an overview of different dominant theories and lenses; addresses the issue of whether progress is being made; and suggests approaches and actions that each of us can take. In contrast to the other chapters in Part I providing different 'approaches' to corporate sustainability, ecological perspectives emphasise the interrelationships of organisms and their environment. While its roots are in biology, when we speak of ecology we take into consideration a range of perspectives across different sciences. Our focus is broadly speaking on examining how firms relate to and are embedded in their natural environments. Before moving forward, let us start with a thought experiment: If you were to imagine an environmentally sustainable company, what would it look like? Can you name such a sustainable company?

A good place to start the discussion of ecological aspects of sustainability is the Brundtland (1987) Commission's classic definition of sustainable development as 'development that meets the needs of the present without compromising the ability of future generations to meet their own needs'. This definition makes sustainability inter-generational and thus adopts a longer time horizon than the quarterly or yearly targets or planning cycles of many companies. It also clearly links to available natural resources and explicitly calls for meeting needs instead of aiming to maximise societal benefits, thus invoking a sense of balance between social, ecological and economic dimensions of sustainability (or 'people, planet and profit' in corporate sustainability parlance). We should note that the Brundtland report also calls for intra-generational (i.e., within currently existing generations) justice. While sustainable development is commonly understood as anthropocentric (i.e., human-centric), a central aspect to this notion is also inter-species justice (i.e., between different living species beyond humans), bringing in a more bio-centric notion of development. If we have now defined sustainable development, what then is a sustainable corporation? A firm which follows the principles of sustainable development? Yes ... and no. Let's reflect on this question in this chapter. Ultimately (spoiler alert!), we will argue that (environmental) sustainability is not an organisational characteristic, but should be understood as a systemic (inter-organisational) element. We will examine companies not as external actors with a relationship to the environment, but rather as embedded within their natural environments.

For those of you interested in learning more about how social and environmental perspectives have co-evolved in management, but emerged from different origins, we recommend Bansal and Song's (2017) examination of the roots of corporate responsibility and corporate sustainability. For those of you interested in a broader review of the history of environmental sustainability, we recommend the work of Caradonna (2014). In short, the notion and discussion related to sustainability discourse has changed considerably over the years and it has become one of the most prevailing topics of debate and discussion within society.

As a rather broad characterisation, we can speak of contrasting a critical call for having fewer material things (consumption) and using fewer resources (environmental impact) to more positive notions of regeneration at the local level and flourishing at the societal level. At the company level, we have seen a more internally oriented enterprise integration (focusing on environmental management) being complemented with a more externally oriented market transformation (focusing on the purpose and sustainability impact of the firm) (see Hoffman and Roy in Chapter 23 of this book). We should note while we focus on the corporate perspective to environmental sustainability, the role of other societal sectors such as governments' environmental legislation and regulation (see Chapters 6 and 12 of this book) and civil society contributions (including environmental non-governmental organisations) (see Chapter 13 of this book) are invaluable. Next, let's turn to a more detailed review of important trends and challenges.

7.2 Ecological Trends and Challenges

In 1992, over 1,700 independent scientists, including the majority of living Nobel laureates in the sciences at the time, published a 'Warning to Humanity' (Union of

Concerned Scientists, 1992). This warning began with the words: 'Human beings and the natural world are on a collision course.' This call outlined dangerous trends regarding climate change, population growth, freshwater availability, ozone depletion, overfishing, deforestation and biodiversity. In the over three decades that have passed since this warning, have we been able to address these major environmental challenges? The answer is, as you may have guessed it, a resounding 'no'. The assessment of the world's scientific community is alarming (Ripple et al., 2017). While there have been some successes – most notably regulation addressing atmospheric ozone depletion and increasing the area of land dedicated to conservation, as well as a changing global awareness of pressing environmental challenges – the broader trends have continued and in many cases intensified. Quite simply, there are more of us (increasing population), we are using more resources (increasing affluence) and we are severely harming our natural ecosystems (increasing impact). We should also note that, from the perspective of environmental justice, those with high socio-economic status have a disproportionally high environmental impact (see Nielsen et al., 2021).

In fact, human beings' impacts on the planet are considered so vast that we have started calling this epoch the Anthropocene, the age of humans. The Anthropocene refers to the proposed name of the current geological epoch in which we are living. For more on the Anthropocene as it relates to climate change, see Chapter 23 of this book and its Figure 23.6 depicting the 'Great Acceleration' of environmental, social and economic trends. Rising population, greenhouse gas emissions and temperature go hand in hand with deforestation, loss of biodiversity and decrease in freshwater resources (Ripple et al., 2017). What is common to all these trends is that they indicate either very rapid growth or very rapid decline, each involving significant environmental impacts.

Impacts of human beings on the planet abound, ranging from subtle but significant changes in the composition of the atmosphere (causing climate change), to large changes to the surface of the planet due to agriculture, deforestation, urbanisation and mining (leading to less than 3 per cent of the world's land area to be ecologically intact; see Plumptre et al., 2021), and to impacts on oceans and marine ecosystems, ultimately humans becoming the main cause of the ongoing sixth mass extinction period that our planet has seen. We have now come to a point where human-made objects (from cell phones to buildings and T-shirts to aeroplanes) outweigh all living things (meaning all plants, bacteria, animals and, well, us) (Elhacham et al., 2020).

It is important to note that human societies have seen incredible developments over the past century. World population has more than quadrupled in this time and is likely to stabilise and plateau in the future. During the past century, average life expectancy has more than doubled, literacy rates have more than quadrupled, the world economy has increased by a factor of 80, the share of people living in extreme poverty has dropped by a factor of 8 and we have seen astonishing developments in science and technology. Unfortunately, this human development has most often come at a significant ecological cost. While we see the economy growing (produced capital), the social aspects (human capital) have not grown at the same pace and the ecological consequences have been severe (natural capital) (Managi and Kumar, 2018). Business and its sustainability can be seen as both a (main) culprit and as (part of) a solution to these challenges.

7.3   Ecological Principles of Corporate Sustainability

Before trying to define sustainability for a firm, it is good to determine key ecological principles and aspirations of how we should look at the topic area in general. The discussion of sustainability as it pertains to business firms is founded on some key principles which are listed and briefly presented below. Here we echo and revisit some of the more general principles as listed in the introductory chapter of this book, but from an environmental perspective.

Science-based. Corporate sustainability is deeply rooted in sustainability science and engineering as well as management studies. In essence, the foundation of sustainability thinking and action is evidence-based. It is only through evidence of ecological impact that we can start to tackle sustainability assumptions or myths, such as the idea that it is individual material consumption choices that will save the world or that the rising wealth of the poorest on the planet will have the largest negative environmental impact in the future.

Practical. While much of this chapter is dedicated to specific ways of seeing or understanding the topic, corporate sustainability is inherently a practical problem of how to minimise the negative environmental impacts and maximising positive environmental impacts of a business model (for a discussion of business models, see Chapter 19 of this book).

Contextual. The old adage from town planning – 'Think global, act local' – has a lot of truth to it. Universal solutions to sustainability are rare and all approaches should be adapted to the local context. Environmental innovations or practices that work in Cairo might not work in Copenhagen or Caracas.

Just. A central consideration is the inclusive nature of participation to environmental sustainability. Important questions include: Who gets to participate and who gets to sit at the table where decisions about environmental rules are made? Are different stakeholders part of the conversation or are they being 'talked at'? Is the discussion only between friendly stakeholders or are 'hateholders' also invited to join? Ultimately, environmental issues such as climate change have important social justice elements which are important to consider when assigning costs and thinking of solutions.

Systemic. Systems thinking is a popular term within sustainability, but it is easier said than done. When we look at business, not only individuals and organisations, but as a broader system with interrelated parts, we can have a better understanding of sustainable change over time. This allows us to see the embeddedness of social and economic activity into ecological systems, to move away from only looking for silver-bullet (typically technological) solutions to every environmental problem, to design for resilience, and appreciate the perspectives and contributions of different actors within the system. While climate change and carbon dioxide gets a lot of attention (with several companies pledging to go carbon neutral, net zero carbon or carbon negative/climate positive), it is good to remember that climate and carbon dioxide are just one piece of the puzzle, alongside biodiversity and biochemical flows, among other concerns.

Balanced. Corporate responsibility and sustainability literature has traditionally been based on the notion of triple bottom line – the economic, environmental and social responsibilities of firms (Elkington, 1997). Many business decisions include an interplay of these elements. To use a simple example, producing a safer car (social benefit) typically involves more materials making the car heavier and less fuel-efficient (environmental cost) and is more expensive (economic cost). While the trade-offs are often more difficult to estimate in practice, a balance between economic, environmental and social considerations needs to be reached at the individual, organisational and societal levels. Ultimately, what these balances at different levels look like is heavily influenced by normative, ethical, political and ideological considerations. In this chapter on ecological approaches, we emphasise that ecological sustainability is the fundament and that social and economic sustainability cannot thrive without it.

Transformational. Sustainability is all about transformation and change. We often contrast incremental change with a more transformational one. While the discussion in practice is often about how to be 'a little less unsustainable', the imperative of sustainability is for wider systemic change. Hence, the contemporary calls for energy transitions and aggressive climate goals. In fact, many if not most of the tools and approaches we need for sustainable change already exist. In this way, cultural change becomes essential alongside technological change.

Now that we have a set of ecological principles that we can utilise to start looking for solutions (building on the introductory chapter and the other approaches presented before this chapter), let's evaluate different lenses that have been proposed to approach (corporate) sustainability.

7.4 Lenses in (Corporate) Sustainability

Over the past decades, a range of ecological paradigms, theories, concepts and approaches have been proposed and developed to examine the role of corporations and business in general in environmental sustainability. Here, we will refer to them as lenses. Several fields as diverse as environmental and Earth system sciences, economics, philosophy and indigenous (in itself interdisciplinary) studies have contributed to this endeavour and developed their own related sub-fields (such as environmental economics and environmental ethics). Since it would not be feasible to provide a comprehensive overview, for the purposes of this chapter, we select twelve lenses especially prevalent in the field of management and categorise these according to their nature. These include progress indicators, critiques of growth, social science and indigenous contributions, sustainability innovation concepts and approaches for sustainable organising.

7.4.1 Progress Indicators

As the famous saying goes: 'you can't manage what you can't measure'. Well, in the case of sustainability, countless ways to measure it have been proposed over the decades. Here, we will look at three interrelated frameworks which aim to measure progress on a set of themes or indicators: the UN Sustainable Development Goals, Planetary Boundaries and Doughnut Economics.

As presented in Chapter 1, the UN Sustainable Development Goals (SDGs) are a roadmap for global sustainability. They consist of a set of seventeen goals and 169 more specific targets. The SDGs are part of the so-called Agenda 2030, meaning that the UN General Assembly set these goals to be achieved by the year 2030. The SDGs were preceded by the Millennium Development Goals, targets intended to be achieved between 2000 and 2015. The SDGs were designed based on multi-stakeholder consultation and thus bring in the perspectives of different societal sectors and actors. The SDGs are all interconnected and even partially contradictory. For example, industrial development (SDG 9) can go against climate action (SDG 13) without a deep transformation and decarbonisation of the economy. Ultimately, the Stockholm Resilience Centre (2015) has argued that the SDGs should be rearranged as a 'wedding cake' as depicted in Figure 7.1. This means that the biosphere-related goals related to life on land, life below water, clean water and sanitation, and climate action should be non-negotiable and thus have priority over societal and economic goals. From a corporate sustainability perspective, the SDGs have become a popular way for larger multinational firms, such as health technology conglomerate Philips and multinational consumer goods company Unilever, to describe their social and environmental responsibility. Nonetheless, we should note that many other firms promoting their contributions to the SDG targets have also been accused of greenwashing (i.e., overselling or overemphasising the environmental benefits of their products or services).

A second progress indicator are the Planetary Boundaries. We already learned about them in Chapter 1, setting the scene for this book, but they are worth re-examining here. The planetary boundaries are a set of science-based indicators aiming to determine a 'safe operating space for humanity' (Rockström et al., 2009). They were

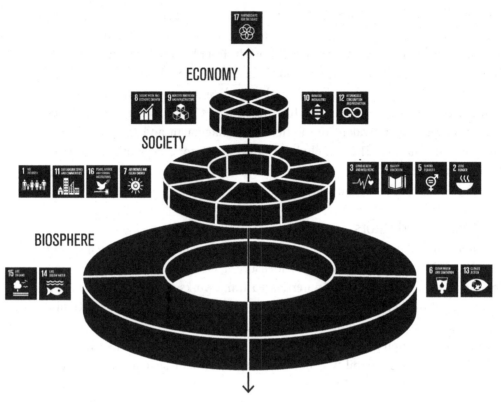

Figure 7.1 Ecological sustainability as a foundation for social and economic sustainability
Designed by Azote for Stockholm Resilience Centre, Stockholm University (CC BY 4.0).

originally proposed in 2009 and have since become an influential way to understand sustainability from an Earth systems perspective. The basic premise of this framework is that we can scientifically identify and evaluate progress on key planetary boundaries that we should stay within to avoid catastrophic abrupt environmental change. These nine boundaries are listed in Figure 7.2 and include environmental issues such as climate change, ozone depletion, ocean acidification and biosphere integrity. Alarmingly, we have already surpassed the safe operating space on five boundaries: climate change, loss of genetic biodiversity (i.e., species extinction), land-system change (i.e., humans transforming natural landscapes through, for instance, deforestation), biogeochemical flows (i.e., related to our use of phosphorus (P) and nitrogen (N)) and novel entities (chemicals and plastics). While these sound like separate environmental (and quite technical!) topics, they are all interconnected and act as both a warning system and a dashboard to manage these planetary risks. In terms of corporate sustainability, the planetary boundaries can be difficult to adapt to an organisational context. Typically, they can be used to explore firm activities in a geographically contextualised way (see Whiteman et al., 2013), but can be difficult to adapt to the company context.

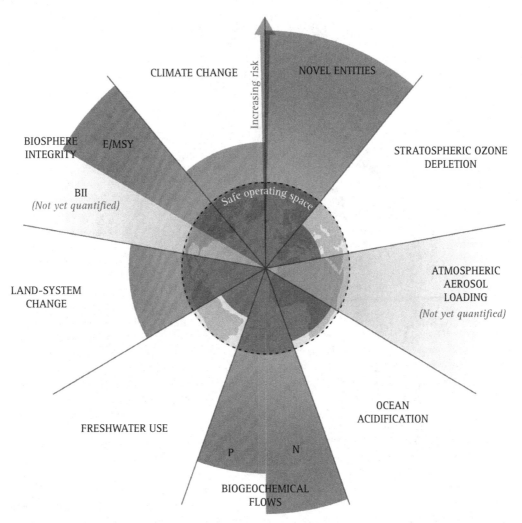

Figure 7.2 Planetary Boundaries. These boundaries characterise the conditions that are necessary for planet Earth to remain stable. Five boundaries have already been crossed.
Designed by Azote for Stockholm Resilience Centre 2022, based on analysis in Persson et al. (2022) and Steffen et al. (2015) (E/MSY: extinctions per million species-years, BII: Biodiversity Intactness Index, N: Nitrogen, P: Phosphorus) (CC BY 4.0).

A third progress indicator is Doughnut Economics, which is an extension of the planetary boundaries framework combined with insights from scholars such as Amartya Sen and Martha Nussbaum. Doughnut Economics is a framework developed by Professor Raworth (2017). Its visual representation is presented in Figure 7.3. What makes the doughnut interesting is that it is able to depict both social ambitions and planetary boundaries in one framework. The outer circle or edge of the doughnut is formed by the planetary boundaries that were described above. The inner circle or edge represents basic social needs which are seen as

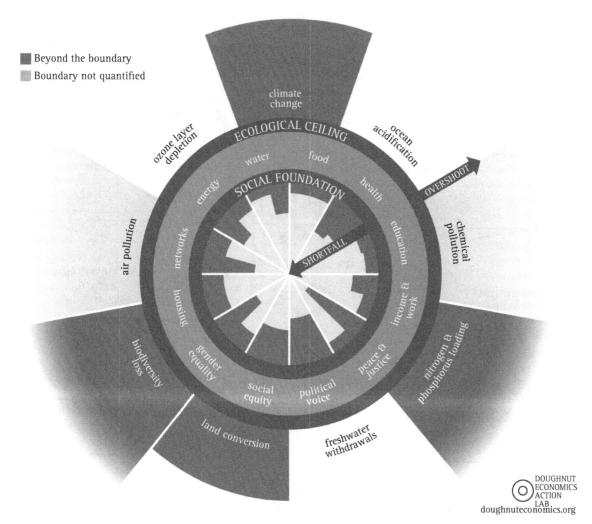

Figure 7.3 The Doughnut of social and planetary boundaries

essential to human life (for instance, water, food, education and healthcare). The main idea is that we need to meet the social floor without surpassing the ecological ceiling. While the Doughnut Economics framework is used by companies to a lesser extent than, for instance, the SDGs, it can be a useful tool to see interconnections and understand systemic impacts. Other organisations, such as the City of Amsterdam in the Netherlands, have adopted Doughnut Economics as a central framework to assess sustainability.

We selected three fairly recent influential lenses that aim to present progress indicators. We should note that a wide range of broad as well as specific indicators of development (including an environmental component) exist. These include the Ecological Footprint, the Genuine Progress Indicator, the Happy Planet Index and many more which we do not review for the sake of space and clarity.

7.4.2 Critiques of Economic Growth

Is economic growth necessary for sustainable development? A large academic and practical movement has come to question what has been taken for granted ever since the post-World War II reconstruction period: Economic growth is the best measure of societal development and gross domestic product is the best measure of progress. Ideally, what we want to see is that economic growth leads to societal growth (i.e., a coupling of both as they go hand in hand) and that ecological impact and resource use decreases as the economy grows (i.e., that we are able to decouple economic growth and environmental impact by dematerialising our economies). These debates go back to the 1970s (Meadows et al., 1972; Easterlin, 1974) and unfortunately the collective evidence thus far seems to point to the contrary (see Figure 7.1; Parrique et al., 2019). First, social welfare increases alongside economic growth only up to a point, after which social welfare ceases to increase despite economic growth. Second, Western societies have not been able to decouple economic growth from material consumption: production has merely moved elsewhere while material consumption has stayed the same or typically increased.

This critique of economic growth takes many forms, but has crystallised into a movement called Degrowth. Degrowth, or in French *décroissance*, initially strikes as a negative term, being 'against something' (even if the original idea has a positive connotation). Certainly, this lens takes a strong stance against the ecological harm caused by the pursuit of continuous growth, problematises the idea that the purpose of human organisation is economic productivity and growth, and speaks against a Western notion of development. Nonetheless, it also aims to provide alternatives, including better metrics of prosperity, a mindset of sufficiency and a focus on participatory local economies. Degrowth does not imply a reduction of well-being (quite the contrary!), but involves a rethinking of how we see and measure well-being. This broad and varied lens has many nuances and has taken multiple forms, coining terms such as degrowth, steady state economics, prosperity without growth, post-growth and agrowth (the latter referring to being agnostic about growth) (see Borowy and Schmelzer, 2017; Jackson et al., 2020). Ultimately, it may be that the future ideological battle lines of sustainability may be drawn between degrowth (a critique of the global capitalistic system advocating for social and ecological well-being), green growth (a business-friendly, sustainability-oriented and technology- and innovation-focused vision of sustainability) and forced green (a regulatory-driven transformation towards sustainable societies).

7.4.3 Social Science and Indigenous Contributions

Next, we turn to social sciences and indigenous studies and selectively pick lenses that can be insightful to our understanding of corporate sustainability: ecological economics; environmental justice; and indigenous knowledge. Ecological economics is a field of research which sees economies and natural ecosystems as interdependent and co-evolving. This lens is often critical of mainstream economics and grounds its analysis in physical reality within a specific temporal and spatial context. In this sense, natural resources flow through the economy instead of the economy being separated from the natural world.

A related lens to ecological economics is the notion of environmental justice. This notion underscores the social-justice-related elements of the governance and implementation of environmental laws and regulations. It includes elements of distributive and procedural justice. If we take climate change as an example, a distributive justice perspective highlights that the most vulnerable populations are typically the least culpable in producing the broader changes affecting them. From a procedural justice perspective, we can examine what roles and responsibilities different national governments take in global climate agreements in light of their current and historical greenhouse gas emissions. These perspectives beg the question: Are certain aspects or forms of development acceptable to some nations and not to others?

Indigenous studies (an interdisciplinary field in itself) and knowledge offer a broad spectrum of insights on sustainability originating from different contexts. Through thousands of years, indigenous systems of knowledge have been based on a profound connection between humans and nature, often subjugated by colonial powers. Banerjee and Arjaliès (2021) argue that as our current ecological crisis is a product of human–nature dualism and Enlightenment thinking, these cannot be the basis of looking for solutions to the crisis.

7.4.4   Sustainability Innovation Concepts

Within the field of innovation, several popular concepts have been launched throughout the years to examine sustainable change. Here, we discuss the circular economy, sustainability transitions and sustainable business models.

A circular economy is an industrial system that is restorative by design. It is a redesign of the current mode of production and economy from a take-make-waste culture to a circular one. The central idea is not only to recycle waste, but to stop producing waste in the first place. The key principles of the circular economy are to design out waste and pollution, keep products and materials in use, and regenerate natural systems (Ellen MacArthur Foundation, 2013, 2019). From a business perspective, circularity can involve a range of different business models, such as eco-design, sharing or virtualising products or services. For an overview of sustainable (including circular) business models, see Chapter 19, and for a discussion of social and sustainable entrepreneurs, see Chapter 9.

Another innovation-related lens which examines corporate sustainability from an ecological perspective is the sustainability transition lens. A sustainability transition is defined as a 'radical transformation towards a sustainable society, as a response to a number of persistent problems confronting contemporary modern societies' (Grin et al., 2010). In short, this lens posits that the environmental problems we face (such as climate change, biodiversity loss and resource depletion) constitute grand challenges that will not be solved by incremental improvements. It involves a fundamental rethinking and radical shifts to how socio-technical systems are configured and function, basically how our societies function. The key insights of a sustainability transition lens are the involvement of multiple dimensions (e.g., technology, culture, markets, infrastructure and policy) and multiple actors (across the public sector, the corporate sector and civil society) coming together in co-evolutionary and uncertain long-term processes of stability and change aiming at sustainability (Köhler et al., 2019). As sustainability transitions are deeply rooted in culture, in Table 7.1 we provide examples of how different cultural perspectives of justice can be linked to sustainability transitions (Köhler et al., 2019).

New regulation and legislation also play a key role in (environmental) sustainability transitions. We should note that sustainability transitions realistically involve winners and losers: as the landscape changes, we can see stranded assets (suffering from unanticipated devaluation) and stranded business models. Firms with advanced environmental capabilities are likely to be the winners. At the individual level, these broader transitions are likely to face a major barrier in psychological resistance.

7.4.5   Approaches for Sustainable Organising

In going through the above perspectives, you may have noticed that the corporation is mostly absent. Sustainability innovation concepts come closer to the business firm, although typically still systemic in nature. While business schools and the field of management put the company front and centre, ecological lenses rarely operate within (corporate) organisational boundaries or focus on commercial products. Let's turn to more corporate- and product-oriented lenses by examining how organisational level approaches to environmental sustainability developed over the past decades.

As environmental problems of corporate activity began to surface in the 1960s (see, e.g., Rachel Carson's book *Silent Spring* in 1962), they were first tackled through regulation and legislation by national governments until the 1980s. Since then, the economic philosophy of neoliberalism combined with deregulation and globalization gained more ground. This involved the idea that business enterprises' voluntary environmental action would be more effective than command-and-control legislation. The first incarnation of this thinking was the environmental management systems (EMS) approach which began to emerge in the late 1980s, taking after the quality management movement. The aim of the EMS approach was to control risk and reduce the harm caused by existing business (Welford, 1999).

EMS were not perceived to be entirely satisfactory by business, regulators or the environmental movement. They were seen as incremental and not sufficiently

Table 7.1 Culture and sustainability transformations

Concept	Definition	Application to transitions
Ubuntu	Emphasises the act of building community, friendship and oneness with the larger humanity	Neighbourhoods' efforts to promote energy efficiency, decisions about food resources within a community
Taoism and Confucianism	Emphasises virtue and suggests that the means to an end is more important than the end in itself	Respecting due process in transition decisions, adhering to human rights protections when implementing infrastructural projects
Hinduism and Dharma	Caries the notion of righteousness and moral duty and is always intended to achieve order, longevity and collective well-being	Seeking to minimise the extent and distribution of externalities, offering affordable access to technology to help address poverty
Buddhism	Expounds the notion of selflessness and the pursuit of individual salvation and nirvana	Respecting future generations, minimising harm to the environment and society
Indigenous Perspectives of the Americas	Recognises interdependence of all life and enables good living through responsibility and respect for oneself and the natural world, including other people	Technologies developed cautiously through long-term experience and sovereign cultural protocols, avoiding dramatic transformation of ecosystems, requiring restoration
Animal-centrism	Values and recognises rights of all sentient life	Promoting transition processes or practices such as veganism, vegetarianism or waste reduction that avoid harm and provide benefits to all sentient animals
Biocentrism	Values and respects the will to live and the basic interest to survive and flourish	Promoting transitions that adhere to a fair share of environmental resources among all living beings
Ecocentrism	Gives moral consideration for human and non-human communities and the basic functioning and interdependence of the ecological community as a whole	Advocating technologies or transitions that preserve the integrity, diversity, resilience and flourishing of the whole ecological community

Source: Adapted from Köhler et al. (2019), modified from Sovacool and Hess (2017).

tackling the environmental problems at hand. What followed was eco-efficiency thinking, introduced to business management by Schmidheiny in the 1990s (Fritsch et al., 1994). The idea was to develop new products, services and eventually business models that 'do more with less'. In other words, eco-efficient solutions would provide the same customer and user needs fulfilment (often called the service unit) with less materials, energy and water, and at the same time, be as or more profitable for the firm providing them. Eco-efficiency thinking kick-started the broader 'win-

win' paradigm of corporate sustainability, moving beyond the environmental sphere. Perhaps the most well-known incarnation of this view is Porter and Kramer's (2011) creation of shared value, which posits that companies should strive to identify and exploit situations where both the company and society can benefit. This has been dubbed the 'win-win paradigm' of corporate sustainability. While intuitively appealing, it is good to approach a world of win-win opportunities with a healthy dose of scepticism (see King and Pucker, 2021).

Eco-efficient products, services and business models abounded, delivering relative reduction of ecological footprint per service unit. But they did not lead to absolute reduction of negative environmental impacts, but instead to rebound effects where increasing production and consumption overtook the environmental savings gained through efficiency measures. As a result, absolute consumption and absolute use of material kept growing so that material extraction tripled from 1970 to 2015, considerably so during the years when the eco-efficiency ideas were already known (International Resource Panel, 2019). Paradoxically, at a global scale, material productivity, a rough equivalent to absolute material efficiency, dropped (see Figure 7.4), apparently due to large-scale outsourcing of production to countries with lax environmental regulation and minimal incentives for best available technologies and efficiency. Unfortunately, ultimately, the environment cares only about absolute reduction of environmental impacts and not relative decoupling or reduction.

When evaluating corporations' sustainability impacts, corporate sustainability has taken many forms. Corporate sustainability's triple bottom line has become a

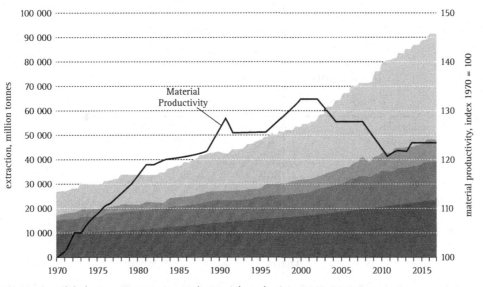
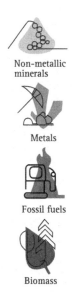

Figure 7.4 Global resource extraction and material productivity 1970–2015.
Source: International Resource Panel (2019: 18).

dominant way for companies to report on sustainability (see Chapters 1 and 17 of this book) and it has been translated to Environmental, Social and Governance (ESG) within the investor community (see Chapter 11). In this sense, the ecological aspects of corporate sustainability are categorised as one bucket, typically examined only insofar as they translate to economic risk.

7.4.6   Categorisation of Ecological Lenses

Now that we have reviewed a selected sample of influential lenses to understand corporate sustainability, we can bring them together into one framework depicted in Figure 7.5. We categorise the lenses on two axes: first, whether they prioritise an eco-social or economic perspective; and, second, whether the related discourses focus on environmental opportunities or more critical perspectives related to environmental limits. Each of the twelve lenses discussed above are depicted in this framework. As a caveat, we should note that many of these lenses, such as degrowth and indigenous knowledge, are not easily categorisable as they represent broad perspectives which do not neatly fit into boxes.

When we look at all these lenses, one thing becomes clear. We need to see the so-called triple bottom line of companies – the economic, social and environmental responsibilities and impacts of firms – not as separate spheres, but as deeply interconnected. We need to see the economy, society and environment in a concentric way. This means that we need to have an economy which is for the benefit of

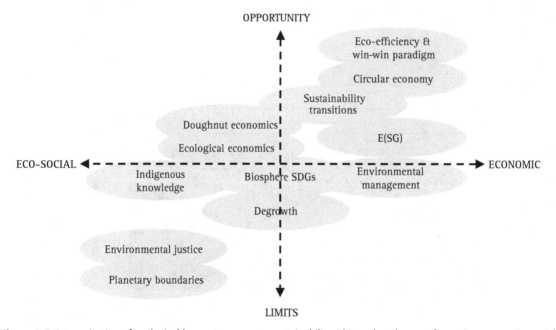

Figure 7.5 Categorisation of ecological lenses to corporate sustainability. This makes the case for seeing economic, social and environmental responsibilities and impacts by firms as deeply interconnected.

society and an economy and society which operate within planetary boundaries. Ecological sustainability is the fundament upon which sustainable societies and economies can thrive. If ecological sustainability collapses, human life on Earth becomes endangered. Ultimately, the ecological perspective to corporate sustainability calls for this form of balance.

7.5 Chapter Summary

Given all of the largely negative and worrying environmental trends that we have covered, is there any room to be optimistic? Granted, a fair deal of realism is in order and the task(s) ahead can seem daunting. Nonetheless, we should also celebrate prior successes, understand different lenses as ways of seeing the problems, systematically analyse our actions, acknowledge opportunities and (at least we choose to) remain cautiously optimistic. Three things should be kept in mind. First, while (slightly) changing consumption habits will not save the world, small actions do add up. Two popular proverbs come to mind: 'every journey begins by a single step' (a version of a Chinese proverb by Lao Tzu); and 'there is no path, the path is made by walking' (a Spanish poem by Antonio Machado). At the same time, these small actions need to be coupled with bigger transitions, such as a transition in energy sources. Relatedly, we actually do have the technologies with which to implement major sustainability transitions and these transitions will influence how we lead our daily lives. Second, change is constant. While many changes have involved the deterioration of our natural environment, there are countless positive trends related to, for instance, developments in literacy, health, average life expectancy, scientific discoveries, technological development and increasing wealth. Furthermore, while changing some things around us may seem impossible, it is surprising how fast what has been considered impossible, becomes inevitable. Third, and relatedly, some transitions can happen (surprisingly) fast. In fact, the time after the mid twentieth century up until today has been dubbed 'the Great Acceleration'. We tend to overestimate change in the short term, but underestimate it in the longer term. When we take a slightly longer time perspective, the pace of change is often overwhelming.

So what can each of us do? We can put into practice the principles listed in this chapter. We can evaluate alternative lenses and actions and their outcomes in an evidence-based manner. We can listen to and try to understand the local context. Without including the people affected by a particular environment problem, an 'external' solution is unlikely to work. We can think in the systems in the sense of appreciating the interconnectedness of the different elements of the system. Ultimately, systems thinking is not sufficient, but we need what we call 'systems action' leading to positive change. The following sections and chapters of this book on actors, processes and issues will hopefully provide you with both food for thought and ideas for systems action.

CHAPTER QUESTIONS

1. What principles act as the foundation of corporate sustainability?

   We list several principles related to corporate sustainability. We suggest picking an example and investigating it to see how these principles have or can be implemented in practice. There is a tendency to pick an organisation, but it is good to remember that sustainability is typically understood to be an inter-organisational or systemic element. Furthermore, you can reflect how you can develop and implement these principles in your own thinking and actions.

2. What are the key environmental trends and challenges and which ones should we prioritise?

   The chapter provides many graphs about environmental, social and economic trends and developments. You can reflect which of these are the most central and how all these trends are interconnected. Ultimately, you can think about the consequences of living in the Anthropocene.

3. What are the dominant lenses of theories of how we approach corporate sustainability?

   You can learn the basic features of each of these lenses and theories and think about what makes each valuable. Each will have their limitations and you can reflect on what types of tensions are inherent across these perspectives. As a common aphorism states: 'all models are wrong, but some are useful'. You can also reflect which of these lenses can lead to actionable and useful outcomes.

FURTHER RESOURCES

- Sustainable Development Goals (SDGs), https://sdgs.un.org/goals.

  The United Nations (2022a) SDGs offer a framework for understanding sustainability through seventeen broad goals and 169 more specific targets. This framework can be considered a multi-stakeholder action plan for addressing sustainability and it calls on all institutions, organisations and individuals to participate. The SDGs have also become a popular way for companies to categorise and organise their sustainability activities.

- Dasgupta Review, www.gov.uk/government/publications/final-report-the-economics-of-biodiversity-the-dasgupta-review.

  The Dasgupta Review is a global review on the Economics of Biodiversity led by Professor Sir Partha Dasgupta (University of Cambridge), supported by an Advisory Panel drawn from public policy, science, economics, finance and business. The Review calls for changes in how we think, act and measure economic success to protect and enhance our prosperity and the natural world. Grounded in a deep understanding of ecosystem processes and how they are affected by economic activity, the new framework presented by the Review sets out how we should account for Nature in economics and decision-making.

- The Lazy Person's Guide to Saving the World, www.un.org/sustainabledevelop ment/takeaction/.

This is part of the United Nations (2022b) website for the SDGs. These macro-level goals can seem at times daunting – ending world hunger and fixing climate change. This useful guide provides tips on how to have impact at the individual level, translating global challenges into everyday meaningful actions.

- *Breaking Boundaries: The Science of Our Planet*, www.netflix.com/title/ 81336476.

This powerful documentary examines how humanity has surpassed several of the planetary boundaries and how collapse can still be averted. What makes this documentary particularly interesting is its science-based analysis of human impact on the planet and its systems thinking showing how the different planetary boundaries are interconnected.

- Doughnut Economics Action Lab, https://doughnuteconomics.org/.

Kate Raworth's doughnut economics has become a popular way to understand and evaluate organisations' or institutions' (such as cities) sustainability impact. The framework aims to depict a balance between social needs and planetary boundaries and the Doughnut Economics Action Lab aims to bring people together to take sustainable action.

PART II
Corporate Sustainability: Actors

8 Multinationals, Small and Medium-Sized Enterprises and Sustainability

METTE MORSING AND LAURA SPENCE

LEARNING OBJECTIVES

- Provide a platform to understand the differences between multinational corporations (MNCs) and small and medium-sized enterprises (SMEs) in terms of sustainability and responsibility.

- Give an account of how sustainability research, policy and practice predominantly focus on MNCs, while neglecting SME practices.

- Clarify the need to understand SME sustainability and responsibility.

- Provide five key differences between MNC and SME approaches to sustainability and responsibility.

- Encourage you, that is, our future leaders, to critically assess how to promote sustainable development in different ways, whether engaging with an MNC or an SME.

8.1 Introduction

Imagine you have graduated from university, you have a job in business but there is something missing from your life – you always have to report to your boss on what you are doing, your work doesn't turn out to be as exciting as you had hoped, and you have a burning ambition to align your own interests and values with your work, or you just want to feel that you are making the world a better place. Over a drink one evening with friends, you decide, there and then, to open your own business. After painstakingly developing your product, you insist on high quality and sustainable inputs, sticking to your values and committing to high ethical standards in how you run your business, and especially how you treat employees, and giving large chunks of any profit to charity. After ten years, you are still a pretty small firm, but you are prospering and have an enviable media profile as a new breed of 'ethical' firm. After just fifteen years, the business has become so successful that it is bought out by Coca-Cola. Twenty years after that initial idea, the business converts to being a B-Corporation, certified with the highest social and ethical standards (see Chapter 9). As a founder you leave an ethically respected business, and move on to new pastures, laying the groundwork for a sustainable charitable foundation. This is somewhat of a mythical story. But it is pretty much based on the story of Innocent Smoothies, which went from a tiny start-up, to a thriving and ethical small business, to part of huge business conglomerate and then a social enterprise. The Body Shop is another example of a business that started small but used their commercial success to leverage their sustainability and responsibility. The Body Shop was established on the founding CEO's personal passion for social and environmental change, addressing an emerging audience of environmentally concerned consumers. It was one of – if not the – world's first SME to deliver a substantial sustainability report in 1984 – long before some larger firms had done so. Later, The Body Shop was acquisitioned by the French MNC L'Oréal and is today owned by the Brazilian MNC Natura, being an example of how MNCs and SMEs are often interconnected and stimulate each other's development. In addition, every supply chain is made up of a mixture of types of firms, and these will all include smaller businesses. So whatever industry you are in, understanding the MNC *and* the SME perspective is important. Plus, companies may not always be what they seem – outsourcing can mean that apparently larger firms are actually quite small because they attend to very little of their business in-house. For example, Finnish gaming company Supercell has only 340 employees and could be considered a medium-sized firm, but has a revenue of over €1 billion. While businesses change their form over their lifecycle – and certainly all are bound to grow and decline in size at some stage – most will remain stable as SMEs. In this chapter, we focus on these fascinating smaller firms either in their early start–up stage, which are on a path to growth, as part of supply chains, or as stable enterprises that stay smaller in size throughout their lifecycle.

For many people, the default position when we talk about business is to think of the large MNCs which dominate the media, stock exchanges and business school curricula. But business is not all about companies like Alibaba, Amazon, Apple, Maersk, Tata or Walmart. Making this assumption is an error for many reasons, missing out the vast majority of businesses, which are SMEs. Some of you will work in an SME when you finish your studies, or perhaps you already do so, or indeed your own family may have a small business with which you are involved. All of us buy products and services on a daily basis which are delivered by SMEs or involve SMEs in their supply chain, for some products such as textiles and clothing, from around the world. While many of these are invisible in terms of the final product, think about your bicycle shop, bakery, hairdresser, local boutique or favourite restaurant – unless they are part of a chain, these are likely to be the SME businesses that keep you functioning on a daily basis. Being a customer of, or experiencing working in, an SME gives you some clues as to how sustainability and responsibility are distinctive in these kinds of organisations.

So how do SMEs differ from MNCs? SMEs are less bureaucratic, more personal and informal, more flexible and differently structured from their larger counterparts (Spence, 2016). This is neither better nor worse than MNCs, just different. But these things influence business practice, and in this chapter we will spell out some of the distinguishing contrasts between MNCs and SMEs where sustainability and responsibility are concerned. Understanding SMEs could not be more important whatever country you are doing business in. They constitute over 90 per cent of private sector business and are perhaps even more important in developing economies than developed ones, where reliance on the economic benefits generated for individuals and communities is a fundamental part of poverty alleviation (Jamali et al., 2009). Policy-makers understand this economic importance, but often overlook the different approach needed to support the sustainability and responsibility of SMEs.

In this chapter, we start by defining SMEs and the role they have. In the main part of the chapter, we work through five points of difference between MNCs and SMEs in terms of sustainability and responsibility. These are motivation, communication, operations, organisation and stakeholder scope. We conclude by encouraging the reader to be aware of the distinctive and important contributions of SMEs and MNCs to sustainability and responsibility.

8.2 Definitions

Statistics on numbers of SMEs won't necessarily convey the relative differences of MNCs and SMEs, but some basic details are perhaps helpful in developing an insight into the scale of the importance of understanding small as well as large firms.

Quite simply, as we have already suggested, SMEs are the normal organising form for private business. They generate the majority of new jobs and are frequently seen as the backbone of the economy (El Madani, 2018). In the European Union, where definitions are relatively stable for SMEs, they are a focus of policy, not least because they are 99.8 per cent of private enterprises, employing two-thirds of private sector employees and generating over 50 per cent of private sector value added. It is also worth noting that the forgotten component of many economies, informal businesses which are not legally registered, are also likely to be SMEs, so official figures of their contributions are probably an underestimate. Much of our discussion in this chapter also has relevance with small social enterprises, which are presented in more detail in Chapter 9.

In every economy, as we have said, SMEs are critically important and there are often some local community distinctions that give character to different regional perspectives (Kraus et al., 2020). For instance, definitions vary of what an SME actually is. Most definitions use number of employees as at least part of the parameters, as well as financial measures such as turnover. The US Small Business Association defines smallness in relation to sector, so for petroleum extraction a small firm might have over 1,000 employees, whereas in Europe the sizing is the same across sectors, with all those businesses having fewer than 250 employees being considered SMEs. In India, where there are tens of millions of SMEs, the Micro, Small & Medium Enterprises Development Act 2006 definition focuses on investment levels, being up to Rs.10 Crore (approx. €1.2 million) for manufacturing SMEs, and Rs.5 Crore (approx. €0.6 million) for service SMEs. For smaller firms, what size category they are in is important because different legal requirements can apply, and access to government financial support can be determined by business size. In addition, size can be relevant for a chance to win some types of contracts, for example, where the public sectors seek specifically to expand their procurement from SMEs as a way of stimulating the economy.

Keep in mind that just as MNCs vary – they may be national, transnational, global, family owned, publicly listed – so too do SMEs. Captured in this very diverse group are sole traders, start-ups, couple-run businesses, family firms, owner-managed firms and so on. In this chapter, we will try to capture some of the *common* characteristics of MNCs and SMEs, but you should be aware of the variations within these groups, and reflect on the differing cultural and political contexts of firms you study.

Finally, in thinking about issues of sustainability and responsibility, we have to be careful about the language used. 'Corporate sustainability' and 'corporate social responsibility' make sense for the larger firms which take on the legal form of a corporation, where the business is 'incorporated' to form an entity with a separate legal personality, where shareholders are not legally liable for the firm. The 'corporate' terminology makes less sense for businesses which are not incorporated (therefore not 'corporations'), which applies to most SMEs. The minute smaller firms see the word 'corporate', they are likely to think 'that doesn't apply to us', and they have a point. SMEs identify more as firms or 'enterprises', that is, a for-profit business that is associated with entrepreneurial ventures and often run by a single individual or family with unlimited liability. As we will show, the majority of knowledge and research on sustainability-related issues assumes a corporate perspective and uses the corporate label. Hence, in this chapter, we will talk in more inclusive terms of sustainability and responsibility. In addition, we should note some small-business-specific language that has emerged in the research literature in order to try to pinpoint the differences for SMEs, that of Small Business Social Responsibility (SBSR) (Guillén et al., 2021). SBSR can be defined as 'those activities of smaller organizations that result in positive social change' (Soundararajan et al., 2018: 935), and is closely related to the values of the owner-manager and the sector in which the business is engaged.

8.3   Five Points of Difference between MNC and SME Sustainability and Responsibility

We have selected five key points of difference between MNC and SME sustainability and responsibility that have emerged from prior research and business practice: motivation, communication, operations, organisation and stakeholder scope. We introduce these as a platform for you to start thinking about some of the fundamental variations in what it means to engage in sustainability and responsibility towards society. These can vary when you are a manager for a large corporation with many employees and possibly spanning many geographies versus when you are a director or owner-manager of a small business with few employees, a less formalised structure, strong connections to the local community and often with a family reputation and legacy to consider (Randerson, 2022). Our selected key points are not an exhaustive list of distinctions, but serve as a basis for you to reflect on how we may engage MNCs and SMEs to support sustainability. You will find a few selected quotes in the text from research interviews with SME managers in Denmark throughout the chapter using pseudonyms to illustrate some of our points (Morsing and Spence, 2021), as well as examples from other published research. We summarise these points of difference in Table 8.1. You may like to reflect on their relevance for countries and industries with which you are most familiar.

8.3.1   Motivation

We know more about what businesses do to try to act sustainably and responsibly than we do about *why* they do it. MNCs are governed by bureaucratic systems and structures and these also direct corporate sustainability and social responsibility. Hence, drivers relate to how corporate sustainability and responsibility practices can contribute to the smooth running of the corporate goals. These often take the form of complying with regulatory requirements and voluntary international standards (sometimes referred to as hard law and soft law) (Jackson et al., 2020). Meeting the requirements of the UK Modern Slavery Act, for instance, means that the business is mitigating against various risks, including being exposed for very weak labour standards in the supply chain, avoiding scandal in the media and possible loss of shareholder and consumer loyalty. Signing up to the UN Global Compact on the implementation of universal sustainability principles might be seen as a way of building a positive image and reputation which can contribute to a profitable business (Schembera, 2018). In the SME, drives to be sustainable and responsible are much more likely to be intrinsic to the business and relate to the personal perspective and values of the owner-manager and their ethics, because of their pivotal role in the business (Grimstad et al., 2020). Frederik Nielsen, who is the owner-manager of a small catering and food processing company, puts it this way:

Table 8.1 Summary of five key differences between MNC and SME sustainability and responsibility

Sustainability and responsibility	Key areas	Multinational corporations	Small and medium-sized enterprises
Terminology		Corporate social responsibility/sustainability	Small business social responsibility
1. Motivation		External orientation	Internal orientation
		International and governmental stakeholder demands	Ethical leadership values
		Promotion of image and reputation	Protection of customer relations, business partners and employees
		CSR to support profit maximising	CSR to support profit satisficing
		Influenced by (financial) media, stock market, media, market	Influenced by trade association, trade press, industry peers, local media, family values
		Risk and compliance	Values
2. Communication		Explicit	Implicit
		Based on company values, codes of conduct	Based on owner-manager values, personal integrity
		Complying with regulatory frameworks and standards	Embedding in culture
		CSR/sustainability in branding – central in communication campaigns	CSR is silent – ingrained in organisational culture
		Formal annual reports, dedicated staff	Informal, ad hoc, word-of-mouth or social media, non-specialised
3. Operations		Transactional	Relational
		Global outreach and impact	Local outreach and impact
		For example, public–private partnership; philanthropic projects; staff volunteering	For example, sponsor local sports club; pay suppliers promptly; school donations; small charitable donations
	Culture orientation	Efficiency, growth, commercial	Authenticity, identity, legacy
		Quarterly time horizon	Intergenerational time horizon
		Strategies and policies 'to drive and support corporate value proposition'	Informal engagement 'that makes local sense now'
		Social responsibility/sustainability as professional risk management	Social responsibility is identity and trust

Table 8.1 (*cont.*)

Sustainability and responsibility	Key areas	Multinational corporations	Small and medium-sized enterprises
		International legitimacy – visible projects and societal engagement	Local purpose – small-scale activities sponsorships
	Place in Global Value Chains	Focal firm, brand vulnerability	Distant from focal firm; relatively anonymous supplier, vulnerable to over-reliance on customer requirements
4. Organising		Formal	Informal
	Senior leaders	CSR endorsed by CEO	CSR lived by owner-manager
		Bureaucratic, formalised structure	Paternalistic informal structure
		CSR professionals and Department	Non-specialised staff
		Professional managers	Product specialists
	SR/sustainability Implementation	Relatively costly and difficult to achieve	Relatively cheap and achievable
	Metric of SR/ sustainability success	Economic growth	Survival for next generation
	Relationship to formal social standards	Standard makers	Standard takers
5. Stakeholder scope	Primary stakeholders	Shareholders, customers Impersonal, anonymous	Family, employees, community, customers, suppliers, small local competitors Personal, social proximity
	Stakeholder management	Transactional, contractual	Relational, personal
	Familial	Separation of work and family is usual	Family employment, ownership and influence common
	Ownership	Shareholders appoint a CEO to run the firm on their behalf	Owner-manager as both principal and agent

'I always had a distinctive feeling about right and wrong, caring and compassion for others who are less strong. A central motivation for me is empowering others' (Morsing and Spence, 2021).

Since SME life is driven by personal relationships and values, these are also the basis for their approach to SBSR (Oldham, 2021). So rather than following formal standards, SMEs are much more likely to be interested in how their own practices affect those with close proximity to the business (Lähdesmäki et al., 2019). While not all SMEs are locally orientated – some may have employees that work remotely all over the world, or are focused on international markets – it is common for SMEs and their owners in particular to be quite strongly linked to their location, and looked to for support of local charities and community leadership (Kraus et al., 2020). Indeed, SMEs might even be distracted from their own sustainability and responsibility goals if they are required to sign up to external standards – something which corporate customers sometimes compel their small suppliers to do (Baden et al., 2009). In practice, this means a close dialogue with employees, industry peers, local media and even friends and family. Motives for responsibility for SMEs are personal, in contrast to the dominant financial motivations for the MNC.

8.3.2   Communication

In the MNC, the sustainability and responsibility activities are most often explicitly communicated as a strategic dimension of the company values and articulated in company codes of conduct (Christensen et al., 2013). Novo Nordisk, a pharmaceutical company, has over the past thirty years systematically made social responsibility and sustainability a core focus for all global communications. They were among the first MNCs asking their suppliers including SME suppliers to also communicate their social responsibilities in order to remain a preferred supplier to Novo Nordisk.

Over the past decades, we have seen an increasing demand for MNCs to demonstrate explicitly how they serve as 'responsible corporate citizens' by employing their economic capacity and expert competence to help address global challenges such as climate change and rising inequalities – in short, the elements of the UN Sustainable Development Goals. An increasing number of global and local governments and industry associations have developed regulatory frameworks and standards with expectations to offer systematic MNC reporting on corporate sustainability activities. Many MNCs use this as an opportunity to integrate their sustainability programmes and action into their marketing and branding campaigns to appear as a legitimate and desirable actor for central stakeholders such as consumers, policy-makers or investors. Such explicit statements about the corporate contributions to social and environmental betterment help also to create an internal alignment among employees across the MNC's many departments and geographies. A professionalisation of sustainability communications has occurred in the MNC and today you will find dedicated staff experts in the MNC with a focus only on sustainability communications (see Chapter 10: Sustainability Professionals).

In often stark contrast to the overt MNC sustainability communications stands the SME's more subtle and implicit approach. The SME owner-manager's personal ethics serve as guiding principles for the SME sustainability and responsibility, providing a blueprint for the business which is imprinted on business practice

(De Cuyper et al., 2020). These guiding values may not be written down anywhere, nor articulated in codes of conduct or strategic programmes (Morsing and Spence, 2019). They are 'lived' in daily practices and embedded in the organisational culture. Alfred Rasmussen is the CEO of an SME cleantech business and he points to how social responsibility is the backbone of the business and that his business ascribes to some certifications, but that they do not have many written instructions: 'the biggest thing is to show those values on a day to day basis'. Even clearer is the statement from Felix Dahl, who heads up an SME fashion business: 'We try not to communicate our values. Values is what you *do*' (Morsing and Spence, 2021; emphasis in the original). The SME owner-manager will often feel uncomfortable having their personal values used for branding purposes and will experience a sense of 'selling out' of personal integrity if s/he is asked to use the SME's sustainability or responsibility credentials for marketing purposes (Morsing and Spence, 2019). Our research records SME owner-managers who argue: 'I am quite a modest guy so we have not been advertising our approach.' Another explains that his SME business spends no resources on advertisement or branding, and he refers to their website and LinkedIn communications in the following way: 'this is our window to the world'. For the SME, social responsibility is experienced in a much more informal way in the daily interactions with customers, employees, local society and other key stakeholders. Accordingly, SME communications about social responsibility are much more tacit and informal and are experienced ad hoc in online or in-person relationships and interactions rather than in strategic programmes and reporting.

It is important to pay attention to how global and local society's low expectations of SME communication and reporting on sustainability and responsibility are starting to change. In the future, it is possible that new reforms to increase expectations of SME standards and reporting will influence and challenge the SME implicit communication approach to sustainability and responsibility.

8.3.3   Operations

As is probably becoming clear, the basis for operating can be very different between large and small firms. For MNCs, the business is likely to be run on a transactional basis, guided by contracts and formal agreements (Spence, 2016). For the SME, the dominant approach is instead likely to be governed by the relationships, networks and sometimes friendships that are most important to them. SMEs can be said to be 'relational' in their business operations, and Jamali, Zanhour and Keshishian (2009) have argued that this is a particular strength in terms of sustainability and responsibility. Some of these MNC/SME differences are influenced by the more likely global reach of an MNC and more likely local reach of the SME. But there are plenty of firms which don't fit this pattern, being locally orientated large firms or global SMEs. Linking back to the motivations in the business, whereas the orientation in the MNC might be to achieve corporate responsibility guided by commercialisation, efficiency and growth, in the SME, the much more personalised goals of authenticity, identity and the legacy of the firm are key (Morsing and Spence, 2019). Longer-term time horizons are likely to be normal for the SME, with intergenerational family legacy a relevant time frame, especially for family firms (Randerson, 2022). Instead, they can build up local connections and reputation. Frederik Nielsen says very clearly that he feels it is not sustainable to run a business just for the sake of pursuing profit:

> My responsibility is to think about bottom line for the environment and for social things for my employees. I have an obligation as a business leader to think longer term. I want us to be here in ten years' time, and – 'I just have a feeling it is the right thing to do' for me as a citizen and a business.

This manifests in the types of responsible practice engaged with, for example. In research in the United Kingdom, a jewellery company similarly spoke of how their values influenced their operational practices, leading them to focus on local business supply as far as was possible, saying: 'We're very keen to source . . . as locally as possible . . . We like to support local business . . . we've just bought some shop fittings which actually come from Italy, that wasn't so much by choice . . . we couldn't source that locally. That is sort of a sadness' (Oldham and Spence, 2021). This personalisation of business issues is typical of small firm owner-managers. Whereas the MNC may invest in a particular strategically rewarding project which offers shared economic and social value (Crane et al., 2014), the SME is more likely to engage at a practical grass-roots level where they can. An outstanding example of this is the Danish SME 'RICE', which is an interior design and accessories firm known for its joyful designs alongside its socially responsible approach taken to production. RICE has been working closely with women producers of raffia products in Madagascar over many decades, through good times and bad, following their guiding principle that while they can't solve all of the world's problems, they should do practical things through their business to help others.

A further difference in operations relates to the expectations that apply to MNCs and SMEs respectively. Many, though not all, SMEs are suppliers and an important part of global value chains. However, they are unlikely to have very powerful roles in these so may have to follow the requirements of their corporate customers (Spence, 2016). In contrast, large MNCs may find that they are the focal firm in value chains, and carry risks for the whole supply chain. So, for instance, when Boohoo was found to be selling clothes made in factories with slave labour, the media and consumer attention was focused much more on Boohoo needing to take responsibility than the supplying company. Rarely are the names of the suppliers at fault even if included in media reports of the scandal (see, e.g., Sillars, 2021).

8.3.4   Organising

Organising for responsible and sustainable business reflects the other organisational systems and structures for MNCs and SMEs respectively. Larger firms are usually highly bureaucratic, with multi-level hierarchies, clear individual responsibilities and written guides and codes for practices (Spence, 2016). These might take the form of a sustainability manager, a code of conduct and a sustainability report. The global technology firm Fujitsu, for instance, has all such structures in place. These systems make the internal cost of implementing social responsibility relatively high for large firms (Wickert et al., 2016). In contrast, since the informal approach within smaller firms and the lack of need for written codes and declarations to make clear what the businesses' values are, organising for sustainability and responsibility is relatively low cost. Agnes Anselm, the founder and owner-manager of a family fast-food-catering business focused on sustainable food, hired a professional marketing person after several years of operation, but still insists that she does not want a brand strategy. Instead, she focuses on hiring the right people with the right values, who believe in the product and the business model. 'We don't really care about strategy. We just want the customers to eat our sustainable food', as they put it. This means that implementing social responsibility is less problematic in a small firm (Wickert et al., 2016). Employees already 'live' the SME responsibilities. However, when we look outside the boundaries of the firm, MNCs are more likely to have the chance to influence standards such as the ISO26000 social responsibility international standard, whereas small firms won't have the resources to get involved individually in setting standards (relying on business associations to represent their viewpoint); they are on the whole standard-takers, having to follow rules designed primarily with MNCs in mind (Morsing and Spence, 2019).

While SMEs may not have the luxury of professional managers with higher-level qualifications and training for their roles – whether marketing, HR or sustainability specialists – they *are* likely to be experts on the service or product that the firm offers, and this gives them the skill set to relate what they do to their core business. Frederik Nielsen is a good example of the informality of organising and leadership that characterises an SME. Nielsen's primary organising principle is his personal values: 'I don't need Ferraris. Purpose is to give people a good life and good food.' As he states it: 'We practice what we preach, and even [if we don't have more formally recognised credentials] experienced waiters want to work for us because of our reputation for caring for our employees.' This implies that when Nielsen and other SME owner-managers recruit new staff, they will prioritise that personal values are aligned with their own. This is often not formalised or described in any detail, but such 'values alignment' serves as a platform for a shared orientation of 'how to do things around here' and supports informal organising principles based on trust (Oldham, 2021). For SME owner-managers, the focus is on the long-term survival of the business as a measure of success and the reputation of the firm, and this plays directly through to their organising practices.

8.3.5   Stakeholder Scope

Stakeholders (see Chapter 4: Stakeholder Approaches to Corporate Sustainability) – those who affect and are affected by a business's operations – give important clues to those groups to whom the business feels ties of responsibility, and stakeholder theory is very closely related to social responsibility research and practice (Freeman and Dmytriyev, 2017). While to understand stakeholders in detail each organisation needs to draw its own bespoke stakeholder map, there are some commonalities between core stakeholders for MNCs, as indicated in Figure 8.1. Figure 8.1's MNC stakeholder map draws on Coca-Cola's stated main stakeholders. They claim a responsibility to their owners (shareholders), their customers and consumers, governments, suppliers and other business partners, their employees and non-governmental organisations. In the case of a company like Coca-Cola, water usage and packaging are major issues, so they have partnerships with groups like the World Wide Fund for Nature (WWF), the Water Resilience Coalition and Ocean Conservancy. How large companies are represented by media and international media is an important part of their reputation (and affects their value directly on occasion – if a scandal erupts, for instance), so alongside customers, suppliers and employees, the media are important stakeholders. Finally, large MNCs are often engaged with governments, working with and seeking to influence their policy-making.

Of course, some SME core stakeholders will be very similar – suppliers and customers are bound to be a part of business life (Kraus et al., 2020). Let's consider a microbrewery, for instance, making a popular range of beer tied to a local identity, such as the Windsor and Eton Brewery in England. Being located in a residential area, they are reliant on goodwill with the local community, and their workers, suppliers and customers all come largely from that same community, so these local stakeholders are bound to be important. For small firms, the business is very often personal as we have noted, and family members may well be involved formally or informally with the business. Importantly, given the close association between the owner-manager of the firm and the firm itself, it is more likely to be a person than the firm as a whole at the centre of an SME stakeholder map as depicted in Figure 8.1 (Spence, 2016). For many SME owner-managers, employees are the key stakeholder. The well-being and the mindset of the employees are key for the success of the SME. As Frederik Nielsen states: 'my biggest responsibilities are to my employees. Also my employees are my best marketing tool.' Stakeholder relationships are probably individually negotiated and based on trust and reputation, rather than dictated by transactional, contractual arrangements as could be expected in MNCs.

Figure 8.1 Comparison of standard MNC and SME core stakeholders.
Source: Developed from Spence (2016).

8.4   Chapter Summary

In this chapter, we provide an overview of some of the main areas that you should
pay attention to with regard to how MNCs and SMEs have different starting points

for approaching and engaging with sustainability and responsibility. There has been an overwhelming emphasis from governmental regulators and industry associations on MNC engagement with sustainable practices and much less attention paid to SME engagement. We point to how SME sustainability is a central source of improving environmental and social improvements. And with this chapter we demonstrate how it is important to understand in what ways SMEs differentiate themselves specifically vis-à-vis their MNC counterparts to influence sustainability through their responsible practices for the betterment of the world. We are not suggesting that one way is better than the other. We have seen how both types of organisations can have a positive impact. We aim to encourage you to consider how to support carefully the development and maintenance of sustainability and responsibility with regard to the very different motives, operational, communicative, organisational and stakeholder structures that the MNC and SME offer. And we specifically invite you to be critically alert to how governments and policy-makers may seek to promote sustainability and responsibility by influencing businesses. Any initiatives should be relevant and responsive to the different types of business in operation.

CHAPTER QUESTIONS

1. Why is it important to understand the differences between MNCs and SMEs where responsibility and sustainability are concerned?
2. What are the five key points of difference between MNCs and SMEs in terms of responsibility and sustainability? Illustrate your answer with examples.
3. Using an SME you are familiar with, outline examples of their sustainability and responsibility practices. Which stakeholders are most important and why?
4. Look at the social media or website of a large and a small firm in the same sector (both in marketing, or construction, or food processing, for example). What similarities and differences do you see in how, or whether, they communicate about sustainability or responsibility?

FURTHER RESOURCES

- Morsing, M. and Spence, L. J. (2019). Corporate Social Responsibility (CSR) Communication and Small and Medium-Sized Enterprises: The Governmentality Dilemma of Explicit and Implicit CSR Communication. *Human Relations*, 72(12), 1920–1947. And accompanying video: www.youtube.com/watch?v=18VICoDhov0

  This article provides insights into how SMEs are contributing to sustainability and how SMEs are challenged in their sustainable activities, especially when it comes to their communication about it.

- Soundararajan, V., Jamali, D. and Spence, L. J. (2018). Small Business Social Responsibility: A Critical Multi-Level Review, Synthesis and Research Agenda. *International Journal of Management Reviews*, 57(7), 1301–1336.

  This article provides a critical overview of how some SMEs engage in sustainable development.

- Responsible Jewellery Council, Small Business Sustainability Toolkit, https:// responsiblejewellery.com/wp-content/uploads/RJC-SME-Toolkit-June-2021 .pdf.

  This toolkit for CSR developed for the jewellery industry is of much wider relevance, focusing on SME responses to the SDGs.

- Business in the Community, Case Studies, www.bitc.org.uk/case-study/.

  Lots of case examples of responsible and sustainable business in small and larger firms are available on the Business in the Community website. The focus is rather UK-oriented, so see if you can find equivalent resources in other countries.

- International Labour Organization, Global Business Network for Forced Labour, https://flbusiness.network/listen-to-ilo-gbnfls-first-podcast-series/.

  The International Labour Organization's Global Business Network for Forced Labour has a podcast series on responsible business conduct in SMEs. This resource is particularly global in scope.

- European Commission, An SME Strategy for a Sustainable and Digital Europe, https://ec.europa.eu/info/sites/default/files/communication-sme-strategy-march-2020_en.pdf.

  This strategy aims at engaging SMEs in sustainable and digital business practices to make Europe the most attractive place to start a small business.

- The Responsible Innovation Compass, https://innovation-compass.eu.

  The Responsible Innovation Compass offers support to SMEs from emerging technology industries to manage their research, development and innovation activities in a responsible and inclusive manner. This online platform contains a number of tools and services tailored to SME needs.

Alternative Types of Organising for Corporate Sustainability

CAROLIN WALDNER AND ANDREAS RASCHE

LEARNING OBJECTIVES

- Learn about hybrid organisations, which combine commercial activities with a social mission, as alternatives to traditional forms of businesses.

- Distinguish different types of organising for corporate sustainability that range between purely for-profit firms and non-profit organisations.

- Discuss foundation-owned businesses as well as different types of cooperatives as organisational forms that combine commercial and social value creation.

- Shed light on the role of social businesses as a common form of hybrid organisations that aims at achieving sustainability goals through market mechanisms.

- Reflect on B Corps as a legal form and certification mechanism for social businesses.

9.1 Introduction

> I think the circumstances have changed, and I think . . . more people see
> the urgency of creating businesses that actually deal with the social
> and environmental crises that we face.
>
> Vincent Stanley, co-founder and director of philosophy at Patagonia

Most of you probably know – or even own products – of the outdoor retailer Patagonia, whose co-founder and director of philosophy said the words that are mentioned in the introductory quote in a recent podcast (Brave New Work, 2021). According to Stanley, the business world is slowly changing: More and more business leaders and entrepreneurs are becoming aware of their responsibility to not only reduce the harm but actively contribute to people's well-being and the protection of the natural environment. Patagonia's leaders started the business in 1965 as a retailer for climbing equipment; however, they soon realised that they were not able to be financially independent in this niche sector. Hence, they started to expand their product portfolio to the clothing sector, distributing primarily outdoor sportswear. While their aim has always been to only produce and sell clothes that do not harm the environment and to provide fair conditions for workers, they soon realised how challenging it is to maintain their sustainability standards while operating as a market-oriented business (Patagonia, 2022). For example, their stewardship towards the environment only allowed them to use natural dying colours for their garments; however, such colours were failing to meet Patagonia's quality standards, threatening the income flow of the business (Ryan, 2021). Despite such challenges, the company stayed true to its initial goal of reaching social and environmental sustainability through market activities. As such, Patagonia is a typical example of a social business.

Social businesses are defined as organisations that 'pursue a social mission while engaging in commercial activities that sustain their operations' (Battilana and Lee, 2014: 399). These businesses are different from traditional for-profit corporations as they combine social/environmental and economic goals, allow for a broader stakeholder participation in corporate decision-making, and provide alternative ownership structures that replace the traditional shareholder-focused models (Luyckx et al., 2022). Such types of businesses are not new. In fact, organisations that aim to create social welfare by relying on business activities have been existing and thriving for centuries (see Chapter 2). Along with social businesses, such organisations also include foundation-owned companies, like the Danish Carlsberg brewery, or cooperatives, like the National Cooperative Bank in the United States. These businesses date way back in time to eighteenth-century industrialisation, and sometimes even further. With the increasing dynamics around corporate sustainability, these 'alternative types of organising' have gained in importance and hence should not be overlooked.

In this chapter, we discuss such alternative types of organising, that is, business operations which are situated between social/environmental value creation and commercial activities. We start with an overview of the underlying organisational hybridity of these businesses. We then discuss four alternative types of organising in more detail: foundation-owned businesses, cooperatives, social businesses and B Corps. For each of these four types, we define the respective organisational form, introduce different characteristics and shed light on relevant advantages and challenges. We also provide a range of examples, which will help you to (a) understand the differences between the four types and (b) distinguish them from traditional for-profit businesses as well as pure non-profit organisations.

9.2 Organisational Hybridity

Businesses that are based on alternative types of organising put their missions to address societal challenges at the core of the company, for example, by producing agricultural goods that are in line with current standards of fair working conditions, environmental protection and animal welfare. Moreover, individuals that seek such alternative types of organising often engage in collaborative organisational mechanisms that enable them to team up with like-minded others, which helps them to embed sustainability-oriented goals into their organisational structure.

Alternative types of organising operate at the crossroads between the private and the civil society sectors. As organisations that combine the underlying logics of more than one sector, they are often called 'hybrid organisations' (Battilana and Lee, 2014). Social businesses, for example, are hybrid organisations that combine mission-driven elements of non-profit organisations with profit-driven practices of commercial enterprises. Such combinations can be a source of creativity and are an important way of enabling businesses to pursue sustainability-related goals. However, they are also highly complex and difficult to manage. Pache and Santos (2013) argue that these organisations are confronted with conflicts that are inherent to the attempt to follow multiple sector logics, stemming from, for example, contradictory stakeholder demands. Hybrid organisations sometimes deal with such conflicts by decoupling or compromising:

- Decoupling refers to complying to only one logic and supporting the second one only through symbolic practices. This can lead to 'greenwashing' if an organisation claims to pursue social goals while primarily focusing on profit maximisation.
- Compromising implies that organisations comply with the institutional logics of both sectors, but only to the minimum of the expected standards to avoid misaligning with either logic. Such compromising, however, is unlikely to satisfy stakeholders in the long term, as 'their' logic is never fully met by the organisation.

Hence, both strategies bear the risk of losing legitimacy and stakeholder support. In order to fruitfully adhere to different logics and avoid conflicts, Pache and Santos (2013) suggest a strategy they call selective coupling. This strategy requires organisational members to be aware of the pool of configurations and opportunities that the logics from multiple sectors allow them to access and then choose the solution that fits the specific situation.

This chapter focuses mainly on hybrid organisations that combine logics from the private (for-profit) and the civil society (non-profit) sectors. The degree of hybridity in such organisations does, however, differ (Shepherd et al., 2019). Some alternative types of organising lean more towards the for-profit logic, while others are more aligned with the non-profit logic. Table 9.1 shows the resulting continuum of alternative types of organising. The two extreme ends of the continuum are traditional for-profit businesses (e.g., Fortune500 giants like Amazon, Apple or Walmart) and pure non-profit organisations (e.g., the Red Cross Movement or the

Table 9.1 Three main groups of hybrid organisations in support of corporate sustainability

	For-profit business	Socially responsible business	Social business	Non-profit social business	Non-profit organisation
Sector logic	Private sector logic (for-profit orientation)	Private sector logic (for-profit orientation)	Hybrid logic (for-profit and civil society sector)	Civil society sector logic (social/ ecological orientation)	Civil society sector logic (social/ ecological orientation)
Business purpose	Profit maximisation	Socially responsible profit maximisation	Social mission in accordance with profit generation	Social mission, supported by profit generation	Social mission
Focus	Shareholder primacy	Shareholders, plus some stakeholders	All stakeholders equally	All stakeholders equally	All stakeholders equally

Source: Adapted and modified from Unterberg et al. (2015).

Bill & Melinda Gates Foundation). Between these two extreme ends, we have three different *groups of hybrid organisations* in support of sustainability: socially responsible businesses, social businesses and non-profit social businesses (displayed as the grey-shaded areas in Table 9.1).

1. *Socially responsible businesses*, which follow the principles of the private sector, aim at profit maximisation and are accountable to their shareholders and stakeholders. In contrast to traditional for-profit businesses, however, their sustainability efforts exceed commonly acknowledged standards, as their social and ecological goals are deeply rooted in their business models. An example is Werner & Mertz GmbH, a German family business which manufactures and sells household chemicals such as cleaning and dishwashing products. The company is best known for its brand 'Frosch'. Since its creation in 1986, the company is highly committed to sustainability, especially circular economy and Cradle2Cradle approaches. The company continuously strives to innovate and improve its products to reduce its eco-toxicological footprints, aiming at a complete biodegradation. As such, the business is seen as an 'eco-pioneer in its industry' (Hansen and Schmitt, 2021: 635) and the brand 'Frosch' is the company's sustainability flagship. The firm's financial profitability is steady (Brück, 2019).

2. *Social businesses* are organisations which balance their aim to maximise financial profits with their attempt to pursue a social (or ecological) mission. An example is Tony's Chocolonely. The Dutch chocolate manufacturer pursues the

goal of reducing the amount of modern slavery in cocoa production, following the mission to achieve a 100 per cent slave-free chocolate production. Considering that currently more than 460,000 workers are doing forced or unpaid labour on cocoa plantations in the Global South (Blom et al., 2015), this is an important and timely goal. The company works towards a systemic change of industry standards and produces only sustainably sourced chocolate bars. However, the company is aware of and openly communicates that not even their chocolate bars are completely slavery-free as current market structures and the use of additional ingredients, such as cane sugar, makes fully sustainable production difficult. The firm's authentic engagement nevertheless improved their success: In 2021, Tony's Chocolonely was repeatedly ranked as most the sustainable brand in the Netherlands. With a turnover of €70 million (2019), it is also the biggest chocolate brand in their home country (Sustainable Brand Index, 2020). Along with improving the sustainability of their own value chain, the company also raises awareness for labour rights violations in the cocoa industry – for example, through unconventional products that disrupt traditional product patterns (e.g., colors and flavours). They are thus able to reach the masses and make their chocolate bars a trending product, not only in the Netherlands, but also in European neighbouring countries, as well as in the United States and Japan (Kraaijenbrink, 2019).

3. *Non-profit social businesses* are organisations that are rooted primarily in the civil society sector. Such organisations follow a social mission and are equally accountable to all their stakeholders, including their beneficiaries. Non-profit social businesses are often non-profit organisations which try to become more business-like by adapting 'languages, practices, and funding mechanisms of the private sector' (McKay et al., 2014: 339). This is done in order to deal with the increasing competition for private and corporate donations, as well as public funds (Maier et al., 2016). While their main revenue stream still comes from donations, non-profit social businesses sell products or services to create a market-based pillar of support. An example is Hard Feelings, a Canadian non-profit social business, which aims at tackling mental health issues by offering low-cost mental health counselling services for a broad range of needs. To do so, Hard Feelings relies mainly on grants and donations, but additionally rents out office space to counsellors as well as therapists (who can thereby provide low-cost counselling) and sells well-being products. This way, the company is able to link the profits from their sales and the rental fees directly to their beneficiaries who receive the mental health support (Turpin et al., 2021). Considering that these organisations are rooted mainly in the non-profit sector, which goes beyond the focus of this textbook, we will not further discuss them in this chapter.

9.3 Alternative Types of Organising for Corporate Sustainability

In the following sections, we discuss four alternative types of organising that fall within the remaining two groups of hybrid organisations outlined in Table 9.1 (socially responsible businesses and social businesses). These four types occur on a continuum between entirely for-profit businesses and fully non-profit organisations. Figure 9.1 plots the four types on the continuum of hybrid organisations that was outlined above. It is important to note that we use the term social business to denote both a specific group of hybrid organisations and an organisational type occurring within this group. Furthermore, we delineate B Corps from the organisational type of social business, even though it can be seen as a specific form of this type – that is, a social business which passed the B Corp certification process. However, we treat them as a distinct alternative form of organising for corporate sustainability in this chapter due to their growing importance in the business and academic world.

9.3.1 Foundation-Owned Businesses

Some large firms such Hershey (the United States), Tata Group (India), Robert Bosch (Germany) and Rolex (Switzerland) are owned by foundations. In these cases, the company is not (solely) owned by investors who possess the publicly traded shares of the company. Rather, the company is either fully or partly owned by an industrial foundation. Industrial foundations have a non-profit (charitable) purpose and need to be distinguished from other types of foundations (e.g., public charity foundations that receive their money from different sources and provide grants). Industrial foundations are primarily set up to have majority ownership of a business or multiple businesses.

Some foundation-owned companies are traded on the stock market. In these cases, the foundation holds the majority of the voting shares (e.g., as in the case of Danish pharmaceutical giant Novo Nordisk), while other investors can hold minority shares. In many cases, the foundations that own the companies were set up by the founders of the company. The founders donated their stock to the foundation, which then subsequently owned the company. For many founders, this

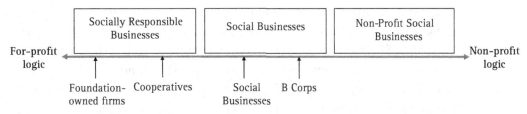

Figure 9.1 Alternative types of organising for corporate sustainability seen on a continuum from for-profit logic to non-profit logic.

Source: Adapted and modified from Unterberg et al. (2015).

change in ownership was a strategic move to secure the long-term future of their business. If a foundation owns a company or owns most of the voting shares, the likelihood of a hostile takeover is reduced (because the shares are not traded publicly, and the foundation does not sell its shares to any bidders).

This type of corporate ownership is especially widespread in the Nordic economies, particularly in Denmark, with companies such as Novo Nordisk, Carlsberg, Mærsk and Velux being owned by large foundations. The foundation that owns the company usually serves a twofold purpose (Børsting and Thomsen, 2017). On the one hand, the foundation works for the good of the company and is supposed to ensure stability. On the other hand, the foundation is also obliged to fulfil a societal mission that is fixed in its charter. For instance, the bylaws of the Novo Nordisk Fonden, which owns Novo Nordisk as well as Novozymes, state that the foundation is supposed to 'provide a stable basis for the commercial and research activities' of the two companies and also 'support other scientific as well as humanitarian and social purposes' (Novo Nordisk Fonden, 2020).

Although foundation-owned businesses are for-profit companies, their underlying ownership structure enables a proactive handling of corporate sustainability in a variety of ways.

- *Long-termism*: Companies that are owned by foundations have truly long-term owners and hence can better work against short-termism, which, in turn, is important when addressing ESG issues. Thomsen et al. (2018) show that foundation ownership is very stable when compared with other ownership structures. This creates several positive effects, such as that managers are replaced less frequently and that decisions are made with a longer time horizon in mind.
- *Higher Reinvestments*: Due to lower pressure from short-term-oriented shareholders, foundation-owned companies often shift a significant part of profits back into improving their products/services and investing in their people. Such a strategy aligns well with corporate sustainability, as it frees up resources to proactively manage ESG issues. It also helps to strengthen the social profile of the company (e.g., in terms of employer branding).
- *Connection between Benefits and Challenges*: Foundation-ownership allows for a better connection between the benefits that a company creates and the challenges it must answer to. In a traditional company structure, the benefits of the company (i.e., its profit) are privatised and usually only serve a few investors, while the ESG challenges that the company faces are often socialised (as in the case of firms that create negative externalities). Foundation ownership also privatises profits (they go to the foundation), but this foundation then works towards addressing some of the socialised challenges (Stenfeldt, 2019).
- *Stronger Corporate Culture*: Grennan (2013) finds that if firms have access to long-term investors and thus face less short-term shareholder pressure, they can

create more productive corporate cultures that focus on personal integrity, customer satisfaction and collaboration. Hence, foundation ownership is not just very stable, but also fosters the creation of shared values and beliefs that in turn can support the integration of ESG issues into the company.

Empirical knowledge on the relationship between foundation ownership and corporate sustainability is still scarce. Børsting and Thomsen (2017) found that foundation-owned firms have a better reputation and better labour relations than other firms. However, the authors also caution that their results do not support a view that foundation ownership per se causes these types of effects. For instance, it may also be possible that particularly socially minded founders created industrial foundations in the past, which would then imply that most foundation-owned firms today were set up as sustainable and responsible businesses (but not that foundation ownership turned them into such companies).

Foundation-owned companies also face challenges. Although Børsting and Thomsen's (2017) study found that such firms have good labour relations because they pay higher average wages, they also uncovered that these higher wages come at the expense of lower profitability. Another problem relates to the high costs of capital that firms, which are partly foundation-owned, may face. Such firms need to raise capital beyond that provided by the foundation. However, since the foundation will not reduce its ownership stakes, new investors will have to accept limited control of the company that they invest in (Børsting and Thomsen, 2017). This, in turn, can make it more difficult to attract investors and hence increases the cost of capital. While the precise effects of such increased costs on sustainability management are unclear, they need to be weighed against some of the possible advantages mentioned above. Finally, we need to remember that foundation-ownership implies that there is a need to align the preferences of the foundation with the activities of the corporation. Although traditional companies also need to do such investor alignment, foundation ownership can create specific challenges due to ownership being concentrated in the hands of one organisational entity.

9.3.2 Cooperatives

Cooperatives are community-based organisations that take the form of associations of different individuals who voluntarily decide to join forces to serve the social and economic needs of their community. A prominent example relates to farmer cooperatives, especially in the Global South. These cooperatives (e.g., coffee cooperatives like delosAndes) are owned and controlled by local smallholder farmers. By managing their business activities unitedly and by combining their bargaining power, farmers in such cooperatives are able to maintain a high level of autonomy, while at the same time participating in the global market (Webb and Cheney, 2014; Tefera et al., 2017).

This tradition of individuals uniting their labour to serve their community can be traced back to medieval times, when peasants worked together to achieve the most efficient harvesting outcomes and share the risk of crop losses. A couple of centuries later, in the eighteenth century, when industrialisation dominated the business world, cooperatives provided an alternative form of organising compared to the traditional factory structures by focusing on decent working and living conditions (Forno, 2013). Today, a cooperative still differs from traditional limited liability companies as it pursues social value creation along with financial profitability and emphasises participatory decision-making as well as joint ownership (Luyckx et al., 2022).

Various types of cooperatives exist. One example are producer cooperatives, which include individual smallholder farmers or other producers (e.g., fishermen or handicraft makers) who voluntarily unite to access a larger market and hence ensure economic and social stability for their communities. By collaborating in the cooperative, producers can get better access to resources (e.g., fertilisers and seeds), approach trainings and peer learning opportunities, and share their equipment and materials. A producer who is member of a cooperative is less vulnerable to market instabilities, which means that producers can start to invest in long-term and sustainable production practices (e.g., crop-rotation, natural fertilisers and mixed cultivation). Producer cooperatives are nowadays particularly common for farmers in developing countries (Webb and Cheney, 2014; Mazzarol et al., 2018), but we also find large producer cooperatives in the Global North. For instance, the Danish dairy cooperative Arla Foods enables milk farmers to produce high quality milk while receiving competitive prices to sustain and grow their farms. Arla Foods is a good example for how large cooperatives can grow: In 2020, Arla consisted of almost 10,000 owners in seven European countries, and as such it is one of the largest milk producers worldwide. The company's revenue amounted to over €10.6 billion, which shows the profitability and growth potential of cooperatives (Mazzarol et al., 2018; Arla Foods, 2021).

A second example are customer cooperatives – for example, in the banking sector (e.g., cooperatives such as the National Cooperative Bank in the United States). Like producer cooperatives, customer cooperatives are owned and managed by its members, which in the case of banks are the customers who have deposits with the bank or hold shares in it. Many cooperative banks were founded in the nineteenth century with the aim of serving people and small businesses by offering loans with low interest rates. Customers participate in the cooperative's governance by voting for a board of directors. This board must ensure that the bank places the customers' needs over pure profit maximisation. This member-oriented system, however, also implies that the profit, which can be generated by a cooperative bank, is usually limited. Most members of cooperative banks are individuals and small businesses, which implies that the total value of the assets under management that such banks handle is often rather small (Goglio and Kalmi, 2017). Another example of customer cooperatives can be found in the retail sector (e.g., food cooperatives like Coop Norden in Scandinavia). The cooperative's members in this case are the retailers or customers. By joining forces, they can improve their purchasing power, generate economies of scale and strengthen their marketing strategies.

The participatory and member-oriented structure of all kinds of cooperatives brings various advantages that help these organisations to pursue a social mission and combine it with commercial value creation, particularly in the long term. Nevertheless, cooperatives also face a range of challenges. Often, members struggle to define their property rights clearly and fairly. Because the distribution of positive outcomes is equal for all members, regardless at which point in time a member joined the cooperative, newer members are treated more beneficially as their total investment is usually smaller in comparison to early members. Hence, early members are treated disadvantageously (in relative terms). Another problem for cooperatives occurs when the investment portfolio does not represent the risk preferences of each member – for example, when a highly risk-averse individual must go along with a rather risky strategic decision because the community decided to pursue it. In such situations, members are less likely to perform at their best. They either take more risk than they are comfortable with, or they feel being held back by the community, if they would be willing to take more risks (for more challenges, see Cook 1995).

9.3.3   Social Businesses

Social businesses are organisations that pursue a social mission while simultaneously engaging in commercial business activities (Battilana and Lee, 2014; Doherty et al., 2014). While setting up commercial business activities, such businesses work towards social objectives (e.g., reducing inequality, poverty and unemployment) and/or address ecological objectives (e.g., minimising greenhouse gas emissions, deforestation and fighting the loss of biodiversity). Social businesses that aim at ecological objectives are often referred to as 'environmental enterprises' (or 'eco-preneurs'; Cohen and Winn, 2007). In academia and practice, you also find the term 'social enterprise', especially in the entrepreneurship-related literature that focuses on innovative solutions for social problems. Several other terms exist, which may differ slightly in their definitions, yet refer to the same type of organisation (for a recent review, see Vedula et al., 2021). In this chapter, we use the term 'social business' as it is widespread among practitioners and academics. Because they are rather wide in scope, the terms social business and social value creation usually also include a consideration of environmental objectives.

While all social businesses have in common that they strive to create social and economic value simultaneously, they differ in *how* they do so. Saebi et al. (2019) found that social businesses can be differentiated into four different types, depending on two factors. The first factor is the inclusion of beneficiaries in the value creation process. Social businesses can create the social value *for* their beneficiaries or *with* their beneficiaries. Social value is created for the beneficiaries when companies generate some form of commercial revenue to cross-subsidise their social/environmental engagement. Social value is created with the beneficiaries when beneficiaries are seen as part of the value-creation process (e.g., as employees). The second factor is the integration of social and economic value creation. In the differentiated approach, social and commercial value creation are independent from each other. Commercial profits are generated completely unrelated to the social or environmental mission, but they are used to fund this mission. In the integrated approach, commercial and social value creation are entangled – for example, when beneficiaries are the paying customers of the social business and receive products/services at a low price. This differentiation results in four business models for social businesses (see Table 9.2).

1. The *two-sided value model* in which the social value is created for beneficiaries and differentiated from the economic value. An example is the US-based shoe manufacturer TOMS, which donates one pair of shoes to children in need for each pair sold to regular paying customers. In this business model, commercial activities cross-subsidise the social mission and beneficiaries are recipients outside of the value-creation process.
2. The *market-oriented work model* in which the social value is differentiated (i.e., cross-subsidised) by the economic value that is created. In contrast to the first business model, the social value is now generated with beneficiaries. The German social enterprise Auticon, for example, employs autistic people as IT consultants. The beneficiaries are thus part of the value-creation process. The commercial value in this business model is differentiated, as companies pay Auticon for its IT services to access the specific skills of people with autism.
3. The *one-sided value model* in which the social value is created with beneficiaries as employees, and where this value is entangled with the business's commercial

Table 9.2 Different business models for social businesses

Social/environmental mission Commercial activities	For beneficiaries (beneficiaries as recipients)	With beneficiaries (beneficiaries as part of value creation process)
Differentiated (commerical activities cross-subsidise social mission)	Two-sided value model	Market-oriented work model
Integrated (beneficiaries are paying customers)	One-sided value model	Social-oriented work model

Source: Adapted and modified from Saebi et al. (2019).

activities. Such business models are prevalent with many social businesses in the Global South. People in remote rural areas are offered products that improve their health or living standards. These people are thus paying customers, who do not actively engage in value-creating processes.

4. The *social-oriented work model* in which beneficiaries are both customers and at the same time employees. The commercial activities are entangled with the social mission, and the beneficiaries are part of the value-creation process. As such, this business model is a combination of the market-oriented and the one-sided value models. An example is VisionSpring, which sells high quality glasses to poor communities at affordable prices, while employing people from these communities in their sales department (Saebi et al., 2019).

Despite the different approaches, a common goal of all social businesses is to use market-based activities to address needs in society. The profit- and growth-oriented commercial activities serve as a means to achieve the social mission of the business. The range of social missions is vast. It ranges from dealing with rather small-scale societal challenges in local neighbourhoods to large-scale approaches that address market failures which other actors – such as commercial businesses, public institutions or non-profit organisations – leave unattended (Zahra et al., 2009).

The hybrid nature of social businesses and their inherent opportunity to deal with social and economic goals simultaneously presents a range of benefits, which other organisations may not have. In contrast to traditional non-profit organisations, social businesses are often financially independent due to their commercial activities (Doherty et al., 2014). Moreover, social businesses can benefit from a positive reputation and stakeholder support when promoting their social mission (Waldner, 2020). Nevertheless, social businesses also face a range of challenges. Their hybrid nature and goal duality present organisational leaders with tensions (Smith et al., 2013). Such tensions may originate from the organisation's internal structures and practices – for example, when organisational members are trying to focus on profit-oriented elements and social mission-related values simultaneously. In some cases, tensions are also triggered by social businesses' external environment, such as when stakeholder demands (e.g., from investors, customers, employees and beneficiaries) are not well aligned.

Such tensions can challenge the decisions that social business leaders need to make – for example, when deciding who to hire (the person with a business background or the person with expertise in the social field), how to communicate the dual identity to stakeholders (focusing on financial independency or social value creation) or which performance metrics to use (financial measures that show short-term success or social impact measures that are long-term oriented) (Smith et al., 2013). If such tensions are not addressed adequately, they can result in an imbalance of the social and commercial goals. Such an imbalance can threaten the organisation's legitimacy and ultimately bears the danger of mission drift. Mission drift means that the business's stakeholders perceive an inconsistency between the organisation's actions and its stated mission. Such drift usually occurs in the form of a loss of focus on the social mission for the gain of financial performance (Grimes et al., 2019). Mission drift is mainly associated with negative outcomes for a social business, including the decline of the business's authenticity, which may lead to a decrease in stakeholder support and jeopardise the survival of the organisation (Battilana and Lee, 2014).

One way to respond to mission drift is to integrate participatory governance mechanisms, which allow the employees or customers of the social business to influence decisions. For example, the German online bank Tomorrow Bank invites its stakeholders to share ideas and provide feedback via a publicly available virtual whiteboard. Another mechanism to avoid mission drift is a more binding non-distribution constraint, which legally forbids social businesses to distribute profits to shareholders. In many social businesses, this constraint is included in the governance structure and serves to avoid profit-maximising behaviour (Defourny, 2014).

Mission drift can also be avoided by becoming a certified social business (see the B Corp discussion below) or by giving the entire business a different legal status. The latter option, however, depends on the business's location, as not all national regulatory frameworks grant social businesses the possibility to register a suitable legal status. In the United States, social businesses can legally register as a public benefit corporation (PBC). Businesses with such status have social/environmental benefit as well as financial profit as legally defined goals. As of 2022, the PBC status is available in thirty-nine US states (and the District of Columbia) (Social Enterprise Law Tracker, 2022). Similarly, in the United Kingdom, social businesses can register as community interest companies and in Belgium as social purpose companies. In other countries, where no suitable legal form exists, social businesses usually register as a traditional for-profit company, as a charity or as a cooperative. Mair (2020) analysed over 1,000 social businesses in nine countries and found that: (1) more than half of them had the legal status of a non-profit organisation; (2) more than one-quarter had the legal status of a for-profit organisation; (3) 5 per cent were registered as cooperatives; and (4) only the remaining businesses had a legal status that allowed them to lawfully combine non-profit and for-profit logics. Hence, most social businesses still have a legal status that inadequately reflects their hybrid organisational character.

Another relevant challenge for social businesses is access to financial capital. Social businesses often have unfavourable risk and return characteristics, which makes raising capital through mainstream investor channels difficult. The long-term focus on social value creation does not align well with the demand for quick returns by many investors. Social businesses therefore face a dilemma. On the one hand, mainstream investors often look for quantifiable performance metrics that are not always available when addressing social problems. On the other hand, donors and investors in non-profit organisations (such as providers of public grants or fellowships), which usually step in to support mission-driven organisations, often refrain from investing in social businesses because of their engagement in commercial activities (Lyons and Kickul, 2013).

Many social businesses therefore look for specific investment opportunities that are geared towards creating social and environmental impact. Impact investing funds, for instance, specifically aim to create a measurable social or environmental impact and financial returns at the same time (see also Chapter 11). Impact-oriented investors are increasingly starting to target social businesses with additional funding options (e.g., the Social Innovation Fund). Social banks also provide funding to organisations aimed at social value creation and thus reflect a valid financing option for social businesses. In other cases, social businesses have raised money through social venture capital and venture philanthropy; funding sources that often also provide non-financial support to social businesses (e.g., through consulting). Finally, crowdfunding platforms like Kickstarter (www.kickstarter.com) are offering more and more possibilities to invest in social businesses, and even platforms that focus exclusively on social crowdfunding have evolved more recently (e.g., www.causes.com).

9.3.4   B Corps

B Corps are for-profit businesses that explicitly follow a hybrid logic and hence reach beyond the profit maximisation logic. B Corps are designed so that they explicitly include the interests of stakeholders into their governance structures. In fact, the consideration of stakeholder interests is a *legal requirement* for a profit-oriented business to carry the label 'B Corp'. Yet, not every corporation can simply turn itself into a B Corp. B Corps are those firms that have passed a certification which is conferred by B Lab, a global non-profit organisation. Understood in this way, we can see B Corps as social businesses that have passed a specific certification process.

To be awarded the B Corp certification companies must achieve a minimum score during an assessment of their social and environmental performance. The certification must be renewed every three years. The certification process consists of two essential steps:

1. *Eligibility*: Companies are asked to make an impact assessment of their own social and environmental performance. This self-assessment is measured against the B Lab standard and firms must reach a minimum score to count as eligible for certification. Exemplary topics that are assessed include: the firm's governance (e.g., whether management is evaluated according to ESG criteria), community

relations (e.g., the percentage of management positions given to underrepresented minorities) and environmental impact (e.g., how waste is recorded and handled). Companies that aim for certification need to prove that they have included stakeholder commitments explicitly into the governing documents of the company (e.g., its bylaws). This is an important change from a corporate governance perspective. Once stakeholder commitments are part of a firm's governing documents, managers are *legally* required to consider the rights of relevant stakeholders. Finally, firms must be transparent about their social and environmental performance to be considered eligible for certification (e.g., by making such performance publicly available).

2. *Evaluation and Verification*: The submitted information is then evaluated and verified by B Lab. This happens through an analysis of the submitted documents, as well as through talks between the company and B Lab's analysts. One advantage of certification via B Lab is that the evaluation and verification of documents is done by the non-profit entity itself. By contrast, other certifications (e.g., factory certifications in global supply chains; see Chapter 24) outsource these tasks to third parties, which usually creates less reliable results.

The number of certified B Corps has grown steadily throughout recent years. In 2007, the initiative started with nineteen certified businesses, while today more than 4,000 firms in over seventy countries are certified. Most of the certified companies are small and medium-sized enterprises (SMEs). The SME focus of the B Corp movement is noteworthy, as corporate sustainability is often viewed as being mostly a topic for larger (multinational) corporations (see Chapter 8). However, some larger firms have also turned into B Corps, including Patagonia, Ben & Jerry's, The Body Shop and Danone (North America). For larger companies, it is either possible to certify the parent company directly (if the parent organisation can ensure that the performance targets are met for 95 per cent of operations) or to certify each subsidiary individually. The latter approach is more 'organic', in the sense that subsidiaries can slowly become familiar with B Corp certification and thus build momentum. The more decentralised approach is also better if a company has subsidiaries in various countries with different legal requirements. Companies that receive more than 1 per cent of their revenue from the following sectors cannot become a B Corp: coal, pornography, gambling, weapons (including ammunition) and/or tobacco (B Corp, 2022).

One benefit of the B Corp certification is that the certificate can act as a branding tool. Companies can signal to relevant audiences that they are 'B Corp certified' and thereby increase stakeholder trust. As legal changes to a company's governing documents are a precondition for certification, the B Corp label also signals to stakeholders a certain degree of seriousness related to a company's ESG efforts. However, B Lab's certification model also creates costs. Although the costs of certification depend on the annual sales of the company, these costs can still impede the interest in becoming certified, especially among SMEs who usually do not have significant financial resources devoted to corporate sustainability management. Another drawback of the B Corp model is that certification itself does not grant any legal status (unless a B Corp is registered as a benefit corporation in the United States; see below). Although B Corps have a legal requirement to change their governing documents in favour of stakeholder considerations, they are not granted a different legal status compared to other corporations.

Critics have argued that the B Corp model remains too focused on certification, and that such certification cannot substitute for good governance (O'Regan, 2019). Just changing the governing documents of a firm does not always lead to a different way of governance, even if well intentioned. Corporate governance intersects with corporate sustainability in many ways (see Chapter 15). For instance, the board of directors and executive management also need to have the right mindset so that the firm can make an impact on social and environmental problems. Another criticism relates to the fact that corporations can easily drop the B Corp certification. While there is a directory of active B Corps (i.e., firms that are currently certified), there is no directory of firms that used to be certified but did not renew their certification. Certified companies can walk away from the B Corp model if they believe it no longer suits their needs or beliefs. CouchSurfing is a good example. The company was certified as a B Corp in 2011, but it did not maintain this status in the long run (O'Regan, 2019).

One widespread misunderstanding is that becoming a B Corp will hurt managers' control in the sense that some stakeholder groups can dictate the corporate agenda. This is not true. Becoming a B Corp means that managers and directors will have to consider social and environmental performance criteria alongside financial performance criteria when making decisions. Of course, meeting and maintaining the performance requirements for a B Corp certification is likely to influence the decisions that managers and directors will make. However, it does not affect the control that a company has over its own operations and strategic direction.

B Corps need to be distinguished from PBCs, which were introduced above. PBCs were first established in the United States in 2010 and reflect corporate entities that have a separate legal status under US law. Although B Corps and PBCs share some similarities, they are not the same thing. In the past, there has been quite a bit of confusion about the relationship between PBCs and B Corps. It is therefore important to bear in mind the following:

- PBC reflects a legal status (which is difficult to change), while B Corp certification can be taken away from a firm or the firm cannot apply for recertification.
- It is possible to be a PBC with a B Corp certification.
- It is not true that only PBCs can receive B Corp certification status.
- B Corp certification is not a precondition to become recognised as a PBC.
- Being recognised as a PBC meets *some* of the requirements of the B Corp certification.

The main difference between both organisational types is that PBCs reflect a legal status, while B Corp certification is awarded by a non-profit entity (B Lab) outside of any legal framework. In both organisational types, directors on the board are required to consider the firm's impact on a broad range of stakeholders – not just on shareholders. While the B Lab certification outlines certain performance requirements in the sense that firms need to reach a minimum score during the assessment, PBCs face less stringent performance requirements and are only asked to disclose self-reported metrics.

Table 9.3 summarises the four alternative types of organising for corporate sustainability and digests challenges, different types and examples.

Table 9.3 Summary of alternative types of organising for corporate sustainability

Type of organising	Foundation-owned firms	Social businesses	B Corps	Cooperatives
Description	For-profit companies that are owned by non-profit industrial foundations	Organisations that pursue a social mission while relying on commercial activities to sustain their operations	For-profit firms that are certified by B Lab; there is a legal requirement to consider stakeholder interests	Voluntary union of individuals or entities that pursue the same goal and join their forces in order to act more efficiently
Who influences decisions?	The foundation who owns the company (if they own majority of voting shares)	Social business leaders, sometimes employees and other stakeholders	Managers and the board of directors (like in traditional companies)	Members of the cooperative (e.g., producers, customers, employees)
Different types	Differentiation along two factors: - Foundation fully owns vs. partly owns business - Foundation owns publicly listed company vs. private company	Differentiation along two factors: - Social value creation for beneficiaries and with beneficiaries - Economic value creation integrated or differentiated from social mission	Differentiation along two factors: - B Corps that are SMEs versus MNCs - B Corps where each subsidiary is certified vs. parent company is certified	Many different forms, such as: - Producer cooperatives - Credit unions - Consumer cooperatives - Worker cooperatives - Purchasing cooperatives

Table 9.3 (*cont.*)

Type of organising	Foundation-owned firms	Social businesses	B Corps	Cooperatives
Exemplary challenges	- Possible higher costs of capital - Need to manage foundation-company interface	- Tensions due to goal duality - Diverse stakeholder demands - Mission drift - Funding	- Over-focusing on certification - No guarantee of impact - Easy to drop out (not renewing certificate)	- Definition of property rights - Free riders - Diverse risk preferences of individual members
Examples	Novo Nordisk, Carlsberg, IKEA, Tata Group, Hershey, Rolex	Too Good To Go, Auticon, Werner & Mertz GmbH	Tony's Chocolonely, Patagonia, TOMs	Arla Foods, DelosAndes Coffee Cooperative, The Cooperative Bank, Mondragon
Recommended literature	Børsting and Thomsen (2017) Thomsen et al. (2018)	Battilana and Lee (2014) Smith et al. (2013) Saebi et al. (2019)	Pollack et al. (2021) Villela et al. (2021)	Webb and Cheney (2014) Mazzarol et al. (2018)

Source: Own table

9.4 Chapter Summary

The key take-away from this chapter is that there are alternative types of organising for corporate sustainability that operate as hybrid enterprises between for-profit businesses and non-profit organisations. These alternative types do not just define ESG practices, but they often integrate social and environmental concerns deeply into their business models. Often, these organisations reach beyond a reactive 'do-no-harm' approach towards sustainability and instead aim to create positive social as well as environmental impact.

Some of the discussed alternative types of organising are not new; they have a long history of creating social and ecological value. Foundation-owned companies and cooperatives date back to the eighteenth century, and even social businesses have a long tradition in enabling organisations to combine commercial activities and social mission achievement. Being certified as a B Corp, in contrast, is a promising novel organisational form that emerged from 2007 onwards. All the discussed alternative types of organising are confronted with a range of challenges, such as dual mission achievement, diverse stakeholder expectations and getting access to financial capital. Nevertheless, these types have proven as promising pathways to integrate sustainability into the business sector and are therefore an important part of corporate sustainability.

CHAPTER QUESTIONS

1. From the lens of organisational hybridity, how can alternative types of organising be differentiated from one another and what do they have in common?
2. How do alternative types of organising contribute to corporate sustainability?
3. What kinds of different social businesses exist?
4. What are the main challenges of social businesses, foundation-owned companies and cooperatives? Where do you see 'dark sides' and what criticism would you raise?
5. How would you criticise the B Corp movement? Do you see it as an idea that could help to repurpose a larger set of corporations? Why/Why not?

FURTHER RESOURCES

- Battilana, J., Besharov, M. and Mitzinneck, B. (2017). On Hybrids and Hybrid Organizing: A Review and Roadmap for Future Research. In R. Greenwood, C. Oliver, R. Suddaby and K. Sahlin-Andersson. (Eds.), *The SAGE Handbook of Organizational Institutionalism* (2nd ed., pp. 133–169). London: Sage.

  This book chapter sheds light on antecedents, challenges, opportunities and management strategies of hybrid organisations.

- B Corp website, www.bcorporation.net/.

  You can learn about the B Corp movement and current certified companies on this website.

- Strine, L. E. (2014). Making It Easier for Directors to 'Do the Right Thing'? *Harvard Business Law Review*, 4, 235–253.

  An article by the (now former) Chief of Justice at Delaware Supreme Court (2014–19), Leo E. Strine, about the potential of and pathways for the benefit corporation movement to lead a sustainable systemic change of the corporate world.

- Ted Salon: US Airforce (2019). The Crisis of Leadership – and a New Way Forward. With Halla Tómasdóttir, www.ted.com/talks/halla_tomasdottir_and_ bryn_freedman_the_crisis_of_leadership_and_a_new_way_forward.

An interview with Halla Tómasdóttir, former B Lab CEO and presidential candidate for Iceland, about the potential of leadership to guide a transformation towards sustainability.

- The Flanders Show. (2021). The New Cooperative Business Model Could Change Everything, www.youtube.com/watch?v=nRgZQHqb07A.

  A video that shows how cooperatives are becoming increasingly relevant in current times, especially in the tech industry.

- Volkmann, C., Tokarski, K. and Ernst, K. (2012). *Social Entrepreneurship and Social Business: An Introduction and Discussion with Case Studies.* Wiesbaden: Gabler.

  This textbook provides a comprehensive overview of social entrepreneurship (and social businesses) based on current theoretical stances and various practical examples.

- Yunus Social Business Hub, www.yunussb.com.

  On this web page you can learn more about social businesses as a tool to foster sustainable development in the Global South. The hub's name refers to Muhammed Yunus, Nobel Peace Prize laureate and founder of the micro-finance institution Grameen Bank.

10 Sustainability Professionals

CHRISTINE MOSER AND EVGENIA I. LYSOVA

LEARNING OBJECTIVES

- Learn about the emerging profession of sustainability professionals.
- Learn about their work and characteristics.
- Discuss the specific skill sets and competencies required.
- Zoom in on the motivations, values, tasks and practices of sustainability professionals.
- Reflect on possible future pathways for sustainability professionals.

10.1   Introduction

The past years have seen an unprecedented increase in attention to sustainability issues. While other chapters in this book will tell you all about what sustainability is, we pay specific attention to the crucial role of *sustainability professionals* in driving sustainability change. Sustainability professionals are people who are tasked with advancing and implementing sustainability in organisations. You may come across different terms that are used to refer to sustainability professionals, for example: *CSR managers, CSR professionals, sustainability managers, ESG (environmental and social governance) managers* and similar. Despite these different terms, they tend to conduct similar activities, which typically include analysing, controlling and advancing sustainability in organisations (Spraul et al., 2019). Figure 10.1 provides an overview of the profession's main facts.

The job title *sustainability professional* is very recent. As a profession, it was established in 2007, with the creation of the largest professional association: the International Society of Sustainability Professionals (ISSP). Other associations, such as sustainabilitypractitioners.org, followed. With the development of the professional status for sustainability work in the context of organisations, there was a need to introduce sustainability in higher education in order to prepare qualified sustainability professionals. As a result, the past decade has seen an increased number of academic institutions offering a variety of courses, certificates and

SUSTAINABILITY PROFESSIONALS

They earn €50–€100K	47 per cent hold the title 'CSR manager'	66 per cent interact with their CEO at least four times/year
34 per cent report to the communications department	The average team size is one to two	Climate change is their biggest challenge

Figure 10.1 Common traits of sustainability professionals at a glance.
Source: Developed based on De Bernardi and Pedrini (2019).

programmes in sustainability. An increasing number of consultancy firms now specialises in sustainability. In the early 2020s, most multinational companies and other large and small organisations have by now created the position of sustainability professional or manager.

The role of sustainability professionals in present-day organisations cannot be overstated. Faced with gigantic challenges regarding CO_2 emissions, climate change, human rights violations and a myriad of other staggering problems, companies count on their sustainability professionals to somehow come up with a way out of this labyrinth. However, in practice, when pursuing goals that address sustainability-related issues and problems in the context of organisations, these professionals have to deal with tensions that arise when sustainable goals are in conflict with the commercial goals of organisations. Although achieving commercial goals while at the same time safeguarding sustainability goals is a challenging task, many people recognise the necessity and meaningfulness of succeeding in these efforts and are attracted to work as sustainability professionals. The industry provides them with jobs: 2019 has seen an increase of 10 per cent of sustainability job postings on LinkedIn, and there was a 7.5 per cent increase of people with a sustainability job title on LinkedIn (Makower, 2020).

In this chapter, you will learn about who sustainability professionals are, what they do, what motivates them and what can help them to continue with their important work.

10.2   Who Are Sustainability Professionals?

In this section, we describe the pathways into the profession and the characteristics and position of sustainability professionals in organisations, and we discuss how the profession is different from others. We will then describe the skill set that sustainability professionals need, as well as their competencies.

10.2.1   Different Pathways into the Profession

There are different pathways of developing sustainability work within an organisation. Sustainability professionals can be recruited for a sustainability-focused job, accompanied by the creation of a separate department or team that is tasked with the promotion of sustainability in a company. In this case, the sustainability department represents a fully autonomous function within the company. A different pathway is to naturally grow within the company, being previously based in another department. Employees who grow into sustainability professions in the company often come from the communication departments, investor relationships, accounting, health-safety quality or human resources management (HRM) departments. The management of sustainability in a company can be located within any single one of these departments, or it can be shared across departments. For example, one department would focus on managing the environmental dimensions of sustainability, whereas another department would cover the social dimensions of sustainability (Gond et al., 2011a).

10.2.2   Characteristics and Position

You may come across different labels of sustainability professionals, namely, the labels of CSR manager, sustainability manager, sustainability consultants and similar. Although these different labels do not usually imply big differences in what these sustainable professionals actually do, we can differentiate two main characteristics. The first difference is with regard to their *status* in relation to the organisation: they are either *insiders* or *outsiders*. Those sustainability professionals who are insiders are usually (middle) managers whose task is to put sustainability into practice. In contrast, outsiders such as sustainability consultants are, like other consultants, hired for particular and temporally bounded projects or to coach employees.

Second, the *formality* of their role can differ. In the case of their role being *explicit*, they are designated as sustainability professionals (independent of how they are called). They typically work at a CSR or sustainability department. In the case of their role being *implicit*, they engage in sustainability work independently of their current job title (which can be something quite unrelated) as long as they promote sustainability in the organisation (Spraul et al., 2019). The overview of classifications is summarised in Table 10.1.

In addition to sustainability professionals being classified into insiders and outsiders, and their job titles being made explicit or not, we can distinguish sustainability professionals based on the role they take in promoting sustainability in the company. Roughly corresponding with more generic roles used in HR, we can differentiate between *experts, facilitators and collaborators, catalysts and strategists*, and *activists* (Visser and Crane, 2012; MacDonald et al., 2020). The respective category refers to 'the mode of operating in which they felt most comfortable, fulfilled or satisfied' (Visser and Crane, 2012: 11–16). Table 10.2 summarises this typology. While this categorisation of sustainability professionals builds on the meaning they find in their work, which is a subjective criterion, it is possible to differentiate sustainability professionals based on objective criteria such as hierarchical position in an organisation (e.g., line managers, senior managers, etc.), salary level (e.g., different salary grades) and location within an organisation (e.g., separate department, within another department such as marketing or HR). The

Table 10.1 Classification of sustainability professionals

Label of sustainability professionals	Status in relation to the organisation	Role formality
CSR manager, sustainability manager, CSR professional	Insider	Explicit or implicit
Sustainability consultant	Outsider	Explicit

Table 10.2 Types of sustainability professionals

Type of sustainability professional	Characteristics
Expert	Gives expert input, focuses on technical excellence, seeks uniqueness through specialisation, derives pride from problem-solving abilities
Facilitator and collaborator	Focuses on people development, creates opportunities for staff, changes attitudes or perceptions of people, likes team building
Catalyst and strategist	Gives strategic direction, influences leadership, tracks organisational performance, birds-eye view and perspective
Activist and change agent	Motivated by broader social and environmental issues, is part of the community, fights for a just cause, wants to achieve improved conditions in society

Source: Based on Visser and Crane (2012) and MacDonald et al. (2020).

latter categorisation allows comparison with other occupations and the creation of statistics and overviews (e.g., ISSP, 2016; De Bernardi and Pedrini, 2019).

A key characteristic of this emerging profession is that it is ripe with tensions (Mitra and Buzzanell, 2017), as described in Box 10.1. Sustainability professionals face struggles in their everyday work. In particular, the strain between commercial goals (i.e., profit maximisation and financial performance) and sustainability goals (i.e., conducting business in a responsible and sustainable way) is inherent in their everyday experiences. They need to address important but often contradicting goals and aspects of work. Moreover, working towards achieving one goal will affect if and how another goal can be achieved. The tensions faced by sustainability professionals are not easy to address due to the fact that these conflicting goals cannot be addressed separately: they need to be addressed simultaneously as the triple bottom line is what defines sustainability (people, planet, profit). Therefore, sustainability professionals often perceive their task as very difficult and in the context of limited resources and support within an organisation, they may even find these tasks impossible to achieve.

In part because of the complexity of their job, sustainability professionals continuously struggle to affirm their status and recognition in the company (Risi and

---

INSIGHTS | BOX 10.1 Tensions in supermarket chains around sustainability

Imagine a supermarket chain. As for most businesses, achieving commercial goals (i.e., making money) is at the forefront of most supermarket chains' corporate strategies.

However, and again as for most businesses, supermarket chains are under mounting pressure from society, stakeholders and increasingly shareholders to engage with sustainability issues. This tension is especially apparent for supermarkets as their core value proposition – food – impacts the environment and societies in many different, and often damaging, ways. The people responsible for somehow navigating these opposing goals are sustainability professionals. And although their profession is increasingly recognised as essential for realising sustainability goals, their task is very difficult and at times seemingly impossible. Reconciling commercial and sustainability goals is difficult to achieve in practice: there is an inherent tension between throwing away food (which is bad for the environment and thus does not meet the company's sustainability goals) and losing commerce because of under-stocked shelves (the understocked shelves would be good for sustainability, but bad for commerce).

(Moser, 2020).

Wickert, 2017). They aim to do so by showing that pursuing sustainability goals can solve essential business-related problems. For example, a sustainability professional who wants to implement an environmentally friendly way of production needs to convince internal stakeholders (e.g., employees, management, etc.) that despite the investment this change requires, once implemented it can help by saving resources and receiving a return on investments. This is important as not every internal stakeholder may sense the urgency for this change, limiting their readiness for it. Like with any change, this convincing communication is therefore critical for driving sustainability changes in the organisation. Affirming status and earning recognition for their work is crucial for sustainability professionals because it helps them to win the competition for resources such as funding or staffing (Carollo and Guerci, 2018). This internal competition is with the other occupational groups (e.g., HR, IT or Marketing) in the organisation, who are often much more experienced (and also better staffed) than sustainability departments. This difference in experiences and resources is related to the fact that, being a rather 'new' occupational group, sustainability professionals still need to claim their territory in an organisation. As one of the interviewed CSR professionals in a study of Gond et al. (2011a: 123) explains: 'With HRM like with other departments, there are logics of territory and power. They see this guy with his "CSR hat" which is not very well defined but which is broad and interdepartmental, and they ask: where does he come from? What does he tell us? What is his legitimacy?'

The characteristics and position of sustainability professionals will differ depending on the context of the organisation they work in. In particular, professionals as managers can be often found in multinational corporations (MNCs), where they are challenged to go through the different layers of bureaucracy and multi-level hierarchies to succeed in pursuing their sustainability goals. In contrast, in small and medium-sized enterprises (SMEs), the role of sustainability professional will be taken by the expert on the service or product (see Chapter 8).

10.2.3 Hard and Soft Skills

Needless to say that sustainability professionals are expected to have certain *skills* that enable them to address the complex job challenges described above. The most desired hard skills include strategic planning, project management and sustainability reporting; and the most desired soft skills include communication, influencing change, problem-solving, and team-building and collaboration (Figures 10.2 and 10.3; Atwood et al., 2016). For example, 68 per cent of sustainability professionals are expected to be skilled in strategic planning, and 67 per cent are expected to be skilled in communication. Interestingly, the preferred hard and soft skills also signal the necessity for sustainability professionals to be good strategic organisers who are able with their communicative efforts to promote organisational change. This can often be a tricky and extremely difficult balancing act: being good at strategic

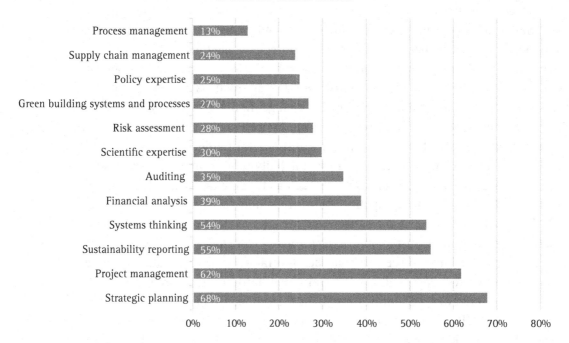

Figure 10.2 The hard skills sustainability professionals are desired to have.
Source: Based on Atwood et al. (2016).

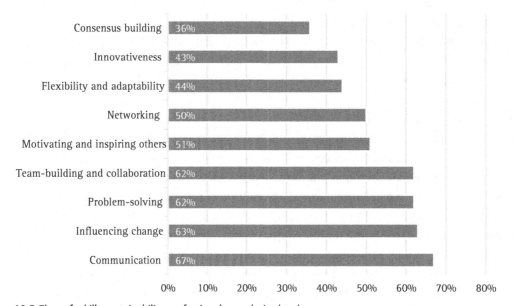

Figure 10.3 The soft skills sustainability professionals are desired to have.
Source: Based on Atwood et al. (2016).

Table 10.3 Competence domains of sustainability professionals

Competence domain	Skills, characteristics and motivations
Cognition-oriented	Foresight thinking, systems thinking, instrumental understanding
Functional-oriented	Management and leadership skills, good at identifying and realising CSR-related business opportunities, good at implementing CSR
Social-oriented	Facilitates interpersonal CSR processes, good at supporting people
Meta-oriented	Value-driven, affective, strong ethical and normative understanding, good at reflecting

Source: Osagie et al. (2016) and Spraul et al. (2019).

planning, project management, reporting and auditing, to name but a few desired skills, *and at the same time* being good at communicating, problem-solving and motivating others. Like a sheep with five legs and a golden coat, ticking all the boxes often leaves sustainability professionals lost or confused. It may be that they do not know what to prioritise, and often they fulfil certain requirements but not others. This suggests that sustainability professionals need their intrinsic motivation also for coping with the high and diverse job demands.

10.2.4 Competencies

Combinations of the above-mentioned hard and soft skills have been described in *competence profiles*. Here, it becomes crystal-clear that a sustainability professional 'has to be an "allrounder", covering a wide variety of requirements' (Spraul et al., 2019: 19). They have to become experts on all of the following four competence domains: cognition-oriented; functional-oriented; social-oriented; and meta-oriented (Osagie et al., 2016; Spraul et al., 2019). These different competence domains require different skills, characteristics and motivations. Table 10.3 provides an overview. In practice, this means that the daily activities of sustainability professionals are full of various tasks spanning from making strategic plans and showing leadership how sustainability initiatives are being implemented, to communicating and convincing internal stakeholders of the need for these initiatives. This suggests that a successful professional is someone who is a social thinker and a practical executer.

10.3 Motivations, Values, Tasks and Practices

In this section, we will outline what drives sustainability professionals and discuss their personal motivations and values. Next, we discuss their typical tasks and practices.

10.3.1   Motivations and Values

In their work, sustainability professionals are guided and motivated by *values* - the vision they have on how they ought to behave, and what their positive goals in life are (Hemingway and Maclagan, 2004). These values also determine the direction in which sustainability professionals would like to see sustainability practices and strategic changes being implemented in the organisation. For example, a sustainability professional may strongly value equality. Therefore, she would specifically bring about sustainability-driven changes in an organisation that can be aimed at addressing different aspects of inequality currently present in the organisation. Being able to act following their personal values is important for sustainability professionals. This is because following their personal values ensures that they will feel they are authentic in their work and, thus, will experience their work as personally significant and worthwhile (Tams and Marshall, 2011; Mitra and Buzzanell, 2017). Having the opportunity to act in accordance with their personal values will also help them to experience a greater fit with the organisation they work for. Greater perceived fit will add to their willingness to commit, stay, and contribute to bringing about positive change in their organisation.

Sustainability professionals can differ in the kind of *drivers* that motivate their engagement in sustainability work. These motivational differences can be seen across the above-identified four types of sustainability professionals. In particular, experts are motivated and derive meaning from developing and offering specialist input, providing quality improvements in processes and products. Facilitators are motivated and derive meaning from using their knowledge and skills to empower other people. Catalysts are motivated by their dedication to a cause and derive meaning from creating and influencing change. Lastly, activists are motivated by and derive meaning from contributing to improving the lot of others at a broader societal level (e.g., fighting poverty, inequality and other broad society-focused causes) (Visser and Crane, 2012). The latter group of sustainability professionals is likely to find it hardest to derive meaning from their work as their often 'radical' cause-pursuit efforts may not be addressed by narrowly defined organisational views on sustainability (Girschik et al., 2022). Check Box 10.2 for some examples of how different sustainability professionals talk about their motivations.

10.3.2   Tasks and Practices

Despite the profession still emerging, we have a good overview of the *tasks* that sustainability professionals usually execute (Table 10.4). As you can see, being a sustainability professional is no mean feat: responsibilities and activities concern the entire organisation and value chain. These professionals have to engage in formulating relatively abstract strategies and visions and making a business case; formulate and implement interventions; innovate; broaden the organisation's

INSIGHTS | BOX 10.2 Sustainability professionals talking about their motivations

'I usually get that sense of meaning in work when I've finished a product, say like an Environmental Report and you see, I've really put in a lot and here it is. Or you have had a series of community consultations and you now have the results.' (*Expert*)

'The part of my work that I've enjoyed most is training, where I get the opportunity to work with a group of people – to interact with people at a very personal level. You can see how things start to get clear for them, in terms of understanding issues and how that applies to what they do.' (*Facilitator*)

'I like getting things changed. My time is spent trying to influence people. The real interesting thing is to try and get managing directors, plant managers, business leaders and sales guys to think differently and to change what they do.' (*Catalyst*)

'That gave me satisfaction ... I can go back to a workplace and people say, "Since you've been here there's been a change, we're now treated like human beings, we actually now get rewarded for the work we do, our working environment it's much better, there's fresh air and there's life, we actually enjoy it, we feel happy to come to work", and for me that's a big difference.' (*Activist*)

(Visser and Crane, 2012).

Table 10.4 Responsibilities and activities of sustainability professionals

Responsibilities	*Activities*
Sustainability vision, strategies and interventions	Identify, select and plan strategies and interventions based on a shared vision and predefined goals
Business case for sustainability	Identify possibilities for risk and cost reduction, profit increase and employee motivation
Sustainability performance	Implement interventions (project management, fundraising, organise meetings and events); monitor and evaluate intervention performance
Support, buy-in and approval	Educate and consult colleagues, advocate and promote sustainability goals; convince top management of sustainability vision, strategies and interventions
Innovation	Initiate and promote sustainability innovations (products, processes, behaviours); business model innovation
Sustainable supply chain	Integrate sustainability aspects into the entire value chain
Organisational knowledge base	Support and advise leaders, teams and relevant co-workers
External stakeholders and communication	Reporting to external stakeholders about vision, strategies and interventions

Source: Adapted from Spraul et al. (2019) and MacDonald et al. (2020).

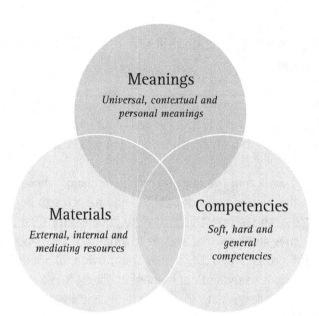

Figure 10.4 Practices of sustainability professionals can be understood in terms of meanings, competencies and materials.
Source: Based on Salovaara and Soini (2021).

knowledge base; and communicate with stakeholders; while at the same time 'selling' their issues to top management in order to ensure their buy-in.

Sustainability professionals' practices are characterised by three main elements: meanings, materials and competencies (see Figure 10.4). Meanings refer to universal meanings captured in ideas and aspirations, which generally give a boost to sustainability issues. Contextual meanings refer to things like the organisational mission or vision. And personal meanings are derived from core values and motivations. To be able to carry out their work practices, sustainability professionals need different materials and tools. External resources refer to their networks; they use internal resources such as their personality to convince others of their cause; and they also use tools such as certification schemes. Finally, competencies include soft (e.g., interpersonal competencies) and hard (management and leadership) skills. It is also important for sustainability professionals to be generally competent, for example, to be able to think critically, have strong analytical and interpersonal skills, and being well-educated in terms of underlying regulations. The intersection of these three elements makes this profession different from many others: especially the meaningfulness of their work and their personal values strongly motivate sustainability professionals, which is in contrast to many other professions and managerial roles.

Bringing about sustainable change in organisations requires sustainability professionals to think about how to communicate the need for the change, as well as how to implement sustainability strategies in practice. We know from sociological research that communication and daily work practices are contextual – that is, they are shaped by the context in which they are conducted. In addition, these practices are often contested in political struggles, adding to the complexity of the sustainability professionals' jobs. Finally, we should understand sustainability work as a collective effort: sustainability professionals never act in isolation, but are part of a network of professionals from different occupational groups (for an overview, see Gond and Moser, 2021). Box 10.3 describes possible ways of integrating tasks and practices in the wider organisation.

SNAPSHOTS | BOX 10.3 Story of Carola Wijdoogen, Director of Sustainable Business at NS Netherlands National Railways

In her 2016 book *MVO doe je zo* ('CSR works like this'), Carola Wijdoogen, Director of Sustainable Business at NS Netherlands National Railways, talks about her vision and understanding of being a sustainability professional. With a background in procurement and innovation, she asked herself when starting the new job: 'What's the added value of the sustainability manager?' And: 'What does a sustainability manager actually do?' According to her, there is no one-size-fits-all approach, but across organisations, sustainability professionals fulfil similar roles. She describes seven such roles:

1. Engage and grow the network
2. Lead for strategy
3. Support implementation
4. Challenge to inspire and connect
5. Empower others for success
6. Innovate for continuous renewal
7. Learn from reporting

'For anyone in the sustainability management role, the book offers insightful perspectives and concrete examples in each of the outlined roles. In a way that enables sustainability managers to critically assess their roles, their focus and their action plan for impact. So while perhaps not a linear roadmap with consecutive action steps for success, the book certainly offers a map of some kind as well as guidance to better navigate the context of your own industry and organization.'

(Baghuis, 2017).

There are different ways in which sustainability professionals can pitch their projects (Wickert and De Bakker, 2018). This pitching is often referred to as *issue-selling*: presenting sustainability issues in a way that can win the attention of the top management to allocate resources and make strategic changes. First, sustainability professionals seek to strengthen their internal influence within an organisation by creating a network of internal allies who support sustainability issues. Then, they start to 'sell' those issues that could be easily implemented to show their contribution to organisational performance. Second, they seek to make sustainability issues emotionally appealing for people in different functions (e.g., HR and IT). Third, sustainability professionals try to adapt their language: they want to understand others' viewpoints so that they adjust how they speak about particular issues in ways that align with these other viewpoints.

As sustainability professionals engage in issue selling, they have to craft their way of *communicating* about their work. While positioning themselves and talking about their work as idealists or those who 'enlighten the business' reflects the importance sustainability professionals place on values, most sustainability professionals do not present them in this way. Also, they often have to use the language that positions them as business-oriented managers who can show how addressing sustainability issues contributes to the profitability of the organisation. This can be done by emphasising their deliverables, extensively using numbers and referring to the weight of sustainability efforts in company outcomes.

Sustainability goals of the organisation are often at odds with the mainstream strategy (Hengst et al., 2019) – which is often mostly business- and profit-oriented. What often happens is that the two strategies – sustainability and mainstream strategies – become *decoupled*, meaning that they are not connected (anymore). This decoupling of strategies is often a root cause of sustainability professionals' difficulties with implementing their ideas in practice. While the mainstream strategy is widely accepted in the organisation as the legitimate strategy, the – mostly new – sustainability strategy can face severe challenges in terms of acceptance and legitimisation. Sustainability professionals, who fight to implement sustainability strategies, are caught in between. Moreover, they are often made responsible for the failure of the sustainability strategy, despite their rarely being in a powerful position that could ensure their success.

In addition, it can be difficult to implement sustainability strategies for three more reasons:

1. Sustainability can be very hard to implement as it is something that cannot always be easily measured. Although the past decades have seen a dramatic rise in standards, tools, codes of conducts, policies, key performance indicators and reporting schemes with regard to sustainability (Gond and Brès, 2020), it can still be *difficult to measure* and put into words just what it means to be 'sustainable' (see also Chapter 1).

2. While it can be relatively easy to measure sustainability with external tools, changing the internal organisation or *creating new sustainable practices* before they can be measured can be difficult. This is because organisational change typically meets resistance throughout the organisation; often, employees, managers and even CEO suite members are against changes that may threaten their tried-and-trusted business practices.

3. Sustainability is a complex phenomenon that requires organisations to address at the same time ethical, social and environmental concerns. And while a business might decide to work on these concerns internally, businesses are usually embedded in large *networks of stakeholders* – such as other businesses, governments and NGOs – all of whom might have their own take on these concerns.

In sum, implementing sustainability is a tricky job, and sustainability professionals are the people who are in charge of it: without sustainability professionals, sustainability strategies would rarely get implemented in practice.

10.4 The Future of Sustainability Professionals

Being a sustainability professional is a tough job: they are often deeply and intrinsically motivated, and engage with different tasks and practices, yet are often caught in intense situations that require tailor-made approaches and solutions. Realising that we will need sustainability professionals now more than ever, we need to think about how they can go about doing their job in a way that fulfils their personal needs and dreams, while at the same time serving their organisation in the best possible way – to make it more sustainable.

10.4.1 How to Safeguard One's Motivations and Personal Values

Sustainability professionals have different opportunities to integrate their motivations and personal values in their job – Box 10.4 is a short narrative about one such professional. First, they may decide to *compromise* by giving up or taking some distance from some of their personal values (Carollo and Guerci, 2018). This can enable them to have a more pragmatic approach towards the implementation of sustainability initiatives in their organisation. Second, they could *engage* in crafting how they view their work to still being able to see themselves as professionals who make a difference in the organisation. We know that people who are flexible in how they view themselves at work and how they pursue their personal values and goals can experience greater meaningfulness in what they do (Lysova and Khapova, 2019). Third, sustainability may *constrain* their emotional expressions reflecting their particular personal values. For example, sustainability professionals who are passionate about climate change may decide to constrain how expressive they are in

INSIGHTS | BOX 10.4 Sustainability professional's motivations and personal values

One has to wonder: what is my ultimate goal? Do I want to live in total respect for the environment or do I want to have an impact? Because to do my job I have to take the car, go to the office, submit to rules and constraints ... I have to make a compromise by giving up some personal values. However, since my ultimate goal is to produce a change, even though a small one, I chose to be a sustainability manager in a big company like this one, with all the consequent problems and inconsistencies, because I think I can really make the difference here.

(Carollo and Guerci, 2018: 257).

their communication about climate change with internal stakeholders. This is because their perhaps radical ideas, driven by their passion and needs, may raise stakeholders' expectations of their companies' performance beyond the aspirations of the company itself (Wright and Nyberg, 2012). This could eventually have negative consequences for how their ideas are accepted and their feasibility in the eyes of internal stakeholders. This means that it is sometimes wiser in the corporate context to hold back – even if such constraint feels uncomfortable or unfamiliar. However, instead, they may engage in the extensive emotional expression of commitment and passion to these issues when they talk about their profession to others.

10.4.2   How to Execute One's Tasks and Practices

How can sustainability professionals go about doing their job in a way that does justice to all the different stakeholders, organisational needs and job demands? We suggest that there are at least three possible ways forward.

First, it can be difficult to receive the necessary acceptance and resources and engage in practices that facilitate achieving sustainability goals. One way to resolve this tension is to *build a network of internal allies* (Wickert and de Bakker, 2019). This means that sustainability professionals should find like-minded colleagues with whom they can team up. Indeed, 'you have to invade the system and, basically, establish flagship projects to give people an orientation and then scale things up' (Wickert and de Bakker, 2019: 2).

Second, the espoused sustainability goals of the organisation may be at odds with its mainstream strategy. This leaves the sustainability professional in the uncomfortable position of having to reconcile two opposing, decoupled strategies. This issue can be resolved: sustainability professionals can adopt a so-called *paradoxical cognitive frame* (Hahn et al., 2014), which can help them to accept (instead of reject) problematic issues and at the same time accommodate conflicting interests (instead of eliminating them). Accepting that problematic issues exist is a first step as it allows them to find out what exactly the problem is. Once they have become aware of the issues, it will be easier to accommodate the conflicting interests.

A third possible way to address the demanding job needs is to work in a *task-by-task* manner (Hengst et al., 2019). Here, the professionals work to legitimise the new sustainability strategy vis-à-vis the mainstream strategy in action cycles. In other words, they try to integrate the new strategy with the mainstream one by instilling it in their daily tasks and in small portions. Such daily tasks may include the sharing of relevant knowledge (Moser, 2020) which can broaden the organisational knowledge base.

It is important to note that in all three scenarios, sustainability professionals would need the backing of senior management, and most of all the board of directors. This is because senior management and the board of directors allocate resources which, as for all other professions and departments, are needed to develop and realise projects.

10.5   Chapter Summary

In this chapter, we have covered a lot of ground about the emerging sustainability profession and how it differs from many others. We have summarised the work of the people who are the professionals, their characteristics, required skill sets and competencies, underlying values and motivations, the tasks and practices that are part of their work and possible future ways forward. What can you take away from this chapter? You now know that this profession is heavily driven by intrinsic motivation and personal values, and is demanding. On the one hand, that means that a position as sustainability professional could be a meaningful job: if you care for sustainability, you would on a daily basis work on projects that are important and meaningful to you. On the other hand, you may expect to be met as the above-mentioned sheep with five legs and a golden coat: people may rely on you for delivering hard and soft skills, being an expert on all issues related to sustainability (and there are many issues that meet this criterion) and balancing all these demands in a patient fashion. And whatever developments this job will see, it is clear that the position of sustainability professional is here to stay and will most likely consolidate in the future.

CHAPTER QUESTIONS

1. What skills are sustainability professionals expected to have?
2. What is the background of sustainability professionals, and in which departments are they located?

3. What are tasks and practices of sustainability professionals?
4. How can sustainability professionals safeguard their motivations and values?
5. Describe an example of the tensions that sustainability professionals can experience in their daily tasks and practices.

FURTHER RESOURCES

- Carollo, L. and Guerci, M. (2017). Between Continuity and Change: CSR Managers' Occupational Rhetorics. *Journal of Organizational Change Management*, 30(4), 632–646.

  In this article, the authors show CSR professionals' change potential in organisations.

- Greenbiz (2020). State of the Profession, www.greenbiz.com/report/state-profession-2020-report.

  This report provides you with a complete and thorough overview of the state of the profession of CSR professional.

- Hunoldt, M., Oertel, S. and Galander, A. (2020). Being Responsible: How Managers Aim to Implement Corporate Social Responsibility. *Business & Society*, 59(7), 1441–1482.

  This article speaks to the question of how CSR professionals can manage tensions between social, environmental, economic and technical issues. It provides four actionable strategies that CSR professionals can use in their work.

- Snider, J. (March 2019). Sustainability Professionals Must Shine Brighter than Their Peers: Here's How to Do It, www.greenbiz.com/article/sustainability-professionals-must-shine-brighter-their-peers-heres-how-do-it.

  This online managerial article has great tips for how to be the best CSR professional that you can be.

- Wright, C., Nyberg, D. and Grant, D. (2012). 'Hippies on the Third Floor': Climate Change, Narrative Identity and the Micro-Politics of Corporate Environmentalism. *Organization Studies*, 33(11), 1451–1475.

  This article highlights some of the dark sides of being a CSR professional, and helps you to overcome potential tensions and conflicts.

11 Investors and Sustainable Finance

ANDREAS RASCHE

LEARNING OBJECTIVES

- Learn about the significance of investors for corporate sustainability.
- Distinguish between different approaches that investors use to incorporate sustainability into their investment decisions.
- Discuss the integration of sustainability into equities and other asset classes.
- Reflect on the role of data and data providers that are used in sustainable finance.
- Learn about how investors actively engage with companies on sustainability issues.

11.1 Introduction

Investors are usually not the first group of actors that come to mind when thinking about change agents for corporate sustainability. Usually, we think of investors as being interested in short-term profit maximisation and shareholder value. Corporate scandals in the financial world abound, ranging from the discussion of irresponsibility during the 2007–08 global financial crisis to more recent misconduct related to the manipulation of interest rates and money laundering. But a significant part of financial markets is increasingly interested in long-term value creation and thus actively considers sustainability-related issues when making investment and lending decisions. Of course, this interest is not always driven by ethical considerations. Rather, it often relates to investors' aim to reduce their own investment risks.

Thinking now about sustainable investing matters ... Every one of us is an investor, either directly or indirectly. You do not need to have a big savings account for sustainable investing to matter. Our money is often invested on behalf of us – for example, by pension funds, banks and the institutions which we are part of (e.g., some universities have significant endowments that are invested).

This chapter discusses why and how investors embed sustainability-related concerns into their decisions. While sustainable investing covers social and environmental issues, it also emphasises corporate governance-related factors. Investors therefore talk about 'ESG' (environmental, social and governance) factors. The focus on corporate governance is understandable, as many investors have traditionally seen weak governance practices (e.g., exaggerated executive pay) as a risk (see Chapter 15). The 'G' within ESG, however, also reaches beyond corporate governance considerations and includes issues like a firm's tax strategy, political donations and corruption.

Throughout this chapter, we use sustainable finance as an umbrella term that includes reflections about how to relate ESG factors to lending as well as investing decisions (Schoenmaker and Schramade, 2019). While sustainable investing focuses primarily on integrating ESG factors into investment analysis and decision-making (GSIA, 2018), sustainable lending is also about considering ESG factors within lending decisions. Sustainable finance affects both asset owners and asset managers: asset owners (e.g., foundations, pension funds, insurance firms or high-net-worth individuals) own the underlying assets and they usually entrust the management of these assets to asset managers.

We start by discussing what motivates investors to enter the sustainability field (section 11.2). We debate different reasons for their engagement, ranging from concerns for securing competitive returns to changes in the regulatory landscape and client demand. Next, we discuss how ESG factors are integrated into different asset classes. Investors refer to the term 'asset class' to describe a collection of investments that behave similarly. For instance, equities (stocks) and fixed income (bonds) are prominent asset classes. We first discuss how ESG considerations are integrated into equity investing (section 11.3). We then look at other ways to consider ESG-related information in investment decisions, focusing on impact investing and fixed income (section 11.4). While sections 11.3 and 11.4 discuss how ESG issues can be incorporated into investment decisions, section 11.5 looks at how investors that *have already* invested in companies can improve these firms' ESG performance, either via active engagement and dialogue or via voting on shareholder resolutions. Next, we discuss what different kinds of data can shape investors' consideration of sustainability issues (section 11.6). Finally, we look at the new European legislation (Sustainable Finance Disclosure Regulation, SFDR) which requires investors to disclose the level of sustainability risks and adverse sustainability impacts associated with their investment decisions (section 11.7). Figure 11.1 provides an overview of this chapter.

11.2 Why Does Sustainability Matter to Investors?

Investors care for sustainability for different reasons. One reason relates to the belief that these factors are 'material' when judging the value of a corporation. Materiality, a concept that originated in financial accounting (see also Chapter 17), refers to the

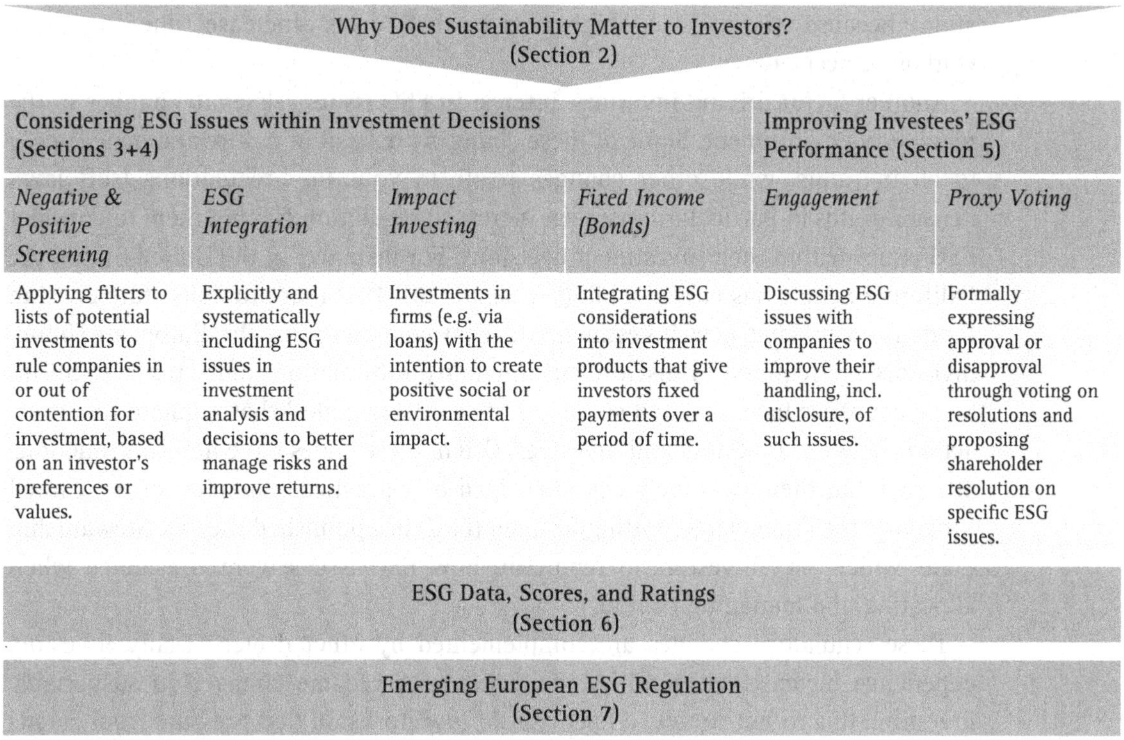

Why Does Sustainability Matter to Investors? (Section 2)					
Considering ESG Issues within Investment Decisions (Sections 3+4)				**Improving Investees' ESG Performance (Section 5)**	
Negative & Positive Screening	*ESG Integration*	*Impact Investing*	*Fixed Income (Bonds)*	*Engagement*	*Proxy Voting*
Applying filters to lists of potential investments to rule companies in or out of contention for investment, based on an investor's preferences or values.	Explicitly and systematically including ESG issues in investment analysis and decisions to better manage risks and improve returns.	Investments in firms (e.g. via loans) with the intention to create positive social or environmental impact.	Integrating ESG considerations into investment products that give investors fixed payments over a period of time.	Discussing ESG issues with companies to improve their handling, incl. disclosure, of such issues.	Formally expressing approval or disapproval through voting on resolutions and proposing shareholder resolution on specific ESG issues.
ESG Data, Scores, and Ratings (Section 6)					
Emerging European ESG Regulation (Section 7)					

Figure 11.1 Different intersection points between sustainability and finance.
Source: Adapted and modified from Principles for Responsible Investment (2020).

belief that a certain ESG issue is relevant and also significant for a given firm. Materiality is judged relative to a firm's context, especially its industry and country of operation (see also Chapter 5). For instance, while employee health and safety are material to firms operating in the extractive industries (e.g., mining), it is less material to firms from the financial services sector. Investors believe that material ESG issues impact the value of a firm because it influences the risks and opportunities that a company is exposed to. A firm that manages its ESG factors well is believed to reduce its risks (e.g., reputational or litigation risks) and enhance its opportunities (e.g., gaining access to new markets).

The link between ESG factors and companies' value drivers aligns with the discussion of the 'business case' for corporate sustainability and has been the subject of much empirical research (see Chapter 1). By now it is accepted that this link is at least non-negative. Friede, Busch and Bassen (2015) report that 90 per cent of research studies in this area find either a positive or a neutral link between a firm's ESG factors and its financial performance. Hence, there seems to be evidence that ESG factors matter to investors when they judge what drives the value of a firm. For instance, an investor who recognises that a firm in the extractive industries has poorly developed health and safety practices might adjust her/his company valuation because there is a higher risk that costs increase due to more workplace accidents.

Another factor driving investors' interest in ESG issues relates to changes in the regulatory environment. Some of these changes are legal in nature and hence apply to all investors, while other changes relate to voluntary regulations (soft law). Pension funds in particular have seen increased regulation forcing them to consider ESG issues within their investment decisions. For instance, in the United States, the California Senate has passed a bill (CA Senate Bill 185) that prohibits state pension funds from making new investments in coal companies. In the European Union, investors are required to disclose sustainability information under the new SFDR. Some countries have updated so-called 'stewardship codes' that regulate the interactions between investors and investees. Often, these codes have no legal sanctions attached, but they are widely acknowledged best practice examples. In the United Kingdom, the Financial Reporting Council (FRC) has published the 'UK Stewardship Code' which asks investors to report on how ESG issues were considered when allocating and managing capital.

These regulatory changes are complemented by other drivers. Many investors experience increased demand by their clients to become engaged in sustainable investing. In a recent survey, 23 per cent of investors said that pressure from clients (e.g., people who have their retirement money going into a pension fund) is influencing their adoption of sustainable investing practices (State Street Global Advisors, 2019). Especially larger asset owners, such as foundations or high-net-worth individuals, can push asset managers towards considering ESG factors in their decision-making. Finally, it is important to note that some investors also consider ESG factors simply because they believe it is the right thing to do. Religiously motivated investors put faith-based considerations above concerns for materiality or client demand. For example, investors that seek to follow Islamic religious principles do not put money into pork-related businesses and also avoid investments in firms that profit from gambling, pornography and alcohol.

These drivers have pushed sustainable investing into the mainstream. In 2021, the Global Sustainable Investment Alliance estimated that sustainable investing assets stood at $35.3 trillion when considering five major markets (i.e., Europe, the United States, Canada, Japan, and Australia and New Zealand; see GSIA, 2021). This accounts for a 15 per cent increase when compared to 2018 and shows that around one-third of all professionally managed assets across regions incorporated sustainability considerations in some way. By far the largest geographic markets for sustainable investment were Europe ($12 trillion) and the United States ($17 trillion). A prior GSIA (2018) survey also showed that about half of all assets that relate to sustainable investing decisions refer to public equity (i.e., stocks bought through the public market). In other words, most investors focus on publicly traded stocks when trying to incorporate ESG considerations into their portfolios. About 36 per cent of all assets that relate to sustainable investing decisions are put into fixed income products (mostly bonds).

11.3 Strategies to Incorporate ESG Factors into Equity Investing

Investors use different strategies to incorporate ESG factors into their equity investment decisions. Equity investors are those who invest with an ownership stake, either because they buy publicly traded shares of a company (public equity investors) or because they invest in firms that are not listed on a stock exchange (private equity investors). So far, sustainable investing has mostly focused on public equity investors, while private equity investing seems less affected. One reason for this is the lack of standardised data and ratings for privately held firms, as these have different disclosure requirements when compared to publicly listed companies.

11.3.1 Negative Screenings

Screenings are a frequently used tool to incorporate ESG factors into investment decisions. The popularity of screenings is mostly due to their simplicity. To 'screen' means to either exclude or include certain stocks from a portfolio based on ESG considerations. Negative screenings (exclusions) are a widely used strategy in the sustainable investing universe (GSIA, 2021). Typically, investors exclude companies that operate in controversial ('sin') industries, such as tobacco, alcohol, gambling, pornography and the production of weapons. More recently, a number of investors have also excluded companies related to fossil fuels (e.g., coal-mining companies). In 2020, BlackRock, the largest asset manager in the world, announced that it would divest from companies that earn more than 25 per cent of their revenues through thermal coal. By now, a number of major global asset owners are applying negative screens (e.g., pension funds or insurance companies).

Practically speaking, there is the question of what to do with diversified firms which may produce a controversial product, but which are also producing other, non-controversial, products. For instance, the French multinational company Thales Group has a major involvement in the rail industry and provides air traffic management systems. However, it also produces defence systems, such as short-range missile systems. While there is no official rule how much a firm can earn from controversial products, most investors apply a 10 per cent revenue threshold – that is, firms are excluded if at least 10 per cent of their revenue comes from the excluded product or activity.

Do negative screenings impact investment returns? When viewed in isolation, one may be led to believe that negative screens harm returns. For instance, tobacco companies are very profitable and outperformed the UK and US markets by more than 3 per cent annually between 1900 and 2014. However, we need to remember that most investors operate large portfolios within which controversial stocks only account for a small percentage. If we consider this, the effect of negative screens is almost negligible. To continue the tobacco example, only 1.7 per cent of the MSCI World benchmark index relates to tobacco stocks. When comparing the performance of the MSCI World index (including tobacco) and a tobacco-free version of it, the performance difference is minimal (Schroders, 2017). Negative screens will mostly have negative performance implications if they remove bigger parts of the investable universe and if the investment horizon is rather short.

11.3.2   Positive Screenings/Thematic Investing

It is also possible to apply a reverse strategy by picking stocks from companies that show a particularly good ESG performance. Some investors screen companies against minimum ESG standards and international norms. Usually, these investors believe that a minimum level of ESG performance is required before they would consider a stock at all for investment. For instance, Arabesque – an investor that only considers firms with a strong ESG profile – determines its investment universe (i.e., the pool of companies from which to choose stocks) by assigning firms a 'GC Score'. This score indicates how well a company aligns with the UN Global Compact's ten principles, and it is used before any further filters are applied to narrow down the investment universe.

Over the years, many 'ESG funds' have emerged. In 2020, Bloomberg tracked more than 2,800 funds that focused on ESG-related issues. These funds contain stocks of companies with a strong ESG profile (usually measured through ratings) or they include stocks that align with a particular ESG-related investment field (e.g., clean energy). Interestingly, ESG funds seem to be more resilient than other types of funds. During the COVID-19 crisis, the average ESG fund only fell 12.2 per cent, which is approximately half of the decline of the S&P500 benchmark index during this time (Bloomberg, 2020). In terms of overall long-term performance, research shows that ESG funds neither outperform conventional funds nor do they underperform (Renneboog et al., 2008). An analysis by the International Monetary Fund (IMF) reached a similar conclusion, arguing that 'the performance of sustainable and conventional funds is comparable' (IMF, 2019: 87).

Another way to positively screen stocks for ESG performance is through sustainability-adjusted stock market indices such as the Dow Jones Sustainability Index (DJSI) at the New York Stock Exchange or the FTSE4Good Index at the London Stock Exchange. Such indices follow a 'best-in-class' approach – that is, they include in the index those companies they consider to be the highest ESG performers in a given industry. For instance, the DJSI assesses the sustainability performance of around 2,500 firms in over fifty industries each year. Out of these, the index selects the top 10 per cent of each industry for the index, resulting in 323 firms being listed as part of the DJSI World Index in 2020.

11.3.3   ESG Integration

While negative and positive screenings imply that certain stocks are deliberately included or excluded when building an investment portfolio, ESG integration means that investors integrate social and environmental considerations into the 'fundamental analysis' of *all* firms within their portfolio. Investors perform fundamental analysis whenever they assess the estimated future financial performance of a company they either have already invested in or plan to invest in. Such analysis uses financial and non-financial data from different sources and is usually also based on an investor's dialogue with company representatives. ESG integration means that investors consider those sustainability factors within their fundamental analyses that they deem to be relevant and significant (i.e., 'material') for judging the value of a company. The belief is that once material ESG factors are considered within investment analyses, investors are better able to predict the future performance of a firm. Consider the following example. Union Investment analysed a company from the apparel industry and found that this firm had improved labour conditions at its supply factories. The analysts concluded from this that the company faced lower levels of reputational risk, which in turn had implications for the investor's stock valuation model (PRI, 2016).

ESG Integration does not put investors' own beliefs and values into the focus of the analysis, such as when stocks from certain sin industries are excluded from a portfolio. Rather, it considers the entire investment universe (i.e., all possible stocks) and tries to find out how material ESG issues affect a firm's estimated future financial performance. ESG Integration is usually seen as one way to mainstream sustainable investing – to make it relevant for the vast majority of investors by including it in the 'normal' everyday analyses of companies that investors perform in any case.

11.4   Other Ways to Integrate Sustainability into Investment Decisions

While integrating sustainability considerations into equity investing remains an important focus, investors have also used other ways to consider ESG criteria within their decision-making. This section explores two additional ways: (1) impact investing; and (2) integrating ESG criteria into fixed income products, especially bonds.

11.4.1   Impact Investing

Whether or not a specific equity investment creates a positive impact on sustainability issues remains a topic of heated debate. Based on our discussion above, it is fair to assume that most ESG-related investment approaches are either used because they help investors better address risks and opportunities or because they help to express certain personal or religious values. The actual impact on sustainability problems does not seem to be the key driver of the investment approaches discussed thus far, perhaps except for some thematic ESG funds that fall under the positive screening umbrella.

Impact is a tricky topic in the context of sustainability. In the context of sustainable finance, we need to distinguish 'investor impact' from 'company/investee impact'. Investor impact refers to the change that investors create in the social and environmental impact generated by their investee companies (Kölbel et al., 2020). In other words, investors' impact is less direct.

Impact investing assumes that investors are first and foremost motivated by their intention to create a positive impact on ESG issues. They put the estimated impact on ESG factors above other considerations within their decision-making. Figure 11.2 outlines the spectrum of impact capital, ranging from approaches that

	Traditional Finance	Finance-first (Risk-only)	Finance-first (Opportun.)	Thematic	Impact-first	Philanthropy
FOCUS	Limited or no focus on ESG factors underlying investments	Focus on ESG risks and reputational risks	Focus on ESG opportunities through investment selection	Focus on one or a cluster of issue areas where growth opportunities create at least market-rate returns	Focus on one or a cluster of issue areas (*may* require some financial trade-off and below-market returns)	Impact-Only: focus on one or a cluster of issue areas (usually with financial trade-off)
EXAMPLE		Negative screenings	Positive screenings ("Best in Class") ESG integration	Clean energy mutual fund	Fund providing debt or equity for social enterprises	Foundations / charity

Impact Investment

Competitive Returns

ESG Risks

ESG Opportunities

Figure 11.2 The spectrum of impact capital. This ranges from approaches that primarily focus on risks and returns to approaches that are exclusively concerned about social and environmental impact.
Source: Adapted and modified from Novak et al. (2018: 2).

use sustainability in an instrumental way to achieve better returns (e.g., ESG integration) to approaches that consider impact to a larger extent (e.g., thematic ESG funds or funds providing capital for social enterprises). Impact investing is not philanthropy (e.g., through charities). The latter assumes a sole focus on impact and does not attempt to create market-rate returns. Impact investing aims for market-rate returns. Yet, investors usually accept that in some cases their desire to create impact will mean that they must tolerate below-market returns, at least for some time.

Impact investing is an investment approach that operates across a variety of asset classes. Only 5 per cent of all investments made under the umbrella of impact investing focus on public equities (GIIN, 2019). In such cases, impact investors would buy stocks of companies that they believe create a positive impact on selected ESG factors. Such a strategy, however, assumes that investors have access to impact-related data at the firm-level. Some investors have started to use criteria to assess the ESG impact that firms create and to also benchmark these impacts across companies. For instance, one criterion is intentionality – that is, whether the impact was intentionally created or whether it occurred as a by-product of a firm's activities (Schoenmarker and Schramade, 2018: 240).

The most common asset class affected by impact investing is private debt. In 2019, 69 per cent of impact investments were related to private debt. Investors loaned money to enterprises that they believed would create a positive impact on selected ESG factors. Impact investors focus on a range of sectors, including energy, housing and agriculture. At the receiving end there are often small and medium-sized enterprises that want to grow their activities but do not yet have access to other forms of financing. Several impact investors focus their activities on emerging and developing economies – for instance, by providing microfinance schemes to local communities or by financing start-ups that aim to provide products or services to the poor. For instance, Acumen, a non-profit investment fund, has supported a company – Aarusha Homes – that builds safe and affordable homes for migrant workers in India. Access to such housing creates a positive impact, as it increases the stability of workers' lifestyles and thereby enhances the likelihood that they can retain their jobs.

Impact investing still faces several challenges. One problem is the measurement of ESG-related impact. As investments are often made into smaller enterprises that do not have a well-developed ESG data infrastructure, it is often not possible to assess in detail what impact has been made, by whom and on which stakeholder groups. Another problem relates to impact investing still being seen as new and unfamiliar. The unfamiliar nature of such investments can lead to prejudices. One widespread prejudice is that impact investors only reap low returns; a belief that has, however, not been confirmed by empirical research (GIIN, 2019). Finally, there is a problem with scale. Impact investing usually focuses on smaller projects that are often financed through private debt or private equity. Due to the relatively small scale of the needed investments, asset owners that are used to making large-scale investments (e.g., pension funds) usually have problems entering the world of impact investing.

11.4.2   Fixed Income/Green and Social Bonds

Fixed income refers to investments which give investors fixed payments over a predefined period. Bonds are one type of investment approach under this asset class. In its most general sense, bonds reflect 'certificates of debt issued by a government or a corporation that promise payment of the borrowed amount, plus interest, by a special future date' (Schoenmaker and Schramade, 2019: 253). While some debt is private (e.g., when taking out a bank loan), bonds reflect public debt. They allow the issuer of the bond to borrow from different investors at once. Most bonds come with a rating giving investors information about the risk they are taking and the likelihood that the issuer of the bond will pay back the money. Most bonds are either given out by governments or corporations.

Why does sustainability matter to bonds? The short is answer is that ESG-related factors influence the risk that a bondholder takes. The argumentation is similar to that for equities: ESG issues contain information that are relevant for assessing the perceived value of a bond. For instance, the rating agency RobecoSAM assesses the sustainability profile of countries along ESG criteria. RobecoSAM (2015) found that for sovereign bonds (i.e., bonds that are issued by governments) there is a negative relationship between a country's ESG score and the insurance premium that investors are asking for. In other words, a stronger sustainability profile of a country corresponds to lower risks for bondholders. Research has shown a similar relationship for corporate bonds. Firms with low ESG ratings pay higher interest rates for their bonds (Barth et al., 2020) because investors require compensation for risks they feel are not yet properly addressed by the company.

Looking beyond the link between bonds and ESG ratings, we can also view bonds as one important way to raise money for sustainability projects. In recent years, so-called 'green' or 'social' bonds have proliferated. These bonds are tied to specific sustainability themes (e.g., clean energy or sustainable agriculture) and they raise money for projects in these areas. The volume of green and social bonds has increased throughout the last years. As of 2019, the ICE BofAML Green Bond Index listed bonds worth $345 billion, which was up from $55 billion in 2015.

One challenge with green and social bonds is to ensure that their proceeds are really used for sustainability-related purposes. Some bonds may be labelled 'green' or 'social', but only use a part of their proceeds for the intended social or environmental purpose. Although green and social bonds are increasingly 'ring-fenced' on the issuers' balance sheets (i.e., they are set aside exclusively for the intended purpose), there is still a need to signal that this investment approach is not misused.

This has sparked the creation of the *Green Bond Principles* and the *Climate Bond Initiative*. Both initiatives have released standards that bond issuers can comply with on a voluntary basis, including the requirement that proceeds are exclusively used for the intended environmental or social purpose and the need to properly manage proceeds and to report on them in a timely manner.

11.5   Active Ownership: ESG-Related Investor Engagement

So far, we have explored ways to integrate ESG factors into investment decisions across different asset classes. Yet, investors can also consider ESG factors by encouraging those companies in which they *have already invested* to improve their sustainability performance. This approach is called 'active ownership'. Note the difference between active ownership and ESG investment: Whenever investors consider ESG factors within their own analysis and decision-making, sustainability is seen as a criterion that determines whether an investment is made at all (e.g., in the case of screenings or impact investments). By contrast, active ownership assumes that an investor has already made the investment decision and now wishes to improve the ESG performance of the investee company.

Active ownership relies on investors' legal rights as partial owners of corporations. Investors that follow an active ownership strategy try to convince companies either to better manage their material ESG issues or to improve their disclosure of ESG-related information. Both aspects are important for investors. Better management of ESG issues minimises a firm's exposure to risks and thereby enhances its potential financial performance (see above), while enhanced disclosure of ESG-related information fosters transparency and therefore allows investors to make better decisions.

There are two strategies for pursuing active ownership: (1) engagement and (2) proxy voting.

11.5.1   Engagement

Engagement implies that investors seek to have a dialogue with selected companies on ESG factors – for instance, to get more information about how exactly firms address material issues and what likely performance implications this may have. Engagement can happen through different channels (e.g., in-person meetings, emails or conference calls). Gond et al. (2018) find that engagement can create value for corporations as well as investors (see Table 11.1). First, engagement can be valuable because it improves communication between both parties. It helps investors to signal ESG-related expectations vis-à-vis investees, and it also helps investees to clarify potential misrepresentations of sustainability topics. Second, engagement

Table 11.1 How ESG engagement creates value

Value creation dynamics	Corporations	Investors
Communicative (exchanging information)	• Clarifying expectations and enhancing accountability • Managing impressions and rebalancing misrepresentations	• Signalling and defining ESG expectations • Seeking detailed and accurate corporate information
Learning (producing and diffusing knowledge)	• Anticipating and detecting new trends related to ESG • Gathering feedback, benchmarking and gap spotting	• Contextualising investment decisions • Identifying and diffusing industry best practice • Building new ESG knowledge
Political (deriving political benefits)	• Enhancing the loyalty of long-term investors • Elevating sustainability and securing resources • Enrolling internal experts	• Meeting client expectations • Building long-term relationships • Advancing internal collaboration and ESG integration

Source: Adapted from Gond et al. (2018: 7)

can also be valuable because it creates learning effects for both parties. Investors usually profit because it helps them to build up new ESG knowledge and contextualises investment decisions. Corporations learn because engagement gives them feedback about their own ESG practices (and omissions), which in turn improves their ability to better anticipate emerging sustainability trends and topics. Finally, engagement can also create what Gond et al. (2018) call political value. For investors, such value can be expressed through improved long-term relationships with companies they invest in, while for companies, successful engagement can imply having a pool of loyal investors who are interested in the long-term success of their business.

Increasingly, engagement is happening as a coordinated activity that is driven by coalitions of investors. The main reason behind such collective action is that the likelihood that a company will change its ESG practices increases if more investors join an engagement campaign. Coalitions usually pool the interests of investors: together, investors can have a more significant share of stocks which helps when trying to be heard by a firm's senior management. One important investor coalition is the Principles for Responsible Investment (PRI), which emerged as a sister initiative of the UN Global Compact (see Chapter 20). Collaborative engagement is at the heart of the PRI. For instance, between 2010 and 2013, a group of twenty-one investors (representing US$1.7 trillion in assets under management) approached twenty companies that had poor anti-corruption systems and hence faced increased risk of corruption. The group of investors sent letters to the companies requesting further information on the firms' anti-corruption systems. Based on this, an independent research provider assessed the anti-corruption measures in more detail. Overall, 85 per cent of the targeted companies engaged with the investors and jointly worked towards improved practices on corporate transparency and anti-corruption (PRI, 2013).

11.5.2 Proxy Voting

Investors which hold shares in publicly traded companies have the right to vote their shares on topics that are presented for vote during the annual general meeting (AGM). Investors can also file shareholder resolutions themselves and hence put a topic on the AGM agenda. For most resolutions, the management of the company will give a recommendation on how it thinks shareholders should vote. The agenda and supporting material for the AGM are mailed to all investors prior to the actual meeting. These materials are called 'proxy statements' and the term 'proxy voting' emerged because of this.

More and more investors file shareholder resolutions that address ESG-related topics. For instance, US-based Arjuna Capital filed multiple proposals asking technology companies to reduce the gender pay gap in 2016. Although the number of ESG-related resolutions is increasing (e.g., in 2020, over 400 resolutions on ESG-related topics were filed in the United States alone), it is still rare for such resolutions to win the support of the majority of a firm's shareholders. However, there is a trend that more and more shareholders vote in support of ESG resolutions *against* the recommendation of management (Morningstar, 2019). This implies that investors are forming more independent viewpoints on ESG issues, and that they are prepared to vote against management in support of stronger social and environmental agendas. Even if the majority of ESG resolutions remains unsuccessful, their mere existence shows that sustainability topics are on shareholders' minds. Also, given the public nature of AGMs, companies are eager to avoid negative publicity and therefore try to settle ESG disputes with investors before they turn into a shareholder resolution.

As investors with large stock portfolios need to respond to many ESG-related resolutions, they often seek help from third-party advisors (e.g., companies like ISS and Glass Lewis). These so-called 'proxy advisors' are for-profit firms that provide voting recommendations which are based on their own research about a company and its sustainability profile. The influence of proxy advisors has grown due to increased pressure on mainstream investors to show active ownership on ESG issues. However, the precise impact of such advisors is fiercely debated. On the one hand, there is critique that some investors blindly rely on proxy advisors' recommendations and hence do not form their own opinions on ESG-related topics. On the other hand, research also shows that larger investors often ignore proxy advisors' voting recommendations by 'voting down' possible actions on ESG issues (Chuan et al., 2019).

Most investors see proxy voting as a possible escalation strategy if attempts to engage with a company fail. Ultimately, investors can always divest from companies that they believe do not live up to their ESG expectations and/or which are not interested in having a constructive dialogue (see Box 11.1). For instance, the Norwegian Sovereign Wealth Fund excluded the Brazilian mining company Vale in 2020 because it believed that the company was responsible for serious environmental damage in the region. However, such divestment decisions remain contentious among investors. While some believe that divestment is an appropriate tool to pressure firms, others argue that retreating from a firm also implies that investors completely lose their influence on companies with a poor sustainability track record. Also, other investors are likely to step in and buy the shares that activist investors put on the market.

INSIGHTS | BOX 11.1 'Should I Stay, or Should I Go?' – Divesting from Fossil Fuel Companies

With the debate on climate change gaining traction in recent years, different stakeholder groups, including NGOs and politicians, have called for investors to divest from companies that are directly linked to fossil fuels. Most of these companies are connected to the coal, oil and natural gas industries. The hope is that by selling shares in these companies, investors can (1) send a strong public message which helps to stigmatise fossil fuel investments, (2) lower their own risks associated with fossil fuel investments (e.g., reputational risks) and (3) redirect capital flows into cleaner industries to help finance renewable energy sources.

Some investors, however, caution that such an approach also has its limits. First, selling shares does not really address climate change, because the ownership would only be transferred to another investor (and probably someone who does not care as much about climate-related issues). Second, some investors have argued that one should not generalise too much. Many 'brown firms' (i.e., fossil fuel companies) actually produce 'green patents' (i.e., innovations that are needed for renewable energy to grow). In other words, divesting from fossil fuel could also imply divesting from innovation. Finally, some investors have pointed to the enormous emissions created by other industries, which, at least in some cases, have escaped public attention. For instance, semiconductor and cement companies release enormous volumes of emissions within their respective production processes.

So, what are the implications for practitioners? It shows that exclusion and divestment decisions can be tricky when adopting a more holistic perspective. Just excluding firms or divesting from them is unlikely to produce much change. According to Edmans (2021), what is needed is an approach where investors comprehensively check firms' positive ESG impacts ('actively doing good') versus their negative contributions ('do no harm').

11.6   Types and Limits of ESG Data

Investors use different strategies to receive information on companies' ESG performance. After all, the data that investors use during screenings, ESG integration and also for exercising active ownership needs to come from somewhere. Some investors engage directly with firms to see how they perform vis-à-vis certain sustainability issues. This approach has the advantage that the investor gains first-hand and contextualised information on ESG issues. It also helps investors to better understand the reasons behind a firm's ESG performance. However, this personal approach is labour intensive and can only be performed for a small set of investee firms. Most investors base their investment decisions on standardised ESG data – that is, data that exists in a predefined format and that is available either through companies themselves or through other organisations.

Table 11.2 gives an overview of the sources of ESG data. It is important to distinguish ESG raw data (i.e., newly created data) from aggregated scores and ratings (i.e., approaches that use existing raw data and combine it in new ways). The vast majority of ESG raw data comes from companies themselves via their sustainability reporting (Chapter 17). As such reporting has matured in recent years, the data is increasingly useful to investors. However, there are also external providers of company-specific ESG raw data. Some of these providers offer raw data on certain topics (e.g., South Pole providing emissions data), while other providers deliver data that is less tied to any specific topic but more comprehensive in scope (e.g., RepRisk providing data on firms' reputation).

Providers of scores and ratings use this raw data to assess companies' ESG performance, either vis-à-vis certain topics or across a range of different ESG issues. Well-known rating providers are Sustainalytics, RobecoSAM and Refinitiv. These firms aggregate raw data in a way that firms' final sustainability score is based on the weighted average of their score on dozens of ESG items.

Table 11.2 ESG data can come from external or internal sources

	ESG raw data (internal)	ESG raw data (external)	ESG scores and ratings
ESG data focused on specific issues	Through firms' ESG reports	e.g., Southpole (firm-specific emissions data)	e.g., Equileap (ratings related to gender equality)
ESG data cutting across topics	Through firms' ESG reports	e.g., RepRisk (tracking company news based on big data)	e.g., KLD, Refinitiv, Sustainalytics, Vigeo-Eiris

Source: Adapted and modified from Schoenmaker and Schramade (2018: 171)

Although the quantity of ESG data has increased in recent years, there are still problems with the perceived quality of this information. Quality problems are particularly challenging for investors who use this data to identify sustainability leaders and laggards and thus base investment decisions on it. One specific problem is the lack of standardisation in raters' methodologies. Berg, Kölbel and Rigobon (2019) have reported a significant divergence of rating scores among ESG rating agencies. While one rating agency may assess a company as being very sustainable, another agency may assess the same company as being unsustainable. The main sources of such divergence are differences in how certain ESG attributes are measured (e.g., the quality of labour practices can be measured by workforce turnover or by the number of labour cases against that firm) and which attributes are included in a scoring model in the first place (e.g., some raters include lobbying as a measure of governance, while others do not). Finally, there is also a problem with how certain ESG attributes are weighed in a scoring model. Even if different raters use the same ESG attributes and also measure them by using the same indicators, they may still weigh attributes in different ways. For instance, labour rights may enter the final rating with greater weight than lobbying depending on how important both topics are seen by a rating agency.

Another problem is that ESG ratings rarely consider the products that a company offers and the industry that it operates in (Schoenmaker and Schramade, 2019). A tobacco company may still earn respectable ESG scores if its sustainability performance compared to industry peers is good. Many ESG ratings remain industry-neutral and 'just' provide sustainability-related information without questioning the ethical qualities of the underlying products or services. In 2021, Hargreaves Lansdown, a British financial service company, looked at the five most highly ESG rated firms in the FTSE 100 (according to Refinitiv data) and found that British American Tobacco (BAT) turned out to be the third highest ranked company (Lund-Yates, 2021). While BAT is criticised for selling a product that causes addiction and that can create significant negative effects on consumers' health, the very good ESG score was mostly due to the company's well-managed environmental impact (e.g., regarding the use of renewable energy) and its good human rights track record (e.g., with regard to tobacco farmers).

11.7   Emerging Legislation in Europe: The Sustainable Finance Disclosure Regulation

Recently, the European Commission has started to regulate what counts as a sustainable financial product. In 2019, the Commission launched an ambitious Green Deal. This Green Deal introduced several policy initiatives that were designed to contribute to making the European Union climate neutral by 2050. For investors, one specific policy initiative is of special relevance: the so-called Sustainable Finance Disclosure Regulation (SFDR). The regulation reflects binding European law that is equally relevant for all EU member countries.

The first part of the SFDR, the so-called level 1 implementation, came into effect in March 2021. The SFDR forces financial market participants (i.e., all parties interacting on the financial market, including financial advisors, asset owners and asset managers) to disclose how they account for sustainability risks as well as adverse sustainability impacts of those companies they have invested in. For instance, an investment fund offered by a European asset manager will have to disclose the level of sustainability risks and adverse sustainability impacts that are embedded in the investment portfolio. Consider this example: If the asset manager invested in firms with high greenhouse gas emissions, the level of these emissions will need to be reported. The European Union has defined specific reporting templates that investors will need to follow, so that the disclosed information is comparable and can be benchmarked across investor companies and across time. The hope is that the SFDR will enhance transparency, so that those who buy financial products can better judge the level of sustainability that is attached to a certain financial product.

Why is a regulation like the SFDR needed? The main reason is that some financial products that claimed to offer sustainable investments (e.g., certain ESG funds) were not sustainable at all. In the past, it was easy to offer ESG-related financial products, because there was no common definition standardising what counts as a sustainable financial product. According to data from Morningstar (2019), over 250 investment funds were repurposed in 2020 (up from 179 the year before). Such repurposing implies that existing non-ESG funds are transformed into ESG-related funds. This is mostly done to avoid having to build entirely new ESG funds from scratch. However, this strategy also runs the risk of not making deep enough changes to the investment portfolio to fully consider ESG criteria, causing a situation in which repurposing rather implies 'rebranding'.

The SFDR will make such repurposing or rebranding of funds more difficult, because investors will have to disclose for each fund the level of sustainability risks as well as potential adverse sustainability impacts that result from investment decisions. Based on this data, investors will have to classify whether an investment product they offer is 'light green' or 'dark green' (Table 11.3). Light green financial products would only promote certain ESG characteristics, but they do not directly have a sustainable investment objective. We can expect that the bulk of ESG-related products would fall within this category (e.g., funds that apply negative screens).

Dark green financial products are those that directly have a sustainable investment objective attached to them. So far, the SFDR has defined dark green financial products as those investments into economic activities that support certain

Table 11.3 Light and dark green products under the SFDR

	Light green financial products	Dark green financial products
Product category	• Products that promote environmental or social characteristics, but do not have as their objective a sustainable investment • Investment follows 'good governance' • It is possible that the products invest partially with the objective of sustainable investments	• Products that explicitly have sustainable investment as their objective • an investment in an economic activity that *contributes* to an environmental or social objective, provided that the investment does *not significantly harm* any environmental or social objective • Investments follow 'good governance'
Exemplary financial products	• Majority of ESG-related financial products • Products using screenings, exclusions, best-in-class	• Products that are sustainability-themed investing (e.g., a fund specialising in cleantech) • Impact investing (e.g., funds with a focus on impact investing)

predefined economic and social objectives without, at the same time, significantly harming other environmental or social objectives. At first, this definition sounds broad, but it is rather clearly defined through an emerging EU-wide classification system for sustainable economic activities (the so-called EU Taxonomy). In the end, we can expect dark green financial products to be mostly linked to impact investing strategies as well as sustainability-themed investments (e.g., a fund that was only set up to invest in cleantech companies).

11.8   Chapter Summary

The key take-away from this chapter is: Sustainable investing matters when thinking about how a transition towards an economy that considers ESG-related factors can be achieved. What started out as a fringe practice some forty years ago and mostly concerned religiously motivated investors has moved into the mainstream of investment practice. The main driver of this transformation is the recognition that investors have to address ESG issues in order to fully recognise the risks that a firm is exposed to and possible opportunities that are created through a transformation towards sustainable business models. While sustainable investment affects all asset classes, the focus remains on equities and bonds.

Although many investors use different screening techniques to either exclude or include companies in their investable universe, the integration of ESG issues into the fundamental analysis of firms within a portfolio has gained traction in recent years. Impact investing is also a quickly growing market for investors seeking to put the social and environmental impact of their investments at the heart of the investment decision. However, sustainable investing also still faces many challenges, the biggest being that ESG data is not fully reflecting firms' sustainability performance.

CHAPTER QUESTIONS

1. What motivates investors to engage in sustainable finance? What do you think limits their engagement?
2. In what ways can equity investors integrate ESG concerns into their investment decisions?
3. How does impact investing differ from other sustainable investment approaches? What do you see as the advantages and disadvantages of impact investing?
4. What does active ownership imply for ESG investors? How can such investors exercise active ownership?
5. What different types of ESG data exist? What problems are associated with ESG data? How would you overcome these problems?

Case Study: *Negative ESG Screenings – Should We Invest in 'Sin Industries'?*
Available from Cambridge University Press at www.cambridge.org/rasche2

FURTHER RESOURCES

- Schoenmaker, D. and Schramade, W. (2019). *Principles of Sustainable Finance.* Oxford: Oxford University Press.

  An introductory textbook on sustainable finance that gives a good overview of different approaches to sustainable investing. It also embeds sustainable finance into the larger discussion of sustainability transformations.

- The Principles for Responsible Investment (PRI) website, www.unpri.org.

  This website gives a lot of additional information on topics covered in this chapter, ranging from discussions of equity investments to reflections on social and green bonds. The website also contains publications that feature many mini-cases.

- The Sustainable Finance portal of the European Commission, https://ec.europa .eu/info/business-economy-euro/banking-and-finance/sustainable-finance_en.

  A website that gives information on developments around sustainable finance within the European Union. It also lists information on corporate ESG disclosure, as well as legislative proposals to further standardise sustainable finance (linked to the EU Taxonomy).

12 Government and Corporate Sustainability

JETTE STEEN KNUDSEN AND JEREMY MOON

LEARNING OBJECTIVES

- Understand different perspectives on government and corporate sustainability (including corporate social responsibility – CSR).
- Identify the types of corporate sustainability issues that governments address.
- Identify different types of government policies for corporate sustainability.
- Identify ways in which corporations respond to government regulation for corporate sustainability.
- Understand how and why boundaries are changing between public (government) and private (business and civil society) regulation of corporate sustainability through interactions in 'governance spheres'.

12.1   Introduction

Much in corporate sustainability focuses on business and society relations, particularly as it is rooted in the overlapping concept of corporate social responsibility (CSR). In this chapter, we therefore draw on research on regulation for CSR and corporate sustainability to show how government regulates these activities. As indicated in Chapter 1, we see corporate sustainability as an extension of business ethics and CSR, reflecting the greater involvement of corporations in the governance of broad societal issues, and especially those arising from the various environmental challenges facing the planet. So, in the context of this chapter, our interest is in government regulation in an area of public policy vital to society, for which corporations retain some discretion.

Our purpose is, first, to outline the different perspectives on the topic of government regulation of corporate sustainability (i.e., including from literature expressly on CSR), in order to indicate that this has been a contested subject, and to outline reasons for, and dimensions of, this contestation. Second, the chapter presents the different issues to which governments direct regulation for corporate sustainability in order to indicate their changing nature and range over time and differences among political systems. Third, it outlines the types of public policies and their regulatory strength that have been devised for corporate sustainability. The chapter then turns to examining how corporations respond to government regulation for sustainability, focusing particularly on the discretion that corporations have to conform with the law, but also to act sustainably beyond the requirements of the law, and even to enhance the law by pursuing its spirit and logic beyond the parameters specified in particular regulation. This is illustrated in the presentation of four vignettes of regulation for corporate sustainability on: corporate philanthropy, ethical trade, corporate sustainability reporting and corporate taxation. A final section illustrates the complementary interactions of public and private regulation for corporate sustainability with reference to the regulation of, first, working conditions in the Bangladesh ready-made garment industry and, second, the transparency of payments to governments by corporations in the extractives sector.

We should note that governments are of fundamental importance for corporations more broadly. They frame the legal context for the corporate form (Avi-Yonah, 2005) and they are crucial to setting the institutional framework in which norms and expectations of business emerge (Matten and Moon, 2008). Governments are the focus of much corporate political participation, as business, individually or in associations, lobby to have their interests and values enshrined in law, or supported by public recognition and financial resources. Business looks to government to advance its collective interests (e.g., the provision of physical and social infrastructure) and to regulate collective action problems (e.g., competition law) as well as to establish and administer judicial and fiscal systems on which markets depend. Governments provide physical infrastructures (e.g., roads, rail, communications), economic services (e.g., export credits, subsidies or lender of last resort), social welfare (e.g., education, research, health) and security on which corporations and markets depend. And, of course, government is for many businesses a valued customer. But our interest is beyond this and, more particularly, on how governments and corporations interact in addressing business responsibility and sustainability agendas.

12.2   Perspectives on Government and Corporate Sustainability

Despite our positioning of government regulation for corporate sustainability as of fundamental importance, there has been controversy about this relationship.[1] We reproduce this controversy by summarising and juxtaposing different perspectives

---

[1] This section draws on Knudsen and Moon (2022).

on the question of government regulation for CSR which apply equally to questions about the status of corporate contributions to sustainability. The objections to, or anxieties about, such regulation have largely hinged on the perceived threats of such regulation to 'corporate discretion' – that is, the assumption of freedom of corporations to make their own decisions about their social responsibilities – and by extension, their contributions to sustainability. We distinguish the 'dichotomous' perspective (Moon and Vogel, 2008; i.e., that government and CSR are/should be independent of each other) and the 'related' perspective (Knudsen and Moon, 2017; i.e., that government and CSR are/should be connected with each other).

12.2.1   The Dichotomous Perspective on Government and Corporate Sustainability

We explain the dichotomous perspective on government and corporate sustainability with reference to four views as to why government and CSR should be/are removed from each other: the 'definitional', 'normative', 'empirical' and 'implied' views.

The *definitional* view is found when scholars exclude governmental and legal influences on corporations for their definition of CSR because their inclusion would undermine the distinctive corporate motivation for CSR (e.g., Davis, 1973). The distinction was echoed by Frynas: '[T]he voluntary aspect forms the key distinguishing characteristic between CSR and mandatory regulation in that CSR establishes certain standards and rules of behaviour that are followed by companies voluntarily, even though there is no mandatory requirement to do so' (Frynas, 2012: 2). The definitional argument for dichotomising government and corporate sustainability also occurs when scholars need to stipulate boundary conditions for statistical evaluations of the value added by corporate investments (e.g., Flammer and Luo, 2017; Flammer et al., 2019). Other scholars theoretically modelling CSR also adopt a definitional view of the dichotomous perspective. Thus, McWilliams and Siegel's (2001) theory of the firm analysis of CSR defined it as 'actions that appear to further some social good beyond the interests of the firm and that which is required by law' (2001: 117). Despite their different inherent methodologies, what unites these two definitional views is that governmental mandates are *ipso facto* incompatible with corporate discretion for CSR, and by extension for corporate sustainability.

Second, some scholars take a *normative* or ethical view that governmental regulation of CSR and corporate sustainability would necessarily be a bad thing. In some cases, it is assumed that it is a bad thing for society and for government if, through CSR, corporations seek governmental roles (e.g., Levitt, 1958). The fear here is that the relationship with government would inappropriately empower corporations to subvert or even take over government. Echoing the definitional view, but on moral grounds, Levitt (echoed in Friedman, 1970) posited a 'natural division between economic [of business] and social functions [of government]' (1958: 48).

Other arguments for the dichotomous perspective have reflected the rather different *normative* view that regulation is unwelcome for the quality and performance of CSR. So, in this view, and in contrast to Levitt (1958), the threat is to corporations from government. This view is shared in Porter and Kramer's (2011) advocacy of 'creating shared value' in which they argue that: 'Government and civil society have often exacerbated the problem by attempting to address social weaknesses at the expense of business ... Companies must take the lead in bringing business and society back together' (Porter and Kramer, 2011: 64). Third, scholars have adopted an *empirical* view on the dichotomous perspective such that they have extrapolated from their observations of CSR filling in governmental voids. This features in accounts of CSR before the development of the welfare state (e.g., Husted, 2015; Djelic and Etchanchu, 2017; Etchanchu and Djelic, 2019); in the context of remote extractive industries (e.g., Muthuri et al., 2008); and in the context of globalisation whereby corporations, often with civil society actors (Matten and Crane, 2005; Scherer and Palazzo, 2007; 2008), take on governmental roles in the absence of accompanying state capacity (e.g., Locke, 2013). This empirical view has featured in the Political CSR literature because '[o]n the global level, neither nation-states nor international institutions alone are able to sufficiently regulate the global economy and to provide global public good' (Scherer and Palazzo, 2011: 900). Fourth, perhaps reflecting the fact that CSR and corporate sustainability have been principally subjects for business and management scholars, the dichotomy is often *implied*, rather than stated (e.g., Margolis and Walsh, 2003). Here, the accounts given of corporate initiatives underestimate or overlook the roles of government, the law or public policy which often frame such corporate departures. It could be reasonably concluded that for the hundreds of papers on CSR and corporate sustainability which make no mention of it, government simply appeared unrelated to the analysis by virtue of this disciplinary perspective. One, presumably unintended, effect is that it has compounded the impression of government being of little relevance to corporate sustainability.

Thus, for four rather different reasons (definitional, normative, empirical and implied), the dichotomous perspective has had a powerful effect on the CSR, and by extension, corporate sustainability literatures. These views need to be understood in order to appreciate the reasons for the relative neglect of government in the analysis of CSR and corporate contributions to sustainability.

12.2.2   The Related Perspective on Government and Corporate Sustainability

In contrast, we present and explain views as to why government and corporate sustainability should be/are related. Studies of government and corporate sustainability obviously include in their definitions corporate policies and actions which reflect government regulation. We focus on the 'normative' view for the related perspective, which simply proposes that in certain circumstances there may be good reasons for regulation of CSR and corporate sustainability, be it for government, corporations, society or the natural environment (Preston and Post, 1975). Second, the 'embedded' view brings a different empirical/institutional approach to the question, reflecting insights into the historic embedding of corporate behaviour in the institutions shaped by government (Moon and Vogel, 2008). Likewise, the third, 'agential' view also brings empirical evidence to support the related perspective, particularly reflecting the recent wave of regulatory approaches by government to business conduct in pursuit of societal agendas (Kourula et al., 2019).

First, the *normative* view contends that, contrary to its dichotomous counterpart, corporate engagement with government is good for public policy and indeed for corporate sustainability. Preston and Post (1975) offered *normative* support for business involvement in, and accountability for, public policy and thus coined the term 'public responsibility' to distinguish this from 'ad hoc managerial policies and practices' (1975: 9). Such a view would extend to corporate sustainability that is intended to address societal challenges in reflection of government policies (Vogel, 1996; Marens, 2008). Such normative arguments also feature in accounts of relationships between corporations and *new governance* on the grounds that the forms of engagement that this participatory model of governing brings serve governments and the quality of CSR (Moon, 2002). Such assumptions also feature in the corporate citizenship literature (e.g., Moon et al., 2005; Crane et al., 2008) which sees corporate engagement with government positively, notwithstanding caveats on power and accountability.

Our second and third views both reflect empirical assessments of corporate sustainability. The *embedded* view of government and corporate sustainability is found in research revealing that corporations – much as markets – reflect the long-term shaping effects of government (e.g., Avi-Yonah, 2005) and more specifically that different national approaches to corporate sustainability reflect inherited government policies and institutions (Matten and Moon, 2008). This reflects the tradition of historical institutionalism (e.g., Thelen, 2014) in which focal policy commitments and actor behaviours are explained in terms of structures of the economy which are shaped by decades and centuries of government. Thus, the state acts as an enabling condition of corporate sustainability (Schrempf-Stirling, 2018) and by providing structures for remedying alleged legal sustainability shortcomings (Schrempf-Stirling and Wettstein, 2017).

Third, there is the *agential* view of government and corporate sustainability which focuses on public policies introduced by governments using their agency rather than reflecting the effect of inherited institutional norms. Such policies have not necessarily achieved the institutional status of those in the aforementioned view and may reflect the specific agendas of the times, such as the 'CSR and public policy' period in the United States from 1978 to 1986 (Gerde and Wokutch, 1998); and in the context of economic downturns in the United Kingdom in the 1980s (Moore et al., 1989); and in Australia (Moon and Sochacki, 1996) and Denmark in the 1990s (Vallentin, 2015b). The volume of research into agential relationships between government and corporate sustainability has increased since the turn of the twenty-first century, including: aggregate studies on European government policies for CSR (Albareda et al., 2008; Steurer, 2010; Knudsen et al., 2015); analysis of specific governmental instruments (Giamporcaro et al., 2020); and studies of national government approaches to corporate sustainability (e.g., Gond et al., 2011b; Midttun et al., 2015).

Table 12.1 presents a summary of the perspectives and views analysed hitherto concerning government regulation for corporate sustainability.

The related perspective on government and corporate sustainability requires us to reflect on the four views in the dichotomous perspective. Regarding the definitional view, for certain sorts of argument and analysis it is clearly desirable to distinguish governmental and corporate variables; but heuristics should not obscure realities of government regulation for corporate sustainability. With regard to the normative view, there may be circumstances where corporate involvement with government is detrimental to business responsibility and sustainability, but equally it may enhance such private initiatives. So, rather than conclude one way or another, the merits of particular policies will need to be judged on a case-by-case basis. Clearly, the

Table 12.1 The dichotomous and related perspectives on government regulation for corporate sustainability

	Dichotomous perspective	Related perspective
Views within each perspective		
Definitional	Government regulation of the corporation is excluded in definitions of corporate sustainability	*By default*, corporate sustainability can reflect government regulation
Normative	Government regulation for corporate sustainability is bad for government and for corporate sustainability	Government regulation for corporate sustainability is good for government and for corporate sustainability
Empirical	Based on evidence of corporate sustainability in the absence of government regulation	Based on evidence of corporate sustainability as a reflection of government regulation *Either* in **Embedded** institutions *Or* in **Agency** reflected in specific policies
Implied	Absence of reference to government regulation in analysis of corporate sustainability	*By default*, presence of reference to government regulation in analysis of corporate sustainability

empirical view on the dichotomous perspective has an element of empirical validity – sometimes government roles are not obvious. But often their roles are latent, as evidenced in the 'implicit' institutional contexts in which corporations operate (Matten and Moon, 2008). In any case, there is abundant evidence of government agency for regulation of corporations' responsibility and sustainability as we shall see (section 12.4). The implied dichotomous view is understandable given the conventional focus and training of management scholars; but we suggest that more interdisciplinary analysis would be appropriate for evaluating the roles of corporations in the sustainability challenges we face. By default, there is no equivalent to the implied view in the dichotomous perspective. The related perspective expressly recognises the relationship of corporate sustainability with government regulation.

So, notwithstanding the specific explanations for the dichotomous perspective, we conclude here that government regulation for CSR and corporate sustainability is long-standing and widespread. The remainder of the chapter explores these relationships more closely. Our next task is to examine: the manifold corporate sustainability issues that such regulation addresses; the types of policies that governments address to corporate sustainability; and issue and policy preferences of different types of government.

12.3   Recent 'Agential' Government Regulation for Corporate Sustainability

In this section, we indicate and illustrate: the types of issues that governments address in their corporate sustainability regulation; the types of regulation that governments provide for corporate sustainability; and the different overall approaches used by government.[2]

12.3.1   Corporate Sustainability Issues Addressed by Governments

This section explores the types of issues that governments have addressed through their regulations for corporate sustainability. It does so first with reference to policies of European governments, and then more broadly with reference to government policies in other political systems.

In their study, Knudsen et al. (2015) investigate the issues to which EU member governments addressed CSR regulation between 2000 and 2011. The issues were classified according to the different government ministries, which had responsibility for the respective regulation in twenty-two countries. Knudsen et al. (2015) report that in broad terms there was a shift from social (e.g., community, education) and

---

[2] This section draws on Knudsen et al. (2015).

environmental issues (e.g., pollution) through to economic (e.g., employment, local development) and international issues (e.g., ethical trade, human rights, climate change). Thus, overall, there appears to be no major area of public policy to which at least one European government has *not* deployed corporate sustainability regulation.

However, some comparisons about issue range of different governments can be made. First and foremost, not all the countries have deployed regulation for the full range of issues. Denmark, France, Germany, Italy and the United Kingdom stand out as addressing corporate sustainability across Social/Employment, Environmental, Economics, and Foreign and Development policy areas. More generally, the breadth of the application to policy issues increases as one moves from the former Communist and the Mediterranean countries (Italy aside), all of which had a relatively partial application of such regulation, to Northern Europe, Scandinavia and the United Kingdom, which have applied their corporate sustainability policies relatively broadly. It is also significant that the European Union has also introduced policies for corporate sustainability. The 2015 Directive on Non-Financial Reporting (Directive 2014/95/EU) brought requirements for disclosure on corporate policies, risks and outcomes concerning environmental, human rights, employee issues, anti-corruption and bribery, and gender diversity on boards of directors (Jackson et al., 2020). More recent amendments extend the areas covered to six environmental objectives, including climate change adaptation, sustainable water use and prevention of pollution. If a corporate activity meets the criteria and contributes to these goals, it can be classified as compliant. In 2020, the European Union also adopted a Sustainable Finance Taxonomy Regulation (EU) 2020/852 that is a system to classify which parts of the economy can be marketed as sustainable investments. It establishes environmental criteria that an economic activity has to meet in order to qualify as environmentally sustainable. (European Commission, 2020b).

Outside Europe, other governments have also introduced regulation for corporate sustainability, but have often differed in their issue focus and the strength of regulation. For example, reflecting its more legalistic tradition, in the area of tax transparency the United States adopted legislation in the form of Dodd Frank Section 1504, requiring that US firms specify taxes paid from extractives on a country basis. In contrast, the UK government supported and endorsed the creation of a multi-stakeholder initiative called the Extractive Industries Transparency Initiative, which also highlighted tax transparency (Knudsen, 2018).

Although much of the corporate sustainability literature focuses on business in liberal and democratic political systems, governments in a range of other types of system also regulate corporate sustainability. The government of the People's Republic of China introduced regulation to raise environmental and safety standards of products in its export market in response to publicity of product shortcomings (Hofman and Moon with Wu, 2017). Another example is the 2013 amendment to the Indian Companies Act that requires large companies to spend 2 per cent of their average net profits of three years on CSR (Gatti et al., 2019).

Of course, the regulatory agendas are also changing very quickly and in recent years we have seen many governments developing policies to assist or require corporation sustainability in global supply chains and, specifically, related to climate change. In 2019, for example, the European Union launched the European Green Deal. One of the ambitions is to put the goal of a climate-neutral European Union by 2050 into legislation. In December 2020, EU environment ministers agreed, for example, to reduce EU greenhouse gas net emissions by at least 55 per cent by 2030 compared to 1990. European companies have a major role to play if Europe is to reach these goals. In 2021, the United States rejoined the Paris Agreement and China doubled down on its objective to be carbon neutral by 2060. Under the Paris Agreement, 196 countries have committed to reducing greenhouse gas emissions. Domestic climate change initiatives will also have international reach. The European Union, for example, is moving forward with a carbon border-adjustment that allows the Union to set the same carbon price for imported goods as it does for its own domestic production. This means that EU companies will need to set carbon targets for goods produced outside of the Union. Most recently at the November 2022 COP27 meeting countries reaffirmed their commitment to limit the global temperature rise to 1.5 degrees Celsius above pre-industrial levels. Most importantly the meeting countries for the first time agreed to establish a dedicated fund, to assist developing countries in responding to loss and damage.

This is a significant departure as it signals that, contrary to some of the assumptions about corporations going beyond the reach of their governments with globalisation (Scherer and Palazzo, 2011), governments have been prepared to regulate their corporations abroad. This was pioneered in the United States when the Alien Tort Claims Act was used against corporations (not just individuals) for complicity in human rights violations and for environmental crimes. In the area of anti-corruption, the United Kingdom introduced the Bribery Act to address bribery of foreign officials in 2010. Another more recent area of focus has been regulation for corporate sustainability in international supply chains. France, the Netherlands and Germany have all adopted new legislation that requires home country firms to undertake a due diligence investigation of their supply chains aimed at preventing risks and serious abuses of fundamental rights, health, personal safety and the environment (Sharma, 2021). France's 2017 Duty of Vigilance Act (*Loi de Vigilance*) requires all large French companies – with over 5,000 employees in France or over 10,000 worldwide – to undertake due diligence with regard to the companies they control and all their contractors and suppliers. The Dutch Child Labor Due Diligence Act (*Wet Zorgplicht Kinderarbeid*, 2019) obliges companies to investigate whether their goods or services have been produced using child labour and whether they have planned to prevent child labour in their supply chains. The German government has adopted a new 'Supply Chain Act (*Sorgfaltspflichtengesetz*, 2023) that obliges companies to conduct human rights and environmental due diligence in their supply chains. In February 2022, the EU Commission adopted a proposal for a Directive on corporate sustainability due diligence.

Finally, we should note the role of international governmental organisations in regulating CSR and corporate sustainability. As a rule, such organisations do not have the power of mandate (see below), but in endorsing appropriate corporate policies through codes and standards and collaborating in international partnerships, they bring their imprimatur to bear on the regulatory environment, particularly for multinational corporations. The UN Global Compact introduced ten principles, which its signatories are expected to comply with in the areas of human rights, labour rights, the environment and anti-corruption. The Compact was followed by the UN Guiding Principles on Business and Human Rights, which are a set of guidelines for states and companies to prevent, address and remedy human rights abuses committed in business operations. The United Nations' Sustainability Development Goals, devised as a basis for governments' sustainability policies, have been adopted as a form of guidance by many corporations – and in some cases (e.g., in Denmark) with the express encouragement of national governments.

12.3.2 Types of Regulation Used by Governments to Address Corporate Sustainability Issues

Having outlined the issues to which government policies are directed, we now turn to the sorts of policies governments deploy, and specifically what regulatory strength they employ in regulating corporate sustainability. We adopt the framework of Fox et al. (2002) and Knudsen et al. (2015) to distinguish four types of government policy to encourage corporate sustainability: endorsement, facilitation, partnering and mandate (Table 12.2).

Governments can *endorse* corporate sustainability in order to raise awareness of this approach and promote good practices. Examples of endorsement policies include the approval and affirmation of principles and standards, general information campaigns and websites, political rhetoric, awards and labelling schemes.

Table 12.2 Forms of government regulation for corporate sustainability

Type of regulation	Description
Endorse	Political support through general information campaigns and websites, political rhetoric, awards.
Facilitate	Incentives for companies to adopt corporate sustainability policies through subsidies or tax incentives; public procurement.
Partner	Collaboration of government organisations with business organisations to develop and promote principles, standards, guidelines.
Mandate	Regulation of minimum standards for business performance (i.e., UK Anti-Bribery Act; mandatory non-financial reporting).

Source: Adapted from Knudsen et al. (2015).

This approach presumes a degree of responsiveness of businesses and their primary stakeholders to government signalling, and it values giving businesses flexibility to innovate as to their best method of achieving the governmental policy goal.

Governments can also *facilitate* corporate sustainability by offering subsidies and tax expenditures to companies which pursue specified policies (e.g., charitable contributions, employment of marginalised sections of the workforce, introducing a clean technology). An increasingly common approach is for governments (including sub-national) to build corporate sustainability criteria into public procurement conditions. This can have a profound effect on the policies of corporations supplying governments and can also contribute to the establishment of these standards into business more widely. Such policies clearly bring more material government resources than do the endorsement policies and thus will usually be associated with more precise targeting (e.g., of the companies addressed, the criteria for receiving public resources, the terms of such receipt).

Governments can also support corporate sustainability *partnerships* by encouraging and joining (e.g., for ethical trade – see section 12.4.3, below) business and other actors in partnerships to raise business standards, deliver public goods and signal the legitimacy of new practices. Partnership approaches can assist in disseminating knowledge about sustainability issues (e.g., to service users and product consumers), and can even support the development of guidelines, standards or codes. This form of regulation will also bring more material government resources (e.g., financial, organisational) and may well entail some specification of the obligations on all parties of entering the partnership.

Finally, governments can *mandate* corporate sustainability. A common recent example is the introduction of rules for mandatory non-financial reporting, which requires firms to disclose in their annual report which social and environmental activities they have been involved in (see section 12.4.4, below, and Chapter 17). Other policies include requirements for building materials and emissions to meet minimum environmental standards, for due diligence for supply chain labour standards and for diversity in company boards. Policies that mandate behaviour involve the specification of some minimum standard for business performance embedded within the regulatory framework. This may also bring the presumption that governments monitor compliance with their regulations which demands other types of organisational and financial resources. Mandating involves governments taking the most definitive role in corporate sustainability through regulations and decrees.

12.3.3   Government Policy Approaches to the Regulation of Corporate Sustainability

On the basis of the two dimensions of analysis we have reported – issues addressed and regulatory type deployed – we are able to distinguish different broad approaches of government to corporate sustainability. Not all European governments use the full range of regulatory forms to address CSR which can also be taken to apply to policies for corporate sustainability. The Mediterranean countries tend to mainly use endorsement as their means of regulating corporate sustainability. This is a relatively weak regulatory form, mainly consisting of the imprimatur and legitimacy of government. At the other end of the spectrum, the countries which utilised a full range of endorsement, facilitation, partnership and mandate policies were most notably the United Kingdom, Northern Europe and Scandinavia. Knudsen et al. (2015) therefore see these as embedding CSR most 'deeply' by use of the full regulatory range. Together, these regulatory forms reflect the fact that a range of legal (mandate), fiscal (facilitation) and organisational (partnership) can be deployed for corporate sustainability government resources along with those of the governmental endorsement.

We have outlined the very wide – and expanding – range of issues to which governments address policy for corporate sustainability, home and abroad; we have outlined the range of regulatory measures that governments have applied for this purpose; and we have outlined the distinctive approaches that different governments have taken in this endeavour. We now turn to the responses of corporations to such regulation.

12.4 Corporate Responses to Government Regulation for Sustainability

12.4.1 Corporate Discretion in Relation to Public Policy for Corporate Sustainability

Just because governments regulate for corporate sustainability, this does not guarantee corporate reactions. Corporations retain choices even in the face of mandated law (see McBarnet, 2007).[3] They can ignore regulation and risk punishment. However, in keeping with the related perspective, corporations also have choices as to how they 'take' regulation. On the one hand, they can 'conform' with the law or act 'through the law' by responding to government incentives for responsible or sustainable business behaviour. Businesses can also go further and 'enhance' the law by following its spirit and act 'for the law'. This can include, for example, refraining from creative compliance to avoid exploiting competing regulatory standards. It can also include engaging in policy advocacy conducive to wider business responsibility and sustainability, or applying the logic of the law more widely in their business operations.

We now turn to illustrate how corporate discretion for engagement with public policy, and the strength of the public policy itself, can evolve across different cases.

---

[3] Section 12.4 draws on Knudsen and Moon (2022).

Our vignettes are: corporate philanthropy in the United States; ethical trade in the United Kingdom; corporate non-financial reporting in Denmark; and corporate taxation internationally following the release of the Panama Papers in 2016. For three of the four cases (philanthropy, ethical trade and reporting), the literature has often understated the significance of government. In the fourth case (tax), the literature has often understated the significance of corporate discretion for responding to government regulation for corporate sustainability.

12.4.2   Corporate Philanthropy in the United States

Corporate philanthropy is a long-standing and widespread form of corporate sustainability, particularly in the United States (Maignan and Ralston, 2002; Carroll et al., 2012; Reisman, 2019). While this has been assumed to be a voluntary activity, it has been underpinned by tax incentives for corporate charitable donations reflecting the inheritance of the 1601 English Charitable Uses Act by the American colonies and later by state and federal governments. This does not mean that philanthropy is any more or less responsible or sustainable because it attracts a subsidy, but simply that this form of corporate sustainability is related to government regulation. This logic also extends to the provision of health insurance and other corporate benefits to US employees that corporations often include in their CSR and sustainability policies which can also reflect subsidies provided by the US government (Rein, 1982) and thereby conform to the related perspective, illustrating how corporations can respond positively to a public policy framework to deliver welfare outcomes. Indeed, tax incentives are deployed by governments throughout the world, whether for charitable donations, for employment stimulation or for clean technology. Corporations can ignore such regulation, adopt its logic in their sustainability policies, or integrate the logic of such regulation more deeply or more widely.

12.4.3   Ethical Trade in the United Kingdom

Ethical trade refers to the sourcing of products and services under conditions that confer workers' labour and human rights and that are otherwise responsible (Blowfield, 1999: 753–754). Although the issue has been a long-standing one, in the last twenty years, corporations and business associations, partnerships and multi-stakeholder initiatives have adopted and developed private standards for working conditions and living wages (see Chapter 20). However, governments have also played a role in developing ethical trade policies. The Ethical Trading Initiative (ETI) was instigated by the UK government in 1998. It is a CSR multi-stakeholder institution of eighty-plus companies, NGOs and trade union bodies, claiming coverage of 10 million workers. Subsequently, UK governments facilitated the ETI (e.g., in the form of finance, secondments, network access) and some aspects of this collaboration reflect a partnership relationship. This was further complemented by the Modern Slavery Act (2015), which includes *Transparency in Supply Chain*

Provisions, requiring large businesses to publish a statement of the steps they have taken to ensure that there is no slavery and human trafficking in their supply chains. Yet, in this mandated public policy, corporations retain some discretion not to publish the statement if they declare that no such steps have been taken. Moreover, they can also choose how to conduct and publish their due diligence.

The UK cases are not isolated. As noted in section 12.3.1, there are numerous public policies for more responsible international supply chains, often through endorsement and facilitation of CSR organisations, and as already noted, there is also a growth of mandate for due diligence regarding abuses in MNCs' international supply chains.

12.4.4   Corporate Sustainability Reporting in Denmark

Corporate sustainability reporting (also known as non-financial or environmental, social and governance [ESG] reporting) has become pervasive among corporations (Ioannou and Serafeim, 2011 – see Chapter 17). It brings expectations of accountability both to company stakeholders and to society, and an opportunity for corporate communication. This partly reflects societal demands for greater 'transparency of corporate social and environmental impact, together with delivering enhanced levels of accountability to organizational stakeholders' (Owen and O'Dwyer, 2008: 385). While this form of corporate reporting emerged voluntarily, numerous countries and the European Union have introduced reporting policies. We focus on Denmark, known as a leading CSR and corporate sustainability country (Knudsen et al., 2015; Knudsen and Brown, 2015; Vallentin, 2015a).

Following Danish companies' initiatives to report voluntarily in the 1990s, the government lent its support. The Foreign Ministry collaborated with the UNDP Nordic Office to form a taskforce to organise outreach activities and advise companies about the UN Global Compact. Subsequently, the Non-Financial Reporting Act (Section 99a of the Danish Financial Reporting Act, 2008) and its further amendments brought a mandate, requiring publicly traded or publicly owned companies and large private companies to report on their social responsibility policies, how these are translated into action, and their evaluation of these initiatives and prospects for future initiatives. The Act was extended in 2012 to require reporting of initiatives to reduce the impact of climate change, human rights protection and prevention of irresponsibility. Beyond these requirements, complying companies had considerable discretion over *what* issues they reported on and *how* they presented their reports. However, whereas the corporation's decision as to *whether* to report was initially voluntary (report or explain), now failure to report can result in fines. A study concluded that 'companies are reflexive and selective ... they do not just passively conform to new CSR guidelines' (Pedersen et al., 2013: 366). So, while corporations had the choice to simply comply with the mandate, many of them embraced the regulation and reported much more fully than the legal minimum.

12.4.5   Corporate Taxation Internationally

Corporate tax barely featured in accounts of CSR historically, on the assumption that responsibility was confirmed by compliance with mandated requirements (Carroll, 1979). Following critiques of extractives corporations' lack of transparency about their tax to host governments in the 1990s, and evidence of legal corporate tax avoidance following the 2008 financial crisis, responsible tax payments emerged as a more explicit issue. The Panama Papers (*The Guardian*, 2016) revealed the extent of corporate discretion over how they complied with corporate tax law. In this light, tax authorities now provide advice to MNCs regarding their choices between multiple tax authorities, transparency and anti-avoidance in general. They invite tax negotiation and encourage corporations to adopt the fairness principle in their tax strategies (Hilling and Ostas, 2017). Accordingly, business associations have developed responsible tax principles to inform that discretion. The B Team has developed an approach reflecting corporations' discretion to enhance tax law through their *tax management, tax relationships*; and *tax reporting* (B Team, 2018 – see also CSR Europe, n.d.). Individual corporations have also developed their own tax principles and practices (e.g., Starbucks, 2017; Maersk, 2019). Rather than simply complying, including through legal loopholes, the approach is to embrace the spirit of the law (McBarnet, 2007; Moon and Vallentin, 2020).

Together, our vignettes illustrate the operation and dynamics of the dichotomous and related perspectives on government and corporate sustainability. Certainly, the dichotomous perspective seems apposite in the origins of some spheres of corporate action, yet the vignettes are mostly reflective of the related perspective as various government regulations encouraged, scaled up and institutionalised private initiatives. In the case of corporate philanthropy, the institutionalisation appears so effective that it is often misrepresented as unrelated to public policy.

But it would be a mistake to conclude that this is a simple sequencing story from private initiatives followed by public policy. The literature has often understated the significance of interactions of government policy with company philanthropic, ethical trade and non-financial reporting initiatives. Moreover, corporations not only use their discretion *through* and *for* public policy, but also further raise the quality of their initiatives *beyond* public policy. In the case of taxation, there is some interplay between the related and dichotomous perspectives. Public policy now includes overtures to corporations to exercise their discretion and to do so responsibly and in the spirit of the law. Private initiatives set out approaches to taxation entailing ethical principles, tax management practices, and reference to the framing for responsible taxation provided by national and international regulators. In this case, the literature has often understated the significance of corporate tax policy in any way beyond compliance.

12.5   Interactions of Government and Private Regulation: Corporate Sustainability through 'Governance Spheres'

In light of the weight of government policies for corporate sustainability and the varying responses of corporations to these, it becomes obvious that there is a variety of interactions between governments and corporations concerning sustainability. Cashore et al. (2021) argue that these take place in governance spheres which are distinguished by focal problems, extant institutions and actors able to bring regulatory power to bear, whether public (i.e., governmental) or private (i.e., business and civil society). They set out a typology of different sorts of interactions between public and private authority, ranging from their being complementary, to competitive, to co-existent. In this section, we set out two examples of complementary interactions between government regulation and corporations: interactions of government regulation with private supply chain governance of international supply chains focusing on garments in Bangladesh; and interactions of public and private regulation in tax transparency.

12.5.1   Supply Chain Governance in the Bangladesh Ready-Made Garment Sector

A wide range of problems including violations of labour rights, factory fires and building collapses has plagued the Bangladeshi garment sector. In April 2013, Rana Plaza, an eight-storey building, collapsed, killing over 1,200 apparel workers and wounding more than 2,500. The disaster led to an international outcry and to demands for initiatives to ensure that a similar tragedy would not happen again. We focus on two private corporate sustainability initiatives which were related to extant domestic regulation, and which were supported in different ways by European and North American national governments.

In 2013, two monitoring regimes establishing fire, electrical and building safety programmes emerged in Europe and North America: respectively the multi-stakeholder-oriented *Accord* and the business-dominated *Alliance*. Importantly, in both cases, the corporate initiative is to ensure compliance with extant Bangladesh government regulation – not to impose another safety code. Union organisers and anti-sweatshop activists persuaded the big European brands such as H&M to sign an Accord to police safety conditions and allow access to trade unionists. The Accord's brands engage with more than 1,500 factories that employ more than 50 per cent of the Bangladeshi garment workers engaged in the export sector. Although the Accord had company and union representatives on its board, significantly, it also had a representative of an international governmental organisation – the International Labour Organization (ILO) – as board chair and tiebreaker. While most North American retailers and brands would not sign the Accord due to liability fears, a group of apparel companies, retailers and brands led by the Gap and Walmart founded the Alliance for Bangladesh Worker Safety, an internally binding five-year undertaking with the intent of improving safety in Bangladeshi apparel factories. The Alliance has a governing board that consists of prominent leaders from major brands and was criticised for having no union representation. However, the Accord and Alliance factories do not appear to differ substantially in their occupational safety and health (OSH) performance (defined as fire safety, electrical safety and building safety), and they shared audit reports when they sourced from the same factories. Significantly, although the Accord and Alliance were ostensibly private initiatives, they were supported financially by national governments which also contributed to capacity building of building inspectors and have implemented training programmes on the ground in Bangladesh.

Moreover, in the background to these initiatives, the EU and US governments used trade policy to drive change. The United States has a long tradition of using trade policy to promote social change in the exporting country. In 2013, President Obama adopted a foreign trade policy initiative, suspending Bangladesh's trade benefits under the Generalized System of Preferences (GSP) in view of insufficient progress by the government of Bangladesh in granting Bangladeshi workers internationally recognised worker rights. That decision followed an extensive review under the GSP programme of worker rights and worker safety in Bangladesh during which the US government encouraged the government of Bangladesh to implement some needed reforms. While US trade policy restrictions may only affect a minor share of Bangladeshi exports to the United States, the significance of the termination of the GSP should not be underestimated. Moreover, the European Union put pressure on the Bangladesh government itself to address worker safety and rights issues by threatening to suspend its policy of unconditional trade access for Bangladesh (the 'Everything But Arms' programme).

In sum, government policies complemented corporate initiatives to promote better labour standards, ranging from top-down hierarchical trade regulation to promote better labour standards (government regulation of CSR in a firm's host country), to soft regulation in the form of endorsement and facilitation of multistakeholder initiatives such as the Accord and business collaborations in the form of the Alliance.

12.5.2 Corporate Tax Transparency in the Extractives Sector

Extraction of oil, gas and mining resources can lead to economic growth and social development. However, poorly managed extraction has been known to lead to corruption and conflict. This phenomenon has come to be known as the 'resource curse': corruption, conflict and poor management of revenue in many resource-rich economies, and the use of commodity sales to finance violence and conflict (Frynas, 2009). More openness around how a country manages its natural resource wealth is therefore seen as necessary to ensure that these resources can benefit all citizens. A long-standing issue in international business responsibility has been to ensure transparent payment of taxes and charges by, usually Western, companies in the extractive sector to their host, usually developing, country governments (Knudsen and Moon, 2017). This case highlights a privately run multi-stakeholder initiative called the Extractive Industries Transparency Initiative (EITI), and its relationship with public regulation in the form of the US Dodd Frank Act's Section 1504, as well as the European Union's revision of its Accounting Directive.

The UK government launched the EITI in 2003 (https://eiti.org/). Stakeholders involved in the EITI included, first, extractive companies and civil society organisations such as Global Witness, the Publish What You Pay Coalition, Transparency International and Oxfam, and later national governments of countries with the respective natural resources. The background to the EITI illustrates complementary regulatory interactions. In 1999, Global Witness published a report on the lack of transparency and government accountability in the oil industry in Angola such that the Angolan civil war was financed by oil money. This led to the 'Publish What You Pay' campaign, which focused on the need for transparency to make explicit how much each mine paid in taxes as a way to empower local communities and their demands for public services. In February 2001, John Browne, Chief Executive Officer of BP, responded to the campaign and committed to publish payments made to the government of Angola (Browne, 2010). When the Angolan government threatened BP with reprisals, Browne started looking for a collective action solution. The UK government followed the lead from BP to enhance transparency and Prime Minister Tony Blair launched the EITI to make corporate payments to host governments transparent. The responsibility for launching and coordinating the initiative in its early years rested with the British Department for International Development. This included hosting a crucial EITI Conference in London, 2003, where initial signatories (national governments, companies, industry groups, international organisations, investors and NGOs) agreed on the basic principles. The UK government contributed £1 million at the outset for technical aspects related to developing the initiative. However, the EITI was very quickly internationalised with an endorsement by the 2004 G8 Summit, the 2005 Commission for Africa Report, the formation of an international board and the location of the international secretariat in Oslo in 2006.

By launching the EITI, the UK government set in motion a process to 'level the playing field' for its significant extractive industry sector. If a country decides to become an EITI member, then all companies operating in the country, including state-owned companies, are required to publish what they have paid to host governments (taxes, royalties, etc.). The EITI requires a reconciliation of what a government discloses it has received with what companies say they have paid. Most importantly, the EITI establishes a mechanism for debate about the resources inside the host country, which includes the government, corporations and civil society organisations. In short, the EITI is not just about publishing the numbers, but also about creating a platform for dialogue and enhanced accountability in countries rich with natural resources. The EITI requires companies to report their payments to governments, but also requires governments to report on revenues received. Currently, fifty-five national governments are signatory to the EITI, and sixty-four companies (e.g., oil and gas, mining and metals, commodity traders, financial institutions) and eight major NGOs are supporters of the EITI.

The pioneering work of the EITI has been built upon by other governments. For example, the Norwegian government has adopted legislation that makes it mandatory for Norwegian extractive firms to report on taxes paid for each project and by country. The European Union and the US government have also pursued complementary mandatory regulation in order to promote tax transparency in the extractive sector. The European Union in 2013 revised its 1978 Accounting Directive and now requires oil, gas, mining and logging companies to publicly disclose the payments they make to governments for the extraction of natural resources. The Accounting Directive requires large public companies incorporated in the European Union to report such payments – the list of companies includes Shell, BP, Total, Anglo American and others. For example, since Shell is listed in the United States and in the European Union, the new mandatory regulatory requirements will require a company such as Shell to provide information to the US and EU authorities about payments made in all ninety countries where it operates. The US government sought to promote tax transparency in the form of Section 1504 of the Dodd-Frank Wall Street Financial Reform Act, which focused on ensuring financial transparency and in particular on natural resource transparency. It was adopted following a public outcry in the United States over conflict minerals in the Democratic Republic of Congo and requires publicly listed oil, natural gas and minerals companies to file reports to the Securities Exchange Commission on project-level payments to foreign governments. In both cases, the governments were seeking to build on what they understood to be the achievements of the EITI.

12.6   Discussion

Our focus on collaborative interactions highlighted the role that governments can play in shaping corporate sustainability initiatives. The UK government, for example, played a key role in the inception of the EITI and the European Union supported the creation of the Accord. Furthermore, companies have discretion in terms of how they engage with these policies. Government policy for corporate sustainability does not necessarily coerce companies. Companies are free to decide whether they join initiatives such as the EITI and the Accord. Furthermore, the

Danish non-financial reporting regulation initially left it to corporations to decide whether to report (although this has been amended to require large firms to report) and how they wanted to develop a sustainability report. Our cases illustrated that private and public governance realms are not distinct nor static. Instead, they are policies built upon one another. As the authors have noted elsewhere (Knudsen and Moon, 2017: 200), 'Although the hands of government are visible, they are not solely orchestrating corporate sustainability ("CSR"); rather, they are part of an ensemble of improvisation'. Following Hatch's (1997)´ analysis of organisational processes, we note how government–corporate relationships reflect the improvisation of jazz, with elements of '"soloing" or taking the lead; "comping" or supporting others' lead; "trading fours" or switching between leading and supporting; "listening" or opening the space for others' lead; "responding to or accommodating others"' ideas'.

While our two examples of interactions between public and private initiatives – supply chain governance and tax transparency – focused on collaboration, it is important to note that interactions can also take other forms and be competitive or simply coexist, for example, with conflicting goals (see Cashore et al., 2021). An example of the former is industry environmental self-regulation in an attempt to pre-empt more stringent regulation (Vogel, 2005). An example of the latter is the 2021 US Congress adoption of the Uyghur Forced Labor Prevention Act that requires companies to prove that goods imported from China's Xinjiang region are not produced with forced labour (BBC, 2021a). The Act has been criticised by major companies that do business in the area, including Coca-Cola, Nike and Apple, which argue that this could create havoc in their supply chains as the region produces cotton (Nike) and sugar (Coca-Cola) and supplies workers to factories.

We close with some reflections on implications that follow from our analysis of the close relationship between corporate sustainability and public policy. First, from a legitimacy point of view, it is important to distinguish what are the roles of government and private actors. It is important that corporations are not seen as having unduly influenced public policy-making in ways that bring inappropriate advantages to them collectively and individually. But it is also important for the integrity of corporations that their sustainability initiatives are not seen as mere extensions of government policy. Striking such a balance is a delicate ongoing act.

12.7 Chapter Summary

The chapter has explored government policy for corporate sustainability, and the relationship between public policy and private initiatives for corporate sustainability. It has made a distinction between the dichotomous perspective that sees government and corporate sustainability as separate, and the related perspective that sees the two as closely intertwined. The chapter has identified a range of different sustainability issues that governments address and has highlighted a range of public policy approaches to that effect. While governments play a key role in shaping corporate sustainability, the chapter has also pointed out that corporations have some discretion in how they respond to government initiatives as they can conform with, expand or even sometimes break government regulation. The chapter provided some illustrations of complementary interactions in governance spheres between public and private regulation.

CHAPTER QUESTIONS

1. Why have governments become interested in regulating (international) corporate sustainability?
2. Why have government policies for corporate sustainability been contentious?
3. What sort of corporate sustainability issues do governments focus their policies on?
4. What types of government policies can you distinguish (think regulatory strength)?
5. How can corporations respond to government regulation for sustainability?
6. How can government policies complement private initiatives for corporate sustainability?

> **Case Study:** *Tax Transparency in the Extractive Sector*
> Available from Cambridge University Press at www.cambridge.org/rasche2

FURTHER RESOURCES

- Abbott, K. W. and Snidal, D. (2000). Hard and Soft Law in International Governance. *International Organization*, 54(3), 421–456.

  This article provides a general overview of different forms of regulation in international governance which frames this chapter. It is a reference point for much international relations and CSR literature.

- Andonova, L. (2014). Boomerangs to Partnerships? Explaining State Participation in Transnational Partnerships for Sustainability. *Comparative Political Studies*, 47(3), 481–515.

  This is one of the, still rare, contributions which recognises the significance of national governments for international sustainability agendas.

- Jackson, G., Bartosch, J., Avetisyan, E., Kinderman, D. and Knudsen, J. S. (2020). Mandatory Non-Financial Disclosure and Its Influence on CSR: An International Comparison. *Journal of Business Ethics*, 162(2), 323–342.

This article provides an international comparison of twenty-four OECD countries to examine if CSR reporting requirements leads to more CSR. It finds an increase in CSR activities, but not a decrease in Corporate Social Irresponsibility.

- Knudsen, J. S. and Moon, J. (2022). Corporate Social Responsibility and Government: The Role of Discretion for Engagement with Public Policy. *Business Ethics Quarterly*, 32(2), 243–271.

This article investigates the relationship between CSR and government and presents an integrated framework for corporate discretion for engagement with CSR.

- Knudsen, J. S., Moon, J. and Slager, R. (2015). Government Policies for Corporate Social Responsibility in Europe: A Comparative Analysis of Institutionalisation. *Policy and Politics*, 43(1), 81–99.

This article provides an overview of CSR policies of twenty-two European governments from 2000 to 2011.

- Vogel, D. (2021). The Politics of Preemption: American Federalism and Risk Regulation. *Regulation & Governance*, 2 June, https://doi.org/10.1111/rego .12414.

This article explores four cases of risk regulation in the United States. Regulations were initiated at the state level despite business opposition. When faced with a range of state product regulations, firms decided to support expanding federal regulation in order to pre-empt even stronger state regulation.

NGOs, Activism and Sustainability

FRANK G. A. DE BAKKER AND FRANK DEN HOND[*]

LEARNING OBJECTIVES

- Learn about the role of activism in sustainability.

- Distinguish the characteristics of different types of activist NGOs, their tactics and (aspired) outcomes.

- Develop an overview of interactions between activist NGOs and firms over issues of sustainability.

- Understand which firms are likely to be targeted by NGO activism and how firms respond to such activism.

13.1 Introduction

A decade ago, few people would have heard about *fracking*, a technical process for the extraction of natural gas from rocky undergrounds that is based on creating fissures in the rock to allow for the extraction of the gas. The imminent depletion of more accessible natural gas supplies has made the technique an attractive supplement to more conventional extraction technologies. Yet, fracking has met with a lot

[*] This chapter contains sections that are adapted from earlier work by both authors. The details are listed below.

de Bakker, F. G. A. and F. den Hond. (2008). Activists' Influence Tactics and Corporate Policies. *Business and Professional Communication Quarterly*, 71(1), 107–11. Copyright 2008 by Association for Business Communication. Reprinted by permission of SAGE Publications, Inc.

de Bakker, F. G. A. and F. den Hond. (2008). Activist Groups Tactics to Influence Companies. In: C. Wankel (ed.), *21st Century Management: A Reference Handbook*, pp. 927–37. Copyright 2008 by SAGE Publications, Inc. Reprinted by permission of SAGE Publications, Inc.

de Bakker, F. G. A. and F. den Hond. (2008). Introducing the Politics of Stakeholder Influence: A Review Essay. *Business & Society*, 47(1), 8–20. Copyright 2008 by SAGE Publications, Inc. Reprinted by permission of SAGE Publications, Inc.

den Hond, F., S. Stolwijk and J. Merk (2014). A Strategic-Interaction Analysis of an Urgent Appeal System and Its Outcomes for Garment Workers. *Mobilization*, 19(1), 83–111. Copyright 2014 by Mobilization. Reprinted by permission of Mobilization.

of protest. In many countries, activist NGOs have pointed out the various risks associated with the technology, including environmental pollution, occupational health hazards and earthquakes. They organised rallies, started petitions and took legal action. Their targets have been the companies that (intend to) use fracking technology and the authorities that issue the required licences. Not all protest was successful, but some projects were reconsidered, some large investors withdrew and it has surely sparked heated debate. Today, many people know about fracking.

This is just one example of the many issues on the agendas of activist NGOs. Many of their issues involve the conditions and consequences of corporate activities; think of climate change, biodiversity, child labour, workers' rights, product safety, inequality or pollution. Whether activist NGOs seek to stop contested corporate practices or prefer to collaborate with industries and businesses in order to push for better alternatives, NGO activism has become a lasting element in the discourses and practices around sustainability.

Understanding how NGO activism offers opportunities and poses challenges to firms is important to appreciate the broader question of what makes businesses more sustainable and more socially responsible. This chapter discusses the role of NGO activism as a driver of sustainability. We first provide an overview of what activist NGOs are. Next, we explore ways by which activist NGOs seek to influence corporate policies, ranging from collaboration and partnerships to contestation and protest. We then discuss which firms are more likely to encounter NGO activism, and how they may respond to such activism. At the end of this chapter, readers should be able to explain the role of NGO activism in sustainability; to distinguish the characteristics of different types of activist NGOs, their tactics and the outcomes of their activism; and to develop an overview of interactions between activist NGOs and firms.

13.2 Activist NGOs: What Are They?

Over the last decades, interactions between firms and their multiple stakeholders have attracted considerable attention. Among these interactions, those with activist non-governmental organisations (NGOs) have assumed an increasingly prominent position. Whereas previously activist NGOs typically would have turned to governments in order to get their claims on businesses honoured through legislation or law enforcement, more recently they have addressed their claims directly to businesses. This development is related to globalisation:

1. As a consequence of their policies of liberalisation and deregulation, governments have become reluctant to directly regulate business, preferring other policy instruments such as self-regulation.

2. The unprecedented internationalisation of production and trade has reduced the possibility for national governments to effectively regulate internationally operating firms.

3. The availability and widespread adoption of information and communication technologies has facilitated the fast transfer of information across the globe, including information about firms' externalities and alleged wrongdoings in faraway countries.

For example, issues such as climate change and labour conditions in supply chains are highly complex, crossing the jurisdictional boundaries of national authorities, rife with uncertainty, and riddled by multiple, often incompatible interests and value orientations. They have no easy solutions and are often referred to as wicked problems. Under such conditions, when climate change and other issues can no longer be effectively addressed by national regulation and policy-making only, many NGOs and businesses have come to realise that their involvement is needed. Some firms have taken proactive roles, perhaps out of perceived self-interest or because they sincerely believe they can contribute to addressing the issue. Others have been more sceptical and reluctant, at the risk, however, of subsequently receiving sharp criticisms and being put under pressure to change their posture by a vocal public opinion – for example, in social media and activist NGOs.

Yet, *who are these activist NGOs*? How can we define these groups, collectives, movements and organisations that seek to influence firms' policies and practices? To define 'activist NGOs', we first need to define what are NGOs, non-governmental organisations. That is not an easy task. In part, they are defined by what they are *not*: they are organisations, but not associated with the (national, regional or local) state structure, hence the label 'non-governmental'. So are most business firms, but unlike firms, NGOs are not interested in making a profit; their *raison d'être* is in advancing some cause – for example, related to environmental, social and governance issues (ESG) or the United Nations' Sustainable Development Goals (SDGs). When that cause is largely a private matter, such as (in many countries) the organisation of religion or sports, they are usually referred to as civil society organisations; when their cause is in advancing a common or public good or the interests of a third party (but not commercial or business-related; think of Amnesty International who campaign for the rights of individuals who are detained as political prisoners), they are called NGOs. Often, a distinction is made between different types of NGOs: 'direct aid' NGOs aim to support those in need, 'empowerment' NGOs aim to strengthen local communities in achieving their objectives, and 'advocacy' NGOs attempt to influence the decision-making processes and policies of governments and businesses. Of course, these categories are not mutually exclusive: some NGOs are of a mixed type – for instance, when they combine (local) empowerment and international advocacy.

Many organisations that operate independently from government and business are not driven by a profit-motive and pursue a public good. They vary according to whom they are accountable (if at all: members, constituents, donors, beneficiaries, etc.) and go by labels that emphasise some particular characteristic. We have civil society organisations, secondary stakeholders, social movement organisations, public interest groups and many others. All these labels are problematic as they are not mutually exclusive. Many actual organisations fit more than one label or they are hybrids. For example, consumer leagues such as automobile clubs AA in the United Kingdom and ADAC in Germany are private interest groups, yet they not only advance the interests of their members, but also (claim to) work for a common good; as not-for-profit organisations they nevertheless have substantial commercially profitable activities. Table 13.1 provides an overview of related terms and some examples.

In this chapter, we narrow our focus to what we call 'activist NGOs' in order to emphasise, on the one hand, their willingness to organise collective action in the pursuit of their objectives and, on the other, their independence from state structures and commercial interests. They can also be referred to NPOs, NGOs, INGOs (when they operate internationally), CSOs, secondary stakeholders and/or public interest groups. Some may consider them to be private interest groups; what is a 'public' and what is a 'private' interest can sometimes be debated and often is ideologically laden. Activist NGOs not only lobby national, regional and/or local governments, but they also organise media campaigns to influence public opinion around the themes that they find important and actively engage with others in collaborative and/or contentious ways in order to realise their objectives. In the context of this chapter, they muster supporters and resources which they use to stimulate companies to become more sustainable (or less unsustainable). In the following sections, we characterise activist NGOs in greater detail.

13.3   NGO Activism: Some Characterisations

There are many possible grounds for characterising activist NGOs. Obviously, they vary in their domain of interest, objectives and scale of operation: from environmental pollution to worker rights and child labour, from local to transnational. Rather than going into detail on all the varieties of activist objectives here, we introduce three important distinctions: preferred mode of operation, ideological position and tactical repertoire (den Hond and de Bakker, 2007).

First, regarding their preferred *mode of operation*, we distinguish between collaboration and contention. Many activist NGOs engage in collaboration with corporations, enter in dialogue and agree to participate in corporate initiatives, such as

Table 13.1 NGOs, activists and related organisational concepts

Label	Definition, characteristics, examples
Not-for-profit organisations, or non-profit organisations (NPOs)	Organisations that do not have as their main objective the provision of income for their owners or shareholders.
Non-governmental organisations (NGOs)	Organisations that are not controlled by the state. Strictly speaking, business firms are NGOs when they are not state-owned, but usually business firms are not considered to be NGOs: the term is reserved for organisations that are neither a part of a government nor a conventional for-profit business. Often, a distinction is made between the following: - 'direct aid' NGOs seek to provide assistance to people in need: Red Cross, MSF/Médécins Sans Frontières; - 'empowerment' NGOs seek to stimulate emancipation of local communities and minorities: OXFAM; - 'advocacy' NGOs seek to influence government or business policy: Greenpeace.
International non-governmental organisations (INGOs)	NGOs that operate in international arenas and have offices in several countries.
Civil society organisations (CSOs)	Organisations that do not operate in the realms of the state or the market. 'Civil society' is therefore considered the 'third' sector of society, associated with family and the private sphere, emphasising voluntary action, as distinguished from political and economic action. Examples include sports clubs, churches, neighbourhood committees, human rights organisations.
Secondary stakeholders	Organisations or groups upon whom a business firm does not in a direct way depend for its economic survival, such as media, communities and regulators.
Private interest groups	Organisations that seek to advance the private interests of their members, such as business associations, labour unions and consumer leagues.
Public interest groups	Organisations that seek to advance some public interest, or common good, beyond the private interests of their members.
Activist groups, and social movement organisations (SMOs)	Organisations or groups of people that exhibit a propensity to mobilise and organise campaigns around themes they deem important, typically in opposition to some political, legal, cultural, religious or other kind of authority. The members of some activist groups are willing to run personal risks and to make certain sacrifices in order to reach their goals. Examples include Greenpeace, PETA and Friends of the Earth.

stakeholder engagement and cause-related marketing. A vast literature has developed on cross-sector partnerships (cf. Clarke and Crane, 2018) and related concepts such as social alliances (cf. Seitanidi and Crane, 2014) and multi-stakeholder initiatives (cf. de Bakker et al., 2019). This literature examines how actors from different backgrounds collaborate in order to establish some shared objectives, pool resources and develop joint standards or approaches to issues of shared concern, such as those relating to sustainability and corporate social responsibility (CSR). Collaboration can be an effective way for activist NGOs to influence corporate activities as joint projects and partnerships offer them the possibility to exert influence over corporate initiatives.

Other activist NGOs pursue more contentious engagements with corporations: they target corporations in adversarial ways, such as through naming-and-shaming campaigns, the organisation of boycotts and other means of publicly visible protest. Their preference for contentious engagements is related to a conviction that collaboration is not an effective means to establish their goals of driving corporations towards greater levels of sustainability and social responsibility. They argue, for example, that collaboration would jeopardise their independent position and reduce their options to remain critical of corporate sustainability initiatives: they fear being co-opted. Nevertheless, collaboration and contention are not mutually exclusive: some activist NGOs entertain both collaborative and antagonistic relationships with the same firms, depending on the topic or the geographical setting.

Another way to characterise the different types of interactions between activist NGOs and firms is by considering the ideological position of the NGOs involved. We distinguish between radical and reformist activist NGOs. According to social movement theory, radical groups are the ones that 'offer a more comprehensive version of the problem and more drastic change as a solution' (Zald and McCarthy, 1980: 8). They strive for fundamental change in their area of concern and think that companies cannot be part of their envisaged solution, as in their view corporate 'success' is closely tied to the very problem they seek to address. On the other hand, reformist groups are inclined to work with business to evoke corporate social change – for instance, on sustainability. Although they see current business practices as part of the problem, they also think business can, and should, be part of the solution by reforming their ways of operating. Obviously, radical and reformist are the two poles of a spectrum and many intermediate positions are possible. Yet, to understand the different tactical approaches NGO activists use at the operational level, this distinction is helpful.

A third way to distinguish different activist NGOs is by looking at their tactical repertoire. Building on the work of della Porta and Diani (1999), we suggest that three dimensions categorise the deployment of tactics by activist NGOs. Their tactics can aim at inflicting damage or gain onto the target; both damage and gain in turn can be either symbolic or material. A boycott is an example of a tactic aimed at exerting pressure on a targeted firm or industry through inflicting material damage; a massive media campaign in support of an alternative practice is an example of a tactic aimed at establishing symbolic gain. Tactics aimed at a material impact directly affect the cost or revenue structure of a firm, either positively or negatively, whereas tactics with a symbolic impact affect its reputation, again either positively ('gain') or negatively ('damage'). The first dimension is thus the nature of the tactics' intended effect on corporations.

The next dimension to categorise the deployment of tactics is in the amount of effort that is needed to make a tactic effective. Some tactics only require a limited number of committed people in order to be effective. For example, maintaining a website, a social media account or a blog to expose corporate misdoings only requires the efforts of a relatively small number of dedicated people. Similarly, preparing legal action can be done by just a few highly competent individuals. Yet, in both examples, the activists need specialised knowledge (and funds to finance their work). Other tactics rely on the participation of a large group of people: a boycott can only succeed if a very large number of people decide not to buy a certain product or service. As involving large numbers of participants in tactics can be difficult to organise, activist NGOs typically start off using tactics that require only a small number of dedicated participants; staging a social media campaign, negotiating a collaboration and conducting research to underscore the salience and urgency of an issue are examples of such tactics.

Time is a third dimension to characterise the deployment of tactics. Activist NGOs' campaigns may last for long periods of time. For example, ever since 2012, the Dutch animal rights organisation Wakker Dier has run its 'plofkip' campaign to phase out the sales and use of industrially grown broiler chickens in supermarkets and restaurants. Broiler chickens are raised, in extremely densely populated cages, within six weeks to a weight of 2.3 kg; they have become symbols of industrialised meat production. The campaign has been successful in gradually improving the conditions of production, through its consistent use of a combination of naming-and-shaming and naming-and-praising tactics. However, not all activist NGOs are able to successfully use the same tactics over a prolonged period of time. When the use of some tactics turns out to be ineffective, there is a likelihood of escalation. Many activist NGOs initially choose tactics that require relatively small numbers of participants to be effective, but when these are to no avail they may seek to escalate. Escalation can be sought in various ways, such as moving from collaboration to confrontation, from tactics that require few participants to those that depend on large numbers of participants, from using 'carrots' (and 'sermons') to using 'sticks', or from inflicting symbolic to material damage. Radical and reformist activist groups are likely to differ in how they seek escalation, as their ultimate objectives and worldviews are very different. Diverging ideological positions imply different views on what tactics are desirable, appropriate and effective. For example, radical activist NGOs are more likely to escalate towards tactics that increase material damage, but are less likely to rely on large numbers of participants; reformist activist NGOs are more likely to escalate towards tactics that increase symbolic damage and that require large numbers of participants for their efficacy.

13.4 How NGO Activism Affects Corporations

NGOs deploy a wide variety of tactics in their attempts to make businesses more sustainable or more socially responsible. Several studies have examined the tactical repertoires that NGO activists have at their disposal (cf. den Hond and de Bakker, 2007; Doherty and Hayes, 2019); in this chapter, we group their tactics according to how they affect corporations. We distinguish tactics working through (corporate) governance, such as shareholder activism; through financial means, such as affecting operational costs and revenues; and through collaboration, such as in the form of partnerships. Whereas these three sets of tactics imply direct engagement with firms, a fourth set of tactics works in an indirect manner, by creating alternatives to the provision of services and products by corporations.

13.4.1 Shareholder Activism

A firm's corporate governance structure may provide opportunity for a particular kind of activism. Shareholder activism makes use of the principal–agent relationship between a firm's shareholding owners and its management in order to influence top management decision-making in privately held corporations – that is, they make use of the firm's corporate governance structure in the pursuit of their interest. A distinction should nevertheless be made between shareholder activism on social issues versus financial shareholder activism. Although both are types of shareholder activism, the focus of this chapter is on shareholder activism on social issues. For example, activist NGOs may find allies among a firm's shareholders who can voice their claims. Potential shareholder allies include large financial institutions such as banks, insurance companies, pension funds and socially responsible investment (SRI) funds. Or, activist NGOs can become shareholders themselves and use the associated rights in shareholder meetings. One example is the activist NGO Follow This (www.follow-this.org/) that specialised in using shareholder activism to pressurise the oil industry to get serious about climate change. Shareholder activism offers activist NGOs the option to exert influence through the threat of damage, either by generating negative publicity for the firm (i.e., symbolic damage) as shareholder meetings are typically well covered by financial media, or by stimulating institutional investors to invest in (or divest) the shares of particular companies, which is thought to decrease (or increase) the cost of capital for these companies (i.e., material gain/ damage) (see Chapter 11).

Shareholder activism in the form of SRI was introduced by religious communities in the United States, such as the Quakers and Methodists. Early examples include their abstaining from investing in companies that undertook activities they disproved of for religious or moral reasons, such as making use of slave labour, the production and selling of tobacco, guns or alcohol, or gambling (Guay et al., 2004; Goranova and Ryan, 2014). Today, such negative screening is still a prevalent strategy, but it has been complemented by positive screening: investments are made solely in firms that meet certain criteria regarding their ESG policies and performances (see Chapter 11). These criteria are typically of a relative nature (e.g., 'best in class', 'showing improvement'). Positive screening not only requires criteria, but also the production and processing of large amounts of verified data on how well various companies perform on these criteria; an entire industry has emerged around ESG reporting by companies (see Chapter 17), the verification of reported data, the rating of companies and the creation of a large number of subtly differentiated investment portfolios to meet the various preferences that are found in the market (Avetisyan and Hockerts, 2017; Crifo et al., 2019).

Investors that use negative screening to inform their investment decision may feel little need to engage with a firm's management. However, when they use positive screening, there may be clear reasons for them to do so. For example, when a firm they have invested in (or that they consider investing in) creates great value for its owners and almost meets their criteria for investment, they may wish to point the firm's management to its performance on the wanting criteria. This mechanism, that a (major) shareholder uses its ownership rights to influence decisions of the company it has invested in, offers plenty of options to activist NGOs. When firms are publicly traded, NGO activists can use shareholder meetings to communicate their demands. Such meetings are attended by senior management, shareholders and the financial press. Attracting attention for their cause at such events hence is one way to spread their demands among a wider audience; financial press covers these events and other shareholders may be triggered by the calls, while senior management may feel (or be, through voting) required to formally respond. This is certainly the case in the United States, where 'proxy voting' has become very common (Agrawal, 2012). Once a proposal had been submitted and met certain criteria, firm management has two options: either to reply to the proposal and put that resolution up for voting in the shareholder meeting, or to negotiate with the filers of the resolution. When an announced proposal is withdrawn, this can be seen as a signal of success for the filers: apparently the need to put the proposal up for vote has disappeared because management has given in to their demands or because it has reached a compromise with the filers (Graves et al., 2001). How exactly the mechanisms to exert pressure on the top management operate may vary across countries and corporations depending on national corporate governance law and firm-specific procedures. Yet, the underlying principle remains the same: use the principal–agent relationship in the interest of the principal by performing in the shareholder meeting and working with other shareholders as allies.

Although social shareholder activism nowadays is booming, the impact of this type of activism is difficult to determine. Some research, for instance, suggests that more politically active firms are 'more likely to challenge socially oriented share-holder proposals and less likely to arrive at agreements with social activists than their less politically active counterparts' (Hadani et al., 2019: 656). (Ironically, it must be noted that recent research suggests that financial shareholder activism, such as that by hedge funds, may assess a firm's involvement in sustainability even as a signal that excess resources are being spent: the firm is judged to have wasteful intentions and capabilities, which prevent it from maximising shareholder value in the short term [Desjardine et al., 2020: 1]. This may drive activist hedge funds to target firms with higher levels of CSR engagement, punishing them for not maxi-mising shareholder value in the short term.) Furthermore, while this tactic may work with large firms that are listed on the stock market, it is less obvious how it would work vis-à-vis firms with different ownership structures, including many small and medium-sized enterprises. Hence, it is important to look beyond these tactics to the other ways by which activist NGOs can exert influence on firms.

13.4.2   Operational Costs and Revenues

When we discussed shareholder activism, we already pointed at its potential influence on firms' cost of capital. Yet, there are more ways in which activist NGOs can impact the financial situation of a firm: they can try to influence its operational costs and revenues, both positively and negatively. There are two main routes to do so: directly through the marketplace and indirectly through the mobilisation of public opinion.

13.4.2.1   Marketplace Tactics

Our starting point to consider how activist NGOs can affect operational costs and revenues is in the field of political or ethical consumerism. The main tenet, here, is that consumption is fraught with ethical and political issues: buying a piece of cloth is not just to purchase some functionality, or to express one's identity or adherence to some fashion, but also to financially support a firm that pollutes the environment and exploits workers, either directly or through its supply chains, and to contribute, when the piece of cloth is no longer worn, to the production of household waste. Forms of political consumerism include boycotts, increased preferences for organic or Fairtrade products and lifestyle choices (Boström et al., 2018). Political and ethical consumers seek to change firms, markets, industries and supply chains through their choice of products, services and producers (Micheletti, 2003). Which products, services or producers they select is informed by their evaluations of the supplier. Activist NGOs play important roles in developing and disseminating such evaluations, by promoting standards for environmentally or socially sustainable products or otherwise inform consumers of what is 'behind a company's label' (e.g., https://labourbehindthelabel.org/). Consumers can thus leverage activists' claims as they have a direct impact on a firm's sales: informed by activist NGOs' claims, consumers are politicised to use the marketplace as an arena for change.

Consumers' buying power is thus critical in political consumerism. By withholding their buying power, that is, by *not* buying certain products or services, consumers can exert influence over firms, provided they do so in sufficient numbers. After all, in order to be effective, a boycott needs substantial numbers of participants and thus the problem of collective action needs to be overcome. Activist NGOs need to make sure they reach and convince a substantial number of consumers in order to make a boycott successful. This requires considerable effort in overcoming collective action problems and has proven difficult (Delacote, 2009). Just as activist NGOs can call for a boycott to demonstrate that they disapprove of a certain issue, they can also call for a 'buycott': calling upon consumers to use their buying power in support of certain products or producers that are preferred for the values embedded in them.

Boycotts have been around for a long time. Well-known examples include the boycotts of multinationals that had invested in South Africa during the times of the Apartheid regime, and the boycott of Shell in Germany over its plans to sink in the North Sea a decommissioned oil rig in the mid-1990s. Examples of buycotts can be found in movements that seek to support local ('buy local'), fair trade and ecological products in the market. Beyond these, buycotts are more difficult to find, probably because they are less media savvy. One high-profile example in the Netherlands is the already-mentioned animal rights activist NGO 'Wakker Dier', who have been running media campaigns against intensive animal husbandry, praising (or shaming) those supermarket chains that had (or had not yet) made a significant step towards banning 'factory farmed meat' from their shelves. Campaigns such as these are examples of how activist NGOs may 'reward' or 'punish' companies through the market mechanism, by seeking to influence consumers' purchasing behaviour and thereby to shape markets.

Additionally, activist NGOs have been highly involved in advancing standards as a way to influence 'value' and 'valuation' in the market. Through their involvement in standards, activists can have an impact on what is considered a product or service that has been produced in an environmentally or socially sustainable manner. The Marine Stewardship Council (MSC), for instance, was established from the collaboration between a company (Unilever) and an activist NGO (WWF). After the collapse of cod fishery in parts of the Atlantic Ocean, both had a joint interest: WWF was concerned about the loss of biodiversity, whereas Unilever was concerned about its long-term supply of fish. Together, they took the initiative to start the MSC, which soon thereafter became independent of its founders. Nevertheless, this initiative is a clear example of collaboration between a firm and an activist NGO that worked through the marketplace, signalling to consumers that fish products labelled with the MSC logo had been brought to the market in a more sustainable way than non-labelled fish.

According to Micheletti (2003), the use of boycotts, buycotts and standards has flourished since the 1990s and their effect on firms' operational costs can make them successful. Yet, as these tactics require the participation of large numbers of consumers, they are difficult and costly to organise for activist NGOs. Hence, they are usually not among the tactics that activist NGOs initially select in their efforts to increase firms' sustainability practices.

It is important to note that there is another set of tactics that may or may not be legal and that can have the effect of increasing a firm's operational costs. Sabotage and obstruction of facilities – for example, by the blocking of gates and hacking computer networks – are some of the tactics that more radical activist NGOs sometimes resort to. These tactics are not only highly visible in the media and thereby draw public opinion to the issue at stake (see the next section), but they can also be very disruptive for the daily operations in firms and thereby increase costs. Yet, compared to the other tactics discussed in this chapter, these more extreme tactics are used only sparsely.

13.4.2.2 Public Opinion Tactics

A key factor for the success of boycotts and buycotts is the widespread dissemination of information regarding which ones are ongoing, why they are called for and what their purposes are. Lists of current boycotts can be found on websites such as www.ethicalconsumer.org/. Public opinion tactics, the use of mass media and social media channels to spread information and emotion on industries, firms and their products and services are key in NGO activism that seeks to affect operational costs and revenues.

Mass media have the possibility to influence public opinion, and thereby to add to, or distract from, the reputation of those people, organisations or entities on which they put the spotlight. Working through mass media offered a range of new means to NGO activists. They use media campaigns to support firms that work in line with their objectives, and to inflict symbolic damage on firms that don't. A firm's reputation is considered to influence its sales and market shares (Minor and Morgan, 2011) and the overall attractiveness as an employer (Turban and Greening, 1997). Hence, reputation has become so important for many firms that they are eager to bolster or protect their reputations. Firms' heavy reliance on reputation thus gives activist NGOs a lever to gain influence: if their tactics support corporate reputations then that might be a selling point; if their tactics potentially harm a firm's reputation then this strengthens the activists' position vis-à-vis the firm.

The wide variety of public opinion tactics all use communication about corporate policies, plans and activities in an effort to influence both business and the general public. These tactics can be contentious, non-contentious or involve a mix of both. By endorsing certain firms, products or practices, NGO activists can provide symbolic gain to firms and strengthen their reputations; by engaging in negative publicity (in press, online or at meetings), NGO activists can exert pressure on firms and damage their reputations. An interesting example of the latter tactic is 'culture jamming': corporate symbols and logos are taken out of context, transformed and released to the public. The subversion of well-known symbols or logos is supposed to disrupt the general public's positive attitude by questioning and criticising the firm and its behaviour (e.g., adbusters.org). Rather than calling for action, this tactic aims to generate negative publicity. As Bennett (2003: 152) noted: 'unlike boycotts, many contemporary issue campaigns do not require consumer action at all; instead, the goal is to hold a corporate logo hostage in the media until shareholders or corporate managers regard the bad publicity as an independent threat to a carefully cultivated brand image'. Starting off as a threat of symbolic damage, such a tactic thus could well develop into one that inflicts material damage.

Over the last decade, several studies examined the impact of protest on market value. King and Soule (2007: 38) found that the staging of protest did have a negative impact of stock price, but also that 'the most powerful feature of protest vis-à-vis stock price lies in its ability to upset image management, not in its ability to threaten direct costs to firms'. Bartley and Child (2011) investigated the effects of anti-sweatshop campaigns on firms. They found 'compelling evidence' that only 'specialized and recognizable firms experienced notable declines in sales as they faced anti-sweatshop campaigns' (2011: 439). They also found a significant effect on stock price, but only a limited effect on corporate reputation (2011: 445). Both studies were conducted in the United States. These, and other studies, thus find mixed evidence of the impact of boycotts and activist campaigns. In individual cases, however, the impact may be substantial. That is, of course, what activist NGOs hope for, while the overall mixed evidence poses a dilemma to firms facing activism about whether and how to respond.

13.4.3   Partnerships

Yet another way for activist NGOs to exert influence over firms is to collaborate with a corporation – for example, in the form of a partnership or alliance (see also Chapter 18). Influence through collaboration is based on the 'giving and taking' between the parties that may be needed to develop common ground and shared objectives. Cross-sector collaborations have grown in prominence. Within the literature a whole range of partnerships is distinguished, ranging from cross-sector partnerships to social alliances and multi-stakeholder initiatives (de Bakker et al., 2019). Although such partnerships and initiatives differ in their exact focus and composition, they all involve a willingness to foster cross-sectoral collaboration (Seitanidi and Crane, 2014). Some of these partnerships involve the transfer of resources, while others focus on establishing change in corporate policies and/or products. The development of standards and labels is one example (think of the MSC label mentioned earlier); collaboration on new products or services is another. For example, several NGOs have teamed up with firms to increase the use of solar power. There also exist partnerships in which activists and firms collaborate to impact other firms – for example, in the agri-food or clothing and shoes industries, aiming to help other firms in the supply chain to reduce their environmental impact or to improve their labour conditions (McDonnell, 2016).

Radical NGO activists are less likely than reformist groups to engage in partnerships or collaborations with firms. After all, as they typically consider firms not to be part of their desired solution, they will not be much inclined to engage in partnerships. Reformist groups, on the other hand, are more likely to work with firms in trying to change their behaviour because, in their worldview, reform can be an effective way to accomplish change: their presence in a partnership gives them the possibility to influence a firm's policies and practices. Many partnerships are presented as successful initiatives that create 'win-win situations'.

Yet, there is also criticism of the positive tone in which cross-sector partnerships are discussed. One may wonder what their actual contribution is: Do partnerships really contribute to social change? Critics argued that partnerships can be used, and indeed are being used, by firms for window-dressing or greenwashing: they show off with a partnership, but do not really change their operations or strategies (Wu et al., 2020). Finally, it is feared that NGOs jeopardise their independence when entering a partnership, by being co-opted (Baur and Schmitz, 2012). Co-optation refers to processes by which authorities (e.g., government agencies, leadership teams, and business firms) absorb critics into their policy- or decision-making structures as a means of neutralising the threat that critics may pose to their stability or existence. For some activist NGOs, the risk of being co-opted is a reason for refraining from positive engagement with corporations. Notwithstanding such critique, partnerships can have far-reaching consequences in changing markets and organisations. Some standards and labels have led to the widespread adoption of new 'rules of the game' and therefore partnerships are likely to remain an important tactic for many activist NGOs.

13.4.4 New Business Systems

For some activist NGOs, partnerships are not a viable option. The more radical activist NGOs may well argue that entering into collaboration or negotiation with companies confers legitimacy to the entities whose very legitimacy they fundamentally contest. Others refrain from collaboration with firms because they feel that doing so would limit their ability to publicly criticise them. If, furthermore, their analysis is that protest is unlikely to fundamentally change the behaviour of companies – for example, because the problems they seek to address are systemic and inherent to the prevailing corporate capitalist system, or if they would rather invest their energy in a positive way to create something new – they may turn away from engaging with firms. Instead, they may choose to contribute to developing some alternative economic order. Rather than challenging individual corporations, it is the institution of corporate capitalism that they challenge and that they seek to replace with one that, in their view, is not oppressive, exclusive, exploitative and polluting, but democratic, liberating, inclusive, respectful and sustainable. Such has been the thrust of the Occupy and alter-globalisation movements.

There are many and widely diverging examples of initiatives that subscribe to such an agenda, including worker-owned factories and shops, local exchange trading systems and networks (LETS), such as time banks, food collectives, etc. Time banks, for example, are self-organised collectives in which members exchange services of which the value is measured in units of time instead of money (Laamanen et al., 2020). The common denominator in all these initiatives is a desire of their participants to become less dependent on the dominant corporate capitalist system. While there is the awareness that complete autarky is probably an ephemeral dream, participating in them is for many participants both an act of self-fulfilment and a way of showing that some alternative is actually possible. This is not a new idea. Whereas the idea and the term 'LETS' was coined in the early 1980s, various sorts of workers', consumers' and producers' cooperatives were already set up in the mid nineteenth century to counter corporate power in areas such as agriculture, finance and retail, resulting in, for instance, cooperatively owned and managed sugar refineries, banks, supermarkets and – more recently – facilities for the production of wind power. The long and successful history of many such cooperatives suggests that multiple ways of organising economic exchange can be viable, and indeed can compete head on with more ideal-typical capitalist firms that are dominant in Western industrialised markets. Some of the alterative practices that cooperatives developed have been adopted by conventional firms: the organic agriculture movement, for example, has contributed to the mainstreaming of organic products in food markets. Yet, this development involves a risk as it might lead to the crowding out of organic producers by large industrialised producers and retailers (Sikavica and Pozner, 2013).

Another form of new business systems is found in social enterprises. These entrepreneurial organisations link their activities to a social mission and offer a business-like contrast to traditional non-profit organisations through a hybrid organisational form (Battilana and Lee, 2014). Some social enterprises highlight the link with the local community in which they operate, such as the so-called community-based enterprises that have become more prominent in the United Kingdom, whereas others aim to improve social and environmental sustainability within the supply chain. Activist NGOs, for instance, have been engaged in the emergence of social enterprises such as Fairphone (Akemu et al., 2016), or in enterprises active in markets as diverse as medicine, water or food. Much of these initiatives, the contexts in which they operate, and their organisation are studied in the domain of entrepreneurship, where a dedicated literature has emerged on social enterprises and social entrepreneurship. Yet, as Luke and Chu (2013) note, the concepts of social enterprises and social entrepreneurship are different as not every enterprise is entrepreneurial. In their view, research on social enterprises emphasises the commercial business activity, and research on social entrepreneurship highlights opportunity recognition, innovation and risk. Both are important to develop an alternative economic activity. Through the provision of resources (such as time, knowledge, legitimacy or financial support), activist NGOs can use this route to contribute to demonstrating the viability of their ideas, creating an alternative product or service offering.

All in all, creating alternatives to current business systems provides the opportunity to establish new norms and standards that better fit the objectives of the activist group and that establish links between local communities and business initiatives. Yet, the mainstreaming of these alternatives can also be a risk for the original initiatives.

13.5 Which Corporations Are Likely to Encounter NGO Activism?

In a chapter highlighting NGO activism and sustainability, it is also important to discuss which corporations are likely to encounter NGO activism. In the literature, some attention has been given to the question of which factors increase the likelihood that firms are targeted by activist NGOs. This explanation may well be symmetrical: the same factors are relevant for explaining why NGOs select particular firms as partners.

According to Hendry (2006), a firm is more likely to be targeted by NGO activism when: (1) it is a proven, repetitive trespasser of social or legal norms; (2) it is visible to consumers in the value chain or through brands and is an important player in the industry; or (3) it operates in an industry that is under high levels of scrutiny by activist groups. If a firm is a repeated wrong-doer, it will be easier to mobilise support for activism; if a firm operates in an advertising-intensive industry, reputational threats or support will provide leverage to the activist NGO; and if a firm is operating in an industry that is already considered socially or environmentally sensitive, then it is more likely to be targeted by activist NGOs, either for collaboration or for contestation. Firm size might be another influential factor, although research is inconclusive on whether larger or smaller firms are most likely to respond positively to activists' calls for change.

Obviously, activist NGOs will make choices in targeting firms. They will be selective in picking their targets as campaigning may require substantial resources (money, time, energy) and hence they will try to select those targets that look most promising to help them reach their own objectives. Yet, as Rowley and Moldoveanu (2003) suggest, pursuing their interests is not always the sole reason for activist groups to target a firm. Strengthening their own position vis-à-vis their constituencies and reaffirming their social identity may be additional reasons: as targeting large, visible firms is more likely to attract media attention, activist NGOs may therefore decide to do so, even if the chance of success in terms of change in firm behaviour is small.

In addition to pursuing its interests and confirming its identity, ideology will also be an important factor in an activist NGO's targeting decisions, as we suggested in section 13.3. Radical activist NGOs will select a different set of potential targets than reformist activist NGOs because this fits in with their desired worldview: radical activists will be less inclined to collaborative interactions, whereas collaboration can be a fruitful tactic for more reformist activists, especially if the target firm is open to reassessing its sustainability behaviour, or is performing better than its industry peers on the issues at stake. Whereas reformist activist NGOs will be inclined to work with such leading firms, more radical activist NGOs are much less likely to do so. Taking these considerations into account, it seems quite clear that certain firms are more likely to attract the attention of activist NGOs and to become a target, either for collaborative or for contentious interactions. Then how do firms respond?

13.6   Strategic Response or Taking Responsibility?

As the upheaval around fracking and many other examples show, business activities can be contested. Not everyone agrees that all activities undertaken by firms are legitimate. Following Suchman (1995), contested business activities can be considered to lack moral legitimacy, in the sense that the activities themselves, or their consequences, are considered to violate some moral principle. Think of paying bribes, the use of child labour or the Volkswagen scandal over its software manipulations to simulate better performance on emission tests. Firms may also be considered to lack pragmatic legitimacy, in the sense that their activities, or the consequences thereof, are contrary to the interests of some of their stakeholders. Although many food companies are considered to have moral legitimacy, some of the products they offer have been scrutinised for possible health risks to consumers, which may affect these firms' pragmatic legitimacy with consumers.

Hence, even if a firm operates in such a way that its activities are legally permissible – it operates within the conditions set by law and regulation, it has obtained all the required licences and permits, and it adheres to their provisions – its activities, or the organisation as such, may still be contested. Legality and legitimacy are not the same. While being perfectly legal, some activities of the company might still be considered illegitimate by outsiders – for example, because the activities or their consequences are associated with pressing social or environmental issues.

Activist NGOs have become main protagonists in articulating the social and environmental sustainability issues in which companies can be implicated, in mobilising people around the issues they find important and in putting pressure on firms to effectively address these issues. The inability or unwillingness of national governments to directly regulate business activities regarding sustainability has been a driver behind NGO activism towards firms, as we argued in section 13.2. Moreover, some of these issues, such as climate change, labour rights issues in upstream supply chains and poverty alleviation, are highly complex, involve radical uncertainty as to their causes and consequences, and are infused with multiple and opposing values and interests; to such an extent that they are beyond the capacity of governments and firms to resolve them. Many people have come to see NGOs as crucial agents in helping firms (and governments) to address these issues (Reinecke and Ansari, 2016).

Many companies have experienced, or are likely to experience, NGO activism. As we have seen above, NGO activism may take various forms but always makes some claim on the firm. Some firms will just sit and wait until they are targeted by activist NGOs, but others may decide to be more proactive. A range of studies has examined the various ways in which firms can respond to, or anticipate, NGO activism. These responses vary from seeking allies and partnering with NGOs to defending their own positions and partnering with peers. Relevant questions for targeted firms include: Which claims to respond to, and how to respond, if at all?

Building on stakeholder theory, Mitchell, Agle and Wood (1997) proposed a model to predict under what conditions a firm's management is more likely to respond to claims made by stakeholder groups, such as activist NGOs. They argued that management is more likely to respond as the stakeholder's salience increases. Salience, in turn, is seen as a function of the urgency of the claim ('do we, as a firm, need to respond swiftly?'), its legitimacy ('is this a claim that is widely supported?') and the power of the claimant ('how potent are the means that the claimant can deploy to force us to respond?'). Cast in these terms, one strategic question for activist NGOs is how to increase their salience vis-à-vis their target firms. Rowley (1997) extended the notion of power by considering the position of the firm in the social network structure of its stakeholders. He argued that when the network of the firm's stakeholders is denser – for example, the activist NGO has secured many allies to its cause – the firm faces a stronger claimant. However, when the firm's centrality is higher – that is, there are several disconnected groups of stakeholders making claims on the firm – it has a stronger position, as it can 'play off' one group against another.

These two classical models depart from the situation that firms have multiple stakeholders, including activist NGOs, each having different, potentially incompatible or even contradictory claims on the firm. But even when the claims are not incompatible or contradictory, their sheer numbers may be such that a firm cannot attend to all of them; some prioritising will need to be done. Having decided *which* claims to attend to, a next strategic question for the firm is *how* to respond. There is a considerable literature on 'response' to 'institutional pressures' which is relevant. As can be inferred from section 13.4, some of the tactics that activist NGOs deploy, such as public opinion tactics, can be understood in terms of increasing institutional pressure on firms. Moreover, NGO activism in itself can be seen as an expression of societal expectations about what companies should do. Much of this literature on how companies respond to institutional pressures builds on the seminal framework developed by Oliver (1991). Her framework was one of the earliest formulations of the idea that institutional pressures can be resisted. Oliver's framework comprises five different response strategies that range from 'giving in' to 'resisting' institutional pressures. For example, acquiescence, or compliance, refers to a response in which companies accede to the claims posed upon them. Defiance, on the other hand, is a resisting response strategy in which claims are denied, dismissed, challenged or counter-attacked. Other response strategies on the continuum from acquiescence to defiance include compromise, avoidance and manipulation. Compromise is a response strategy that encompasses bargaining, negotiating or creatively working together to develop some solution that is acceptable to both the firm and the activist NGO. Avoidance is a strategy by which firms conceal their non-conformity, buffer themselves from NGO activism or otherwise seek to escape from the claims upon them. To publish a CSR report that selectively highlights successes but omits failures or ongoing problems is an example of an avoidance strategy. Another example of avoidance can be found in Whelan, de Bakker, den Hond and Muthuri's (2019) account of how the UN Global Compact made it more difficult for activist NGOs to challenge its policies and practices by 'deflating' its own standards. Finally, manipulation is a response strategy in which firms seek to change or exert power over the content of the claims they face or over the activist NGOs that make these claims. Examples of manipulation strategies include co-opting activist NGOs, influencing public opinion, lobbying politicians and regulators, and seeking to prosecute activist NGOs by legal means.

While typologies such as these are helpful to classify and describe firms' responses to NGO activism, they cannot be used as normative frames to guide how firms should deal with NGO activism. Their formulation and presentation seem to emphasise (and legitimise) rationalised and instrumental self-interest on the part of the firm. They offer a set of highly instrumental frameworks for developing a 'strategic response'. For example, they appeal to 'bottom-line' thinking and the economic calculus of costs and revenues, as well as to risk management approaches that are associated with a discourse of maximising shareholder value. But they do not easily open up to 'taking responsibility', because they disregard the values, and hence the morality, that are implied in the issues that NGOs seek to address.

For a firm to take responsibility implies that it moves beyond the defence of its own economic interests to consider the questions of what kind of corporation the firm wishes to be, what role in society it aspires to fulfil and how to relate to its various stakeholders. Despite all the talk of 'win-win solutions' and 'creating shared value' (Porter and Kramer, 2011), such opportunities remain rare events, and even the concept itself has been criticised (Crane et al., 2014). Acquiescence may be a rational response strategy when it is inevitable that the firm has to address a societal demand as expressed or amplified in the claims by activist NGOs, or when the approach that the firm has developed to address a societal issue, perhaps in collaboration with activist NGOs, is going to strengthen its competitive position. But in other instances, the issue at stake may be less unequivocal: there may be disagreement about its causes and consequences of the issue and multiple values and interests may be involved. If this is the case, it might be appealing to consider the salience of the activist NGOs that bring the issue to the firm, and to wait and see if the NGOs' salience increases to critical levels (instead of considering it as a weak signal of how the society in which the firm operates may change). It might be tempting to the firm to seek to defy, avoid or manipulate the claims from NGO activism in an effort to defend its own interests, because doing so is not challenging to the status quo. Yet, if the words and phrases such as 'responsibility', 'respect', 'sustainable' and the 'integration of economic, environmental and social considerations into business decision-making' – words and phrases that are often found in the 'core values', 'mission statements' and other expressions of firms' purposes – are to have any meaning, they imply and demand an openness on the part of the firm to other voices that may be dissonant with its own talkings and doings. If the meaning and intent of a firm's sustainability policies and practices are to be anything other than an instrument to the maximisation of shareholder value, it needs to be open to the values and interests of its other stakeholders and broaden its scope to its wider sustainability impacts. Expressing such other voices, values and interests is exactly what activist NGOs do. By shaping firms' views of potential alternative solutions, they may help in creating forms of sustainability activities and CSR as 'aspirational talk' (Christensen et al., 2013) that sets a more complete version of corporate activities in motion. Engaging with activist NGOs can be difficult, especially if there is hostility in how they approach the firm. Then again, sometimes these contentious interactions can, in the end, lead to changes in practices. It will be the task of activist NGOs to ensure that a firm's responses develop beyond window-dressing to ensure real change.

13.7 Chapter Summary

Starting from the premise that the wish of non-traditional stakeholders to engage with corporate policies, processes and outcomes is there to stay, the chapter has first sought to clarify some notions about how to talk about them. As noted, these actors have been conceptualised as NGOs, civil society organisations, social movements and several other terms. All these terms have particular connotations that emphasise some of their traits and characteristics while downplaying others. We used 'activist NGOs' for two reasons: to highlight their willingness to organise collective action in the pursuit of their objectives, and to focus on their efforts in furthering their take on environmental and social sustainability.

Drawing on social movement literature, we argued that activist NGOs can leverage their claims by showing that many people share them ('logic of numbers') or by using positive and negative incentives to make corporations change ('logic of damage'). Elaborating on these distinctions, we refined the idea of 'activism': we showed how collaboration and confrontation are often closely related, and how the most visible forms of activism typically have a longer history. Next, we discussed various ways by which NGO activism may knock on corporate doors. We focused on tactics working through corporate governance, through operational costs and revenues in direct and indirect ways, and through collaboration, as these are common routes that NGO activists apply. These three sets of tactics were supplemented with a fourth one that does not imply direct engagement with firms: creating alternatives to the provision of services and products by firms.

Not all firms are equally susceptible to NGO activism. We reviewed literature that suggests which conditions increase the odds that a corporation will be facing NGO activism. Firm size, industry and visibility to consumers are important elements, as well as their historical record on CSR and sustainability issues. Furthermore, activist NGOs may also target firms to strengthen their own position vis-à-vis their constituencies by reaffirming their social identity or because doing so fits with their own ideological position.

Finally, in discussing how corporations may respond to NGO activism, we linked up with other chapters in this textbook. More fundamentally, we put the onus on corporations by suggesting that how to respond to NGO activism – or how to prevent it popping up in the first place – involves corporate management and staff to ask some tough questions about their identity, mission and values, policies and processes, and their role in a globalised society that confronts major challenges, such as climate change. Ultimately, these are questions of ethics. While it will be impossible to get rid of NGO activism, we suggested that considering the corporation not as a vehicle for maximising profit or shareholder value, but as a means for shaping society for the better, will open up possibilities for constructive engagement with all sorts of ideas and preferences, including those held by activist NGOs.

CHAPTER QUESTIONS

1. How can the ongoing attention of activist NGOs for labour conditions in Chinese electronics factories be characterised in terms of the tactics they apply?
2. Sample a major newspaper for recent examples of different activist NGO tactics on issues of sustainability.
3. Provide an overview of characteristics of activist NGO–business interactions.
4. Write a recommendation for a firm being targeted by activist NGOs, based on a worked real-life example.
5. Examine under which conditions partnerships between NGOs and firms may work out well.

> **Case Study:** *Clean Clothes Campaign*
> Available from Cambridge University Press at www.cambridge.org/rasche2

FURTHER RESOURCES

- Seitanidi, M. and Crane, A. (Eds.). (2014). *Social Partnerships and Responsible Business: A Research Handbook*. New York, NY: Routledge.

  This edited volume presents a wide range of perspectives on cross-sector partnerships and critically examines the motivations for, processes within, and expected and actual outcomes of cross-sector partnerships from a variety of disciplines.

- Soule, S. A. (2009). *Contention and Corporate Social Responsibility*. Cambridge: Cambridge University Press.

  This book presents a rich overview of anti-corporate activism over time, combining insights on social movements, private politics and their consequences.

- Yaziji, M. and Doh, J. P. (2009). *NGOs and Corporations: Conflict and Cooperation*. Cambridge: Cambridge University Press.

  These authors provide an overview of interactions between NGOs and corporations, both contentious and collaborative, illustrated with a range of examples.

- Business for Social Responsibility, http://bsr.org

  Business for Social Responsibility (BSR) is a global non-profit organisation that works with a large network of member companies to build a just and sustainable world by developing sustainable business strategies and solutions through consulting, research and cross-sector collaboration.

- Center for research on Multinational Corporations, www.somo.nl

  The Center for research on Multinational Corporations (SOMO) is an independent, not-for-profit research and network organisation working on social, ecological and economic issues related to sustainable development. Since 1973, the organisation investigates multinational corporations and the consequences of their activities for people and the environment around the world. Their website provides a rich overview of research on CSR issues and activists' efforts to influence these issues.

14 Consumers and Corporate Sustainability

SANKAR SEN

LEARNING OBJECTIVES

- Understand the behaviours of consumers in response to corporate sustainability actions.

- Learn about the psychological forces (the 3 U's) underlying consumer responses to corporate sustainability.

- Consider the contingencies that determine how consumers understand, evaluate and embrace corporate sustainability information.

- Assess the successes and struggles of corporate sustainability efforts in reaching consumers and converting them to loyal customers.

14.1 Introduction

Think back to the last time you went shopping in a store or on the Internet. Did any of the brands or products you came across or searched for have an eco-label or a Fairtrade certification? Were they made from recycled materials? If so, how much did such information feature in your decision? Did you choose the brand based on this information? And if this information was not apparent, did you search for it before deciding what to buy? Did you consider how well products minimised their impact on the environment, how ethically a company sources their raw materials or whether a portion of their profits goes to some charity? If you didn't consider these things, is it because you did not have the time or inclination to do so?

Consumers are the *raison d'être* of companies. The success of companies hinges on consumers buying from them (in the case of business-to-business companies, buying from the businesses such companies sell to), often repeatedly. To get consumers to buy their products, and do so happily and consistently, companies, particularly successful ones, need to understand, make and sell what their consumers need, want and demand. This is the very crux of marketing.

It is not surprising, then, that companies pay close attention to what they think consumers want them to do in the domain of sustainability, such as tackling environmental and social issues. Understanding the hopes, wishes and wants of this key stakeholder group allows companies to respond in ways that make their businesses successful and sustainable. The more consumers like a company's sustainability efforts, the more likely they are to buy its products and talk it up to other consumers.

So, does sustainability have a place in the worldview of most consumers today? The answer would seem to be an emphatic *yes*. Survey upon survey in recent years points to increasing consumer concern, and for many, alarm, about both the physical state of our planet (i.e., the environment) and the well-being of the people inhabiting it. In a recent poll, 86 per cent of consumers from the United Kingdom, the United States and China expect businesses to help tackle the challenges of climate change and social justice, with 75 per cent saying that the COVID-19 crisis has raised their expectation that businesses will help fight climate change and other big problems facing the world today (Wunderman Thompson, 2021). This is also reflected in the beliefs of companies about the positive business returns to sustainability (Capgemini Research Institute, 2020).

Yet, a good amount of research tells us what many companies also bemoan: consumers are not putting their money where their mouths are. While consumers want sustainability from the companies they buy from, there is credible evidence of an intentions-behaviour gap in their patronage of these companies. Simply being sustainable is not enough to get consumers to buy their products over those of their competitors. In short, when it comes to consumers and sustainability, companies are faced with a paradox.

How, then, are companies to make sense of this paradox? Do consumers truly not care about sustainability, although they insist they do? Or do they care some, but not enough to change their behaviours? Think about how you responded to the opening questions in this chapter. Do you imagine your friends would respond similarly? What if the entire class was surveyed about its buying habits and corporate sustainability? The more people we survey, the more kinds of answers we are likely to get.

This paradox that companies face is at the heart of what this chapter is about. When companies consider sustainability and their customers, they need not wonder, 'Do my customers care?' The answer is: they generally do. What they need to ask is, 'When, how and why do my consumers care that I do good for the planet and its people?'

We see, then, that the relationship between consumers and corporate sustainability is as complex and nuanced as are consumers themselves. For corporate sustainability to both benefit from and do right by this critical stakeholder group, companies need a systematic understanding of the psychological forces guiding and underlying consumer responses to sustainability. Thus, this chapter takes a psychological perspective to help us understand consumer engagement with sustainability. The chapter lays out the key psychological processes that underlie consumer demand for and responses to corporate sustainability. Understanding these processes and how they come together will allow us to evaluate the effectiveness of a company's corporate sustainability strategy and also formulate and implement corporate sustainability initiatives that elicit the most favourable responses from consumers.

This chapter is divided into three sections. We begin by outlining consumer behaviours that a company's sustainability actions impact or seek to change (section 14.2). These can be divided into two broad categories: pro-company behaviours and pro-sustainability behaviours. Because the former is more directly critical to the survival and success of companies, this chapter focuses primarily on pro-company behaviours. Next, we introduce the three psychological processes that guide these behaviours (section 14.3). We call these the 3 U's (Bhattacharya et al., 2011). Understanding is how well consumers understand a company's sustainability efforts. Utility is the value consumers get from such efforts. Unity is the sense of connection consumers feel with a company based on these efforts. The 3 U's need to work synergistically, as levers, for the key sustainability-guided behaviours to be obtained.

In the final section of this chapter (section 14.4), we introduce the key contingencies that determine the extent to which each of the 3 U's are realised and come together to drive the pro-company behaviours. How well the three levers work together to produce favourable pro-company behaviours is likely to depend on many factors, including consumer demographics, traits and values; key aspects of specific sustainability initiatives; the company in question, including the industry it belongs to and the competition it faces, and the context in which consumers interact with corporate sustainability (see Figure 14.1).

14.2   Consumer Behaviours

Companies are in the business of creating value for themselves and for their stakeholders. This is also the basic premise of sustainability, as reflected in the notion of the triple bottom line (i.e., people, planet and prosperity), which uses accounting terminology to drive home the imperative that being a force for good has to be good for business, and vice versa (Elkington, 1994). In other words, if a company is not profitable, it cannot, by definition, be sustainable in the longer term. This is consistent with the popular notion of creating shared value, defined by business strategists Porter and Kramer (2011) as 'policies and operating practices that enhance the competitiveness of a company while simultaneously advancing the

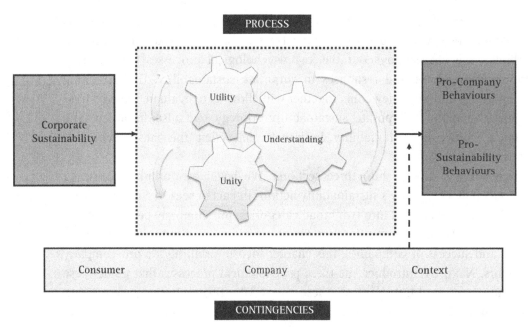

Figure 14.1 The 'levers' of Utility, Understanding and Unity (The 3 U's Framework). The 3 U's need to work together to bring about sustainability-guided consumer behaviors.
Source: Adapted from Bhattacharya et al. (2011).

economic and social conditions in the communities in which it operates' (2011: 66). Key to the creation of such value, then, are consumers' pro-company and pro-sustainability behaviours, driving the success of corporate sustainability.

14.2.1   Pro-Company Behaviours

Companies can be successful only if, ultimately, consumers support the company by engaging in a range of pro-company behaviours. The most basic and important of these behaviours is, of course, purchase. So, a critical question companies ask about consumer responses to their sustainability efforts is, 'Do my consumers buy (more of) my product?'

After years of debate over whether a company's sustainability efforts cause consumers to actually buy its products, there is a growing consensus that consumers do preferentially buy from sustainability-focused companies, ranging from apparel companies (e.g., Patagonia, Stella McCartney) to candy companies (e.g., Theo Chocolate, Justin's). Notably, sustainable products often cost more. Thus, an important question is, are consumers willing to pay more for sustainable products and services? More than half of 6,000 consumers in eleven countries across North America, Europe and Asia surveyed by Accenture in 2019 said they would pay more for sustainable products designed to be reused or recycled (Widlitz, 2020).

The same survey showed that more than half of all consumers are willing to pay more for sustainable products. An interesting study by Trudel and Cotte (2009) identified that merely knowing that a company is being sustainable is a bigger driver of consumers' willingness to pay more than exactly how sustainable it is. However, consumer willingness to pay more may become moot as the streamlining and optimising of sustainable production processes and supply chains, along with employee efficiency, bring traditionally higher prices of sustainable products more in line with their conventional counterparts. More generally, while sustainable products often cost more upfront, many may cost less in the long run, such as high-efficiency dishwashers and washing machines that use less water and electricity.

Consumers can also be loyal to sustainable companies over the longer run, buying from them again and again, and spreading positive word-of-mouth. Sustainable companies, such as Ben & Jerry's, Patagonia and Lush Cosmetics, all have loyal customers who act as evangelists for these brands. For example, Twitter users recently praised Patagonia for boycotting Facebook over the latter's prioritising of profits over consumer welfare. Particularly intriguing is consumer resistance to negative information about a sustainable company or its products. This can even turn to forgiveness if the company has truly transgressed. More generally, a reputation for sustainability reduces consumer anger and negative feedback following service failures, mitigating the potential for such actions to damage corporate image and credibility. Not surprisingly, consumers are forgiving when a company responds to a service failure through sustainability-related actions, such as donating money to a charity on behalf of the consumer (Thomassen et al., 2020).

Consumers may also impose penalties on companies they believe to be behaving unsustainably or deceiving people about their sustainability actions. Penalties come in the form of not buying from them and spreading negative publicity about the company. In some cases, this culminates in larger-scale boycotts of such companies (see Chapter 13). For example, high-end department store Fortnum & Mason stopped selling foie gras, made through the force-feeding of ducks and geese, after several years of protests against their sale of this luxury food. While minimising anti-company behaviours are crucial to the success of a company, in this chapter we focus on consumer responses to the efforts of companies to be sustainable, rather than to lapses in sustainability.

14.2.2   Pro-Sustainability Behaviours

A company's sustainability efforts can also alter a broader set of consumer behaviours, helping the company create societal value. While these behaviours do not necessarily contribute as directly to a company's success as do behaviours such as purchase, loyalty and positive word-of-mouth, they are consequential and essential positive outcomes because they reduce unsustainable modes of consumption and, ideally, increase regenerative modes of consumption (i.e., ones that restore, renew or revitalise the world's resources). Such behaviours go beyond choosing products with sustainable sourcing, production and features to include not only the sustainable use and disposal of products, but also a broader set of sustainable consumption behaviours ranging from reducing power, fuel and water waste to contributing, through time, money or human capital/expertise, to social and environmental causes and movements.

Clearly, it is difficult to draw a hard line between the two basic kinds of behaviours we have discussed so far. A case in point is the movement towards waste-minimising, closed loop supply chains, in which a company buys back its products when these are no longer functional or needed by the consumer, employing reverse logistics to repair and resell the products or reuse parts in future products. Clothing companies such as Arc'teryx and The North Face, for example, take back their consumers' old clothing in exchange for a credit towards future purchases, refurbishing these used items for reuse. Such regenerative consumer-to-business (C2B) transactions are both pro-company, in that they may contribute to a company's economic success, and pro-sustainability. In fact, the same could be said for the purchase of sustainable products, through which the consumer contributes to the well-being of the planet and its people. However, the two types of behaviours differ along the prosperity dimension because the economic benefits to the company are more direct and apparent in pro-company behaviours – the focus of this chapter – than in the more generally sustainable ones.

14.2.3   Summary

A company's sustainability efforts can change its consumers' behaviour in two ways. The first, pro-company behaviours, are directed at the company, helping it succeed, whereas the second, pro-sustainability behaviours, include consumers' embrace of sustainability behaviours in general.

14.3   Psychological Drivers of Pro-Company Behaviours: The 3 U's Framework

Now, we turn to an examination of the three processes that jointly determine how consumers respond to corporate sustainability. The psychological engine that drives consumers' reactions to sustainability is made up of the 3 U's: Understanding, Utility and Unity. We discuss each of these U's in more detail in the sections that follow.

14.3.1   Understanding

Today, sustainability information is everywhere. Think back to the opening set of questions. It is likely that one or more of the products you looked at conveyed sustainability information. Perhaps a product or the company website prominently featured that the company is environmentally conscious (e.g., uses eco-labelling), is made with fair-trade ingredients, uses recycled materials or packaging, donates money to specific causes or contains all-natural/organic ingredients.

You may also have been exposed to such information through advertising. On Earth Day 2021, for instance, many companies, including P&G, Apple, Budweiser and SodaStream, released ads to get consumers to care about the environment. Similarly, the sustainability strategies and achievements of more and more companies are also available to consumers on company websites, often as comprehensive sustainability reports. A recent KPMG survey reveals that 80 per cent of companies worldwide now report on their sustainability actions (KPMG Impact, 2020).

At the same time, media reporting on sustainability is at an all-time high, with global coverage of climate change at its highest level in over a decade (Media and Climate Change Observatory, 2021). Pieces on corporate sustainability range from everyday reports of different initiatives companies are engaging in, general surveys about the importance of sustainability to companies today and, importantly, overall rankings of companies on sustainability (e.g., Newsweek, 2019). In short, consumers today are continually exposed to corporate sustainability information from a range of company and non-company sources.

Critically, though, exposure does not equal understanding. Understanding hinges on consumers' active attention to sustainability information and reflects the extent to which they deliberate on this information, and what kinds of meanings they generate. And, in general, many consumers still have a fairly limited understanding of sustainability itself, let alone the engagement of companies with it.

There are three basic reasons for this. First, for many consumers, sustainability is still not a major consideration in deciding what to buy or who to buy from. For instance, an Earth Day, Ipsos Global Advisor (2020) survey showed that while consumers are concerned about the environment, their willingness to make an effort to consume sustainably has not evolved much since 2014. As a result, curiosity about such information among many consumers remains fairly low.

Second, sustainability information, while plentiful, is often delivered to consumers in a fragmented, piecemeal manner, with different sources providing a diversity of perspectives and sometimes contradictory opinions. This is complicated by the fact that a company's sustainability actions span a range of domains, with often uneven and sometimes conflicting sustainability performance across these domains. For example, Walmart has committed to reaching zero emissions across its supply chain by 2040, and yet has been criticised for its labour decisions, such as cutting worker hours while increasing workload. This makes it difficult for consumers to come up with clear assessments of how sustainable a company really is. At the same time, many consumers are not familiar with the vocabulary of sustainability, ranging from the often-technical information conveyed on product packaging, such as unpronounceable sustainability-oriented product features and obscure third-party certifications, to even terms such as SDGs and B Corps.

Third, focusing on sustainability information can sometimes be psychologically aversive for consumers because such information often centres on the ills of the world. In addition, consumers sometimes have trouble combining a company's sustainability information with more basic, critical product information such as price and quality. Together, these can actually cause consumers to sometimes actively avoid acquiring such information about products when making choices.

Generally, then, many consumers tend to process sustainability information rather heuristically and idiosyncratically, using available and often simple inputs such as an eco-label on a product, or information they glean from other people, the media or advertising. Such processing tends to be based more on what the company is doing rather than what exactly it has achieved (i.e., its sustainability effectiveness) and produces binary yes/no appraisals of sustainability (e.g., a company is sustainable or not sustainable) rather than a more nuanced sense of the extent to which a company is sustainable.

Central to this understanding, however cursory, are the inferences consumers make based on a company's sustainability actions. These inferences are of two kinds. The first involves inferences about the regular (i.e., performance-based) features of a sustainable product. The second involves inferences about the company's motives for being sustainable, and what that says about the company.

14.3.1.1   Product Performance Inferences

Research has shown that consumers often use their knowledge of a company's sustainability actions, both general and product-specific, to make inferences about how well its products might perform in terms of their basic functions. Interestingly, such inferences can be both positive and negative. Sustainable products sometimes seem to suffer from what some researchers call a sustainability liability, wherein consumers infer weaker performance for products with one or more sustainability features. This is reflected, more generally, in research that documents an adverse influence of product sustainability information on product efficacy judgments. For instance, green products can be deemed less rather than more effective by consumers for whom environmental concerns are a high priority. Such inferences are based on consumers' underlying sense that the resources companies devote to sustainability are diverted from those devoted to maximising or enhancing product performance on the more conventional dimensions, causing companies to sacrifice the latter for the former.

At the same time, a company's sustainability actions seem to sometimes enhance perceptions of product performance. For instance, across a diversity of product categories (e.g., wine, a hair-loss treatment, a teeth-whitening product and resolution-enhancing software), a study found that consumers rate products as more efficacious when they are produced by companies engaged in sustainability initiatives even when they can directly observe and experience these products (Chernev and Blair, 2020). Similarly, consumers, particularly those who care more about sustainable consumption, rate even the non-environmental features of green products more positively (Haws et al., 2014) and ascribe greater healthiness (Minton and Cornwell, 2015; Peloza et al., 2015) to sustainable food products. Interestingly, these positive performance inferences based on sustainability seem most likely to happen when consumers view the company as a moral entity, doing good for the world and the people in it.

14.3.1.2 Company Motive Inferences

When a company tells consumers about how good their products are, consumers do not ask, 'Why is a company telling me this?' However, when consumers learn about a company's actions in the sustainability domain, particularly when they hear it from the company itself, consumers wonder why a company is engaging in these actions and telling them about it. This is because while consumers expect companies to extol the virtues of their products, they do not necessarily expect companies to extol their own virtues. In other words, consumers continue to see a contradiction between the inherent self-interest – including profit-seeking – of companies and their motivations to do good for the planet and its people, making them suspicious of corporate sustainability. A recent survey showed that while 73 per cent of consumers expect brands to be sustainable, 71 per cent don't believe that brands will actually deliver on their sustainability promises (Havas Group, 2021).

This ambient scepticism can manifest in consumer perceptions of company deceit, for example, greenwashing, which refers to consumers' beliefs that a company cares more about presenting itself as environmentally friendly than on actually minimising its environmental impact. As an example, Allbirds is facing a class-action lawsuit alleging that its claims that its running shoes have a low carbon footprint are misleading because of the narrow tools it used to measure environmental impact (Truth in Advertising, 2022). Interestingly, such scepticism can be instrumental in making companies withhold their sustainability credentials from consumers, a phenomenon known as green-hushing.

Consumers also make inferences about the motives of specific companies based on sustainability information about them. These are of two basic kinds. The first of these, not surprisingly given the sceptical backdrop against which consumers make these inferences, are to self-serving motives; consumers infer that the company is engaging in sustainability to selfishly boost revenues, profits or reputation. This is sometimes referred to pejoratively as green-selling, when a company highlights the greenness of its offerings to sell more products. On the other hand, consumers may ascribe altruistic motives to a company, inferring that the company genuinely cares about helping the planet and its people. Attributions can vary even within these two

Figure 14.2 Factors determining the fit between a company and its sustainability initiatives

basic types. For instance, consumers can infer that the company is acting in line with its values, that sustainability is part of its strategic objectives (e.g., targeting a new customer group) or that is doing what is demanded by stakeholders. Notably, these two categories of causal inferences are not mutually exclusive; consumers increasingly infer mixed (i.e., self-serving and altruistic) motives.

These causal inferences are based on many different characteristics of a specific sustainability effort (e.g., its perceived fit with the company's core competencies, customer base and/or competitive positioning), which we will discuss later in this chapter (Figure 14.2). For now, it is important to be aware that these motive inferences are not only subjective, but have also been shown to guide consumers' pro-company behaviours. While inferences of other-serving, and even mixed, motives can produce positive responses from consumers, they are less inclined to support a company when its sustainability actions are attributed to purely selfish motives. This is consistent with consumers' inferences about the authenticity of a company's sustainability efforts, or the extent to which it is honest and transparent about these efforts, which is becoming increasingly important in driving consumers' pro-company behaviours.

14.3.2 Utility

Consumers want their products to be useful to them. They look for not just functional benefits, which are the more tangible outcomes associated with product use (e.g., being able to run faster with a pair of sneakers), but also more abstract, psychosocial benefits, which refer to the psychological self-expressive or social outcomes associated with product use (e.g., being admired by others for a pair of sneakers). Products also provide emotional benefits, in the form of positive emotions experienced by consumers because of product ownership and use (Peter and Olsen, 2009).

Not surprisingly, then, consumers respond more positively to sustainability initiatives that provide functional, psychosocial and/or emotional benefits. These can come from the consumption of sustainable products themselves or by purchasing from companies that prioritise sustainability. We discuss each of the three benefits in more detail in the sections that follow.

14.3.2.1 Functional Utility

On average, the current prices of sustainable products are almost double those of their conventional counterparts. Given that most consumers look to get their money's worth from their product purchases, it might be tempting to conclude that the functional value of sustainable products is generally low. However, consumers do sometimes glean functional benefits from corporate sustainability endeavours. For instance, while the upfront costs of certain green products (e.g., appliances such as washing machines or dishwashers) are higher, over time they consume fewer resources (e.g., electricity, water), making them cost-efficient in the longer run. A good example is LED light bulbs, which cost about five times as much as incandescent bulbs to purchase, but consume less than 25 per cent of the energy of their incandescent counterparts and last fifty times longer.

In the close association of sustainability with the environment and society, what sometimes gets lost is the product dimension of corporate sustainability. To elaborate, the notion of corporate sustainability is not just restricted to the protection of the environment and attention to the world's social problems, but also, more basically, the provision of high quality, healthy, safe and durable products, which maximise consumer benefits and minimise consumer harm. This is particularly true for categories such as food, personal hygiene, clothing and household goods, including electronics (Speed Queen washers and dryers, to give but one example).

Functional benefits can also come through participation, more specifically, in social programmes that companies engage in as part of their sustainability efforts. For instance, the Crest Healthy Smiles programme was implemented by Procter & Gamble to help improve the oral hygiene and health of children in disadvantaged communities in the United States. In a study of this programme, it was evident that participants received functional benefits in the form of healthier teeth and gums (Du et al., 2011).

14.3.2.2 Psychosocial Utility

Consuming from sustainable companies is a moral act because you are not just thinking about yourself, but also about others, putting the longer-term well-being of other people ahead of your own shorter-term gains. Thus, many of the psychosocial benefits of consuming from sustainable companies are tied to the ability of a consumer to signal that they are a moral person, not just to others, but also, importantly, to themselves.

14.3.2.2.1   Self-Signalling and Self-Expression Engaging in behaviours that help others can help us signal our goodness to ourselves, letting us know that we are good people. Since sustainable products carry in them the promise of helping the planet and its people, consuming such products allows us to signal our goodness to ourselves. Put differently, consuming sustainable products allows us to enhance our sense of who we are (i.e., I am a good person), making us feel better about ourselves. You may not be surprised to learn, then, that consumers are more likely to consume sustainably after they have engaged in some morally/ethically questionable behaviour or are, more generally, not feeling so great about themselves and their abilities.

Related to self-signalling benefits are the self-expressive benefits certain consumers get from consuming sustainably. Consumers who already know themselves as socially or environmentally conscious and are, more generally, concerned about the well-being of the planet and its people can be motivated to consume sustainable products because that is consistent with, and expresses, their sense of who they are. In that, they are not so much trying to become a better person by consuming sustainably as they are trying to be consistent with their sense of being a good person. Such self-expressive benefits also help consumers avert the negative feelings that can arise when they experience a discrepancy between who they think they are and how they consume.

14.3.2.2.2   Other-Signalling Buying sustainable products can also help consumers signal their goodness to others, fulfilling our needs to belong and for status. For example, shopping at Patagonia or carrying a Trader Joe's-branded tote bag signals that you support sustainability. This is particularly true of sustainable products that cost more, and can sometimes even be of lower quality, as the higher cost and possibly lower quality can make such products costly, and can therefore be a credible signal of goodness. Our desire to let people know that we are a moral person who cares about others is critical to our inclusion, acceptance and even respect within not only our network of family and friends, but also, often more crucially, our wider social circles and communities.

These distinct but related benefits consumers can get by consuming from sustainable companies interact to produce some interesting dynamics. For instance, consumers seem to prefer the more altruistic self-expressive and self-signalling benefits to the more instrumental functional and other-signalling benefits. As a result, when sustainable products are marketed using a combination of such appeals (e.g., this water bottle is good for the environment – which is an appeal to one's own environmental consciousness – and helps signal your green-friendly values to others), the more instrumental appeals can 'crowd out' or reduce the persuasiveness of the self-expressive appeals, causing consumers to want the product less than if it has been advertised with only a self-expressive appeal (Edinger-Schons et al., 2018). Second, the psychosocial benefits consumers receive from consuming sustainably can, ironically, make them behave less ethically after they have consumed such products. This is because most people find it challenging to be good and moral all the time, and feel that the moral credit they accumulate by consuming sustainably gives them the licence to be selfish, by consuming in non-sustainable ways or behaving antisocially.

14.3.2.3 Affective/Emotional Utility

For most people, consuming in a way that is good for the planet and its people feels good. For instance, the purchase of a reusable S'well water bottle may 'feel' better than purchasing several single-use water bottles. Many studies document the warm glow consumers feel after they consume sustainably (Capgemini Research Institute, 2020). These warm, fuzzy positive feelings of satisfaction and joy come from consumers' sense that they are 'doing their part' to help others and can be distinct from the positive emotions that can accompany the achievement of the more specific functional and psychosocial needs we discussed earlier. Interestingly, a recent study shows that these feelings of warm glow can come from merely using a sustainable product, regardless of whether or not the consumer actually chose it (Tezer and Bodur, 2020).

The emotional benefits of using sustainable products can also come from emotions that are linked to the well-being of others, as opposed to oneself. These emotions, often called moral emotions, range from negative to positive. Negative moral emotions are guilt, embarrassment and shame, whereas positive moral emotions include elevation – that warm, fuzzy optimistic feeling we get when we witness the kind acts of others – gratitude, admiration and pride. As we would expect, sustainable consumption can help reduce any negative moral emotions we feel, or anticipate feeling, if we care about sustainability but do not end up consuming sustainably. Similarly, consuming from a sustainable company can make us feel elevated, grateful and proud of both the company and ourselves. An interesting study of consumers' vindictive behaviours towards a company following a product failure shows that such anti-company behaviours are mitigated by the gratitude consumers felt towards the company when it was engaged in sustainability prior to the product failure (Kim and Park, 2020). Furthermore, studies show that the elevation consumers feel in response to the sustainability actions of a company drives a variety of pro-company behaviours (Xie et al., 2019).

14.3.3 Unity

At a fundamental level, a company's engagement in sustainability says something about who it is and what it stands for. A company's actions in the sustainability domain reveal its values, or its 'soul', particularly if such actions are genuine or at least deemed as such by consumers. These values can connect consumers to companies in strong and deep ways, creating an enduring and rewarding bond between the two. In that sense, corporate sustainability can produce a sense of unity between consumers and a company, based on the perception that the company and consumers stand for the same things. Many consumers, for instance, are loyal to Ben & Jerry's both because they like their ice cream and they like the causes the company supports, which include addressing climate change and disclosing GMOs in food labelling. This is particularly true for certain groups of consumers, such as those belonging to Generation Z.

As you might imagine, this deep, values-based sense of unity produced by corporate sustainability can make consumers feel more strongly positive about a company than how they feel based on the functional and psychosocial utility they gain. In that sense, we can think of this U as not only the most powerful of the 3 U's in producing sustainability-based pro-company outcomes, but also as critically dependent on the precise nature of consumers' Understanding and Utility. If, for instance, consumers perceive a company's sustainability to be motivated by pure self-interest, then they are unlikely to feel a sense of unity with the company, regardless of the values its sustainability actions embody. Similarly, this sense of unity is more likely to emerge from self-signalling and self-expression benefits consumers derive from corporate sustainability than from the functional or other-signalling motives we discussed earlier.

We can think of Unity as the ultimate driver of consumer response to corporate sustainability. This raises two questions. What is the exact nature of this Unity? And why do consumers connect in this way with certain companies? As humans, we have three kinds of fundamental needs related to our identity, or our sense of who we are and how this makes us feel. First, we want to have a clear sense for who we are, which is an identity-definitional need. Second, we want to feel good about ourselves, which is an identity-enhancement need. Finally, we want to feel special and unique, which we can call an identity-distinctiveness need.

One way we fulfil these needs is by affiliating with other people, groups and organisations, incorporating these social identities into our own in ways that allow us to use parts of those identities to meet our three identity-related needs. Studies show that we may also incorporate appealing social identities from companies that we support. When a company embodies values and traits we want to acquire or emulate, we make it part of our own identity. Through this process, known as identification, the company becomes a part of who we are and how we see ourselves and, therefore, very important to us.

Genuinely sustainable companies are prime candidates for such identification, as their values can help consumers meet their self-definitional and self-enhancement needs, and often even their self-distinctiveness ones. When this happens, consumers put great trust in the company and its actions and feel very strongly about it, seeing its successes as their success. Naturally, consumers who identify with such a company become strong advocates of it and its products, taking on the role of a brand evangelist, such as in the case, as we discussed earlier, of Patagonia.

Consumers identify with only a small number of companies. In fact, the Havas Group's Meaningful Brands (2021) report, which is based on a survey of about 400,000 consumers from around the world, shows that while consumers crave transparency and authenticity from brands, 75 per cent of brands could disappear without consumers really caring. Certain brands, however, stand out in this sea of consumer cynicism and indifference. Some usual suspects in the United States are Patagonia, Ben and Jerry's, TOMS Shoes, Warby Parker and Dr. Bronner's. As more and more brands start to engage with socio-political activism, by taking a stance on controversial socio-political issues such as abortion, same-sex marriage, immigration and gun control, this relatively new, powerful and values-revealing dimension of sustainability has the potential to arouse consumer passions and increase their identification with brands whose socio-political values match their own.

14.3.4 Summary

In this section, we learned about the three psychological processes that guide consumers' pro-company behaviours towards companies engaged in sustainability: Understanding, Utility and Unity. These three processes are highly interdependent, as represented in the 3 U's framework.

Now that we have learned about the 3 U's and how they work, a key question remains: What factors determine how well these three processes work synergistically to produce pro-company outcomes? In this chapter's final section, we discuss the different aspects of the consumer, the company and the context in which the consumer interacts with corporate sustainability that affect the specifics of each U, determining ultimately their joint efficacy in driving pro-company behaviours.

14.4 Contingencies that Impact the 3 U's and Consumer Behaviours

As in all domains of human life, no two consumers react exactly the same way to what companies do in terms of sustainability. Specifically, what consumers understand about a company's sustainability efforts, what types of and how much utility they get from these efforts, and whether this produces in them a sense of unity all vary with many different aspects of the consumer herself, the company in question and the context in which a consumer interacts with corporate sustainability. In this section, we go through some key aspects of the consumer, the company and the context that have been shown to determine how consumers process and embrace corporate sustainability information, and the extent to which it guides their pro-company behaviours.

14.4.1   Aspects of the Consumer

Traits that influence consumer reactions can be separated into two categories. The first is demographics, which is the objective characteristics that are used to describe a population. These include physical characteristics such as age (and, more broadly, generation), gender, race and ethnicity, and socio-economic ones like income level, employment, location, homeownership and level of education. The second category is psychographics, which pertains to the psychological characteristics of consumers, such as their attitudes and opinions, aspirations, values, lifestyles and interests. Demographics help us understand who the consumer is, whereas psychographics help us understand what, how and why they think, feel and behave the way they do. Naturally, different demographic groups are likely to also vary on their psychographics.

14.4.1.1   Demographics

The age of consumers greatly impacts their relationship to corporate sustainability. Given its ongoing evolution, it is not surprising that younger generations are more attuned to corporate sustainability than are older ones. Surveys show that millennials and Generation Z exhibit a greater preference for sustainable consumption and also a greater willingness to pay for such products than do Gen X and baby boomers. Younger generations are more sensitive to the authenticity and trustworthiness of sustainability, demanding that the sustainability actions of companies are not only clearly rooted in their overall purpose and values, but also reflect those of their consumers. Along with their greater monitoring of sustainability information in general, younger consumers, then, are likely to differ from older generations in terms of all three of the U's we discussed earlier.

Similarly, gender, household income and formal education all affect consumers' thoughts, feelings and behaviours pertaining to corporate sustainability. Women, for instance, are more likely than men to consume sustainably, due in part to their greater agreeableness, interdependence and openness to experience. Men, on the other hand, often consider sustainable consumption to be less masculine and tend to avoid sustainable products, causing a male-oriented brand such as Jack Daniel's to integrate sustainability thoughtfully into its core messaging. Thus, the social and self-expressive benefits to women are likely to be greater. Similarly, the finding that middle-class consumers have a greater desire for green products than their lower- and upper-class counterparts can be understood in terms of the greater other-signalling value of such products to this social class, allowing this group to both assimilate with its own class and differentiate from the lower class.

Finally, consumers from different parts of the world have different relationships with corporate sustainability. A recent study suggests that consumers in Asia/ Pacific and Africa/Middle East report higher sustainability concerns than those in Europe and the Americas (PwC Global Consumer Insights Pulse Survey, 2021). A study involving sustainability in luxury markets found that differences in consumer knowledge about sustainability as well as their association of this with the concept of luxury (i.e., differences in understanding and utility) influenced how German versus Korean consumers reacted to luxury and non-luxury products that communicated their sustainability on social media (Kong et al., 2021).

14.4.1.2 Psychographics

Underlying many of the demographic differences discussed above are differences in the psychological make-up of consumers. These include differences in beliefs, preferences, behaviours and values both general, and specific to sustainability. For example, consumers vary in the extent to which they believe a company's sustainability efforts detract from (i.e., trade-off belief), rather than reinforce (i.e., win-win belief), its core business endeavours. These beliefs alter consumers' inferences about the extent to which sustainability has a positive or negative effect on the more functional features of products (i.e., Understanding), causing those with trade-off beliefs to want sustainable products less than consumers holding win-win beliefs.

Turning to preferences, consumers vary in their affinity for the different dimensions of sustainability and the specific issues that companies focus on, such as environmental protection or social causes. These preferences determine not only the utility consumers obtain from a company's sustainability initiatives, but also their chances of feeling a sense of unity with it. More generally, consumers also vary in the extent to which they care about sustainability itself. A recent global survey revealed that most people are either value-driven consumers or purpose-driven consumers (Haller et al., 2020). While value-driven consumers care most about getting their money's worth, focusing on price and convenience in their brand choices, purpose-driven consumers consume based on how well the brands match their personal values and who, importantly, 'walks the talk' when it comes to sustainability. Naturally, purpose-driven consumers are not only more likely to consume only from companies that get sustainability right, but also their 3 U's are likely to be different from their value-driven counterparts.

On the topic of values, as we discussed earlier, sustainability done right ultimately speaks to the values of the company and its consumers. Thus, consumer responses to corporate sustainability hinge critically on the type of values a consumer embodies. These range from sustainability-specific ones like green consumption values to a wide range of general ones like altruism, social consciousness, political ideology (i.e., conservative versus liberal) and what is called the collectivism/interdependence orientation, which espouses giving greater importance to the social collective than to the individual. For instance, communally oriented consumers, who care for the welfare and needs of others, value corporate sustainability more than exchange-oriented consumers, who subscribe to reciprocity or quid pro quo relationships. Similarly, altruistic and biospheric (i.e., always taking into consideration the costs or benefits to the biological balance on Earth) values increase consumers' choice of sustainable products due to the greater utility they derive from such products (White et al., 2019).

More broadly, consumers who are chronically focused on the future, seeing the world around them in more abstract and interconnected ways, likely understand sustainability differently and see more utility in it than do other consumers. As a result, future-focused consumers like sustainable products more than those who are more present-focused. Similarly, differences in mindfulness and connectedness to nature – which reflect how consumers like to lead their lives – increase environmental concern and sustainable behaviours. On the other hand, consumers vary on how materialistic they are (materialism values), and more materialistic people prefer sustainable products if the products and their marketing focus on the benefits to themselves rather than to others (White et al., 2019).

A final point: demographics and psychographics do not work in isolation; each consumer is a complex mixture of the two. For instance, the 'green consumer' has certain demographics and psychographics that work together to drive pro-company behaviours, such as a relatively high level of education, social consciousness, health consciousness and spirituality. Similarly, we can think of a consumer's political ideology, which has been shown to affect their 3 U's and subsequent pro-company behaviours, as a coherent collection of values, rather than as a single factor.

14.4.2   Aspects of the Company

As we discussed earlier, one of the most crucial parts of Understanding are the inferences consumers make about a company's motives for engaging in sustainability. Not surprisingly, then, several aspects of the company, and its relationship to the specific sustainability issues it engages in, determine the extent to which consumers infer altruistic, other-serving motives as opposed to primarily self-serving motives, raising concerns about 'sustainability-washing'.

One of the most studied among these aspects is consumers' perceived fit between the company and the sustainability issue in which it engages (Figure 14.2). To decide whether this fit is low or high, consumers appraise this fit routinely, based on dimensions ranging from brand positioning (e.g., Dove's Real Beauty campaign) and target market (e.g., Avon's support of breast cancer treatment) to the colour schemes of the company's and cause's visual materials. A higher fit perception typically produces more other-serving motive inferences, based in part on consumers thinking that the issue 'makes sense' for the company and is one in which the company can actually make a difference. Sometimes, though, high fit runs the risk of backfiring, especially when consumers are unable or unwilling to ascribe altruistic motives to a company's actions, as in the case of tobacco companies promoting respiratory health or even urging its consumers to smoke less, and alcohol companies encouraging their consumers to drink responsibly. For example, Philip Morris received significant backlash for supporting a youth smoking prevention campaign.

More generally, consumers' motive inferences, along with other aspects of their Understanding, and even the Utility they obtain, help consumers decide whether the company is basically good, caring and genuinely concerned about the well-being of the world at large. Thus, the same sustainability actions of a company can be understood differently based on different characteristics of the company. For instance, when a company is positioned on sustainability (e.g., Stonyfield Farm yogurt), rather than engaging in sustainability (e.g., Dannon), consumers are more likely to see the company as genuinely caring and are more likely to feel a sense of Unity with it and engage in more pro-company behaviours. This is reflected at the product level in higher 'green' judgments of a product when the same environmental benefits are associated with its central features (i.e., defining characteristics) rather than its peripheral ones. More generally, knowledge about a company's sustainability lapses can, naturally, diminish the positive Understanding and Utility of a company's sustainable actions.

This 'goodness' halo, which we learnt about earlier, is more likely to arise from the 3 U's if the sustainability is associated with the company (i.e., corporate sustainability) rather than its specific brands. Furthermore, this halo is more likely to accrue to companies that are pioneers in sustainability, setting the trend (e.g., Stella McCartney), rather than ones following the trend. This points, more generally, to the key role played by the competitive context in how consumers understand and discern value in a company's sustainability actions. The same sustainability actions are going to be understood differently depending on the industry a company belongs to. Consumers' Understanding of and Utility from the sustainability actions of tobacco and oil and gas companies, or more generally vice product categories, such as pornography, will be different from those of more inherently sustainable virtue categories. Thus, the 3 U's consumers derive from the pro-environmental campaign of a pornography company such as Pornhub's recent one are likely to be different from those if such a campaign was launched by a health food company. Similarly, studies show that consumers' responses to sustainability in luxury product categories are more complicated than those for, say, consumer packaged goods, since many see an inherent contradiction between what sustainability means and what luxury stands for. Thus, the increasing number of luxury fashion companies trying to be sustainable (e.g., Prada, Gucci) may face an uphill battle convincing consumers that they are believable.

Finally, the more a company involves its consumers in its sustainability efforts, the more positively consumers will respond in terms of both the 3 U's and the pro-company behaviours that follow. For instance, one study showed that when a company allows consumers to choose the specific sustainability issue(s) it engages with, their sense of a heightened personal role (a benefit) and greater sense of Unity make them behave more positively towards the company (Robinson et al., 2012).

14.4.3   Aspects of the Context

Consumer- and company-specific characteristics aside, aspects of the specific situation or context in which the consumer interacts with the company and its sustainability actions are also likely to impact consumer responses. Thinking back to the opening example, how much time you had to make your choice would be an example of the decision context. As you might imagine, if you had more time and were making your purchase on a desktop computer or even at a store rather than on a small mobile device, you might be more likely to focus on, or even seek out, sustainability information about the brands you considered.

In section 14.4.1, we discussed many enduring and relatively permanent aspects of the consumer (e.g., their age, income and values) that alter their responses to corporate sustainability. However, some other aspects can be temporarily activated by the context. For instance, aspects of the context that heighten consumers' sense of self-accountability, or the extent to which they feel they should adhere to the standards they set for themselves, can increase their guilt over not consuming from sustainable companies, drawing them to the products of such companies. More generally, because sustainability centres on taking care of the future, any aspect of the context that gets consumers to think more abstractly or focus on how sustainability provides longer-term benefits can make them see more Utility in such actions. Such a future mindset also reduces the Utility consumers see in the more economic benefits to themselves of consuming from sustainable companies.

Much of this context is determined by how sustainability information is communicated to consumers by companies. Many studies have shown that consumers' responses to corporate sustainability are very sensitive to the precise – and often subtle – variations in the message, the copy and the media through which such information is communicated. For instance, while more and more companies are using the communication tactic of storytelling to engage consumers with their sustainability messages, the general scepticism consumers have towards corporate sustainability can make them see selfish motives in a company's use of such a potentially manipulative ploy, pushing them away from such messages and pro-company behaviours. Along these lines, message and copy elements such as message frames and the number of claims, the communicated gravity of the CSR issue, the future versus present framing of both the CSR issue and the company's response and the abstractness of the sustainability information have been shown to influence one or more of the 3 U's and behaviours (White et al., 2019). The source of the communication matters as well: to consumers, non-profit partners in a sustainability initiative are more credible than their corporate counterparts. And, given our discussion of greenwashing, it is not surprising that consumers react negatively to high spending on sustainability-related advertising and, more specifically, to communications that contradict a firm's sustainable actions, such as a positive corporate environmental policy statement, but negative environmental behaviour.

Even incidental aspects of the context can influence consumer responses to corporate sustainability. For instance, in the opening example, if you settled on your final set of brands by disqualifying certain brands (i.e., process of exclusion) as opposed to qualifying certain brands (i.e., process of inclusion), studies suggest that you probably focused more on sustainability information (Irwin and Naylor, 2009). And if you happened to shop on a hot day, you were probably more conscious about global warming and more likely to take the products' environment-friendliness into account in deciding which brand to purchase (Li et al., 2011).

14.4.4 Summary
The 3 U's process through which corporate sustainability influences consumers' pro-company behaviours is likely to hinge critically on several aspects of both the consumer and the company whose sustainability involvement the consumer is responding to. Furthermore, many aspects of the specific context in which the consumer responds to a company can determine how consumers respond.

14.5 Chapter Summary

This chapter presented a detailed and nuanced psychological account of when, how and why consumers respond to corporate sustainability. To see what we have learned, and how we could use this knowledge to make better decisions about corporate sustainability, let us circle back to the example we opened the chapter with, but view it now through the eyes of a company. If our product was one of the options the consumer in the opening example was considering, then what would our sustainability strategy need to be to maximise our chance of being chosen by the consumer?

To answer this question, we would need to start at the end of the chapter, and consider all the relevant aspects of our target consumer, who we are as a company and the context in which our consumer is most likely to be making her decision. This understanding would come from both secondary and possibly primary market research, and form the foundation of an effective and enduring sustainability strategy. This research would need to provide accurate insights into the nature and extent of our target market's Understanding of not just our corporate sustainability efforts, if any, but those of our competitors as well, the types of Utility consumers derive from these, and whether or not this Understanding and Utility produce Unity with us or our competitors.

Armed with this essential understanding, we can start to assemble a sustainability strategy that optimises our target market's Understanding, Utility and Unity. What sustainability issues does our consumer care the most about? How do they understand it? What actions do we need to take so that consumers ascribe our involvement to genuine concern, rather than just a cynical business move, which they are quick to see through? What sustainability-based benefits would be best for our consumer, and how might we best communicate those? How best can we foster a sense of Unity based on our sustainability strategy, through the issue we support, the difference we make through our support, and our communication thereof?

When the 3 U's have been optimised, both pro-company and pro-sustainability behaviours will follow. But we end with an important qualification. As we have learned from this book, consumers are only one of many stakeholders that companies need to heed in coming up with their sustainability strategies. And, ultimately, our understanding of the responses of consumers – and, indeed, all other stakeholders – to corporate sustainability needs to be in the service of ensuring that businesses are a genuine and effective force for the good of our planet and its people.

CHAPTER QUESTIONS

1. Define Unity in the context of consumers and corporate sustainability initiatives. How do Utility and Understanding affect a consumer's sense of Unity?
2. What are the three types of Utility? Explain how companies can tap into each type of Utility to successfully promote their sustainable products and sustainability initiatives.
3. Identify and describe the three reasons why many consumers lack a full and meaningful understanding of sustainability and corporate sustainability initiatives.
4. What factors might make a consumer sceptical about a company's claims that it engages in sustainable business practices?
5. What is the goodness halo? Think of some examples of products/brands for which such a halo might exist.
6. What are three pro-company behaviours that consumers exhibit in support of a company's sustainability efforts?
7. You and your team are designing a marketing campaign about your company's carbon-neutral, zero-waste line of clothing.
   a. What demographic and psychographic traits should you consider?
   b. Why should you be concerned about the inferences that consumers make about your sustainability claims?

c. How would you convince consumers that there is a good fit between the company's values and your sustainable clothing line?

d. Describe three ways that you can create a favourable context to drive sales of your sustainable clothing line.

FURTHER RESOURCES

- Bhattacharya, C. B., Sen, S. and Korschun, D. (2011). *Leveraging Corporate Responsibility: The Stakeholder Route to Maximizing Business and Social Value.* Cambridge: Cambridge University Press.

A psychological perspective on consumer and employee responses to corporate sustainability that fleshes out the 3 U's framework with recommendations for company action towards successful corporate sustainability.

- Smith, M. E. (2021). *Inspiring Green Consumer Choices: Leverage Neuroscience to Reshape Marketplace Behavior.* London and New York, NY: Kogan Page.

A neuroscience, behavioural economics and experimental psychology perspective on the behaviour-intention gap in sustainable consumption, and how companies can leverage these insights to get consumers to actually consume more sustainably.

- Triple Pundit (2020). The Top Eleven Must-See Sustainability Documentaries, www.triplepundit.com/story/2020/sustainability-documentaries/709211.

This website contains links to eleven documentaries that focus on different aspects of, and approaches to, sustainability. As you watch these, think about the role consumers might play in each, and how our learning from this chapter can help us better understand these roles, with the goal of achieving a more sustainable world.

PART III
Corporate Sustainability: Processes

15 Corporate Governance and Sustainability

ANDREAS RASCHE

LEARNING OBJECTIVES

- Learn about the different elements of the corporate governance system and how they affect corporate sustainability.

- Understand how boards can be designed so that they better consider ESG issues within their discussions.

- Study which challenges related to corporate governance represent issues that are addressed as part of a firm's sustainability strategies (e.g., board diversity).

- Review how corporate governance issues that are relevant to sustainability are regulated through mandatory and voluntary frameworks.

- Reflect on what a new, more sustainability friendly, paradigm of corporate governance could look like.

15.1 Introduction

On 18 June 2020, Wirecard – a firm specialising in payment transaction services and one of Germany's FinTech success stories – faced a problem. The *Financial Times* reported that the company's auditor EY refused to sign off the 2019 accounts, because €1.9 billion were 'missing' from the balance sheets (McCrum and Storbeck, 2019). Four days later, Wirecard put out a warning that the €1.9 billion likely never existed in the first place. Two banks in the Philippines, which allegedly were supposed to hold the money, said that they never had an account with this sum. On 22 June 2020, the firm's CEO, Markus Braun, was arrested and another three days later Wirecard filed for bankruptcy. Investigations revealed a number of irregularities, including opaque accounting techniques and failures of prior audits. First reports about possible irregularities at Wirecard already occurred months earlier. On 28 April 2020, one of the major investors in the company argued in an open letter that 'we are of the view that the supervisory board is legally obliged to intervene. In our opinion, the necessary intervention is now to remove the CEO from all management duties' (TCI Fund Management, 2020). Yet, the CEO stayed until 19 June 2020, leading to questions about whether the board should have acted earlier and with more force. Many observers attributed the scandal to poor corporate governance. Because of the scandal, Peter Dehnen, the chairperson of the Association of Supervisory Boards in Germany, called for more dialogue-based governance and a stronger involvement of stakeholders. He said: 'With the rules presently in place, I feel we are still back in the last century' (Browne, 2020).

As this opening case shows, poor corporate governance can threaten the very existence of firms. Yet, it can also be an important driver to steer companies in a more sustainable direction. This chapter looks at both perspectives. There are many definitions of what corporate governance is (and is not). As a start, let us use a broad definition and refer to the well-known *Cadbury Report* that was published in the United Kingdom in 1992. The report defined corporate governance as 'the system by which companies are directed and controlled' (The Committee on the Financial Aspects of Corporate Governance, 1992: para. 2.5). With the growth of corporations in the twentieth century, it became clear that such directing and controlling was needed. In many cases, the quick growth of corporations eroded the influence of owners. Hence, there was increased need to control what managers were doing and to control the risk that they were taking through their decisions and omissions. Corporate governance therefore aims at creating structures, processes and systems that enable a balanced consideration of the interests of a firm's stakeholders.

Well-designed corporate governance ensures that the firm is led in a responsible and sustainable way and that it is focused on long-term value creation. On the other hand, poorly designed corporate governance can quickly undermine a firm's perceived integrity and the transparency of its decisions. Almost all major corporate scandals throughout the last decades were in one way or another related to poorly exercised corporate governance. According to the Organisation for Economic Co-operation and Development (OECD), the financial crisis that hit the global economy in 2008 can be 'to an important extent attributed to failures and weaknesses in corporate governance' (Kirkpatrick, 2009: 2). Before and during the crisis, risk management systems failed and important information on firms' risk exposure did not reach boards and senior management. Also, companies' remuneration systems were not aligned with their strategic goals and therefore created an unhealthy risk appetite that undermined long-term thinking.

This chapter discusses the relationship between corporate governance and corporate sustainability. We will first look into the different components of the general (and to some extent idealised) corporate governance system. This gives us a good overview of the players involved in corporate governance, and it also allows us to revisit a central tension: shareholder- versus stakeholder-oriented governance. We then move on to discuss how well-designed corporate governance can support firms' sustainability efforts. We label this debate 'corporate governance *for* sustainability', and we discuss how sustainability topics can be integrated into the discussions of boards of directors. Next, we show that some aspects of corporate governance can themselves pose challenges that need to be discussed under the environmental, social and governance (ESG) umbrella. We label this debate 'corporate governance *as* sustainability', and we focus on topics that reflect the 'G' in ESG (e.g., executive compensation and CEO duality). Finally, we discuss elements of a redesigned corporate governance system, which would allow sustainability-related debates to be addressed better.

15.2 The Corporate Governance System

Before we start to explore how corporate governance and corporate sustainability are interrelated, it is important to reflect on two basic questions: (1) Who participates in corporate governance? and (2) What is the relationship between shareholders and stakeholders within corporate governance?

15.2.1 Who Participates in Corporate Governance?

Corporate governance practices and regulations differ across countries and regions. Despite these differences, we can outline a general corporate governance system (Figure 15.1) that explains which actors exist and what their roles are. Note that the precise nature and role of these actors within corporate governance depends on relevant national regulations and on institutionalised practices within a country. One important component of each corporate governance system are the firms' stakeholders (see Chapter 4). Much of the literature adopts a limited view and only considers a firm's shareholders as those with a legitimate place in governing the corporation. Legally speaking, shareholders can exercise more influence on the firm than other stakeholder groups, because they provide the capital. Shareholders usually elect the board at the annual general shareholders meeting. The board, in turn, reports to the shareholders before or during this meeting.

The board of directors is supposed to oversee the decisions that are made by executive management. It is the highest decision-making body within a company, and the management of the firm usually reports to the board. The composition and role of boards differs across regions. In the Anglo-Saxon corporate governance model (e.g., used in the United States and the United Kingdom), boards have executive and non-executive directors. Executive directors are managers within the company, while non-executive directors come from outside. In this model, the Chief Executive Officer (CEO) often acts as Chairperson of the board. In the continental corporate governance model (e.g., used in Germany and the Netherlands), the board is entirely composed of non-executive directors which can represent investors, unions or also the government. Because the CEO and executive management have no seat on the board, the

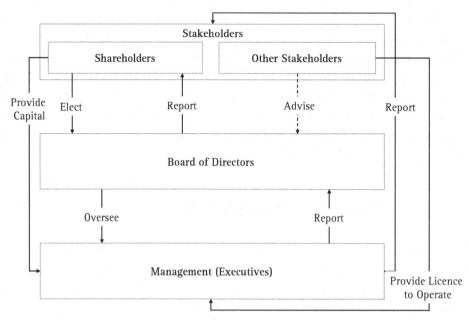

Figure 15.1 The corporate governance system demonstrates actors and roles across countries and regions

continental model better separates operational management from the board's oversight function. However, due to the exclusion of executives, boards under the continental model often lack first-hand business insights.

The corporate governance system outlined in Figure 15.1 deviates from some of the shareholder-focused systems. Shleifer and Vishny (1997: 737), for instance, see corporate governance as being exclusively concerned with '[t]he ways in which suppliers of finance assure themselves of getting a return on their investment'. The system outlined in Figure 15.1 acknowledges the role of shareholders, but it also highlights the role of other stakeholders. Although the role of stakeholders in corporate governance is, legally speaking, still not specified in most jurisdictions, they can influence the direction in which a firm is heading. On the one hand, some stakeholder groups participate directly in the board. For instance, German law stipulates that employee representatives must make up 50 per cent of all directors at board level (for firms with more than 2,000 employees). This gives unions a strong voice on German boards, although the Chairperson, who represents the investor side, has two votes in case of a draw. On the other hand, some firms have created advisory councils that allow them to include wider stakeholder opinions in board-level discussions. Although these councils have usually no formal authority and only provide recommendations, they are often used to compensate for skills and knowledge that do not exist within the board. For instance, Unilever has set up an external Sustainability Advisory Council that consists of seven independent external specialists who provide feedback on the development of the company's sustainability strategy (Lawrence et al., 2019).

15.2.2   The Shareholder-Stakeholder Nexus

Most firms acknowledge that they need to earn a societal licence to operate. Firms cannot just operate because shareholders are providing the necessary financial capital. They also operate because governments provide a legal framework for them to operate in (e.g., securing property rights), customers are willing to purchase their products and unions engage with them during collective bargaining processes. Shifts in societal expectations or corporate misconduct can threaten or even erode this licence, as the many corporate scandals related to sustainability issues show. To secure their licence to operate, many firms have started to disclose information not only to shareholders, but also to other stakeholder groups (see Chapter 17). The idea of producing an integrated corporate report is exactly about disclosing financial *and* non-financial information that is relevant to a firm's shareholders as well as to other stakeholder groups.

Looking at the shareholder-stakeholder nexus within corporate governance throws up one essential question: For whom should a firm create value? Not surprisingly, this question has sparked some controversy. Some have argued that shareholders should be given primacy and firms should be governed in ways that shareholder value is maximised (Rappaport, 1999), while others have suggested that corporations need to be governed in the interests of a wider array of stakeholders (Stout, 2012a). At the heart of this debate is the concept of 'fiduciary duties'. Such duties specify that board members must act in ways that put the interest of the organisation above any self-interest. Acknowledging one's fiduciary duties implies to act with care and remain loyal to the firm (Robé, 2011). For many decades, the dominant view was that the existence of fiduciary duties implies that directors are legally obliged to maximise value for shareholders *only*. However, with the rise of stakeholder thinking, this view became increasingly challenged. In 2009, the former CEO of General Electric, Jack Welch, even famously declared shareholder value to be 'the dumbest idea in the world' (Guerrera, 2009).

Recent interpretations of directors' fiduciary duties take a more holistic perspective, arguing that boards need to promote the overall value of the corporation and act in ways that are in the best long-term interest of the firm. The *Harvard Law School Forum on Corporate Governance* has summarised this shift in thinking as follows:

> The fiduciary duty of the board is to promote the value of the corporation. In fulfilling that duty, directors must exercise their business judgment in considering and reconciling the interests of various stakeholders – including shareholders, employees, customers, suppliers, the environment and communities – and the attendant risks and opportunities for the corporation. (Lipton, 2016)

In other words, fiduciary duty creates a positive duty on boards to consider sustainability-related issues. What justifies this broader interpretation of fiduciary duties? First, there is widespread agreement by now that in many cases ESG issues affect the risks that firms must cope with and the market opportunities they need to respond to (see Chapter 11). For instance, climate change poses new material risks for insurance companies, while it also pushes other companies to improve their resource productivity (e.g., in terms of energy efficiency). Second, legal frameworks increasingly ask corporations to consider stakeholder interests and to be transparent about how they do so. For instance, in the European Union, companies with more than 250 employees must disclose information about their ESG performance. Exercising care therefore implies fully aligning with these emerging legal require-ments. Stout (2012a: 3) summarises the debate by saying that 'the shareholder value ideology is just that – an ideology, not a legal requirement or a practical necessity of modern business life'.

Drawing a clear line between shareholder and stakeholder thinking is also not possible when considering the heterogeneity of shareholders. Many shareholders have interests beyond short-term wealth maximisation (Buchholtz et al., 2009: 328). Shareholders vary in terms of their underlying goals and investment horizons. Some institutional investors, like pension funds, explicitly invest in companies that have superior ESG performance (see Chapter 11), mostly because these companies are believed to follow a long-term orientation in their decision-making and hence expose investors to less risk. Other investors exercise 'active ownership' strategies in which they engage with companies on ESG-related topics and try to convince them to improve their sustainability strategies and the disclosure of information. The behaviour of these investors creates a situation in which managers cannot view shareholders and stakeholders as opposing forces, because addressing shareholders' interests inevitably implies also respecting and protecting stakeholders' rights.

The remainder of this chapter discusses the relationship between corporate gov-ernance and corporate sustainability in two interrelated ways: (1) it is possible to reflect on how a corporate governance system should be designed so that it can better address corporate sustainability (*corporate governance for sustainability*); and (2) it is possible to discuss how corporate governance itself can pose a challenge to corporate sustainability (*corporate governance as sustainability*). The first point relates to a management challenge – for instance, by asking: How do we create board-level structures that allow the firm to identify and address ESG issues? The second point relates to the 'G' in ESG and asks: Which governance-related problems reflect sustainability challenges?

15.3   Corporate Governance *for* Sustainability

Corporate governance can account for sustainability-related questions in different ways. We first reflect on the role of the board and then discuss how a firm's ownership structure can impact the management of ESG issues.

15.3.1 Designing Board Oversight of Sustainability

The relevance of boards of directors for corporate sustainability has long gone unnoticed. However, when looking at the classic tasks that boards perform, one quickly realises that almost all of these tasks have consequences for how sustainability is managed within a firm (see Table 15.1). One key task for each board is to oversee the strategy of the company and to discuss relevant risks and opportunities. Well-managed sustainability strategies are exactly about addressing such risks and opportunities, as long as firms address material sustainability topics and therefore move beyond generic social and environmental projects. Also, boards decide which C-level executives (i.e., senior executives in charge of entire departments and making company-wide decisions) are hired and how they are paid. This gives boards significant influence over whether sustainability is taken seriously or whether it remains detached from the core of the corporation. For instance, Unilever intensified its sustainability efforts after Paul Polman was hired as .CEO in 2009. Due to the progressive nature of the company, it introduced a Sustainability Progress Index in 2017. The Index makes up 25 per cent of executives' performance-based share incentive scheme, which itself is a part of the overall remuneration structure (Unilever, 2020).

Yet, implementing this new agenda at the board-level remains a challenge. In a survey, 86 per cent of managers believed that boards *should* play a strong role in overseeing the firm's sustainability efforts, while the survey also indicated that only 42 per cent of boards were engaging with such issues (Kiron et al., 2015). Few boards have specially dedicated committees that would address corporate sustainability. Paine (2014) argues that no more than 10 per cent of boards of major US public companies have established committees to discuss ESG topics. How can this gap be closed? One important aspect is to improve how boards organise themselves (Grayson and Kakabadse, 2013; Rasche and Lawrence, 2016). Sustainability often

Table 15.1 A comparison of the classic role and a sustainability-enhanced role of the board

	Classic role of the board	Sustainability-enhanced role of the board
Strategy Oversight	Oversee corporate strategy and identify relevant opportunities and risks	Oversee how material ESG factors influence firms' opportunities and risks
Succession Planning	Succession planning for C-level executives within the firm	Hiring executives who have experience with and knowledge of sustainability
Compensation	Determine and review executive compensation	Align executive compensation with sustainability objectives
Resource Allocation	Review and approve budgets and discuss financial resources	Review and approve resources to proactively manage ESG issues within firm

Table 15.2 Structural options for integrating sustainability into boards of directors

Structural option	Description	Possible benefits	Possible problems
Specialised Sustainability Committee	Develop a stand-alone committee at board level that discusses sustainability-related issues	Gives clear visibility to sustainability at board level	Isolates sustainability to this one committee – risk of 'silo mentality'
Tasking Entire Board with Sustainability	Puts sustainability frequently onto agenda of discussions of the entire board	Ensures buy-in by all directors and enables holistic assessment	Requires skills and knowledge by all directors
Adding Sustainability to Existing Committee	Add sustainability discussions to agenda of existing committees (e.g., risk management committee)	Better integration into existing discussions and easy to set up	Sustainability issues may fall off agenda and struggle for attention
Below-Board Committee on Sustainability	Develop a committee below the board (with non-board members) to provide a focal point for accessing knowledge	Easy to set up and less of a burden for already packed board agendas	Can only support (but not substitute for) board-level discussions

falls off the agenda, because boards are organised in ways that do not put ESG topics 'on the agenda'.

Table 15.2 summarises four different options to structure boards in a way that sustainability is considered.

- *Specialised Sustainability Committee*: One option is to develop a specialised board-level committee that explicitly deals with sustainability questions. As much as boards have committees that discuss remuneration or risk management, they can also have a committee for sustainability. While such specialised committees give visibility to sustainability-related topics, they also depend on directors having sufficient knowledge to discuss relevant ESG problems and opportunities.
- *Tasking the Entire Board with Sustainability*: Another option is to task the entire board with discussing sustainability. Although this option ensures that all directors are engaged in relevant discussions, there is a risk that sustainability falls off the agenda during busy and less frequent board meetings. On the positive side, if the entire board addresses sustainability, it is easier to see the interrelatedness of topics. The board therefore develops a less siloed perspective on sustainability. For instance, ESG issues often throw up compliance questions, which are usually addressed by a separate committee.

- *Adding Sustainability to an Existing Committee*: Some firms also add sustainability topics to the work of an already existing committee. For instance, the compliance and audit committee could look into cases where firms may violate commitments to voluntary standards such as the UN Global Compact. Even though this structural option helps to integrate sustainability discussions with other strategy-related aspects, there is the risk that sustainability falls off the agenda because most committees already have busy schedules and a full workload. Further, there is the risk that ESG topics will be exclusively interpreted from the perspective of the committee (e.g., solely looking at risks when integrated into the risk management committee).
- *Below-Board Committee on Sustainability*: Finally, there is also the possibility to integrate sustainability into below-board committees which then support the discussions at board level. Such committees are usually staffed with *non*-board members. Below-board committees ensure that boards have a focal point where they can get relevant insights. However, such committees by themselves do not ensure that ESG issues are considered by the board. Rather, they can be used in combination with another structural option (e.g., a below-board committee supporting the work of a board-level sustainability committee).

Ideally, of course, boards would not need to create specific organisational structures to acknowledge sustainability, because relevant discussions would be naturally embedded into all aspects of board-level work.

What may be even more important than structural considerations is the mindset with which a board approaches sustainability. Grayson and Kakabadse (2013) argue that shifting the mindset of a board requires two fundamental developments. On the one hand, boards need to start thinking of sustainability as a strategy for risk mitigation and opportunity maximisation. Many directors still associate terms like 'sustainability' or 'CSR' with charity or work on isolated 'feel-good' projects within the corporation. Framing sustainability in terms of risks and opportunities changes how directors view the underlying debates, because it emphasises that the scope of sustainability is much broader and affects the very core of the business. On the other hand, boards must reflect on how they understand their own role. Boards that view their role exclusively as being about monitoring and auditing will mostly *react* to sustainability issues. However, boards that view their role also as one of mentoring a firm's executives to enable corporate sustainability management are more likely to support the creation of proactive strategies that address ESG issues.

15.3.2 Ownership Structures and Their Effect on Corporate Sustainability

Corporate governance can also support corporate sustainability because the ownership structure that a firm chooses enables or limits how sustainability can be addressed. *Publicly listed firms* usually face regulations which shape their attention towards ESG topics. In particular, the disclosure of ESG information is regulated by stock exchanges and hence reflects an inevitable factor of such firms' sustainability strategies. So far, fifty-five stock exchanges around the globe have issued some form of guidance on ESG reporting (Sustainable Stock Exchange Initiative, 2020). Some exchanges have even made ESG reporting a listing rule – for instance, the Singapore Exchange, Euronext Paris and the Bombay Stock Exchange. However, we should not conclude from this that the actual ESG performance of publicly listed firms is better than for other types of firms. Baumann-Pauly, Wickert, Spence and Scherer (2013) caution that larger, publicly listed firms face, relatively speaking, lower costs for communicating their ESG performance, while they have higher costs to implement sustainability strategies due to their size.

When looking at publicly listed firms, the concentration of ownership also matters. Wider ownership in which stocks are distributed among many shareholders is associated with higher levels of ESG performance, mostly because the demands of more heterogeneous shareholders need to be taken into account by management (Kiliç et al., 2015). As indicated above, shareholders reflect a diverse set of actors, ranging from short-term-oriented investors to activist investors that deliberately push firms towards improving their ESG performance (see Chapter 11). Prior research in this area suggests that long-term institutional ownership is connected to higher levels of ESG performance (Neubaum and Zahra, 2006).

Foundation-owned firms are another type of ownership structure that is important in the context of sustainability (see also Chapter 9). Often, these are publicly listed firms where a non-profit foundation holds the majority of voting shares and hence exercises control. This type of ownership structure is particularly widespread in Northern Europe. For instance, the majority of voting shares of the Danish pharmaceutical company Novo Nordisk A/S are in the hands of the Novo Nordisk Foundation. In many cases, the associated foundations have a strong societal mission and therefore ensure that the firms they control have a long-term orientation and strong ESG track record. Børsting and Thomsen (2017) give substance to this claim. They find that foundation-ownership is associated with better labour relations in terms of being a more stable employer and paying employees better. However, they also caution that this does not imply that such firms per se show stronger ESG performance. A bias may exist insofar as that some of the firms that are foundation-owned today were originally set up as businesses with a strong social and/or environmental mission, and foundation-ownership was then selected by the founders to sustain this original mission.

Finally, it is important to also look at firms where ownership and management are exercised by the same individual(s). These *owner-manager firms* often reflect small and medium-sized enterprises (SMEs) and family businesses (see also Chapter 8). From a corporate governance perspective, the existence of owner-manager firms reduces agency problems. The interests of managers and owners cannot diverge, even though conflicts among founders or family members can exist, of course. Owner-managed firms tend to face less pressure from investors to maximise short-term profits and can therefore devote more resources to ESG topics. Further, how sustainability is practised in these firms is usually influenced by the personal values of the owner-manager (who often is also the founder). Some famous sustainability-minded firms were shaped in this way, at least in their early days: consider companies like Ben & Jerry's ice cream and cosmetics by The Body Shop.

15.4   Corporate Governance *as* Sustainability

The way in which corporations are governed throws up problems and challenges that fall under the ESG umbrella, in particular the 'G' (governance) dimension. Firms with poor corporate governance often lack transparency and accountability. Addressing the governance dimension within ESG is therefore a key driver of good corporate sustainability.

15.4.1   Prominent 'G' (Governance) Issues within the ESG Universe

Board Diversity: One area of concern has been the composition of boards. Unbalanced boards can undermine the independence of decision-making. For instance: Do boards that are dominated by insiders (i.e., directors who are recruited from within the company) behave differently from boards that are dominated by outsiders (i.e., directors who have no further affiliation with the firm)? Kesner and Johnson (1990) argued that companies that have boards with a strong presence of insiders are more likely to face lawsuits, especially if the CEO also chaired the board. One explanation for this finding is that a strong presence of outside directors pushes the independence of the board and avoids conflicts of interest, although there is no systematic evidence that outsiders in general make for better board members (Fox, 2012). Prior research has also looked into the diversity of boards and the representation of women and minorities. Some have argued for a positive link between board diversity and firms' ESG performance (Harjoto et al., 2015). Diverse boards reflect a range of experiences and hence better understand the different needs of multiple stakeholders. By contrast, homogenous boards are more likely to be trapped in groupthink and may not challenge the mindset that has shaped their underlying decisions (Buchholtz et al., 2009).

Board Accountability: Another question that is often debated refers to the accountability of the board itself. Many have argued that the accountability of a board – that is, in what way and to whom it is answerable for its actions and omissions (Hale, 2008) – is limited to shareholders. Buchholtz et al. (2009: 335), for instance, argue that stakeholders often lack communication channels through which they could express their preferences or ask questions. A board cannot claim to be accountable to stakeholders without such channels, as it becomes impossible for certain groups to interact with directors on ESG issues. In other words, if boards remain 'closed clubs' that only interact with a firm's executive management, they cannot form truly independent opinions on ESG challenges.

CEO Duality: Yet another area of concern is CEO duality – a situation in which the CEO of a company at the same time acts as the chair of the board. It gives the CEO undue power and may undercut the monitoring function and independence of the board, because the person who heads up the governance organ that is supposed to oversee executive management's decisions is itself part of the management team. Others have argued that CEO duality also has its positive sides – for instance, that there is a 'unity of command at the top' (Finkelstein and D'aveni, 1994: 1102) which can help to make swift decisions. So far, academic research has not pointed in a consistent direction regarding the effects of CEO duality. While some studies have claimed that CEO duality does not affect the operating performance of firms (Baliga et al., 1996), others have found that a separation of both roles had positive performance effects if it followed a time of weak financial performance (Krause and Semadeni, 2013).

Executive Compensation: An area that has received significant public attention is the compensation of executives. On the one hand, there are complaints about the excessive nature of compensation. In 2019, Tesla's CEO, Elon Musk, earned $595 million according to the Bloomberg Pay Index. On average, CEOs were paid $21.3 million in big US-based companies (in 2019), 320 times more than the typical worker in a firm (Mishel and Kandra, 2020). One problem with such exorbitant pay is that most of CEO compensation is stock-related and therefore does not reflect any gains in productivity. On the other hand, there is also discussion around whether executive compensation is well enough aligned with sustainability objectives. So far, only a minority of firms explicitly tie ESG objectives to executives' compensation schemes. A survey by consultancy Pearl Meyer (2017) showed that only 36 per cent of firms tied executives' compensation plans to ESG-related metrics. One key challenge is to define clear metrics that cover those ESG issues that are material to a firm. While ESG metrics are increasingly appearing within executives' performance frameworks, such metrics are often still limited to areas where measurement is easy and non-controversial (e.g., emission targets). It is therefore important to fully align the ESG issues that a company identifies as material in its sustainability report and those issues that are integrated into executive pay packages.

15.4.2   Treatment of ESG in Corporate Governance Legislation

The topics mentioned above form part of a larger universe of corporate governance issues that can be regulated. In general, we can distinguish two different types of regulation for corporate governance. Some issues are regulated through hard law (i.e., legally enforceable). For instance, the Sarbanes-Oxley Act of 2002 (SOX) outlines several compulsory corporate governance requirements for firms. A number of issues are also regulated through soft law (i.e., voluntary corporate governance codes). Such codes are 'formally nonbinding and voluntary in nature, issued by multi-actor committees, flexible in their application, built on the market mechanism for evaluation of deviations and evolutionary in nature' (Haxhi and Aguilera, 2014: 2). These codes outline what can be considered best practices in the area of corporate governance.

Table 15.3 summarises how three corporate governance instruments treat the four topics that were discussed above. It compares the US-based SOX (mandatory) with

Table 15.3 Coverage of corporate governance issues in corporate governance legislation

	Sarbanes Oxley Act (US)	UK Corporate Governance Code (2018)	G20/OECD Principles of Corporate Governance
Legal Basis and Scope	Compliance: mandatory (with few exceptions) Scope: all publicly-traded U.S. firms	Compliance: principles are mandatory; provisions need to be observed Scope: all listed firms in the UK	Compliance: voluntary Scope: predominantly for listed companies; but all companies are encouraged to comply
Board Diversity	Boards have to have a majority of independent outside directors (employees are not considered independent, §303A.02)	Diversity (incl. gender) to be considered for board appointments; annual evaluation of board needs to consider diversity (Princip. J & L)	Need for balanced and qualified board (Anno. II.C.3); countries may consider measures to enhance diversity (VI.E..4)
Board Accountability (Role of Stakeholders)	Not covered	Firms should understand views of key stakeholders and report on how their interests are considered (Provision 5)	'... recognize the rights of stakeholders ... and encourage active cooperation between corporations and stakeholders.' (IV)
CEO Duality	Not covered	'The roles of chair and chief executive should not be exercised by the same individual.' (Provision 9)	Separation of the two posts is regarded as a good practice and is encouraged to enhance accountability (VI.E)
Executive Compensation	Determining long-term CEO compensation via firms' performance and shareholder return (§303A.05)	Remuneration should be designed to promote long-term sustainable success and be aligned with long-term strategy (Princip. P)	'[a]ligning remuneration with the longer term interests of the company and its shareholders.' (Principles VI.D.3–VI.D.4)

the UK Corporate Governance Code (mix of mandatory and voluntary), and the G20/OECD Principles of Corporate Governance (voluntary). From an ESG perspective, the picture that emerges is rather sobering, with the UK Corporate Governance Code (revised 2018) providing the most detailed and advanced guidance. SOX does not explicitly cover the accountability of boards to broader stakeholder groups, and it also makes no specific statements around CEO duality. While the UK Code and the OECD Principles encourage firms to recognise the interests of broader groups of stakeholders, their provisions remain either limited (the UK Code emphasising to understand and report on stakeholder views) or vague (the OECD Principles not specifying who exactly counts as a stakeholder). When it comes to board diversity, the SOX's coverage remains rather vague (highlighting the general need for director independence). The UK Code and the OECD Principles outline more specific provisions in this area, and in the case of the UK Code even explicitly acknowledge the need for gender diversity. One area highlighted by all three instruments is the need for long-term executive compensation. Given that the nature of executive compensation has been at the heart of numerous corporate accounting scandals (e.g., the Enron scandal in 2001; Spiro, 2002), this is a positive development. However, none of the three instruments explicitly asks firms to tie executive compensation to ESG performance.

15.5   Towards Sustainable Corporate Governance

Our discussion up to this point has shown that corporate governance, as it is practised right now, has a hard time to fully support well-articulated sustainability strategies. Bower and Paine (2017: 51) argue that the key 'error at the heart of corporate leadership' is our understanding of what we believe managers are supposed to do. Our idea about the role of managers and management is still much shaped by the traditional, shareholder-focused model of corporate governance, which is based on agency theory (Jensen and Meckling, 1976) and which has several flaws that make it unfit to fully incorporate ESG considerations. Under the shareholder-centric model, shareholders are understood as 'principals' and managers are assumed to be the 'agents' who make decisions on behalf of shareholders. But, this principal–agent model is at odds with forward-looking managerial thinking.

The shareholder-centric model of the firm is not aligned with corporate law. As Bower and Paine (2017: 53) argue: 'From a legal perspective, shareholders are beneficiaries of the corporation's activities, but they do not have a "dominion" over a piece of property'. In other words, shareholders are not owners of the firm, also because they do not have the incentive to exercise care. Exercising such care would require having a long-term investment horizon. Yet, the bulk of company shares are held by institutional investors (e.g., mutual funds) and therefore managed by individuals who are rewarded on a quarterly basis. This short-termism becomes obvious when looking at shares' holding period. On average, a stock at the NYSE is held for approximately nine months (as of 2018), while investors were holding stocks for nearly six years in the mid-1970s (Maloney and Almeida, 2018).

The shareholder-centric model sees managers and directors as agents who are 'obliged to carry out the wishes of a principal' (Bower and Paine, 2017: 53). This makes these groups order-takers who exercise what shareholders tell them to do. However, corporate law does not see managers and directors in this way. Under law, managers and directors have a fiduciary responsibility and are assumed to make *independent* judgments. This implies that executive management and also directors are by far not just obliged to do what shareholders tell them to do. Their decisions are autonomous and discretionary, and they have a duty to act in the best interest of the company, which is different from arguing that they need to exclusively serve shareholders' interests. How, then, can corporate governance be redesigned so that sustainability is taken more into consideration?

15.5.1 'The New Paradigm' – A Voluntary Framework

A corporate governance model that addresses these flaws needs to move away from an exclusive focus on a firm's shareholders to acknowledge that managers also have duties towards the corporation itself as well as its stakeholders. One promising new model of corporate governance was outlined by Martin Lipton (2016). His thinking around *The New Paradigm* shows a roadmap for creating a corporate governance model that reaches beyond short-term-oriented shareholder value thinking. *The New Paradigm* is built on three major pillars:

- *Governance*: Boards and managers are explicitly asked to reflect on the firm's purpose and to develop strategies for sustainable, long-term value creation. A firm's governance structure should support the organisation in making a positive contribution to society – for instance, by recognising relevant stakeholder needs. Boards must set the right 'tone at the top' and promote an ethical corporate culture. The board should encompass directors with diverse backgrounds, experiences and expertise. *The New Paradigm* also emphasises that '[t]he board of directors and senior management should integrate relevant ESG matters into the company's strategic and operational planning, budgeting, resource allocation and compensation structures' (Lipton, 2016: 16).
- *Engagement*: Companies are asked to make disclosures to shareholders based on relevant ESG matters (e.g., including how compensation packages stimulate long-term growth). Investors are asked to seek proactive engagement with firms on matters that are of long-term interest to the company and its stakeholders.

Engagement is built around the idea of true dialogue and lasting relationships; there should not be any dominating voices. Also, investors should support the long-term interests of firms and their stakeholders.

- *Stewardship*: Asset managers are asked to promote sustainable, long-term value creation for those parties whose money they invest and also for the firms they invest in. Further, asset managers should foster companies' long-term growth and highlight whenever short-term conflicting goals endanger such growth. In terms of voting on shareholder resolutions, asset managers are asked to vote in such a way that the long-term success of the firm they invested in is secured. In general, investors are asked to consider ESG factors when they develop their investment strategies.

The New Paradigm does not reflect legislation. It is a framework that firms, investors and other stakeholders can use as a point of orientation when thinking about what a less short-term-oriented corporate governance system could look like. The three pillars highlight some of the issues discussed in this chapter (e.g., the need for board diversity and the importance of integrating ESG topics into board-level discussions). As a whole, the framework moves towards a corporate governance model that is less centred on a firm's shareholders and rather puts the company itself and its numerous stakeholders into focus. All three pillars explicitly emphasise the need to deeply root long-term thinking into the behaviour of different corporate governance actors. Of course, *The New Paradigm* will not magically solve all problems that occur at the interface of ESG and corporate governance. But it is a step in the right direction, and it is specific enough to be implemented by companies and investors in different countries.

15.5.2 The European Union's Proposal for a Sustainable Corporate Governance Directive

While *The New Paradigm* reflects a voluntary framework, the EU Commission has recently started discussions around adopting a new *Sustainable Corporate Governance* (SCG) Directive. Although precise and final details of this Directive are not yet known (as of October 2022), the overall rationale motivating such a Directive is known. The SCG Directive aims at tackling the problem of 'short-termism' within corporate governance. It will create rules that reduce pressure for short-term decision-making and incentivise companies to consider the long-term development and sustainability of business operations. Under EU law, Directives are not direct regulation. Rather, they provide a legal framework which EU Member States must translate into relevant national law.

Based on what is known about the SCG Directive at this stage (e.g., through the consultation period), we can look at some of the topics that the EU Commission is considering regulating:

1. *Mandatory Due Diligence*: The Commission considers imposing a legal duty on firms to conduct due diligence vis-à-vis ESG topics. According to the European

Parliament, such due diligence should reflect 'a process put in place by an undertaking in order to identify, assess, prevent, mitigate, cease, monitor, communicate, account for, address and remedy the potential and/or actual adverse impacts on human rights, including social, trade union and labour rights, on the environment, including the contribution to climate change, and on good governance, in its own operations and its business relationships in the value chain' (European Parliament, 2021: 21).

2. *Duty of Care Obligation*: The EU Commission further considers imposing a duty of care obligation vis-à-vis ESG issues on members of the board. Such a change would revise and extend existing fiduciary duties. An extended duty of care would imply that members of the board are legally obliged to consider stakeholder interests, which are relevant for the long-term sustainability of the company, into their own decision-making (European Commission, 2020a: 3). In practice, such an obligation would imply that boards will have to integrate broader stakeholder interests when discussing the strategy and risk management of a company.

3. *Regulating Remuneration of Board Members*: Finally, the European Union also considers including board members' remuneration in the SCG Directive. Changes to remuneration could be seen as one way to enforce the extended duty of care obligation. Practically speaking, firms could be asked to align the remuneration of board members more explicitly with longer-term perspectives.

Although the EU SCG Directive is not yet adopted, there will be changes to how corporate governance is practised within European companies.

15.6 Chapter Summary

This chapter has taken you on a journey to explore the relationship between corporate governance and corporate sustainability. We saw that the way in which corporations are governed still impedes progress on corporate sustainability, mostly because some elements of existing governance systems remain too focused on the role of shareholder wealth, which in turn reinforces short-termism. The key controversy underlying this debate is the one between shareholder value thinking and a wider stakeholder orientation. One key message of this chapter is that, while an explicit stakeholder orientation is desirable and would support a more holistic corporate governance system, few firms have embedded such a stakeholder orientation in their governance systems. Also, most mandatory regulations (e.g., SOX) do not force companies to adopt an explicit stakeholder orientation.

However, we also discussed areas of progress. We showed that there are different options for boards to organise oversight of corporate sustainability, and that such oversight also rests on the mindset that the members of a board develop over time. We also saw that governance challenges, such as CEO duality and executive compensation, increasingly appear on firms' ESG agenda and hence are getting more and more attention. Finally, we discussed: (1) a voluntary framework – *The New Paradigm* – that outlines what firms can do in practical terms to create a governance system that has an explicit long-term orientation; and (2) the very recent EU initiative to create a Directive on *Sustainable Corporate Governance.*

CHAPTER QUESTIONS

1. What are the key components of the corporate governance system? In what ways does the current system limit the uptake of ESG topics by corporations?
2. How can boards of directors organise oversight of corporate sustainability?
3. What are typical governance challenges included in the 'G' dimension of the ESG agenda? How would you address these challenges?
4. In what ways does the ownership structure of a corporation affect its corporate governance? What could be possible consequences for addressing ESG topics?
5. Which areas of corporate governance should be reformed according to *The New Paradigm*? What would be possible consequences of such a reform for addressing sustainability?

FURTHER RESOURCES

- Barton, D. and Wiseman, M. (2014). Focusing Capital on the Long Term. *Harvard Business Review*, 92(1/2), 44–51.

  An article discussing how long-term capitalism could work. The main argument is that change needs to start with investors who need to adopt strategies that aim at maximising long-term results.

- Paine, L. S. (2014). Sustainability in the Boardroom. *Harvard Business Review*, 92(7/8), 86–94.

  An article discussing how boards of directors can address sustainability. It builds on the experiences of Nike, which created a dedicated committee already in 2001. The article reflects on possible roles that such a committee could have (e.g., being a stimulus for innovation).

- Stout, L. (2012). *The Shareholder Value Myth: How Putting Shareholders First Harms Investors, Corporations, and the Public.* San Francisco, CA: Berrett-Koehler.

  A book discussing the flaws underlying shareholder value thinking. The book includes many reflections relevant for corporate governance, including reflections on the legal challenges of shareholder value thinking.

16 Reputation and Corporate Sustainability

CHRISTOPHER WICKERT AND JOEP CORNELISSEN

LEARNING OBJECTIVES

- Discuss why corporate reputation is an important asset for firms and how to distinguish reputation from related things like identity, image and legitimacy.

- Describe how companies across industries manage their reputation in relation to corporate sustainability (CS).

- Critically reflect on symbolic ('talking') versus substantive ('walking') approaches to CS and show how this may create both opportunities and threats for companies.

16.1 Introduction

When deciding to buy a product, what do people usually think of? Probably the price, the quality of the product and maybe also whether they like the brand. Or would consumers also consider how well this company treats its employees, how ethical it is and whether it shows environmental sustainability? Most of us would probably relate to the former. But, according to research by the Reputation Institute (2015), people's willingness to buy, recommend, work for and invest in a company is driven by about 60 per cent by their perception of the company – in other words, by its reputation – and only about 40 per cent is driven by how people perceive the product itself or the price alone. Many firms, in particular global brands from around the world, such as Adidas, H&M, IKEA, Lego, Nike, Coca-Cola, Apple and the like often consider brand reputation their most important asset, besides other resources like financial or human capital. For instance, H&M's reputation for being a fashionable but low-priced clothing brand has enabled the company to outperform its rivals for many years. Coca-Cola's reputation for being *the* global beverage of good taste and reliable quality has allowed the company to sustain its market share in the face of fierce competition.

16.2   Reputation and Corporate Sustainability

What is corporate reputation? The Reputation Institute, a well-known consultancy and market research firm, identifies seven dimensions as constituting a reputation: workplace, governance, citizenship, financial performance, leadership, products and services, and innovation. On reflection, out of these seven, three can be directly related to corporate sustainability (CS) – namely, citizenship (how a company behaves in relation to the natural environment and the local communities where it operates), workplace (how a company treats its own and its suppliers' employees) and governance (what a company does to ensure ethical conduct and prevent wrongdoing, such as corruption). What the institute's analyses over the years have shown is that more than half of how people feel about a company (i.e., the strength of that firm's reputation) is based on their perceptions of a firm's sustainability practices. According to Kasper Ulf Nielsen, executive partner at the Reputation Institute, 'Corporate sustainability speaks to who the company is, what it believes in and how it is doing business', which makes CS a

> core element of reputation and [it] can be used to help establish trust and goodwill amongst stakeholders. [Almost half] of people's willingness to trust, admire, and feel good about a company is based on their perceptions of the company's sustainability, so this is a key tool for companies to improve support from stakeholders like consumers, regulators, financial community, and employees. (Smith, 2013)

CS thus seems to have moved centre stage as a key component of what makes a good corporate reputation. However, the rules of the 'reputation game' have become a little trickier when looking at some of the companies that have recently scored high in reputation rankings. In 2021, among the top-10 are companies such as Microsoft, The Walt Disney Company and Adidas. All of these companies, according to Reputation Institute's survey, are extremely proactive in terms of the dimensions that drive CS reputation. But – critical voices may wonder – how can companies that have repeatedly been accused by NGOs, industry analysts and governments of exploiting their monopolistic market position (Microsoft), of prohibiting employees from joining labour unions and remunerating them with poor wages (Disney), or being frequently accused of doing too little to uphold safe working conditions in their supply chains (Adidas), have such a positive reputation for sustainability? The question is whether reputation rankings accurately reflect the sustainability efforts of companies, and if their performance in other areas (such as financial performance, or marketing and branding) may actually by association suggest to stakeholders that they make an equally sterling contribution in sustainability terms. Notably, reputation is not about a company's products or how they are produced, but about the company behind the products, and how people *perceive* this company.

How, then, do stakeholders perceive and evaluate a company in terms of sustainability? And what are companies doing to manage such perceptions with their stakeholders?

The picture becomes even more complicated when comparing those companies scoring high in reputation rankings, including the one from the Reputation Institute, but also other rankings such as *Fortune* magazine's ranking of the world's most admired companies. Apple, for instance, frequently tops the *Fortune* ranking, but is constantly being criticised by NGOs for acts of corporate social *ir*responsibility in relation to issues like human rights, labour norms and selling products that create massive amounts of hard-to-recycle waste. Surprisingly, in contrast to Apple's case, companies that are applauded even by critical NGOs like Greenpeace for their substantive efforts to make products and processes more sustainable, including Unilever, or Marks & Spencer, score much lower and hence appear to not reap the benefits of having the best CS reputation, despite their investments.

The overall question that emerges is the following: When is CS reputation more a form of *symbolic impression management* (in other words, empty 'talk') and when is it reflective of *substantive efforts* (in other words, 'walk') to truly promote social and environmental sustainability? What are the opportunities connected to building a reputation for CS? And what are the potential risks when not caring at all about building a good reputation for sustainability?

In order to answer these questions, we will first explain the foundations of corporate reputation, delineate it from related concepts such as identity, image and legitimacy, and explain its relationship to CS. We will then show how CS management can be an opportunity to enhance reputation, but which – if poorly managed – can also present itself as a risk that might damage a company's reputation. We will propose that the effects of CS on reputation can be better understood if examined against two key dimensions: first, whether a company is sincerely 'walking' CS by substantially integrating socially and environmentally responsible business practices, or if a firm is rather 'talking' about CS by engaging in symbolic impression management in order to construct an unsubstantiated façade of CS without much substance. Second, whether CS activities are aligned with a company's core business operations, or whether they remain at the periphery in non-core activities. These two dimensions together provide a framework that classifies different ways in which companies approach CS, and how they use their CS activities for reputation-building purposes. Furthermore, the framework sensitises us to advantages and pitfalls associated with each approach. We conclude the chapter by reflecting on some of the dynamics and controversies related to a company's CS reputation.

16.3   Defining Corporate Reputation

In one of Shakespeare's most famous plays, Othello bemoans that reputation is 'oft got without merit, and lost without deserving' (*Othello*: II, 3: 260). When we apply this insight to the corporate level, two important questions arise: how is reputation granted or built, and how can it be lost, or, perhaps less dramatically, damaged? These questions have brought considerable attention to the topic of corporate reputation, both among academics and practitioners. Studying reputation is theoretically meaningful because it contributes to our basic understanding of fundamental social processes and resources that are important to the corporate world, and it is practically important because reputations can also create substantial value for companies.

Most understandings of corporate reputation focus, broadly, on Shakespeare's *merit* part. They describe how reputation is built, and what the benefits are that having a good reputation entails. This includes gaining and sustaining competitive advantage, being able to charge a price-premium on products, and attracting talent and investors. In general, reputation is conceived as the product of substantive and symbolic corporate actions over time, in which companies send information to external observers and observers use this information to form impressions of the company.

Scholars have not yet agreed on a commonly accepted definition of reputation, but the most basic understanding is that, as an important intangible asset, reputation refers to 'observers' collective judgments of a corporation based on assessments of the financial, social and environmental impacts attributed to the corporation over time' (Barnett et al., 2006). Reputation hence reflects 'that over time an organisation can become well known, can accrue a generalised understanding in the minds of observers as to what it is known for, and can be judged favourably or unfavourably by its observers' (Lange et al., 2011: 154). Central to reputation in all definitions is that it implies an *evaluation* and *comparison* of organisations to determine reputation relative to one another. For any two organisations, they will either have the same reputation, or more likely, one will have a better reputation than the other. That is why a good reputation is perceived as an essential and distinctive firm competitive advantage.

Seeing reputation as a source of competitive advantage in turn requires companies to behave and act consistent with their past performance and with the public's expectations. In this sense, reputation can be viewed as a solution for asymmetric information that market participants usually have about product quality, adequate pricing and, importantly, whether sustainability messages of the company are symbolic or substantive. When faced with a lack of information on a product or on a firm's activities, stakeholders rely on the firm's reputation to judge its products or intentions. Reputation thus functions as a signal to external observers that allows grasping the firm's key characteristics. Assuming that, for instance, consumers make their buying decisions after scanning a firm based on its past behaviour and actions, such as product quality, reputation provides assurance that the same firm will behave and act consistently in the future.

Accordingly, having a good reputation can be a considerable advantage to a company when dealing with its various stakeholders, such as consumers or investors. However, reputation is also often issue and stakeholder specific. A company may have a particular, and potentially different, reputation for different issues, including its profitability, social and environmental sustainability, employee treatment, corporate governance and product quality. Goldman Sachs is a company that exemplifies this in its most extreme form because it is both 'well loathed' and 'well loved' by stakeholders. It has an excellent reputation for profitability, but its ethics and sustainability are considered very poor, or virtually non-existent. A corporation may also have a different reputation for each of its stakeholder groups. For example, while much of the general public is sceptical of Goldman Sachs's behaviour that reflects a particularly ruthless kind of capitalism, investors and clients may see the company in a much better light because it is able to deliver superior returns.

More generally, different stakeholder groups base their reputational judgments on a different set of outcomes. This means that, for instance, a company's reputation from the point of view of employees will be based primarily on workplace outcomes such as wages, career opportunities or healthcare benefits; that of consumers on product, service and marketing outcomes such as price, quality and branding; and that of investors on business and financial outcomes, such as dividends or share price. Thus, members of each group would form their own specific evaluation of a certain company.

This issue and the stakeholder specificity of corporate reputation may also explain the inconsistency that is often experienced in attempts to measure reputation, such as by the *Fortune Most Admired Companies* (http://fortune.com/worlds-most-admired-companies) ranking which represents probably the best-known reputation ranking in the world. However, the ranking is largely a self-assessment, where managers of participating companies and financial analysts rate one another (except their own company). As such, the ranking reflects what *managers* think of a company, while other stakeholders, such as journalists or NGOs, do not directly participate and share their views. In short, what we have suggested so far is that reputation rests in the minds of its beholders and is a subjective concept, because it is essentially what different internal and external stakeholders believe about a company (Cornelissen, 2021).

The observation that reputation is socially constructed and based on the *perception* of stakeholders, and not factual or objectively provided by a 'neutral' party, renders it particularly likely for manipulation by those that aim to gain advantage by having a favourable reputation, including the company itself. To better account for manipulative efforts, we distinguish between *symbolic* commitments of companies in pursuit of a good reputation, and more *substantive* efforts around investments and resource commitments. To understand these counter-poles better, however, it is important to first delineate reputation from related concepts. We will then delve into the relationship between sustainability and reputation and shed light on what companies do to manage their reputation.

16.3.1 Corporate Reputation and Related Concepts

Identity, image and legitimacy are concepts that are often seen as closely related to reputation. They share some of the same ground, but important differences remain: *Identity* describes the perception that employees and managers – those inside the firm – hold of the nature of their firm and which comprises the underlying core character of the firm. In other words, it relates to those features of the company that employees and managers believe are central, enduring and distinctive to their firm. Identity asks the question: 'Who/what do we believe we are as a company?' For instance, employees and managers can perceive their company as 'environmentally and socially responsible' or 'acting according to the highest ethical values'.

In contrast to identity, *image* is the perception that external observers, such as investors, consumers and the general public, have of a company. Image describes what comes to mind when one hears the name or sees the logo of a company, and hence refers to observers' general impressions of a particular firm. Image answers the question 'What/who do we want others to think we are?' For instance, a company may want to create an image of being an environmentally responsible company or being a very attractive investment for shareholders.

What becomes clear when comparing image and identity is that consistency in how a company sees itself and how others see the company is important when successfully managing reputation. This is because reputation is the aggregation of these perceptions of image and identity. Besides being an aggregation of identity and image, reputation also involves a more considered evaluation of a firm, whereas image is typically seen as a more immediate perception or response – for example, to an advertising campaign. As such, where images may be more subject to change, and change from moment to moment when impressions are formed, reputation is, on the other hand, more inert, and thus often more stable over time, as it involves a gradually built up accumulation of experiences and impressions.

There are also many similarities between reputation and *legitimacy*, because both concepts result from similar social construction processes when stakeholders evaluate an organisation. However, while reputation is about a comparison among different organisations, legitimacy concerns the social acceptance resulting from adherence to social norms and expectations. For example, a company can have a superior reputation for delivering the highest quality products, or being the most environmentally friendly producer in its industry, but it may also have a reputation for poor labour relations. In contrast, a company would be considered legitimate if it respects the law and fulfils the general purpose of what a business is and should do. Thus, it appears that a central element of legitimacy is meeting and adhering to the expectations of a society's norms, values, rules and meanings – in other words, conformity to a social category. Reputation, in contrast, is an evaluation of a firm by stakeholders in comparison to other firms. Based on this distinction, reputation is related to competitive advantage, whereas legitimacy is more like a 'hygiene factor', a necessary condition for long-term survival and the so-called social licence-to-operate. Having defined reputation more generally, we now turn to the question of what it means to have a 'CS reputation', and how engaging in CS may impact a company's overall reputation.

16.4 How Corporate Sustainability Impacts Reputation

Most people would probably agree that today we simply feel differently about the role of business in society than some generations before. Almost two decades ago, Lewis (2003) reported that, in the late 1970s, two-thirds of the British public agreed that the profits of large companies benefited society at large. However, what became apparent in the early 2000s is probably even more evident today: the large majority of the public seems to disagree that society benefits if companies focus on nothing else than creating profits and maximising shareholder value (Lewis, 2003). This means that the trust of the general public in companies to look after society has gradually eroded. At the same time, the large majority of the public believes that companies have a moral obligation to society. Interestingly, many also believe that in particular large multinational companies 'don't really care' about the long-term environmental and social impact of their actions. In their perception, business falls short of paying proper attention to exactly those issues that are of increasing interest to the general public and society at large.

This observation reflects a broader trend that immediately speaks to the relationship between CS and reputation. It underscores that, out of the seven dimensions that constitute reputation as mentioned above, those that can be related to CS are becoming increasingly important for stakeholders. For example, whereas in the past *the* major components that were necessary to gain and sustain a superior reputation were financial performance, good prices and high product quality, sustainability has been receiving increasingly more importance. While the former components are obviously still considered important, the sustainability impacts of business have moved centre stage. This process is fuelled by a more powerful civil society and

NGOs such as Greenpeace and Amnesty International that use social media channels such as blogs, Twitter or Facebook to raise attention about how companies behave with regard to sustainability. They even launch boycotts against companies, which can considerably impact their reputation. For example, the famous campaign that Greenpeace launched against Nestlé in 2010 to stop the unsustainable production of palm oil and the damage this caused to the habitat of endangered species had a massive impact on Nestlé's reputation, including among consumers (a drop in sales of the Kit Kat bars) and investors (Nestlé's plunging share price).

Stakeholders can now more easily find information about how sustainable the processes and products of a company are – for instance, with regard to their CO_2-emissions, water usage or toxic releases. Consumers are nowadays more concerned, or at least aware, about the social conditions such as workers' rights in supplier factories, and ethical breaches in the context of corruption make it to the media much quicker. However, not only consumers take sustainability more into account when making reputational judgments about a firm. Prospective employees are also asking about the sustainability activities of their future employers, and many don't want to work for an irresponsible company. Financial investors alike now see socially responsible investing (SRI) as an important market segment and include sustainability issues in their evaluations (see Chapter 11). CS can thus be seen both as an important *component* of reputation and as something that influences the *overall* reputation of a firm.

While these examples suggest that corporations can improve their reputation by paying close attention to sustainability, cases also abound where reputation is threatened when companies do *not* pay sufficient attention to CS. Likewise, reputation can be harmed when there is 'too much of a good thing' – in other words, a firm makes more symbolic than substantive commitments to sustainability. We will therefore discuss CS as an *opportunity* for enhancing reputation, as well as a *risk* that may damage reputation.

16.4.1   The Quest for CS Reputations

Before we get into detail on how firms manage their CS reputation, we explain how individual stakeholders form the reputation of a firm, specifically in relation to CS. Reputation involves a considered evaluation of a firm vis-à-vis its rivals, where stakeholders consider its main and distinctive attributes (such as its profitability, the quality of services and products, and labour relations), which together make up a profile image. They in turn attribute that reputation to an organisation, and if asked (in a survey, for instance) rate it accordingly. What is at the heart of these dynamics is the twin challenge for firms to be seen as doing the right things (e.g., to behave sustainably), and as doing things somewhat differently (and relatively better) from their competitors. Marketers, communication scholars and practitioners refer to this challenge as points of similarity and points of difference between a firm and its rivals on key aspects of its identity, image and reputation. Organisational sociologists and strategic management scholars use the more specific language of legitimacy (sameness) and reputation (distinction). Legitimacy and reputation are as mentioned distinct but closely related constructs in the context of CS. Legitimacy refers to general norms and values in society that imply certain standards around what is acceptable behaviour of firms (or not). As far as CS is concerned, it is clear from numerous studies that firms are

> transformed by new pressures to look like responsible actors. They are increasingly obligated, by law and public pressure, to take on expanded concerns such as environmental protection, corporate social responsibility and philanthropy, employee rights and job satisfaction, workplace diversity, community engagement, and consumer safety. (Bromley and Meyer, 2017: 945)

There are thus significant pressures on firms to meet public expectations and standards of legitimacy as far as their CS engagement is concerned. Indeed, for many firms, there is now something like a legitimacy base-line for CS, in terms of what generally speaking is expected of them by their stakeholders. Such expectations may, however, vary depending on the size, visibility and sector of the company, but nonetheless the pressure for legitimacy is surely felt by many firms around the world. Reputation is distinct from, but builds on, legitimacy in that besides a base-line expectation, it is about what firms do differently specifically in terms of CS, and what they are therefore known for, or rated more highly on, vis-à-vis their direct competitors.

One useful way of looking at this is to consider a firm as an individual actor, who needs to act responsibly towards its stakeholders and society at large and wants to build a specific reputation. This kind of personification is one that is common in the communication, management and sociological literatures, where organisations are seen to have 'identities' and 'reputations' akin to human beings. In addition, research across marketing, consumer research, communication and organisational sociology confirms that stakeholders attribute a 'corporate identity' to an organisation, and also form a reputation of that organisation in ways that closely resemble how individuals form impressions of other human beings (Chun and Davies, 2006). As such, the responsible actor notion is not just a metaphor, as it resembles how stakeholders form reputations of firms.

Two specific implications arise when stakeholders attribute person-like images and reputations to organisations: first, stakeholders will relate the various direct encounters and impressions that they have of an organisation into a singular image or reputation, as if the various messages and actions of the members of the organisation actually came from a single embodied person. In other words, they integrate and compress different impressions into that of the actions of a single actor, who operates (and is seen to operate) in a particular environment where it attempts to differentiate itself from rival firms to gain reputation and legitimacy. As a result, stakeholders will think of a firm as a single unitary actor (rather than a loosely connected collective) and will, for example, refer to a particular bank or retailer as having taken a particular stance on a given issue, as having expressed certain opinions or as having done certain things.

Second, firms, like human agents, are seen to be capable of taking deliberate, reflective and goal-directed action. Stakeholders in effect attribute to firms the capacity of taking deliberate action, akin to how human beings have intentionality and agency. King et al. (2010) stress that such stakeholder attributions are commonplace, in part because firms have been legally and institutionally endowed with agency, and with individual rights and responsibilities. The broader implication here is that in modern societies organisations are by law but also in the minds of stakeholders and the general public treated as if they are individuals – granting them analogous powers to act and assigning them analogous responsibilities and rights.

The two implications together – the fact that stakeholders integrate their impressions into a single 'corporate' reputation and attribute intentions and actions to the firm – provide a useful starting point to consider how firms approach sustainability, in their actions and communication, and how accordingly stakeholders form a reputation of that firm. Sticking to the image of the organisation as an actor (in the minds of their stakeholders), we make a distinction between a firm's CS 'talk' and 'walk', which according to recent research accounts for differences in how firms practise CS (Wickert et al., 2016).

CS talk, akin to the kind of symbolic impression management tactics we have sketched above, involves the various ways in which an organisation communicates with its external audiences, such as customers. CS talk by itself mirrors a form of advertising or 'a strategic variant of marketing aiming to promote a company's image and reputation ... as well as the sales of its products' (Eisenegger and Schranz, 2011: 6). In comparison, *CS walk* encompasses substantive and behaviourally oriented activities inside a firm, such as adjusting production methods to mitigate environmental impacts, or improving working conditions across the firm's supply chain. Firms that 'walk' CS invest in responsible business behaviour and implement CS along core business processes in order to achieve measurable outcomes.

Together, 'walk' and 'talk' make up the overall profile of a firm in terms of its CS engagement. They are obviously not mutually exclusive, as good behaviour (walk) will be broadcasted and reported by most firms (talk), and in some cases talk itself can be seen as a substantial investment (e.g., in stakeholder dialogue platforms addressing CS standards and issues). Yet, we use this rough distinction here to develop a framework on CS reputation management. In particular, when we see the two dimensions as separate but related scales, we can identify different approaches to CS reputation management. For example, in particular, large and well-known multinational corporations may be overselling their CS efforts (talking), by framing and spinning good stories about themselves and in a way that is not reflective of their actual investments and changes in behaviour (walk). In the literature, this phenomenon is termed as 'greenwashing'. Similarly, a firm may be actually making substantial progress on CS targets internally, but without sufficiently broadcasting or communicating the results. This may be the case when firms are focused on CS goals in themselves, and may as a result besides some basic reporting decide not to communicate much with their stakeholders about the real progress they are making. The latter can be observed in particular among many small and family-owned firms (Wickert, 2016).

Obviously, an ideal state for firms is to be 'walking the talk', where they engage with their stakeholders, implement sustainable activities, and transparently and collaboratively communicate about the results. In what follows, we sketch these different approaches, discuss when they are used and what the consequences may be in terms of a firm's CS reputation – being an opportunity to enhance reputation or leading to a risk that may damage reputation.

Theoretically, this difference between walking and talking CS can also be seen to describe different approaches to how companies communicate about their sustainability efforts. Morsing and Schultz (2006) describe three core strategies, based on public relations theory. The first strategy, titled the 'stakeholder information strategy', involves a blanket information dissemination process in which companies do a lot of 'telling', but little 'listening'. It is a one-way, directed process of communication with the purpose of informing external stakeholders about CS-related actions and achievements. One core assumption here is that managers know best and may indeed be 'walking the talk' as far as substantive actions on CS are concerned. However, with this communication strategy they do not open up themselves and their organisations to actual discussions with stakeholders around important CS topics. They instead just give their own, one-sided take on CS and make this public.

The second strategy, the 'stakeholder response strategy', is still a directed one, from organisation to stakeholders, but here the organisation is more two-way in its approach in trying to gather feedback from stakeholders and then using that feedback strategically to frame and persuade them more effectively. For example, an organisation may set up consultation exercises with key stakeholder groups to gauge how they feel about certain sustainability issues. In addition, they may also gather feedback on what way of presenting their progress or achievements on CS is most likely to persuade their stakeholders, or otherwise limit opposition to the company's plans and actions. As the main aim with this strategy is to frame things in the best possible light and to persuade stakeholders, the way in which such stakeholder consultation is organised may itself take on a

Table 16.1 A comparison of three communication strategies for corporate sustainability

	Stakeholder information strategy	Stakeholder response strategy	Stakeholder involvement strategy
Model of communication	One-way and asymmetric (centred around interests of the organisation)	Two-way and asymmetric (centred around interests of the organisation)	Two-way and symmetric (balancing the interests of organisations and stakeholders in society)
Aim of communication	Informing stakeholders of CS activities and achievements	Persuading stakeholders of CS activities and achievements	Involving and deliberating with stakeholders about CS activities, targets and achievements
Engagement of stakeholders	Non-existent (only as audience)	Limited (only as part of surveys, consultations and opinion polls)	Extensive (centrally involved in CS strategy and actions)
Walk vs. talk	Mostly talk (and in the form of simply declaring or pronouncing actions taken)	Mostly talk (and in the form of framing messages to prime preferred readings of actions taken)	Walking the talk (and in the form of openly discussing and substantiating any talk of actions and achievements)

Source: Adapted from Morsing and Schultz (2006).

symbolic form – as 'smoke and mirrors' and as of legitimising decisions in CS where some limited form of consultation has taken place.

Finally, the 'stakeholder involvement strategy' is one that is a more dialogic, two-way process of communication in which organisations truly listen to their stakeholders and engage and deliberate with them what actions and goals regarding CS the company should pursue. If this strategy is honestly and deliberately used by organisations, it allows them to set progressive targets for the CS, and to 'walk the talk' as they do so. They incorporate the voice of their stakeholders (e.g., in the form of materiality assessments), solicit feedback and alternative viewpoints, and are conscious of openly reporting how well they are doing (i.e., aligning substantive action and talk), as well as where the areas for improvement might be. Table 16.1 below outlines these three communication strategies.

16.5   Walking Corporate Sustainability: An Opportunity to Enhance Reputation

Broadly speaking, companies that aim to walk CS attempt to seriously implement sustainable business practices as part of their core operations. This can create opportunities to enhance their reputation. What does research tell us about how companies should and actually are walking CS in order to improve their reputation?

Yoon et al. (2006) argue that the positive reputation effects of CS with an important stakeholder group they analysed – consumers – are stronger if the motives for CS are perceived as sincere; in other words, the company is able to show that it is indeed taking substantial steps towards integrating CS in core business operations, rather than making symbolic commitments. Consumers also tend to grant more reputation credits if they perceive a lower salience of firm-serving benefits from CS activities. This means the firm is seen to engage in CS not only for instrumental reasons and because there might be a business case, resulting in higher profits, but also because paying attention to a particular CS issue, such as child labour or climate change mitigation, is the right thing to do and does not depend on direct payoffs. Yoon et al. (2006) further show that consumers consider CS activities to be even more credible if they receive information about them from an independent, neutral source, rather than only from the company itself – for instance, through advertising or CS reports. This means, for instance, that sincere CS walk further benefits a company's reputation if it is endorsed by certification organisations such as the Forest Stewardship Council (FSC), which stands for sustainable forestry, or the Fairtrade label, which aims to ensure responsible sourcing of raw materials such as cocoa or coffee.

While research suggests that reputation effects are generally higher if companies manage to sincerely walk CS, other studies also show that industry matters. Different sectors usually have different environmental and social impacts, which moderate reputation effects. While metals, mining, oil extraction and power generation, for instance, have a significant impact on soil, water, climate and other environmental aspects, textile production, food processing and agriculture often go along with significant violations of labour and human rights of the involved workers, for instance, in factories or on plantations. Other industries, in contrast, particularly the renewable energy industry, information and communication technology, and the service sector are generally seen as causing much lower environmental and social impacts and are associated with fewer highly visible environmental issues.

Brammer and Pavelin (2004) argue that stakeholders such as local communities, regulators, the media and environmental pressure groups tend to observe those firms that create significant environmental externalities much closer and they expect firms to reduce or make reparations for their impacts. At the same time, 'good' environmental performance, in other words, walking CS, is more likely to contribute to enhanced reputation in those sectors where environmental or social impacts are present and if a company makes credible efforts to mitigate these impacts. What this also means is that companies are ill advised if they focus on

CS activities that are unrelated to the potentially harmful impact their operations have, assuming they aim to secure the positive reputation effects of CS.

Examples abound both of companies that either fail to connect their social and environmental impacts to their sustainability activities and thus have a hard time reaping the reputational benefits, or companies that have managed to tackle those sustainability issues that are material to their core business. For instance, supporting cultural events may be considered a social contribution by utility companies, yet stakeholders are unlikely to grant significant reputation credits if these companies engaged in such CS activities. Their carbon emissions, on the other hand, cause massive environmental impacts and these companies are thus much better able to enhance their reputation by focusing on the development of climate change mitigation strategies or investing heavily in renewables. In contrast, for the textile industry and companies like H&M, carbon emissions are perhaps less salient, while CS activities that are related to the improvement of working conditions in their supply chain may have a huge impact on workers' lives, thus providing a better lever to influence their reputation. Likewise, the AIDS pandemic in Africa may be a marginal social issue for a retailer like Carrefour or Metro, but pharmaceutical companies like Bayer or Novartis are much closer connected, as are mining companies like Anglo American or DeBeers that depend on the local labour supply for their operations.

Effectively managing CS, therefore, also implies taking into account that if sustainability impacts are less apparent, reputational benefits that are expected to result from CS might be marginal, because stakeholders simply care about other things. If a company like Shell provides recyclable paper cups on its oil platforms and exploration ships in the Arctic – a probably well-meant but at the same time somewhat ironic attempt to be sustainable – but simultaneously continues dangerous deep water drilling in zones where endangered species are near extinction, few would be surprised that this did not significantly enhance their reputation as a sustainable company. Rather, such behaviour makes the company even more likely to be accused of greenwashing. Moreover, there is also an administrative cost associated with those CS activities that are peripheral to a firm's business operations and that do not fit with their real environmental and social impacts, which in turn may harm its financial performance and thus can even harm the reputation in the eyes of other stakeholders such as investors.

Research has also pointed to a positive correlation between corporate giving (making donations to charitable organisations, such as childcare, culture or sports) and corporate reputation. In general, it is argued that companies which donate more enjoy a better reputation than those who donate less. However, other scholars have criticised these findings. They doubt whether such philanthropic activities are really beneficial to reputation and suggest that CS activities need to be consistent with the company's overall strategy and attached to core business activities in order to have a positive effect on reputation (see, for instance, Becker-Olsen et al., 2006). At the same time, focusing on philanthropy as an instrument to enhance corporate reputation may not be a viable strategy in the future. As we have shown above, stakeholders and civil society in particular are increasingly distrustful of business, and shift their attention from corporate support of childcare, museums or festivals to more material issues such as working conditions, climate change mitigation or corruption. This basically means that stakeholders are paying more attention to how sustainable the actual value-creating activities are – 'how the money is made' – when evaluating CS, and are less concerned to which charitable causes some percentages of profits are allocated – in other words, 'how the money is spent'. In turn, CS activities that are largely unrelated to a firm's core business may no longer work to position itself in a favourable light (Wickert and Risi, 2019).

Besides the importance of ensuring that CS activities focus on what stakeholders generally expect companies to do, scholars studying corporate reputation have also argued that walking CS can help to protect a company's reputation from damage. While companies can use other means to improve their reputation, such as innovative products, engaging in CS can also help create a buffer against reputation losses in times of scandals or when facing allegations of wrongdoing. Several authors argue that in situations of a reputational crisis, sincere CS engagement offers protection against negative publicity in the media. Companies with credible CS activities are thus exposed to lower reputational risks than those who are not perceived as sincerely walking CS (Eisenegger and Schranz, 2011). This is because stakeholders are more likely to believe that the questionable issue at hand was rather an accident that can be resolved, instead of being a more systematic part of how the company is doing business. Minor and Morgan (2011), for instance, have studied the link between reputation and CS among US firms over a period of fifteen years and conclude that stock prices, used as a proxy for a company's reputation as perceived by investors, declined considerably less after an adverse event, such as a product recall, if a firm has been perceived as sincerely managing sustainability. We conclude that walking CS, along core business operations and issues where social or environmental impacts are visible and substantially addressed, offers a significant opportunity for companies to both enhance and protect their reputation.

16.6 Talking Corporate Sustainability: Risking Reputational Damage

In contrast to walking CS, companies that are not 'walking the talk' cannot be considered to be seriously engaging in CS. Instead, an emphasis on only talking CS involves unsubstantiated and symbolic impression management in order to create a façade of sustainability that is not, however, connected to a firm's core-business operations, trying to wash business practices green in the eyes of stakeholders. However, this approach may backfire and therefore brings serious reputational risks. Cases abound where consumers have started to boycott a company if they find out that its CS messages are not sincere, NGOs might launch campaigns and 'name and shame' particular firms, and sustainability-oriented investors might divest their money (see Chapter 13). Oil and gas companies like BP and Shell are frequently accused of deceiving consumers with their advertising. For instance, according to *The Guardian*, some of BP's advertising campaigns had misled the public by focusing on the company's low carbon energy products, when more than 96 per cent of its annual spend was on oil and gas. In consequence, BP withdrew the ads before the complaint was assessed by courts (2021). Websites like the 'Seven Sins of Greenwashing' (http:// sinsofgreenwashing.com/) aim to make people aware of some of the worst forms of greenwashing among consumer products – and stop them from buying such products.

As we have shown above, companies face increasing stakeholder pressure to act in a sustainable manner, while at the same time having a good reputation is critical to success. This situation, however, confronts many corporations with a problem: while walking CS is considered the 'better' choice in terms of long-term reputation building, it is also very costly, and it is often difficult to directly measure outcomes and thus to evaluate short-term gains. Companies would have to roll out sophisticated CS management schemes, policies and operating procedures, which could include installing expensive measures and monitoring processes in their operations, or rearranging supply chains in order to uphold adequate working conditions and pay fair wages. Focusing instead on talking CS without corresponding integration of non-marginal CS activities to core business operations, in contrast, is rather cheap, in particular for large multinational corporations. As long as stakeholders do not discover the 'empty' CS façade, companies may reap short-term reputational gains (Wickert et al., 2016). This brings about a fundamental dilemma for the relationship between corporate reputation and CS.

Consider the case of an automotive company like BMW and its CS activities to become sustainable. Dowling and Moran (2012) examine this case and pose the question how a company should respond to environmental concerns when many of its operations, products and services can be easily construed as causing exactly this concern, such as pollution. They suggest that this is a dilemma with which major automobile, oil and other companies around the world have been struggling with, that 'the success of their business models makes the natural environment more congested and polluted' (2012: 30). Admittedly, most of these companies are well aware that many of their stakeholders are concerned about their environmental impacts. However, as Dowling and Moran assert, 'to date, the response to this dilemma has been to bolt-on some CS activities, many of which are only marginally related to their core activities … [while] … these activities can easily be construed as a cynical attempt to deflect attention from the underlying problem' (2012: 30). The authors hence are very concerned that many CS activities address rather marginal problems and are often aimed to direct attention away from more serious issues. Such behaviour can, however, be very risky in terms of long-term reputation effects.

Despite the arguments we have presented about the reputational risks of the talk-walk misalignment, some research suggests that if we consider this misalignment as dynamic, rather than static, it should not necessarily be condemned (e.g., Haack et al., 2012; Christensen et al., 2021; Haack et al., 2021). This is because the talk-walk mismatch might only be a temporary phenomenon at the beginning of a company's sustainability journey and which can start with ambitiously voiced aspirations and commitments which then need to be put into practice. When judging a company's presumed greenwashing, it is thus important to take a long (er)-term perspective and consider whether a certain company is making serious efforts and is on track to close, over time, the talk-walk gap by living up to its commitments.

Overall, we conclude that a company that is not walking the talk over extended periods of time can generally encounter significant reputational risks. What our discussion so far suggests is that two dimensions are important when making judgments about the effects of CS activities on reputation. First, are these activities reflective of *substantive* efforts to promote social and environmental responsibility (CS 'walk'), or are they rather a form of *symbolic* impression management that aims to construct a façade of CS without much substance (CS 'talk')? Second, are CS activities connected to a company's *core business* activities and do they address those areas of concern in its industry and in society that have considerable impacts, both positive when specific CS activities are promoted, and negative when CS activities are aimed to avoid or mitigate such impacts? Or are CS activities only peripheral to a company's operations and can thus be considered a *non-core activity*? Table 16.2 summarises the relationship between these dimensions and indicates the expected reputation effects:

Table 16.2 Corporate sustainability and effects on the reputation of a company

	Core business activity	Non-core activity
CSR walk: Substantial efforts	*Reputation effects: high opportunity to enhance reputation, and on a long-term basis*	*Reputation effects: probably ineffective in the long-run enhancing reputation*
CSR talk: Symbolic impression management	*Reputation effects: Risky, because no substance, but high expectations (backfire)*	*Reputation effects: probably ineffective in protecting reputation from damage*

16.7   Chapter Summary

In this chapter, we examined the relationship between corporate sustainability and reputation. We have shown that sustainability in business moved centre stage in the reputation landscape and is a critical component that influences the overall reputation of a company. We started by introducing key terms, and by defining reputation alongside other related constructs such as identity, image and legitimacy. We then discussed CS as an important part of a company's reputation, and illustrated different ways in which companies engage in CS to enhance and protect their reputation. Specifically, we distinguished between walking and talking CS, the first referring to substantive commitments and the latter involving symbolic public relations efforts. The two dimensions together provide a framework to analyse the CS approaches of different companies, and to identify the potential risks and rewards for their reputation. Based on an overview of these risks and rewards, we generally advocate that companies 'walk the talk' and transparently communicate about and report on their commitments to, and progress on, substantial CS activities, such as reducing their carbon emissions and enhancing worker welfare.

CHAPTER QUESTIONS

1. Does CS really have an effect on reputation? Think about the latest product you bought. What did you take into account other than price and general product quality? Did you think about any CS-related aspects?
2. If you were a manager responsible for corporate reputation, to which stakeholder group(s) would you pay most attention? Why?
3. Assuming that walking CS is costly, and talking CS is cheap, why should companies 'walk the talk'?
4. Think of an industry and the different players within it; what would be in your opinion core versus peripheral CS activities, and what approaches are companies in this sector taking in this respect?

Case Study: *Beyond Control? Managing Reputation after the BP Deepwater Horizon Oil Spill*
Available from Cambridge University Press at www.cambridge.org/rasche2

FURTHER RESOURCES

- Forbes. The 10 Companies with the Best CSR Reputations, www.forbes.com/pictures/efkk45mmlm/the-10-companies-with-the-best-csr-reputations/.

Forbes's ranking of companies with the best CS reputations adds to Fortune's ranking (below) by focusing specifically on CS. This allows a comparison of companies which scored similarly/differently in the two rankings, and gives insight into which criteria are considered to compile this CS-based ranking.

- Fortune. World's Most Admired Companies, http://fortune.com/worlds-most-admired-companies/.

Fortune magazine's ranking of the world's most admired companies gives an overview of those companies considered to have the best reputations worldwide, and gives insight into which criteria are considered to compile the ranking.

- RepRisk, www.reprisk.com.

RepRisk is a leading provider of dynamic business intelligence on environmental, social and governance risks for an unlimited universe of companies and projects.

- Reputation Institute, www.reputationinstitute.com.

Reputation Institute is a leading private sector research and advisory firm for corporate reputation that measures reputation and associated risks. This report will be interesting for those who want to gain a practical and hands-on perspective on the importance of corporate reputation.

17 Reporting, Materiality and Corporate Sustainability

CHRISTIAN HERZIG

LEARNING OBJECTIVES

- Enhance appreciation of corporate sustainability reporting (CSRep), its historical development and the different forms it can take.

- Raise critical awareness of rationales advanced to explain the phenomenon of CSRep.

- Impart understanding of potential problems and challenges with CSRep.

- Develop knowledge of guidelines and regulatory frameworks that govern CSRep and enable students to critically evaluate their effectiveness in enhancing transparency and accountability.

- Familiarise students with the concept of materiality and the most widely accepted standard for reporting, the Global Reporting Initiative.

- Foster understanding of country- and industry-specific developments in CSRep.

17.1 Introduction

Corporate sustainability refers to the expectation that business is responsible for its impact on society and the environment. Society expects companies to take responsibility for avoiding, reducing or, at best, compensating for negative externalities, as well as contributing to social welfare while being held accountable for these impacts and explaining externalities transparently. However, such responsibility is articulated through a complex set of means and is constantly changing. The importance of understanding these complexities and dynamics and the need for transparency and accountability has provoked considerable interest in the field of corporate sustainability reporting (CSRep), the subject of this chapter. In essence, CSRep reflects a company's responsibility to portray – in printed reports or on corporate websites – an account of its ecological, social and economic performance and impact, and inform its stakeholders to what extent the company can contribute to sustainable development. The number of companies that have published a dedicated corporate sustainability report has increased considerably in recent decades, as has the criticism of the reluctance and inability of some companies to provide a full and fair account of their performance and impact on society and their stakeholders. This debate reflects the different approaches to regulating CSRep and the roles that society and stakeholders might play in enhancing the engagement in and quality of CSRep.

The chapter begins with a general definition of CSRep, an overview of its historic development and the various forms it can take (Section 17.2). Then, rationales for and challenges to companies' engagement in CSRep are outlined (Section 17.3). In Section 17.4, different alternatives for governing CSRep are explored, distinguishing voluntary standards from legally binding measures such as disclosure regulations introduced by governments and stock exchanges in European and other countries. Particular attention is paid to the most widely applied standard for CSRep, the Global Reporting Initiative (GRI) Standards, and the concept of materiality. Finally, in section 17.5, countries and industries in which reporting has turned into a more institutionalised practice are described in more detail. The chapter ends with a conclusion in Section 17.6.

17.2   Definition, Development and Assurance

In this section, we look at three interrelated questions: (1) What is corporate sustainability reporting? (2) How has corporate sustainability reporting evolved? and (3) How can corporate sustainability reports be externally assured?

17.2.1   What Is Corporate Sustainability Reporting?

With corporate sustainability reports, companies endeavour to demonstrate their wider responsibility to society and inform stakeholders to what extent they might contribute to sustainable development. There are various rationales which serve to provide an argument for a company's engagement in CSRep (see Section 17.3.1). Generally, the global demand for transparent, reliable and accountable forms of socially responsible business has increased in recent decades due to increased stakeholder activism, growing media coverage, numerous business scandals and various corporate governance failures. Large and multinational companies have become particularly vulnerable to public pressure by consumers, social and environmental activists and other groups interested in responsible and sustainable business. Thus, they have engaged in communicating the social and environmental effects of their economic actions to particular interest groups in society and to society at large, thereby claiming that corporate sustainability reports provide a nuanced picture of their ecological, social and economic activities and performance.

However, although CSRep has increasingly become a subject of regulatory approaches, it also remains vague, ambiguous and contested alongside the entire concept of socially responsible business (Gond and Moon, 2011). In particular, the meaning of corporate responsibility can vary according to the context in which businesses operate. The idea of corporate responsibility is dynamic in that its meaning, application and use has significantly changed over time. This makes reporting on corporate sustainability difficult. The dynamic nature of the concept in tandem with ideas such as 'corporate citizenship' and 'social accountability' adds to this complexity, and the fairly fast and often changing terminology applied to non- or extra-financial reporting initiatives is just as obstructive. There is currently a plethora of labels for non-financial reports (e.g., sustainability report, corporate social responsibility report, corporate citizenship report, sustainable development report and integrated report). For the sake of clarity, this chapter refers to 'corporate sustainability reports' and 'corporate sustainability reporting' (CSRep) when addressing any form of a company's self-presentation that goes beyond the traditional role of providing solely financial accounts to the capital owners.

To get a better sense of what constitutes CSRep, two other characteristics and developments need to be examined: its discursive formation within the process of stakeholder engagement and its increased embeddedness in a new public sphere, namely the virtual reality created by the Internet.

There is a general recognition of the vital importance of stakeholder engagement and dialogue, as well as their place within the context of the overall CSRep process through which companies decide on the report's format and what to disclose in their reports (Rinaldi et al., 2014). This is reflected in various reporting principles most prominently established in guidelines and standards published by the GRI and AccountAbility (see Table 17.1 and Section 17.4.1). According to these frameworks, a corporate report should cover a company's significant economic, environmental and social impact by detailing the most relevant issues to stakeholders and society and providing a comprehensive assessment of the company's performance. Besides these principles of materiality and completeness, there is also a strong expectation that a company examines and reflects on how it identifies and engages with stakeholders and responds to their reasonable expectations and interests (stakeholder inclusiveness and responsiveness). This is also discussed within the context of institutional reform designed to improve the structure within which CSRep takes place and stakeholders are empowered through greater participation (Cooper and Owen, 2007; Gray et al., 2014). Such institutional reform goes beyond what is understood as 'administrative' (or technical) reform, which primarily looks at how CSRep is used to enhance the level of transparency. With regard to guidelines, standards and regulations, administrative reform is often expressed as both a comprehensive set of environmental, social and economic indicators framing the content of reports and guidance on technical topics in measuring and reporting on

Table 17.1 Overview of selected voluntary frameworks for corporate sustainability reporting

Initiative (launch year)	Focus of reporting	Description	Core subjects	Application and further information
Eco-Management and Audit Scheme/EMAS (1993) EU regulation	- Management process - Reporting content (themes and indicators)	- Represents a European standard to establish a certifiable environmental management system and related reporting scheme ('environmental statement') - Requires regular environmental reporting on specific themes and based upon some general types of indicators every three to four years depending on business size (further specified through sector guidance documents) - Addresses reporting principles (e.g., comparability through benchmarking), but does not specify principles	- The environment (water, energy efficiency, material efficiency, biodiversity, waste and emissions) - Environmental policy and management system - Environmental programmes and objectives - Environmental performance and compliance with legal obligations	- 3,851 organisations and 12,856 sites in Europe - EMAS Global allows for using the scheme outside Europe - All types of organisation across sectors - Additional sectoral reference documents (e.g., best environmental management practices) Further information: www.emas.eu
AccountAbility: The AA1000 Series of Standards (1995) Global consulting and standards firm	- Management process - Reporting quality (principles)	- Principle-based standards to develop a sustainable business model and strategy, actively engage with stakeholders and foster public disclosure - World's first sustainability assurance standard - Publishes guidance notes - Offers training and consulting	- Stakeholder engagement - Governance, strategy and accountability - Assurance of sustainability management, performance and reporting	- North America, Europe, the Middle East, Asia and Africa - All types of organisations - Sectors such as financial services, energy and extractives, consumer goods, food and beverages, and pharmaceuticals Further information: www.accountability.org

Table 17.1 (*cont.*)

Initiative (launch year)	Focus of reporting	Description	Core subjects	Application and further information
Global Reporting Initiative/GRI (1997) Global, not-for-profit organisation governed by multi-stakeholder network	- Management process - Reporting quality (principles) - Reporting content (indicators)	- Details reporting principles and entails general disclosures about the reporting organisation and material topics - Details specific information about material topics across three categories: economic, environmental and social - Provides implementation guidance, a sustainability disclosure database, a support suite and training programme	- Process of reporting and stakeholder engagement - Analysis and assessment of materiality - Governance, strategy and policies - Economic performance, market presence, anti-corruption, tax, etc. - Environmental assessment of suppliers, materials, water, biodiversity, etc. - Employment, labour relations, training and education, local communities, etc.	- Over 10,000 organisations in over 100 countries - All types of organisations across sectors - 40 additional sector standards under development Further information: www.globalreporting.org
The Greenhouse Gas/ GHG Protocol (1998) Global NGO-business partnership	- Reporting content (indicators) - Reporting quality (measurements and principles) - Management process	- Supplies the most widely used international accounting standards for companies to measure, manage and report on greenhouse gas emissions (GHG) - Standards cover GHG inventories, including emissions from a company's value chain, a product's full life cycle and climate change mitigation projects - Develops guidance documents (e.g., how to engage with suppliers) which sometimes include reporting principles	- The environment (climate change)	- More than 460 global members in developed and developing countries - All types of organisations across sectors - Additional sector-specific tools Further information: www.ghgprotocol.org

Carbon Disclosure Project/CDP (2000) Investor-led, not-for-profit initiative	- Reporting content (indicators)	- Enhances disclosure of environmental information in order to accelerate carbon reduction and protect natural resources - Provides access to supplementary analytical tools and best disclosure practices	- The environment (including climate change, water, forests and environmental risks in supply chains)	- More than 9,500 organisations in developed and developing countries globally - All types of organisations (except not-for-profit) across sectors Further information: www.cdp.net
Organisation for Economic Co-operation and Development/OECD (2006)	- Management process	- The risk awareness tool for multinational enterprises in weak governance zones helps multinationals to identify risks and ethical issues - Complements the 'OECD Guidelines for Multinational Enterprises'	- Organisational governance - Ethical wrongdoing - Human rights - The environment - Labour - Health and safety	- 50 member countries, including advanced and emerging countries - All types of organisations across sectors Further information: www.oecd.org
United Nations Global Compact/UNGC (2009) UN initiative and global company-based network	- Reporting content (themes)	- Requires participating companies to comply with ten UNGC Principles and produce an annual Communication on Progress (COP) report to inform stakeholders about companies' efforts to uphold the principles - Provides guidance on developing COP reports, including software tools, policy documents, COP trends and list of active UNGC reporters - Enhanced digital platform for COP will be launched in 2023	- Human rights - Labour practices - The environment - Anti-corruption	- More than 12,000 corporate participants in over 160 countries - All types of organisations across sectors Further information: www.unglobalcompact.org

Table 17.1 (cont.)

Initiative (launch year)	Focus of reporting	Description	Core subjects	Application and further information
ISO 26000 (2010) International standard-setting body	- Management process	- The non-certifiable standard provides organisations with guidance on how social responsibility can be integrated throughout an organisation based on seven principles, seven core subjects and stakeholder engagement - Addresses the need for communicating commitments and performance, but works together with other reporting initiatives (such as the GRI and the IIRC) to specify concrete links between the initiatives	- Organisational governance - Human rights - Labour practices - The environment - Fair operating practices - Consumer issues - Community involvement and development	- More than 80 countries adopted the standard - All types of public, private and non-profit organisations across sectors Further information: www.iso.org
International Integrated Reporting Council/IIRC (2011) Global coalition of regulators, investors, companies and accounting bodies	- Reporting content (themes) - Reporting quality (principles) - Management process	- Framework describes the process of how value can be created, governed and reported - Details guiding principles for reporting and the process of engaging with stakeholders - Provides an example database, various guidance documents and various networks	- Stocks of value in form of financial, manufactured, intellectual, human, social and relationship, and natural capital - Strategy, governance and performance - Business model and activities - Risks and opportunities	- More than 2,500 companies in over 75 countries - All types of organisations across sectors Further information: www.theiirc.org

Note: Management process – guidance on how to design the management processes underlying CSRep; reporting quality – guidance on how to attain a standard quality for CSRep (principles for the way of reporting and/or measuring); reporting content – guidance on the content of CSRep (themes only or detailing indicators).

issues related to corporate responsibility. The possible tension which can emerge from different motives for and levels of stakeholder engagement and dialogue as well as their influence on the potential power of CSRep to serve as an accountability mechanism will be discussed in Section 17.3.1. Rinaldi et al. (2014) and Gray et al. (2014) provide a comprehensive overview of different forms of engaging with stakeholders in practice and key issues in the implementation of stakeholder engagement and dialogue.

A related and emerging element of CSRep is the use of the Internet for disclosing information and engaging with stakeholders about corporate sustainability. Greater use of the Internet for CSRep promises advantages in information provision, accessibility and comprehensibility (Herzig and Godemann, 2010). This is due to its manifold advantages in providing access to a large quantity of information, presenting an integrated view of different aspects of sustainability through links to other information sources related to the company or other organisations, 'customising' reporting through individual access for stakeholders and using a combination of different media elements (e.g., audio, images or videos). Thus, the Internet can support the reporting process in various ways to overcome problems such as information overload or lack of target group orientation (see Section 17.3.2). In practice and despite disadvantages to using the Internet (e.g., the exclusion of some stakeholders from the reporting process due to limited web accessibility or the difficulties in assuring web content), the combined use of printed reports and online reporting has become the primary means of CSRep. Some companies have now abandoned printed reports completely and rely exclusively on internet-based CSRep.

Advantages of internet-supported CSRep include a range of communication possibilities for engaging and communicating with stakeholders. An increasing number of companies has started to interact with stakeholders regarding sustainability issues through blogs, discussion forums and more synchronous forms of dialogue (e.g., instant messaging, chat boxes). However, dialogue-based online relationships established and largely influenced by companies have also been criticised as being a public relations exercise rather than a means for meaningfully enhancing the role of stakeholders in corporate decision-making and reporting. The concern over deficiencies in stakeholder engagement and reporting processes in the critical accounting community will be explored in Section 17.3.2, but it is worth noting here that the emancipatory power of the Internet has paved the way to another form of reporting: the so-called counter or shadow accounting, which usually challenges companies that provide a high level of self-presentation on corporate sustainability.

Having looked at one of the most recent developments in CSRep, the use of the Internet, the next section will explore the historical development of CSRep (an enlightening historical review is given by Owen and O'Dwyer, 2008; see also Herzig and Schaltegger, 2011 and Buhr et al., 2014).

17.2.2   How Has Corporate Sustainability Reporting Evolved?

Although companies already disclosed social information primarily regarding their employees and communities in earlier decades of the twentieth century, considerable interest in non-financial reporting among practitioners and researchers did not arise until the 1970s. At that time, changing societal expectations and needs imposed new demands on companies and sparked a debate on companies' responsibilities towards society's well-being. To counter public and governmental criticism, several large US and Western European companies started publishing *social reports*. Companies used these reports to inform their stakeholders about the company's activities, products and services, as well as related positive and negative social impacts. This report also included new social accounting techniques, such as the value added statement, which presents the added value generated by an organisation and its source and distribution among the contributors (e.g., to the state via taxes and duties, to employees via salary and benefits and to shareholders via dividends). Social reports demonstrated how company value was created and attributed to a larger number of stakeholders rather than just the shareholders. The emergence of these new forms of accounting and reporting can be seen in the light of rising income levels that shifted the focus of society and politics to objectives such as overall quality of life. However, by the end of the 1970s, social reporting was in decline again. Among the reasons for the decline were inadequate target group orientation, a mismatch between the information interests of most stakeholders, social reports often being scientifically designed and remote from the reality of most people's lives, a misuse of social reporting as a public relations tool that reduced its reliability and credibility, an insufficient integration of social and financial reporting and the positive economic and political development of Europe with job movements to the services sector and improved working conditions (Herzig and Schaltegger, 2011).

During the late 1980s and 1990s, non-financial reporting regained importance. However, the focus shifted from social to environmental issues due to various environmental incidents and catastrophes (e.g., Bhopal, India; Schweizerhalle, Switzerland; and Hoechst AG, Germany). Companies were held responsible for the consequences of these environmental disasters. In response to the increased pressure for greater transparency and accountability, companies, particularly those operating within environmentally sensitive industries, started to publish *environmental reports* to inform stakeholders about the organisational activities' impacts on the natural environment (e.g., air and water emissions, types and amounts of wastes, etc.) and their approaches to managing environmental issues and impacts. These environmental reporting activities were partly enforced by new laws (compulsory reporting) and partly voluntary. The following years saw different attempts to integrate environmental and social issues within corporate reporting (e.g., safety, health and environment reports). Overall, environmental reporting began to supersede companies' early social reports. By the turn of the century, the number of environmental reports and the attention they received in the media and society increased considerably. Meanwhile, their average quality improved from being primarily green glossaries and one-off reports to emerging as more comprehensive environmental reports published on a regular (e.g., annual) basis. An example of a voluntary approach to environmental reporting is the *European Union Eco-Management and Audit Scheme* (EMAS; see Table 17.1).

In the mid-1990s, attention shifted towards *sustainability reports* and 'multi-issue reporting' (Kolk, 2004). Sustainability reports reflect companies' claims to depict an overall picture of their ecological, social and economic sustainability activities and performance and to inform stakeholders as to what extent and how companies contribute to sustainable development (Herzig and Ghosh, 2017). One of the earlier examples is Shell's 'Triple P-Report' (People, Planet and Profits) published in the late 1990s, whose title already indicates the multidimensional reporting style. Compared to social reporting in the 1970s, which emphasised employee-related issues and value creation for various stakeholders, social aspects within sustainability reports hold global importance and are more comprehensively dealt with in terms of moral and ethical questions of sustainable development (e.g., child labour in the supply chain, human rights, poverty alleviation, gender issues and trading relationships). However, while generally integrative in nature, these reports do not necessarily address financial figures or performance measures in a comprehensive way, but often concentrate on corporate ecological and social strategy and performance.

Companies vary in their approach to reporting extra-financial subjects. While some companies integrate all information into one report, other companies opt for publishing either individual reports (e.g., environmental, social, community or ethical supply chain reports) or a combination of these reports as separate documents. Such reports are heterogeneous with regard to their title, length, content, standard and external assurance applied. As a whole, there has been a continuous increase in the number of extra-financial reports. Between 2008 and 2020, the percentage of the world's largest 250 corporations that provided some sort of a stand-alone corporate sustainability report increased from 80 to 96 per cent (KPMG, 2020).

Besides these developments in extra-financial reporting, environmental and social information has also been increasingly integrated into primarily financial reports. Two main developments include the extension of annual reports and the rise of the integrated reporting concept. In many countries, companies are required by law or by the respective stock market to produce and publish an annual financial report. The annual report is regarded as the most formal corporate reporting document and traditionally focuses on companies' key financial and performance figures. However, there has been an increased focus on selected environmental and social aspects of corporate performance in financial reports driven by the increasing interest of investors, analysts and regulatory requirements. In Europe, the implementation of the EU Accounts Modernisation Directive with the reformed law regulating the balance sheet (European Parliament and European Council, 2004) was the beginning of the *extension of annual reports*, forcing shareholder companies to include non-financial performance indicators, specifically environmental and labour-related indicators, in the prognosis reports included in their annual reports. The Accounts Modernisation Directive was followed by new European Reporting Directives on CSRep in the following years (see Section 17.4.2). The coverage of issues related to corporate sustainability in annual reports has increased worldwide from 4 per cent of the top 100 companies in 2008 (twenty-two countries), to over 20 per cent in 2011 (thirty-four countries) and to 61 per cent in 2020 (forty-five countries) (KPMG, 2020). The extent to which companies' annual reports address financial, governance, social and environmental performance and corporate sustainability evaluations, however, still varies.

There is the expectation by some (particularly professional accounting bodies, consultancies, regulators and corporations) that a more consistent approach to reporting can be promoted through the most recent CSRep initiative: *integrated reporting*. Integrated reports are based on the idea of reporting on the relationship between companies' financial results and sustainability impacts in the form of one 'holistic' and complete report. According to the International Integrated Reporting Council (IIRC), an integrated report is 'a concise communication about how an organization's strategy, governance, performance and prospects, in the context of its external environment, lead to the creation of value in the short, medium and long term' (IIRC, 2013: 7). By effectively linking these often isolated aspects, companies can provide disclosure on past performance and comment on their long-term goals for future value generation. According to the IIRC's Integrated Reporting Framework released in December 2013, an integrated report should provide information on a company's impact on the communities in which it operates and how it intends to strengthen its positive effects and eliminate or mitigate its negative impacts. The framework was updated in January 2021 to enable more decision-useful reporting. The revision resulted in improved insight into the quality and integrity of the reporting process and a clearer distinction between outputs and outcomes. Another part of the revision was the simplification of the required responsibility statement for the integrated report and a stronger focus on balanced reporting of conservation of value and erosion scenarios (IIRC, 2021). The impact the initiative will have on the reporting environment and the extent to which it will serve various stakeholders and contribute to sustainable development is still unclear. A notable number of scholars has evaluated the integrated reporting initiative critically, especially with regard to its objective and practice (de Villiers et al., 2014; Rinaldi et al., 2018), and there seems to be variety in the ways in which integrated reporting is understood and used within institutions. There have been difficulties with the implementation of the new framework (e.g., with regard to selecting and linking non-financial information (NFI) with financial key performance indicators (KPIs)) and concerns have been expressed about whether the initiative is managerially captured by mostly financially interested stakeholders. A global consultation conducted by the IIRC in 2017 aimed to explain the challenges of integrated reporting. One of the key findings was the lack of guidance and leading practice examples, which led to complications in implementing integrated reporting in organisations (IIRC, 2018).

17.2.3 How Can Corporate Sustainability Reports Be Externally Assured?

Notable developments have not only been evident in the changing forms and rising numbers of reports, but also in the number of reports assured by external bodies. As stakeholders expect companies to publish accurate, reliable and credible corporate sustainability reports, companies face a dilemma: the unavailability of one universal reporting standard puts the validity, reliability and comparability of the reports into question. The inconsistent and voluntary reporting in substantial parts therefore requires a reliable external source to assess the credibility of CSRep. Accordingly, and in line with the GRI's recommendations to externally assure the reliability of CSRep, an increase in *external assurance statements* has been observed in recent years. Whereas only 30 per cent of the top 250 companies from the Global Fortune 500 conducted assurance on their corporate sustainability reports in 2005, the number of companies that used third-party assurance rose to 59 per cent in 2013 and to nearly 71 per cent in 2020 (KPMG, 2020).

There are two main standards for facilitating the assurance of corporate sustainability reports: the International Standard on Assurance Engagement (ISAE) 3000 and the AA1000 Assurance Standard (AA1000AS). The ISAE 3000 was initiated by the International Auditing and Assurance Standards Board in 2003 and is primarily used by accounting firms. The Assurance Standard, revised in 2013, addresses assurance engagements that are not audits or reviews of historical financial information. The AA1000AS was proposed in 2003 by AccountAbility. The most recent iteration of the standard, AA1000AS v3, was enforced in January 2021. It is rooted in AccountAbility's (2018) principles of inclusivity, responsiveness, materiality and impact. The core principle of impact means that organisations monitor and measure and are accountable for their actions that affect the ecosystem. Whereas the ISAE 3000 relies on fixed assurance procedures to provide a certain extent of security to the profession, the AA1000AS concentrates on the quality of the reporting process and leaves room for more individual adjustments. The ISAE 3000 and AA1000AS can be regarded as complements rather than substitutes and are often simultaneously obtained by companies and assurance providers.

External assurance is generally considered to enhance the credibility and quality of the report, the related reporting process and companies' operations and risk management. However, in practice, concern has been raised about the effectiveness of current assurance practices. As the GRI and all other reporting standards do not prescribe the extent of the examination, the external assurance can vary considerably among companies. Evidence on which to base conclusions from the review of corporate sustainability information is also often restricted – that is, a *limited assurance* engagement is often used in preference to the more comprehensive reasonable assurance. Further concerns emerge from ambiguities and inconsistencies in current approaches to sustainability assurance, such as independence and degree of thoroughness of audits (Owen and O'Dwyer, 2008).

17.3   Rationales, Problems and Challenges

This section explores why companies do or should engage in corporate sustainability reporting and which kinds of problems and challenges can be associated with disclosing sustainability information.

17.3.1   Why Do or Should Companies Engage in Corporate Sustainability Reporting?

Numerous rationales have been proposed to explain the existence of CSRep (for a comprehensive review, see Gray et al., 2014). The phenomenon has been explored from a meta/meso or systems perspective (e.g., political economy and critical theory), an organisational perspective (e.g., resource dependency and organisational change theory) and an individual perspective (e.g., psychology and anthropology). At each level, CSRep has been theorised to provide complementary and overlapping explanations, albeit much more emphasis has been placed on the first two perspectives. As is the nature of theory, some theoretical lenses have proven to be helpful in exploring and enhancing understanding of CSRep at more than one level. For example, *discourse theory* has been used to explore both organisational transformation towards sustainable development through text or visual analysis of corporate sustainability reports (intra-organisational perspective) and the advance of local democracy and moral consensus in the light of certain corporate sustainability practices (meta perspective). Viewing the various theories as overlapping and closely interlinked concepts rather than in isolation facilitates a fuller understanding of the phenomenon of CSRep. A joint consideration is also often suggested for three of the most common theories in CSRep literature: institutional theory, legitimacy theory and stakeholder theory. These three theoretical lenses are placed at the intersection of the organisational and the meso/sub-system levels.

From the perspective of *institutional theory*, institutional pressures create a specific institutional environment in which companies make decisions regarding what to disclose and how to disclose it (Higgins and Larrinaga, 2014). These external pressures can be coercive (e.g., mandatory CSRep; see Section 17.4.2), mimetic (e.g., following reporting practices of competitors) and normative (e.g., fulfilling professional expectations such as compliance with reporting standards and guidelines published by professional accounting bodies; see Section 17.4.1). In the case of globally operating organisations, possible tensions can arise between the integration of reporting 'infrastructures' mandated by the headquarters of a company and subsidiaries' responsiveness to local expectations at the host-country level ('institutional duality' in the case of CSRep; Beddewela and Herzig, 2013). *Legitimacy theory*, by contrast, builds on the idea that there is an implicit social contract between companies and society. Hence, society grants legitimacy to companies as long as they comply with societal norms and expectations and CSRep corresponds with actual corporate activities and performance. While institutional theory broadly discusses how reporting practices and changes bring legitimacy to a company, legitimacy theory investigates how a company mobilises its reporting to legitimise its relationship with society and how CSRep assists a company in managing threats to its organisational legitimacy. However, this corporate legitimacy is put into question if the corporate and societal value systems diverge. For example, companies have been accused of pursuing strategies to change perceptions of responsibility without changing actual behaviour, deflecting attention in reports onto other issues or even seeking to change external expectations of performance through reporting. Overall, strategies to manage threats to organisational legitimacy and establish, maintain or repair legitimacy through CSRep have been investigated in a large body of accounting research. (An overview and future directions for using legitimacy theory to examine CSRep is provided by Deegan, 2014, 2019.)

Stakeholder theory also views companies as embedded within a business environment, which is composed of a diverse range of stakeholders (interest groups and individuals) who, directly or indirectly, can affect or are affected by companies' business operations (Freeman, 1984a; see Chapter 4). Companies are thus considered to be bound by various social contracts with divergent stakeholders. These stakeholders hold different perspectives on corporate business conduct and vary in their ability to impact corporate activities and legitimacy. Examples of stakeholders threatening companies' legitimacy or licence to operate include consumers boycotting products and services and employees withholding their loyalty, and petitioning the government to impose fines or legal restrictions on the company.

Depending on the level of the importance assigned to stakeholder engagement, two competing perspectives on CSRep – stakeholder accountability and business cases – have increasingly been distinguished from each other because their power to enhance the accountability of organisational activities and impact is seen to differ considerably (Brown and Fraser, 2006; Gray et al., 2014). *Stakeholder accountability* focuses on increasing the transparency and accountability of companies to their stakeholders. Assuming that companies do have wider responsibilities than simply generating money for their shareholders, the accountability of companies is extended beyond the traditional role of providing financial accounts to the capital owners. CSRep thus serves the process of communicating the social and environmental effects of companies' economic actions to stakeholders to enable them to meaningfully participate in corporate decision-making and reporting. This is based on the notion that, in a democratic society, stakeholders have certain information rights that need to be protected from abuses of corporate power and the enhanced accountability of companies encourages wider democratic processes of discourse and decision-making. Meaningful engagement with relevant stakeholders through reporting (irrespective of the power they might possess) approximates to what various scholars view as 'true', 'real' or the normative approach to accountability.

This view of accountability contrasts with the second variant of stakeholder engagement and reporting, where stakeholders are consulted or managed by companies through and around reporting processes to gain their support and approval. Here, engagement with CSRep takes place only when benefits are created for both the stakeholders and the business itself ('win-win paradigm'). The range of reasons for businesses to produce corporate reports includes the creation of competitive advantage through the development and penetration of new market segments, creating financial value through, for example, business efficiency or the identification of possible cost savings, and motivating and raising awareness among staff. Reasons also relate closely to the above mentioned three theoretical lenses: using CSRep as a means for companies to legitimise their activities and their impacts and to manage their relationships with stakeholders to further their own interests. Employing stakeholder theory and reporting in such an organisation-centred way resonates in the production of corporate sustainability reports for reasons of reputation, impression and risk management.

The *business case* for sustainability is, overall, a widely recognised motive underlying CSRep. From the perspective of stakeholder accountability proponents, however, using CSRep as a tool to primarily look after its powerful (i.e., often financially oriented) stakeholders and to report the extent to which it benefits the company's profits only leads to 'soft' accountability and does not promote participatory governance.

17.3.2   What Are the Problems and Challenges of Corporate Sustainability Reporting?

A key problem with CSRep is the concern that the predominance of the business case perspective in practice deflects attention from social change and the current problems to be addressed in corporate sustainability reports. There is criticism that companies may take the role of powerful 'elites' that steer society in a direction that reinforces their own dominance without making sufficient contributions to sustainable development (Brown and Fraser, 2006; Cooper and Owen, 2007). This concern is manifested in the 'performance–portrayal gap' (Adams, 2004), which reflects the view that reports often convey a favourable rather than a representative picture of the company and fail to establish relationships between environmental and social disclosure and actual performance. Corporate sustainability reports are thus often accused of assisting management in controlling the perceptions of stakeholders and seeking legitimacy or reputation rather than enhancing stakeholder accountability for the real societal impact of companies' activities.

To confront managerial capture of the social and environmental agenda and to reveal possible contradictions between a company's self-presentation and stakeholder perspectives, the concept of *shadow reporting* has been put forward. Shadow reporting can be viewed as a technology that collects, compiles, showcases, represents and communicates evidence from external sources, including newspaper articles, NGO reports, direct testaments from workers, ex-employees, trade unions, suppliers and public pollution registers (Dey, 2007). The purpose of these *'external' accounts* (also referred to as 'anti-reports', 'counter accounts' or 'social audits') is to reveal contradictions between what companies disclose in their corporate reports and what they suppress in order to reveal problems with companies' activities and to provide additional insights into the environmental and social impacts associated with these activities. Overall, shadow reporting can be understood as an attempt to challenge CSRep and move away from an organisation-centred perspective of reporting using independent but not necessarily objective sources (Dey et al., 2011).

Wider criticism of CSRep includes concerns as to whether the company might be the wrong boundary to report on sustainability and demonstrate accountability for material social and environmental impacts. As Gray (2006: 73) states: 'Sustainability is a planetary, perhaps regional, certainly spatial concept and its application at the organisational level is difficult at best.' Another criticism is that CSRep can be non-specific, aiming at a diffuse and excessively wide group of potential readers. Besides uncertainties in boundary setting, this concern may stem from the voluntary nature and somewhat overwhelming range of reporting guidelines and standards (despite some notable tendencies of convergence; see Section 17.4). A lack of orientation towards a target group is also associated with the risk of creating an information overload. In the 1990s and early 2000s, some companies tended to flood their readers with increasingly extensive corporate sustainability reports. While this problem has generally diminished with the increased use of online reporting, the quality of reports leaves much to be desired at times. Companies are being criticised for putting incorrect and irrelevant data into corporate sustainability reports and considering environmental, social and economic aspects of organisational activities in an additive rather than integrative manner. They thereby fail to recognise and mention possible and actual tensions across competing social, environmental and economic objectives and challenges embodied in companies' approaches to sustainability (Haffar and Searcy, 2020).

Overall, it seems there is considerable room for improvement regarding the level of accountability provided by corporate sustainability reports, the quality of their content, the stakeholder engagement process and the practices of external assurance. While there is a growing number of large, typically multinational companies producing corporate sustainability reports, it appears that many small and medium-sized enterprises and family companies still do not engage with this topic to a great extent despite playing a significant role in markets, communities and society. Some reasons for this lack of engagement are the high and disproportionate costs associated with the production of reports and the inadequacy of reporting schemes to address companies' needs and routines for managing their relationships with local customers and communities. However, knowledge about how these companies practise reporting and discharge accountability is rather limited as most research and publications (including texts such as this one) concentrate on the impacts and role of large and multinational companies in governing sustainability issues at a global level.

17.4   Approaches to Governing Corporate Sustainability Reporting

The rise in CSRep can largely be attributed to the continuous development of guidelines, standards and regulations. They provide guidance to companies in the development of reports and aim at governing and spreading CSRep within and across countries and sectors. Guidelines are non-binding and often used as a basis for the voluntary development of corporate sustainability reports. They reflect the practical experiences encountered by companies and other organisations and institutions. Organisations engaged in the development of these guidelines are governmental (both national and supranational) as well as non-governmental (e.g., industry associations, multi-stakeholder initiatives and research institutions). These guidelines have been followed by the development of standards for reporting and assurance and by the introduction of new regulations (mandatory reporting). Standards are issued by standardisation organisations and often form a basis for certification processes. By contrast, regulations on various forms of CSRep have a binding character and have been enforced by associations and ministries in various parts of the world.

The following section explores voluntary and mandatory frameworks for CSRep and critically reflects on their role in disseminating CSRep and enhancing transparency and accountability.

17.4.1 Voluntary Corporate Sustainability Reporting

A growing body of national and international guidelines for CSRep has evolved in the last two to three decades to support companies in developing reports and externally communicating their social, ecological and economic performance to satisfy the information needs of different stakeholder groups. A review of seventy-one countries and regions identified approximately 135 voluntary standards, codes and guidelines for CSRep in 2016 (KPMG et al., 2016). The number of voluntary standards has doubled over the last few years, and the 2020 review showed more than eighty countries and regions (GRI et al., 2020; see also Chapter 20).

Table 17.1 portrays a selection of key voluntary frameworks for CSRep with their most important characteristics. As summarised in the table, the guidelines address different aspects of corporate sustainability, differ with regard to the sector and the size of companies they can be applied to and vary in that some of them focus on the reporting content (themes and/or indicators), the reporting quality (formulating principles for the way of reporting and/or measuring), the management process (providing guidance on how to design management processes underlying CSRep) or all factors.

The most generally accepted and universally applied CSRep framework is provided by the GRI, an international, network-based non-profit organisation representing an international multi-stakeholder initiative involving businesses, civil societies, academia and public institutions worldwide. The GRI reporting framework can be considered the de facto standard for CSRep. According to KPMG's survey in 2020, 67 per cent of the top 100 companies in fifty-two nations applied the GRI reporting framework and for stand-alone corporate sustainability reports, and its application rate was at 73 per cent. Moreover, the 'Carrots & Sticks' (GRI et al., 2020) study cites it as the most frequently referenced CSRep standard by governments, financial market regulators and stock exchanges (see also Table 17.3).

The GRI reporting framework has gradually evolved since its initial inception in 2000 for a variety of reasons, including the need to incorporate additional disclosure requirements as gathered from the stakeholder consultative method, improve companies' understanding of material issues, remove ambiguities in interpretation of concepts and principles, and reach harmonisation with other major guidelines and initiatives related to CSRep. The reporting framework was renamed the 'GRI Standards' in 2016. The new GRI Standards build on the G4 Guidelines previously developed by the GRI (2017) and effectively replace them from 2018. The update primarily changes the structure and format, but leaves the main content, concepts and requirements untouched. The guidelines have been restructured into a set of modular, interlinked reporting standards, consisting of three Universal Standards (Foundation (GRI 101), General Disclosures (GRI 102) and Material Topics (GRI 103)) and thirty-one Topic-specific Standards (reduced from thirty-four in 2016), which are organised into economic (the GRI 200 series), environmental (the GRI 300 series) and social (the GRI 400 series) categories. This structure enables the GRI to update the individual standards regularly and to give organisations the possibility to refer to individual standards. As a recent development, the family of GRI Standards will be extended through the Sector programme to develop standards for forty sectors over the next few years. The Sector Standards do not include new topic-specific indicators, but rather, they help companies identify material topics by contextualising CSRep (i.e., describing a sector's most significant impacts and stakeholder expectations) and report on these by listing disclosures that are relevant for the sector to report on. Sectors' priority is based on the significance of their environmental, social and economic impacts. The first Sector Standard, Oil & Gas (GRI 11), was published as part of the revised Universal Standards 2021, and will be followed by a second standard for the agricultural sector.

In contrast to some changes introduced by the new GRI Standards, the principle of *materiality* remains a key characteristic of the GRI reporting framework (as it is for IIRC's Integrated Reporting framework). By aiding in identifying material issues, companies are encouraged to focus on the most important impacts on the economy, environment and society in their CSRep. The materiality principle also includes the concept of boundaries. Companies are not only asked to determine the most material aspects, but are also required to describe whether the impact – making an aspect material – occurs occurs inside or outside the organisation and where the impact ends. Reporting companies need to delineate the reason for an aspect's materiality and outline how the material aspects are managed (Universal Standard GRI 103 'Material Approach'). The materiality principle also determines the selection of the content for the topic-specific disclosures and requires companies to thoroughly report on how they deal with the material impacts within their organisation and their supply chains.

The focus on materiality creates various opportunities for reporting organisations and their stakeholders. It enables companies to emphasise what their essential sustainability-related impacts are. By concentrating on and limiting their reports to critical topics and key risk impacts, companies can not only shorten their reports, but they can also increase their clarity, relevance and credibility. This reduction in information redundancy can enhance transparency and understanding regarding the selection, prioritisation and management of core topics selected for the report. Stakeholders are assumed to better process and respond to fewer but more relevant CSRep. Companies disclosing more material reporting might be more likely to engage with and receive feedback from stakeholders, as their reports are likely to become more meaningful and comprehensible to their stakeholders (Adams et al., 2014). Additional benefits arise from the process of defining material aspects. By justifying why certain information is included or excluded and how on the impact boundaries for each material aspect are set, companies must reflect on the importance assigned to sustainability in the sector and organisation and rethink their sustainability structures.

Overall, with the help of the GRI Standards, the CSRep initiative attempts to further simplify and standardise companies' reporting of non-financial and economic impacts, make the information more comparable and consistent and ensure the disclosure of relevant, useful and timely information that reflects the organisations' sustainability activities and impacts. Regarding the increasingly mature but still diverse international frameworks for CSRep (see Table 17.1), the GRI plays a key role in strengthening the synergies and complementarities between these initiatives (particularly regarding the largest and most commonly used ones). Associated with the enhanced convergence and harmonisation of the numerous reporting schemes is the expectation that this will further strengthen their adoption and implementation. The strategic alliance of the GRI and the UN Global Compact (UNGC; see Table 17.1) was one of the first initiatives to reduce the complexity of reporting practices. Since 2010, the UNGC has encouraged its participants to use the GRI when demonstrating progress towards attainment of the ten principles of the UNGC within their annual Communication on Progress reports. Easier understanding of the multitude of reporting schemes is especially facilitated by the complementary characters of the GRI Standards, UNGC principles, OECD Guidelines and ISO 26000 norm, as well as through closer cooperation between CSRep standard-setting bodies as announced by the GRI, Sustainability Accounting Standards Board (SASB), IIRC, Carbon Disclosure Project (CDP) and Climate Disclosure Standards Board (CDSB) in 2020. Generally, mutual participation in development processes and the joint production and publication of documents and reporting resources characterises standard-setting. For example, through their joint Action Platform for Reporting, the GRI and UNGC joined forces in 2017 to foster and provide guidance for future reporting towards the United Nations' Sustainable Development Goals (SDGs). In a similar vein, the IIRC and SASB have recently announced that they are merging to form the Value Reporting Foundation.

Despite working towards the convergence and harmonisation of the current reporting standards, concern has been raised about the effectiveness of voluntary frameworks for CSRep in enhancing transparency and accountability, as will be discussed in the following section.

17.4.2   Mandatory Corporate Sustainability Reporting

For many years, there has been extensive debate concerning the role governments should play in CSRep. Some researchers have called for governments to enact at least a minimum regulatory framework to overcome the incompleteness of voluntary non-financial reporting and the reluctance of a vast majority of companies to make any kind of CSRep. It is argued that mandatory reporting would prevent companies from conveying a misleading view of their activities and seeking to influence public impressions in their own interests through the provision of false or incomplete information (Adams and Narayanan, 2007). By generating a more balanced CSRep, mandatory reporting is further assumed to foster the quality and, subsequently, the credibility of the information disclosed. Mandatory reporting is also expected to provide more consistent disclosures, thereby enabling a year-on-year comparison of corporate non-financial performance against set objectives and across various companies (Cowan and Gadenne, 2005).

However, concerns have been raised about relying on government regulations to prevent all the shortcomings of voluntary disclosure (Larrinaga et al., 2002). Sceptics question whether regulations (alone) can have a significant impact on both corporate accountability and the quality of CSRep (Cooper and Owen, 2007). It has also been argued that command and control regulation may be costly and stifle innovation. In addition, mandatory reporting might remove any corporate incentives to do more than what's legally necessary, could be too inflexible to adjust to changes in the complex business environment and generally contradicts the voluntary nature of corporate responsibilities. Table 17.2 summarises the advantages and disadvantages of voluntary and mandatory approaches to CSRep as discussed in the literature.

Despite the controversial debate about the role of mandatory frameworks for enhanced transparency and accountability, corporate sustainability issues have become the subject of a growing body of regulations. According to a study by

Table 17.2 Advantages and disadvantages of voluntary and mandatory corporate sustainability reporting

	Voluntary CSRep	Mandatory CSRep
Disadvantages	• Reluctance in reporting behaviour • Focus on positive content • Incomplete reporting • Less transparency • Less credible disclosure • Fewer comparable reports	• No empirical evidence that mandatory reporting significantly impacts corporate accountability and the quality of corporate sustainability reports • High cost of command-and-control regulations • Stifles innovation, which might limit innovation and creativity in reporting • Inflexible to changes in business environment • Contrary to the idea that corporate responsibilities are voluntary
Advantages	• Coincides with the idea that corporate responsibilities are voluntary • More creative reporting • More adaptable to changes in business environment	• More complete and consistent disclosure • Holistic reporting of positive and negative content • More balanced reporting • Higher quality of reporting • More credible disclosure • Better year-on-year comparison of sustainability performance against set objectives • Better comparability of reports among companies

KPMG et al. (2016), 65 per cent (or 248 policies) of the 383 CSRep frameworks identified in seventy-one selected countries and regions can be classified as (at least partially) mandatory.

Table 17.3 presents recent CSRep initiatives in various countries and regions, most of which are mandatory, although each country and individual legislation concentrates on different issues with varying scopes of application (see also Section 17.5.1). The overview by KPMG (2020) illustrates that, besides governments and other regulatory bodies (e.g., financial market regulators), stock exchanges have become a key player in actively fostering CSRep in various countries (see also the overview by The Hauser Institute for Civil Society, 2014; Herzig and Kühn, 2017). Table 17.3 provides only a list of selected developments in CSRep at the global level from 2017 to 2020. There have already been several examples of stock exchanges taking responsibility for encouraging CSRep in previous years. In 2014, the Sustainable Stock Exchanges (SSE) Initiative, which aims at enhancing corporate transparency through cooperation among investors, regulators and companies, reported that over one-third of the fifty-five participating exchanges offer CSRep guidance or training for their listed companies. Twelve of the fifty-five exchanges required aspects of environmental and/or social reporting for at least some of their companies, with seven of those exchanges requesting reports from all listed companies (e.g., Johannesburg Stock Exchange, Shanghai Stock Exchange, Shenzhen Stock Exchange and Taiwan Stock Exchange), and five exchanges requiring reports from companies of a specific size or industry (SSE, 2014). Against the background of the developments shown in Table 17.3, it is not surprising that, four years later, the number of SSE partner exchanges increased to seventy-eight, the number of exchanges offering training on ESG issues increased to forty-eight and the number of exchanges with mandatory ESG listing requirements increased to sixteen (SSE, 2018).

With regard to developing countries, South Africa was one of the first countries to request CSRep from listed companies. According to the King III Code on Corporate Governance, companies listed on the Johannesburg Stock Exchange have been required to produce a report which integrates financial and sustainability performance since 2010. The updated King IV Code on Corporate Governance, which came into force in April 2017, is more concise and places responsibility on the governing body to enforce governance. The Code goes beyond a 'comply-or-explain' regime, a common feature of CSRep frameworks in which companies can decide to comply and disclose NFI or explain their reasons for not disclosing. Instead, it adopts a 'comply-and-explain' approach, which refers to the recommended practices that a company has adopted or will adopt in the coming financial year (KPMG, 2016).

A key development in Europe has been the implementation of the *EU Accounts Modernisation Directive*, in which the reformed law regulated the balance sheet

Table 17.3 Global efforts by governments and stock exchanges to foster corporate sustainability reporting

Argentina	In 2019, the general regulation (797/2019) of the National Value Commission (NVC) required public companies to report on their environmental or sustainability policies.
Australia	The revised ASXCGP 4.3 and 7.3 stated companies should, where a company report is not audited, disclose their process and report material climate risks in their annual report (RG247).
Belgium	In 2017, legislation came into force on non-financial reporting for public interest entities (PIEs). This legislation resulted from the European Non-Financial Reporting Directive (NFRD).
Canada	The Large Employer Emergency Financing Facility programme instituted by the Canadian Government provided short-term liquidity assistance as interest-bearing term loans to large employers affected by the COVID-19 outbreak. The borrower is subject to publishing annual climate-related financial disclosure.
China and Hong Kong (SAR)	December 2019: the Stock Exchange of Hong Kong Ltd published new requirements in its 'Consultation Conclusions on Review of the Environmental, Social and Governance (ESG) Reporting Guide and Related Listing Rules', coming into force after the 1 July 2020 financial year. The amendments represented a shift away from reporting to management, with an emphasis on the board's role in the corporate governance structure for ESG matters.
Colombia	In 2018, the GRI and the Colombian chapter of the World Business Council for Sustainable Development and others, such as the Colombian Ministry of Finance, implemented the 'Competitive Business Program for GRI SMEs'. It seeks to improve the reporting capacity of 500 Colombian SMEs.
Costa Rica	In June 2017, the 2017–30 National Policy for Social Responsibility was launched to promote a responsible and sustainable management approach between public and private companies and organisations, public administration and civil society entities, and it attributed a high priority to social responsibility reporting based on internationally recognised models. Additionally, a report prepared by the Ministry of Economy, Industry and Commerce proposed that Costa Rican organisations begin a maturity process on sustainability reports and that transnational companies report local indicators in their consolidated global reports.
Czech Republic	In 2017, the updated Accounting Law came into force, stating that any large entity, which is also a PIE, with more than 500 employees has to report NFI (in a separate or consolidated annual report).
Finland	In 2017, the Finnish Government's Ownership Steering Policy came into force, expecting state- and majority-owned companies to integrate sustainability into their business operations and management. They need to report in general meetings on their progress towards measurable targets, implemented and planned measures, and in their annual report on sustainability and their tax footprint on a country-by-country basis (while prohibiting aggressive tax planning). In 2020, the State Treasury published its guidance on responsibility reporting and framework. The long-term objective is to make responsibility reporting a fixed

Table 17.3 (*cont.*)

	part of the annual reports of ministries, government agencies and institutions. In 2018, Finance Finland created a reporting framework to monitor climate work in the financial sector. Companies can use the framework to describe their actions in mitigating climate change and to help track results over several years. In 2019, Nasdaq Nordic updated its ESG Reporting Guide.
France	In 2017, the '1180 Ordonnance' transposed the European NFRD into French law. In the same year, the Duty of Vigilance law was introduced, requiring large French companies to implement a vigilance plan with extraterritorial scope intended to identify risks and prevent serious harm in three areas: human rights and fundamental liberty, health and safety and the environment.
Germany	From 2017, the 'CSR-Richtlinie-Umsetzungsgesetz' (German implementation of the European NFRD) requires all listed companies and all financial companies with more than 500 employees to report on certain sustainability information.
Greece	Greek law 4403/7-7-2016 transposed the European NFRD. This was then included in a 2018 law (4548/13-6-2018) for the Société Anonymes. In addition, the Athens Stock Exchange in 2019 issued a voluntary ESG reporting guide.
Hungary	The European NFRD has been transposed to Act C of 2000 on Accounting, effective from 2018 and applying only to certain PIEs. Exemption applies to subsidiaries where the NFI is published in the consolidated annual report of the parent company.
Iceland	In 2018, the European NFRD was transposed into Icelandic national law. Many reporting companies are using the ESG Nasdaq Nordic guidance for KPIs to fulfil the requirements.
India	Since 2017, the Securities and Exchange Board of India (SEBI) has published a mandate encouraging the voluntary adoption of Integrated Reporting by the top 500 listed companies. In 2019, SEBI extended the Business Responsibility Reporting requirements to the top 1,000 companies.
Ireland	The European NFRD took effect on 21 August 2017.
Italy	As a result of the European NFRD, there is a new Legislative Decree 254/2016 that requires all large PIEs to disclose information about social, environmental, human rights, anti-corruption and diversity policies, risks and KPIs. The law came into force on 1 January 2018.
Japan	The Japanese Ministry of Economy, Trade and Industry started a Task Force on Climate-related Financial Disclosures (TCFD) study group in 2018; in December 2018, it published TCFD guidelines for companies which include supplementary explanations, sector-specific guidance and model case studies. The Japanese Ministry of the Environment revised its Environmental Reporting Guidelines in 2018.
Kazakhstan	In 2018, the Sovereign Wealth Fund, Samruk-Kazyna, enhanced ESG disclosure with consolidated reporting on sustainable development based on the GRI principles. The Fund took the lead in the implementation and integration of sustainable development principles in the activities of the fund and portfolio companies. The Kazakhstan Stock Exchange presented an updated methodology for preparing an ESG report, developed with the support of the International Finance Corporation. The social and corporate governance sections were expanded.

Table 17.3 (*cont.*)

Malaysia	In 2018, Bursa Malaysia updated the Sustainability Reporting Guide & Toolkits. The guide includes case studies, reference to the SDGs and the TCFD recommendations, guidance on integrated reporting and a new assurance chapter to provide guidance on how it may be conducted.
Mexico	New federal laws include the General Law on Sustainable Forest Development in 2018.
Netherlands	In 2017, the non-financial information (NFI) decree came into effect for annual reports in the Netherlands, whereas on 31 December 2016, the diversity decree was entered into force for annual reports on the same date. The NFI decree was developed in 2001 to help 'sustainable' companies distinguish themselves from other companies in the sector.
Nigeria	The Securities and Exchange Commission (SEC) approved the Nigerian Stock Exchange's Sustainability Disclosure in November 2018 for listed companies. The guidelines include a stepped approach to integrating sustainability into organisations, indicators to be considered for annual disclosure and relevant timelines.
Pakistan	In 2018, Pakistan introduced the SDGs National Framework (Pakistan One United Nations Programme III (OP III) 2018–22).
Panama	The government has defined a plan to prepare and reduce impacts due to climate change and is preparing ESG guides for different sectors. Different professional organisations and government have worked on initiatives to strengthen corporate governance practices.
Poland	Under the European NFRD, about 300 of the largest companies in Poland are required to publish a non-financial report. The statements may constitute an integral part of the annual report or a stand-alone document. This applies to companies and capital groups of more than 500 people.
Romania	In 2018, Romania extended its regulatory requirements regarding the disclosure of NFI. All companies with more than 500 employees have to disclose NFI starting in the financial year 2019. The level of disclosure is similar to the European NFRD.
Saudi Arabia	In 2018, the Saudi stock exchange joined the SSE Initiative.
Singapore	The Monetary Authority of Singapore (MAS) issued three consultation papers on its proposed Guidelines on Environmental Risk Management for banks, insurers and asset managers. The guidelines aim to enhance financial institutions' resilience to environmental risk and strengthen the financial sector's role in supporting the transition to an environmentally sustainable economy in Singapore and in the region. This is part of the MAS Green Finance Action Plan to become a leading global centre for green finance.
South Korea	The National Pension Service of Korea adopted the Stewardship Code in 2018 and has announced ESG investment guidelines to expand responsible investment practices and corporate engagement. Since 2019, the Korean Stock Exchange has requested listed companies (with total assets over 2 trillion Korean won) to submit an annual corporate governance report. The report requires information disclosure on shareholders, the board of directors and a supervisory committee.

Table 17.3 (*cont.*)

Spain	In 2018, Law 11/2018 transposed the European NFRD into Spanish law.
Switzerland	Switzerland has mandatory disclosure requirements for specific ESG topics, such as management remuneration and specific sectors (e.g., the extractive industry).
	On 1 July 2020, the Equality Act was amended to include a new section related to equal pay requirements between female and male employees. Organisations with 100 or more employees should complete the first equal pay analysis by 30 June 2021 and public entities will need to publish the results.
	The Swiss administration has also laid out plans regarding sustainable finance, which might align with future EU rules.
Taiwan	Taiwanese companies in the food sector, financial insurance, chemical industries and companies with paid-in capital of over 5 billion New Taiwan dollars must follow the Financial Supervisory Commission's 'Rules Governing the Preparation and Filing of Corporate Social Responsibility Reports by TWSE and TPEx Listed Companies'. They must publish an annual sustainability report. According to the rules, companies are required to
	- cover ESG risk assessment in sustainability reports to strengthen disclosure of the connection between relevant performance indicator and management;
	- disclose the management of climate-related risks and opportunities, actual and potential climate-related impact and how to identify, assess and manage climate-related impact, as well as indicators and targets used to assess and manage climate-related issues;
	- disclose the number, average and median salary of full-time employees who are not in supervisory positions and their difference from the previous year.
Thailand	The Stock Exchange of Thailand released its sustainability reporting guideline in 2018/19. However, this remains voluntary.
United Arab Emirates	The Abu Dhabi Stock Exchange (ADX) made a formal commitment to drive sustainability in financial markets by becoming a partner exchange of the UN-led initiative: the SSE. The ADX has also created ESG disclosure guidance to support its listed issuers' sustainability reporting journeys, as part of the UAE National Vision 2021 and Abu Dhabi Economic Vision 2020. The voluntary guidance provides listed companies with thirty-one indicators that are mapped against GRI Indicators and the SDGs and that are considered essential to report in alignment with the SSE Initiative and World Federation of Exchanges.
	The Dubai Financial Market ESG Reporting Guidelines assist listed companies to incorporate ESG information into their reporting processes. The guide aims to promote transparency and disclosure among listed companies by highlighting the key benefits of sustainability reporting to meet the demanding requirements of institutional investors for ESG information. It is aligned with the recommendations of the SSE initiative and the World Federation of Exchanges.
United Kingdom	In 2019, the United Kingdom committed Net Zero 2050 to law. Companies are expected to report on their own contribution and progress to achieve the law's goal of bringing all greenhouse gas emissions to net zero by 2050.
	The Energy Savings Opportunity Scheme until December 2024 is mandatory energy assessment legislation in the United Kingdom to report energy consumption and identify energy efficiency measures for the purpose of reducing energy usage.

Table 17.3 (*cont.*)

	In 2019, streamlined energy and carbon reporting with mandatory requirements for greenhouse gas reporting were updated and extended to cover large unquoted companies (excluding subsidiaries).
	The TCFD recommendations will apply to UK listed companies in the financial and non-financial sectors from 2022. Large asset owners must also disclose in line with the TCFD.
	In January 2019, the United Kingdom integrated the European NFRD into the Companies Act, Section 172. Companies must disclose NFI that is necessary for an understanding of the development, performance, position and impact of a company's activity.
	In 2019, under 'engagement with employees and others', directors must issue a statements on engagement with employees and with suppliers, customers and others in a business relationship with the company.
	In 2018, the PRA Pension Disclosures stated that trustees of defined benefits and defined contribution pension schemes must disclose companies' policy on taking account of 'financial material' considerations, including ESG factors, such as climate change.
	In 2018, the UK Corporate Governance Code, which is required by premium listed companies, aims to help investors evaluate company practices, which should include those relating to climate risk. The Code also requires (since October 2014) disclosure of the company's longer-term viability statement. Climate risk is expected to form part of this statement.
	In 2020, the FRC Stewardship Code for asset managers and asset owners stated that signatories need to publish a Stewardship Report that sets out how they have applied the Code Principles (including ESG) in the preceding 12 months.
United States	There is investor pressure on the SEC to require ESG disclosure and to regulate the naming of ESG funds as 'sustainable' or 'green'. The US Congress has also proposed bills on carbon reporting and human capital reporting.

Source: The KPMG Survey of Sustainability Reporting 2020 (KPMG, 2020: 56–60). See: https://assets.kpmg/content/dam/kpmg/xx/pdf/2020/11/the-time-has-come.pdf.
Note: This selection of global developments in CSRep is non-exhaustive and covers new regulations, initiatives and programmes launched between 2017 and 2020.

(European Parliament and European Council, 2004). This directive forced shareholder companies to include non-financial performance indicators, specifically environmental and labour-related indicators, in the prognosis reports included in their annual reports. In 2014, the European Parliament and European Council enacted mandatory disclosure of a larger range of NFI by large companies. Because of the new Directive 2014/95/EU, also called the NFRD, approximately 10,000 European companies have been required to report on their corporate responsibility polices, the associated results and risks and risk management in their annual reports since 2017 (European Parliament and European Council, 2014). A proposal by the European Commission to amend the existing reporting requirements of the

NFRD was adopted in 2021 and will expand this group of affected European companies starting in 2023. According to the new Corporate Sustainability Reporting Directive (CSRD), all capital market-oriented companies, regardless of their size, will fall within the scope of the regulation (with the exception of micro enterprises). In addition, large non-capital market-oriented companies will have to prepare a corporate sustainability report if they meet at least two of the following three criteria: (1) total assets of €20 million, (2) turnover of €40 million, and (3) 250 employees. Around 50,000 European companies are expected to be affected by the updated CSRD. An important change is the inclusion of non-financial reporting in the consolidated management report to improve the integration and accessibility of non-financial reports. Other important factors of the new law will be the development and implementation of uniform and binding reporting standards and an external audit requirement (starting with limited assurance) to increase the quality and comparability of CSRep. Finally, the new CSRD strengthens double materiality as an important concept (see Section 17.4.1), which was first proposed by the European Commission in their guidelines on reporting climate-related information in June 2019. The concept includes reporting on sustainability factors affecting the company beyond what is already recognised in financial reporting (financial materiality), as well as how the company impacts the environment and society through its own operations and its value chain (impact/outward materiality; Adams et al., 2021; EFRAG, 2021). The implementation of the new directive into national law will be required as of 1 December 2022.

It remains to be seen what impact the CSRD will have on reporting practices. The translation of previous European Directives on CSRep into national laws has provided mixed results. While some European countries have kept the translation of the basic requirements of the NFRD into national laws to a minimum, other countries (particularly those who began to engage in CSRep before the European Directive was developed) have created more comprehensive mandatory frameworks (Herzig and Ghosh, 2017). In addition to the CSRD, further pressure to disclose sustainability information originates from legislation on transparency in supply chains (see Box 17.1). Individual states in Europe, such as France, the Netherlands and the United Kingdom, have already passed laws against child labour and human rights violations in supply chains. According to the Supply Chain Act in Germany, companies with at least 3,000 employees will have to report on their activities throughout their supply chain starting in 2023 to ensure that they comply with existing human rights, social and environmental standards, and to identify the internal and external risks of their entire value chain. Mandatory transparency through a common legal framework at European level will come and increase the due diligence of companies with regard to their practices and relationships abroad.

> **INSIGHTS | BOX 17.1 Supply Chain Information in Sustainability Reports**
>
> Kenneth Pucker, in his 2021 *Harvard Business Review* article, 'Overselling Sustainability Reporting', outlines the shortcomings of CSRep practices. Pucker highlights the fact that large multinational companies can include low-cost labour locations in their supply chains, resulting in a long distance between where goods are produced and where they are consumed. For example, Timberland, an American footwear company, initially had most of its factories located in the United States; today, approximately 85 per cent of their product production occurs overseas, mainly in Asia. This change shows the increasingly complex web of supply chains and commodity flows. As more contractors outsource work to subcontractors, supply chains have become multi-tiered, leading to traceability issues. These increasingly evolving, global and interconnected supply chains make it extremely difficult for companies to manage and for consumers to understand the supply chain ethics.
>
> When it comes to sustainability reports and the information they contain, issues with understanding arise in the same way. Environmental units of measurement and impact categories, such as grams of phosphorus, tonnes of CO_2 and global warming potential, are difficult to interpret and have no intuitive point of reference. Even sustainability information that is easy to understand at first glance can confuse consumers. For example, Coca-Cola's estimate of how much water is needed to produce a one-litre bottle varies from two to seventy litres of water, depending on the production method used.
>
> Although most of the world's largest companies produce sustainability reports, only a fraction of these businesses has their reports validated by a third party. Furthermore, most companies appear not to be overly transparent about which framework they follow or what information they do and do not include in their sustainability reports (Pucker, 2021). Considering the examples given above, do you believe that the amount of misleading and incomplete data is a result of the lack of mandates and auditing?

We now turn to country and sector developments in CSRep.

17.5   Country and Sector Developments

Although CSRep is a worldwide phenomenon, there are various regional and sectoral differences regarding its maturity.

17.5.1 How Has Corporate Sustainability Reporting Developed in Countries and Regions?

CSRep has steadily increased in various parts of the world. Table 17.4 gives an overview of the publication of reports in fifty-two countries from 1996 to 2020. Not only has the number of countries featuring CSRep considerably increased, but so has the percentage of the largest companies producing reports in every country. Whereas on average 18 per cent of all 100 largest companies surveyed by KPMG in 1996 engaged in CSRep, this percentage increased significantly to an average of 77 per cent in 2020 (KPMG, 2020).

Institutional and legitimacy theories were introduced earlier to explain the phenomenon of CSRep and may serve as an explanation of the country-level differences in reporting (see Table 17.4). The countries that achieve the highest reporting frequencies have enforced regulations on mandatory CSRep by government regulations, stock market listing requirements or both. Moreover, companies from more developed countries seem to provide higher reporting rates than companies from developing countries. This is commonly explained by the weak institutional frameworks of developing countries, low stakeholder pressures (e.g., consumers, legislators and society at large) and lack of resources and capacities. These factors lead to the low implementation of corporate sustainability initiatives and accountability measures. Furthermore, whereas Asian countries have been well represented in KPMG's review of CSRep and in extant literature, knowledge about CSRep in Latin American countries is increasing rather slowly (e.g., Argentina, Brazil, Columbia and Mexico). Information from other parts of the world, such as Africa (excluding South Africa, Nigeria and Angola), is still very limited. However, some studies indicate that the concepts of responsible and sustainable business and related reporting activities are more extensive in these countries than is commonly perceived (Fifka, 2013).

17.5.2 How Has Corporate Sustainability Reporting Developed in Sectors?

Industry affiliation is another institutional determinant assumed to impact CSRep. Research suggests that sectors involved in more direct risks to society and the environment publish more corporate sustainability-related information than those from less-polluting sectors. Environmentally sensitive companies face stronger stakeholder pressure and public scrutiny. As a result, these corporations have become more involved in sustainability considerations alongside their production and supply chains and intend to avoid possible future environmental regulations, boycotts and protest movements. Table 17.5 provides an overview of the sectoral developments of CSRep from 1996 to 2020. This overview shows that companies in 'polluting sectors', such as mining, utilities, electronics and computers, and automotive, tend to engage in CSRep more frequently and reflect a longer time of

Table 17.4 Two decades of corporate sustainability reporting: developments in selected countries

Country	1996	1999	2002	2005	2008	2011	2013	2015	2017	2020
India	–	–	–	–	–	20	73	100	98	98
Indonesia	–	–	–	–	–	–	95	99	–	–
Malaysia	–	–	–	–	–	–	98	99	97	99
South Africa	–	–	1	18	45	97	98	99	92	96
United Kingdom	27	32	49	71	91	100	91	98	99	94
France	4*	4	21	40	59	94	99	97	94	97
Japan	–	21*	72	80	93	99	98	97	99	100
Denmark	10*	29	20	22	24	91	99	94	–	–
Norway	26*	31	30	15	37	–	73	90	89	77
Sweden	36*	34	26	20	60	72	79	87	88	98
United States	44	30	36	32	74	83	86	86	92	98
Brazil	–	–	–	–	78	88	78	85	85	85
Nigeria	–	–	–	–	–	68	82	85	88	85
Hungary	–	–	–	–	26	70	78	84	77	83
Singapore	–	–	–	–	–	43	80	84	84	81
Spain	–	–	11	25	63	88	81	84	87	98
Australia	5*	15	14	23	45	57	82	81	77	92
Canada	34*	–	19	41	62	79	83	81	84	92
Portugal	–	–	–	–	52	69	71	81	80	72
Chile	–	–	–	–	–	27	73	80	–	–
The Netherlands	31*	25	26	29	63	82	82	80	82	88
Italy	–	2*	12	31	59	74	77	79	80	86
China	–	–	–	–	–	59	75	78	73	78
Colombia	–	–	–	–	–	–	77	78	83	83
Taiwan	–	–	–	–	–	37	56	77	88	93
Switzerland	19*	–	–	–	39	64	67	75	82	80
Finland	7*	15	32	31	44	85	81	73	82	90
South Korea	–	–	–	–	42	48	49	73	73	78
Ireland	–	–	–	–	–	–	–	70	78	88
Germany	34*	38	32	36	–	62	67	69	73	92
Peru	–	–	–	–	–	–	–	69	66	81
Romania	–	–	–	–	23	54	69	68	74	66
Russia	–	–	–	–	–	58	57	66	–	–
Belgium	27*	16	11	9	–	–	68	59	62	72
Mexico	–	–	–	–	17	66	56	58	90	100
Poland	–	–	–	–	–	–	55	54	59	77
New Zealand	0*	–	–	–	–	43	47	52	69	69
Slovakia	–	–	–	–	–	63	57	48	55	76
Greece	–	–	–	–	–	33	43	46	54	59
Czech Republic	–	–	–	–	14	–	–	43	51	66
Oman	–	–	–	–	–	–	–	37	–	–
UAE	–	–	–	–	–	–	22	36	44	51

Table 17.4 (*cont.*)

Country	1996	1999	2002	2005	2008	2011	2013	2015	2017	2020
Angola	–	–	–	–	–	–	40	34	32	30
Israel	–	–	–	–	–	18	19	28	–	–
Kazakhstan	–	–	–	–	–	–	25	23	25	59
Bulgaria	–	–	–	–	–	54	–	–	–	–
Ukraine	–	–	–	–	–	53	–	–	–	–
Pakistan	–	–	–	–	–	–	–	–	–	90
Thailand	–	–	–	–	–	–	–	–	67	84
Argentina	–	–	–	–	–	–	–	–	–	83
Austria	–	–	–	–	–	–	–	–	62	74
Sri Lanka	–	–	–	–	–	–	–	–	–	66
Luxembourg	–	–	–	–	–	–	–	–	59	65
Panama	–	–	–	–	–	–	–	–	–	60
Costa Rica	–	–	–	–	–	–	–	–	–	56
Turkey	–	–	–	–	–	–	–	–	50	56
Iceland	–	–	–	–	–	–	–	–	–	52
Saudi Arabia	–	–	–	–	–	–	–	–	–	36
Ecuador	–	–	–	–	–	–	–	–	–	31
Cyprus	–	–	–	–	–	–	–	–	13	23
Kazakhstan	–	–	–	–	–	–	–	–	25	59
N 100 that report (average in %)	18	24	28	41	53	64	71	73	75	77
Number of countries surveyed	13	11	19	16	22	34	41	45	47	52
Global 250 that report (average in %)	–	35	45	64	83	95	93	92	93	96

Source: Adapted from Buhr et al. (2014); KPMG (1996, 1999, 2002, 2005, 2008, 2011, 2013, 2015, 2017, 2020).
Note: Table shows the percentage of the largest 100 companies producing corporate sustainability reports.
* Fewer than 100 countries surveyed.

involvement than companies in 'lower-polluting sectors', such as finance, securities, insurance and service. Another observation is that differences between sectors have diminished over time. This might partially be due to a growing number of sector-specific reporting guidelines (e.g., the 'Sectoral Reference Documents on Best Environmental Management Practices' of EMAS). However, it should be stressed again that a high level of disclosure does not automatically correspond with high performance. For example, the finance sector was seen for a long time as a laggard in CSRep. A commonly cited reason for the non-disclosure of environmental and social information was that financial institutions would not generate substantial environmental and social impacts themselves. Ironically, the financial crisis brought

Table 17.5 Two decades of corporate sustainability reporting: sectoral developments

Sector	1996	1999	2002	2005	2008	2011	2013	2015	2017	2020
Mining	25	45	36	52	67	84	84	84	80	84
Utilities	40	55	50	61	62	71	79	82	74	78
Electronics & computers*	33	30	24	35	58	69	78	79	–	–
Communication & media*	7	16	20	29	47	74	75	–	–	–
Technology, Media & Telecommunications*	–	–	–	–	–	–	–	–	79	84
Automotive	–	38	28	32	49	78	77	77	79	83
Oil & gas	43	53	39	52	59	69	72	76	81	81
Food & beverage	17	22	26	29	47	67	72	76	73	73
Financial services, securities & insurance	5	8	12	31	49	61	70	76	71	78
Personal & household goods	–	–	–	–	–	–	65	74	70	77
Chemicals & synthetics	74	59	45	52	62	68	65	74	81	80
Forest, pulp & paper	56	55	43	50	65	84	77	72	77	80
Construction & building materials	13	18	17	28	32	65	66	71	69	72
Healthcare & pharmaceuticals	41	50	30	30	25	64	69	69	76	72
Transport & leisure	22	33	37	38	39	57	69	69	70	71
Metals, engineering & manufacturing	25	17	24	25	41	61	69	68	68	78
Trade & retail	11	7	15	22	26	52	62	58	63	67
Other services	5	4	6	18	36	53	–	–	–	–
Total companies in survey	903	1,100	1,900	1,600	2,200	3,400	4,100	4,500	4,900	5,200
Top 100 companies from each of N countries	13	1	19	16	22	34	41	45	49	52

Source: Adapted from: Buhr et al., 2014; KPMG, 1996, 1999, 2002, 2005, 2008, 2011, 2013, 2015, 2017, 2020.

Note: Table shows percentage of the largest 100 companies producing corporate sustainability reports.

* The sectors 'Electronics & computers' and 'Communication & media' were merged into 'Technology, media & telecommunications' in 2017.

about dramatic consequences for our economy and society only shortly after the sector caught up with other sectors regarding its CSRep intensity in 2008.

17.6   Chapter Summary

This chapter has outlined and discussed key developments in CSRep and demonstrated that the nature of CSRep and its governance have been subjected to fundamental changes. Companies have extended the scope of their reports in terms of content (e.g., multi-issue reporting of global reach) and changed or amended their reporting medium (e.g., new forms of reports and use of the Internet). These developments have been driven and guided by emerging frameworks for reporting and assurance, strengthened concepts such as materiality, changes in standard-setting and, most recently, a maturing regulatory environment for mandatory CSRep.

There seems to be great interest by large and multinational companies to engage in this agenda. The number of corporate sustainability reports is increasing, across both countries and sectors, and differences in reporting rates between countries and sectors have diminished. By relying on some crucial theoretical lenses at the organisational and meso-level (e.g., stakeholder, legitimacy and institutional theories), this chapter has attempted to shed light on how these involvements can be explained and how practices in CSRep can be evaluated.

It should also become clear from this chapter that criticism of a misuse of reporting for the self-interest of companies, commonly known as green or blue washing, has persisted. In fact, it has not changed much since CSRep's inception. The key problem of CSRep lies in its struggle to achieve a sufficient level of accountability to stakeholders and society at large. This problem has accompanied developments in reporting for a long time, and is likely to continue in the future if rights to information and ways of empowering stakeholders and engaging them more meaningfully in corporate decision-making and reporting do not become more strongly institutionalised. Overall, it seems that although CSRep forms the basis of a constantly growing body of literature and enjoys wide attention in practice, much remains to be done to fully appreciate and realise the importance of transparency, accountability and the role CSRep can play within this context.

CHAPTER QUESTIONS

1. Why do you think companies should (or do) participate in CSRep?
2. We discussed the various advantages and disadvantages of voluntary and mandatory frameworks for CSRep. Which argument(s) do you find more difficult to follow than others?

3. In your opinion, what would be a reasonable approach to governing CSRep? Does the concept of materiality help to overcome limitations in CSRep?

4. Choose a company that interests you, consult its website and search for the electronic version of its corporate sustainability report. What can you learn about the way in which the company engages with its stakeholders and identifies the most material issues for reporting on sustainability? To what extent are stakeholders' views and expectations recognisable and considered by the company in its report? You can also include other information provided on the website in your analysis.

FURTHER RESOURCES

- Gray, R. H., Adams, C. and Owen, D. (Eds.). (2014). *Accountability, Social Responsibility and Sustainability: Accounting for Society and the Environment.* Harlow, UK: Pearson Education.

  This textbook is aimed at students who want to gain comprehensive views on the developments in accountability, social responsibility and sustainability theories and practices. It represents a critical account of the tensions between the way in which organisations are controlled and the need for greater responsibility and accountability to society.

- Hopwood, A., Unerman, J. and Fries, J. (Eds.). (2010). *Accounting for Sustainability: Practical Insights.* New York, NY: A. G. Carrick.

  This book provides rich insights into the different tools and techniques that companies use to advance their engagement in the area of sustainability reporting. The book features case studies from eight organisations, including HSBC, Sainsbury's, Novo Nordisk and BT.

- Laine, M., Tregidga, H. and Unerman, J. (2021). *Sustainability Accounting and Accountability.* New York, NY: Routledge.

  This textbook provides probably one of the most comprehensive and contemporary accounts of the theory and practice of sustainability reporting and accountability.

- Centre for Social and Environmental Accounting Research, www.st-andrews.ac .uk/csear.

  The Centre for Social and Environmental Accounting Research (CSEAR) is an international membership-based network that aims to mobilise accounting scholarship to enable a more sustainable society, as well as to encourage and facilitate high quality, relevant research, teaching and external engagement with practice and policy through developing knowledge, expertise, resources and a supportive network for mentoring and career development.

- CorporateRegister, www.corporateregister.com.

  The Corporate Register is a global online directory of sustainability reports that is counting over 150,000 reports across more than 22,000 organisations.

- Global Reporting Initiative, www.globalreporting.org.

  The Global Reporting Initiative (GRI) is an independent international organisation that provides businesses and other organisations with the most widely used sustainability reporting standards in the world, known as the GRI Standards.

- Integrated Reporting, www.theiirc.org.

  The International Integrated Reporting Framework and Integrated Thinking Principles are used around the world to advance communication about value creation, preservation and erosion, as well as to enhance accountability and stewardship for the broad base of capitals (financial, social, human and natural) and promote understanding of their independencies.

- KPMG, www.kpmg.com.

  KPMG offers audit, tax and advisory services in 145 countries and territories across the globe and has been monitoring global trends in CSRep since 1993. In its latest survey, KPMG analysed sustainability reports from more than 5,000 companies in over fifty countries and jurisdictions.

- Sustainable Stock Exchanges Initiative, www.SSEinitiative.org.

  The SSE Initiative is a UN Partnership Programme with the mission to provide a global platform for exploring how exchanges, in collaboration with investors, companies (issuers), regulators, policy-makers and international organisations, can enhance performance on environmental, social and corporate governance issues and encourage sustainable investment.

18 Sustainability Partnerships

LEA STADTLER AND ARNO KOURULA

LEARNING OBJECTIVES

- Examine sustainability partnerships along the questions of 'what', 'when', 'why' and 'with whom'.

- Investigate the different stages of the partnering process, including critical questions to ask and best practices to consider, and see what this process can look like in practice.

- Discuss the key challenges involved and look at the potential dark side of sustainability partnerships.

- Explore which individual skills will help you successfully engage in sustainability partnerships.

18.1   Introduction

> Partnering is easy to talk about but invariably somewhat harder to
> undertake. It requires courage, patience, and determination over time.
> It is rarely a 'quick fix' solution to a problem and can ... fall short of
> initial hopes and expectations. (Tennyson, 2011: 1)

Sustainability necessitates partnering. By partnering we refer to the joint development and implementation of formal and planned sustainability activities and programmes involving organisations across the sectors of government, corporations and civil society. For example, international coffee shop chain Starbucks and environmental non-governmental organisation Conservation International collaborate to promote ethically sourced coffee around the world. Likewise, the large consumer goods company Unilever engages in the Unstereotype Alliance, led by UN Women, to tackle the prevalence of stereotypes that are often perpetuated through advertising and media content. In 2015, 90 per cent of the managers participating in a large international survey agreed that collaboration is critical for sustainability (Kiron et al., 2017). While depending on the context, governments, the corporate sector, civil society and media are regularly seen to lack either expertise, morality or capacity (Edelman, 2022), partnerships across sectors are commonly seen to offer a potential solution where different sectors complement one another's strengths. Covering the period from 2015 to 2030, the United Nations has provided the world with the Sustainable Development Goals (SDGs), with goal number 17 explicitly calling for more partnerships for sustainability. The SDG partnership platform estimates that thousands of larger partnerships exist and countless small-scale partnerships at the local level are flourishing.

However, with great promise comes also many challenges. As the above quote indicates, implementation and innovation can be difficult. In this chapter, we aim to assess both the promise and problems of partnerships, citing some influential and classic work on the topic along the way. We start by defining partnerships and describing them vis-à-vis alternatives to address sustainability challenges. We outline why and when to partner and discuss who are appropriate partners ranging from collaborating with industry actors, governments, non-governmental organisations (NGOs) or communities or collaborating across multiple sectors. We then turn to addressing the process of partnering and evaluating the key challenges faced when implementing partnerships. In terms of the dark side of partnering, we discuss the relevant risks for partners, beneficiaries and society at large. We end by considering what skills you as an individual and professional may need to engage in sustainability partnerships.

18.2   When and Why to Partner?

Let's start with considering when a company might want to engage in sustainability partnerships and what the alternatives are. Imagine a company that, alarmed by the business implications of climate change, wants to take action. It might start by reducing its greenhouse gas emissions and its use of natural resources. If it lacks a specific set of knowledge, technology or equipment to do so, it may buy it (e.g., contract a consultancy) – on the condition that a suitable market offer exists. The company may also decide to give a donation to an environmental organisation, such as to an NGO, and in this way support their actions. Alternatively, if the company thinks it is a question of governments stepping in, it may decide to engage in lobbying and, for instance, push for stricter regulations.

The idea of partnering comes in when the company wants to engage beyond giving donations, lobbying and adopting simple programmes to integrate sustainability in its own operations. For example, when it seeks more ambitious product and process innovations for which no blueprints exist and for which missing knowledge or technologies cannot be bought. Likewise, the company may consider sustainability partnerships when it wants to embrace more encompassing climate actions that also include other industry and societal actors. Partnering with one or more organisations may here allow to bring together partners with similar interests in solving the underlying sustainability issue (e.g., climate change) and unite the required expertise, technologies, legitimacy, access and/or networks. Thus, from an organisational perspective, partnerships emerge when multiple organisations are interdependent in addressing a sustainability challenge and can realise a collaborative advantage by working closely together. From a societal perspective, partnerships emerge when sustainability problems are not addressed by regulators and also when no market solution can be found (e.g., because there is no market).

18.3   What Are Partnerships?

But what are sustainability partnerships? We should start by noting that different terms are used for these partnerships (e.g., social, environmental, cause-based, or multi-stakeholder alliances, collaboratives or partnerships) and it is good to be clear about their main features. Core to sustainability partnerships is the concept of collaboration. Collaboration, as Barbara Gray noted already in 1989 (5), 'is a process through which parties who see different aspects of a problem can constructively explore their differences and search for solutions that go beyond their own limited vision of what is possible'. As this definition suggests, by working with others, companies can get a better (i.e., more holistic) understanding of the problem, as well as forge more innovative and potentially more successful solutions than they would be able to do on their own.

Within the larger landscape of collaboration, sustainability partnerships are characterised by the active interaction and involvement of the partner organisations in the planning and implementation of joint activities to achieve a common, sustainability-related goal. This means that there is a degree of sharing the decision-making and the implementation responsibilities and risks, as well as agreeing on common values in addressing the targeted goal (Waddock, 1991). Partnering revolves around an underlying reciprocity and interdependence of the partners in line with the doctrine 'you need me, and I need you'. For example, a focal company may choose to collaborate with a set of partners if it needs their expertise, networks, legitimacy, assets and capabilities and/or the prospect of sharing the risks and costs involved to address a sustainability challenge. The partners, in turn, may agree to join a partnership when the sustainability challenge is of common interest and the resources and competencies that the company could bring to the table would provide unique value for addressing it.

As the partners jointly implement the targeted activities, sustainability partnerships are different from purely philanthropic relationships where companies give donations, for example, to an NGO which subsequently implements the funded activities. Likewise, partnerships differ from innovative sustainable business models described in Chapter 19 as they are not focused on the creation of value for a single organisation (although note that business model analysis can, however, be a very good foundation for developing a partnership model). Partnerships also differ from sustainability standards such as developed in multi-stakeholder initiatives (see Chapter 20), where each company unilaterally implements a jointly defined standard. Finally, we see partnerships as including a handful to a dozen organisations instead of broader alliances or networks of 100 or more organisations.

18.4　With Whom Do You Partner?

Sustainability partnerships come in different forms and one way to make sense of the emerging partnering landscape is to identify with whom companies work together in these partnerships. The partnerships we focus on can thus include only the business sector, business–NGO (e.g., cause-based partnerships), business–community (e.g., firms' community engagement and partnership programmes), business–government (e.g., public–private partnerships) and multi-sector (i.e., involving more than two sectors) elements.

Inter-Firm Business Partnerships: A company can collaborate with one or more other companies to exchange, share or co-develop resources and capabilities as part of a project or business operation. These partnerships often aim to create economic value for the companies by jointly exploiting sustainability-related opportunities and/or neutralising related threats. However, firms increasingly combine economic and social and/or environmental objectives when engaging in partnerships with their suppliers (see Chapter 22), business customers, competitors or with firms from other industries. For example, the multinational alcoholic beverage company Diageo and corporate venture management company Pilot Lite together developed a PET plastic-free paper bottle which is subsequently being used by a consortium of global Consumer Packaged Goods companies, such as Unilever, PepsiCo and GSK Consumer Healthcare.

Civil Society–Business Partnerships: Civil society can be considered a space of pluralism, with actors ranging from large NGOs, social movements, local grassroots organisations and anything from religious organisations to labour unions, and sports clubs to university student unions. In this respect, companies can, for example, collaborate with an NGO, such as the WWF or Save the Children, and benefit from the specialised knowledge, capabilities, networks and legitimacy that the NGO has established around the targeted sustainability challenge. An example is the Starbucks–Conservation International partnership we mentioned in the introduction. The objectives of such NGO–business partnerships often involve social, environmental and economic value creation for the partners and societal benefits that accrue to the targeted beneficiary group(s). Companies can also engage with community-based organisations or associations, and thus get access to the different perspectives, ideas and potential support of, for example, the local community in which the company operations are positioned. Larger international NGOs and local grassroots organisations typically have different aims and resources.

Government/International Organisation–Business Partnerships: Companies can further join partnerships with governmental agencies to support the provision of public goods (e.g., health, water and education) or address a common problem (e.g., climate change). Besides the sustainability benefits, partnering with a governmental agency may help the firm get access to public institutions and citizens and learn new skills. It may also be a means for companies to maintain close relationships with public institutions. Beyond just engaging with national or local governments, companies can also join partnerships with international organisations, such as the United Nations' agencies, and benefit from their international expertise and networks. For example, organisations such as UNICEF (UN Children's Fund), an agency responsible for providing humanitarian and developmental aid to children around the world, partners with several large firms to achieve this aim.

Multi-Sector Partnerships: Finally, it is often not enough to collaborate with other firms, civil society or governmental agencies alone, but the sustainability challenge requires integrated approaches across all these actors, especially when the challenge is particularly complex and dynamic (i.e., 'wicked'). The resulting multi-sector partnerships can build on a large portfolio of resources to address the sustainability issue and trigger encompassing change. As you can imagine, these partnerships are, however, also the most complex to manage. An example would be governments, international organisations, NGOs, plastic producers and users, entrepreneurs and scientists coming together in a formalised partnership to tackle plastic pollution in oceans.

Common to the latter three partnership types is that companies collaborate with organisations from other sectors and, hence, these are called cross-sector partnerships (CSPs). The diversity in organisational backgrounds, goals and ways of working in CSPs can be a great source of innovation, yet must be well managed.

18.5   How Does the Partnering Process Work?

Moving on to the question of 'how', let's take a process perspective and consider the main partnering stages, the managerial questions to be asked and some best practices. While our depiction of the partnering process is clear and circular (see

The Partnering Process

Figure 18.1 Zooming into the partnering process.
Source: Based on Tennyson (2011).

Figure 18.1, based on Tennyson, 2011), note that, in practice, the process is more 'messy' where stages may overlap and unexpected external and internal factors may turn neat planning ambitions upside down.

To give a practical illustration of the partnership preparation, set-up and implementation, as well as adaptation stages, we will draw on a partnership called the Logistics Emergency Team (LET) (Logistics Cluster, n. d.). The LET partnership acknowledges that, with climate-related humanitarian crises on the rise and, in view of the warnings of irreversible, worldwide climate-change effects, large-scale relief solutions have become critical. Hence, this partnership brings together four of the largest global logistics and transportation companies, Agility, UPS, Maersk and DP World, to jointly support the Logistics Cluster led by the UN World Food Programme during emergency response to large-scale natural disasters. The partnership is designed to unite the capacity and resources of the logistics industry with the expertise and experience of the humanitarian community to provide more effective and efficient disaster relief.

18.5.1   Stage 1 – Preparing

At the beginning of a partnership endeavour should stand a solid *scoping* exercise aimed at scrutinising the sustainability challenge. This includes the gathering of information and consultation with diverse stakeholders to fully understand the challenge's different facets and potential solutions. On this basis, answers to some fundamental design questions can be sketched: Does this challenge call for a partnership or can it be addressed differently (e.g., with unilateral or market-based actions)? At what scale does the company and potential partners want to address the challenge – at a local, national, international or global level? And what will be the partnership purpose? Will the partnership focus on raising awareness and mobilising resources, offering an operational solution, developing coping capacity and/or developing policies for the sustainability challenge?

The answers to these questions may guide the *identification of suitable partners* in line with the 'three-C' criteria: complementarity, commitment and compatibility. Complementarity means identifying partners whose resources and competences are critical for realising the defined partnership purpose. If each organisation contributes something critical, the partners will be mutually interdependent in reaching the partnership goal and will need one another also in difficult times. Second, the partnership goal must be of strategic interest to all the partners, otherwise they might not sustain their commitment over the long term. For example, for the company, this means creating internal awareness of how the partnership will benefit its own business operations, such as by helping the company manage risks, develop unique knowledge and expertise it can use in its operations and value proposition, and/or promote market transformation and related opportunities. Finally, compatibility relates to the organisational similarities and differences among the potential partners. If several organisations fulfil the complementarity and commitment criteria, companies may decide to choose the one(s) with more organisational similarities. In any case, it is advisable to anticipate and discuss how to best cope with the organisational differences. This analysis will also help move the partners to the next step in terms of systematically *analysing the benefits and risks* that the partnership may entail for each partner organisation, the partners together, for the target group and for society at large.

Now we turn to illustrating the preparing stage with the LET partnership. After the 2004 tsunami in South Asia, a discussion at the World Economic Forum highlighted the important resource constraints that the international community faced in the immediate aftermath of large-scale natural disasters. Many of the companies participating in this discussion had an international presence and could help with their local capacities. Such help would, however, require prior coordination and standing relationships with the humanitarian actors – hence, an international cross-sector partnership was called for. The emerging 'Humanitarian Response Initiative' brought together companies from the engineering, construction, transportation, logistics, healthcare and telecommunications industries – but the negotiations stalled. Despite the members' enthusiasm, their divergent interests and priorities made it difficult to agree upon what support to offer, and when and at what level to intervene. As a result, the focus shifted towards more targeted, industry-based approaches, and four global logistics companies, the World Food Programme as leader of the United Nations' Logistics Cluster and the World Economic Forum started to investigate options to provide coordinated, logistics-focused emergency support to humanitarian organisations in the immediate aftermath of natural disasters. For example, the companies could help with customs clearance, warehousing, transportation and distribution support. In turn, these activities would help bring their local communities back to normal business as soon as possible, offer opportunities to learn to operate in dynamic and difficult environments, and help express their long-term commitment vis-à-vis governments, local communities and customers. An unprecedented partnership idea thus started to take shape.

18.5.2 Stage 2 – Setting Up and Implementing

As you have experienced in group work and work life, for moving any collaborative idea to practice, *building relationships* in terms of developing mutual understanding, respect and trust is important. This is even more critical when competitors and/ or organisations from different sectors come together. The partners may not only talk 'different languages' by using different terminologies, but may also have different priorities and assumptions attached to the partnership idea. To create common ground and develop trust, ongoing and open communication and active listening are essential, as are committed and trustworthy individuals. These individuals then become so-called boundary spanners functioning as facilitators between the involved organisations, often since the beginning of the partnership. It may also help to involve a third-party facilitator who guides the meetings and ensures that the defined process and interaction rules are followed. In addition, structural features may help, such as designing for 'trust building loops' (Vangen and Huxham, 2003: 12). This implies aiming initially at realistic but modest projects and, based on their successful implementation, reinforcing trusting attitudes and gaining underpinnings for more ambitious collaborative projects.

From a structural perspective, setting up a partnership requires agreeing on questions of *governance and coordination*. Governance relates to how decisions are being made and who would be held accountable for what. Coordination relates to the process of integrating the partners' different resources, tasks and activities. Depending on the number of partners, the partnership's scope and complexity, and the level of trust and goal consensus, the partners may decide to delegate main governance and coordination tasks to one partner organisation or decide to always involve all partners in decision-making and coordination. In large and complex partnerships, they may also mandate a separate administrative entity to manage the operational coordination, and govern the partnership more formally based on a board and committees with partner representatives (Provan and Kenis, 2008). The reflections and decisions agreed upon during the set-up stage commonly lead to the definition of a partnership agreement. The agreement specifies the partnership's objectives, clarifies the roles and responsibilities of each partner, and describes the

Table 18.1 Different criteria by which to distinguish sustainability partnerships

Criteria for distinguishing sustainability partnerships				
Challenge addressed	Actors involved	Scope of partnership	Purpose of partnership	Structure of partnership
Which sustainability challenge is addressed? (e.g., poverty, decent work, health, safety, carbon emissions, biodiversity loss)	Governmental organisation *or* Companies *or* Civil society organisations (e.g., NGOs) *or* Multi-sector	Local/ sub-national *and/or* National *and/or* International *and/or* Global	Advocacy and resource mobilisation *and/or* Operational solution *and/or* Capacity building *and/or* Policy (setting and implementation)	Informal governance ↑ ↓ Formal governance

governance and coordination procedures, including the monitoring and reporting mechanisms and the delegation of authority. It should further specify the financial obligations and resource commitments, record the agreed-upon evaluation and assessment objectives, and foreshadow a process to resolve conflict and, in the worst case scenario, to terminate the partnership. Once these details are agreed upon and set in place, the *implementation* process can start – working along a pre-agreed timetable and towards the set deliverables.

As the above discussion has shown, the preparation and setting-up stages can lead to very different forms of sustainability partnerships. While we already introduced different partnership forms in line with the 'with whom' question, we invite you to have a look at Table 18.1. This builds on the key questions you learned about in the partnering process so far and helps bring some structure into the diverse partnering landscape. The table outlines key criteria by which you can further distinguish sustainability partnerships. Under the 'who' part of the table (i.e., the actors involved), we can consider any combination of these actors.

Now we turn to illustrating the setting up and implementing stage with the LET partnership. The idea of LET partnership required first and foremost developing a minimum level of trust and mutual understanding between the companies and the humanitarian actors. While the partners benefitted from having the World Economic Forum as a third party facilitating the numerous meetings, a real milestone was met when the partners put their partnership concept to test in a 'controlled' run, as they called it. Specifically, by helping the humanitarian actors with logistical support in a refugee camp, the companies could prove their commitment to the cause and, together, the partners could use the feedback and learnings from this small-scale intervention to further improve their partnership set-up. After overall three years of continuous work of defining the interaction principles, setting up the partnership structures, and defining, testing and refining the operational processes, the partnership was officially announced. The LET joint Steering Committee with a rotating chair position would have monthly conference calls and meet at least twice a year in person. A detailed disaster relief processes planning with precise standard operating procedures would back their engagement while the partners would use the time between disasters to improve their partnership, discuss challenges and remove obstacles. By 2020, building on fourteen years of collaboration, the LET had provided humanitarian assistance to twenty-two major natural disasters and complex emergencies (Logistics Cluster, 2020).

18.5.3 Stage 3: Adapting

Once in place, how can the partners effectively *review* their partnership, such as to identify areas for improvement? In view of the partnership's social or ecological (rather than solely economic) goals and its potential direct and indirect effects at multiple levels, such analysis requires a systematic approach. Building on Kolk et al. (2008), you may adopt a systems perspective and investigate the partnership's inputs, throughputs, outputs and outcomes. The partnership outputs relate to the tangible goal-related results that can be measured in numbers, such as the number of products or services delivered. They are a result of the inputs (e.g., the committed time, financial investment and in-kind resources) as well as the throughputs (i.e., the partnership's processes, structures and strategies). In this regard, the partners may investigate how to improve the partnership's efficiency; that is, the relationship between inputs and outputs: Do they have the right inputs? What can they change in terms of structures, processes and strategies to become more efficient? Besides assessing the partnership outputs, such as the products and services delivered, the partners may also want to know the partnership's outcomes; that is, the targeted changes or sustainability impact. An assessment of the partnership effectiveness thus includes questions such as: Did their services/products/actions trigger the desired change? Are there better ways to achieve the targeted change? This assessment is complex, given that the partnership actions not only trigger direct effects, but also have indirect (i.e., ripple) effects. For example, does the partnership engagement distract the partners from taking more ambitious actions individually? Or does it encourage and empower the partners and beneficiaries to take additional actions? The direct and indirect partnership effects may thereby emerge at the individual level (e.g., inspired employees), the organisational level (e.g., a company's improved risk management), the inter-organisational level (e.g., greater trust leading to greater coordination within and across the partnership boundaries) and the societal level (e.g., reduction of greenhouse gas emissions of an industry, city or community).

Overall, the evaluation process may lead the partners to *revise* their partnership, such as its design and goals, and adapt it to changing environments. It may further back decisions of whether to continue, maybe even scale, the partnership or to consider a closing down. But how could you *scale the impact* of a partnership? This can be done by increasing the size and/or scope of the partnership by adding new partners, expanding to new geographies and/or adding new activities. For example, the 'Collaboration Continuum' by James Austin and May Seitanidi (2012) suggests that value creation in partnerships is a dynamic process that may increase as the partners' relationship strengthens. Specifically, over continued commitment, the level of engagement, the importance to mission, the magnitude and type of resources, the scope of activities, the levels of interaction, trust, internal change and complexities, as well as strategic nature, co-creation, synergies, innovation and systems change outcomes may grow. Besides increasing the partnership's own value creation, the partners could also spread the partnership 'model' through the partner organisations, share the partnership experience with other organisations, sectors and countries and push policy adaptation, and/or review how their partnership approach can be used to tackle other sustainability challenges. An important yet often not addressed question further is: What comes after the partnership (i.e., *closing down*)? Is the partnership the final solution? If yes, should it develop into a fully fledged organisation? Or is it about building the capacity of the company, the government, the NGO or the community to take over in the long term? Answers to these questions would in turn influence the partnership strategies and design.

Now we turn to illustrating the adapting stage with the LET partnership. Evaluating the LET with the suggested framework would start with reviewing the inputs, hence the partners' contributions. The partnership has considered input measures such as the existence of appropriate and sufficient expertise, time and logistics assets and the need to invite more companies to join the partnership (thereby also taking into account the potential risk of weakening the partner relationships and throughputs). Further, the partners monitored the outputs, for example, in terms of number of relief items stored and/or transported, whereas measuring the outcomes implied the extent to which the LET help has speeded up relief operations, how many lives were saved and/or what benefits finally occurred to the disaster victims. With regard to enhancing the partnership's efficiency, for example, after some years of operations, the LET partners decided to invite a professional process facilitator who would help prepare the partner meetings, follow up on the different agenda items, and help with other coordination tasks. With regard to enhancing the LET's effectiveness, the companies learned from their humanitarian partners that one dollar spent on reducing people's vulnerability to disaster would save around seven dollars in disaster response and reconstruction (UNDP, 2015). This encouraged the LET to start expanding their joint work towards disaster preparedness, such as working with the Logistics Cluster organisations towards greater capacity building, the creation of preparedness networks and the mitigation of logistics bottlenecks ahead of time. Over the years, the partners had learned many lessons that they openly shared with other partnerships, such as at events organised by the World Economic Forum and at the UN World Humanitarian Summit.

18.6   Key Partnering Challenges

> Relishing the diversity that very different partners can bring to the table is key to achieving a wide range of outcomes and benefits. If the goal is to have transformational impact, partners need to be willing to push boundaries, challenge unhelpful mindsets, and speak truth to power. This means ceding some level of control, being prepared to adopt some new practices and thinking imaginatively where listening is more important than talking, learning is more important than being proved right, and taking action is more important than strategising.
>
> (Ros Tennyson – Founder, Associate & Strategic Advisor, Partnership Brokers Association)

By working together, the partners can develop new ideas, build on their pooled financial and in-kind resources for more encompassing and innovative solutions, work towards empowering diverse stakeholders involved, and achieve broad reach based on their combined networks and greater legitimacy. To get there, and as the quote by Ros Tennyson illustrates, partnering requires embracing the unknown, experimenting together and, hence, leaving behind entrenched assumptions and routines. Partnering is therefore often more difficult than expected. Main challenges often occur due to the partners' different backgrounds and the difficulty of sustaining the partners' commitment over time. Let us consider these challenges more in depth.

First, practical and cultural obstacles may emerge as the partner organisations have different overarching goals, norms and values, ways of working and organising, timescales, expectations and languages. These differences become even more difficult in a partnership that operates at the national and international levels. Partnering is a complex process that, in practice, does not always follow rational principles, but is also influenced by emotions and unconscious dynamics, thereby leading to important conflicts. For example, Berger et al. (2004) reveal six categories of predictable problems, including misunderstandings, misallocation of costs and benefits among the partners, mismatches of power, mismatched partners, misfortunes of time and mistrust.

Another major challenge is that of ensuring the necessary resource commitments in the implementation phase. Already in 1988, Sandra Waddock (22) pointed to partnerships' inherent fragility because 'the individuals involved have their own organisational affiliations, agendas and concerns. The partnership may be of secondary concern to most of them.' Furthermore, the commitment must be sustained and potentially adapted as the partner organisations experience staff turnover, face organisational constraints or changes, and witness changes in the social, environmental and institutional context in which the partnership is embedded.

These difficulties led Huxham and Vangen (2004) to juxtapose two interrelated as well as opposing concepts of collaboration. Collaborative advantage evolves around the synergy argument that through partnering something can be achieved that could not have been achieved by any one of the organisations acting alone. Collaborative inertia, in turn, reflects what frequently happens in practice: the collaborative outputs are negligible, the process is lengthy and stories of painful moments or periods are integral to successes achieved. Table 18.2 presents key partnering facets leading to collaborative advantage or collaborative inertia.

The question then arises of what may help the partners realise the potential of collaborative advantage rather than to succumb to collaborative inertia. While a full discussion would exceed the chapter format, let us consider some of the best practices discussed in the literature. First, there are structural facilitators, such as the partners' strategic motivation to join the partnership and address the focal sustainability challenge, their organisational backing and support rather than having one or two committed, yet isolated, individuals involved, and the definition of clear partnership principles, accountability structures and coordination processes. From a relational perspective, frank and constructive communication is critical as mentioned beforehand, as well as the acknowledging and respecting of sectoral

Table 18.2 The opposing concepts of collaborative advantage and inertia

Collaborative advantage	Collaborative inertia
• New ideas	• Endless discussions and power battles
• Pooled resources	• Misunderstandings, inflated expectations and frustration
• Innovative solutions	• Cheating and freeriding
• Greater scope and strengthened networks	• Scepticism and lack of participation
• Increased legitimacy	• Organisational and/or personal limitations
• Empowerment	• Changing external environments

Source: Adapted from Huxham and Vangen (2004).

differences. Rather than trying to change a partner organisation's beliefs or way of working, the idea is to pragmatically find common ground, nurture trusting relationships at personal and organisational levels which often prove very important, and promote collaborative leadership in guiding, facilitating and empowering joint actions. Therefore, a range of individual skills are required from partnership participants. But before we review these personal skill sets, we first need to take a look at the potential dark side of sustainability partnerships. On this basis, you will also see that critical thinking skills are important in the partnership context.

18.7   The Dark Side of Sustainability Partnerships

As our chapter has shown so far, sustainability partnerships provide important potential to address complex sustainability challenges. Yet, they are by no means simple endeavours. At a time where the concept of 'partnering' risks is becoming a new buzzword – as if partnering was the silver bullet to all sustainability challenges and hence an end on its own – we would like to draw attention to the potential dark side of this partnership movement as well. For the companies involved, sustainability partnerships pose risks that are rarely considered. This may involve the risk of harming deployed staff and assets, facing negative repercussions on the corporate reputation if problems occur within the partnership (e.g., when a scandal affects one of the partners) or when the partners do not reach their desired outcomes. The partnership may also raise too high expectations among employees, beneficiaries and partners, thus leading to frustration expressed vis-à-vis the company.

There are also important risks for the so-called 'beneficiaries' (e.g., the targeted disadvantaged communities of disaster victims) when the partnership builds on a 'push' rather than a 'pull' approach and offers products and services that do not match the beneficiaries' or the broader sustainability needs. In this case, the partnership may even tie up civil-society and governmental resources that would otherwise be used in more effective and beneficiary-tailored programmes. Likewise, each failed or underperforming partnership drains the partners' willingness to adopt collaborative approaches and may spur disengagement from the side of beneficiaries and public and/or non-profit partners with implications also for future partnerships. You have to remember that partnerships take a lot of time and effort to set up and manage. In this respect, a study on 330 sustainability partnerships found that 38 per cent of them were not active or had no measurable output (Pattberg and Widerberg, 2014). Moreover, 26 per cent of the partnerships showed activities that did not directly relate to their publicly stated goals and ambitions (Pattberg and Widerberg, 2014).

As larger firms prefer working with larger and well-branded international NGOs, there is also a very real danger of marginalising local communities and grassroots organisations. Finally, partnerships pose a more systematic risk if they are emphasised over other governance approaches, such as stricter regulation. Through partnerships, companies enter spheres formerly reserved for the government and/or civil-society sectors, such as education, public health and humanitarian concerns. They can help bridge important resource gaps, but their involvement also shifts their sphere of influence. Which interests do the partnerships finally pursue? May they increase the power of already powerful players as it is up to the founding partners to decide who should be included in the partnership and how decisions will be made? And how can we control what is happening inside partnerships given that it is up to the partners to decide what kind of partnership information they want to share with the wider public and what they don't? In addition, just like philanthropic donations, if partnerships tend to focus on popular and media-friendly targets or issues, what happens to more controversial and stigmatised challenges as they are not given the spotlight? Ultimately partnerships are typically based on collaboration and agreement and can potentially undermine some actors and perspectives and diminish the possibility of voicing critical and opposing opinions.

18.8   What Individual Skills Are Required?

After describing both the potential bright and dark sides of partnerships, now let's imagine you want to get involved in sustainability partnerships. Certainly, positive drive and critical thinking are both needed, as we have emphasised. Which other skills, then, would help you in sustainability partnerships? When investigating this question together with Adriane MacDonald (MacDonald and Stadtler, 2017), we identified four broad skill sets as being critical: interpersonal, communication, entrepreneurial and systems thinking skills. Interpersonal skills are essential because, to a large extent, sustainability partnerships build on human interactions. This 'human' side of partnerships implies being able to work in teams, to convene and network, to negotiate and empower, and to constructively manage arising conflicts. Interrelated are communication skills, such as active listening, effective communication and knowledge integration skills to enable shared meaning and coordinatation, and to find agreement across the sustainability partners. Entrepreneurial skills are important as well because there is commonly no blueprint for the partnership to follow. Individuals engaging in partnerships may hence benefit from visionary thinking and implementation skills, and need to be able to navigate complexities and paradoxes. Finally, as partnerships are complex organisational entities embedded in even more complex societal environments, systems

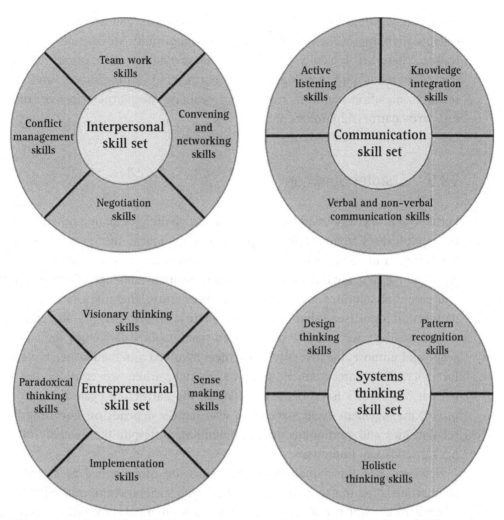

Figure 18.2 Cross-sector partnering skill sets: engaging in partnerships requires a multiplicity of skills. *Source:* Adapted from MacDonald and Stadtler (2017).

thinking skills help partnership practitioners think holistically and analytically, and practise design thinking. As a result, engaging in partnerships requires a multiplicity of skills (see Figure 18.2 for an overview), but you should not feel discouraged. These skills can be learned and, as you work in partnership teams, you can build on one another's strengths and bridge individual weaknesses as long as everyone believes in the partnership approach.

The skills required for successful partnering, especially analytical skills and innovation, active learning, complex problem-solving and critical thinking, also feature among the Top 10 Job Skills that the World Economic Forum (2020) considers critical for the 2025 era. Hence, partnerships provide a pivotal platform for learning and sharpening skill sets required far beyond the sustainability space.

Finally, if you feel like these are your strengths and you are a core believer of collaborative approaches, there is also the opportunity to become a partnership broker. These are typically third parties mandated by the partners to facilitate the negotiation and development of partnership arrangements and to help research, maintain, monitor, review and evaluate the partnership over time (see, e.g., www.partnershipbrokers.org).

18.9   Chapter Summary

Partnering is one way to address sustainability challenges among others. In view of the complexities involved in the partnering approach, the question of whether partnering is necessary must be carefully considered. It is a viable option indeed when the partners are interdependent in addressing a challenge of common interest and potential solutions are shrouded in uncertainty. There is a large diversity in partnership forms (see Table 18.1), hence, there is no one-size-fits-all approach, but a need to adapt according to the targeted sustainability challenge, the partnership scope and purpose, the diversity of partners involved and the partnership's level of formality. There are common patterns, though, when we consider the typical partnership process (see Figure 18.1). While the partnering cycle may look like a project management cycle, partnering also largely depends on nurturing trusting relationships and continuous partner commitment despite the diversity of partner backgrounds and interests.

However, while sustainability partnerships are often hailed as a silver bullet solution bringing together the strengths of each societal sector and different types of organisations, it is critical to reflect on their potential dark side and keep these points in mind when joining or creating a partnership. We outlined potential negative consequences of partnerships and partnership thinking for companies, beneficiaries and society at large. All things considered, we should see sustainability partnerships as hard work requiring sustained commitment and not as an end in themselves, but as a means to achieve the ultimate goal of sustainable impact.

CHAPTER QUESTIONS

1. What are sustainability partnerships and what types of actors can be involved? We suggest researching a sustainability partnership in an area that is interesting to you, such as reduction of poverty, climate change, clean energy or circular economy. It could be a very local partnership in the area where you live or an international and highly visible one with multinational firms and public sector or civil society organisations.
2. How should we manage and evaluate partnerships?

After researching a specific partnership, you can explore how it developed (see Figure 18.1) and what are its key features (see Table 18.1).

3. What are the possible obstacles and challenges that partnerships face?

You can examine your specific partnerships in light of collaborative advantage and collaborative inertia (Table 18.2) and think of the potential negative effects on companies, beneficiaries and society at large. Reflect on whether partnering was the appropriate approach given the context of the challenge or whether other approaches could/should have been used.

FURTHER RESOURCES

- Gray, B. and Stites, J. (2013). Sustainability through Partnerships: Capitalizing on Collaboration, https://nbs.net/sustainability-through-partnerships-a-systematic-review/.

  Access this report for a visually appealing systematic overview of the literature on multi-sector sustainability partnerships. You will get more detailed insights into the partnership landscape, the challenges of alignment and evaluation, and the role of the social context shaping sustainability partnerships.

- Koschmann, M. (2012). Whiteboard animation on YouTube, 'The Collaborative Challenge: Making Quality Decisions Together in the Age of Complexity', www.youtube.com/watch?v=iN_A7keXtVg.

  In this approximately 16-minute whiteboard animation video, you can explore the topic of sustainability partnerships with a view on, for example, their benefits and challenges, and learn how a constitutive communication approach helps improve our understanding of such partnerships.

- Tennyson, R. (2011). The Partnering Toolbook. The International Business Leaders Forum (IBLF) and the Global Alliance for Improved Nutrition (GAIN), 3rd ed., https://thepartneringinitiative.org/publications/toolbook-series/the-partnering-toolbook/.

  Structured along the different stages of the partnering process, The Partnering Toolbook offers a concise overview of the essential elements that make for effective partnering. It also presents eight partnering tools for practical application.

Business Model Innovation for Sustainability

FLORIAN LÜDEKE–FREUND AND STEFAN SCHALTEGGER

LEARNING OBJECTIVES

- Briefly discuss how innovation can help achieve corporate sustainability.
- Explain how business models and business model innovation support corporate sustainability.
- Introduce principles that guide business model innovation for sustainability.
- Give an overview of patterns and tools that support business model innovation for sustainability.
- Discuss how companies can engage in sustainable value creation for themselves and their stakeholders.

19.1 Introduction

Companies striving for corporate sustainability (i.e., contributing to sustainable development through business activities) are faced with the challenge to integrate ecological and social issues into their organisations, production processes, products and services, and many more (Schaltegger and Burritt, 2005). These challenges include achieving higher efficiency and effectiveness in ecological, social and economic terms – for example, by reducing greenhouse gas emissions per product sold and by reducing overall greenhouse gas emissions year on year. It is immediately clear that such goals can go against common customer expectations for more and better products as well as market expectations for more and growing revenues and profits. Striving for corporate sustainability is therefore about balancing different goals and stakeholder interests.

As companies learn how to do this, they develop the ability to engage in sustainable value creation (Freudenreich et al., 2020; Lüdeke-Freund et al., 2020). A rather new way of approaching the challenge of sustainable value creation is to develop so-called business models for sustainability. In essence, business models describe and influence how companies create value for their customers and owners, and for themselves. If ecological and social issues are considered as well in the development of business models, these can turn into business models for ecological and social value creation (Evans et al., 2017). We argue that a proactive stance on corporate sustainability (i.e., an entrepreneurial and innovative way of tackling the integration and balancing challenges of corporate sustainability) is best suited to come up with business models that support sustainable value creation. This leads to the notion of business model innovation for sustainability, which is introduced in this chapter. After reading it, you should be familiar with these five key assumptions:

- *Innovation alters the ability of companies to act.* This includes the ability to integrate ecological and social concerns into business activities and hence the ability to act for corporate sustainability.
- *Innovation for corporate sustainability can take different forms.* That includes small changes to production processes and products as well as fundamentally new ways of how companies do business and create value (i.e., more radical forms of business model innovation).
- *Business model innovation for sustainability helps companies to create value* for themselves and their stakeholders and to preserve or maybe even regenerate the natural environment (i.e., to create sustainable value).
- Business model innovation for sustainability can be supported by following certain *guiding principles*. Following these principles increases the likelihood that the business models of companies support sustainable value creation.
- We can distinguish *various types of business models* with the potential to contribute to corporate sustainability. These can be described as 'patterns' of green, social and fully integrative business models. Various tools to develop such business models do exist as well.

Figure 19.1 gives an overview of the chapter structure and the main topics that will be discussed.

19.2 Managerial and Entrepreneurial Views on Corporate Sustainability

The understanding of the role of companies regarding sustainability, and whether and how they can contribute to sustainable development, has changed considerably in the last three decades (Bansal and Song, 2017). *Reactionary views* assume that sustainability is not part of the duty of managers beyond what is legally required (Friedman, 2007) and *passive views* see companies as regulation takers, process optimisers and adapters to societal pressures from various stakeholders. Representing

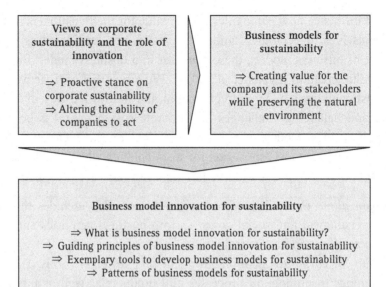

Figure 19.1 Business model innovation for sustainability: chapter overview

a distinctively different view on the environmental and social responsibilities of business, some managers actively seek excellence in their operations and for their products. Here, with an *active view* on corporate sustainability, sustainability engagement is seen as a field to express the strive for highest quality while applying best available technologies and implementing best practices, including zero waste and zero emissions goals or advanced accounting and management control approaches. *Proactive perspectives* broaden the management scope of sustainability engagement even more towards actively contributing to solving grand sustainability challenges, such as staying in the 'safe operating space' of planetary boundaries (Rockström et al., 2009) and global social problems as expressed in the UN Sustainable Development Goals (SDGs) (UN, 2015).

This is where corporate sustainability management and sustainable entrepreneurship start to overlap. Sustainable entrepreneurship is entrepreneurship for sustainable development in the sense that it aims to discover, create and exploit opportunities for sustainable development with social and technological innovations leading to market and societal transformations (e.g., Schaltegger and Wagner, 2011; Johnson and Schaltegger, 2020). With the fundamental approach to assess all direct and indirect effects of the core business and to question existing key products and business models, sustainable entrepreneurs aim to transform existing unsustainable markets (Hockerts and Wüstenhagen, 2010) by contributing to more sustainable consumption patterns and lifestyles with the most radically sustainable products and services imaginable (Schaltegger et al., 2016b). When sustainability management takes on traits of sustainable entrepreneurship and when radically new ways of doing business are needed, innovation comes into play.

19.3 Innovation as a Means to Achieve Corporate Sustainability

There is the general sentiment that being innovative and being able to contribute to sustainable development are somehow related. The proactive stance on corporate sustainability introduced above includes this assumption, as do many of the ideas discussed nowadays, such as cleaner production, sustainable product design, circular economy, sharing economy, green information technologies, etc. The relationships between innovation and contributions to sustainable development are captured by various terms, including eco-innovation, social innovation, sustainable innovation, sustainability innovation, and many more. Adams and colleagues, in their comprehensive review of this topic, use the term sustainability-oriented innovation: 'Sustainability-oriented innovation (SOI) involves making intentional changes to an organisation's philosophy and values, as well as to its products, processes or practices, to serve the specific purpose of creating and realising social and environmental value in addition to economic returns' (Adams et al., 2016: 181). This understanding of innovation resonates well with the notion of business model innovation discussed below. Both point to the importance of sustainable value creation. Before discussing the specifics of business model innovation for sustainability, let us briefly look into other types of innovation that are typically discussed in theory and practice, and how these types of innovation relate to the goal of contributing to corporate sustainability.

Innovation in processes – for instance, based on learning from nature – can improve companies' capabilities to produce with different or even fewer resources and less ecological harm. Process improvements that reduce resource consumption are an almost natural approach for most companies. Less resource consumption typically means reduced production costs. Several companies are changing their production processes and are experimenting with new materials, such as Nike and their Flyknit shoes, where production waste is being reduced and materials increasingly circulate (Nike Circular Design, 2022).

Innovation in products can give new capabilities to customers – for example, their capability to repair and maintain products. Fairphone, a smartphone producer that has become famous for their socially and ecologically driven approach to managing its supply chains, offers modular smartphones that can be easily repaired (Fairphone, 2022). Screens, batteries and other components can be replaced, so that the lifetime of the smartphones can be extended by the customers themselves. Repair guides and community forums contribute to creating a repair culture among otherwise passive customers.

Innovation in services can alter the capabilities of suppliers to interact with their customers – for example, by adding new services to existing physical products – that is, by moving towards product-service systems. Physical products have in many cases significant impacts on the environment. Just think of the ecological footprint of cars. Steel, plastic and other materials are needed to produce cars and emissions occur as they are used. Using cars more efficiently, by moving from owning to sharing, and combining them with public transportation systems allows rethinking 'mobility as a service'.

These examples help understand that innovation changes established capabilities and allows companies, their customers, their suppliers and various others to act in new ways – 'innovation alters our capabilities to act' (Breuer and Lüdeke-Freund, 2017: 57). This is what innovation is good for. This is its purpose. Innovation leads to new means-end combinations, and in doing so it alters our capability to act for corporate sustainability. But whether innovation is always a good thing is a very different question. We may argue that the illustrations above (reducing resource use in production, developing socially responsible supply chains and moving towards services instead of products) point to innovations that aim at making the world a better place. Yet, this does not happen automatically or accidentally. It is a deliberate choice of managers and entrepreneurs to steer their innovation projects towards more sustainable value creation (Breuer and Lüdeke-Freund, 2017; Lüdeke-Freund et al., 2020). In the following, we will see what this means with regard to business model innovation for sustainability.

19.4   Business Models for Sustainability

Helping mankind operate within the planetary boundaries and achieve the UN SDGs is obviously a huge challenge – many would even say *the* challenge of the twenty-first century. Needless to say, companies play an important role both as cause of the problems we face and as part of the solutions we need.

19.4.1   Why Think about Business Models?

A rather new way of thinking about how companies relate to the natural environment and society is by taking a business model perspective (Schaltegger et al., 2016a; Upward and Jones, 2016; Lüdeke-Freund, 2020; Pedersen et al., 2021). But why is thinking about business models useful? Because business models are essentially about how companies create value (Massa et al., 2017). And value creation, in turn, relates in manifold ways to the natural environment and society (e.g., using resources, employing people). Hence, the value creation, respectively business model, perspective is very useful from a sustainability point of view.

The general focus on value creation is expressed in the assumingly most popular *conceptual* definition, proposed by Osterwalder and Pigneur (2009: 14): 'A business model describes how an organisation creates, delivers, and captures value based on a particular value proposition.'

On a more detailed level, this is typically described by referring to several business model components. Following Osterwalder and Pigneur (2009), these include the following: value proposition, key partners, key resources, key activities, customer relationships, customer channels, costs and revenues. While we refer to 'companies' most of the time, the business model concept also applies to many other organisations, such as non-profit or public organisations.

On a *practical* level, business models refer to what companies do and the characteristics they have (Massa et al., 2017). A famous business model found in practice is the so-called 'Razor and Blade' pattern (Gassmann et al., 2020). The idea behind it is to decompose an offering into a basic device (e.g., a razor handle, a coffee machine) and consumables (e.g., blades, coffee capsules), and to create a lock-in effect for customers. They must buy the basic device *and* the consumables to enjoy the product and the value it creates (e.g., a well-shaved face, high-quality coffee). While the basic device creates a lock-in because customers will not buy another razor handle or coffee machine that often, most of the revenue is generated with the consumables (i.e., blades or coffee capsules). These are rather expensive, but at the same time very attractive because they are convenient. Obviously, this way of applying the 'Razor and Blade' pattern is questionable from a sustainability point of view. It creates strong incentives to over-consume resources and to create a large amount of waste (e.g., Nestlé alone sells billions of Nespresso coffee capsules per year, leading to thousands of tons of additional aluminium waste). We present a 'greener' way of using the 'Razor and Blade' pattern later. (We explain the concept of 'business model pattern' in section 19.5.4, below.)

Suffice to say, business models describe (conceptually) and influence (practically) how companies create, propose, deliver and capture value. If we are able to describe and understand how companies do this, we should also be able to describe and understand how companies can create ecological and social value in conjunction with financial and customer value – that is, how companies can engage in *sustainable value creation* (Evans et al., 2017; Lüdeke-Freund et al., 2020). This requires a shift in perspective and going beyond conventional business model definitions.

19.4.2   What Is a Business Model for Sustainability?

By combining both notions, on the one hand an entrepreneurial and innovative stance on corporate sustainability and, on the other, business models as an expression of how companies create value, we get to the core concepts of this chapter: *business model for sustainability* and *business model innovation for sustainability*.

As a first approximation, we can say that a business model for sustainability is about solving ecological and social challenges through a company's value creation activities. A company operating a (theoretically) perfectly sustainable business model would restore the natural environment, create social value and make a profit with every product or service it sells. Can you imagine such a business model? There is an interesting example: Fairphone (see Box 19.1).

> **SNAPSHOTS | BOX 19.1 Fairphone – combining sustainable product design and social responsibility**
>
> Fairphone offers an alternative smartphone that is designed to last. It is easily repairable and updatable, so it does not become obsolete too fast. Beyond sustainable product design, Fairphone is heavily investing in socially responsible supply chains. The company deeply cares about the working conditions of their suppliers, most importantly miners, and actively works on improving these. Taken together, Fairphone is considering the ecological and social effects of their products from cradle to grave and is turning this approach into a very successful business model. Profits are used to improve the product's quality and the working conditions in the supply chain. Fairphone's business success perpetuates the company's engagement for a more sustainable electronics industry. As of 2022, 400,000 Fairphones were sold – just imagine if this company operated on a similar scale to Apple or Samsung ...

Two questions immediately emerge: First, what is a business model for sustainability? And, second, how can business models for sustainability be developed to help companies perform better in ecological and social terms? We can answer the first question straightaway: 'A business model for sustainability helps describing, analyzing, managing, and communicating a company's sustainable value proposition to its customers, and all other stakeholders, how it creates and delivers this value, and how it captures economic value while maintaining or regenerating natural, social, and economic capital beyond its organisational boundaries' (Schaltegger et al., 2016a: 6). We see that a business model for sustainability is about serving the needs of many stakeholders and finding new ways to serve these needs through, for example, new production processes, supply chains, products or services. And at the same time, it is about doing no harm to the natural environment and communities. Ultimately, it is about positive contributions to saving the natural environment and allowing people to prosper and flourish.

This understanding of a business model is very different from the traditional understanding of business models and value creation in at least four aspects (Breuer et al., 2018):

- first, it starts from an orientation towards sustainable development;
- second, it builds on a much broader and much more inclusive notion of value creation that includes ecological and social value;
- third, it is about stakeholders and not only customers, investors or business partners; and
- fourth, it takes a systems perspective by considering various relations to the natural and social environments.

We will come back to these principles later. As a first exercise to familiarise yourself with these principles, you could try to find out whether and how Fairphone or any other company you like applies them in their way of doing business. Regardless of the company and what it is doing, the capability to innovate is needed in one way or another to transform conventional business models into business models for sustainability or to come up with completely new ones.

19.5 Business Model Innovation for Sustainability

Building on our definition of innovation, we can say that *business model innovation* improves the capabilities of organisations to create value. Business model innovation is a more systemic approach to innovation than, for example, process or product innovation. Business model innovation changes how companies propose, deliver, capture and finally create value (Lüdeke-Freund et al., 2019d). While product innovation involves activities such as product design and testing, business model innovation typically involves more complex and more systemic changes and challenges.

19.5.1 What Is Business Model Innovation for Sustainability?

The e-mobility example tells us that business model innovation integrates various types of innovation, typically new processes, offerings and ways of organising.

INSIGHTS | BOX 19.2 Moving towards e-mobility business models

Take e-mobility as an example. If e-mobility were just understood as using different kinds of engine to drive cars, the real scope of the necessary changes would remain too narrow. E-mobility involves changes in car design, charging infrastructures, pricing and revenue models, customer preferences and behaviour, and much more. It requires *systemic innovation* not only in terms of car production, but also, and maybe more importantly, in terms of which infrastructure is needed to use the cars. At the same time, the value proposition to customers changes. For them, it might become a little greener by reducing local emissions or more fancy by offering nice technical features and apps to turn driving an e-mobile into a new mobility experience. The way value is delivered changes as well – for example, by adding new digital services related to using and maintaining e-vehicles, such as route planning, payment services or software updates for cars. This in turn has an influence on the sources from which car producers can capture value for themselves. Finally, we can say that the whole *system of value creation* changes by moving from traditional to e-mobility.

Because of this special quality, some people refer to business model innovation as the 'fourth dimension of innovation' as it goes far beyond classic product, process or organisational innovations in isolation (Massa et al., 2014). If a new business model is meant to help companies in creating sustainable value, things are becoming even more complex, as we have seen with the business model for sustainability definition and examples presented at the beginning of this chapter.

We are now ready to integrate the concepts and arguments heard before and come up with a more formal definition of business model innovation for sustainability: 'Business model innovation for sustainability improves a company's ability to create, maintain, or regenerate natural, social and economic capital beyond its organisational boundaries by changing the value proposition for its customers and all other stakeholders and/or the way how value is created, delivered and captured' (Lüdeke-Freund et al., 2019d: 105). Let us look at a very prominent and radical case of business model innovation for sustainability to illustrate this concept: US carpet manufacturer Interface.

19.5.2   Guiding Principles of Business Model Innovation for Sustainability

So far, you have read about business models for sustainability and what it means to engage in business model innovation for sustainability. But how can you make sure

---

SNAPSHOTS | BOX 19.3 Interface – from selling products to offering services

Interface's initial business model focused on conventional ways of producing, marketing and selling carpets. The company sought to sell as many carpets as possible. The fundamental drivers of growth were sales volume and frequency. It was a linear industry-age business model based on obtaining physical inputs and processing these into physical outputs. What is happening before and after the production of their products was not a big concern. But when Interface's founder Ray Anderson decided to embrace sustainability, he made a profound shift in his company's business logic. Instead of selling carpets, Interface began offering a floor-covering service. The company went from selling to leasing carpets, which allowed the company to control much more of the supply chain (Anderson, 2009). The carpets were redesigned as tiles, so that only damaged or worn parts required replacing. They were also designed to be highly recyclable because the company could save money by reintroducing them in the manufacturing process. The recyclable carpets significantly reduced total material and energy consumption, allowing Interface to deliver a better service at lower cost.

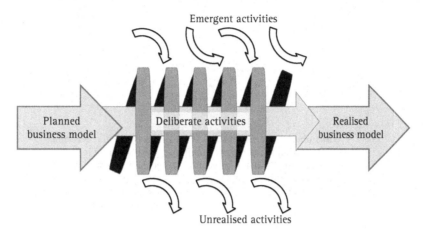

Figure 19.2 Planned vs. realised business models. It's impossible to completely foresee at the planning stage what a business model will be like in reality.
Source: Breuer et al. (2018).

that you are really on the path towards sustainable value creation? How can you increase the likelihood of getting as close as possible to your vision of an ecologically and socially sustainable business model?

The problem is that it can never be determined in advance what a business model will look like in reality. Using a business model tool, such as the famous business model canvas, putting ideas on it and then implementing the business model exactly as it was sketched is a very unlikely scenario (see Strategyzer, 2022, for an introduction to the business model canvas)! And here is why: There will always be a difference between a *planned* and a *realised* business model (Figure 19.2). Imagine a business model canvas (or any business model innovation tool you are using) full of sticky notes with fancy ideas:

- You will turn these ideas into a serious business model design and make a plan for its implementation. You will test it with clients, business partners and further stakeholders. What you are holding in your hands is a *planned* business model.
- Once you start implementing it, you realise that some parts of this plan do not make sense or simply do not work – these turn into unrealised activities. For example, because this one crucial supplier went bankrupt. Or because the actual willingness to pay of your target customers is much lower than their initially stated willingness to pay.
- At the same time, alternative ideas emerge, partly replacing those that are not realised, partly introducing completely new aspects such as a completely new target group – emergent activities come up.
- Only some parts of your original plan are finally realised as deliberate activities. Time, uncertainty and the complexity of business models make sure that your planned and realised business models will always deviate.

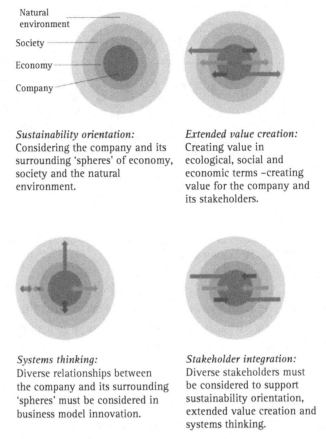

Sustainability orientation:
Considering the company and its surrounding 'spheres' of economy, society and the natural environment.

Extended value creation:
Creating value in ecological, social and economic terms –creating value for the company and its stakeholders.

Systems thinking:
Diverse relationships between the company and its surrounding 'spheres' must be considered in business model innovation.

Stakeholder integration:
Diverse stakeholders must be considered to support sustainability orientation, extended value creation and systems thinking.

Figure 19.3 Guiding principles of business model innovation for sustainability

Now imagine what this means for the development of business models for sustainability. You might start with the best of intentions, but you end up with a horror version of your initial plan – instead of saving the planet, you are destroying it! We have many names for this problem: for example, unintended consequences, rebound effect, paradox or simply uncertainty (e.g., Endregat and Pennink, 2021). To help managers and entrepreneurs avoid such a horror scenario, researchers were looking for guiding principles that help navigate business model innovation processes towards the right direction. They found four major guiding principles (Breuer et al., 2018; see also Figure 19.3).

19.5.2.1   Principle 1: Sustainability Orientation

Sustainability goals should be defined as a reference point, vision or mission for processes of business model innovation for sustainability. This requires openness to various stakeholders' values, needs and expectations. Examples are innovation guidelines building on efficiency, consistency, sufficiency or justice. If you are, for instance, concerned about using natural resources such as water, resource efficiency might be an important guideline. Explicitly following the notion of resource efficiency, your business model will take on certain traits, such as water-efficient production processes, that would not necessarily occur without this orientation. Ask yourself, which overarching concerns, ideals and goals should be guiding your business model innovation process?

19.5.2.2 Principle 2: Extended Value Creation

Business models for sustainability are expected to create value beyond financial value for firms, shareholders or customers. Extending the value concept requires negotiating the relevance of financial *and* non-financial values of various stakeholders. Challenges result from tensions and trade-offs between different bottom lines. While there might be opportunities for simultaneous increases, for example, in customer value and ecological value (e.g., by selling organic and biodegradable products), there will always be a point where you can only improve the one by sacrificing the other. These tensions and trade-offs can only be solved by values-based decision-making – that is, decisions that consider what stakeholders really care about (e.g., health, family, justice or nature) and that are grounded in subjective and even ethical or moral judgments. Ask yourself, what do you and your stakeholders deeply care about (i.e., what are your values) and what type of outcome (i.e., value) do you want to create with your business model? Extended value creation requires reflecting on stakeholders' values (with plural s) and how these relate to desired outcomes in terms of value creation (Breuer and Lüdeke-Freund, 2017).

19.5.2.3 Principle 3: Systems Thinking

Business models are systems of interdependent elements and activities, such as production processes, products and customers. But they also relate to things coming from nature, such as resources, and others coming from society, such as public infrastructures, policy-making, the tax system and many more. Therefore, a holistic view is required to grasp all these elements and activities and to reflect, inter alia, on intended and unintended consequences of business models. For example, if a new production facility is set up in a rural area, what are the consequences for the region and those living there? While positive things like job creation will always be emphasised, what about the consequences for the local infrastructure, the water body or the cosy village nearby? Ask yourself, what is the wider system your business model is embedded in, and how does it relate to different parts of that system?

19.5.2.4 Principle 4: Stakeholder Integration

This brings us to the fourth principle: stakeholder integration. Acknowledgement of the diverse and potentially conflicting interests of your stakeholders is crucial in business model innovation for sustainability. However, stakeholder integration is not a simple linear process. It requires social responsiveness and cultural competencies as conflicts can occur between various stakeholders and can refer to unexpected aspects of a business model. Different stakeholders are related to different cultures, hold different values and have different expectations. These are often expressed as different interests – your employees want safe jobs, your customers want great products and Greenpeace wants you to respect biodiversity and the climate. Ask yourself, who are the relevant stakeholders for a business model innovation process, and how can these be integrated early on and on a continuous basis?

These principles can be used to frame business model innovation processes for all involved stakeholders in a meaningful way. It is important to consider that these principles do not guarantee or automatically lead to business models for sustainability. They are only meant to provide some direction and to increase the likelihood that a realised business model resembles the initially envisioned and planned business model for sustainability as much as possible. Below, we introduce some tools and so-called business model patterns that can help with this.

19.5.3   Exemplary Tools to Develop Business Models for Sustainability

Several tools are available to support business model innovation for sustainability. They combine the strengths of modern innovation approaches such as Design Thinking, Lean Start-Up and Open Innovation with the guiding principles discussed above. Let us begin with a class of tools that focus on the development of sustainability-oriented value propositions.

The so-called *Value Mapping Tool* (see Figure 19.4) allows mixed stakeholder groups to engage in processes of value proposition design. It explicitly considers multiple forms of value – for example, value for customers, value for suppliers and partners or value in ecological and social terms. This helps companies to create more sustainable value propositions. In addition, this tool also considers forms of value that are maybe missed or even destroyed by companies. Different versions of this tool are nowadays available (Bocken et al., 2013; Vladimirova, 2019).

Other tools allow working on complete business models, beyond value proposition design. These are in most cases based on the standard business model canvas.

Take, for example, the *Flourishing Business Canvas* (see Figure 19.5). This tool positions the business model within its wider ecological, societal and economic environments. By doing so, it helps you to model the different contexts in which your business is embedded and to think about how your business model relates to these contexts (Upward and Jones, 2016). The Flourishing Business Canvas is one of the most ambitious tools we have seen so far. It considers all normative guiding principles of sustainable business model innovation and emphasises the various relationships between business activities and their ecological and social contexts in a very clear way. In doing so, ecological aspects such as the use of water, minerals or

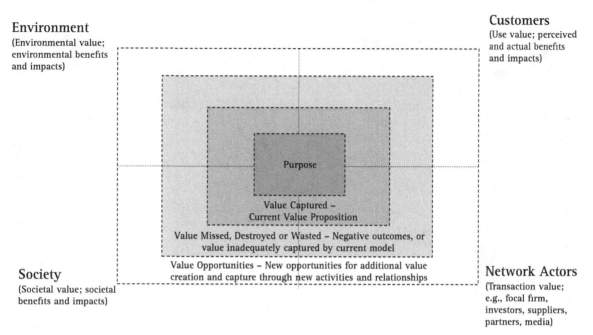

Figure 19.4 The Value Mapping Tool considers multiple forms of value.
Source: Adapted and modified from Bocken et al. (2013).

energy are considered, as are social aspects such as the dependence on stakeholders like employees, local communities or civil society organisations. Since business is nested within these contexts, we can refer to this as the 'systemic embeddedness' of business models (cf. Massa et al., 2018).

The *Triple-Layered Business Model Canvas* (see Figure 19.6) follows a different approach. It adds two more layers to the original Business Model Canvas: one layer for the natural environment and another one for stakeholders. This tool helps you to think about the ecological, social and economic aspects of business in separation, and then to explore the various relations between these different layers (Joyce and Paquin, 2016). The underlying idea is to see business model innovation as taking place simultaneously in multiple dimensions, so the job of managers and entrepreneurs becomes to integrate these dimensions and make sure that their business models are designed consistently across all three dimensions. This tool does also respond to all four guiding principles, but does it in a different way from the Flourishing Business Canvas.

Yet another approach to supporting business model innovation for sustainability is represented by the *Business Innovation Kit* (see Figure 19.7). This toolkit provides a process to facilitate business model development from understanding the values of the involved stakeholders to refining the various elements and activities that make up a business model (Breuer, 2013; Breuer and Lüdeke-Freund, 2017). The Business Innovation Kit makes use of gamification by 'playing cards' and allows mixed

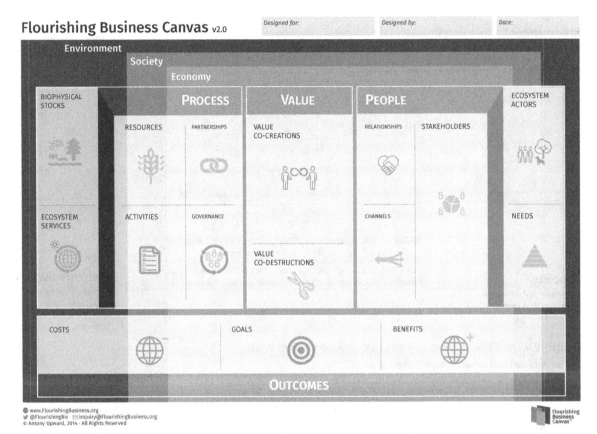

Figure 19.5 The Flourishing Business Canvas. This positions the business model within its wider ecological, societal and economic environments.
Source: www.flourishingbusiness.org/.

stakeholder groups to run their own business model innovation processes. The Business Innovation Kit has been extended by the *Sustainability Innovation Pack* – a tool that integrates sustainability issues directly into the business model development process by raising several questions related to, for example, the effects of ecological and social measures on the efficiency, costs or reputation of the organisation in question.

Finally, we can also refer to a fully digital tool, the *Smart Business Model Canvas* (Venturely, 2022). This tool is based on a completely digital version of the original Business Model Canvas and has been extended by adding various smart and algorithm-based functions such as auto-business-modelling and using an extensive database of business model examples and patterns, which even include various patterns for sustainable and circular business models.

All of these tools are available for free. The references and websites related to these tools will guide you to further materials that you can download and use in your own business model innovation projects.

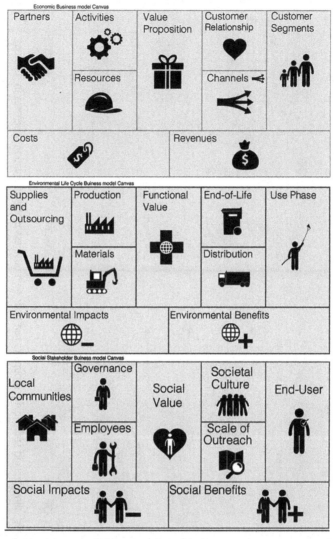

Figure 19.6 The Triple-Layered Business Model Canvas. This adds the natural environment and stakeholders to the original Business Model Canvas.
Source: Joyce and Paquin (2016).

19.5.4   Patterns of Business Models for Sustainability

Throughout this chapter, we have already referred to some examples of business models for sustainability. There is a lot of variety. Some come along as green business models introducing highly eco-efficient processes, products or services (e.g., Interface). Some take the shape of social business models pursuing missions of social inclusion and justice (e.g., Aravind Eye Care System). And others are introducing new understandings of our economy and promote ideas such as circularity and sharing. Looking at all these examples, you were no doubt asking

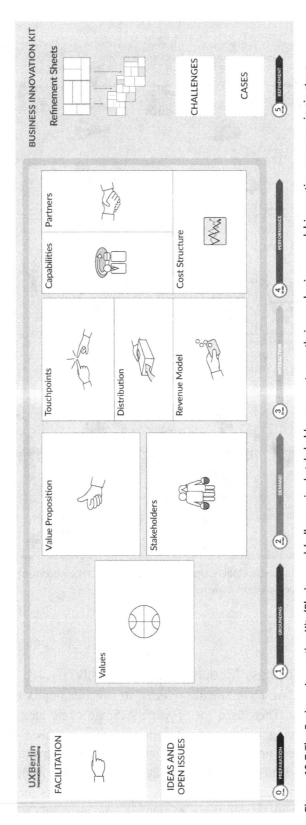

Figure 19.7 The Business Innovation Kit. 'Playing cards' allows mixed stakeholder groups to run their own business model innovation processes in six steps.

Source: www.uxberlin.com/businessinnovationkit/.

yourself: What types of business models for sustainability do exist? We were asking ourselves the same question and developed an overview of this new breed of business models.

Just like biologists crawling through woodlands in search of new insect species, we were systematically searching the business jungle for business models with the potential to contribute to sustainable development (Lüdeke-Freund et al., 2018, 2022; Lüdeke-Freund et al., 2019a, 2019b, 2019c). Just as with new insect species, these business models were systematically described and classified to be clear and useful to others. We came up with a classification of forty-five business model patterns covering various sustainability-related challenges in ecological, social and economic terms (Lüdeke-Freund et al., 2018). This classification integrates and standardises many other classifications and is therefore very comprehensive. Nevertheless, it is just a starting point as new business models are emerging all the time.

Let us take a closer look at the forty-five sustainability-oriented patterns and how they are classified. For this purpose, Figure 19.8 shows a so-called sustainability triangle (see Schaltegger and Burritt, 2005; Kleine and von Hauff, 2009). Each corner represents one of the main dimensions of sustainable development: nature, society and economy. These are interpreted here from the perspective of sustainable value creation and hence refer to the potential of business models to contribute to ecological, social and economic value creation.

Each of the forty-five patterns we found is positioned on this triangle; for example, pattern 'P5.6' at the centre of the triangle, which refers to a pattern called 'Shorter Supply Chains', which is about motivating new business model designs based on reducing the scope and complexity of supply chains which typically causes several environmental and social problems (the full set of patterns cannot be described here; see Lüdeke-Freund et al., 2018, 2022, for a complete overview). The positions of the patterns tell us something very important: the closer a pattern is located to one of the corners (e.g., close to the ecological corner), the stronger is its expected contribution to the respective form of value creation (e.g., ecological value creation). Patterns located between two corners are expected to create a mix of these two types of value. And those at the centre of the triangle hold the potential to contribute to all dimensions of sustainable value creation.

As an example of how to read the triangle, we find a group of patterns on the left side of the triangle, positioned between the ecological and economic corner (group 4, 'Closing-the-Loop'). This group consists of nine patterns that help in closing material and energy cycles and hence support business models for the circular economy. Included are patterns such as 'Take Back Management', 'Reuse', or 'Product Recycling'. Business developers trying to make their companies ready for the circular economy can look into this group and find some inspiration.

Pattern Groups

① Pricing & Revenue
② Financing
③ Ecodesign
④ Closing-the-Loop
⑤ Supply Chain
⑥ Giving
⑦ Access Provision
⑧ Social Mission
⑨ Service & Performance
⑩ Cooperative
⑪ Community Platform

Forms of Value Creation

a   Economic
b   Social
c   Ecological
d   Mainly economic
e   Social-economic
f   Mainly social
g   Social-ecological
h   Mainly ecological
i   Ecologic-economic
j   Integrative

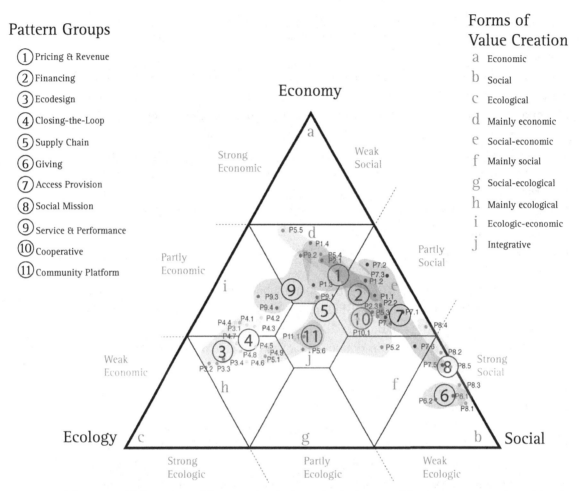

Figure 19.8 The sustainable business model pattern triangle shows that business models can create economic, social and/ or ecological value. For the full interpretative key for P1.1 through P11.1, see Lüdeke-Freund et al., 2018, 2022. A coloured version of the image can be found at https://luedekefreund.com/2018/11/02/45-patterns-to-support-sustainable-business-model-innovation/.
Source: Lüdeke-Freund et al. (2018).

A company that is applying an interesting combination of different circular economy business model patterns is SodaStream. Overall, SodaStream applies a 'Green Razor and Blade' pattern that is supported by various other patterns. The company sells devices to produce sparkling water at home (the 'razor'). In addition, users must buy metal cylinders containing carbon dioxide to make the water fizzy (the 'blade'). Once empty, these cylinders must be returned to get a new one. They are refilled and given to other customers. If a cylinder is broken, its metal is recycled. In this business model, all components are continuously used and reused: the bubble maker, the glass bottles for home use and the gas cylinders. As SodaStream earns most of its revenues from the gas cylinders, the company found a way to make a business based on circulating material, instead of selling goods that are thrown away after usage, such as plastic bottles for sparkling water.

While the SodaStream case is a nice illustration of how different green patterns can be combined, we should also consider the social area of the triangle. Social sustainability challenges are often caused by a lack of access to basic supplies and services such as food, healthcare or education. These social challenges are very often coupled with, or caused by, economic and financial challenges. Families without money cannot afford to send their children to school or to pay for medical services. An iconic example in this regard is Aravind Eye Care System (Seelos, 2014). This Indian eye care hospital chain is maybe one of the pioneers of the so-called 'Social Freemium' business model pattern. Everyone in need of an eye care treatment has access to Aravind. Patients only pay if they are able and willing to pay. If they do not pay, they still get medical treatment, but they do not get the most luxurious hospital room, for example. But this is an acceptable sacrifice. Those who are able and willing to pay get some more amenities on top of their medical treatment. This is 'Social Freemium'. Finally, you could also take a look at another great initiative launched by US American carpet producer Interface, which is called Net-Works. This initiative is about collecting ocean waste and turning it into inputs for new products. At the same time, it creates new income opportunities for local and poor communities as people can join the initiative and earn money by collecting and delivering ocean waste (Interface, 2022).

There is, of course, much more to these cases and the forty-five patterns. If you are interested in ecologically and socially driven business models or even fully fledged triple-bottom-line business models, you will find some inspiration in the full overview of the patterns found in Lüdeke-Freund et al. (2022). You can easily use these patterns together with the tools introduced above. The online *Smart Business Model Canvas* makes use of these business patterns and, in addition, another set of twenty-six patterns that is more specific about business models for the circular economy (Lüdeke-Freund et al., 2019c).

19.6   Chapter Summary

This chapter introduced a new approach to corporate sustainability which focuses on business model innovation for sustainability. We discussed how *innovation alters the ability of companies to act*, and hence their ability to integrate ecological and social concerns into their business activities. We saw that *innovation for corporate sustainability can take different forms*, from small changes in processes and products to radical business model innovation. Building on that, we saw that business model innovation for sustainability can help companies *create value for themselves and their stakeholders and preserve the natural environment* (i.e., to engage in sustainable value creation). Certain *guiding principles* can be identified, based on current research on business models for sustainability, which increase the likelihood that companies engage in sustainable value creation. We finally distinguished *various types of business models for sustainability* and introduced the notion of business model patterns as well as various tools to support their development. All in all, this chapter offers the theoretical and conceptual basics of business model innovation for sustainability as well as a little toolbox that students can explore and even use in their own projects.

Let us conclude by pointing out some important limitations of the introduced approach to business model innovation for sustainability. First, innovation is not a panacea. As noted in section 19.3 on innovation, it is a major trend and buzzword in management and entrepreneurship, and in the field of corporate sustainability as well. There are very good reasons to seriously consider new business models as a means to help companies create sustainable value, but not every problem can or should be solved through innovation. In some cases, less exciting approaches such as administering and managing the activities of a company may suffice – there are many standard routines related to managing people, processes, going to market and many more that companies simply need to function. We should avoid fetishising innovation, and we should always also consider exnovation as an option (Heyen et al., 2017). But we should also be clear about situations and challenges when being innovative and thinking out of the box is required.

Second, the notions of business model for sustainability and business model innovation for sustainability are closely related to the notion of sustainable value creation. The theory is that companies must find ways to create ecological, social and economic value in an integrated manner. They should have positive impacts only. Needless to say that this is hardly feasible. There will always be tensions between different goals and stakeholder interests and there will always be negative effects on the natural environment and people, at least unintentionally (e.g., when highly efficient and resource-saving processes lead to job losses, or when new technologies such as energy storage systems lead to environmental harms through the production of increasing amounts of lithium). The tensions, sometimes even fundamental paradoxes, must be considered and actively detected and managed to not fall into the trap of overly optimistic win-win or triple-win promises (Hahn et al., 2018; Endregat and Pennink, 2021).

Third, as more and more new visions, we can also say paradigms, emerge, such as circular economy, sharing economy, green growth, a-growth or degrowth, we must reconsider the roles and special capabilities of public institutions, civil society and business (cf. Mintzberg, 2015). Market-based, competition-driven and profit-seeking ways of organising value creation definitely have their limitations. Not every human need can or should be solved by relying on 'the market'. There are good reasons for organising certain exchanges via markets. But there are other situations – for example, when it comes to the most vulnerable groups of a society or critical topics such as education and healthcare – in which the division of labour between public, civil and business organisations, and their different purposes, should be reconsidered and adjusted for more proactivity on the side of public and civil organisations.

CHAPTER QUESTIONS

Task 1 – Innovating for corporate sustainability:

- Why is a proactive stance on corporate sustainability needed to tackle grand sustainability challenges? What are the limitations of a purely administrative or managerial approach, and in how far does an entrepreneurial approach go beyond these?
- What is the role of innovation in this regard? Briefly discuss examples of process, product, and service innovation with the potential to mitigate ecological and social problems.

Task 2 – From conventional to sustainable business models:

- What is a business model, and in how far does the notion of business model relate to value creation?
- Briefly discuss at least three conceptual differences between a conventional understanding of business models and the notion of business model for sustainability.
- Can you name a company that represents the idea of a business model for sustainability? In how far is it different from its conventional counterpart? Take, for example, cases from the mobility or electronics sectors.

Task 3 – Guiding principles:

- Can you summarise the four key principles of business model innovation for sustainability in your own words?
- Describe how Interface Inc. (you may also take another company discussed in this chapter) applies the four key principles of business model innovation for sustainability.

FURTHER RESOURCES

Business models for sustainability

- Aagaard, A. (Ed.). (2019): *Sustainable Business Models – Innovation, Implementation and Success.* Cham, Switzerland: Palgrave Macmillan.

This collection of research papers offers a broad overview of current topics of sustainable business model research, including various tools and case studies.

- Aagaard, A., Lüdeke-Freund, F. and Wells, P. (Eds.). (2021). *Business Models for Sustainability Transitions – How Organisations Contribute to Societal Transformation.* Cham, Switzerland: Palgrave Macmillan.

Sustainable business depends on macro-level conditions (e.g., politics, societal trends) and the responses of micro-level actors – for example, in terms of new business models. This edited volume is the first to systematically integrate the macro and micro levels in a systematic way.

- Breuer, H. and Lüdeke-Freund, F. (2017). *Values-Based Innovation Management: Innovating by What We Care about.* Houndmills, UK: Palgrave Macmillan.

Values and what people care about drives entrepreneurs and businesses in various ways. In this book, the influence of values on innovation in general and business model innovation for sustainability in particular is discussed in detail.

- Wells, P. (2013). *Business Models for Sustainability.* Cheltenham, UK: Edward Elgar.

Peter Wells is one of the pioneers in the field of sustainable business model studies. In this book, he summarises his thinking about sustainable business models, including key principles of their development, relationships to larger socio-technical systems, and interesting insights from practice.

Business model innovation for sustainability

- Lüdeke-Freund, F., Schaltegger, S. and Dembek, K. (2019). Strategies and Drivers of Sustainable Business Model Innovation. In F. Boons and A. McMeekin. (Eds.), *Handbook of Sustainability Innovation* (pp. 101–123). Cheltenham, UK: Edward Elgar.

Sustainable business model innovation differs significantly from more traditional forms of business model innovation. This chapter provides a comprehensive overview of specific definitions and guiding principles related to sustainable business model innovation.

- Schaltegger, S., Lüdeke-Freund, F. and Hansen, E. G. (2012). Business Cases for Sustainability: The Role of Business Model Innovation for Corporate Sustainability. *International Journal of Innovation and Sustainable Development*, 6(2), 95–119.

A classic way of motivating sustainable business is searching for so-called business cases – that is, business success achieved by solving sustainability problems. This article provides a thorough discussion of business models and how business model innovation can help companies to develop business cases for sustainability.

- Lüdeke-Freund, F., Breuer, H. & Massa, L. (2022). Sustainable Business Model Design – 45 Patterns. Berlin, Germany: Self-published. www.sustainablebusiness .design.

  This monograph introduces the notion of sustainable business model design and presents 45 business model solutions, called 'patterns', in detail. As a practitioner guide this book offers a lot of practical insights from 100+ case examples and suggestions for using the patterns in practice.

Tools

- Business Innovation Kit, www.uxberlin.com/businessinnovationkit/.
- Flourishing Business Canvas, www.flourishingbusiness.org/.
- Triple Layered Business Model Canvas, https://designbetterbusiness.wordpress .com/.
- Smart Business Model Canvas, https://venturely.io/.
- Sustainable Business Model Blog, https://sustainablebusinessmodel.org/.

Patterns

- Sustainable Business Model Design – 45 Patterns, www.sustainablebusiness .design.

20 Sustainability Standards

ANDREAS RASCHE

LEARNING OBJECTIVES

- Learn what sustainability standards are all about.
- Understand what different types of sustainability standards exist.
- Discuss the input and output legitimacy of sustainability standards.
- Reflect on the (lack of) impact created by sustainability standards.
- Distinguish different types of critique raised against sustainability standards.

20.1 Introduction

In the 1980s, a number of NGOs organised consumer boycotts against major retailers that were selling products based on tropical woods. The main goal was to tackle deforestation. Some NGOs, such as Friends of the Earth, even started to introduce their own labelling and certification schemes. However, as the sourcing of tropical woods is based on long and complex commodity chains, these first attempts to regulate deforestation through voluntary measures remained without much impact. NGOs were convinced that intergovernmental action was needed; they lobbied the International Tropical Timber Organization (ITTO) to adopt a legally binding and government-sanctioned certification scheme. Some hoped that negotiations at the 1992 Earth Summit in Rio de Janeiro would produce such an intergovernmental agreement. Yet, governments showed little interest in adopting a legally binding forest convention that would have helped to tackle the negative effects of deforestation (Gulbrandsen, 2012). As a response, some environmental NGOs (most notably WWF) were convinced that without the voluntary participation of major industry players (e.g., retailers and manufacturers) a wide-ranging certification programme could not be established. In 1993, several parties, including social and environmental NGOs, industry representatives and auditors, met in Toronto to launch the first voluntary certification standard to regulate deforestation: the Forest Stewardship Council (FSC) was born.

The FSC example points to one consequence of the globalisation of business activity. While companies can split their value chain activities across countries (e.g., to reap the benefits of low wages and access to natural resources), governmental regulation is often still bound to national borders, impeding the effective regulation of transnational social and environmental problems. The emergence of such governance gaps (i.e., areas in which governments and intergovernmental institutions do not contribute much, if at all, to problem solutions) has spurred the proliferation of private global business regulation. Such regulation is usually based on the adoption of voluntary sustainability standards like the FSC. Unlike other forms of regulation, governmental actors do not have the capacity to enforce such standards through legal sanctions. Despite them being voluntary, businesses are often keen to join such standards – for instance, because they see them as a way to proactively manage social and environment issues and hence fulfil different stakeholder groups' expectations.

This chapter discusses the nature, legitimacy, impact and critique of sustainability standards. Section 20.2 develops a definition of sustainability standards and distinguishes three different types. This discussion shows that, while standardisation in the field of sustainability has grown in recent years, existing initiatives differ in several important ways. Section 20.3 discusses how the legitimacy of sustainability standards can be assessed. We differentiate between standards' input and output legitimacy. Section 20.4 discusses the impact that sustainability standards can potentially have on adopting firms, end consumers and the regulated issue area. Section 20.5 takes a detailed look at the critique that has been raised against selected standards (e.g., the coexistence of multiple standards with a similar purpose).

20.2 Sustainability Standards: What's in a Name?

In this section, we first want to explore what sustainability standards are and what types of standards have developed over time. We will also discuss how such standards interact with government-based regulation of corporate sustainability (see also Chapter 12 on the role of government regulation).

20.2.1 What Are Sustainability Standards?

Standards, in their most general sense, can be defined as 'rules for common and voluntary use, decided by one or several people or organizations' (Brunsson et al., 2012: 616). Standards represent specific types of rules and hence have a regulative capacity. They reflect one specific type of soft law, because they are voluntary for potential adopters and do not rely on legal mandate or sanctioning mechanisms. In other words, standards are different from laws. Of course, standards could potentially become part of legal obligations, if legislators decide to include a standard in a law, but in their original form they are not part of legal frameworks and rather exist as voluntary commitments.

Legal theory distinguishes between harder and softer forms of law. While hard law is expressed as binding rules (*jus cogens*) and is usually more precisely formulated, softer forms of law reflect non-mandated norms and expectations that are often framed more vaguely. Because soft law does not rest on the authority of states to enforce its rules, it is the various initiatives' perceived legitimacy and, in some cases, pressure by third parties that influence their capacity to regulate sustainability issues. Understood in this way, adopting standards is not a purely voluntary act, but often the result of pressure by competitors, consumers, NGOs, activists and/or business associations.

Sustainability standards is an umbrella term to describe those forms of soft law that promulgate predefined rules and/or procedures to guide, assess, measure, verify and/or communicate the environmental social and/or governance performance of firms (Gilbert et al., 2011; Lambin and Thorlakson, 2018). Such standards need to be distinguished from company codes of conduct. Such codes are usually defined by companies themselves (e.g., to govern their own supply chain or their internal operations). By contrast, sustainability standards are defined 'outside' of those organisations that adopt the rules. Many believe that this gives standards more legitimacy, as firms cannot easily influence the content of the rules they sign up to.

20.2.2   Types of Sustainability Standards

Sustainability standards differ along several dimensions. First, we can differentiate sustainability standards according to the type of standard that is being defined (see Table 20.1):

- *Principle-based standards* reflect broadly defined guidelines to steer participants' behaviour on social and environmental issues. Well-known examples include the UN Global Compact, the OECD Guidelines for Multinational Enterprises, the Principles for Responsible Investment (PRI) and the Equator Principles (Rasche, 2009). These standards reflect a baseline of foundational values and guidelines that businesses can use as a starting point for initiating actions around sustainability. For instance, the Equator Principles represent a framework for financial institutions to determine the social and environmental risks involved in project financing (e.g., for large-scale projects such as the construction of river dams or power plants). In some cases, the underlying principles act as a framework for dialogue, learning and the exchange of best practices among participants. Most firms use principle-based standards as a baseline to develop their own internal policies and management processes around sustainability. Although principle-based standards do not include

Table 20.1 Overview of different types of sustainability standards

	Principle-based standards	Certification standards	Reporting standards
Description	Broadly defined guidelines to steer participants' behaviour with regard to social and environmental issues; foundational values and guidelines that businesses can use as a starting point for initiating actions around corporate sustainability	Focused on verified compliance; verification rests on certification procedures in which auditors assess a single factory or farm; producers that pass the audit are awarded a seal of approval for a specified period of time	Frameworks for disclosing information on a firm's social, environmental and economic performance; reports are usually not verified by standard setters
Exemplary standards	• UN Global Compact • OECD Guidelines for Multinational Enterprises • Principles for Responsible Investment • Equator Principles • Caux Round Table Principles	• Forest Stewardship Council • Marine Stewardship Council • Social Accountability 8000 • Fair Labor Association • Fairtrade • Rainforest Alliance	• Global Reporting Initiative • Carbon Disclosure Project • International Integrated Reporting Framework • Greenhouse Gas Protocol • Sustainability Accounting Standards Board

verification mechanisms, they try to identify non-compliant participants through other, usually 'softer', means. For example, the UN Global Compact and the Equator Principles force their participants to report on implementation progress, while the OCED Guidelines for Multinational Enterprises contain National Contact Points that are supposed to mediate when an external party raises concerns regarding a firm's behaviour.

• *Certification standards* are more focused on compliance with a set of expected practices, behaviours or principles. Verification rests on certification procedures in which auditors assess practices in factories or farms. Such standards define performance criteria for an industry or set of companies – for example, to ensure decent workplace conditions (e.g., the Fair Labor Association (FLA) or Social Accountability 8000), or they specify certain targets in terms of environmentally friendly management (e.g., the FSC or the Marine Stewardship Council, MSC). Some initiatives also require that adopters integrate the specifications of the standard into their management systems (e.g., human resource or supply chain management). Producers that pass the audit are awarded a seal of approval for a specified period of time. Often, such seals act as a precondition to enter into contractual relationships with MNCs.

- *Reporting standards* offer frameworks for transparency – that is, disclosing information on a firm's social, environmental and economic performance. Although some firms reported non-financial information in the 1980s and 1990s, comparing the content of these reports and benchmark companies was difficult. Because reporting was not standardised, businesses disclosed whatever information they felt was appropriate. In 2000, the Global Reporting Initiative (GRI) released its first standard to harmonise the disclosure of non-financial and ESG (environmental, social and governance) information (see also Chapter 11). Although other reporting frameworks exist (e.g., the Carbon Disclosure Project), the GRI quickly emerged as the de facto global standard for communicating around sustainability-related issues (Etzion and Ferraro, 2010). Most reporting standards consist of predefined standard disclosures (telling adopters what information to report) and reporting principles (advising adopters how to manage the reporting process). In the United States, the Sustainability Accounting Standards Board (SASB) helps companies develop, measure and manage material information needed by investors to understand their sustainability.

SNAPSHOTS | BOX 20.1 The UN Global Compact

The UN Global Compact (www.unglobalcompact.org) is a principle-based sustainability standard. Set up in 2000 by former UN Secretary-General Kofi Annan, the Compact positions itself as a framework that corporations can adopt to align their strategies and operations with ten universal principles as well as the Sustainable Development Goals (SDGs). The ten principles are broadly formulated and cover human rights, labour rights, the environment and anti-corruption. The initiative is *not* designed as a tool to monitor corporate behaviour. Rather, participating companies are expected to implement the ten principles and SDGs in their sphere of influence, to share best practices with other stakeholders and to enter into partnerships with other participants (e.g., UN agencies or NGOs).

As of 2022, the Compact has more than 17,000 active business participants. The barriers to entry are rather low. Companies can join the Compact by issuing a 'letter of commitment' to the UN Secretary-General. The letter needs to be signed by the CEO (in order to ensure that there is top-management support for the initiative within the participating firm).

Although the Compact is not designed to monitor or measure participants' performance, it has installed certain integrity measures that are supposed to provide transparency and public accountability. The most important measure is the so-called Communication on Progress (COP) policy, which requires participants to issue a public report on an annual basis. This report is available via the UN Global Compact website and describes what the firm has done to implement the ten principles and support the SDGs. Participants who fail to submit a report on an annual basis are delisted from the initiative. So far, the Compact has expelled more than 15,000 businesses for failure to meet its reporting requirement. This number is surprisingly high, and critics argue that it shows that many participants are not serious enough about their engagement. A 2021 study revealed that 58 per cent of all delisted firms are small and medium-sized enterprises (SMEs) – that is, firms with fewer than 250 employees (Rasche et al., 2021).

Although the three types of standards help us to navigate the landscape of initiatives, there is overlap among them and a single standard may exhibit features of more than one type. For instance, the UN Global Compact also contains a reporting framework (the so-called 'Communication on Progress' reporting). Hence, it is not a pure set of principles, but to some degree also a reporting framework. It is hard to standardise the field of sustainability standards, and we need to keep its heterogeneous nature in mind.

Another way to distinguish standards is by looking at who is involved in their governance – that is, who decides which rules are used and how these rules are enforced (Rasche and Esser, 2006; Gilbert and Rasche, 2007). Most sustainability standards are designed as *multi-stakeholder initiatives* (MSIs). These standards have governance bodies in which the voices of different groups (e.g., NGOs, firms, governments) are heard (de Bakker et al., 2019). Well-known examples are the FSC and the MSC. These governance bodies regulate essential decisions, such as the nature and content of standards, who can join, and which complaint and dispute resolution mechanisms exist. Other standards are designed as exclusive alliances among business actors and are therefore often called business-led initiatives (e.g., amfori BSCI, formerly the Business Social Compliance Initiative). A few standards are also governed exclusively by international organisations (IOs) and therefore reflect *IO-driven initiatives*. For instance, the OECD Guidelines for Multinational Enterprises were developed by the OECD, which also enforces its underlying rules.

20.2.3 Interactions of Sustainability Standards with Government-Based Regulation

Sustainability standards do not work in isolation. Often, they interact with other forms of regulation, most of all with the work of public regulatory agencies. It is possible to distinguish three types of interactions among standards and government-based regulation (Steering Committee of the State-of-Knowledge Assessment of Standards and Certification, 2012). In some cases, governments have *superseded* sustainability standards – for instance, when state-based actors start to require or incentivise practices that were originally established by voluntary standards. The Leadership in Energy and Environmental Design (LEED) certification standard started out as a purely voluntary initiative. It quickly grew into a widely used standard for construction projects; particularly in the United States, LEED-certified buildings demonstrated several environmental and economic benefits (e.g., reduced energy use). Regulators in the United States noted these benefits and started to incorporate some elements of LEED into building regulations and incentivised builders to consider other elements (e.g., via lower fees or tax credits). Governmental regulators thus 'took over' parts of the LEED standard and moved the underlying practices into the domain of hard law.

Governments and sustainability standards can also interact in a more *symbiotic* way. In this case, governments and standard setters reinforce each other's actions, with both maintaining full autonomy. When having symbiotic interactions, state regulators do not integrate the content of a standard into hard law. Rather, standards fill gaps in existing legislation and hence supplement legally binding measures. This type of interaction is particularly relevant when considering the incomplete nature of intergovernmental agreements. For instance, the Clean Development Mechanism (CDM) Gold Standard was established to fill gaps in an existing intergovernmental agreement. The CDM, which was originally established as part of the Kyoto Protocol (defined in Article 12) in 1998, was criticised for multiple shortcomings. This weakened its credibility and undercut trust by multiple stakeholders. In 2002, the WWF launched the CDM Gold Standard as a voluntary certification scheme. The Gold Standard reached beyond the original CDM and certified emission-reduction projects. The CDM and the CDM Gold Standard were symbiotic. The Gold Standard addressed some of the deficits of the original CDM and thus made it more attractive. On the other hand, the CDM managed to become more attractive to investors and thus also increased the popularity of the Gold Standard (Levin et al., 2009).

Finally, there can be *hybrid* interactions between sustainability standards and governmental regulation. In this case, governmental actors and standard setters share the work of regulation (either explicitly or implicitly), such as when a sustainability standard specifies state-based regulations or when it ensures compliance with these regulations. For instance, while national law usually does not require GRI reporting, some countries have recommended that firms refer to the GRI to produce more specific sustainability reports. For instance, the Danish Financial Statements Act requires sustainability reporting for larger businesses; the explanatory notes and guidance documents to the Act encourage the use of the GRI Guidelines.

20.3   The Legitimacy of Sustainability Standards

The proliferation of sustainability standards has created concerns around the level of democratic legitimacy attached to this type of privatised regulation. Government-based regulation through hard law is ideally embedded into a democratic system, in which those who make political decisions are elected to do so. Regulation through sustainability standards does not rest on such democratic mechanisms, as we do not elect those who set voluntary standards. How, then, do sustainability standards establish a level of democratic legitimacy that convinces firms, consumers and other parties (e.g., NGOs) that the underlying rules are appropriate?

A regulator's democratic legitimacy refers to the socially shared *belief* that there is a normative obligation to voluntarily comply with rules of governing authority (Scharpf, 2009). Such beliefs are important as they increase the societal acceptance of sustainability standards in the absence of electoral democratic mechanisms. The legitimacy demands on sustainability standards are more complex than those on governmental regulation, because such standards operate across national borders and hence function against a background of heterogeneous cultural values and traditions. Two different types of legitimacy need to be distinguished. *Input legitimacy* refers to the belief that 'decisions are derived from the preferences of the population in a chain of accountability linking those governing to those governed' (Mayntz, 2010: 10). Input legitimacy deals mainly with questions of stakeholder involvement in the process of formulating a standard. *Output legitimacy*, in turn, is 'derived from the capacity of a government or institution to solve collective problems and to meet the expectations of the governed citizens' (Mayntz, 2010: 10). The output legitimacy of sustainability standards depends on their capacity to provide an effective solution to the policy issues that are being addressed.

20.3.1   Input Legitimacy

The level of a standard's input legitimacy can be judged by four factors (Mena and Palazzo, 2012). First, it is influenced by the degree of *inclusion* of diverse stakeholder representatives in a standard's governance structures. Ideally, representatives of all stakeholders affected by the rules of a standard should also be included in its governance. For instance, the FSC includes stakeholders from the social and environmental domains (e.g., relevant NGOs), as well the economic domain (e.g., companies in the forest and timber industries) in its decision-making structures. Stakeholders from these three sectors are further divided into sub-sectors according to whether they represent the Global North or South. Second, a standard's input legitimacy also depends on whether included stakeholders can influence relevant decisions. Even though stakeholders can be formally included in governance structures, they do not necessarily need to be given the right to impact decisions. A standard's level of *procedural fairness* therefore reflects whether stakeholders are given a voice and whether power differences among them are neutralised as far as possible.

Third, input legitimacy is influenced by whether the included stakeholders are willing and able to change their positions if others present convincing reasons. Sustainability standards that are dominated by one group (such as business-driven initiatives) are usually less prepared to adopt such a consensual orientation. By contrast, standards with a high *consensual orientation* often have formal dispute settlement processes in place. Finally, input legitimacy also depends on whether stakeholders affected by a sustainability standard can evaluate its actions and decisions. Such external evaluation can only take place if standards are *transparent* about how decisions are reached and the performance level of participating companies. The legitimacy of a particular initiative will be higher if it discloses relevant information (e.g., voting procedures, implementation progress).

20.3.2   Output Legitimacy

The level of rule *enforcement* particularly impacts the output legitimacy of sustainability standards (Mena and Palazzo, 2012). In what ways do standard setters ensure that adopters implement their rules? Certification standards usually enjoy higher degrees of output legitimacy, as they involve monitoring procedures to verify compliance with their rules and sanction non-compliant participants. However, the stringency of the underlying rules and the quality of monitoring vary significantly. Business-driven standards are often criticised for relying on less stringent rules, which shield participants from high implementation costs (Auld, 2014). The output legitimacy of sustainability standards is also influenced by their *coverage* – that is, the number of firms that implement the underlying rules. If more firms participate in a standard and obey its rules, then the underlying social or environmental problem can be better addressed. The number of participants is often driven by the so-called bandwagon effect. The more firms participate in a specific initiative, the higher the competitive bandwagon pressure for non-participating firms, because there is a threat of lost competitive advantage.

Finally, a standard's output legitimacy is also impacted by the fit of its rules to the underlying problem (i.e., its *efficacy*). Some standards have been criticised for issuing rules that are either too general to be implemented in any meaningful way or the rules are formulated in ways that do not require significant and costly changes in corporate behaviour. Rules can also be inefficacious regarding the origins of potential adopters. The rules underlying many standards are written for large (often Western) firms, while the specific problems of smaller companies (in the developing world) are not much considered.

The factors influencing the input and output legitimacy of sustainability standards (see Table 20.2 for an overview) are sometimes hard to change. Unequal power among actors involved in standards' governance can impede change. Once a certain set of actors dominates decision-making, it is difficult to introduce fundamental modifications despite criticism. For instance, amfori BSCI (formerly known as the Business Social Compliance Initiative), which is governed by member companies and business associations, has been continuously criticised for a lack of a more balanced governance approach in which all stakeholder groups equally participate

Table 20.2 Input and output legitimacy of sustainability standards

Dimension	Criterion	Definition	Key questions
Input Legitimacy	Inclusion	Involvement of stakeholders affected by the issue in the structures and processes of the standard	Are the involved stakeholders representative for the issue at stake? Are important stakeholders excluded from the process?
	Procedural fairness	Neutralisation of power differences in decision-making structures	Does each of these categories of stakeholder have a valid voice in decision-making processes?
	Consensual orientation	Culture of cooperation and reasonable disagreement	To what extent does the standard promote mutual agreement among participants?
	Transparency	Transparency of structures, processes and results	To what extent are decision-making and standard-setting processes transparent? To what extent are the performance of the participating corporations and the evaluation of that performance transparent?
Output Legitimacy	Coverage	Number of rule-targets following the rules	How many rule-targets are complying with the rules?
	Efficacy	Fit of the rules to the issue	To what extent do the rules address the issue at hand?
	Enforcement	Practical implementation of the rules and their verification procedures	Is compliance verified and non-compliance sanctioned?

Source: Adapted from Mena and Palazzo (2012: 537).

in the standard. Despite these critiques, the standard remains governed by business actors, while other stakeholder groups can only offer advice.

20.4   The Impact of Sustainability Standards

Can voluntary standards effectively discipline the behaviour of firms? Do standards really help to solve the social and environmental problems they are claiming to address? Answers to these questions are context-bound – that is, they depend on what dimension of impact we study and which sustainability standard we analyse (Jellema et al., 2022). The debate around standards' impact is, of course, related to the debate around output legitimacy. Standards that can claim high levels of impact are usually judged to also have high levels of output legitimacy, because they can better meet the expectations that others have vis-à-vis the initiative.

In its broadest sense, impact is about changes in outcomes and behaviours – for instance, when firms modify their production and procurement processes or when coffee farmers change how much fertilisers they use. The debate around impact is therefore multidimensional and we always must ask: impact on which outcomes and impact produced by whom (Haack and Rasche, 2022)? We therefore distinguish three areas in which standards can potentially make an impact: (1) standards can influence how adopting firms change their practices; (2) standards can impact how consumers make purchasing decisions (e.g., through labels) and how other stakeholders behave vis-à-vis the firm; and (3) standards ideally also impact the ESG issues that they were set up to address in the first place.

Figure 20.1 gives an overview. It distinguishes between standards that aim at investors (e.g., the PRI) and standards that aim at other firms. In the case of a standard trying to influence investors' practices, we must differentiate the impact that the standard has on those companies that the investor invests in from the impact that is created by the investee company. Consider the following example. An asset owner does not have direct influence on how an investee company manages its operations. Investor impact is therefore the *change* that investors' activities cause in the impact that investee companies have on ESG-related issues. In other words, investors have a more indirect impact on ESG issues. Chapter 11 discusses investor behaviour in more detail, and we therefore focus here exclusively on standards that are not trying to influence investors.

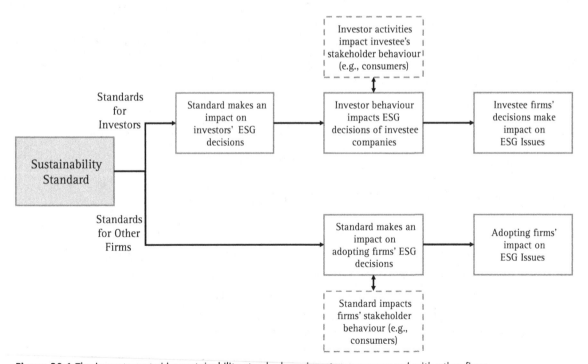

Figure 20.1 The impact created by sustainability standards on investors as compared with other firms

20.4.1   Impact on Adopting Firms

The most widely discussed dimension of impact is whether adopters really implement standards' content or whether they just commit to the standard without making any substantial changes ("greenwashing").

The implementation quality of principle-based initiatives is difficult to evaluate, as there is no clearly defined baseline against which to measure compliance. While these standards can have a high number of participants, their level of compliance often varies significantly. Hence, we need to distinguish between impact through standards' *diffusion* and impact through standards' *compliance*. Sustainability standards can be widely diffused and can have many adopters in quantitative terms. However, when the quality of implementation is low, there will only be limited overall impact on firm behaviour and the ESG issues that are supposed to be addressed.

Impact through diffusion. Impact through diffusion depends on several factors – for instance, the bilateral foreign direct investment (FDI) activities between two countries. Often, home countries, whose firms operate under a specific standard, 'export' this standard via FDIs into host countries. MNCs' subsidiaries may adopt sustainability standards that are also used in their country of origin. It is also possible that standards diffuse in host countries because subsidiaries can create externalities that impact local firms (e.g., when local suppliers are asked to adopt a certain standard). Such FDI-based effects were shown to be relevant in the context of ISO 14001 (Prakash and Potoski, 2007). Trade can also be a driver of standard diffusion. Importing countries' standards are often de facto requirements for firms based in exporting nations. This effect is particularly observable in industries where global brand name companies push certification standards through their supply chain, as in the case of the apparel industry. Given that the bulk of exports from developing nations are motivated by trade relationships with firms from developed countries, trade often creates incentives to ratchet up social and environmental standards in developing countries.

The strength of a country's regulatory environment and its attitude towards international treaties also affect the diffusion of sustainability standards. Firms operating in countries with more stringent social and environmental regulations usually show higher adoption rates. Joining sustainability standards helps businesses to comply with existing regulations and to better anticipate the development of the regulatory environment. For example, the UN Global Compact's tenth principle on anti-corruption paved the way for discussions within firms on how to best cope with newly arising extraterritorial law in this area (e.g., the UK Bribery Act). Some governments have also tied public procurement decisions to the fulfilment of social and environmental criteria. Sustainability standards are often accepted as evidence that these criteria are met. For instance, the diffusion of the FSC in the United Kingdom was supported by the results of a public comparative evaluation of different certification standards. The UK procurement office concluded from this study that the FSC met the highest standards, and that competing initiatives (e.g., the Programme for the Endorsement of Forest Certification) failed on several points.

Impact through compliance. The impact of sustainability standards also depends on whether adopters comply with the underlying rules. Standards are only effective tools for regulation if they improve the social and environmental performance of firms. Although firms cannot freely choose their level of compliance (e.g., because some standardisers enforce rules via inspections), many standards allow for variations in implementation quality. Often, there is a gap between firms' level of compliance and their positive communication about the resulting social and environmental performance, causing claims that businesses greenwash their operations. What, then, influences firms' level of compliance vis-à-vis a standard?

Economic incentives play an important role in this context. Firms usually choose a level of compliance that matches their perceived benefits and costs. High-quality implementation can be costly. For instance, full compliance with ISO 14001 requires maintaining different aspects of an environmental management system, including costs for training personnel, adjusting business processes and documenting outcomes. The exact amount of costs is influenced by the fit of existing corporate practices with the content of a standard. Firms from regions with tight social and environmental regulations often face lower implementation costs and can reach higher levels of compliance without much difficulty. Also, larger firms are usually better equipped to cover implementation costs, as they already have relevant management systems in place and hence face lower costs for corrective actions.

Firms balance costs against the perceived benefits of standard implementation. Market demand is one important consideration in this context. Large corporate buyers often require certain certifications from their suppliers and thus offer them incentives to justify higher costs of compliance. Christmann and Taylor (2006) found that the importance placed by buyers on the issue addressed by a standard influences the quality of implementation by suppliers. Suppliers were willing to invest more in implementation and go beyond what is minimally required if buyers perceived the regulated issue as important. The costs attached to finding alternative suppliers also influence the quality of standard implementation. If buyers face high switching costs when replacing existing suppliers (e.g., in case of non-compliance), they are less likely to punish low levels of compliance. A high level of compliance can also result from the need to manage reputational risks. Especially larger (multinational) firms, which have public images and brand reputations to defend, are more vulnerable to activism that criticises low levels of compliance. For instance, Greenpeace criticised Nestlé in 2010 for ignoring its commitment to the Roundtable on Sustainable Palm Oil (RSPO). After an extensive public shaming campaign, the company agreed to more ambitious targets when it comes to fighting mass deforestation.

20.4.2   Impact on Consumers

Consumer behaviour is mostly shaped by certification standards that have visible product labels attached (e.g., Fairtrade or FSC), while corporate participation in other types of standards remains unknown to the bulk of end consumers. Product labels are one way to overcome information asymmetries in markets. Such asymmetries exist because consumers cannot directly observe the social or environmental characteristics of a good or service. The production of sustainable goods relates to internal business processes (e.g., sourcing), which cannot be observed by individual consumers. Labels transform the unobservable credence attributes of goods (i.e., attributes that need to be taken on faith) into observable search attributes (i.e., attributes that can be assessed prior to purchase). Labels emit market signals and communicate to consumers that a product conforms to the codified requirements of a specific standard. This lowers consumers' search costs, as it helps to compare products and to identify those goods with social or environmental features. However, product labels are only successful if consumers really alter their purchasing behaviour. Do consumers prefer labelled over non-labelled products, and are they willing to pay price premiums for labelled goods?

Several studies have shown that a subset of consumers is willing to pay price premiums for labelled products. For instance, Loureiro and Lotade (2005) found that some consumers were willing to pay a price premium for fair trade labelled coffee. However, the impact of product labels on consumer choice is often overestimated, because there is an observed gap between consumers' *intention* to pay premiums for labelled products and their actual purchasing *behaviour*. A 2021 study found that while 39 per cent of consumers said that it is important for them that a product is produced under safe and ethical working conditions, only 18 per cent of consumers made a conscious decision to purchase a product that meets these characteristics (Strong et al., 2021). There are different reasons for this gap. One reason relates to the way in which research is conducted. Research in this area often suffers from a so-called social desirability bias – that is, consumers publicly declare that they prefer labelled products (because they consider this answer to be the most socially accepted), while they act in a different way when faced with an actual purchasing decision. However, there are also several other reasons for consumers not 'walking their talk'. For instance, some consumers are very price sensitive and cannot afford the price premia associated with product labels.

This is not to say that product labels and their belonging certification standards are without impact. Rather, consumer reactions to labels are heterogeneous and are influenced by several factors, such as: the label itself and consumers' trust in it; consumers' interest in and understanding of the regulated issue; the level of the associated price premium; and the geographic context of consumption. For instance, consumers are often suspicious of standards that are sponsored by industry groups, even when such standards are widely known (Teisl et al., 2002). Consumers' reaction to labels also depends on the product itself and whether they believe that there is a connection between their usage of the product and the underlying social or environmental problem. Some problem areas are complex and consumers need to be educated about the impact of their purchasing behaviour (e.g., the link between palm oil, deforestation and the loss in biodiversity).

20.4.3   Impact on Regulated Issues

Does the adoption of environmental certifications reduce pollution? Do workers really benefit from labour standards? These questions are essential, as it would be possible that a sustainability standard impacts firm behaviour and consumer choice, but remains without much influence on the actual social or environmental issue (e.g., because the standard does not raise the bar very much). Methodologically speaking, it is difficult to establish a causal link between the adoption of a standard and its social as well as environmental impacts. Direct measures of gains do not exist in all cases (and hence proxy measures need to be used). Even if gains can be measured directly, it is difficult to correctly isolate the effects of a certain standard, because social or environmental improvements can also be caused by other factors (e.g., better enforcement of hard law). For instance, if we want to show that farmers are better off because they work on a farm that is Fairtrade certified, we would need to show that farmers' welfare gain was caused by the introduction of Fairtrade and no other potential influencing factors.

Most initiatives address several different policy areas. For instance, the scope of the FSC criteria is rather broad, including workers' rights, indigenous peoples' rights and environmental conditions. In many cases, the impact of a standard on its portfolio of issues is uneven. Barrientos and Smith's (2007) assessment of corporate codes of labour practice, which were aligned with the Ethical Trading Initiative (ETI) Base Code, is a case in point. Their study showed that the ETI influenced outcome standards – that is, those labour standards that are either negotiated or the product of legislated entitlements. Workers benefitted from improved health and safety provisions and reduced working hours. However, the study also revealed that the ETI had little or no effect on workers' process rights – that is, those rights that regulate whether and how employees are incorporated into negotiations around labour conditions (e.g., the right to collective bargaining). Another study looked at whether the RSPO standards for palm oil, discussed above, made a difference, and found that there was no sustainability difference between certified and uncertified plantations (Morgans et al., 2018). A recent review of the impact of sustainability standards therefore concluded that such initiatives have a mixed impact on social and environmental issues (Jellema et al., 2022). While there are clearly some positive impacts (e.g., farmers receiving higher income for certified products), these gains need to be evaluated against negative impacts (e.g., that farmers often have to work longer hours to reap these benefits).

20.5   Critique of Sustainability Standards

Sustainability standards have been criticised from various angles. In this section, we discuss three common critiques: (1) there are too many unconnected standards doing the same or at least similar things (standard multiplicity); (2) there is a lack of inclusiveness when defining standards; and (3) standards can be used as a tool to greenwash corporations' sustainability activities.

20.5.1   Standard Multiplicity

The coexistence of multiple sustainability standards with a similar purpose is often seen as a challenge to the evolution of effective private regulation. Such standard multiplicity has been observed in some industries. Certification standards in the global coffee industry (e.g., Fairtrade, Rainforest Alliance and the Common Code for the Coffee Community [4C]) partially overlap and serve a similar purpose. A comparable situation occurs when looking at the ready-made garment industry (e.g., the Fair Labor Association, Fair Wear Foundation, SA 8000, Clean Clothes Campaign and Worker Rights Consortium). While these standards differ regarding some dimensions (e.g., their historic roots and level of diffusion), there are also considerable similarities among them (e.g., some of the criteria used for certification).

Standard multiplicity creates several problems. It confuses suppliers, who often must comply with multiple standards at the same time (e.g., when supplying buyers who have subscribed to different initiatives). Gaining multiple certifications can also incur substantial costs on the side of suppliers. Standard multiplicity also puzzles consumers, who have a hard time comparing the product labels that are attached to the standards. Similar standards can also lead to competition for business participants among standard setters. Such competition is likely to have negative effects, as it can lead to a regulatory 'race to the bottom' – that is, initiatives try to attract participants by deliberately watering down their standards. Despite efforts to enhance collaboration among standard setters (e.g., through the Joint Initiative on Accountability and Workers' Rights, JO-IN, in the garment industry), there are no signs of convergence. Why do sustainability standards that serve a similar purpose not converge?

One answer to this question relates to the fact that the proliferation of standards has created a market for sustainable goods in some industries (e.g., coffee, tea, apparel). This market offers standard setters a competitive space within which they can coexist through differentiation strategies (Reinecke et al., 2012). This differentiation is partly driven by standard setters' wish to preserve their identity and autonomy. Standards within one industry often position themselves differently on the market. For instance, some standards in the global coffee industry emphasise social justice and price premium for small-scale producers (e.g., Fairtrade), while others highlight biodiversity conservation (e.g., Rainforest Alliance) and superior coffee quality (e.g., Nespresso AAA). Differentiation also occurs because standards stress different levels of stringency, ranging from initiatives with rather strict requirements and implementation procedures (e.g., Fairtrade) to standards with relatively low entry barriers (e.g., 4C). Hence, standards can coexist because they focus on a particular niche in the market and are reluctant to give up what they perceive to be their added value, making consolidation and rationalisation of existing initiatives difficult.

20.5.2   Lack of Inclusiveness

Many standards are explicitly designed as MSIs. This puts much emphasis on the engagement with stakeholder groups while developing and governing standards, not least because the involvement of different spheres of society is perceived as increasing the independence of standard setters. While all individual stakeholder groups reflect a certain interest, and are therefore not neutral per se, the combination of different interests can lead to an image of independence (Boström, 2006). The inclusiveness of standards is therefore important. Inclusiveness can refer to the scope of included stakeholders in terms of involving different types of parties (e.g., representing business, civil society and government) and in terms of engaging with parties from different geographic origins. It can also refer to the quality of participation – that is, how stakeholders are involved in decision-making processes relevant to a standard (Schouten et al., 2012). Critics point out that while many standards claim to be MSIs, in practice there are significant variations in terms of the scope of stakeholder involvement and the quality of participation.

Fransen and Kolk (2007) differentiate two types of sustainability standards, which represent extreme ends on a continuum of inclusiveness. On the one hand, there are standards that follow a strategy of broad inclusiveness and active stakeholder involvement. These initiatives have a balanced representation of different stakeholder interests in their governance bodies (e.g., the FSC). On the other hand, there are standards that follow a narrow approach based on consultation of interested parties (but not active engagement). Stakeholder consultation is mostly found in business-driven standards where non-business stakeholders often just have an advisory function but no formal voting rights. Such initiatives mostly engage with stakeholders from developed countries, while only having indirect links to representatives from the developing world. Within business-driven standards, the demand for inclusiveness usually conflicts with the aspiration of industry players to have a high degree of control over standard development and governance.

Inclusiveness is only useful for standard setters when power asymmetries between participants are reduced. Such asymmetries increase if participants are very dissimilar in terms of their size and their control of financial and non-financial resources. Most sustainability standards face a dilemma: the more stakeholders are involved in standard setting, the more likely will be the existence of power asymmetries among participants, which, in turn, impedes the management of the standard and the creation of legitimacy. Completely avoiding 'capture' by one group of stakeholders is difficult. Most of all, it requires a careful design of the formal structures within the standard-setting organisation. For instance, the above-mentioned three-chamber system of the FSC allows the organisation to balance different interests without allowing one particular group to exert too much influence on decisions.

20.5.3 Greenwashing

One of the most common critiques of sustainability standards is that participating companies use them to greenwash their operations – that is, standards are only adopted for symbolic purposes and do not influence the everyday practices in corporations. This critique is particularly raised against principle-based standards, which contain no monitoring mechanisms and hence cannot verify whether adopters really change their practices.

However, it would be misleading to believe that monitoring processes always ensure full compliance. Boiral's (2007) study of nine ISO 14001 certified organisations shows that managers adopted different strategies to resolve the tension between the need to appear legitimate to external audiences and the need to protect internal efficiency. One strategy was to adopt the standard only superficially. Managers documented and classified existing practices for environmental protection to come into compliance with ISO 14001, but they hardly launched any new activities or substantive corrective actions. In the end, the documented practices were hardly consulted by employees and the adopting organisations only created an internal rhetoric of success around the effective implementation of ISO 14001.

Monitoring of corporate practices remains a challenge in the context of certification standards. One widely documented problem is that auditors are usually paid directly by the brands or factories being monitored. This undercuts their neutrality, as auditing firms have an incentive to soften their monitoring practices to retain client relationships. Further, audits are often announced and hence give factories sufficient time to cover up problems. The FLA has responded to these criticisms and installed a mechanism which uses unannounced audits and does not allow firms to pay auditors directly. We must also keep in mind that many sustainability standards are used in the context of long and flexible supply chains, which makes monitoring a challenging task. MNCs can usually move production quickly to other factories or even countries, and multiple layers of ownership at supply factories make systematic and continuous monitoring difficult. Many standards only cover first-tier suppliers, whereas social and environmental problems are often found further down the supply chain, in the informal sector or in the context of home-based work. Despite all these criticisms, monitoring has raised compliance levels at some factories, especially when it is not used as a stand-alone strategy but combined with other efforts (e.g., better procurement management in global supply chains).

20.6 Chapter Summary

This chapter looked at sustainability standards as one way to practically implement corporations' social and environmental responsibilities. We showed that sustainability standards are part and parcel of a move towards global business regulation through soft law. While this does not mean that intergovernmental regulation is not needed, soft law offers a practical alternative to address those problems where governments could not yet agree on any binding rules. We discussed the heterogeneous nature of sustainability standards, differentiating between principle-based initiatives as well as reporting and certification standards. The discussion showed that sustainability standards often struggle with positioning themselves as legitimate alternatives to other forms of regulation, especially when considering their input and output legitimacy.

Our assessment of standards' impact revealed that some firms show rigorous compliance with standards because there are economic benefits of implementation (e.g., eco-efficiency through process improvements). However, these benefits can usually only be activated when firms reach beyond superficial adoption. It would be misleading to limit the discussion of standards' benefits to things like an increase in reputation and new market opportunities; many standards create indirect effects that often remain unacknowledged (e.g., they generate barriers for new market entrants). We also showed that labels like Fairtrade or the FSC have helped to create a growing market for sustainable goods in some industries (e.g., paper and coffee). Our discussion also revealed that standardisation in the field of sustainability is often criticised, especially for the coexistence of too many initiatives with a similar purpose, lacking inclusiveness in standard development and the unreliability of auditing mechanisms.

The final question, which still remains unanswered, is this: Even if all sustainability standards were fully implemented by all adopting firms, would this make our global economy sustainable? There are many reasons to believe that sustainability standards themselves are not sufficient to achieve such change – for instance, because standard requirements are often only promoting incremental changes which are then adopted by a handful of companies. In the end, the scale of change that is needed can only be achieved when adopting a mix of regulatory measures ranging from national and regional hard law to softer forms of sustainability commitments.

CHAPTER QUESTIONS

1. In what ways, if any, do principle-based standards and certification standards differ regarding their level of input and output legitimacy?
2. What benefits can firms reap from adopting sustainability standards? Do these benefits differ when looking at different types of sustainability standards?
3. Are sustainability standards an appropriate way to regulate those global problem areas where intergovernmental agreements do not yet exist? Why/why not?
4. How would you criticise sustainability standards? Do you think that there are any remedies to address your points of critique?

> **Case Study:** *The UN Global Compact*
> Available from Cambridge University Press at www.cambridge.org/rasche2

FURTHER RESOURCES

- The Ecolabel Index, www.ecolabelindex.com.

  The Ecolabel Index provides a practical overview of 455 standards that are used in 199 countries and across twenty-five industry sectors.

- Greenpeace: Destruction Certified, www.greenpeace.org/international/publica tion/46812/destruction-certified/.

  A well-known study by Greenpeace discussing the role of certification standards in the context of ecosystem conversion and deforestation. The main finding of the report is that certifications reflect a rather weak tool to protect forests and to prevent ecosystem destruction.

- The ISEAL Alliance, www.isealalliance.org.

  The ISEAL Alliance is a standard for sustainability standards. It sets a framework for how credible and transparent sustainability standards should operate.

- The MSI Integrity Project, www.msi-integrity.org.

  A project dedicated to studying whether MSIs protect and promote human rights. Have a look at their report 'Not Fit for Purpose', which discusses the limits of MSIs in the context of global supply chains.

PART IV
Corporate Sustainability: Issues

21 Business and Human Rights

KARIN BUHMANN[*]

LEARNING OBJECTIVES

- Explain the significance of human rights to corporate sustainability, including climate change issues.

- Introduce the normative framework of human rights and explain its relevance for social expectations and regulatory developments on business and human rights (BHR).

- Explain the background, key normative instruments and operational aspects of the BHR regime.

- Discuss the implications for socially responsible business and wider sustainability governance.

21.1 Introduction

Companies can contribute positively to human rights through their activities – for example, through occupational health and safety training or advancing diversity in the workplace. However, we more often associate business activities with human rights abuse, such as child labour, overtime work, workplace accidents, infringements on land rights and many other issues. Companies can cause adverse human rights impacts in multiple ways, ranging from impacts on their own or suppliers' employees, to harm caused by use of products against their intended use that the company could have prevented through its distribution channels, and more indirectly through contributions to climate change that in turn affects human rights. Reports on human rights problems may cause firms reputational problems, resulting in lost contracts with upstream buyers, delays in deliveries and disrupted relations with employees, suppliers and local communities (Ruggie, 2013). Redressing reputational and economic losses requires significant human and financial resources.

---

[*] This chapter builds on the chapter 'Business and Human Rights: Not Just Another CSR Issue?', co-authored by Karin Buhmann and Florian Wettstein, in the first edition of this book.

Consider the following examples:

- When the COVID-19 pandemic forced store closures in Europe and the United States in early 2020, suppliers in garment-producing countries faced extensive order cancellations and extended payment terms. Major apparel brands and retailers cancelled or postponed orders (including some already produced). Following practices in the sector, payments are only made when goods are shipped. Reduced payments resulted in massive lay-off or suspension of factory workers. As workers lost the ability to provide for themselves and their dependants, this reduced their access to or enjoyment of human rights to work, food, shelter and access to health services, putting their livelihoods at risk.
- In a landmark ruling on corporate responsibilities for climate change, the District Court of The Hague in 2021 reasoned its ruling with significant reference to human rights. The court observed that Royal Dutch Shell is responsible for significant CO_2 emissions, which contribute towards global warming and climate change with serious and irreversible consequences and risks for the human rights of those living in affected areas. To inform a standard of care for the company's conduct, the court referred to human rights, especially the right to life and the right to respect for private and family life, and soft law endorsed by the company, including the UN Guiding Principles (UNGPs).

As these examples show, show that business & human rights (BHR) issues can arise in all regions. Some types of problems, typically related to working conditions in mines, factories or industrial production, may be particularly common in low-wage countries with weak institutional set-ups for labour inspections, etc. However, BHR issues – for example, related to adequate involvement of affected stakeholders – also arise in other countries.

BHR has undergone an intensive development over the past decades. It is subject to increasing regulation and formalised public governance, but it remains strongly influenced by moral views and business ethics. Especially throughout the last five years, BHR has solidified significantly as an academic topic and specialised area of business practice. It has also demonstrated strong influence on other governance areas related to corporate sustainability and social responsibilities, in particular due diligence as a management practice to identify and handle harmful impacts.

This chapter first provides an overview of the evolution of BHR, then explains what human rights are and their implications for business, and the connection between BHR and corporate sustainability. Next, it introduces the BHR regime in more detail, with an emphasis on the corporate responsibility to respect human rights and the specific steps set out in the United Nations (UN) Guiding Principles on Business and Human Rights (UNGPs) (UN, 2011). An overview of accountability and remedy mechanisms is followed by a discussion of BHR implications for wider sustainability governance, critical perspectives and a conclusion.

21.2 A Brief Overview of the Evolution of BHR

The international human rights regime, which was mainly developed in the twenti-eth century with a basis in international law, focused on states as duty holders. The international economic regime developed during the same period provided com-panies with extensive rights to make economic profits but few societal obligations. In response to this imbalance, a specialised BHR regime has evolved. This regime recognises that while states clearly have binding duties to protect individuals against business-related human rights harm, companies have responsibilities to respect human rights. Non-binding BHR responsibilities can be argued through ethical views on business conduct, yet in practice they are normatively based on human rights standards set out in international human rights law (including labour law).

In the 1990s and early 2000s, BHR-related ideas were closely related to corporate social responsibility (CSR) and business ethics. More recently, BHR has become subject to detailed normative guidance from international organisations, especially the United Nations. The current BHR regime turns around guidance developed in a multi-stakeholder process, with the UN (2011) Guiding Principles on Business and Human Rights (UNGPs) de facto state of the art in terms of guidance (Wettstein, 2012). The UNGPs apply to all companies in all countries and expect them to establish a human rights policy, apply human rights due diligence as a management process to identify and manage risks and harmful impacts, and provide remedy when harm occurs. Fundamental normative elements of the regime, in particular human rights due diligence, have been adopted by transnational business govern-ance instruments issued by the OECD and the European Union and national law in some countries.

21.3 Human Rights and Their Implications for Business

Human rights derive from the inherent dignity of the human person. They are seen to be unconditional, which means that we have them merely by virtue of being human. Human rights include elements of compassion and charity, which resonate with religious norms in many cultures around the world; ideals on freedom from interference by powerful agents and opportunity to pursue ambitions and personal goals that were argued by political philosophers like Rousseau, Montesquieu and Hobbes; and the ideal of freedom from want that resonates with socialist political philosophy.

Arguing a philosophical justification for human rights, Harvard philosopher and Nobel laureate Amartya Sen (2004) perceives human rights as 'quintessentially ethical articulations' that do not have to be legal claims. This underscores that from the philosophical perspective human rights are inherent, whether or not they are accompanied by rights or claims established in law.

Much of the origin of the notion of human rights is associated with the freedom from interference by a powerful agent, originally the state. Reflected in the French revolution's Declaration of the Rights of Man (1789) and the American Declaration of Independence (1776), human rights ideas played important roles in struggles against absolutism in the seventeenth and eighteenth centuries. Theories by Karl Marx and the evolution of socialism added social and economic rights to civil and political rights. While the liberal human rights notion stressed freedom from interference, the socialist approach perceives human rights as claims held by individuals for specific goods or services to be provided by the state. This applies, for example, to rights to education and access to health services. With BHR, the state-centrist approach to human rights responsibilities has expanded to encompass companies as powerful non-state actors.

The legal regime is a recent development in the history of human rights, which evolved from moral, philosophical and political norms and thoughts anchored in many cultures. It has, nevertheless, become quite defining because it specifies the rights and obligations of societal actors.

With human dignity at its core, the basic idea inherent in what we refer to as 'human rights' is a global concern (see also Shelton, 2014: 1–44). In business contexts (and beyond), human rights issues and problems are frequently not framed as such. Understanding the human rights substance in terms of dignity, freedom from want and protection against abuse by powerful actors, rather than expecting human rights terminology, can help managers appreciate concerns of a human rights character and implement human rights in business practices in the context of a particular firm, sector and/or cultural background.

Human rights issues may arise in a range of conventional management contexts, such as supply chain, contract or human resource management, capital generation, investment, corporate reporting and, of course, risk management. Human rights matter to businesses for business ethics, strategic, managerial, reputational and legal as well as external political and governance reasons.

The Rana Plaza collapse in 2013, which killed more than 1,000 people and maimed many, tragically showcased the adverse human rights impacts of economic decisions to produce under cheap conditions which are frequently accompanied by substandard occupational health and safety, as well as salary, working hours and other working conditions. The ability to operate under such conditions are caused by national 'governance gaps', which enable businesses to formally observe national rules and regulations, but in reality operate under the radar of enforcement.

In addition to private companies, governments across the globe are major buyers of a range of products used for their delivery of services. Examples include medical and personal protective equipment; computers and printers; building and construction materials like concrete, timber, bricks and marble; and services from operations to construction and private security services. This makes public procurement potentially a major economic factor to drive responsible production processes and supplies.

There is no comprehensive and fully inclusive list of human rights. However, the Universal Declaration of Human Rights (UDHR) (UN, 1948) offers a detailed overview (summarised in Table 21.1), which has inspired multiple later international and

Table 21.1 Overview of human rights listed by the Universal Declaration of Human Rights

Article number	Summary of human right in article
1	All are born free and equal in dignity and rights.
2	Freedom from discrimination.
3	Right to life, liberty and personal security.
4	Freedom from slavery.
5	Freedom from torture and cruel, inhuman or degrading treatment.
6	Right to recognition before the law everywhere.
7	Right to equality before the law and equal protection without any discrimination.
8	Right to remedy.
9	Freedom from arbitrary arrest, detention and exile.
10	Right to fair public hearing.
11	Right to be presumed innocent until proven guilty. No retroactive punishment.
12	Right to privacy.
13	Right to freedom of movement.
14	Right to seek asylum.
15	Right to a nationality.
16	Right to marry and to a family.
17	Right to own property.
18	Freedom of thought, conscience and religion.
19	Freedom of opinion, expression and information.
20	Right of peaceful assembly and association.
21	Right to public participation in government; right to free elections.
22	Right to social security.
23	Right to work; right to equal pay for equal work; right to remuneration that is just and ensures a dignified existence for the employee and the employee's family; right to form and join trade unions.
24	Right to rest and leisure, reasonable working hours and holiday with pay.
25	Right to an adequate standard of living, including food, clothing, housing, medical care and social service.
26	Right to education, including elementary education.
27	Right to participate in cultural life.
28	Right to a social and international order supportive of human rights.
29	Community duties.
30	Freedom from interference in the above rights.

national human rights instruments. Studies show that companies are capable of infringing on virtually all human rights (UN, 2007).

Critique of human rights for being a Western construct belongs to the political value struggles of the late twentieth century, but do not reflect the multicultural participation in the group that drafted the UDHR, nor the way in which newly independent countries engage with human rights (Glendon, 2001; Jensen, 2016).

21.4   Human Rights and Corporate Sustainability

Bansal and Song (2017) distinguish between sustainability and CSR. They trace the core concerns in corporate sustainability to perspectives on limits to growth, related to the systemic perspectives on environmental and ecosystem sustainability common in the natural sciences; and those of CSR to ideals on managers' morality and a connection between profit and society.

From this perspective, BHR has a strong leaning towards CSR. This is natural because human rights as such trace their substance and origins to ideas on ethics. Given a heavy focus on labour conditions and impacts on local communities, a social dimension has always been strong in BHR. However, as the second example in the introduction section 21.1 (the Hague District Court ruling) aptly illustrates, enjoyment of human rights is also highly dependent on climate and the environment. We may say that BHR is directly related to social sustainability, and indirectly to environmental sustainability and a sustainable climate, in both cases dependent on economic sustainability with profits made in a manner that respects society as well as the environment. This is further illustrated in Box 21.1.

SNAPSHOTS | BOX 21.1 Corporate sustainability dilemma: wind farms and indigenous rights

Across the Nordic Arctic, Sámi communities are protesting and lodging court cases against the expansion of wind-power farms that the Sámi perceive to have adverse impacts on their traditional reindeer herding. This conflict pitches the urgent need for a transition to low-carbon energy production with the human rights of the Sámi. As Indigenous People, the Sámi enjoy rights to traditional culture and to particularly qualified involvement in decision-making concerning their lands, especially according to International Labour Organization (ILO) Convention No. 169. How should companies, governments and other actors, such as institutional investors who are called upon worldwide to ensure the necessary finance for the transition, respond and act?

Compared to CSR and wider ideas on corporate sustainability, BHR has a distinct character, defined and characterised by a detailed normative foundation in human rights; a recognition of the duties of states and at the same time of the responsibilities of companies to self-regulate when states do not adequately implement and enforce their own human rights obligations with regard to business-related impacts; and a strong emphasis on the necessity of victims to have access to remedy and their grievances addressed.

21.5 The BHR Regime

Like other specialised human rights regimes, the BHR regime is grounded in the UDHR as well as the underlying ethical considerations on which human rights rests.

The UDHR was adopted in 1948 to give flesh to general commitments to respect and promote human rights, which the UN Member States agreed to in 1945. The moral view of human rights is reflected in the opening of the UDHR and the first article, which states: 'All human beings are born free and equal in dignity and rights. They are endowed with reason and conscience and should act towards one another in a spirit of brotherhood' (UN, 1948). The UDHR has given rise to several other detailed international and regional legal instruments on human rights. Typically creating binding obligations for states, these instruments offer guidance for non-state actors, such as companies. The International Bill of Human Rights (IBHR) comprises the UDHR and two international treaties, which set out the rights described by the UDHR in greater detail: the International Covenant on Economic, Social and Cultural Rights (ICESCR, UN, 1966a) and the International Covenant on Civil and Political Rights (ICCPR, UN, 1966b). The IBHR is important in a BHR context, because the principles that it embodies 'comprise the benchmarks against which other social actors judge the human rights impacts of companies' (UN, 2008: para. 58) and therefore inform social expectations of business enterprises to respect human rights. Along with the fundamental labour standards set out by the ILO, the IBHR forms a minimum base line for the corporate responsibility to respect human rights.

The ILO fundamental labour standards comprise the freedom of association (including to form and belong to a trade union) and the right to collective bargaining, freedom from discrimination in the workplace, the elimination of child labour and the abolition of slavery, and involuntary and forced labour. The ILO and the standards covered by the fundamental conventions predate the United Nations by several decades. The ILO was established in 1919 in response to concern with national and transnational exploitation of labour. With a tripartite composition of labour and employers' organisations as well as states and an output of almost 200 binding conventions and over 200 guiding recommendations, the ILO has proven a productive and resilient organisation able to respond to ongoing labour challenges in a globalising world. International labour standards also inform important labour-oriented CSR instruments outside the BHR field.

Launched in 2000 as a voluntary business governance instrument, the UN Global Compact's principles cover human rights (Principles 1–2, based on the UDHR) and labour rights (Principles 3–6, based on the fundamental labour standards). In the early 2000s, a UN initiative, the 'Draft Norms' on BHR, failed to become adopted. A new initiative launched in 2005 led to the UN Protect, Respect and Remedy Framework (UN, 2008). The Framework report built on a three-year comprehensive multi-disciplinary social science study of the causes of business-related human rights abuse and led to recommendations for states and companies and for enhanced access to remedy for victims (Buhmann, 2017). Based on the Framework, the UNGPs spell out those recommendations into operational guidance.

In principle, nothing in international law keeps decision-makers from establishing obligations pertaining to non-state actors, such as companies. Yet, decision-makers (which in international law are states) have generally developed rules without directly binding effect on companies, including the UNGPs. Since 2014, efforts have been underway to develop a binding treaty on business and human rights. The development of international law treaties is usually a protracted process. The drafts so far suggest that the BHR treaty will follow the conventional pattern in international law according to which states are duty holders, with obligations to implement regulation of companies in national law. For this reason, the UNGPs remain the currently most advanced international BHR instrument, but they do not stand alone. The UNGPs, and in particular their due diligence approach, have come to inform human rights and labour provisions in a large range of private and hybrid business governance instruments (Buhmann, 2021) as well as voluntary and mandatory non-financial reporting, including under the EU Non-Financial Reporting Directive that applies to large companies across the European Union. At the national level, a few states (Germany, France and the Netherlands, as well as Norway, an EEA country) have introduced national law mandating certain companies to undertake human rights due diligence with regard to all or some types of activities and/or human rights risks related to their transnational operations. If an EU proposal that was presented in 2022 is adopted, mandatory human rights will become a requirement for many companies in all EU Member States, along with environmental due diligence.

21.5.1 The UNGPs and the Three Pillars: State Duties, Corporate Responsibilities and Access to Remedy

The UNGPs comprise three overarching 'pillars': (1) The *state duty to protect* against business-related human rights abuse; (2) the *corporate responsibility to respect* human rights; and (3) *access to remedy* for victims.

The *state duty to protect* is based on the idea of 'horizontal' human rights obligations. This means that states must protect individuals or communities against human rights abuses by third parties (like companies). They should do this through adequate policies, regulation and adjudication (monitoring and enforcement). Governments already have such obligations under international law – for example, to develop appropriate national legislation and enforce it, but the UNGPs explain the implications in detail with specific regard to business impacts on human rights. Several governments have adopted national action plans (NAPs) on BHR to help them deliver on their duty to protect.

The *corporate responsibility to respect* reflects recognition that societies and stakeholders expect firms not just to comply with domestic law, but, where it is inadequate or even conflicts with accepted human rights standards, to go beyond it by respecting international human rights law. Accordingly, companies are de facto expected to self-regulate to ensure that in addition to the relevant national law they observe, as a minimum, the IBHR and ILO core labour standards. The corporate responsibility to respect human rights applies to any type of business, regardless of size or sector. To ensure the integration into a company's practices, business enterprises should have a *human rights policy*, adopted and communicated by the highest management level. To identify, prevent and mitigate adverse impact and communicate how they do so, they should exercise *risk-based due diligence*. Contrary to the financial and legal liability ('transactional') due diligence approaches that are typically used by firms to identify and assess financial or legal liability risks to the firm, due diligence elaborated by the UNGPs aims to protect society from the harm caused by the enterprise. Of course, if done well, it may also protect the firm against risks, such as reputational or economic. The corporate responsibility to respect human rights has led to rising expectations of other non-state actors to respect human rights, as exemplified in Box 21.2.

SNAPSHOTS | BOX 21.2 Corporate sustainability in practice: FIFA, Qatar 2022 and human rights

In preparation for the 2022 FIFA World Cup, extensive construction work and refurbishment of stadiums was initiated in Qatar. FIFA (Fédération Internationale de Football Association) is a non-profit organisation and the international federation governing football (soccer). Qatar established a Supreme Committee for Delivery and Legacy (SCDL) to contract firms to construct the stadiums. Much of the manual work on the stadiums was undertaken by migrant workers from South Asia. After work on the stadiums had begun, reports emerged of conditions that were problematic from a human rights perspective, related to working hours, occupational health and safety, cramped accommodation, underpayment, fee schemes and retention of employees' identification documents. FIFA came under severe criticism for being connected to those practices. Following initial resistance against assuming responsibility, FIFA in 2017 published a global human rights policy aligned with the UNGPs. The policy notes, for instance, that where the national context risks undermining FIFA's ability to ensure respect for internationally recognised human rights, FIFA will constructively engage with the relevant authorities and other stakeholders and make every effort to uphold its international human rights responsibilities (FIFA, 2017).

Access to remedy for victims of business-related human rights abuse targets both companies and states. Remedy entails both a procedural aspect through access to a complaints (or grievance) handling institution, and a substantive aspect – that is, compensation if harm has occurred. Access to remedy offers an individual or community who perceives their human rights to have been abused the possibility to have their grievance considered. This ideally brings clarity, dialogue and learning to avoid similar occurrences in the future, and reparation in case a violation is found to have occurred.

In elaborating the risk-based due diligence process proposed by the UN Framework, the UNGPs set out guidance for actions that companies should take to identify risks related to adverse human rights impact, prevent such impact, mitigate impact that has already occurred and remedy damage done.

The risk-based due diligence process and its core elements, including impact assessment, meaningful stakeholder engagement and the exercise of leverage vis-à-vis business relationships, are among the most significant contributions of BHR theory in terms of guidance for companies on how to manage the complex relationship between economic activities and their societal impacts. The significance is evident in that leading transnational business governance instruments with a wider CSR focus have adopted the risk-based due diligence approach (e.g., ISO's 26000 Social Responsibility Guidance Standard) and some cases (e.g., the OECD's (2011) Guidelines for Multinational Enterprises and the EU's Non-Financial Reporting Directive) expanded it beyond human rights to also cover the environment, corruption and related issues.

The orientation to societal risk has given rise to the term 'risk-based due diligence', which is applied by the OECD Guidelines. In terms of substance, objectives and steps, human right due diligence and risk-based due diligence are synonymous, but risk-based due diligence may apply other topics than human rights, such as the environment.

21.5.2 'Do No Harm', Human Rights Fulfilment and Connection to the SDGs

The BHR regime based around the UNGPs and UN Framework is fundamentally premised on the objective that businesses should 'do no harm'. Accordingly, human rights due diligence process is generally focused on adverse impacts caused by the company. Business ethics scholars have criticised the focus for being overly instrumental and neglecting opportunities to contribute to human rights fulfilment (e.g., Wettstein, 2012, 2015). The UN Framework recognises that companies may undertake commitments voluntarily to contribute to human rights (UN, 2008: para. 25), but refrains from providing guidance. Contributing to societal needs such as, for example, any of the 17 Sustainable Development Goals (SDGs) does not offset harm caused; however, a company may benefit from its stakeholder engagement and impact assessment undertaken as part of the human rights due diligence to identify salient SDG-related needs that it could address through its wider sustainability policies. An impact assessment involving stakeholder engagement undertaken as part of a due diligence process may serve to identify potential needs of a local community that a company may wish to address (Buhmann et al., 2019).

21.5.3 Operational Aspects of Human Rights Due Diligence

Given the wide adoption of the UNGP's due diligence approach as a key modality for identifying and managing harm, it is important for managers involved in BHR to have a fairly detailed understanding of the elements and steps of due diligence. This is also called for in order to enable companies to document and report on their due diligence processes, as increasingly required by business partners as well as voluntary or mandatory non-financial reporting standards.

21.5.3.1 An Ongoing and Contextual Process

Human rights due diligence should be undertaken as an ongoing process comprising a series of complementary steps: assessing actual and potential human rights impacts, integrating and acting upon the findings, and tracking responses and communicating how impacts are addressed. (Each of those steps is also outlined below.)

Assessments of human rights impacts should be undertaken at regular intervals, such as before a new activity or relationship or major decisions or changes in the operation (e.g., market entry, product launch, or wider changes to the business); in response to or in anticipation of changes in the operating environment (e.g., rising social tensions); and periodically throughout the life of an activity.

Some companies already apply other forms of due diligence targeting risks caused by the company (e.g., to health and safety or the environment). Such processes can be drawn on for human rights due diligence; however, research demonstrates that to be effective these need to be adapted to the particular task of managing human rights risks (McCorquodale et al., 2017).

Companies also need to tailor their due diligence to meet the needs of the specific contexts in which they operate, those for which the particular due diligence is applied and dynamic developments (Guiding Principle (GP) 17). In addition to stakeholder consultation, in particular with affected stakeholders (rights-holders/victims), the process should involve internal and external expertise – for example, on contextual human rights issues.

21.5.3.2 Assessing Actual and Potential Human Rights Impacts

Information gained through the impact assessment process forms the foundation for further steps in the due diligence process.

The initial step in conducting human rights due diligence is to identify and assess the nature of the actual and potential adverse human rights impacts with which the company may be involved. The purpose is to understand the specific impacts on specific people in a specific context of operations. Typically, this includes assessing the human rights context prior to a proposed activity; identifying who may be affected; identifying the relevant human rights standards and issues; and assessing the adverse human rights impacts that the proposed activity and associated business relationships could have on affected stakeholders (GP 18 with commentary).

Accessing interdisciplinary human rights expertise may help the company understand human rights issues in their appropriate context – for example, taking account of cultural specificities and past historical conflicts that affect affected stakeholders' perception of current human rights impacts.

The impact assessment should not only cover adverse human rights impacts that the company may cause or contribute to through its own activities, but also those that may be directly linked to its operations, products or services by its business relationships. The process may vary in complexity with the size of the business enterprise, the risk of severe human rights impacts and the nature and context of its operations. However, it should be open-ended in recognition of the fact that human rights risks may change over time as the company's operations and operating context evolve (GP 17).

The assessment of potential or actual human rights impacts should consider all rights set out in the IBHR and ILO core labour rights, as a minimum (GP 12). However, as these are, precisely, only the minimum level, they do not constrain a company from considering impacts based on additional human rights instruments, whether international or regional. For example, a company may decide to consider whether there is a case for free, prior and informed consent in line with the ILO's Convention No. 169 (ILO, 1989), which is not a fundamental convention, but is nevertheless significant for projects in areas where indigenous peoples might be affected.

The process should be designed to identify and understand human rights impacts even if stakeholders – whether 'affected' or other – are not able to identify them as impacts or in human rights language. This may require extensive training on the part of the company's employees or hired experts who conduct the impact assessment, as actual or potential affected stakeholders may perceive impacts differently from the company. The assessment should pay attention to any particular human rights impacts on individuals from groups or populations that may be at heightened risk of vulnerability or marginalisation (e.g., Indigenous groups), as well as gender differentiations in impacts, such as the different risks that may be faced by women and men.

21.5.3.3   Meaningful Stakeholder Engagement

Meaningful consultation and engagement with affected stakeholders form essential elements of the impact assessment process (GP 18). In order to adequately identify risks and impacts from the perspective of those affected, companies should seek to understand the concerns of these stakeholders by consulting them directly in a manner that takes into account language and other potential barriers to effective engagement, such as genderised roles and cultural norms, as well as other circumstances affecting the communication with actual or potential victims. If such direct involvement is not possible, the company should consider reasonable alternatives – for example, consulting credible, independent expert resources and/or civil society (OECD, 2017; OECD, 2018: 8, 22–23, 28–31). Indigenous people have particular rights to consultation and involvement (ILO, 1989; UN, 2007).

21.5.3.4 Integrating and Acting on Findings – Taking Appropriate Action

When the company has identified risks or actual impacts, it must integrate and act on the findings to take appropriate responses. This means that the company should take necessary steps to prevent risks or cease any adverse impact that it *causes*. If it *contributes* to a risk or an adverse human rights impact, it should take the necessary steps to prevent or cease that contribution. Moreover, it should use its influence ('leverage') to mitigate any remaining impact to the greatest extent possible.

What constitutes appropriate action can be more complex if the company does not cause or contribute to the impact, but the impact is *directly linked to its operations, products or services by their business relationships*. The enterprise may terminate the relationship; however, it is recognised that such a response may not be the best option in view of the wider human rights implications of ceasing collaboration (GP 19; OECD, 2011: Commentary 22). Exercising influence (referred to as 'leverage' in BHR) may have a longer-term positive impact.

If the company lacks influence, it may be able to increase it – for example, offering capacity-building or other incentives to the related entity, and/or by collaborating with other actors, such as other companies, labour unions, civil society organisations or industry associations. If the enterprise lacks the influence to prevent or mitigate adverse impacts and is unable to increase its leverage, it should consider ending the relationship.

21.5.3.5 Tracking Responses

Tracking is necessary in order for the company to know if its human rights policies are being implemented optimally, to know whether it has responded effectively to the identified human rights impacts and to drive continuous improvement. Tracking should be integrated into relevant internal reporting processes applied by the enterprise. It can involve tools that the enterprise already applies for tracking other issues (e.g., environmental impacts). Here, too, special efforts should be made to impacts on individuals from groups or populations that may be at heightened risk of vulnerability or marginalisation in order to track the effectiveness of the company's responses (GP 20 with commentary).

21.5.3.6   Communicating and Reporting How Impacts Are Addressed

Stakeholder communication can occur throughout the due diligence process. Communication during the impact assessment process contributes to explaining impacts or risk factors to stakeholders and understanding their concerns. End-process communication provides feedback to affected and other stakeholders and offers a form of accountability through transparency on the process and how impacts are addressed. This involves communication on the due diligence process, and steps taken in response to its assessments, including to prevent or mitigate harmful impacts and provide remediation (GP 21).

Communication can be undertaken in several ways, including in-person meetings, online dialogues, consultation with affected stakeholders and actual reporting. Reporting typically takes place after other steps have been taken. For the sake of accountability, formal reporting is particularly important where risks of severe human rights impacts exist, whether this is due to the nature of the business operations or operating contexts (GP 21 with commentary; OECD, 2018: 59–61).

In several countries, particularly across the European Union, companies' own decisions to report on a voluntary basis on due diligence and human rights risks have been supplemented (or supplanted) by mandatory non-financial reporting.

21.5.3.7   Remediation

In response to the due diligence process, the company needs to remedy adverse impacts caused. Even with the best policies and practices, a business enterprise may cause or contribute to an adverse human rights impact that it has not foreseen or been able to prevent (GP 22). Of course, remediation is equally important if due diligence has been deficient or not undertaken at all.

Remediation is an expectation in situations where an enterprise causes or contributes to adverse impacts. When adverse impacts are directly linked to its operations, products or services by a business relationship, remediation is not required as part of the company's responsibility to respect human rights. However, the company that was directly linked may take a role – for example, by using its leverage to encourage the entity that caused or contributed to the impact to provide remedy (Ruggie and Sherman, 2017).

Remediation can take several forms, which can be combined. It can include solving the problem, making sure it does not reoccur, and/or providing compensation or rehabilitation for affected stakeholders who have suffered harm.

21.6   Accountability and Remedy

Companies can be held to account informally through the market, when consumers or business partners respond to information on the company's human rights impacts by shifting their buying preferences or investments away from the company.

Several companies have experienced the backlash that transgressions with regard to human rights can have on their reputation. Nestlé's baby-formula marketing disaster in the 1970s, for example, still affects their reputation and image today. Similarly, Shell's role in Nigeria or the revelation of Nike's reliance on child labour and sweatshops in the 1990s are still present in many people's minds today. These companies have had to invest much in improving their human rights records after they experienced the serious public relations repercussions such incidents can cause.

In principle, non-financial reporting can contribute to such market-based accountability. In practice, the evidence of this is limited. Partly as a response, civil society organisations and other actors have been pushing for increased access for victims to formal remedy with courts.

Accountability is often seen as a reactive measure to disclose or punish actions after they occurred. But accountability may also carry proactive or 'prospective' aspects by bringing attention to problems before they arise and thereby helping actors manage change – for example, to avoid causing human rights abuse. In the human rights field, the saying that prevention is better than cure has acute relevance. An arm lost in an occupational accident cannot be replaced, a childhood lost to child labour cannot be relived and a field contaminated by toxic emissions may take years to recover before it can supply its owners with a living. Accordingly, accountability mechanisms that can help identify risk before they cause harm, and/or shape future business action to become more responsible, are of particular significance.

Access to remedy offers an individual or community who perceive one or more of their human rights to have been violated a grievance mechanism, which ideally may bring clarity, dialogue and learning to avoid similar occurrences in the future, and reparation in case a violation is found to have occurred.

The BHR literature considers three forms of remedy institutions: business-based remedy, organised by the company or a group of companies; and state-based, which are either judicial (courts) with powers to adopt enforceable rulings, or non-judicial, such as the National Contact Points under the OECD Guidelines that, in principle, may handle extraterritorial impacts and grievances. By drawing on NCPs as a key and pre-existing accountability mechanism, the UNGPs can be said to strategically 'piggy-back' on to other sustainability governance mechanisms and instruments (Buhmann, 2015).

21.6.1 Business Mechanisms: Operational-Level Remedy

Companies should provide remedy at the operational level – for example, through a concern mechanism and redress. Such mechanisms offer an opportunity for victims to bring human rights impact to the attention of the firm directly rather than having to rely only on court procedures that are often expensive and lengthy. Ideally, operational-level remedy mechanisms enable the firms and the victims to identify and handle a problem before it escalates, and a forum for learning for the management to know more about human rights concerns and risks in the country, region and/or sector of operation so that they may better identify and prevent those in future.

It is important to note that remedy procedures and reparation are often culturally sensitive. Both should be designed to be culturally appropriate and adequate. Monetary compensation is expected and/or adequate in some circumstances, but may be inadequate without an apology in others, or if administered without understanding of the specific context of the victims may lead to further problems.

21.6.2   State-Based Remedy

Courts are *judicial* remedy institutions, empowered to make enforceable decisions. The possibility to apply human rights litigation to sue companies for liability for causing or being complicit in human rights abuse varies between countries. Liability cases may be lodged in most countries, but these are normally limited to companies or torts linked to or occurring *within that state.* This creates major obstacles for victims of transnational business-related harm to obtain remedy. Moreover, lodging cases with courts is often expensive; and a successful outcome generally depends on having access to experienced legal counsel, which can be very expensive. The law of some nation states, especially in the United States, the United Kingdom, Canada and Australia, allow for courts to handle cases of extraterritorial damage under certain circumstances. The mandatory Corporate Sustainability Due Diligence proposal currently (2022) being considered by the European Union includes measures to enhance accountability for victims in non-EU countries with regard to human rights harm caused by an EU-based company in the victims' country, through courts and administrative sanctions in the company's EU home state.

National Contact Points (NCPs) are a remedial and complaints mechanism established at the state level under OECD Guidelines. Unlike many courts, NCPs have *extraterritorial* powers to handle cases in host countries. The wide territorial scope of the Guidelines means that companies may be subjected to grievances with home state NCPs for actions committed in another state without an NCP, and therefore to reputational damage that may result from such a case. NCPs first offer mediation to seek to help the parties find solutions to a case. If the parties do not accept the offer or mediation is not successful, the NCP considers the case and makes findings on the company's observation of the OECD Guidelines. Being *non-judicial*, NCPs do not issue judgments, but they can issue critique of a company and make recommendations. This has important potential to shape responsible business conduct for the specific and other companies.

The numbers and types of cases handled by NCPs vary somewhat across countries. This is likely partly due to the types of business operating in or out of the NCP country, and partly due to levels of independence, resources and forms of composition (see, e.g., OECD, 2016). For example, as cases involving the extractives industries frequently involve multinational companies and transnational operations, they are also frequently subject to complaints with NCPs rather than with bodies with powers limited to national jurisdictions. As a result, NCPs in countries with extractives industries or companies in the sector tend to receive substantial numbers of complaints compared to some others.

The diversity of NCP organisation and resources across various countries means that whereas some NCPs are recognised to be strong and effective remedy institutions and drivers of guidance for responsible business conduct, others are less effective (OECD, 2016). As significantly, there is considerable divergence in the extent to which NCPs use their powers to make recommendations or express critique of company practices (Buhmann, 2018).

Some National Human Rights Institutions (NHRIs) have somewhat similar functions to NCPs.

21.7 Sustainability Governance Perspectives

As we have seen, recent decades' developments in the BHR field have been fast and have substantially changed the form and contents of expectations and requirements on businesses with regard to their impacts on human rights. They have also had implications for wider sustainability governance, and are likely to continue to have so in the years to come as well. The following sections elaborate.

21.7.1 Regulatory and Normative Combinations

The UN Framework recognised that a diversity of factors is at play with regard to shaping business conduct and driving companies to act with responsibility for human rights. In its analysis, the UN Framework report itself drew on several disciplines relevant to BHR – for example, business ethics, management and organisational studies, human rights law and political science. The report recognised the significance of the social licence to operate for the success of a business endeavour. It also recognised political and legal limitations of national law for the regulation of transnational business conduct and related impacts that occur outside of the company's home state. Partly to help address such limitations, the UNGPs explicitly encourage states to deploy a strategy of 'smart-mix regulation', drawing on hard law (binding requirements), soft law (guidance), economic and other incentives, etc. In recent years, civil society actors and others have called for increased deployment of hard law, citing examples of soft law and incentives not being sufficiently effective to drive up business respect for human rights. This has resulted in the current EU proposal for mandatory due diligence and access for victims to EU courts for deficient due diligence and resulting harm.

21.7.2 Strategic Communication

In its choice of language, the UN Framework and UNGPs strategically buy into the specialised terminologies applied in specific academic fields and practice (Buhmann, 2017). For example, the UNGPs deploy the term 'affected stakeholders' when referring to actual or potential victims of business-related harm. In the human rights field, it is common to use the term rights-holders. In applying the stakeholder term, the UNGPs apply a term that managers are familiar with, as stakeholder ethics and stakeholder management are common elements in management training and practice. The aim is not to indicate disregard for rights-holders, but to help managers understand and appreciate the importance of taking seriously the impacts a business may cause and recognise the implications from the perspective of those affected. This is strongly reflected in the UNGPs' guidance on meaningful stakeholder engagement, in particular with affected stakeholders. The language and aims of the guidance can be seen to reflect the recognition of rights-holders in business ethics: rights-holders are obviously included in Edward Freeman's (1984a: 46) definition of stakeholders, as is any group or individual who can affect or is affected by the achievement of the organisation's objectives; and in Evan and Freeman's (1993: 82) recognition of local communities as stakeholders that have a claim to participate in decisions that substantially affect their welfare, and to have their human rights respected (see Chapter 4).

21.7.3 BHR Influence on Wider Sustainability Governance

The UNGPs and UN Framework have influenced several sustainability and CSR instruments and caused revisions of others. The UN Global Compact refers to the UNGPs and the UN Framework in its detailed human rights guidance; the ISO 26000 Social Responsibility Guidance Standard was strongly influenced by the UN Framework and the evolving UNGPs with regard to human rights, labour issues and due diligence. The 2011 revision of the OECD's Guidelines for Multinational Enterprises aimed to ensure coherence with the UNGPs and expanded the risk-based due diligence approach to other issues. The Guidelines are recommendations from governments to MNEs operating *in* or *from* adhering countries (besides OECD countries, some non-OECD countries, including Argentina, Brazil and Egypt adhere to the Guidelines), with the aim of advancing responsible business conduct for human rights, labour, the environment, corruption and other issues.

A 2011 Communication (policy document) on CSR from the EU Commission revised the European Union's CSR definition to offer coherence with the UNGPs and the related 2011 revision of the OECD's Guidelines. Significantly, under the influence of the smart-mix recommendations of the UNGPs and their elaboration of the inter-relationship between public and private CSR governance, the EU Communication changed its definition of CSR to no longer explicitly refer to voluntary action, but simply as 'the responsibility of enterprises for their impacts on society'. This enabled the European Union to begin legislating on CSR, which had not been possible when CSR was defined as voluntary. The European Union's Non-Financial Reporting requirements on CSR and on sustainability-relevant due diligence processes (effective from 2017) are a result of the new definition combined with the adoption of the smart-mix regulatory approach. Moreover, the European Union has adopted reporting and due diligence documentation requirements for institutional investors. The EU proposal for mandatory corporate sustainability due diligence not only covers human rights, but also the environment. And as shown in section 21.1, above, the UNGPs also inform expectations on companies' climate change responsibilities.

These developments demonstrate that the BHR regime is having a significant impact on CSR and wider sustainability governance.

21.8   Critical Perspectives

The UN Framework and the UNGP have been broadly endorsed by companies, governments and civil society organisations, partly as a result of the multi-stakeholder process through which they were developed (Buhmann, 2017). However, there also has been a critical discourse since the publication of the UN Framework. Points of contention refer to the process of the UN mandate, as well as to the form and the content of the UNGP (Wettstein, 2015).

Some business ethicists have criticised the UNGPs for a lack of normative grounding and for an outlook on corporate human rights responsibility that emphasises reputational aspects over moral obligations (Arnold, 2010; Cragg, 2012; Wettstein, 2012). Business ethicists also critiqued the separation and distribution of responsibility as being unclear. Some have called for a more extensive approach, which includes not only a do-no-harm provision, but also positive duties in the realm of protecting and fulfilling human rights (Kolstad, 2012; Wettstein, 2012).

Against this background, it should be kept in mind that the UN Framework and UNGPs were never intended to be the absolute solutions. The UNGPs were a breakthrough in bringing about multi-stakeholder-based agreement on international guidance on business responsibilities for human rights, and through this paved the way for the treaty process. Moreover, while the UNGPs are soft law without their own enforcement and remedy mechanism, they have influenced a wide adoption of due diligence and non-financial reporting on due diligence processes and general management of risks to human rights.

21.9   Chapter Summary

This chapter has introduced several aspects of the idea that businesses hold responsibility for their impact on society with a particular focus on human rights. A topic of global relevance, BHR issues may arise in emergent as well as mature economies. We explained the philosophical and legal background to the modern perception of human rights, its implications for responsible business and connections to corporate sustainability. We explained the evolution of the BHR regime and the key theoretical and normative texts and introduced key elements of the UNGPs that currently serve as advanced guidance for businesses as well as states with regard to business-related human rights harm. We introduced the human rights risk-based due diligence approach and its main elements and explained its importance for responsible management, not least in view of increased due diligence requirements in law and business relations. We discussed accountability challenges and remedy mechanisms; critique that has been levelled against the BHR regime, including the UNGPs, and steps towards a treaty on business responsibilities for human rights; and how BHR has influenced wider sustainability governance, including environmental and climate governance.

CHAPTER QUESTIONS

1. My boss asks me to provide a list of human rights of relevance to business operations. Where do I find such a list – and is there just one list?
2. The UNGPs, as a soft-law initiative, are not legally binding for businesses. Does this make them irrelevant?
3. What is so special about human rights due diligence?
4. Human rights have been defined as obligations for states. If a firm complies with the law in its country of operation, why should it care about human rights?

> **Case Study:** *Lundbeck's Pentobarbital Human Rights Dilemma*
> Available from Cambridge University Press at www.cambridge.org/rasche2

FURTHER RESOURCES

These texts offer additional insights into the challenges and opportunities for business that emerge from working with human rights in a business context:

- Buhmann, K. (2017). *Changing Sustainability Norms through Communicative Processes: The Emergence of the Business & Human Rights Regime as Transnational Law*. Cheltenham, UK: Edward Elgar.

This book analyses the evolution of the BHR regime with an emphasis on communicative strategies and processes, and develops implications for management and wider sustainability governance.

- Buhmann, K. (2015). Public Regulators and CSR: The 'Social Licence to Operate' in Recent United Nations Instruments on Business and Human Rights and the Juridification of CSR. *Journal of Business Ethics*, 136(4), 699–714.

  This article describes the influence of the UN Framework and UNGPs on other transnational responsible business governance instruments and sustainability policies, including those of the European Union.

- McCorquedale, R., Smith, L., Neely, S. and Brooks, R. (2017). Human Rights Due Diligence in Law and Practice: Good Practices and Challenges for Business Enterprises. *Business and Human Rights Journal*, 2(2), 195–224.

  This article offers cases of business engagement with human rights due diligence and an analysis of what due diligence approaches are the most effective with regard to human rights risks and impacts.

- Wettstein, F. (2012). CSR and the Debate on Business and Human Rights: Bridging the Great Divide. *Business Ethics Quarterly*, 22(4), 739–770.

  This article describes and analyses differences, similarities and complementarities between CSR and BHR.

22 Labour Rights in Global Supply Chains

DIRK ULRICH GILBERT AND KRISTIN APFELSTAEDT

LEARNING OBJECTIVES

- Learn about recent developments of globalisation and global supply chains.
- Name the core labour standards of the International Labour Organization (ILO).
- Describe cases of labour rights violations that commonly occur in global supply chains.
- Critically evaluate the arguments for and against sweatshop labour.
- Identify institutional responses at different levels to improve working conditions in global supply chains.

22.1   Introduction

Globalisation is often defined as a process of increasing economic, social, political and cultural interconnectedness. While globalisation is certainly not a new phenomenon, as international trade has always been part of human history, the speed and scope of globalisation has increased substantially in recent years. Over the past three decades, globalisation has particularly manifested itself in the spread of global supply chains. The income generated in global supply chains has nearly doubled over the past fifteen years. Advances in information and communication technology as well as the liberalisation of the global financial system and capital markets have substantially reduced trade and coordination costs and have been important drivers for the increase in global trade and the related growth of global supply chains.

Only recently, rising protectionism and trade wars between the United States and China, as well as the COVID-19 pandemic and the war in the Ukraine, have placed an unprecedented burden on the world economy and the globalisation process of supply chains. Particularly, the virus had a tremendous effect on global supply chains and during the climax of the COVID-19 crisis, many supply lines were cut off due to shutdowns and a decreasing demand throughout the world (Gereffi, 2020). Already existing power asymmetries in global value chains have become even fiercer because some multinational corporations (MNCs) opted for cancelling contracts with their suppliers without paying compensations. As a result, many workers (e.g., in the textile industry in India, Bangladesh and China) lost their jobs and remained stranded without work, food, shelter or means of transportation to their home. This made poor working conditions of workers in the Global South even more visible. Moreover, the COVID-19 pandemic has clearly shown once again that workers and suppliers at the producing ends of global value chains are the weakest and most vulnerable actors in most industries (Carmine et al., 2021).

Despite these recent developments and a decline in international trade, many economies have already partially recovered from the crisis and global supply chains have proved far more robust than expected. At the same time, and in response to changing labour costs, advances in automation and the COVID-19 pandemic, MNCs have already begun redesigning their complex supply chains and exploring ways to build more resilience into them. For example, they have begun to diversify supplier relationships, relocate certain value-chain activities back to their home countries and invest more heavily in robots to substitute labour-intensive production steps.

Nevertheless, countries at all stages of development, ranging from low-income countries to the most advanced, are still involved in global supply chains. The expansion of supply chains has led to a growing specialisation of countries and firms in specific activities or stages in the value chain (Ponte, 2019). Even if the COVID-19 pandemic and the war in the Ukraine have recently caused disruptions, we believe that the underlying principles and mechanisms of global value chains will not change fundamentally. According to Verbeke (2020), the 'governance system [of global value chains] came into existence because it was better suited to serve economic efficiency and to create economic value than other types of governance'. That is why MNCs will continue to outsource a large number of different activities from industrialised countries to international networks of contractors in both developed and less developed countries. In line with Kano and Oh (2020), we believe that recent changes that do occur in global supply chains are not necessarily pandemic-specific. Rather, COVID-19 and the war in the Ukraine have reinforced already existing macro-level trends and tensions such as digitisation, nearshoring or renewed protectionism.

Therefore, a profound division of labour characterises global value chains today and will continue to do so in the future. In the footwear, apparel or electronics industry, for example, MNCs mainly concentrate on value chain activities such as research and development, product design and marketing, while thousands of independent contractors in developing countries and emerging economies focus on the often labour-intensive production of goods. These contractors cobble shoes, sew shirts or assemble mobile phones according to exact specifications of MNCs and are required to deliver high-quality products often according to very tight delivery schedules. International production networks therefore reach across many national and cultural borders and are affected by multiple jurisdictions and different cultural norms and values. While participation in global supply chains provides many developing countries with the chance to enhance economic growth and generate new income opportunities for the population, as will be highlighted in this chapter, the working conditions for many workers in local production facilities frequently are abysmal.

In this chapter, we are particularly interested in the contracting arrangements of MNCs with suppliers in less developed countries which have been labelled as 'sweatshops'. Critical stakeholders from civil society, such as labour and human rights activists, trade unions and non-governmental organisations (NGOs), have charged that large MNCs exploit workers in sweatshops by failing to pay a living wage, tolerating child labour and disregarding basic labour rights. The sharp criticism of sweatshops recently has led not only to an increase in public discussions in the media and a more critical evaluation of the sourcing activities of MNCs; but it has also fostered the development of numerous hard and soft law initiatives addressing human rights and environmental as well as social issues in global supply chains (e.g., the German Supply Chain Law and the UN Global Compact). Against this background, questions arise as to which role sweatshops play in global value chains, how they should be evaluated from an economic and ethical perspective, and what measures can and should be taken to improve poor working conditions.

This chapter proceeds as follows: In the next section, we provide a brief overview of the labour rights frequently affected by the contracts between MNCs and their suppliers before discussing a number of examples for violations of these labour rights in global supply chains. We offer a definition for sweatshops and then continue to critically evaluate the pros and cons of sweatshop labour. Based on these insights, we briefly review opportunities at different levels and by different actors to regulate and improve working conditions in global supply chains. In particular, we discuss the role of MNCs, industry-led initiatives, multi-stakeholder initiatives and governments in improving labour rights in global supply chains.

22.2 Labour Rights

Working and having a job is central to people's well-being all over the world. Work not only provides income, but also paves the way for social and economic advancement of individuals, their families and the communities they live in. Throughout history, workers have tried to express their interests and claim their rights. After World War I, based on the insight that social peace is a crucial prerequisite for peace and economic growth, in 1919, the International Labour Organization (ILO) was established. The ILO is a key player in the arena of labour rights and has developed a system of international labour standards. The ILO promotes opportunities for workers to obtain productive and decent work in conditions of freedom, equality, security and, most importantly, dignity (ILO, 2015). In 1946, the ILO became a specialised agency of the newly formed United Nations. The United Nations also backed workers' interests by incorporating some key labour rights into Articles 23 and 24 of the UN Declaration of Human Rights (see Chapter 21).

The goal of both the United Nations and the ILO is to introduce globally applicable and acceptable minimum standards to protect employees' rights. The labour standards, however, are only legally binding once a Member State has ratified them. Since its inception, the ILO has issued 190 conventions on labour rights (as of 2022), of which eight are considered as the 'core labour standards' being recognised internationally and claiming validity for all countries. The core labour standards are the following:

- Freedom of association and the effective recognition of the right to collective bargaining (Convention No. 87 and No. 98).
- The elimination of all forms of forced and compulsory labour (Convention No. 29 and No. 105).
- The effective abolition of child labour (Convention No. 138 and No. 182).
- The elimination of discrimination in respect of employment and occupation (Convention No. 100 and No. 111).

The most recent convention No. 190 was adopted at the Centenary International Labour Conference in 2019. It focuses on violence and harassment in the world of work and is now open for ratification by ILO Member States. Convention No. 190 and its supplementing recommendations represent the first international standards providing a common framework to prevent, remedy and eliminate violence in the world of work, including gender-based violence and harassment. The Convention requires Member States to define and prohibit violence and harassment in the world of work in laws and regulations and adopt appropriate measures to prevent it.

The United Nations and the ILO are only two of a large number of stakeholders (e.g., consumers, governments, NGOs) who are interested in labour rights, and the core labour standards mentioned above represent only a small fraction of the multitude of labour rights which are possibly at stake. The list of these labour rights is long and covers, for example, the right to a living wage based on a regular working week not exceeding forty-eight hours or a safe and healthy workplace free from violence and harassment. We focus mainly on the role of MNCs regarding labour rights and want to show that labour rights violations are commonplace in global supply chains and mostly happen in the plants of local contractors – the so-called sweatshops.

22.3   Violations of Labour Rights: Sweatshop Labour in Global Supply Chains

While globalisation and the increase in international trade in recent decades has helped to lift numerous people around the world out of poverty, poor working conditions, low wages and associated low standards of living – which have existed throughout human history – continue to prevail in global supply chains. As early as in 1850, the term 'sweatshops' was first used in England to describe production facilities where workers worked for low wages under poor conditions. Workers who performed monotonous and sometimes hazardous work for low wages were referred to as 'sweaters', and so-called 'sweating' was widespread during the height of the Industrial Revolution. Powell (2014) provides a comprehensive overview of the history of sweatshops and assumes that they first existed in England from around 1780 and in the United States from the beginning of the nineteenth century. In the course of industrialisation, sweatshops then spread to parts of South America and Africa, but above all to Asia in the course of the twentieth century.

The definitions of 'sweatshops' vary in the literature. The US General Accounting Office (1988) defines sweatshops as production sites employing workers at low wages, for long hours and under poor conditions. Arnold and Hartman (2006: 677) define the term 'sweatshop' as:

> any workplace in which workers are typically subject to two or more of the following conditions: income for a 48 hour workweek less than the overall poverty rate for that country; systematic forced overtime; systematic health and safety risks due to negligence or the wilful disregard of employee welfare; coercion; systematic deception that places workers at risk; and underpayment of earnings.

Other authors believe that defining a sweatshop only by referring to different aspects of working conditions hampers a substantive debate on the morality of sweatshop labour by definition. They propose to define sweatshops more broadly as industries which violate labour rights in a way that makes their actions prima facie wrong (Zwolinski, 2007). Following this definition, sweatshops exist throughout the world in both developed and less developed countries. The critical discussion of sweatshops in the public and in the academic literature has nevertheless primarily focused on developing countries. These sweatshops are usually legally independent firms that have become part of the global supply chains of large MNCs.

The critical discussion concerning sweatshops mainly focuses on the violation of labour rights and the moral status of sweatshop labour. It is important to note that violations of labour rights are widespread and often happen with the implicit approval of local authorities. In Bangladesh, for example, factory owners in the past have been accused of colluding with state institutions and bribing government officials into defying regulations and building codes. Moreover, factory owners are among the wealthiest people in the country, occupying around 10 per cent of the seats in the Bangladeshi parliament (Zaman, 2014). Table 22.1 provides only a few examples of such labour rights violations to illustrate the magnitude of the problems related to the global contracting arrangements of MNCs.

Violations of labour rights can be found in almost all industries and in nearly every part of the globe. As Table 22.1 indicates, each industry faces particular challenges. Nonetheless, a number of labour rights issues cut across industries and countries. Health and safety issues and freedom of association, as well as wages, range at the top of the most common labour rights violations worldwide. The worst breaches against labour rights are usually recorded at sub-contracting workshops (i.e., second- or third-tier suppliers) as these are much harder to control than those factories that directly supply MNCs.

Over the past years, it has become evident that certain groups of workers are particularly prone to experience violations of their labour rights. Seasonal workers, migrants, refugees or people from marginalised minority groups and in many sectors also women are more vulnerable and particularly at risk of experiencing violations. The ILO further noted that the COVID-19 crisis disproportionately affected those millions of workers that already found themselves in vulnerable situations. These examples highlight that although jobs in international supply networks may be better than other available alternatives in developing countries, the working conditions are often hazardous.

22.4   The Sweatshop Labour Debate

There is a lively debate in the disciplines of philosophy, economics, politics, sociology and business ethics whether and to what extent sweatshop labour is coercive and exploitative. This heated debate around the already negatively connoted term 'sweatshop' has received a tremendous amount of attention not only from theory, but also from NGOs (e.g., Oxfam, Clean Clothes Campaign), multi-stakeholder and standard-setting initiatives (e.g., Fair Labor Association, Social Accountability International), governments, consumers and MNCs. In this chapter, we would like to draw attention to the fact that, with regard to the evaluation of sweatshops, the theoretical perspective from which the topic is analysed is very important. The question of whether sweatshop labour leads to desirable or undesirable consequences heavily depends on the theoretical perspective one adopts. A large body of literature, critical and positive with regard to sweatshops, can be found and we note that the discussion has evolved beyond the superficial objections to sweatshops in the 1990s. Proponents of sweatshop labour mainly argue from an economic point

Table 22.1 Common labour rights violations in global supply chains

Form of labour right violation	Example
Child labour The ILO estimates that, around the world, approximately 152 million children are working instead of going to school. 70 per cent of child labour occurs in the agricultural sector (e.g., in the production of cocoa, tea, cotton and palm oil). Most children labourers face hazardous work environments that are harmful in physical and mental terms. The COVID-19 pandemic is likely to exacerbate the situation for children in many countries and experts fear that child labour may worsen as the pandemic may reduce opportunities in the labour market for parents, pushing their children into hazardous and exploitative work (ILO, 2017a, 2018, 2020).	**Cocoa industry, Côte d'Ivoire/Ghana** Côte d'Ivoire and Ghana account for much of the world's supply in cocoa. While cocoa is lucrative to international traders, farmers in West Africa often receive very low wages. Farmers often cannot hire labourers to harvest and instead draw their children out of school to perform this arduous task. According to a study funded by the US Department of Labor, in the harvest season of 2018–19, an estimated 1.56 million children aged between 5 and 17 were working in the cocoa sector in Côte d'Ivoire and Ghana. Children working on cocoa plantations, for example, find themselves exposed to chemicals and long working hours. Child labour often leads to low educational access and attendance, which again traps families in a vicious cycle of poverty (US Department of Labor, 2013).
Forced labour Forced labour is defined by ILO Convention No. 29 as 'all work or service exacted from any person under the menace of any penalty and for which the said person has not offered himself voluntarily'. In 2017, the ILO recorded around 16 million people as victims of forced labour in the private economy. The sectors most afflicted with forced labour are domestic work, agriculture, construction, manufacturing and entertainment. Besides women and girls, Indigenous People and migrant workers are particularly vulnerable to being forced into labour (ILO, 2017b).	**Electronics industry, Malaysia** Forced labour has been identified as a common risk within electronics supply chains, which around the world employ a high number of migrant workers who are particularly vulnerable to exploitation. In 2014, a study by the human rights NGO Vérité found that in the Malaysian electronics sector, 28 per cent of workers, both female and male, were found to be in situations of forced labour. High recruitment fees, and the debt that workers often incur to pay those fees, leave workers vulnerable to exploitation. A common practice in the Malaysian electronics sector is the retention of passports. As the study reports, for 71 per cent of foreign workers, it was difficult or impossible to receive their passport back when they asked for it (Vérité, 2014; KnowTheChain, 2018).
Living wages In many countries around the world, a considerable gap exists between the wages that workers earn and the cost of their basic needs. While the ILO has set standards on regular payment of wages, and minimum wage levels, often wages are either not paid out or, if paid, are insufficient to meet basic needs. Some governments have set the legal minimum wage below the actual cost of living in order to attract foreign investment. With a living wage, workers should not only be able to satisfy their basic needs, including being able to pay for education of children and transportation, but also receive some discretionary income for unforeseen events such as illness. The lack of a living wage is inextricably linked to other labour rights violations. To increase earning, many workers must do overtime work and cannot take time off when they are sick. In addition, workers often do not fight for better wages, because they fear losing their jobs if they demand their rights or join a union (ILO, 2021; ILRF, 2021).	**Apparel industry, Bangladesh** The apparel industry in Bangladesh has been a key driver for economic growth over the past few years, employing more than 4 million workers, with women making up the lion's share of the workforce. While the sector has contributed significantly to economic and social development over the past few years, it is marked by a number of serious deficits and violations of labour standards, with low wages ranking at the top of the list. In order to quantify what workers would need for a decent living, the Asia Floor Wage Alliance (AFWA) has put forward a worker-led calculation method. In 2018, the Bangladeshi government set the monthly minimum wage at 8,000 Tk (approx. 95 US dollars), whereas the AFWA suggests that in order to provide for a living wage of a family, a wage would need to be set at 37,661 Tk per month, highlighting a fundamental gap in current pay (CCC, 2019; ILO, 2019).

Freedom of association	Electronics industry, China
In many countries, workers are hindered from collectively organising. Intimidations and acts of violence are often used to stop workers from collective action. To undermine unionisation, workers get fired, or imprisoned, or are replaced with migrant workers or children who are often even less able to claim their rights (ILRF, 2021).	The International Trade Union Confederation annually puts forward a report analysing the world's worst countries for workers, documenting violations of internationally recognised labour rights by governments and employers. The 2020 report ranks China among the countries with no guarantee of rights. China is the largest manufacturer of consumer electronics, producing goods for MNCs such as Microsoft and IBM. In China, the only union allowed is the non-democratic 'All-China Federation of Trade Unions' (ACFTU). However, Chinese workers are often unaware of its existence or its mandate. As an audit by the Fair Labor Association at the Apple subcontractor Foxconn brought to light, the majority of the members of the union committee were nominated by the management team and while there were elections, the candidates were often supervisors (SOMO, 2012; ITUC, 2020).
Health and safety	Apparel industry, Bangladesh
The ILO reports that every year about 2.8 million people die from work-related accidents or diseases, while a further 374 million people suffer from non-fatal work-related accidents each year. Most of these accidents are preventable (ILO, 2021).	In 2013, the Bangladeshi garment sector was struck by the worst industrial accident in the country's history. The building complex Rana Plaza, hosting five garment factories, collapsed, burying under it thousands of mostly female garment workers. After the incident, twenty-nine global brands were identified as having placed orders at the factories within Rana Plaza and were accused of having been complicit in creating or maintaining a deadly work environment. In response to the incident, a number of national and international programmes and initiatives were set up to improve safety conditions in the industry. While there have been substantial improvements in the sector, ILO Better Work reports that issues associated with Occupational Health and Safety remain the single biggest area of non-compliance in factories in Bangladesh (Better Work, 2019).

of view (e.g., neoclassical theory) to justify sweatshop labour. Opponents of sweatshop labour usually apply ethical theories (e.g., Kantian Ethics, Rawls's Theory of Justice) to frame the debate in terms of the moral status of sweatshop labour. We will show in the following two subsections that both parties have strong arguments and the debate over what to do about sweatshops is far from being resolved. Drawing the line between right and wrong in terms of sweatshop labour is difficult and basically a matter of balancing economic and moral arguments against each other.

22.4.1   Pros of Sweatshop Labour

Proponents of sweatshop labour usually start from the assumption that individuals working in a sweatshop freely choose to do so. The choice to accept a job in a sweatshop is an exercise of autonomy even if it is not a fully autonomous one. For workers, accepting the (bad) conditions of a sweatshop is probably their most-preferred option among a very restricted set of options. Furthermore, sweatshop workers usually do not accept difficult labour conditions in order to gain an extra income for luxuries, but work to survive and escape the misery of poverty (Zwolinski, 2007; Powell and Zwolinski, 2012; Faraci, 2019). According to the proponents, choices to work in a sweatshop, when they are made autonomously, deserve respect and generate a claim against interventions of NGOs, MNCs, governments and other stakeholders trying to fight or even prohibit sweatshop labour. Although workers' rights may be violated in a sweatshop environment, the abuse of peoples' rights is only a consequence of the autonomy of their own choice and not an objection to it (Zwolinski, 2007: 692–693). Proponents also argue that workers are aware of the difficult working conditions and have much more local knowledge of the particular situation in host countries than scholars and activists in developed countries. Claims by opponents of sweatshops that workers are somehow irrational and will not choose the option which is in their best self-interest would, hence, require considerable empirical evidence, which so far cannot be found (Powell and Zwolinski, 2012).

In the literature, this purely economic rationale for sweatshops is called the choice argument. Famous economists and Nobel laureates such as Milton Friedman and Paul Krugman are proponents of this argument and strongly oppose interventions in the market to ban sweatshop labour (Friedman, 1973; Krugman, 1997). Friedman even points out in his memoirs that his own mother worked as a seamstress in a sweatshop in the United States and yet he believes that this form of labour is an important step in a country's economic development (Friedman and Friedman, 1998). For Friedman or Krugman, a ban on sweatshops would deprive many developing countries of their only chance to exploit their comparative advantages in the (world) market and make them useful for their own economic development. Krugman (1997) expresses this pointedly in his much-cited article entitled 'In Praise of Cheap Labor': '. . . as long as you have no realistic alternative to industrialization based on low wages, to oppose it means that you are willing to deny desperately poor people the best chance they have of progress for the sake of what amounts to an aesthetic standard – that is, the fact that you don't like the idea of workers being paid a pittance to supply rich Westerners with fashion items'.

Based on these assumptions, it would be wrong to deprive workers of the option to choose working in a sweatshop because it would be a violation of the workers' autonomy. All else being equal, sweatshops make their workers better off, even if the conditions are unfair. Sweatshop labour might not be the first choice, but this kind of labour is preferred by most of the workers to any other alternative. The salary earned in sweatshops is typically higher than that paid by alternative sources of employment and better than being unemployed (Zwolinski, 2007). Workers living in poverty often have only a very small list of viable options to improve their living conditions. These options often range from prostitution or theft to sweatshop labour, and removing one option from this very short list, usually the most preferred one, would not be any better for the worker. A comparison of wages paid by sweatshops with those earned through non-sweatshop jobs (e.g., working as a nanny or waiter) even shows that sweatshop jobs seem to out-pay the other domestic rivals significantly (Zwolinski, 2007: 703–704). A study by Powell and Skarbek (2006) found that sweatshop wages in the Dominican Republic, Haiti, Honduras or Nicaragua were three to seven times higher than wages paid elsewhere in the domestic economy, regardless of whether the salaries were paid by MNCs or local subcontractors. The money earned in a sweatshop, even if the salary is meagre, may still help workers to educate their children, feed their families, pay their rents and improve their living conditions. Workers thus seem to be better off than they would have been without sweatshop labour. In light of these arguments, it is not beneficial to prohibit sweatshop labour because it does not make a contribution to solving problems like poverty. On the contrary, without sweatshops, developing countries like Bangladesh or Cambodia would lose a significant amount of their gross domestic product (GDP) and tax revenues that MNCs bring to those countries. The range of currently available options to fight poverty would be even more reduced and governments typically worry that an increase in cost of running sweatshops could lead MNCs to leave or stay away (Zwolinski, 2007: 697).

Following this argument, one can conclude that not only MNCs but also workers benefit from sweatshop labour because they are both better off than without this form of work. The wages paid by MNCs to workers help to increase their standard of living, even if the gain from sweatshop labour does not seem to be fairly distributed between both parties. Proponents argue that MNCs outsourcing to sweatshops at least do *something*, which in their opinion is better than doing *nothing* to make workers in developing countries better off. MNCs not outsourcing their labour to sweatshops and producing under higher standards in their home countries do not benefit those workers at all. Zwolinski (2012) argues that it would be odd to blame MNCs for helping *some* workers while most other firms and individuals are helping *none.* This does not necessarily mean that MNCs in their global supply chains are doing as much as they *should* be doing – from a moral point of view – to improve the living of sweatshop workers. Nonetheless, compared to offering no job alternatives, a job with low labour standards and low wages might be the best option available to most of the workers.

This argument is in line with what Wertheimer (1996) has called the 'Nonworseness Claim', which says that it cannot be morally wrong to engage in a voluntary, consensual and mutually beneficial transaction between an employer and a sweatshop worker, rather than refraining from this transaction altogether (Faraci, 2019; Berkey, 2021). Hence, proponents of sweatshops argue that MNCs should continue to outsource value-added activities to sweatshops – despite public criticism – because this benefits both the workers and the developing countries whose economic growth increases. Customers from industrialised countries should also continue to buy products from sweatshops to stimulate demand for labour in such production facilities. Following this line of reasoning, sweatshops are a necessary step in the process of economic development of developing countries. Without labour in sweatshops, many of these countries would be deprived of their opportunity to increase their prosperity to a level where sweatshops would eventually no longer be necessary. Powell (2014: 129) puts it this way: 'Sweatshops do not just provide a better job than the really lousy other options in these countries. Sweatshops themselves are part of the very process of development that will lead to their elimination.' Powell (2014) cites countries such as the United States, England and Singapore as examples and emphasises that, in the history of these countries, it was primarily work in sweatshops that was a basic prerequisite for their economic development.

If one follows this economically based argumentation, then government intervention in the market that improves working conditions in sweatshops would, *ceteris paribus*, lead to cost increases and thus to lower competitiveness and, ultimately, to the relocation of production to other countries. This would not help workers in sweatshops, host countries or MNEs. Therefore, sweatshop advocates oppose any government interventions that limit the competitiveness of sweatshops in international markets and would strongly reject the recent call for more supply chain regulation (Miller, 2003; Flanigan, 2018). The well-known American economist Jeffrey D. Sachs even went so far as to claim at a panel discussion at Harvard University that there are not too many sweatshops in the world, but rather too few.

While many of these economists repeatedly emphasise that they certainly have sympathy for workers in sweatshops, they still defend sweatshops as the best available alternative for workers and argue that the economic advantages outweigh their disadvantages. Moreover, many authors raise the fundamental question of whether paternalistic measures to combat sweatshops by the state are even effective. Too often, critics argue, government action does not achieve its stated goals and a government does not necessarily know what is in workers' best interests. A closer look at the labour rights affected by sweatshop labour also reveals that wages and other standards regarding, for example, health and safety, workers' right to collective bargaining, or forced labour, must be treated as different kinds of labour rights. The arguments in favour of sweatshops mainly focus on wages and have shown that, although sweatshop wages may not be high enough to lift workers out of poverty, sweatshops can make a significant contribution to improve the standard of living in developing countries.

From a moral point of view, nevertheless, concerns over other labour rights may be distinct from concerns over wages (Zwolinski, 2012). Morally, critics may hold that forced labour or unsafe working conditions violate workers' rights in a way that low wages do not. In practice, however, issues like low wages and other labour standards are inextricably linked and proponents of sweatshop labour usually argue that improvements in both areas lead to an increase in total cost of production. For MNCs and the sweatshops in their global supply chains, the overall costs of a transaction matter and often an increase in worker safety may come at the expense of other forms of compensation (e.g., wage or overtime bonus). This leads to the paradoxical situation that workers themselves are not willing to sacrifice parts of their wages in order to receive, for example, higher health and safety standards. A survey found that only very few Guatemalan sweatshop workers were actually willing to trade any wages for more health and safety standards (Zwolinski, 2012: 164). Nearly 65 per cent of the employees asked in this survey answered that they were not willing to sacrifice any wages for an improvement of their labour standards. Following this argument, one can conclude that both parties affected, the sweatshop and the workers, do not want to put their competitive advantage at risk and implement measures to improve labour standards. However, based on this (purely economic) rationale, it would even make sense to further reduce labour standards to achieve an improved cost position and thus an even greater competitive advantage. From an economic point of view, a profit-maximising firm is indifferent to compensating workers with money or other benefits (e.g., health, safety, leisure) because the firm only cares about the overall cost of the total compensation package.

Powell and Zwolinski (2012) argue that workers think differently because they actually care about the mix of compensation they receive. Economic theory suggests that, the higher the overall compensation, the more likely workers desire non-monetary benefits. Unfortunately, many sweatshop workers only receive low wages because their productivity is low and, hence, their compensation level is low as well. Accordingly, and as indicated above, workers demand most of their compensation in wages and only little in improvements of labour conditions, such as health and safety. This leads to a problem for the opponents of sweatshop labour, who want to separate the discussion about wages from safety and other working conditions. Both workers and firms are limited by the same factor, the worker's marginal revenue product. And if activists only demand to improve safety in sweatshops, then either they are pushing for a reduction in wages (which workers do not seem to prefer) or they will unemploy workers by raising their package of total compensation more than their marginal productivity. Powell and Zwolinski (2012) refer to empirical studies providing (only weak) evidence that an increase of the minimum wage leads to an increase in unemployment. However, the literature on this important question provides mixed results and does not produce clear implications for policy-makers.

22.4.2   Cons of Sweatshop Labour

Contrary to the proponents of sweatshops, opponents claim that sweatshop labour is wrongfully coercive and exploitative. The economists' standard response to this criticism is that sweatshop labour can be mutually beneficial, for the worker and the firm, although it may be coercive and exploitative. In this response lies the core of a first problem, which opponents of sweatshop labour criticise. From their point of view, both of the above-mentioned standard economic justifications for sweat-shops – the choice argument and the argument that sweatshops promote economic development – fall short, precisely because they refer exclusively to the economic consequences for workers and developing countries. Opponents of sweatshops argue that it is a mistake to narrowly focus on the interaction between a worker and the company running a sweatshop and to only focus on the *economic* benefit to the worker relative to which he or she stood prior to the employment (Preiss, 2019).

The choice to accept a job in a sweatshop may be an inevitable move for a worker to improve his or her standard of living, but this does not *morally* justify the unjust conditions that lie in the background of the specific interaction (Kuyumcuoglu, 2021). The economic argumentation in favour of sweatshops thus fails to recognise an essential aspect that goes hand in hand with poverty in many developing countries. People generally only decide to work in sweatshops because they are desperate and have no alternative to escape poverty. In the end, they therefore do *not* make a voluntary decision, which authors such as Friedman and Krugman imply they do. Workers are more or less *forced* to work in sweatshops due to the social structures in developing countries as well as the institutional framework in global supply chains. Lebaron (2021: 3) argues that exploitation is 'a logical outcome of contemporary business models and supply chain dynamics, traceable to stable patterns including those surrounding workers'. These social and economic back-ground conditions can be referred to as *structural injustice*. According to Jugov and Ypi (2019), structural injustice is a distinctive kind of justice, which can be under-stood as a system of formal and informal rules responsible for unjust power positions and the unjust distribution of wealth and resources among the different groups in a society. Sweatshop workers are victims of structural injustices deeply embedded in global value chains, from which MNCs typically benefit the most. According to Berkey (2021), employers of sweatshop workers wrongfully claim an unfairly large share of the benefits generated in supply chains and at the same time fail to implement more favourable working conditions. From this, it follows that the choice argument of the proponents of sweatshops is only weak, because the more desperate the situation of a sweatshop worker and the more pronounced the structural injustice is, the stronger the pressure to come to terms with inhumane working conditions will presumably be. For opponents of sweatshops, workers are wrongfully exploited by their employers and due to the structural injustice have no choice but to accept unjust working conditions (Mayer, 2007; Preiss, 2019; Lebaron, 2021).

Kates (2015) proposes that, even if workers personally choose to work in sweatshops, third parties should interfere with this choice through banning or regulating sweatshop labour, since sweatshop workers are trapped in a collective action problem. A collective action problem is characterised by a conflict of interest of a single sweatshop worker and the interests of the entire group of sweatshop workers. The trouble is that labour is usually an abundant factor in developing countries, so that a single complaining worker can easily be replaced by a worker accepting the conditions of a sweatshop, although they are not in his or her interest either. Sweatshop workers are only able to give effect to their autonomous choices through collective action, which, however, can only come into effect by means of law. Hence, Kates (2015) concludes that, paradoxically in order to respect the autonomy of sweatshop workers, it is necessary to regulate sweatshops.

Critics further argue that a firm, when taking advantage of such structural injustice, fails to show appropriate respect to the worker that he or she deserves. Based on Kantian ethics, Arnold and Bowie (2007) argue that managers of both MNCs and sweatshops have the duty to guarantee the dignity of workers and must neither coerce nor exploit them. Both individuals and firms who contribute to unjust social processes bear a moral responsibility for the processes themselves and the results they produce. These duties may include paying workers a living wage, meeting health and safety standards, and adhering to local labour laws. Arnold and Bowie (2007) claim that workers as human beings with autonomy and dignity are ends in themselves and should not be treated only as means. Coercion and exploitation are wrong, simply because subjects are turned into mere tools and objects lacking the ability to choose for themselves how they want to act. From a Kantian perspective, we have an obligation to respect the dignity of both ourselves and others. Hence, any form of exploitation – for example, wages below a living wage or forced labour – are inherently disrespectful and fail to meet the moral principle of the *categorical imperative*. Take the example of the abuse and exploitation of girls and women workers in the South Indian textile industry. A study by two international NGOs, published in 2014, found that many girls and women working in the Indian textile industry suffer from forced and bonded labour (SOMO and ICN, 2014). Recruiters convince parents to send their daughters to spinning mills or other sweatshops by promising a well-paid job, accommodation and education, as well as a lump-sum payment at the end of three years. In reality, however, the girls have only very limited freedom of movement, face long hours of work, do not get any form of education and only rarely get the lump-sum payment promised to them.

Based on the categorical imperative, managers of MNCs and their suppliers would have a *moral* obligation to ensure that workers do not live under conditions of forced labour and poverty by paying adequate wages for the hard work in sweatshops. In the same vein, Berkey (2021) claims that MNCs as beneficiaries of sweatshop labour have a *positive duty* to the global poor and should use their resources to provide impoverished people with employment opportunities and improve the conditions in sweatshops, at least when doing so will not be extremely costly. From this moral point of view, the cost of respecting workers must be considered as a necessary condition of running a business. In this context, *adequate* wage means the minimum wage required by law or the wage that is necessary to live above the poverty line. Contrary to the arguments discussed above, opponents of sweatshop labour even argue that MNCs usually have a certain degree of latitude when it comes to wages, so that they should be able to voluntarily raise wages in sweatshops without inevitably causing unemployment.

Arnold and Bowie (2007) are also convinced that managers of MNCs and sweatshops should not be seen as subjects to overwhelming economic forces who inevitably must make workers redundant when increasing wages. On the contrary, competent managers should be able to find ways to increase wages while at the same time absorbing additional costs by means of internal cost cutting elsewhere in the value chain or by reducing executive compensation. Interestingly, a study in the Indonesian apparel and footwear industry found that a voluntary increase in wages after massive anti-sweatshop campaigns actually did not lead to an increase in unemployment (Harrison and Scorse, 2006). Rather, the increased wage costs in relation to the total costs of the MNCs were so small that the firms seemed to be able to compensate this investment easily elsewhere in the value chain and that these costs could be successfully passed on to the consumer. In the footwear industry, where companies like Nike, Adidas and Puma heavily compete, labour cost in Indonesia typically accounts for less than 5 per cent of the sales price of a sports shoe. MNCs sell those shoes in New York or London in many cases for US$100 top$200. An increase in labour costs of, for example, 50 cents an hour is not likely to have a dramatic impact on the profitability of a MNC, but rather does have a noticeable positive effect on the sweatshop worker (Harrison and Scorse, 2006). The authors of this study even found that not only wages increased in Indonesia over a longer period of time, but also employment. A reason for this could be that the increase in costs is often cushioned by the fact that product demand is growing as well.

The economic standard argument that rising wages, *ceteris paribus*, lead to an increase in unemployment has another weakness from the point of view of the critics of sweatshops. Not only does it presuppose a direct causality that exists between wage costs and unemployment and that, in the view of some authors, is not empirically demonstrable (see Miller, 2003; Harrison and Scorse, 2006). At the same time, many critics question whether a country necessarily has to go through a sweatshop phase as part of its economic development. This view ignores the fact that, in addition to the presence of the production factor (cheap) labour, there are other variables that are responsible for the development of countries, such as property protection, economic freedom, better social laws, technological developments, improved education or even the work of trade unions. Most importantly, economic development does not necessarily mean the complete elimination of sweatshops. For example, sweatshops today still exist on a large scale in the textile industry in the United States, even though the country has the highest GDP in the world (Ellis and Tran, 2016).

Proponents of sweatshop labour emphasise that MNCs employing contracting arrangements with suppliers in less developed countries only have limited responsibility for the problems associated with sweatshops, because these production sites belong to legally independent companies. MNCs when outsourcing their activities often draw on indirect sourcing via purchasing agents. These agents take over responsibility for handling the purchasing contracts and further subcontract the work, often to a number of different factories. As a result, the sourcing process becomes more and more opaque. Nevertheless, critics of sweatshop labour argue that it is the MNC's responsibility to know the conditions under which their products are being made and that they do have leverage to influence their value chains (Phillips and Caldwell, 2005). In this line of argument, firms like Adidas, Nike and H&M who benefit from international production networks should shoulder more responsibility for the externalities caused by these value chain activities. Moreover, MNCs have distinct duties regarding the workers of their contract factories because of the power and the substantial resources they have at their disposal. MNCs typically dictate the terms and conditions of their orders, such as price, quantity or date of delivery to their supplier network. Increasingly, standards related to health and safety and environmental protection become part of those terms. MNCs consequently have the ability to foster labour rights and fair working conditions in their supply chain (Arnold and Bowie, 2007). Even in cases where a firm is too small to use all of a supplier's capacity and only places orders representing a small percentage of the supplier's total turnover, it is partly responsible for the working conditions in a sweatshop. Although in such cases a single firm cannot directly exert influence over the supplier, a firm that is genuinely interested in respecting labour rights could and should collaborate with other buyers to develop and ensure acceptable standards.

22.5 Regulation and Improvement of Working Conditions in Global Supply Chains

After the critical review of the pros and the cons of sweatshop labour, we now briefly review opportunities at different levels and by different actors to regulate and improve working conditions in global supply chains. Different actors at various levels and through diverse institutional arrangements, ranging from voluntary approaches to hard law, are addressing the labour rights violations as discussed in this chapter. We draw a distinction between measures to regulate and improve working conditions at company level, industry level, multi-stakeholder level and governmental level. Nevertheless, it is important to keep in mind that individual actors alone cannot eliminate the structural injustice in global value chains. Although unjust or even missing regulation by national governments, along with policies of institutions such as the ILO, play a substantial role in determining the background conditions under which MNCs operate, we argue that companies also have obligations to do as much as possible to benefit the global poor and change the unjust conditions in global supply chains associated with their business operations.

22.5.1 Company Level

MNCs have good reasons to actively deal with low labour standards in their supply chains; ignoring such issues may put them at risk of a bad corporate reputation and thus of losing corporate legitimacy and their licence to operate. In the 1990s, Nike became the poster child of the anti-sweatshop movement when the working conditions at its overseas suppliers came to light (Zadek, 2004). As a response to these allegations, Nike, and shortly after many other sportswear brands as well as MNCs from other industries, drew up a code of conduct. A code of conduct can be defined as a set of standards, guidelines or rules for ethical behaviour, which firms impose on their suppliers as a prerequisite for entering into contract with them. The formulated standards and procedures of a code can come in a variety of forms. Codes of conduct can be formal or informal, contain a lot of detail or be rather broad in their application. In its code of conduct, Nike, for example, outlines the minimum standards it expects each supplier factory to meet. Suppliers of Nike are, among other things, expected to employ workers who are at least 16 years of age or past the national legal minimum working age and to pay their workers on a timely basis, as well as at least the minimum wage required by country law (Nike, 2021). Since the

1990s, codes of conduct have become a standard of operation for dealing with labour conditions in global supply chains (Locke, 2013). In order to check whether suppliers actually abide by a certain code, MNCs usually monitor and audit compliance. Such audits are either performed internally (also referred to as first party monitoring) – that is, by the firms themselves – or externally through second or third parties. Second-party monitoring means that an auditing company is commissioned and paid to oversee compliance with a company code. Third-party monitoring means that an independent party, usually an NGO that does not have any business relation with the firm, checks compliance with a certain code.

Supplier codes of conduct and the associated monitoring, auditing and reporting practices have received intense criticism. Kuruvilla, Liu, Li and Chen (2020), for example, note that the increasing use of codes of conduct over the past years has not been accompanied by substantive improvements in global supply chains. Although empirical studies in this respect are still rare, consensus exists that much of the variation in the extent to which supplier codes are actually associated with improvement of working conditions depends on how monitoring takes place – that is, the length of audits, whether audits are pre-announced or not, or whether workers versus managers are used as key information sources (Short et al., 2020). Bartley and Egels-Zandén (2015) further highlight that the effect of codes of conduct vary for different types of labour rights issues: while they identified improvements at factory level with regard to eliminating child labour, other 'enabling rights' such as freedom of association or collective bargaining remained continuously undermined.

While monitoring practices can be improved – for example, through unannounced random visits and sophisticated information-gathering techniques (i.e., by interviewing workers outside of the factory or by gathering information from organisations that workers trust) – in practice, MNCs alone will never be able to completely monitor their global supply chains. Only a more collaborative approach to the governance of global production, including MNCs and their suppliers but also other stakeholders such as NGOs, national governments, trade unions and local communities, can provide realistic insights into local working conditions and improve them. In order to foster cooperation, MNCs can provide incentives to suppliers for improved performance in upholding fundamental labour rights.

The apparel and sports company Puma, for example, offers long-term partnerships to suppliers that perform well on economic, environmental and social criteria (Baumann-Pauly et al., 2016). The rationale behind this long-term strategy is to educate and convince both suppliers and internal stakeholders of the firm, such as the managers of the sourcing department, that sustainability in general and social standards in particular can be improved through true partnerships. Suppliers seem to make improvements to environmental and social aspects of their business voluntarily, because they start to realise that this not only has a positive impact on their workers, but also pays off economically, as they are rewarded from brands with longer-term sourcing commitments (Baumann-Pauly et al., 2016). In order to support such long-term partnerships, MNCs need to invest in capacity development at local level and should not expect the supplier to shoulder all of the costs of compliance with existing codes of conduct.

Another prerequisite for improving social standards at suppliers is that MNCs critically review their own purchasing practices and increase transparency along their supply chains. Purchasing practices relate to all contractual and informal arrangements that global retailers and brands use to do business and interact with their suppliers. Purchasing practices are considered to have fundamental effects on suppliers' ability to comply with company codes of conduct. For example, if MNCs have bad planning and forecasting systems in place and change orders at the last minute, suppliers may need to force workers to work overtime in order to deliver according to their contract. Hence, only if MNCs accept the positive duty to the global poor, review their own practices and pay higher purchasing prices to their suppliers, can suppliers afford to pay higher wages and ensure that fundamental workers' rights are upheld.

Finally, as part of their responsibilities under the UN Guiding Principles on Business and Human Rights (UNGPs), MNCs are also required to undertake human rights due diligence (see Chapter 21). This means that companies have to identify, prevent, mitigate and account for how they address adverse human rights impacts associated with their business operations. Practically, this includes four key steps: assessing actual and potential human rights impacts; integrating and acting on the findings; tracking performance; and communicating about how impacts are addressed. If companies find that fundamental human rights have been violated in their supply chains, they need to provide access to remedy. For example, if an MNC finds that a supplier has made workers redundant due to their engagement in a union, which is an infringement of the right to freedom of association, it needs to ensure, for example, that these workers are reinstated and work with the respective supplier to prevent similar adverse practices in the future.

22.5.2 Industry Level

Besides the efforts by individual companies, issues of labour rights and supply chain transparency are also being addressed at industry level. In this case, MNCs cooperate with other firms in their respective industry in order to commit themselves to industry-specific standards and articulate guidelines for appropriate conduct. Examples include the Responsible Business Alliance (RBA, formerly known as the Electronics Industry Citizenship Coalition), which aims at creating industry-wide standards regarding social, environmental and ethical issues in electronics, retail and automotive industry supply chains, or the International Council of Toy Industries (ICTI), which is the industry association for the worldwide toy industry. In 2004, ICTI founded the Ethical Toy Program committed to improving social standards at toy factories around the world. The benefit of industry codes and standards is that they take the pressure from suppliers to comply with different, and sometimes conflicting, codes of conduct and reduce the burden of multiple inspections. However, industry initiatives are often criticised for not including other stakeholders, particularly trade unions, at governance level, since the governing bodies or executive organs of industry initiatives are usually entirely comprised of business representatives. In contrast to industry initiatives, multi-stakeholder initiatives (MSIs), which will be outlined in the next section, aim at a more substantive engagement of different stakeholders from different spheres of society (de Bakker et al., 2019).

22.5.3 Multi-Stakeholder Level

Over the last two decades, there has been an increase in MSIs. The majority of MSIs generate voluntary CSR standards that are intended to provide MNCs and their respective stakeholders with ways to systematically assess, measure and communicate their social and environmental performance (Gilbert et al., 2011). Many MSIs directly or indirectly address working conditions in global supply chains and aim to contribute to improving labour rights at the global level. The difference between MSIs and the above-mentioned industry-led initiatives mainly lies in the groups of stakeholders involved in the process of fostering accountability (de Bakker et al., 2019). MSIs typically include not only MNCs and associations directly linked to the respective industry, but also many other stakeholders, such as NGOs, unions, government actors, investors and sometimes even consumers. Examples of such MSIs are the UN Global Compact, SA 8000, the Global Reporting Initiative and ISO 26000 (see also Chapter 20).

The proliferation of MSIs can mainly be attributed to the lack of a unified system of transnational regulation for social and environmental issues. MSIs generally aim at filling the omnipresent governance voids related to the manifold activities of MNCs by issuing standards, which define voluntary rules of appropriate conduct. This is why such standards are also often referred to as soft law, since they are not legally binding (Abbott and Snidal, 2000). The standards produced by MSIs are usually considered as having more legitimacy than those of industry initiatives, since MSIs bring together a more diverse set of stakeholders. Research has, however, also indicated that MSIs have limits when it comes to improving working conditions. Barrientos and Smith (2007), for example, in an analysis of the impact of the Ethical Trading Initiative (ETI) on workers' rights, found that while slight improvements could be registered in terms of outcome standards (i.e., tangible issues such as minimum wage and working hours or health and safety standards), no improvements became evident in terms of process rights (i.e., freedom of association and protection against discrimination). Other studies observe that many MSIs have only little or no positive outcome, indicating policy-practice decoupling (Vigneau et al., 2015). Decoupling is the creation and maintenance of gaps between formal policies and actual organisational practices, assuming that adopters do not really implement the standards produced by MSIs despite formally embracing them. Against the backdrop of this criticism of MSIs, we argue that we need both more research on how to design such initiatives and a sincere commitment by MNCs and other stakeholders to avoid decoupling when addressing the manifold challenges of sweatshop labour in global value chains.

22.5.4   Governmental Level

Both proponents and opponents of sweatshop labour emphasise the importance of governmental regulation when reforming working conditions and addressing labour rights. Legal institutions within countries facing labour rights issues are often either weak or absent, or in the worst case exploitative. A primary solution to the problem of sweatshop labour hence lies in a stronger (or at least different) regulation by states and a more successful implementation of labour laws.

Structural injustice in supply chains requires structural solutions and responses at governmental level that can come in three main forms. First, developing country governments can pass laws and regulations regarding, for example, health and safety standards or minimum wages, or improve the enactment of existing laws. Bangladesh, for example, has very elaborate building regulations on the book, but these laws were often disregarded in the past, thus providing the backdrop for the fatal Rana Plaza collapse. Second, wealthier countries can adopt laws relating to wages and working standards in order to regulate the import of products made in factories abroad, or can pass laws to hold 'national' MNCs accountable for human rights violations occurring at their subsidiaries and suppliers abroad. In France, Germany, the United Kingdom and a number of other countries, public debates are ongoing around whether a corporate responsibility to respect human rights should and can be turned into a legal liability through extraterritorial regulation in the future. Finally, at intergovernmental level, a number of organisations such as the European Union, the United Nations and the ILO, whose members are national governments, engage in efforts to regulate labour rights in the global economy. Yet, in the absence of coercive institutions at international level, intergovernmental organisations also rely on voluntary compliance by states.

In this chapter, we cannot discuss the manifold governmental regulations in detail. However, Table 22.2 provides an overview of various laws or legislative initiatives in different countries and the European Union. In light of the ongoing discussion of the Sustainable Development Goals as well as the COVID-19 pandemic, it can be stated that the call for more regulation of global supply chains has gained momentum in recent years. The chances are high that more countries will follow the examples listed in the table and start a discussion on whether and how supply chains should be regulated. The European Union is also currently exploring what meaningful EU legislation on mandatory due diligence and corporate accountability should look like and has invited key stakeholders for consultation.

Table 22.2 Supply chain regulation in selected countries/regions

	UK	Germany		France	USA		EU	
Name	Modern Slavery Act	Supply Chain Law	CSR Directive Implementation Act	Corporate Duty of Vigilance Law	Dodd-Frank Act, Section 1502	Transparency in Supply Chains Act (California)	Conflict Minerals Regulation	Non-financial Reporting Directive
Year	Endorsed 2015 / in force since 2015	Draft in 2021 / entry into force planned for 2023	Endorsed 2017 / in force since 2017	Endorsed 2017 / in force since 2017	Endorsed 2010 / in force since 2012	Endorsed 2010 / in force since 2012	Endorsed 2017 / in force since 2021	Endorsed 2014 / in force since 2017
Target group	Companies doing business in the UK with • global turnover of £36 million by themselves or through subsidiaries	German companies with • more than 3,000 employees (as of the year 2023) • more than 1,000 employees (as of the year 2024)	Capital market-oriented companies, credit institutes and insurance companies operating in Germany with • more than 500 employees • balance sheet total of more than €20 million or turnover of more than €40 million	French companies with • more than 5,000 employees through their French direct or indirect subsidiaries • or more than 10,000 employees worldwide	Companies listed on US exchange • must verify whether tin, tungsten, tantalum or gold are used in the supply chain (also in products from contractual partners)	Companies doing business in California (e.g., generate significant sales or own assets there), even if they do not have a presence there with • more than US$100 million in gross annual sales worldwide • primary business in retail or manufacturing	Companies worldwide that • declare, or have another company declare, a certain amount of conflict materials for import into the European Union	Public-interest entities with • more than 500 employee
Content	Topic: • Slavery, serfdom, forced and compulsory labour and human trafficking Scope: • Own operations, business relationships and entire supply chain	Topic: • Human rights, environmental matters Scope: • Own operations and direct business relationships • Occasion-related for indirect suppliers	Topic: • Environmental, social and employee matters, respect for human rights, anti-corruption and bribery matters Scope: • Own operations, business relationships and relevant supply chains	Topic: • Human rights and fundamental freedoms, human health and safety, environment Scope: • Own operations, business relationships and supply chain (subcontractors and suppliers with established business relationship)	Topic: • Financing of violent conflicts in the Democratic Republic of Congo or its neighbours through tin, tungsten, tantalum and gold (conflict minerals) Scope: • Entire supply chain	Topic: • Slavery and human trafficking Scope: • Direct supply chain	Topic: • Financing of violent conflicts through tin, tungsten, tantalum and gold (conflict minerals) worldwide Scope: • Entire supply chain	Topic: • Environmental, social and employee matters, respect for human rights, anti-corruption and bribery matters Scope: • Own operations, business relationships and relevant supply chains

Table 22.2 (cont.)

	UK	Germany		France	USA		EU	
Name	Modern Slavery Act	Supply Chain Law	CSR Directive Implementation Act	Corporate Duty of Vigilance Law	Dodd-Frank Act, Section 1502	Transparency in Supply Chains Act (California)	Conflict Minerals Regulation	Non-financial Reporting Directive
Obligations	Public annual disclosure • on the measures taken to ensure that slavery and human trafficking are not taking place (report may include: organisational structure, business activities and supply chains, corporate policies, due diligence processes, business units and supply chains with risks and related measures, effectiveness of measures, training)	Due diligence • for own operations and direct business relationships: risk analysis, grievance mechanism, statement on respecting human rights and preventative measures • in event of violation: in own operations remedial action to end violation and preventive measures, in direct business relationships plan for minimisation and prevention • for indirect suppliers (only in case of concrete indication): risk analysis, implement concept for minimisation and avoidance, preventive measures	Annual disclosure • on environmental, social and employee matters, respect for human rights, anti-corruption and bribery matters • related to each topic on business model, pursued policies, results of policies, the main risks (based on materiality analysis) and the non-financial key performance indicators • in addition, description of the diversity policy applied in relation to the undertaking's administrative, management and supervisory bodies	Establishment and implementation of vigilance plan • in cooperation with stakeholders • with regard to mapping of risks, risk assessment, mitigation and prevention actions, alert and monitoring mechanism Annual disclosure • of vigilance plan and implementation report	Due diligence and annual disclosure • if minerals are coming from recycled material or not from the Democratic Republic of Congo or neighbouring countries: only report origin of the conflict materials (including the process of country of origin determination) • in case of suspicion: use a recognised framework to examine in depth and report whether minerals originate from violent groups	Public annual disclosure (on corporate website) • on supply chain verification, supplier audits, certifications, whether and how the workforce and contractors are held accountable when they do not comply with company requirements, trainings (or indicate that the company does not apply measures to each of the aspects)	Due diligence requirements • according to the OECD Due Diligence Guidance for Responsible Chains of Minerals from Conflict-Affected and High-Risk Areas • including management system, risk mapping and assessment, designing and implementing strategy to respond, third-party audits Annual disclosure • of the countries where the minerals come from, the quantities imported, and the minerals imported	Annual disclosure • on environmental, social and employee matters, respect for human rights, anti-corruption and bribery matters • related to each topic on business model, pursued policies, results of policies, the main risks (based on materiality analysis) and the non-financial key performance indicators • in addition, description of the diversity policy applied in relation to the undertaking's administrative, management and supervisory bodies

Enforcement mechanism	Annual disclosure • on the fulfilment of due diligence obligations	Secretary of State may apply to a High Court for an order requiring the company to make the declaration (will be enforced with an administrative fine) • Reputational interest	Review of company reports and investigation of complaints by the Federal Office of Economics and Export Control • Fines in case of violation of the law, companies can be excluded from public procurement for up to three years in the event of serious violations • Reputational interest • Those affected by human rights violations can continue to assert their rights in German courts and can now also file complaints with the Federal Office of Economics and Export Control	Review of the report by the Supervisory Board, which in practice usually commissions external auditors to do so • In the event of non-compliance or misrepresentation, a fine of up to €10 million or 5 per cent of annual sales can be issued • In case of incorrect or exaggeratedly positive representations, competitors and consumer associations can enforce claims for injunctive relief under competition law against the company • Reputational interest	Civil liability for payment of damages • Any organisation or person with legitimate interest may seek a court order to fulfil monitoring obligations (for purpose of enforcing the order, the court may threaten and impose a continuously recurring administrative fine) • Reputational interest	Fines to be imposed by the Securities and Exchange Commission (SEC) • Shareholder lawsuits for damages following misstatements • Maryland and California: Exclusion from the allocation of public orders • Reputational interest	Attorney General receives list of all reporting entities from tax authority each year • It can request that companies be ordered to publish a report, enforceable with a penalty payment • Reputational interest	Authorities review documents and audit reports and conduct on-site inspections • Effective enforcement ensured by each Member State through sanctions (depending on EU-state implementation) • Collaboration of authorities and sharing of information • Reputational interest	Must be transposed into national law (see the example of CSR Directive Implementation Act in Germany)

Table 22.2 (cont.)

	UK	Germany		France	USA		EU	
Name	Modern Slavery Act	Supply Chain Law	CSR Directive Implementation Act	Corporate Duty of Vigilance Law	Dodd-Frank Act, Section 1502	Transparency in Supply Chains Act (California)	Conflict Minerals Regulation	Non-financial Reporting Directive
Critical issues	• No specific minimum information in the report required (and no specifications for structure, content, design of report) • No mandatory minimum requirements for diligence; permits the statement that no measures have been taken • Legislators essentially rely on civil society organisations to critically review company reports and publicly denounce shortcomings	• Due diligence to the full extent relates only to own business activities and direct business relationships • For indirect suppliers, companies only have to take action when a possible violation is pointed out or damage has already been done • No civil liability for foreseeable and avoidable damage • Environmental standards only marginally taken into account	• Narrow scope of addressees • Companies are required to report sustainability risks only if they are material to the company (sustainability impact and economic relevance); reports therefore often remain vague and incomplete • No provision for comparability of reports (e.g. no concrete specifications for structuring or performance indicators) • Application of due diligence is not made mandatory; companies are free to report that they do not pursue any concepts	• Narrow scope of addressees • Leaves many questions up to the practitioners of the law and the courts to resolve • The injured person must prove that the damage could have been avoided if the company had exercised due diligence, which poses an enormous challenge for plaintiffs	• Companies rather tend to withdraw from the conflict region than to seek conflict-free local economic partners • Conflicts in the area are complex and addressing them depends on the integration and support of additional regulatory and political initiatives	• No mandatory minimum requirements for due diligence	• 'Downstream companies' that import metals (not the minerals upstream of them) are exempted from parts of the due diligence obligation (initially to be fulfilled voluntarily) • Certain similarly conflicted materials are not covered, notably lithium, cobalt and jade • Conflicts in the area are complex and addressing them depends on the integration and support of additional regulatory and political initiatives	• Application of due diligence is not made mandatory, companies are free to report that they do not pursue any concepts • Voluntary due diligence approach is insufficient: According to civil society organisations, companies fail to report properly on their human rights risks, impacts and due diligence, while national authorities are not fulfilling their supervisory and enforcement role adequately

Sources: European Parliament and European Council (2014); Bundesregierung (2017); econsense and twentyfifty (2019); Grabosch (2019); EPRS (2020); Bundesministerium für Arbeit und Soziales (2021); Bundesministerium für wirtschaftliche Zusammenarbeit und Entwicklung (2021); Germanwatch (2021); Initiative Lieferkettengesetz (2021).

Regulation at governmental level becomes particularly important when MNCs are unwilling to address labour rights issues and improve the working conditions on a voluntary basis. This appears necessary, because the voluntary implementation of human rights issues in global supply chains is only proceeding slowly. According to a recent study, almost half (46.2 per cent) of the largest companies in the world, surveyed by the Corporate Human Rights Benchmark, did not show any evidence of identifying or mitigating human rights issues in their global supply chains (Business and Human Rights Resource Centre, 2020). In this case, laws may help to improve safe and healthy working conditions and minimum wages for workers in supply chains. However, even if the regulation of labour rights at governmental level would be ideal, governments are usually moving slow or find themselves exposed to conflicting interests. For example, developing country governments often refrain from stricter regulations fearing that they might hamper international investments. High levels of corruption in many of the export-oriented developing countries also prevent the effective implementation of regulatory approaches. In India, for example, labour regulation has been used by government officials to extort businesses instead of protecting workers' rights. Even if developing countries are willing to improve the situation for workers, they are often unable to finance substantive changes due to budgetary constraints. The drawbacks of regulation at governmental level again highlight the importance of soft law approaches and voluntary agreements by MNCs to improving labour rights.

Over the last few years, various actors have argued that, in order to foster business respect for human rights and sustainably improve standards in global supply chains, a so-called 'smart mix' of measures at all of the aforementioned levels – national and international, mandatory and voluntary – will be needed (Shift, 2019). Supplementing traditional forms of business regulation via legislation with incentives and industry as well as multi-stakeholder governance approaches, while at the same time enhancing the role of financial actors in encouraging more sustainable business practices, in our view holds the greatest potential for lasting improvements of labour rights in global supply chains.

22.6   Chapter Summary

Globalisation has primarily manifested itself in the growth and spread of global supply chains. The increased outsourcing of value chain activities of MNCs to developing countries has raised concerns about the working conditions of millions of workers within global supply chains. The ILO core labour standards form an internationally accepted baseline when it comes to protecting workers' rights. Nonetheless, labour rights are frequently violated, for example, in the food, consumer electronics or apparel supply chain. Violations pertain to inadequate pay and long working hours, forced and child labour, health and safety breaches or infringements of the freedom of association, among others. Throughout different disciplines, a fierce debate has emerged whether and to what extent work in so-called sweatshops is exploitative. Arguments in favour of sweatshops have mainly been voiced by neo-classical economists, proposing that sweatshops are mutually beneficial arrangements between workers and a factory and that denying workers the option of working in a sweatshop would disregard their autonomous choice. Arguments against sweatshops largely stem from business ethicists and philosophers who, often based on Kantian ethics, argue that sweatshops fail to respect the dignity of workers and that MNCs have a moral duty to ensure adequate working standards. Attempts to improve working conditions in global supply chains can be found at different levels and involving different actors. In this chapter, we have drawn a distinction between efforts at company, industry, multi-stakeholder and governmental level and argued that a smart mix of these measures is needed to uphold labour rights in global supply chains.

CHAPTER QUESTIONS

1. Are MNCs benefitting the poor when outsourcing value chain activities to sweatshops in developing countries?
2. Can the choice of women working in Indian spinning mills be considered a free one?
3. If it were possible, would you recommend shutting down all sweatshops at once?
4. Should MNCs be held liable in their home countries for the working conditions at their local contractors in developing countries? If so, how?
5. Can labour rights be effectively addressed through self-regulation?
6. Does the setting of social and environmental standards of MNCs for suppliers represent a form of cultural colonialisation?

Case Study: *Labour Rights in the Garment Industry – the Rana Factory Collapse*
Available from Cambridge University Press at www.cambridge.org/rasche2

FURTHER RESOURCES

- Better Buying website, https://betterbuying.org/.

  Better Buying is an initiative that works with suppliers in global supply chains to rate purchasing practices of brands and retailers. The website provides an overview of current rating results and outlines how key purchasing practices impacts working conditions.

- Ponte, S. (2019). *Business, Power and Sustainability in a World of Global Value Chains.* London: ZED.

  An introductory textbook on global value chains that provides a good overview of the current literature. It also discusses power relations in global value chains and a number of case studies.

- The Clean Clothes Campaign (CCC) website, www.cleanclothes.org/.

  This website provides lots of information on the mission, the network and the campaigns of the CCC. The CCC is an alliance of organisations, including trade unions and NGOs. The aim of the CCC is to improve the working conditions of workers in the global garment and sportswear industries.

- The International Labor Organization (ILO) website, www.ilo.org/global/lang-en/index.htm.

  This website provides lots of additional information on topics covered in this chapter, ranging from labour standards and sweatshops to reflections on measures to promote rights at work, encourage decent employment opportunities, enhance social protection and strengthen dialogue on work-related issues.

- The International Labor Rights Forum (ILRF) website, www.laborrights.org.

  This website provides lots of information on the human rights organisation ILRF, bringing strategic capacity to cross-sectoral work on global value chains and labour migration corridors. The ILRF holds global corporations accountable for labour rights violations in their supply chains; advances policies and laws that protect decent work and just migration; and strengthens freedom of association, new forms of bargaining and worker organisations.

23 Business, Climate Change and the Anthropocene

ANDREW HOFFMAN AND SUKANYA ROY

LEARNING OBJECTIVES

- Consider business and the market as both a cause of and solution to the climate crisis.

- Learn about the Enterprise Integration and Market Transformation phases of businesses' adjusting to climate change.

- Situate the challenge of climate change within the broader shift of the Anthropocene.

- Discuss the underlying economic, cultural and societal shifts associated with the Anthropocene.

- Reflect on careers in management as a calling or vocation to rethink the vast power that business has to solve our climate challenges and the role of the executive in managing these.

23.1   Introduction

Since the nineteenth century, with the advent of what has been called the 'industrial era', human activity has been influencing the global climate through the emission of greenhouse gases, most notably carbon dioxide (CO_2), but also methane (CH4), nitrous oxide (N_2O), hydrofluorocarbons (HFCs), perfluorocarbons (PFCs) and sulphur hexafluoride (SF_6). These gases act like a greenhouse, trapping heat in the atmosphere and raising global temperatures, which in turn alters weather patterns. In 2008, scientists set a boundary limit for global average atmospheric CO_2 at 350 ppm to maintain a stable environment. By 2015, concentrations had reached 400 ppm and are still climbing. These elevated concentrations are increasing the frequency and intensity of wildfires, droughts, hurricanes, temperature fluctuations, sea-level rise and more at an alarming rate. Costs to the global economy could amount to a decrease of between 11 and 14 per cent of global economic output by 2050, amounting to as much as US$23 trillion (Swiss Re, 2021).

This chapter will assess climate change as a concern for business, both as a stand-alone issue and as part of the broader shift that scientists are calling the Anthropocene to denote that we have entered a new geological epoch – the 'age of humans' – in which human activity is an animating force within global ecosystems. It will begin by examining the extent to which the market – comprised of corporations, the government and non-governmental organisations, as well as the many stakeholders in market transactions, such as the consumers, suppliers, buyers, insurance companies, banks, etc. – is the cause of the climate crisis, but also discussing the extent to which the market must be the solution. While government policies can spur the market and individual choices can feed it, business, with its extraordinary powers of ideation, production and distribution, is best positioned to bring about change we need at the scale we need it. The chapter will then present two models for examining the role that business can play in addressing the climate crisis. The first is Enterprise Integration, which works by fitting climate concerns within existing business objectives and parameters. The second is Market Transformation, which is based on the premise that systemic change is necessary to address the systems challenge of climate change. Addressing the existential threats of climate change and the Anthropocene will require transformation in several key foundations of the market system and, indeed, our overall culture. The chapter concludes with a call for business students and business leaders to think of their career as a vocation or a calling, one that recognises the vast power that business has to either solve our climate challenges or bring us to ruin.

23.2   Is Business the Cause of, or Solution to, Climate Change and Other Anthropocene Issues?

Before we examine the relationship between business and climate change, we start with a simple question: Do you think business is the cause of, or the solution to, climate problems? How you answer this question places you in one of two camps within the environmental movement. On one side are the 'dark greens', those who see the market as the problem and business as the enemy (Steffen, 2009). On the other side are 'bright greens,' those who see the market as the solution and business as an ally. Dark greens tend to distrust and often confront the corporate sector, while bright greens work within the market system, often in close collaboration with corporations.

Of course, this dichotomy is too stark to recognise more nuanced positions, but where do you stand? The truth is that the two sides are mutually dependent and need each other to accomplish their goals. Scholars of social movements argue that more extreme groups within a movement actually help moderate, consensus-building groups through what is called a 'radical flank effect' (Haines, 1984). When radicals pull the political spectrum further in one direction, they shift the centre of the debate and make previously radical groups seem moderate. For example, Martin Luther King Jr. was at first seen as too radical for many white Americans. But when the more militant Malcolm X became a public figure, he pulled the political flank to a more extreme position and made King's message more 'moderate'. Moderates help move change through incremental gains, while radicals can set the agenda and become the standard bearers for a movement's transformative goals. Radicals focus on deeper, core issues; moderates find ways to gain widespread appeal and spur pragmatic action. The environmental movement needs both.

Yet, dark greens tend to criticise bright greens as having been co-opted by companies to help greenwash environmentally damaging activities. Bright greens tend to dismiss dark greens as out-of-touch radicals who only complicate the environmental agenda with utopian demands. Business needs dark greens to continually warn against compromise and push the frontier of possible solutions to environmental issues like climate change, ecosystem destruction, water scarcity and, most importantly, the flaws in our social and economic systems that have created and amplified these crises. Bright greens can build on that energy to drive change within institutions and organisations.

Taken together, bright greens and dark greens can help shift markets to solve our greatest challenges. Indeed, they must. The market is the most powerful organising force on Earth and business is the most powerful entity within it. Business possesses the resources to develop the buildings we live and work in, the forms of mobility we employ, the clothes we wear and the food we eat. If the market is not developing the solutions we need at the scale we need them, they will not be found.

In the chapter that follows, we consider the business approach to climate change in two phases as shown in Figure 23.1 (Hoffman, 2019a). The first phase, Enterprise Integration, is founded on a model of business increasing competitive positioning in a market shift by integrating climate change into pre-existing business considerations. By contrast, the second phase, Market Transformation, is founded on a model of business transforming the market. Instead of waiting for a market shift to create incentives for climate action, companies are creating these shifts to enable new forms of business practice. Enterprise Integration is geared towards present-day measures of success; Market Transformation will help companies create tomorrow's measures. The first is focused on 'reducing unsustainability'; the second is focused on 'creating sustainability'. The first attends to symptoms; the second attends to causes. The first focuses primarily inward towards the health and vitality of organisations; the second looks outward towards the health and vitality of the market and society in which they operate. The first will help future leaders get a job in today's marketplace; the second will help them develop a lifelong career. The first is incremental, the second transformational.

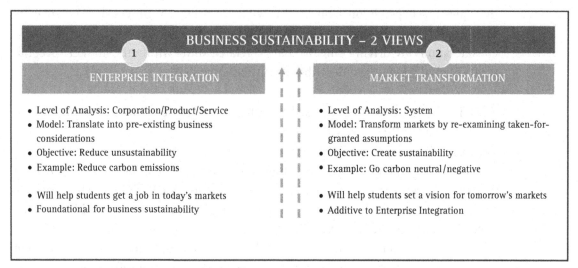

Figure 23.1 The Enterprise Integration view of business sustainability compared with the Market Transformation view. *Source:* Hoffman (2019a).

23.3   Enterprise Integration

Climate change represents a market shift in the form of both systemic risks that span the entire economy and local risks that impact specific sectors, industries and companies. In this framing, business leaders can remain agnostic about the science of climate change, but still recognise its importance as a business issue. Its full scope is a response to key business constituents that are bringing climate concerns to the corporate agenda (Hoffman, 2018).

In some sectors, these market shifts will involve incremental changes like shifting from incandescent lightbulbs to LED lightbulbs. In others, they can be transformational. Just as the computer industry eliminated the typewriter in the early 1980s and the compact disc replaced the phonograph album in the mid-1980s, climate change is poised to create similar upheavals. By 2100, economic damage in the form of declining crop yields, food shortages, premature deaths, damage to homes and critical infrastructure, shortages of clean water, air pollution, flooding, fires and more could reach between US$54 trillion under a warming scenario of 1.5°C and US$69 trillion under a warming scenario of 2°C (Lafakis et al., 2019). Sectors such as fossil fuels, automobiles, energy grids, construction, tourism and many more will feel the brunt of these costs more deeply than others, with many corporations, technologies and markets being eliminated and replaced by others.

In order for corporate leaders to make sense of climate change and direct resources to solving it, this kind of market framing is necessary. As such, this renders the often-asked question, 'does it pay to be green?' irrelevant. In the face of market shifts, companies must innovate to adapt and, at times, to survive. Asking if it 'pays to be green' is the same as asking if it 'pays to innovate': the answer to that question depends on who does it, when and how. Business decision-makers must explore two dimensions of climate-driven market shifts. First, what business considerations are driving climate change-related shifts within the market? Second, what internal frames best describe the business imperative to respond?

23.3.1 What Business Considerations Are Driving Market Responses to Climate Change?

The exact forms of the market shifts around climate change are quite varied, and pressures can emerge from any number of market constituents. As shown in Figure 23.2, these pressures can fall into four categories (Hoffman, 2018). *Coercive drivers* – in the form of domestic and international regulations enforced by courts – compel companies to address climate change as a matter of legal compliance. Regulations alter markets through a variety of methods, whether a direct carbon price or more indirect forms like renewable portfolio standards, efficiency standards for buildings, cars or appliances, net metering or feed-in tariffs.

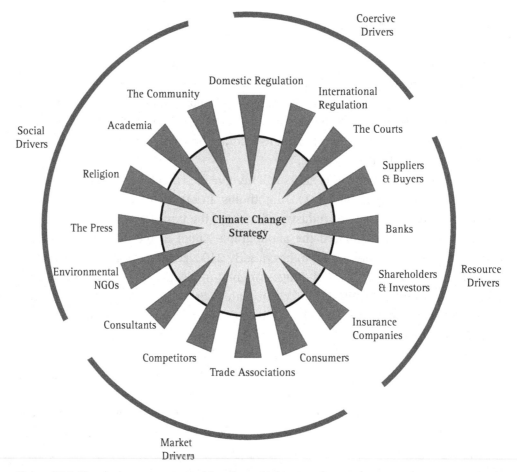

Figure 23.2 Climate change strategy is driven by multiple external pressures.
Source: Hoffman (2018).

Beyond coercive pressures, responses to climate change are also being driven by *resource, market and social drivers*. The first – emerging from suppliers, buyers, shareholders, investors, banks and insurance companies – alter companies' access to raw materials and financial capital. For example, Walmart has driven climate change concerns across the value chain to compel suppliers to reduce emissions related to their product offerings. Similarly, climate change has compelled many companies to re-evaluate the security of their supply chains in the face of destabilising events (such as the Fukushima Daiichi nuclear disaster, which disrupted the flow of materials from many suppliers in Japan). The impact investing movement and sustainable finance sectors have integrated sustainability concerns into financial decision-making such that, by 2020, ESG (environmental, social and governance) investing accounted for US$35.5 trillion, or 36 per cent of global assets under management in 2020, with climate change standing out as the number one concern among investors (followed by plastic reduction, community development, circular economy and the Sustainable Development Goals (GSIA, 2021).

Market drivers – emerging from consumers, trade associations, competitors and consultants – alter competitive dynamics as companies vie for a shifting consumer base. For example, the LOHAS consumer segment (Lifestyles of Health and Sustainability) was estimated in 2016 to be a US$355 billion market in the United States and a US$546 billion market worldwide, and continues to grow (Szakály et al., 2017). *Social drivers* – including environmental non-profit organisations, the press, religious institutions and academia – reflect the extent to which markets will continue to change. For example, the growth of climate change concerns within educational (see the 350.org divestment movement and campus commissions on carbon neutrality) and religious institutions (see Pope Francis's *Encyclical on Climate Change and Inequality* and statements by leaders of other religious denominations) direct attention to the development of societal norms and values. As this list illustrates, businesses are part of a complex web of inter-relationships within which demands for action on climate change are increasingly pervasive.

23.3.2   What Frame Best Describes the Business Imperative to Respond?

Discrete pressures on firms translate climate change into fundamental business concepts. As insurance companies apply climate pressure, climate change becomes a risk management issue for firms. Pressure from competitors becomes an issue of strategic direction. From investors and banks, it becomes an issue of capital acquisition; from suppliers and buyers, an issue of supply chain logistics; and from consumers, an issue of market demand. In effect, climate change becomes a core issue for firms as it is brought to managerial attention through pre-existing avenues related to marketing, accounting, finance, operations, etc. In each case, firms can draw on pre-existing models and language to formulate a response. By realising this 'fit', firms can begin to see climate change as a strategic issue no longer directed by external social considerations, but rather by internal strategic interests as shown in Figure 23.3 (Hoffman, 2018).

The challenge for business leaders is to find the most effective frame to communicate the business imperative for addressing climate change. However, not all frames are applicable in each corporate organisation. The drivers in Figure 23.2 and the frames in Figure 23.3 vary in their importance and influence based on the specific company and issue. For a consumer goods company like Procter & Gamble, consumer demand will be the value frame that will create the most engaged response. For global retailers like Walmart that manage a large supply chain network, operational efficiency (particularly in transportation) will hold the most relevance. Executives at the appliance company Whirlpool admit that they do not use the words climate change to compel action among their employees. Instead, they use energy efficiency, which has been a core concern for the company for decades. This kind of framing puts climate change into a language that the company already recognises as important.

One consideration and frame that is radically altering markets is risk management as driven by the insurance sector. Data from Swiss Re shows a steady increase

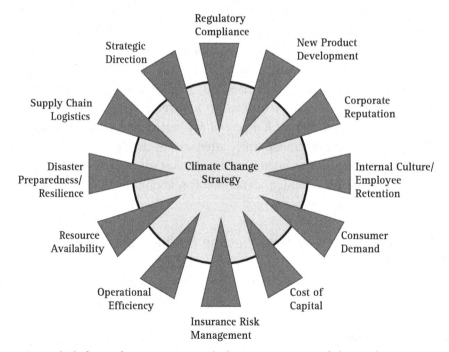

Figure 23.3 Multiple frames for communicating the business imperative of climate change.
Source: Hoffman (2018).

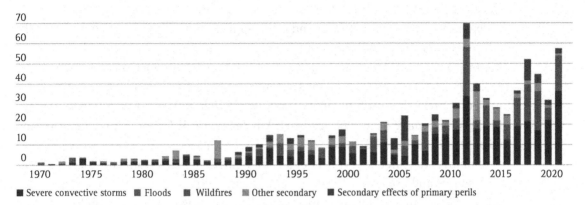

Figure 23.4 Global insured losses from secondary perils since 1970, in US$ billion (2020 prices).
Source: Swiss Re Institute (2018).

in the frequency of natural disasters over the past three decades (see Figure 23.4), which have a corresponding increase in the costs of those disasters. In 2019, Munich Re became the first major insurer to explicitly link California's wildfires to climate change, issuing a white paper that warned: 'Climate trends also show an increase in wildfire hazard, which is arguably higher now than it ever was in the 20th century. This illustrates that the overall risk and loss levels are significantly different than in the past. And as the state's climate continues to change, California will experience a further worsening of these conditions in the medium term' (Faust and Steuer, 2019).

These projections have undeniable financial consequences for the insurance industry, which paid out a record US$135 billion for natural catastrophes in 2017, almost three times higher than its prior annual average of US$49 billion (Howard, 2018). This is not to mention the uninsured losses that typically make up half of the economic impact of natural disasters, a staggering tab picked up by individual citizens and taxpayers. But recognition of these disasters' economic impact is changing the sector as more insurance underwriters begin to both recognise the magnitude and threat of climate risk and change their risk modelling, underwriting practices and policy pricing. Some are even throwing away older actuarial data and hiring climate scientists to develop risk models for what is being called the 'new normal'. The ability to drive a car, buy a house, build an office building, run a manufacturing plant and enter into contracts are all supported by insurance. As the insurance sector continues to factor the growing risks of climate change into coverage and premiums, it will transform the economy.

Insurance is just one of many drivers that are creating market shifts, and the results can be seen in multiple sectors. For example, the automotive sector is being transformed such that the future is both electric and eventually autonomous (with exceptions in certain rural, farm and other applications). Electric car company Tesla enjoyed a market capitalisation of US$640 billion in 2020, ten times that of General Motors, a company that announced in 2021 that its product portfolio would be entirely electric by 2035. Numerous automakers have made similar statements. Even Bill Ford, great-grandson of Henry Ford, warns that 'cars can't continue to operate the way they have been, because we'll kill the world if China just cuts and pastes what we do' (Safian, 2018).

Similarly, the energy sector is being fundamentally transformed in the way we both source and use power. In 2020, renewable energy leaders NextEra Energy, Enel and Iberdrola enjoyed steady market capitalisation growth to rival fossil fuel leaders ExxonMobil, Shell and BP (see Figure 23.5). The US Department of Energy predicts that the future grid will use significantly more clean energy, but also anticipates vastly more consumer control that will allow two-way flows of energy and information (including distributed generation, demand-side management, electrification of transportation and energy efficiency) and holistically designed solutions (including regional diversity, AC-DC transmission and distribution solutions, microgrids, energy storage and centralised-decentralised control) (US DOE, 2020). The days of large baseload power plants and a centralised grid are coming to an end.

Within the food sector, the world's soon-to-be 10 billion people will eat less meat and begin to think about alternative forms of protein, whether vegetarian or vegan diets, plant- or insect-based protein substitutes. The plant-based meat market is expanding with major food producers like Tyson, Cargill, Perdue and JBS joining new entrants like Upside Foods, Impossible Foods and Beyond Meat. The latter had the most successful initial public offering (IPO) of 2019 (Shanker et al., 2019). These products are now selling through fast food outlets and major supermarket chains. Consulting firm A. T. Kearney predicted that, by 2040, as much as 60% of the meat we eat will be either lab-grown or plant-based products that look and taste like meat (Carrington, 2019).

All of the examples just listed represent impressive market shifts that are, at least partially, in response to concerns for climate change. But, while important for reducing the emission of greenhouse gases, they do not solve the problem. Framing climate change simply as a continuing shift in ordinary strategic concerns to meet existing stakeholder demands avoids grasping the full scope of the issue. Market responses will not be dictated by ecosystem constraints or biophysical realities, but rather by internal strategic norms which yield routinised solutions. These responses are generally grounded in strategies for eco-efficiency, which do not fundamentally challenge the underlying economic models that are causing the problem in the first place. These models treat the environment as a limitless source of materials and sink for waste and are built on a belief system that enshrines perpetual economic growth based on continued consumption. So, while framing climate change within existing market logics is important for slowing the velocity at

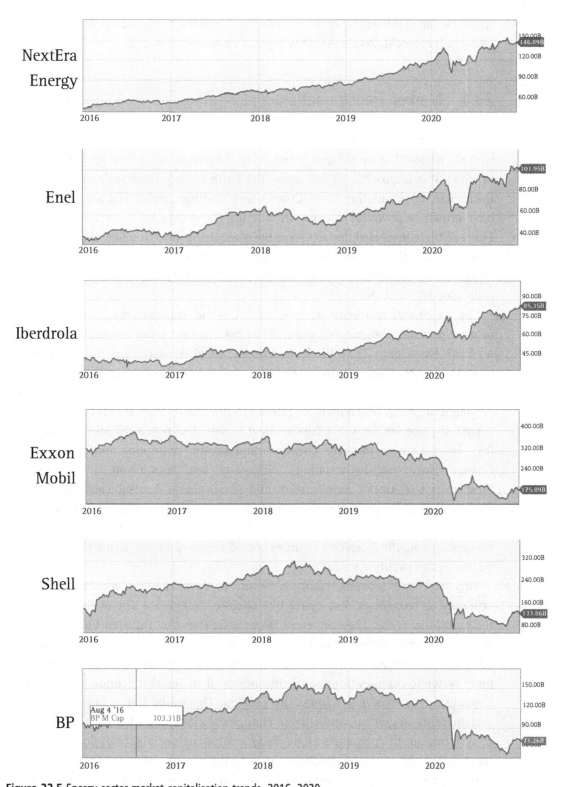

Figure 23.5 Energy sector market capitalisation trends, 2016–2020

which we are approaching systemic collapse, it will not fully address the roots of the problem (Ehrenfeld, 2008). Another type of response is needed.

23.4   Market Transformation

To fully capture the urgent scope of the climate challenge, we must come to terms with the notion that we are now living in the Anthropocene, a new geological epoch in which it is impossible to talk about the Earth's ecosystems without recognising the human role in altering them (Crutzen and Stoermer, 2000). Human technologies have grown so powerful that we are altering the ecosystem on a planetary scale. Many of these increased impacts have been occurring since roughly 1950 or the end of World War II, marking what scientists call the 'Great Acceleration', where the trajectories of multiple environmental and social metrics began to increase dramatically (see Figure 23.6).

Climate change represents just one marker of the Anthropocene; there are a total of nine 'planetary boundaries' essential to maintaining a safe environment for life on Earth (see Figure 23.7). We have crossed out of the safe zone for five already: Climate Change, Biosphere Integrity (BII stands for Biodiversity Intactness Index, a measure of how land-use pressures have diminished wild species' abundance since pre-modern times), which includes Species Extinction (E/MSY stands for extinctions per million species per year), Biochemical Flows of nitrogen (N) and phosphorous (P), Novel Entities (notably chemical and plastic pollution) and Land-System Change (such as deforestation). Scientists are monitoring another three: Freshwater Use, Ocean Acidification and Atmospheric Aerosol Loading (such as particulates). Just one is on the mend: Stratospheric Ozone Depletion has been reversed after the Montreal Protocol on Substances that Deplete the Ozone Layer was enacted in 1987, leading to an expected recovery of the ozone layer near the middle of the twenty-first century.

This dark and looming reality necessitates deep changes within the market economy. It recognises that issues like climate change are not environmental in the traditional sense. They represent systems failures that threaten life on Earth as we know it, and simple solutions based on existing logics, such as operational efficiency or consumer demand, will not address the full scope of the problem. Far more systemic changes in present conceptions of the market economy are needed. Capitalism must evolve to address this problem. One initial step is to recognise that sustainability in general, and climate change solutions in particular, are properties of systems, not of companies alone. Future corporate sustainability leaders will be measured by the extent to which they change the broader systems of which they are part. This examination can begin with a critical re-evaluation of the 'purpose of the corporation', and continue to a reassessment of the role of the government in the

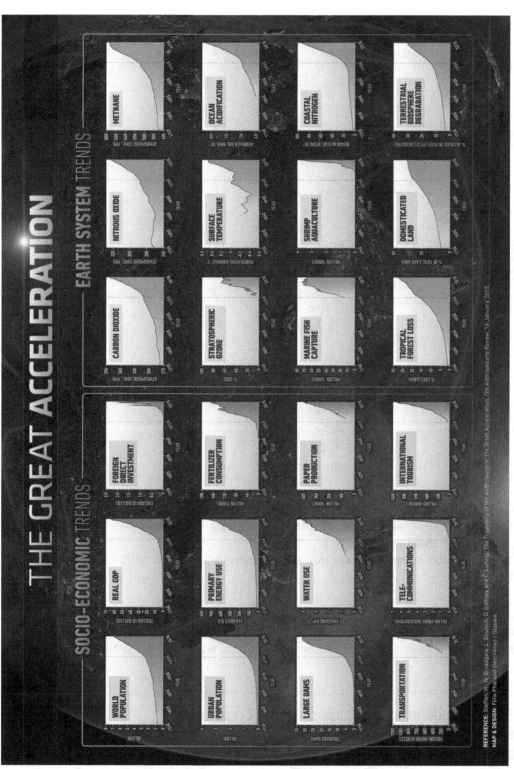

Figure 23.6 The planetary dashboard of the 'Great Acceleration'. (E/MSY: extinctions per million species-years; BII: Biodiversity Intactness Index; N: Nitrogen; P: Phosphorus.). An online version of this figure can be viewed at https://stockholmuniversity.box.com/s/04hq983n7dcer8y7kinw2l77f5kub239.

Source: Steffen et al. (2015a).

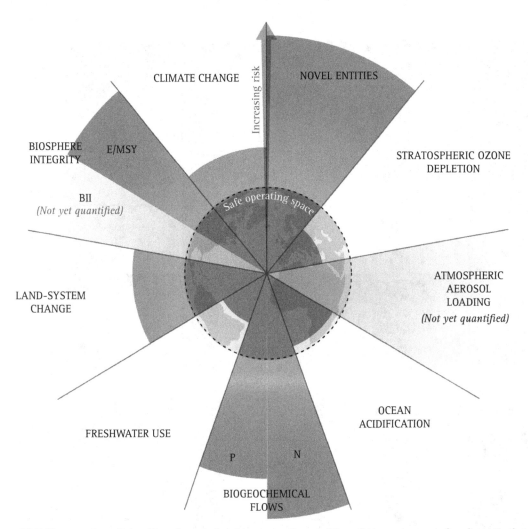

Figure 23.7 Planetary Boundaries. These boundaries characterise the conditions that are necessary for planet Earth to remain stable. Five boundaries have already been crossed. (E/MSY: extinctions per million species-years; BII: Biodiversity Intactness Index; N: Nitrogen; P: Phosphorus.).
Source: Designed by Azote for Stockholm Resilience Centre 2022, based on analysis in Persson et al. (2022) and Steffen et al. (2015a).

market and the models and metrics that guide market activity. Ultimately, new models will develop to guide business behaviour in ways that cut to the core of the challenge.

23.4.1   Redefining the Purpose of the Corporation

In 2019, the CEO of BlackRock sent a letter to CEOs of public companies reminding them of their responsibility not only to deliver profits, but also to make 'a positive contribution to society' (Fink, 2019). That same year, 200 chief executives from the

Business Roundtable, including the leaders of Apple, American Airlines, Accenture, AT&T, Bank of America, Boeing and BlackRock, issued a statement that redefined 'the purpose of a corporation' as investing in employees, delivering value to customers and dealing fairly and ethically with suppliers, not just advancing the interests of shareholders (Yaffe-Bellany, 2019). In 2020, the World Economic Forum published a 'manifesto' that redefined 'the universal purpose of a company' as one that 'serves society at large ... supports communities ... pays its fair share of taxes ... acts as a steward of the environmental and material universe for future generations' (Schwab, 2019).

These statements are in direct contrast to the view that has become mythologised within business and within society that the purpose of the corporation is simply to 'make money for its shareholders', even to the point of believing that US corporate law demands it. No such law exists. This inaccurate notion emerged in the 1970s out of the Chicago School of Economics and has led to multiple problems in the functioning of the market, not least of which include a narrowed focus on quarterly earnings and short-term share price swings, limitations on strategic thinking by decreasing focus on long-term investment and strategic planning, and efforts to offload environmental and social costs on others in the interest of satisfying the specific type of shareholder who is 'shortsighted, opportunistic, willing to impose external costs, and indifferent to ethics and others' welfare' (Stout, 2012b). Business Professor and Management Consultant Peter Drucker took a broader view, arguing in the 1950s that 'the purpose of a company is to create a customer'. Profits are one metric of how well the company performs this purpose, but ultimately, he argued, 'the business enterprise ... exists for the sake of the contribution which it makes to the welfare of society as a whole' (Drucker, 1954).

23.4.2 Redefining the Relationship between the Government and the Market

Another misconception that has taken root among many business leaders is the idea that government has no place in the market and that regulation is an unwarranted intrusion in the market. These views are naïve and destructive. Government is the domain in which the rules of the market are set and enforced, and companies with a mindset towards serving society can participate constructively in policy formation, seeking policies that help to make society and the economy strong and fair in the aggregate, not just for the select and affluent few.

But there is good reason to be concerned about the extent to which corporations influence policy for their own interests. A 2014 study concluded that economic elites and narrow interest groups were very influential in the establishment and form of US federal policy between 1981 and 2002, while the views of ordinary citizens had virtually no independent effect at all (Gilens and Page, 2014). This conclusion would seem to be supported by the amount of money that is spent on lobbying each year, reaching into the billions of dollars in governments around the world. InfluenceMap (2020), a watchdog organisation that tracks corporate influence, found that the largest oil and gas companies spend nearly US$200 million per year in lobbying efforts to delay, control or block policies to tackle climate change. All told, corporate influence strains government's ability to set even the most rudimentary policies (i.e., a carbon price). Such activity is not always visible. ExxonMobil, for example, states on its webpage that the company is 'committed to positive action on climate change' while spending over US$40 million in 2018 to lobby against climate policies (Laville, 2019), and has supported trade groups like the American Legislative Exchange Council (ALEC) and the American Petroleum Institute (API), which also lobbies against climate policy.

Today's business students are entering a world where distrust of the relationship between business and government is at an all-time high. At the same time, many corporations enjoy tremendous power to lobby governments in ways that are often in opposition to public interest. This creates a need for regulation that requires corporations to disclose more details about their political actions both individually and as part of industry associations, make their lobbying stances public and reveal which politicians they have called on to take a given position, what some call 'corporate political responsibility' (Lyon and Delmas, 2018). This idea is less radical than it seems. Many forms of lobbying in the United States were banned until the nineteenth century. The Georgia state constitution at one time read that 'lobbying is declared to be a crime', and in California, it was a felony. It was not until the early 1970s that major corporations began to lobby aggressively on their own behalf.

23.4.3   Misguided Metrics and Models

Climate change also leads to a re-examination of the metrics and models used to understand, explain and set policies for the market. Two of these that have received significant attention are neoclassical economics and principal-agent theory. Both are foundational to management practice but built on extreme and rather dismal simplifications of human beings as largely untrustworthy and driven by avarice, greed and selfishness. Climate change further challenges us to re-examine the unquestioned metrics used in economic calculations. Two notable examples are discount rates and gross domestic product (GDP).

Valuation techniques like the discounted cash flow method are seen by some as 'anchored in arcane ideas' that 'favor short term gains at the expense of future generations' (Cifuentes and Espinoza, 2016). Economist Nicholas Stern (2007) stirred a healthy controversy when he used an unusually low discount rate to calculate the future costs and benefits of climate change mitigation and adaptation. Using a rate of 1.4 per cent, Stern argued that it is inherently unethical to use standard discount rates on certain issues. Most large multinational corporations use a discount rate between 5 and 10 per cent in cash-flow analyses. But a discount rate of 10 per cent assumes that anything ten years out or more is worthless. Is that true? That is the future of your children and your grandchildren.

Similarly, GDP measures national health only in terms of the movement of money as a proxy for societal welfare. This limits its usefulness as a full measure of human prosperity. For example, someone may choose to eat all their meals at Krispy Kreme Doughnuts and McDonald's, and GDP will go up. If they have a heart attack and go to the hospital, GDP goes up. If they die and their family pays for a funeral and burial, GDP goes up again. Are all these positively contributing to societal welfare? Of course not. And yet this logic guides decisions about economic policy: for instance, the country of Madagascar sought to increase GDP by increasing its production and export of wood. But in the process, the country deforested at such an alarming rate that it hampered future cash flows from this resource. The goal of GDP growth sent them in the wrong direction (Ehrhardt-Martinez, 1998). To find alternatives to GDP, Bhutan has instituted the Gross Happiness Index, and former French President Nicolas Sarkozy formed a commission whose report (Stiglitz et al., 2010) recommended new metrics shifting economic emphasis to a broader measure of overall well-being that could overcome GDP's neglect of the environmental impacts of economic decisions, economic inequality (such that most people can be worse off even while average income is increasing) and the value of wealth to be passed on to future generations.

23.4.4　Developing New Business Models

Ultimately, systems change in market transformation requires compelling new business models. Recognising that mankind's 'throughput' – the sheer weight of materials, including fuel, that feed the world's economies – increased by 800 per cent in the twentieth century (Krausmann et al., 2009), many have begun to consider new ideas such as steady-state economies or even economic 'degrowth'. According to economics Nobel Laureate Robert Solow, the United States and Europe might soon find that 'either continued growth will be too destructive to the environment and they are too dependent on scarce natural resources, or that they would rather use increasing productivity in the form of leisure' (Stoll, 2008). Systemic corporate strategies to address this involve the optimisation of operations and supply-chain logistics to move away from linear production models where raw materials are extracted, turned into products, sold to consumers and disposed of at the end of their life. Instead, new models are being used to reduce the need for raw materials and the creation of waste, including life-cycle analysis, which examines the total environmental and economic costs of products from 'cradle to grave'; industrial ecology, which seeks to link waste streams from one company that may be used as a feedstock in another; and the circular economy, which is a framework for reducing material and energy use among all constituents in a supply chain by designing recyclability into initial designs and recycling in a way that keeps materials at their highest value (rather than, for example, merely burning them for fuel).

Ultimately, this kind of model re-examination challenges business leaders to be more critical about capitalism both as it exists currently and as it evolves (Hoffman, 2021). While many take the form and function of capitalism as a given, capitalism is actually malleable and dynamic. Throughout the nineteenth and twentieth centuries, the emergence of new policies to block monopoly power, collusion, price-fixing and unsafe or exploitative working conditions all required businesses to adapt. Addressing twenty-first-century challenges of reducing or eliminating greenhouse gas emissions will require similar transformations. Consider also the many existing forms of capitalism: Japanese, American and Scandinavian capitalism approach issues such as government collaboration and the societal responsibilities of companies very differently. Future business leaders must consider these variants as well as their historical origins, the underlying models on which they are based, and the ways in which they both serve and harm society if they are to assume any kind of role in shaping necessary improvements (Hoffman, 2021).

23.4.5   Asking New Questions

Ultimately, systems change to address climate change and the Anthropocene must move beyond *reducing unsustainability* towards *creating sustainability* (Ehrenfeld, 2008). To do that, business leaders must ask new kinds of questions. For example, many companies have shifted from thinking about carbon reductions to instead focusing on strategies that strive to be carbon neutral or even carbon negative. The kind of thinking and logics in the former are more in line with Enterprise Integration, using existing models and frameworks to make incremental advances in addressing climate change. But the latter requires a whole new way of thinking. Toyota's goal, for example, of going 'beyond zero environmental impact' by reducing and eventually eliminating CO_2 emissions from vehicle operation, manufacturing, materials production and energy sources to become carbon neutral by 2050 will require answers to tough questions about the connection between materials and profit ('making money by pushing steel out the door'), a focus on services and not just products (the service of 'mobility' to move people and goods, rather than the product of an automobile), new kinds of partnerships and a renewed role for government in driving systemic change. Solutions to climate change require these new types of aggressive thinking, and the number of companies that are announcing similar programmes to achieve carbon neutrality is growing. Entire countries, including Iceland, Costa Rica and New Zealand, have set goals to be carbon neutral by the middle of the twenty-first century. Some companies like Ikea and Microsoft have even pledged to go carbon negative, effectively undoing the carbon emissions they have created in their lifetimes. These efforts will set the world on a different path over the next fifty to a hundred years.

Another question that some have begun to ask is whether one can solve the climate change problem in a society and market that is built on consumerism. The World Business Council for Sustainable Development, for example, is examining notions of what 'sustainable consumption' might look like (WBCSD, 2011). Patagonia is exploring this question with its Common Threads and Worn Wear initiatives, which encourage people to buy used clothing or repair damaged clothing in order to make it last. Dell, Adidas, Method and others have taken steps to address the critical issue of ocean plastics by developing programmes to stop plastics from entering the environment, making new products with recycled ocean plastics and developing alternatives to plastics such as biomaterials (Lear, 2018). Actions like these are driving shifts not only in how businesses operate, but also in our culture, how we think about nature, ourselves and the connection between the two.

23.5 Climate Change and the Anthropocene as a Cultural Shift

Ecologist Aldo Leopold (1949) warned that: 'no important change in ethics was ever accomplished without an internal change in our intellectual emphasis, loyalties, affections and convictions. The proof that conservation has not yet touched these foundations of conduct lies in the fact that philosophy and religion have not yet heard of it. In our attempt to make conservation easy, we have made it trivial.' By framing the solutions to climate change in the language of commerce, we take steps to address the issue on a technical level. But it is important to recognise the extent to which cultural change must accompany such solutions. While free-marketers and technology entrepreneurs may advertise otherwise, there is no technological or market-based silver bullet to solve our environmental problems (Hoffman, 2019b). Electric cars are promising, but they are still cars that require energy and resources to be built, operated, recycled and disposed of, all of which increase our carbon emissions even if some of that energy comes from renewables. Geo-engineering may ameliorate our impact on the environment, though many fear that it will make things worse. But both geo-engineering and electric cars are designed to preserve prior patterns of consumption: to live in ever-larger homes, drive ever-larger cars and consume as we always have.

Climate change is not just a technological or economic problem. If we continue to desire perpetual economic expansion, endless growth, ever-increasing material objects to purchase and throw away, and an environment that will never cease to provide the resources we want and accept the unlimited waste we dump into it, then we will fall back into the convenient and lazy mindset that technology and policy alone will fix our problems. Without systemic changes in our culture and values, we will never recover from the destructive path on which we are embarked. In the long term, we will have to change how we think and live. Signs of this change are already emerging. There is a good chance, for example, that your children or grandchildren will not get a licence or own a car. This is already happening with the new generation of non-drivers and is likely to continue as conceptions of car ownership morph into considerations of mobility. One extreme projection is that the number of passenger vehicles on American roads could drop by 80 per cent between 2020 and 2030, from 247 million to 44 million (*Forbes*, 2017). This is an entirely different reality from the one that previous generations grew up in.

Life in the Anthropocene is the ultimate 'commons problem', where survival depends on collective actions even as the morality of individual actions takes on new meaning. In a world where the wealthiest 20 per cent of the population account for 77 per cent of total private consumption while the poorest 20 per cent account for just 1.5 per cent (Shah, 2014), the responsibility falls heavier on some than others. Similarly, when the richest 10 per cent of people produce half of the planet's individual-consumption-based fossil fuel emissions, while the poorest 50 per cent contribute only 10 per cent (Oxfam, 2015), the responsibility to protect the commons (i.e., natural resources accessible to all) falls most on those creating the problem. But as the world faces a widening income gap, there is a parallel widening 'climate divide' (Kennedy, 2003), where the poorest of the world are least responsible for climate change (both at present levels and historically) but most at risk, while the affluent of the world are most to blame but have the resources to adapt to its impacts.

As such, the language of economics and commerce may be expedient, but it is incomplete. The market is an important tool for understanding and addressing our challenges, but it is not the only one. What is right and just? How much is sufficient to be happy and fulfilled? These are questions that technocratic thinking alone cannot answer, but philosophy, theology, the humanities and the social sciences, as well as tacit, vernacular and pragmatic knowledge, can help (Hoffman, 2021). This does not suggest a rejection of the scientific method or the power of the market, but of a reductive, purely technocratic approach with excessive belief in the power of scientific knowledge and economic development to pursue an ongoing conquest of nature. It is a rejection of 'scientism', the belief in the superiority of the physical sciences to the exclusion of other forms of knowledge. With its preference for quantifiable measures over qualitative understanding, focus on atomised parts over the collective whole, and pursuit of outcomes like human utility, technical efficiency and political expedience as unquestioned goods, a purely scientific understanding of our relationship to the natural world has limits. Although the development of new technologies to reduce our environmental impact is a good thing, these are only reducing the velocity at which we are running towards a brick wall; they are not changing our course.

23.6 Management as a Calling

Viewing business management through the lens of the Anthropocene calls for a different approach to the education of corporate leaders. Business students must learn the basics of management, but they must also seriously consider the vast power they possess to shape our society. Tomorrow's business leaders must start thinking critically about the societal role of businesses, their positions as managers in guiding those businesses and the overall system in which they will practice their craft. As such, they should consider management a *calling*: not just the pursuit of a career for personal gain, but a vocation based on the values of leading commerce and serving society (Hoffman, 2021). A leader with a calling will think and act in ways that transcend shareholder wealth maximisation. They will focus on influencing the overall market in which business operates, seeking solutions to economic, social and environmental problems that are systemic in nature and bringing together the broad array of market constituents to solve them.

The process of exploring this calling cannot be accomplished simply by adding electives to standing degree programmes. It must allow for guided discernment to develop more focused, balanced and mature students who will be thoughtful about why they are pursuing their path and how they might direct it towards a personally, professionally and socially meaningful career. Similar to the spirit invoked to train doctors and lawyers, business students should aspire to become pillars of commerce who serve not only shareholders, but also employees and society, embracing a revitalised set of professional and moral ideals. If schools do not provide this training in any formal way, students must take the initiative to seek it out themselves. Today, many are doing just that by demanding more course content on sustainability and social impact.

23.7 Chapter Summary

As businesses continue to navigate a world transformed by climate change and the Anthropocene, they face a variety of paths to sustainability. Initial attempts to integrate environmentally friendly products or practices should ultimately lead firms to transform their business models for a warming world, and re-examine many of the assumptions, metrics and relationships that commonly guide economic decision-making. But solutions to the climate crisis cannot be imagined based on technological or economic logics alone. They will also need to centre human values in order to facilitate cultural and societal change. Understanding management as a calling will equip the coming generation of business leaders to pursue the solutions our future demands.

CHAPTER QUESTIONS

1. How do the Enterprise Integration and Market Transformation approaches to addressing climate change differ from each other? What motivates companies to move from the former to the latter, and what obstacles could they face in this transition?
2. Consider the range of external forces that generate pressure on businesses to develop climate strategies. How do these correspond to different internal framings of climate issues?
3. Navigating climate change will require new business models and the re-evaluation of old metrics. What are some of the assumptions on which current metrics and models rely, and how might these be reimagined?
4. What are the limits of a purely technocratic approach to climate solutions? Why does culture matter for addressing the climate crisis?
5. What does it mean to understand management as a calling? How does this perspective differ from current approaches to business education, and how can business schools support students who seek to serve society by pursuing careers in management?

FURTHER RESOURCES

- Crutzen, P. (2002). Geology of Mankind. *Nature*, 415(6867), 23.

  This is one of the first articles that explains the concept of the Anthropocene. It is a good baseline for the idea.

- Gates, B. (2021). *How to Avoid a Climate Disaster*. New York, NY: Alfred A. Knopf.

  This book offers a range of technological solutions to climate issues.

- Havey, N. (2020). *Beyond Zero*, http://beyondzerofilm.com/.

  This documentary describes the path-breaking work of Interface Carpet under the leadership of its visionary CEO Ray Anderson.

- Hawken, P. (Ed.). (2017). *Drawdown: The Most Comprehensive Plan Ever Proposed to Reverse Global Warming*. New York, NY: Penguin, https://drawdown.org/.

  This book offers a very comprehensive catalogue of steps that can be taken to address climate change.

- Intergovernmental Panel on Climate Change. (2018). Global Warming of 1.5°C, www.ipcc.ch/sr15/.

This is a special report on the impacts of global warming of 1.5°C above pre-industrial levels and related global greenhouse gas emissions pathways in the context of strengthening the global response to the threat of climate change, sustainable development and efforts to eradicate poverty.

- Intergovernmental Panel on Climate Change. (2022). AR6 Synthesis Report, www.ipcc.ch/.

The IPCC offers the most comprehensive syntheses of climate science. Anyone interested in the science and data behind this issue should become familiar with IPCC reports. This is the most recent.

- Rockström, J., Steffen, W., Noone, K., Persson, Å., Chapin, S., Lambin, E., et al. (2009). A Safe Operating Space for Humanity. *Nature*, 461(7263), 472–475.

This is one of the first articles to identify and quantify planetary boundaries that must not be transgressed to help prevent human activities from causing unacceptable environmental change.

- Stockholm Resilience Centre, www.stockholmresilience.org/.

The Stockholm Resilience Centre is a research centre that focuses on resilience and sustainability science at Stockholm University. A joint initiative between Stockholm University and the Beijer Institute of Ecological Economics at the Royal Swedish Academy of Sciences, its mission is to advance the scientific understanding of the complex, dynamic interactions of people and nature in the biosphere and train the next generation of sustainability researchers and leaders.

24 Anti-Corruption Governance, Global Business and Corporate Sustainability

DIETER ZINNBAUER AND HANS KRAUSE HANSEN

LEARNING OBJECTIVES

- Introduce you to the concept of corruption, what it is, what different forms it takes and what its consequences are for business and society at large.

- Give you an overview of the key actors, rule frameworks and initiatives that shape anti-corruption governance.

- Familiarise you with how companies approach anti-corruption, how this approach is evolving in the light of new research insights and what shortcomings and criticisms are raised.

- Show how the evolving approach of corporate anti-corruption efforts are part and parcel of a comprehensive corporate sustainability agenda.

24.1   Introduction

Only a few decades ago, it was commonplace to regard corruption as mainly existing in the Global South. By the 1990s, this understanding began to change. Researchers and policy-makers increasingly acknowledge that corruption is much more complex and deeply intertwined with globalisation and wider shifts in legal and social norms across the world.

Corruption affects economic development negatively, weakens the legitimacy of public institutions and the rule of law, and, not least, undermines the credibility of those international businesses involved in corrupt transactions. From early 2000 onwards, anti-corruption has become a global discourse with initiatives addressing the risks that corruption poses, often in conjunction with other initiatives aimed at promoting democracy and economic competitiveness, or in relation to tackling the illegal production of drugs, money laundering, human right violations, etc.

Corruption has also emerged as a central theme for corporate sustainability. Companies have moved from regarding corruption as a business expense to secure or protect business from or as a problem of dealing with a few rogue employees, to viewing corruption as a substantive, systemic business risk that demands comprehensive efforts to build a corporate culture of integrity. As a result, an increasing number of companies attempt to manage their 'corruption risks' and many have begun to collaborate in efforts to agree standards of probity across different industries, markets or countries. The most visible illustration of the rise of (anti-)corruption on the corporate sustainability agenda was perhaps in 2004, with the adoption of a dedicated anti-corruption principle by the UN Global Compact, the United Nations' high-profile business initiative. This principle formally endorsed by more than 12,000 companies in 160 countries unambiguously states: 'Businesses should work against corruption in all its forms, including extortion and bribery' (UN Global Compact, n.d.b).

How and why did all these changes happen? This chapter sets out to investigate the phenomenon of corruption, how it relates to business and particularly the key institutional shifts and mechanisms which have put corruption on the global agenda for corporate sustainability.

We start with a definition of corruption, distinguish between different forms and flag major corruption consequences. We then map key actors, rules and mechanisms of anti-corruption governance, describe how this landscape has evolved over time and present examples of practical initiatives in this area. Next, we switch to the business view, explore how anti-corruption is being approached by companies as a form of risk management, which tools are being deployed and how these are shaped by an anti-corruption service industry. This is complemented by a summary of critical perspectives on the corporate anti-corruption agenda. Finally, we look ahead, flag dynamics on the horizon and explore how anti-corruption fits into broader corporate sustainability issues.

24.2   Defining Corruption, Tracing Its Consequences

Corruption comes in many different forms and shapes and social scientists have debated how corruption can be understood for decades (Johnston, 2005). In the following, we will introduce you to a few key concepts so that you can participate in the corruption debate with a particular focus on the business perspective.

A pragmatic and widely used definition depicts the phenomenon as *the abuse of entrusted power for private gain* (Transparency International, n.d.) As such, it covers a wide range of issues, for example:

- *Service-level corruption* that targets front-end officials to unduly influence the provision of services or enforcement of rules – for example, to jump the queue on connecting a phone line, to fraudulently lower a water bill or to get away with an illicit oil spill. When it comes to paying extra for gaining access to services that one is entitled to or fending off fines that are illegitimately imposed, related payments are often referred to as petty corruption or facilitation payments – labels that misleadingly connote a rather harmless, if not benign, character (Argandoña, 2017). See Box 24.1 for details on why this is so.

- *Procurement corruption* that relates to unduly influencing the award of contracts – for example, through side-payments or bid-rigging (Søreide, 2002).
- *Political corruption* that targets illicit benefits at policy-makers and the policy-making process to shape laws and regulations in one's favour (to be distinguished from legal and regulated means of partaking in policy-making, such as through lobbying) (Heywood, 1997).
- *State capture*, which refers to a systematic hijacking of all important state and accountability institutions, including the judiciary, for personal enrichment with impunity (Hellman et al., 2000).

As this short enumeration shows, many forms of corruption involve the government and public sector and thus the abuse of 'public power'. As a consequence, they are often called 'public corruption'. Yet, the definition of corruption has evolved to embrace a broader notion of 'entrusted power' that, for example, also includes corruption inside or between two businesses (so-called private-to-private corruption, Argandoña, 2003) – for instance, when a company procurement officer is being bribed by a contractor, a senior executive steers business to a company her family partially owns (self-dealing) or a union leader receives lavish benefits to agree to a big redundancy scheme (Zinnbauer et al., 2009). Broader conceptions of corruption in business as used in policy debates have also come to cover other types of illicit corporate behavior, such as tax evasion or technical fraud – for example, the cheating on vehicle emissions colloquially known as *Dieselgate* (Bouzzine and Lueg, 2020).

The 'tools' to achieve corrupt influence are equally diverse and include bribery (direct payments, in larger transactions dressed up as fees to go-between agents), nepotism and cronyism (the use of kinship or friendship ties) or patronage (the handing out of contracts or jobs in exchange for political support or other benefits) (Scott, 1969).

Another useful distinction that you may encounter is between *collusive* (both parties conspire and gain) and *coercive* (one party is being extorted) types of corruption, which come with different incentives and different anti-corruption responses for the parties involved (Mawani and Trivedi, 2021).

None of these typologies is clear-cut; some are contested or raise additional problems. For example, it is a major concern that some practices that are informal in nature, rooted in particular cultural or social norms or evolve in the context of a weak and dysfunctional state do not comport with narrow legalistic and often Western-centric ideas of order and bureaucratic impartiality and are thus automatically and lazily condemned as corrupt (Zinnbauer, 2020). Such a judgment fails to consider how these practices might be a reaction to broader structural injustices (consider, for example, informal slum dwellers who pay off police as they have been deprived of their land rights) or how they offer alternative ways to organise public authority or to diffuse violence in the absence of a fully functional state (consider, here, gifts to village elders to facilitate communal permission for building a health clinic in a remote village) (de Sardan, 1999).

It is important to keep these concerns and borderline cases in mind and apply the label of pernicious corruption carefully. Yet, such grey zones should also not distract from two important considerations:

- most incidences of corruption in mainstream business life are much easier to categorise and can usefully be explored with the help of the above definition and typologies; and
- even seemingly minor corrupt infractions can cause significant harm, as the case in Box 24.1 illustrates.

INSIGHTS | BOX 24.1 The myth of harmless petty corruption or facilitation payments

The logic is compelling: you need to clear mission-critical medical equipment at a customs point. The equipment is meant to help tackle a Cholera outbreak and needs to get there without delay. So there cannot be much harm in topping up the meagre salary of a border official who cannot otherwise feed his or her family in order to clear the customs procedures as swiftly as possible, right?

But consider this: such payments may in the longer run encourage officials to set up more burdensome regulations (red tape) and also offer the breaking of other, more consequential rules (maybe hygiene inspections) in order to extract more payments. What's more, a lucrative side income can induce superiors in the customs administration to sell such jobs to the highest bidder or demand a cut of each extra payment for themselves. This can even result in a pyramid scheme in which jobs are being sold at every level of the administration and small cuts of the money collected are funnelled upwards to fill the coffers of the ruling party that appoints the most senior officials and sets the scheme in motion. The outcome over time is a gradual corrosion of integrity throughout the entire bureaucracy, the erosion of functioning rule-based governance, illicit political funding for the incumbent government to hold on to power and impunity for any ruthless business or individual prepared to violate the rules. These are not hypotheticals. All these dynamics have been empirically documented (e.g., Carr, 2009; De La O et al., 2015). The aggregate volume and effect of petty bribery is far from petty and such payments cannot be ignored as a negligible cost of doing business. The challenge is to redesign the entire system in ways that curb both the supply and demand for these payments. And business has a role in this as well: see section 24.4.

24.2.1   The Consequences of Corruption in a Business Context

The diversity in corruption types has often also led scholars to assess their consequences differently. As mentioned above, there might be a specific social, economic or political function related to corrupt practices, which can help cut through red tape, stabilise fragile communities, organise business transactions or deflect violence in the absence of fully functioning formal governance arrangements. Yet, even the seemingly most innocuous acts of corruption may lead to harmful consequences further down the road (see Box 24.1). And even if it is sometimes not quite clear what causes that, the weight of empirical evidence suggests that in the long run and in the aggregate corruption evolves to destabilise societies and destroy trust in government, and diminishes the chance for a fair and prosperous future. More specifically in relation to the business context, more corruption seems to be bad for the business environment as it is associated with lower institutional quality, higher barriers to trade, fewer foreign direct investments and less market openness (Rodrik et al., 2004; Ali and Mdhillat, 2015). At the level of individual companies, corruption is linked to weaker firm performance, depressed productivity and lower firm valuation (Dal Bó and Rossi, 2007; Wieneke and Gries, 2011). Corruption inside a company, between companies and in business–government relations abets unfair competition and personal enrichment and more broadly undermines the ability of a business entity to govern itself effectively. Against this backdrop, controlling corruption is not just one important element of corporate sustainability in its own right, but also a necessary condition for achieving other ambitions for corporate sustainability.

A string of major and highly visible corporate corruption scandals from Siemens, Telia and Rolls Royce to Goldman Sachs, Alstom and Odebrecht (for case summaries, see, for example, Stanford Law School, n.d.) exemplifies the many direct and indirect costs for companies, from enormous fines (see Box 24.2 on Airbus) and substantive reputational damage to a painful diversion of precious management time and scarce organisational resources in the clean-up phase.

In a nutshell: some possible immediate social or economic functions notwithstanding, corruption is a big net negative for business.

So what can be done about it? The following sections present the major milestones and players in the evolution of anti-corruption governance that you should be familiar with and then zooms in on how business does and can engage.

24.3   Anti-Corruption Governance: The Big Picture

The project of controlling corruption (henceforth anti-corruption governance) has become an increasingly important issue on the global agenda since the early 1990s.

It has moved out, so to speak, from national space and now entangles a much broader set of actors, relations and activities across borders. The growing focus on corruption and its control is driven by a continuous string of corruption scandals featuring prominent politicians, bureaucrats and business people. It can also be partly attributed to recent developments in media technologies (big information leaks, virality of stories and scandals), as well as political and economic dynamics (populism and rising inequalities reinforcing a feeling of corrupt elites conspiring against the common citizen). As a result, opinion surveys resoundingly list corruption as a one of the main concerns of citizens and experts around the world and many political parties and candidates are at a minimum paying lip service to strong anti-corruption commitments (e.g., Transparency International, 2021b).

In the following, we use the term anti-corruption governance to refer to the complex process of detecting, curbing and preventing, within and beyond national space, the misuse of public office and other forms of entrusted power for private or organisational benefit (Hansen, 2011).

The key feature of anti-corruption *governance* is not only that it acts directly on such transactions, but rather that it also seeks to shape the conduct of the categories of actors that purportedly are engaged in or affected by them: industries, corporations, intermediaries, public sector agencies, international organisations, etc. Governance is therefore not just about government and its actions, but it is also the product of a broader set of actors, and the formal as well as informal rules and norms that govern their conduct with regard to corruption from individual micro- to system-wide macro-level.

Many acronyms for key laws and initiatives swirl around in the anti-corruption literature and in this section we would like to familiarise you with a handful of the most important ones that you will inevitably encounter.

The first building block of global corruption governance was in fact laid by a traditional and national regulatory initiative: the passage of the US Foreign Corrupt Practices Act (FCPA) in 1977 (see Figure 24.1). This law took shape in the aftermath of the political scandals in relation to then President Nixon when policy-makers and shareholders realised that many companies were keeping off the books budgets for covert political donations and bribe payments overseas (Koehler, 2012). The FCPA criminalises bribery on the part of US citizens and firms conducting business overseas, and on the part of companies based elsewhere in the world, but listed in the United States or using US payment infrastructures. It thus sets standards for combatting corruption based on an extraterritoriality principle. It also introduces mandatory company self-regulation by requiring corporations to set up internal control mechanisms and to improve their accounting practices.

During the 1980s, US corporations lobbied the US government to seek international cooperation in suppressing bribes with a view to creating a level playing

Figure 24.1 Legislation landmarks in the fight against corruption

field. Over time and rocked by their own high-profile corruption scandals, other countries grew more sympathetic to this idea and the 1990s marked the emergence of a string of international conventions against corruption. The most far-reaching is the 1997 OECD Convention on Combating Bribery of Foreign Public Officials in International Business Transactions (OECD Convention). It draws heavily on the FCPA. Bribing a foreign public official is now a crime to be punished in all OECD countries and bribes can no longer be eligible for tax deduction. The OECD Convention seeks to ensure enforcement of legal requirements through a comprehensive monitoring system based on countries peer-reviewing one another (Heidenheimer and Moroff, 2017).

During the 1990s and early 2000s, a number of regional anti-corruption agreements also took shape and the focus expanded from transnational bribery to a broader regard for more comprehensive anti-corruption measures and standards at the national level. During the same period, anti-corruption moved up on the international policy agenda and a thriving advocacy community developed around these issues. The World Bank and the international development community began to more strongly recognise corruption as an impediment to sustainable human development. Non-governmental organisations (NGOs) working on environmental and justice issues developed work streams on corruption and in 1993 Transparency International was founded as the first globally active NGO specifically dedicated to corruption issues.

All of these efforts culminated in the UN Convention against Corruption (UNCAC), adopted in 2003. The UNCAC is the most comprehensive legally binding anti-corruption instrument to date, signed by 140 countries as of 2022. It includes a large set of provisions that parties to the convention are expected to implement, covering corruption prevention (e.g., transparency and training mechanisms), criminalisation (making all forms of corruption a criminal offence), international cooperation and asset recovery (repatriating funds that have been stolen through corruption and transferred abroad) (Hechler, 2010).

Existent legal frameworks have come to be complemented by other legally based arrangements. Official anti-corruption agencies have been established in a wide range of countries in the Global North and South (De Sousa, 2010) and national legislations, often with some extraterritorial reach, have proliferated across the globe. Importantly, the UK Bribery Act of 2011 draws on the extraterritorial principle like the FCPA. It regards the failure to prevent bribery as a corporate offence and facilitation payments are prohibited.

24.3.1 From Making Rules to Their Enforcement

With legal frameworks proliferating and the policy community around corruption expanding, attention has gradually shifted towards the problem of effective enforcement, which is widely regarded as a persistent shortcoming of most anti-corruption instruments.

Both the UNCAC and most of the regional agreements, for example, include limited provisions on implementation and monitoring. An assessment of the OECD Convention in 2020 found active enforcement in only four participating countries (Transparency International, 2022).

The first three decades of the influential FCPA also saw very limited enforcement, but US authorities have since the mid-2000s significantly increased the number of FCPA cases against corporations and the severity of the financial penalties issued. In 2019, for example, more than fifty enforcement actions were being filed and total sanctions issues in 2020 reached US$5.8 billion (Stanford Law School, n.d.). In order to further encourage more preventative efforts by companies, direct convictions have been complemented by a broader range of enforcement tools, such as deferred prosecution agreements or expanded settlement options that reward companies with more lenient treatment for putting in place comprehensive anti-corruption programmes inside their organisations and across their supply chains.

24.3.2 Anti-Corruption Governance beyond Laws

Anti-corruption governance for the business sector includes more than the traditional forms of regulation. Industry self-regulation, for example, can emerge when international regulation is absent, partial or ineffective, or as a response to governmental strategies to steer corporate conduct towards public goals without appearing to interfere directly or too much in corporate autonomy. In anti-corruption governance, both forms can be found in the emergence of standards, best practices and codes of conduct, which are developed by

SNAPSHOTS | BOX 24.2 Flying high and above the law? The Airbus global bribery case

In January 2020, Airbus, the largest European aerospace company, eventually reached a settlement agreement that ended a far-flung four-year investigation by anti-corruption authorities in the United States, France and the United Kingdom, with a record fine of close to US$4 billion. Airbus was found to have run an extensive corruption scheme for more than a decade. Through its Strategy and Marketing departments, it employed middlemen to channel millions of US dollars in bribes to officials in sixteen countries around the world, in order to win orders for aircrafts and satellites. Along the way, Airbus violated a number of anti-bribery, arms control and reporting requirements. The case illustrates how, over time, corrupt schemes tend to become routinised and institutionalised inside the business organisation. The resolution of the case is noteworthy not only because of the record fines issued, but also because it indicates a growing international collaboration of anti-corruption enforcement agencies, which has until recently been rather limited and poorly aligned with the increasingly global bribery schemes that large corporate anti-corruption investigations tend to uncover (US District Court for DC, 2020).

business associations. Such collective endeavours also respond to the problem that acting with integrity is made more difficult for an individual company when it knows that its competitors are still engaging in corrupt and thus unfair behaviour. Working together in an industry or across the business sector, developing shared standards and mutual trust that others are also playing by the rules are all measures that help to address this collective action problem and therefore make such joint anti-corruption efforts particularly appealing. One example is the Partnering Against Corruption Initiative (PACI), organised under the World Economic Forum (WEF), whose mission is to develop industry principles and practices in order to establish a competitive level playing field, with fairness and ethical conduct. Another interesting sector-specific example from the shipping industry is described in Box 24.3.

A third category of joint business action against corruption takes the collective approach even further and consists of a growing cluster of multi-stakeholder initiatives. Here, different actors – public, private, NGOs and grassroots, national and international – set out to develop specific regulatory frameworks, to establish standards and goals, frameworks for decision-making and procedures for achieving the standards. A global example of such a multi-stakeholder approach

SNAPSHOTS | BOX 24.3 Collective anti-corruption on the high seas: The Maritime Anti-Corruption Network (MACN)

In 2010, Maersk Line, a globally operating cargo shipping company, sought to convince its peers that all industry players would gain from cooperating on anti-corruption efforts, especially in the light of growing FCPA enforcement and the launch of the UK Bribery Act. In 2011, an informal network between major global shipping industry players was initiated, setting out to map the challenging countries and locations to do business with and through. It was decided to investigate industry issues relating to corruption and geographical 'hot spots' more systematically. The initiative attracted the attention of local and national authorities, international organisations and NGOs, specifically customers and port agents in a number of countries, the UN Development Programme (UNDP) and Transparency International. The MACN was officially born in 2012 and members began to refer to the network on their websites and at official meetings and conferences, capturing further interest from customers, local authorities and suppliers. The cooperation with the UNDP was further strengthened. By 2013, an online platform and an annual in-person meeting process had been established, providing a foundation for sharing best practices and to raise issues with improper demands. The same year, a pilot project in Nigeria was kicked off in cooperation with the UNDP and the UN Office for Drugs and Crime (UNODC). By early 2021, the MACN's membership base has grown to more than 140 companies and its work programme has expanded significantly. The MACN focuses its efforts on capacity building and collective action initiatives, including collaboration with public sector and civil society partners. For example, the MACN has developed an Incident Reporting System through which maritime actors can submit reports of corruption demands in relation to their port operations. The MACN exchanges and uses the information to avoid similiar incidents, as well as to analyse trends in frequency of incidents, allowing the MACN to target collective action efforts and engage with governments.

is the UN Global Compact and its Principle 10 against corruption, which was adopted by the Compact in 2004 and since then has served as one of the progress yardsticks on which participating companies have to report. A first sector-specific initiative along multi-stakeholder lines came into existence in 2002–03 with the Extractive Industries Transparency Initiative (EITI) (see Box 24.4).

SNAPSHOTS | BOX 24.4 Towards transparency below the surface with multi-stakeholder action: The EITI

Designed to bring more transparency and accountability to a sector that is viewed as particularly vulnerable to corruption, the formal governance structure of EITI was established in 2006, with a board consisting of members from governments, companies and civil society. The participation of civil society organisations is regarded as central. The EITI was founded on the idea that transparency on both sides of the transactions – in the financial flows between, on the one hand, resource-extracting companies, who pay royalties and taxes to governments, and on the other, the governments receiving these revenues – will curb the opportunities for rulers and officials to pocket the money for their own use, and for companies to engage in related corrupt practices. The EITI developed a set of voluntary reporting standards for participating countries and companies and incentives implementation through progress validation reviews and reputational pressure. It is therefore different from an international convention where reporting of royalties and revenues would typically be mandatory and non-compliance subject to legal sanctioning. By early 2021, the EITI had fifty-five countries implementing the standard, none of which was assessed to have achieved the highest progress level.

Importantly, the EITI does not rely on a static standard exclusively focused on revenue flows, but has been adapting and expanding its ambitions over time for a more systems-wide approach. As of 2021, for example, the standard also requires reporting on contract specifics and on the natural people who own and control companies (called beneficial ownership disclosure). Considering current debates in the EITI community, further iterations may see stronger reporting on the environmental dimension of the industry and particularly on climate-change-related information.

The rise and visibility of the EITI has spawned a growing number of similar sector-specific multi-stakeholder initiatives – for example, in the construction, medicines and garment sectors. They all share a commitment to developing sector-specific conduct and transparency standards and bring on board different stakeholders to make this happen.

As we have seen, the governance of corruption today can be analysed as driven by a multiplicity of actors – state, non-state and hybrid in-betweens – and a variety of regulatory arrangements spanning from traditional to new forms of regulation on a continuum from hard to soft law. We now turn to a more focused analysis of how corruption is being understood and addressed from a business perspective.

24.4 The Business Approach: Corruption as Risk Management

Describing something in terms of risk has a number of implications for how organisations relate to economic, social and political uncertainties. In the following subsection, we briefly touch on two of these implications.

24.4.1 About Risks and Risk Management

Framing something in terms of risk raises questions about what to do, as well as wider expectations about management and actor responsibility. Uncertainties become risks when they enter into management systems for their identification, assessment and management (Power, 2008). In recent years, corporations' focus on risk has come to tie in with concerns about making explicit and visible the ethical and unethical conduct of organisations. Business responds more actively to a rapidly changing global commercial landscape shaped by a multiplicity of political and social dynamics (O'Callaghan, 2007). At the same time, the phenomenon of reputation in its various forms has come to be seen as an increasingly valuable corporate asset. Risk management incorporates various concerns about reputation loss – for instance, as a consequence of corporate entanglement in corruption scandals. Badly managed risks can potentially destroy a corporation's ability to operate and seriously damage its standing in a community and beyond. In turn, by demonstrating that it has moved into the area of responsible risk management, a company can convert risks into opportunities.

24.4.2 From Adapting to Uncertainty to Managing Corporate Corruption Risks

The process of making corruption risks visible, and calling on the private sector to contribute to addressing them, is closely linked to the efforts by multiple state and non-state forces depicted above. Before the rise of anti-corruption and its ensuing governance mechanisms, Western companies seldom problematised corrupt practices associated with doing business in environments regarded as pervaded by corruption, although there are examples of the opposite. The view of corruption as being standard business practice prevailed in international business, indicating that corruption was rarely considered a risk to be proactively countered, but rather as one among a wide range of uncertainties. In many Western countries, this view was de facto officially supported until the late 1990s by the continuance of governmental tax regulation that allowed the deductibility of bribes.

But the efforts by organisations such as Transparency International and World Bank at making the problem of corruption visible to global publics and decision-makers from the mid-1990s pioneer the de facto construction of corruption as a risk object.

Framing corruption issues as risks has several benefits from a business perspective. As mentioned earlier, it transforms something unknown and potentially threatening into something probabilistic and calculable and thus brings it into the realm of manageability. For a business enterprise, it transfers the task to deal with corruption into the familiar territory and established management systems for dealing with all sorts of business risks. What's more, corruption as risk management animates a proactive approach to prevent corruption from occurring, rather than just a reactive response in crisis mode to an unexpected corruption incident once it has happened. Closely related, framing corruption as risk management and as dealing with something that might happen rather than something that is already happening counters the damaging perception that a company that is active in anti-corruption must be suffering from some serious acts of corruption already, a suspicion with potentially high reputational costs. What's more, talking about the fallout from corruption as corruption risks also makes it easier to map broader linkages to other business risks and thus to understand the consequences and ripple effects of corruption for the broader business model more systematically. In such a perspective, the costs of corruption not only entail reputational risks, but also other damaging consequences for the business operation, such as the earlier-mentioned increasing risks of stiff fines, diversion of management time, downward pressure on company value and debarment from future business opportunities.

24.4.3   Professionalising and Standardising Corporate Anti-Corruption Work

Growing public attention to corruption and growing corporate attention to corruption risks have also given rise to and been further accelerated by a flourishing anti-corruption industry. Many consulting companies and law firms have established lucrative service lines around compliance and anti-corruption. They offer diagnostic analysis and support in designing anti-corruption systems, as well as business intelligence and forensic expertise to help vet business partners or examine suspicious practices. Intensifying efforts to curb money laundering and financing of terrorists in particular have fuelled the growth of business intelligence services – for example, large databases to research politically exposed persons or bespoke investigative services. In addition, anti-corruption service providers carry out surveys and policy research to keep the topic high on the political and business agenda, often working in concert with major anti-corruption NGOs with whom their interests partly overlap.

More and more companies claim to be aware of anti-corruption legislation and corruption risks, and more and more companies have anti-corruption systems in place. A constant feature emphasised is the risk posed to corporate reputation by engaging in corruption, and the potential business opportunities derived from having corruption risk management systems in place.

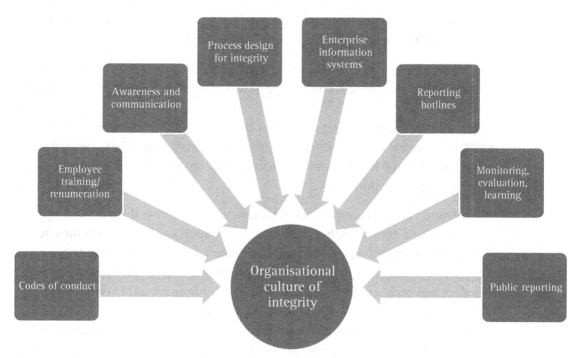

Figure 24.2 The corporate anti-corruption toolbox

The process of making corruption risk visible and framing private sector responsibilities has been accompanied by considerable efforts to introduce specific tools and technologies for managing corruption risk technologies (see Figure 24.2), which include:

- Codes of conducts for employees and suppliers that detail rules for ethical behaviour, tailored to specific industry and company risks.
- Employee training, assessment and remuneration systems that also incentivise and reward integrity.
- Internal awareness raising and communication measures to visibly propagate a culture of integrity and set the appropriate tone from the top.
- Design of key processes to curb corruption risks – for example, through regular staff rotation, the four-eye principle, specific sign-off and delegation authorities, or due diligence vetting of business partners.
- Enterprise information systems that support the screening for and examination of suspicious transactions.
- Reporting hotlines to allow staff and external stakeholders to bring corruption issues to the surface.
- Monitoring, evaluation and learning efforts to track and improve the efficacy of integrity measures.

- Publicly facing reporting and transparency mechanisms to further incentivise good conduct, and instill investor and public trust.

The overall idea is to nurture organisational cultures of integrity that align organisational incentives, norms and practices with this aim (Kaptein, 2011b; Warren et al., 2014).

This shift from focusing on individual bad apples (e.g., employees with corrupt intent) to the barrel (organisational integrity) is also inspired by the growing body of insights on corruption in social psychology and organisational sociology, which stress two key messages:

- Everyone can be corrupt – corrupt behaviour is more shaped by a specific situation and context rather than individual ethical capacity. When the circumstances and organisational contexts are wrong, everyone can slide into corrupt behaviour. And individuals tend to overestimate their capacity to critically reflect and resist corruption (Bazerman and Tenbrunsel, 2011; Haidt, 2012).
- There is a slippery slope towards endemic corruption: corruption scandals time and time again demonstrate how small acts of corruption in a company can morph into systemic, widespread corrupt practices, as bribes need to be covered up on the accounting side, regulators need to be deceived, short-term gains encourage further cheating and the growing scale and gravity of illicit behaviour makes turning back progressively more costly and thus unappealing (Ashforth and Anand, 2003).

24.4.4   Standards, Templates, Benchmarks

Providing guidance for this business approach to anti-corruption is a growing toolbox of standards, templates and comparative assessment exercises.

Transparency International's Business Principles for Countering Bribery, first published in 2003 and refreshed in 2013, have set out a core set of principles that business should adopt for effective anti-corruption efforts. These principles have informed a number of reporting frameworks such as the governance indicators in the Global Reporting Initiative (GRI) or in methodologies put forward by the Sustainability Accounting Standards Board (SASB). A number of specialised data providers (e.g., Sustainalytics or ISS Oekom) apply more granular research and scoring methodologies that also cover business performance in anti-corruption due diligence, while index providers include related information in a number of ESG-oriented products, such as the FTSE4Good or Dow Jones Sustainability Indices. Finally, the International Organization for Standardization developed with ISO 37001 a stand-alone certifiable standard that is directly dedicated to the design and implementation of anti-bribery systems and entered into force in 2016.

24.4.5   Critical Takes on the Anti-Corruption Agenda

The flourishing corporate anti-corruption agenda is not without its critics.

Early criticism revolved around the suspicion that a US-driven anti-corruption agenda rooted in a narrow concept of corruption that privileges a particular Global North idea about how to organise bureaucracies and business was primarily a neoliberal ploy driven by multinationals, in order to gain easier access to markets and government contracts abroad (Brown and Cloke, 2004).

Other critics have taken aim at the lucrative anti-corruption industry and wonder whether the importance and salience of the corporate corruption problems is somewhat inflated by these actors due to the profit opportunities that are attached to this type of work (Sampson, 2010). Estimates suggest, for example, that a large global bank employs more than 20,000 people on compliance and risk-management issues and that globally expenses by financial institutions for the compliance exceed US$180 billion annually (The Economist, 2021).

At company level, questions are at times being raised about the price tag of compliance efforts that may disadvantage smaller, resource-constrained companies, and lead even big players to cut off clients for whom due diligence outweighs the benefits, such as new or smaller bank customers in developing countries. With regard to banks and the practice to drop smaller clients in less transparent markets, this is the so-called de-risking or unbanking problem) (Lowery and Ramachandran, 2015). This means anti-corruption risk management can itself be risky. From an organisational perspective, there is concern related to a potential straightjacketing of organisational flexibility and creativity when anti-corruption leads to excessive rules and over-codified processes and to a loss of diversity in organisational form, when all companies seek to adopt the same compliance and reporting standards without customising them, and when comparative scoring and ranking exercises force them to fall in line.

One may or may not agree with these criticisms and the weight of the empirical evidence may render some more plausible than others. Yet, they all offer valuable food for thought when designing appropriate corporate anti-corruption diagnostics, policies and systems.

24.5   Outlook – Corporate Anti-Corruption and Corporate Sustainability

Tackling corruption has evolved into an integrated and critical part of the overall corporate sustainability agenda. Corruption at the government–business interface undermines corporate compliance with the law and undermines government in the public interest and the rule of law more broadly. It therefore violates a fundamental responsibility of business to society, irrespective of whether one subscribes to a narrow shareholder or more expansive stakeholder model for the company. Corruption between or inside the company destroys fair and competitive markets and diminishes the capability of a far-flung business corporation to effectively execute on other corporate sustainability aims. At a practical level, anti-corruption is a well-established dimension in sustainability assessments and related scoring methodologies and reporting frameworks. And the evolution of corporate anti-corruption trends and programming is closely interlinked with the development trajectory of corporate sustainability. Corporate anti-corruption efforts have moved from a narrow project of doing no harm and avoiding damage to a more ambitious agenda of playing a proactive role in collective action initiatives to promote systemic integrity (Wedel, 2012), to accept responsibilities for anti-corruption across the value chain and to account for the performance in this area in a much more public and reflective way. At the same time, and just like in the broader sustainability arena, many problems remain and new challenges arise. Meaningful enforcement for corporate anti-corruption laws and internal compliance measures is a challenge. Shallow box-ticking compliance with anti-corruption measures – for example, the mere confirmation that a code of conduct exists or a training was carried out, without any information on scope and follow-up – is as much of a problem as shallow application of environmental ambitions that slip into greenwashing.

And impact is still inconclusive. Some forms of corruption at the private–public interface appear on average to be on a modest downward trend. For example, fewer companies across the world report that they feel pressured to pay bribes to tax inspectors, but there is huge variation, and the pace of decline is so slow that it will take another three decades until less than 5 per cent of firms in the average country will be affected (Anderson, 2020). Meanwhile, big corporate corruption scandals keep on surfacing everywhere. And new risks are on the horizon. Crypto-currencies and options for strong anonymity in the Dark Net have the potential to put money laundering on steroids. Crisis situations, such as the onset of the COVID-19 pandemic, amplify corruption risks when supply chains are disrupted, procurements are expedited and large financial support packages are on offer. Perhaps the biggest challenge is how corporations can navigate with integrity political landscapes that exhibit in many places increasingly polarised, populist and autocratic tendencies, as well as business environments that are more politicised and less open.

To forge a successful path ahead in this difficult terrain also requires recalibrating the ethical compass that guides the overall direction of travel. And it is here where the themes of corporate integrity, sustainability and anti-corruption link up in perhaps the most inspiring and productive way.

We started with the common definition of corruption as the abuse of entrusted power for private gain. Revisiting this definition from the vantage point of a fuller notion of responsible corporate citizenship and corporate sustainability suggests approaching 'entrusted power' from a broader stakeholder perspective and assessing its 'abuse' against the social licence to operate and the duties of responsible corporate citizenship. This means corporate anti-corruption efforts can no longer be anchored in a narrow legalistic commitment to comply with laws as imperfect as they might be. Instead, a commitment by business to integrity will have to be rooted in a commitment to not abuse the social licence to operate. Practically, this will require businesses to scrutinise several grey-zone issues that fall outside the purview of classic corruption as bribery. This includes, for example, taking a hard look at whether a company uses its enormous lobbying resources in responsible ways that do not violate fundamental principles of political equality; or whether it exercises its enormous flexibility in arranging its tax matters in ways that do not violate fundamental principles of societal fairness.

These are not easy conversations and there are no easy answers, but the growing salience and public emphasis on a holistic notion of corporate sustainability makes this conversation increasingly inevitable. A strong commitment by business to anti-corruption and corporate integrity is not just about curbing abuse of entrusted power for private gain, but also about activating the use of entrusted power for shared value.

24.6   Chapter Summary

Corruption is frequently referred to as a central challenge for business and society. Yet, the term is very broad and the anti-corruption landscape is very diverse and messy. This chapter hopes to provide some orientation and cut a path through this seemingly impenetrable thicket. Defining corruption as 'abuse of entrusted power for private gain' provides a good starting point and helps us to think through different types and shapes of corruption, as well as the many harms that it can produce, including for business.

At the same time, the chapter sought to highlight that a critical and cautious approach is warranted. A rigid notion of corruption may privilege a particular Northern-centric neoliberal agenda. And a flourishing anti-corruption industry may struggle at times to reconcile the quest for the most appropriate and effective strategies with the objective to preserve and expand the lucrative business opportunities in this area. For the broader anti-corruption governance landscape, we have provided a brief big picture overview of key actors and milestone legislations, and then described the major building blocks for corporate integrity systems from a company perspective.

Three messages stand out (see Figure 24.3): Corruption is important, and a persistent challenge for businesses everywhere. A good response requires working

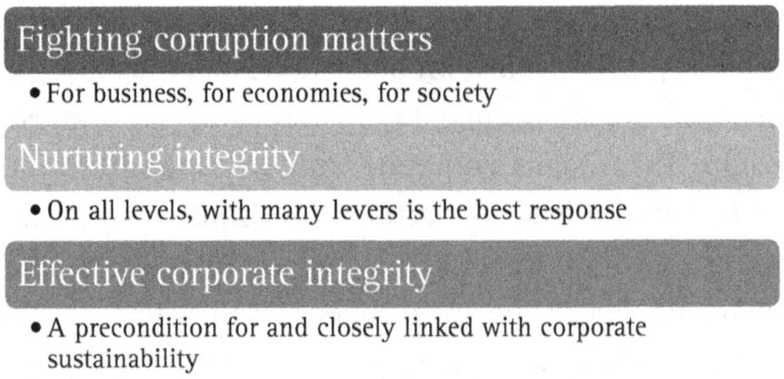

Fighting corruption matters
- For business, for economies, for society

Nurturing integrity
- On all levels, with many levers is the best response

Effective corporate integrity
- A precondition for and closely linked with corporate sustainability

Figure 24.3 Key messages of this chapter: corruption matters, nurture integrity and ensure effective corporate integrity

more broadly on nurturing cultures of integrity. And effective corporate anti-corruption is closely linked with and a basic ingredient for corporate sustainability.

CHAPTER QUESTIONS

1. How can corruption be defined? How do companies come into the picture?
2. What is corruption governance? What types of stakeholders are involved and what dynamics shape its development?
3. How are insights from social psychology and sociology informing our understanding of corruption and how do these insights shape the business response to it?
4. What major concerns and shortcomings are being raised about the way businesses do anti-corruption?
5. How does anti-corruption in the business sector relate to corporate sustainability? Give some practical examples.

Case Study: *Corruption at Siemens*
Available from Cambridge University Press at www.cambridge.org/rasche2

FURTHER RESOURCES

Readings

- Hansen, H. K., Christensen, L. T. and Flyverbom, M. (2015). Logics of Transparency in Late Modernity, special issue of *European Journal of Social Theory*, 18(2), 1–114.

This special issue provides a critical analysis of the transparency debates and movements so central to current anti-corruption efforts.

- Zinnbauer, D., Dobson, R. and Despota, K. (Eds.). (2009). *Global Corruption Report 2009: Corruption and the Private Sector.* Cambridhe: Cambridge University Press.

  A comprehensive collection of contributions on all aspects of analysing and responding to corruption in the business sector.

Various media

- Basel Institute on Governance, https://baselgovernance.org/.

  A research centre with interesting work streams that include, among others, compliance, financial crimes and collective business initiatives in anti-corruption.

- Healy, P. and Djordjija, P. (2012). Fighting Corruption at Siemens, Harvard Business School Multimedia/Video Case, March.

  This multimedia case study provides more details on the Siemens scandal.

- Stephenson, M. (ongoing): The Global Anticorruption Blog, https://globalanticorruptionblog.com/.

  Updated daily, searchable and run from Harvard Law School, this blog offers excellent discussions of a wide range of current corruption issues and developments.

- U4 Anti-Corruption Resource Centre, www.u4.no/.

  A repository of up-to-date anti-corruption research compiled by the Ch. Michelsen Institute Norway.

25 International Development and Corporate Sustainability

AFUA OWUSU-KWARTENG AND SARAH L. JACK[*]

LEARNING OBJECTIVES

- Understand what development encompasses.
- Discuss the role of business in development work.
- Reflect on the impact of business activities on development outcomes.
- Identify the relationship between sustainability and development.
- Identify the conditions under which core business and societal interests are best aligned.

25.1 Introduction

Development studies is a multidisciplinary subject that focuses on the evolution of nations from political, cultural, geographical and socio-economic perspectives. The term 'development' generally represents the process of continuous change in different aspects of the human society. What counts as development is usually extensive, and can include structural transformation, human development, democratic participation and improved governance, and environmental sustainability.

Historically, development studies have focused on developing countries, which have often been referred to as the 'Third World', the 'Global South' or 'developing economies'. Development studies primarily emerged as an academic discipline during the late part of the twentieth century amid growing concerns for developing countries that were struggling to establish themselves in the postcolonial era. It is therefore the shared experience that developing countries have with colonialism, and their desire to advance after the colonial period has ended, that motivates development studies to remain focused on these countries. However, the strong

[*] Funding: This project was supported by the UKRI Collective Fund award UKRI GCRF RECIRCULATE: Driving eco-innovation in Africa: Capacity-building for a safe circular water economy, Grant Ref.: ES/P010857/1.

attention of development studies on developing countries does not mean that the scope and concerns of the field are limited to these countries alone. The issues that development studies seek to address extend beyond developing countries to include the so-called 'developed countries/economies' or 'First World' or 'Global North' countries. For example, most developed countries face challenges with high consumption levels and high carbon dioxide emissions, which not only affects them, but also impacts on developing countries through the global environmental effects of the emissions. Again, both developing and developed countries experienced and were impacted by the COVID-19 pandemic. This has further raised attention to how 'development' and improvement of societies are also a concern for so-called 'developed societies' (see, e.g., IMF, 2020). As the socio-economic issues in Global North countries are equally associated with the concerns of development studies, it is clear that all countries need 'development', in the broadest sense of the word.

The development studies discourse describes the range of projects, schemes, programmes and initiatives that are focused on improving the human society as 'development interventions'. Development interventions are varied and involve a wide range of actors. Recently, the narrative of development agendas recognises the private sector as being integral to the achievement of the global goals. Development thinkers are especially calling on businesses: (1) to be interventional and intentional in their investment decisions; and (2) to give greater attention to the development impact of their activities. In response to such development calls, we see the Coca-Cola Company, for instance, partnering with the Alternative Indigenous Development Foundation Incorporated (AIDFI), a Philippines-based social enterprise, to implement the Blastik Project (see Manila Bulletin, 2021). Specifically, Coca-Cola, through its Coca-Cola Foundation, provided the financial resources needed to scale up the Blastik Project, after AIDFI's successful pilot of a village-scale plastic recycling centre. By funding the Blastik project to help plastic waste reduction as well as create jobs for local communities, we can conclude that Coca-Cola is looking to engage with development work.

While engaging the private sector in development work is admirable, businesses are also known for protecting their own interests. So, then, how can the private sector support the provision of public goods? Can businesses engage in inclusive and sustainable development as current development agendas champion? These are important questions for business and management students to reflect on, especially for individuals who appreciate the idea that economic growth may be slow to benefit the most disadvantaged, and also that growth should be sustainable to achieve long-term development goals.

In this chapter, we examine the role and contribution of business in the attainment of development outcomes, primarily from the perspective of developing countries. The discussion will focus on both the intentional and unintentional ways in which the private sector has influenced development in various contexts.

We begin the chapter by explaining the concept of development and offering a brief history on development studies. In this section, we also discuss some of the notable criticisms against the development field. Next, we will review the ways in which businesses, through their corporate sustainability agendas, have supported or undermined development goals. We provide explicit key case studies to underline the impact of business activities on development outcomes such as gender (in) equality, poverty reduction, democracy promotion and climate change adaptation. In addition, we will discuss how core business can be best aligned with societal interests to achieve development objectives.

25.2   What Is Development?

The term 'development' is relatively broad and vague. The concept has been associated with diverse meanings, interpretations and theories from various scholars, including Todaro and Smith (2003) and Amartya Sen (1999). For example, Todaro and Smith (2003) define development as 'a multi-dimensional process that involves major changes in social structures, popular attitudes, and national institutions, as well as the acceleration of economic growth, reduction of inequality, and eradication of absolute poverty' (17). Their view suggests that development is about restructuring social systems and improving the livelihoods of people through increased economic growth. Amartya Sen (1999), on the other hand, perceives development as 'the removal of various types of unfreedoms that leave people with little choice and little opportunity of exercising their reasoned agency' (xii). For Sen (1999), development is essentially about gaining freedom from definite obstacles, such as poor economic opportunities, repressive states and poverty, that constrain people from achieving their full capabilities. To an extent, both Amartya Sen (1999) and Todaro and Smith's (2003) definitions of development share some similarities regarding the need to eradicate poverty and to improve the economic well-being of people. Interestingly, their ideas of development differ from Reyes (2001), who understands development as 'a social condition within a nation, in which the authentic needs of its population are satisfied by the rational and sustainable use of natural resources and systems' (109). Reyes' (2001) definition of development highlights the need to be judicious about how we utilise the resources available, while attempting to meet people's needs.

These different definitions draw attention to the fact that the concept of development encompasses several components (i.e., physical, economic, environmental, social and demographic). In addition, they implicitly show that there can be implications for the kind of definition one chooses to align with. For example, if one agrees with Todaro and Smith's (2003) explanation of development, then it is possible that such a person may tackle development from a political and economic perspective, as compared to someone following Reyes's (2001) definition, whose primary concern is about environmental sustainability.

Overall, we can see that development is an inherently multidimensional and complex process, involving multiple stakeholders working at different levels to bring about change in the socio-economic conditions of people and societies, especially those that have less favourable conditions. In simple terms, development is bringing about socio-economic change that empowers people to achieve their human potential. Further, it is important to recognise that development has a contextual character – in the sense that people in different contexts can have different understandings of development. So, for instance, *a good and decent life* could be interpreted as 'zero hunger' to a person living in Sub-Saharan Africa, whereas to another person in Europe, this might be 'access to good healthcare'. What this example emphasises is that the nature and extent of development varies considerably across countries and regions. When we understand that development is context-specific, we begin to appreciate the fact that individuals within the same region, country or even household can hold divergent perspectives about development. Moreover, what counts as development changes over time.

In terms of conception and implementation, development can be large-scale and 'top-down' or small-scale and 'bottom-up' (Sanga et al., 2021). We use the notion of top-down and bottom-up to describe how development projects and programmes are organised, and the level at which different stakeholders (e.g., government, local communities, NGOs) participate in the development process. For example, the Three Gorges Dam in China is one of the world's biggest hydropower complex projects (see Gleick, 2009, for further reading), and exemplifies a top-down development initiative. Funded by both domestic and international commercial banks, including the China Development Bank, this dam was mainly constructed to help increase China's electricity through hydroelectric power, and to protect farmlands belonging to local farmers within the Hubei province from flooding. The Three Gorges Dam represents a top-down development initiative because of the relatively higher input the project funders had in the design, implementation and management processes, as compared to the beneficiaries (in this case, the farmers and the local community). Because the beneficiaries were less involved in the development process leading to the construction of the Three Gorges Dam, instead of supporting the local farmers, the project led to their displacement and impoverishment (Wilmsen et al., 2011). This does not suggest that development projects that employ a top-down approach are damaging, because there are several advantages to them. In fact, top-down development approaches can be advantageous in the implementation of complex projects such as the Three Gorges Dam because, sometimes, local communities can overcommit at the project-design stage to plans that may not be realistic (Mukherji, 2013).

With development approaches that are bottom-up, the communities are consulted in the project identification period and throughout the various stages of the project, including the monitoring and evaluation. An example of a bottom-up development project is 'Empowering Girls through Sport and Play in Senegal' (see Right to Play, 2021), which was organised by a not-profit organisation called Right to Play, as part of their development activities to advance gender equality in and through sports. This project is classified as a bottom-up development initiative because the organisation had an objective to empower local actors, and as a result, provided them with equal opportunities to participate in the formulation and implementation of the intervention. The key advantage of the bottom-up approach is its potential to exploit local information to design projects that are needed locally and to distribute its benefits to those who need them the most. Also, by getting communities involved in choosing how funds might be spent and monitoring the progress of projects they choose, bottom-up development approaches can foster local accountability mechanisms. Employing a bottom-up approach is therefore advantageous, to the degree that it allows development interventions to reflect the desires of the project beneficiaries. However, this advantage may not be realised if sub-groups within the community have the power to deprive a project's targeted sub-groups from enjoying the benefits. Also, because bottom-up approaches are more participatory in nature, they can be very slow and labour-intensive to implement, and can sometimes lose momentum along the way.

25.2.1   Development as an Academic Discipline

At its heart, development studies seek to improve the lives of people. As an academic discipline, development studies focus on issues of poverty, resource distribution, gender equality and the like. The discipline was coined in the early 1950s and 1970s after World War II, to transform the economies of countries that had been colonised by Britain, France, Portugal and other European powers (Leys, 1996; Sumner and Tribe, 2008). At the time, it was believed that countries at a 'backward stage' could advance by following the West's guidelines on modernisation (Sylvester, 1999; Bodruzic, 2015). Development studies was therefore birthed from a decolonisation process, as newly independent states sought for policy prescriptions to 'catch up' economically with industrialised nations. For their part, underdeveloped countries were mandated to accept massive support from developed countries, create a thriving democratic environment and make a rational use of their local resources.

In the past, this feature of development studies was guided by modernisation theory, where the state is the principal agent in monitoring development, economic growth and macroeconomic policies. During this period, industrialisation, structural societal change and economic growth were the defining aspects of development. Over the years, modernisation theory has been criticised by dependency theorists for not considering Sen's (1999) view of development regarding freedoms and self-esteem (Mensah, 2019). According to dependency theorists, industrialisation in developed countries rather subjects developing countries to underdevelopment, because often, developed countries tend to exploit the economic surplus of developing countries (Agbebi and Virtanen, 2017). Besides dependency theory, there have been several other theories (e.g., the world systems and globalisation theories) also critiquing the concept of development that modernisation theory proposes (for further reading, see Reyes, 2001).

A key argument against modernisation theory's idea of development as industrialisation is that, although industrialisation may bring about economic growth, another concern is the environmental sustainability of the development that economic growth ushers. The promotion of economic development through industrialisation has seen many investors creating factories in wetlands or destroying forests in order to plant sugarcane, for example, much to the detriment of our environment. Based on the 1987 Brundtland Report's definition of sustainable development, this kind of development, whereby the environment is destroyed for profitmaking, may meet the needs of the present by creating jobs, but the associated impact (such as climate change, soil erosion and global warming) also compromises the needs of future generations. In essence, economic growth is not a sufficient condition for development.

This realisation of the need to protect and preserve our world has been influential in the spread of current global development concepts and paradigms, including 'sustainability' and 'sustainable development' (Mensah, 2019), with development thinkers and practitioners now increasingly emphasising issues of sustainability and climate change, human rights, and local and global inequality, particularly gender inequality. These new features have added to the complexity of the development enterprise because for development to be effective in its interventions, development frameworks must now capture the complexities of the economic, social, ecological and cultural contexts that are specific to social groups, as well as the experiences of these groups with climate change impacts. This has also meant that, nowadays, if you want to engage in development work, you must be careful in the kind of approaches you adopt and utilise.

That said, it is worth emphasising that some of the fundamental changes that have taken place in development studies in these last few years have been led by renowned development economists such as Amartya Sen, Paul Streeten and Ravi Kanbur, to name but a few scholars (Sumner, 2006). The economic backgrounds and works of these scholars, especially Amartya Sen (1999), have been useful in shaping the evolution of development studies into a multi-disciplinarity, and away from purely economic approaches. Amartya Sen's (1999) work on *Development as Freedom*, for example, offered valuable insights about the need to redefine and broaden the concept of development to include freedom, capabilities and well-being. A major contribution that Sen has made to the development discipline is showing that measuring a multidimensional concept such as development with one single (economic) dimension is inaccurate. Sen's redefined concept of development has influenced the World Bank in the adoption of participatory development and community-driven development as its main operational strategy for poverty reduction. Essentially, the contributions of these highly reputed development economists have been instrumental in reshaping the field, in terms of development scholars moving away from using economic indicators as the sole measurement for quality of life, to instead a shift to using more nuanced and holistic indicators of well-being.

In addition to these scholarly contributions, the COVID-19 pandemic has created an awareness among development scholars and practitioners that, perhaps, it is time the field redirected its primary focus on just developing countries to a much broader scope. The pandemic has accentuated the case for understanding contemporary development challenges through a global, rather than a narrower, international development paradigm (Oldekop et al., 2020). Whereas 'international' development focuses on inter-state relations, often via aid, and on problems *of* and *in* the Global South, a broader global development approach should consider processes and problems that cover all countries, including those in the Global North. The COVID-19 pandemic has 'highlighted the falsity of any assumption that the Global North has all the expertise and solutions to tackle global challenges, and has further highlighted the need for multi-directional learning and transformation in all countries towards a more sustainable and equitable world' (Oldekop et al., 2020: 1). In other words, the pandemic has shown that, today, development studies face a very different context from the mid-twentieth century when the field emerged, and it is important that the field widens its international scope beyond developing countries.

25.2.2   Four Distinctive Features of Development Studies

As an academic discipline, development studies has four key features that make it distinct from other programmes (see the overview in Figure 25.1):

1. Development studies has a prime focus on the interest and realities of developing countries. This implies that when development researchers must examine the role and impact of transnational or multinational corporations, for instance, their focus is to understand how the activities of such corporations impact on the developing world.
2. Development studies is interdisciplinary and is built on the notion that development issues are complex. This means that development thinkers whose intention is to understand the developing world and its position in the world economic and political system must acquire collective insights from different academic disciplines.
3. Development studies encourages analysis at the international, national and subnational (regional or local) levels. This suggests that development interventions or initiatives can range from an International Monetary Fund (IMF) programme and private investment in Africa (i.e., at the international level) to a development support programme to a class in a Pakistani village (i.e., at the local level).
4. Development studies is simultaneously theoretical, policy-oriented and empirical. Unlike other academic disciplines, the cross-disciplinary nature of development studies gives it a wide-ranging scope and orientation towards theoretical, empirical and policy issues.

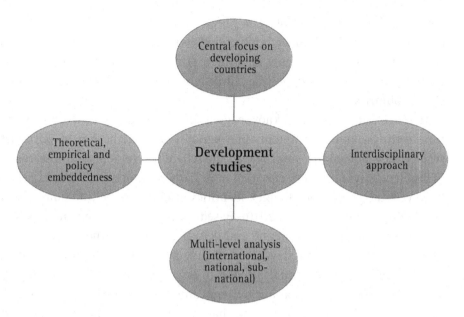

Figure 25.1 The four distinctive features of development studies
Source: Adapted from Loxley (2004).

25.2.3   Criticisms of Development Studies

While development studies is a field of theory and practice that has a good academic and political standing, it also has many internal debates concerning its focus and approaches of achieving development. First, development studies has been criticised for its reduced geographical focus on developing countries, especially Africa. Dambisa Moyo (2009), for instance, argues that Africa's overreliance on aid is because of the unending aid flows to this continent. She and several other scholars believe that the structures of multilateral lending agencies like the IMF and the World Bank are supposed to recolonise previously decolonised countries like Africa (see Abeselom, 2018, on this debate).

The world's experience of the COVID-19 pandemic has further augmented the criticism against development studies' narrowed attention on problems *of* and *in* the Global South. It is now becoming increasingly visible through the COVID-19 pandemic that the so-called 'developed countries' are also in need of 'development'. For example, several reports have shown that many developed countries, including the Netherlands, are struggling to bring the latest wave of COVID-19 infections under control. Similar to most developing countries that are challenged with an efficient healthcare system, reports indicate that the soaring demand for COVID-19 testing in the Netherlands, combined with a shortage of health workers to book them, is pushing the country's health services to its limits (see Moses, 2021). Furthermore, the governments of other developed countries such as Belgium, Austria, Croatia and Italy are dealing with citizen protests because of measures they have put in place to prevent the spread of COVID-19. Most of these protests have involved police interventions with tear gas and water cannons (BBC, 2021b). These ongoing events have increased the criticisms against development studies, as they highlight the limits of the 'development' within Global North countries.

Moreover, developmental knowledge is difficult to apply across diverse sociocultural settings, and in different time periods. During the era of positivist social science, development theory took an un-self-reflexive approach towards its mode of problem-solving, in the sense that most early development thinkers believed that there were no people, no complex identities or mindsets in 'traditional' or 'modern' developing countries (Black, 2010). Based on this logic, development studies gave itself fewer channels to generate and deliver the types of help that local communities might need. Even today, the discipline still makes flawed assessments about the kind of support it should provide to local people. Many times, development studies fail to recognise that one system cannot be adopted by all countries due to their diverse historical and cultural backgrounds. Such shortcomings justify the importance of development scholars and practitioners involving beneficiary communities in the design and implementation of interventions. It is vital to recognise that developmental achievements are notoriously difficult to sustain and, *in extremis*, developmental interventions *can be* severely damaging to the communities they are engaged with, whether by omission or commission (Black, 2010).

Finally, because development studies is still a field whose money and agendas influence the world, there is often an undeniable trend for institutions (especially those focused on development issues, such as the United Nations) to operate according to a market logic. Because the discipline operates in this way, an individual or organisation could face challenges in accessing resources and funding for research that contradicts the Sustainable Development Goals (SDGs), for example, or even for research that tries to assess the SDGs more critically with regard to their relevance and impact. This implies that neoliberal thinking has a significant influence on the research agenda of development studies, which makes it increasingly difficult for the discipline to maintain a critical research focus.

25.3   Understanding the Role of Business in Development Work

Beyond the criticisms, development studies work has made massive contributions to education, health, gender equality, individual and community economic empowerment. Development has been emancipatory in both its meaning and effects, creating at its best new and unprecedented opportunities for historically marginalised people and communities. Even under deficient development regimes, countries like Korea and the Philippines have made significant strides with their gross domestic product (GDP) per capita, literacy and life expectancy. These emancipatory possibilities have been made possible through strategic top-down policies and institutional structures associated with official development agencies like the IMF, the United Nations and the World Bank. The emancipatory sense of development has led to the explosive growth of development studies programmes at universities in many parts of the world, the flourishing of development non-governmental organisations (NGOs) and, more recently, the mounting enthusiasm of the private sector to participate in development work.

In September 2015, the UN General Assembly adopted the 2030 Agenda for Sustainable Development, along with a set of Sustainable Development Goals (SDGs) aiming to eliminate poverty, overcome inequality and tackle environmental degradation in all countries. In contrast to the Millennium Development Goals (MDGs), the SDGs identify the private sector as a key stakeholder in the new global development agenda. For instance, in 2012, the then-UN Secretary-General Ban Ki-moon invited businesses to participate in a high-level panel to advise on the global development framework.

The UN Global Compact website also writes that 'fulfilling these ambitions will take an unprecedented effort by all sectors in society – and business must play a very important role in the process' (see UN Global Compact, n.d.a). The SDGs clearly bring a lot of optimism around the role of businesses in development. But how can businesses fulfil this important role that is expected of them? When it comes to businesses' contribution to development work, there are several ways to achieving this. For instance, businesses can support development through their economic resources, as we see from the case of Coca-Cola and the Blastik project in the Philippines. Businesses can also contribute to development by creating jobs to help reduce unemployment. In the United States, for example, Walgreen Boots Alliance designed and implemented early career programmes, and also provided career support and training to address the high levels of unemployment among young people in Chicago (Jones and Comfort, 2019). Through their expertise in analysing different markets' potentials, businesses can assist development professionals to develop context-specific development interventions. At the same time, businesses can contribute to development through their repeatability and reproducibility (R&R) knowhow, technological expertise, production and scaling experience of businesses to help improve development interventions using technology and innovation. Nonetheless, a significant way in which businesses can contribute to development is by practising corporate sustainability as part of their core business operations.

However, we must understand that the role of the private sector in development is quite complex. First, there is a distinction between 'private sector development' and engaging the 'private sector *for* development' (Byiers and Rosengren, 2012: 9, emphasis in the original). The former basically focuses on the domestic economies in developing countries, whereby their governments design and implement policies to encourage economic transformation through business investments, productivity growth, business expansion and employment. The latter relates to *activities* for development, including those that encourage productive business investment and leverages on private-sector *finance* for development (Pauw, 2015). The 'private sector *for* development' agenda therefore recognises businesses as a key enabler and implementer of development. In fact, it demands a change in how businesses do business – that is, businesses are required to move beyond financial contributions, to instead incorporate poverty eradication and sustainability in their programmes. With this understanding, we use the next sub-section to particularly highlight how businesses can engage in corporate sustainability to help accomplish the 'private sector *for* development' agenda.

25.3.1   Corporate Sustainability and Development

In the past two decades, there has been an increasing awareness among investors, consumers, governments, interest groups and the media about the environmental, social and economic impacts of business activities (Jones and Comfort, 2019). This growing consciousness about business impacts has led to a rise of corporate sustainability movements which are seeking accountability from businesses. It is thus now common to see many companies and organisations embedding sustainability considerations in their investment decisions and activities. Several companies have developed sustainability agendas as an integral component of their business strategies and policies; with most of these targeted at a range of environmental, social and economic issues, including climate change, water and energy conservation, waste management, the conservation of natural resources, employee health and well-being, diversity and equality of opportunity, responsible sourcing and local economic development (Jones and Comfort, 2019).

In general, the efforts and strategies that businesses put in place to promote sustainable development are what we term as corporate sustainability. The idea of corporate sustainability is derived from the concept of sustainable development, and embodies the strategy of business to deliver goods and services in a manner that is both environmentally sustainable and supports its economic growth. Corporate sustainability concerns the different roles that companies can play in meeting the sustainable development agenda, whereby businesses prioritise long-term growth through sustainable methods as opposed to focusing on short-term financial gains.

The concept of corporate sustainability is based on the triple bottom line (TBL), which is basically a model that seeks to balance the economic (profit), social (people) and environmental (planet) priorities of companies. Fundamentally, the TBL model posits that instead of making an impact on just one bottom line, businesses should generate impact on three levels: profit, people and the planet. According to the TBL framework, companies looking to promote sustainability will prioritise: (1) economic models that accumulate and use natural and financial capital sustainably; (2) environmental models that address biodiversity and ecological integrity; and (3) social models that improve political, cultural, religious, health and educational systems, and continually ensure human dignity and well-being (Mensah, 2019).

In terms of acting sustainably, the UN Global Compact (2014) suggests that companies must do the following five things: (1) operate in alignment with the universal principles of human rights, labour, environment and anti-corruption; (2) look beyond their own walls and take actions that support the societies around them; (3) commit to sustainability at the highest level through their leadership; (4) report annually on their corporate sustainability efforts and progress; and (5) engage locally where they have a presence.

Similar to corporate social responsibility (CSR), companies have several reasons for engaging in corporate sustainability and choosing to act sustainably. One of the most common explanations that has been stated is the so-called business case – where corporations implement sustainability policies and practices because they believe that it positively influences their financial bottom line (Rasche et al., 2017). This means that companies practise corporate sustainability to publicly emphasise and demonstrate their commitment to sustainability as a strategy to differentiate themselves from their competitors, and to enhance their brand reputation. Apart from increasing their financial value, firms also adopt corporate sustainability principles simply because they feel that it is the 'right thing to do'. This motivation falls under what we describe as the moral case for corporate sustainability. Some corporations may also engage in corporate sustainability activities as a way of compliance, especially if they happen to operate in places where there exist strong and well-enforced legal regulations. Further, some firms may choose to act sustainably because certain actors (e.g., NGOs, the media, investors) are continually monitoring their behaviour to ensure that they are compliant to the principles of sustainable development. For some businesses also, their efforts at corporate sustainability are mainly because other firms have done the same (coercive and mimetic isomorphism).

In looking to reconcile business and development, we use the next set of case studies to illustrate how businesses can impact on development outcomes such as poverty reduction, gender equality, democracy promotion and climate change adaptation. Specifically, the cases help to highlight how businesses, through their presence, decisions and actions, can directly and indirectly promote or undermine sustainable development.

BOX 25.1: Section overview of the role of business in development work

Summary Points...

The role of firms in development is to do business responsibly, and to pursue opportunities that can help solve societal challenges through business innovation and collaboration. In the business and development literature, there is a distinction between:

- **Private sector development** – refers to how governments in developing countries design and implement policies to encourage economic transformation through business investments, productivity growth, business expansion and employment.
- **Engaging the private sector *for* development** – refers to *activities* for development, including those that encourage productive business investment and leverages on private-sector *finance* for development.

Corporate Sustainability and Development:

Corporate sustainability refers to all the efforts and strategies that businesses put in place to promote sustainable development. The concept is derived from the concept of sustainable development, and represents business strategy to deliver goods and services in a manner that is both environmentally sustainable and supports its economic growth.

Reasons to account for why firms choose to act sustainably:

- Business case
- Moral case
- Compliance
- Coercive and mimetic isomorphism

According to the TBL framework, companies looking to promote sustainability will prioritise:

(i)   Economic models that accumulate and use natural and financial capital sustainably

(ii) Environmental models that address biodiversity and ecological integrity

(iii) Social models that improve political, cultural, religious, health and educational systems, and continually ensure human dignity and wellbeing

To act sustainably, the UN Global Compact (2014) suggests that companies must do the following five things:

- Operate in alignment with the universal principles of human rights, labour, environment and anti-corruption;

- Look beyond their own walls and take actions that support the societies around them;
- Companies must commit to sustainability at the highest level through their leadership;
- Report annually on their corporate sustainability efforts and progress;
- Engage locally where they have a presence.

25.4   Case Studies on Business Impact on Development Outcomes

25.4.1   Poverty Reduction

Poverty severely affects every country's socio-economic development. It not only determines the quality of life of individuals, but it also impacts on the general well-being of a society. When it comes to the ways in which businesses can contribute to reducing poverty, and for that matter promoting development, Vietnam offers a remarkable story.

During the 1990s, Vietnam experienced a substantial and comprehensive socio-economic transformation, which was partly linked to the inflow of foreign direct investment (FDI) (Hemmer and Hoa, 2002). However, the change that occurred in Vietnam was not an overnight success. Its roots can be traced back to the ambitious structural and institutional reforms the Vietnamese government carried out in 1986, which involved promoting the domestic private and foreign sectors, liberalising prices and de-collectivising agriculture. Part of the government's strategies included creating a legal policy on FDI in 1987. This new policy opened the economy to foreign investors, thereby boosting the country's inward investment.

The capital inflows of FDI into Vietnam were extremely significant, such that registered capital of FDI increased from US$371 million in 1988 to US$8,497 million in 1996. In contrast to other developing countries (4.9 per cent in China, 2.2 per cent in Indonesia, 5.2 per cent in Malaysia, 2.4 per cent in Thailand and 1.5 per cent in the Philippines), the implemented FDI levels of Vietnam were remarkably high (7.2 per cent of GDP in 1997). By the end of 2001, Vietnam had around 3,000 foreign investment projects under operation, with registered capital of US$32, 415 million in total. In 2001, FDI contributed up to 30 per cent of Vietnam's investment (10.5 per cent of GDP in 1999) and 21 per cent of export turnover, creating 300,000 direct jobs (Hemmer and Hoa, 2002). The increasing growth that occurred in Vietnam gradually transitioned the country both from a socialist to a market economy, and from an agricultural to an industrial economy.

25.4.1.1   Business FDI and Poverty Reduction

How did FDI become a key ingredient in Vietnam's socio-economic transformation? Well, first, FDI does not automatically reduce income inequality. Also, FDI does not deal with all dimensions of poverty. However, FDI promotes growth, which subsequently reduces income poverty. Specifically, FDI inflows lead to higher per capita GDP, an increased economic growth rate and higher productivity growth. Governments need this economic growth to be able to fund public goods such as water, education and healthcare. This means that FDI is an essential source of capital that complements domestic capital for development. In essence, because growth is the single-most important factor affecting poverty reduction, the FDI of businesses then acts as a channel to achieving that goal.

Often, FDI works through factors such as technology transfer, market expansion, employment creation and innovation in helping to fight against poverty. Foreign capital is only productive, however, when certain favourable conditions have been put in place by the host countries of businesses. Some of these conditions include: a sufficient high level of human capital; complementarity between domestic investment and FDI; a high savings rate and open trade regimes; and a high level of absorptive capacity in a recipient economy. In the case of Vietnam, the country had many of these positive conditions for businesses to operate. The country also had economic and political stability, an untouched large market, a potentially growing economy, hard and competent workers, and low-wage labour costs.

In general, Vietnam provides a good case for businesses' FDI as one of the most effective tools in poverty reduction. On the other hand, it also highlights the relevant role of quality policies and institutions in enforcing business regulation for development. Effective utilisation of capital inflows to raise growth is not possible without appropriate regulatory controls (UNCTAD, 2013). Regulation is therefore critical in understanding both the determinants and impacts of capital flows. All these factors are attractive to both investors aiming at the domestic market or wanting to export. A well-regulated market that is favourable for doing business is relevant to ameliorate poverty in most developing contexts (Dwumfour, 2020).

In the next section, we provide a case study to demonstrate how the absence of business regulations can negatively impact on the attainment of the SDGs on gender equality.

25.4.2   Gender

In the mid-1990s, over 400 women were found murdered in Ciudad Juarez and other neighbouring cities in the state of Chihuahua on the Mexican border (Pearson, 2007). Many of the victims were young women between the ages of 12 and 30, who came from poor neighbourhoods that had substandard housing and other poor services. Through further investigations, it was also found that a significant number of the women were workers in the Ciudad Juarez maquiladora industry, who mostly worked the late shift. Additional investigations exposed that the work-life pattern of the victims involved travelling in unsafe and unprotected areas, either walking or in public or hired transport – which made them very vulnerable to attack. Reports revealed that most of the women disappeared on their way to or from their jobs in the factories, either in early pre-dawn hours or late at night. Findings showed that many of the victims disappeared or were found dead and mutilated after being turned away from their workplace, merely because they had arrived late for their shift.

Interestingly, the management of the export factories in Ciudad Juarez refused to take accountability for what happened outside their factory walls, or the working hours of the factory. Management argued that outside the workplace, the workers were responsible for their own safety and well-being. This meant that the young women were victims of their own circumstances, even when there was a clear link between the murders and the company's activities. What is more interesting is the fact that the Chihuahua state authorities moved slowly on the investigations because they believed that the murdered women were prostitutes – a remark that is popular among those who consider female factory workers as being out of place and out of role. The predictable statements of the factory owners and authorities echo most of the explanations for crimes against women.

25.4.2.1 Business and Gender (In)equality

The case of Ciudad Juarez's maquiladora industry is a good example of the development impact of business activities both nationally and globally. First, it highlights how companies can contribute to gender inequality by downgrading the place and valuation of women workers. At the same time, it reflects a common criticism against engaging the private sector in the development agenda – can businesses be altruistic in the absence of regulations?

In the 1970s, when maquila factories located to Ciudad Juarez and started operating, it was one of the fastest growing cities in Mexico. Ciudad Juarez had a population of about 1 million, and an estimated 60,000 immigrants entering the city every year (Pearson, 2007). The maquila sector alone employed over 25,000 people. At the time of the murders, the physical and environmental infrastructure of the city had deteriorated. Yet, the maquila industry continued to grow. In the business literature, most firms are known to use their corporate sustainability efforts to develop the communities in which they operate. According to the UN Global Compact (2014), the most fundamental contribution a company can make towards achieving societal priorities is to be financially successful *while* upholding a high standard of ethics and treatment of employees, the environment and the community. Through corporate sustainability initiatives, firms can expand access to basic necessities like transport services, infrastructure and secure human and labour rights of citizens. However, this is not the case with the maquila industry. The challenges the women workers faced with transportation, for example, reflects the marginalisation of poor people from entitlements such as utilities, paved roads, adequate police protection, and appropriate and affordable transport. Further, it demonstrates the gendered nature of marginalisation and the vulnerability of women to its consequences. The disconnect between a growing industry and the structural collapse of infrastructure in Ciudad Juarez specifically emphasises a profound stigmatisation and neglect of women's rights by society and the municipality itself. Conversely, the situation represents the failure of businesses to treat the community's well-being as a sustainability goal that is incorporated into the companies' mainline growth strategy and everyday business decision-making.

The UN Global Compact (2014) explicitly mentions that sustainable companies are those that look beyond their own walls and take actions that support the societies around them. For companies that are operating in alignment with the universal principles of human rights, labour, environment and anti-corruption, this would mean taking gender issues into account when designing their organisational and diversity strategies. Yet, many businesses tend to ignore the reasons why they create gendered sustainability policies or even recruit women workers as a central part of their competitive strategy. The narrative of the maquiladora industry shows how companies often engage women workers as a disposable form of labour, and a source of variable capital in the production process that can be used and discarded of easily (Pearson, 2007; Ozkazanc-Pan, 2019). Like the maquiladora industry (and several other companies operating in developing countries), the gendered devaluation of women's work and skills is often seen in how organisations hire and position men in supervisory and technical positions, with women relegated to the lower ranks.

Clearly, a production process that is driven by disposable women's labour contradicts the core ideas about corporate sustainability. Corporate sustainability requires that companies make social investments in the production and reproduction of women's labour power. The deaths of maquila women workers in Mexico highlights the fact that effective and comprehensive corporate sustainability policies and initiatives must extend beyond the factory gate to the population cohort from which corporations recruit women's 'cheap labour'. Rather than implementing narrow and instrumental versions of corporate sustainability initiatives, firms must consider the families and communities of their workers who are dependent on them for their daily and generational reproduction in their policies and initiatives (Ozkazanc-Pan, 2019).

It is important to recognise that companies can have an enormous impact when they decide to tackle sustainability challenges through their core business, mainly because the well-being of workers, communities and the planet is also inextricably tied to the health of the business. By being recognised as a sustainable business, firms can attract and maintain the best workers, as well as increase their corporate reputation. These direct and indirect benefits can in turn translate into financial profits for businesses. So, beyond the moral obligation of companies to implement comprehensive sustainability initiatives, there are also several important reasons for businesses to act sustainably, including the endless advantages it can offer to them.

In the subsequent case studies (i.e., democracy promotion and climate change adaptation), we will discuss some of the efforts that businesses have made to protect their own interests, as well as their operational communities. The case on democracy promotion in South Africa, in particular, reveals how businesses can galvanise support from both local and international actors to maintain their operations.

25.4.3 Democracy Promotion

South Africa became a self-governing dominion of the British Empire in 1910. During this period, only white people had citizenship rights. This was also the time when South Africa was quickly industrialising because of the discovery of gold and diamonds. The Great Depression and World War II, however, shortened South Africa's industrialisation phase, plunging the country into a great economic crisis. In 1948, South Africa ran a general election which was won by the Afrikaner National Party (NP). The NP won mainly because of their promises to improve living conditions, especially for the rural Afrikaans electorate. One of the key political ideologies of the NP was the principle of white minority rule known as 'apartheid' – a system which they used to champion systematic, legislated racial segregation and oppression of all those identified as black, Indian or so-called 'coloured' (people of mixed race).

Before the NP came into power, a group of black South African leaders had formed an alliance in 1912 to establish the African National Congress (ANC), with an aim to defend the political and civil rights of black people in South Africa (Michie and Padayachee, 2019). After the 1948 election, the ANC changed its operations. The ANC started a Defiance Campaign of passive resistance, involving civil disobedience protests against pass laws, curfews and segregation in public facilities. In 1959, some disappointed ANC members separated from the ANC to form another alliance called the Pan Africanist Congress of Azania (PAC). The PAC led a mass demonstration against the Pass Laws system that limited and controlled the movement of black people in South Africa. The PAC also engaged in a series of events to fight against the apartheid regime, many of which resulted in unimaginably aggressive and violent responses (e.g., the Sharpeville massacre of 1960, the Rivonia trial in 1963 and the banning of Mandela) from the apartheid government.

25.4.3.1 Business and Democracy Promotion

For business to survive, the state must function appropriately. Although business may appear to be an unlikely player in a peace process, in South Africa, business was an important catalyst for political transformation, particularly towards the end of apartheid. In 1976, for example, Harry Oppenheimer, who was the CEO of

Anglo-American Corporation (AAC), and Anton Rupert, who was also an Afrikaner business mogul, came together to establish a think tank called Urban Foundation to advocate for reforms to improve the social conditions of black people in urban areas (Smit, 1992; Handley, 2005). Even though the involvement of business in South Africa's transition to democracy started in the 1970s, it became intensified after the 1985 Rubicon speech by the then-Prime Minister P. W. Botha (Wielenga et al., 2021).

The 1985 Rubicon speech was originally supposed to announce major economic and political reforms in South Africa. However, because Botha was not willing to change his position on the apartheid system, he refused to consider making any immediate and major reforms. The speech therefore worsened South Africa's existing economic crisis, leading to continued capital flight, a dropping rand value, trade sanctions and the withdrawal of international business interests from the country. As the apartheid government faced international pressure, businesses operating in South Africa also created an internal conflict resolution 'community' that brought together various political and social forces for meetings, consultations and training at every level of society. The 'community' consisted of labour experts, social activists, clerics, politicians, community leaders and business gurus domestically, as well as practitioners from around the world who supported South Africa in finding a workable solution.

In 1988, the Consultative Business Movement (CBM) was established by Christo Nel, a business consultant who was hired by First National Bank (FNB) director, Chris Ball, to transform attitudes towards race within the bank (Callinicos, 1988). The CBM originally consisted of some twenty businessmen who had the express intention to challenge the NP's propaganda, establish relationships with black leaders and break the 'socio-political logjam' that existed at the time (Wielenga et al., 2021). A tangible result of business's role and contribution in South Africa's transition to democracy was the formation of the Labour Relations Act in 1995. This Act and the 1996 Constitution laid the groundwork for building the kind of society that both employers and labour had been fighting over for decades.

In discussing how businesses can promote democracy, the case of South Africa is unique. For South Africa, the private sector was successful in championing democracy because certain business individuals and groups took 'gutsy' leadership styles. In addition, businesses took a collective approach in pooling resources for a common goal and establishing specific entities to address specific issues. Importantly, during the apartheid era, the South African economy was controlled by six big companies, four of those owned by families, namely, the Oppenheimers (Anglo-American), the Ruperts (Rembrandt), the Gordons (Liberty), and the Menell's and Hersov's (Anglovaal) (Wielenga et al., 2021). These companies owned over 80 per cent of the economy between 1985 and 2004, and, to an extent, it was the huge percentage of the economy that these few companies owned that allowed them to have the influence they did. Moreover, the businesses took a unified approach which empowered them to play a crucial and successful role in South Africa's complex transition to democracy.

In our next case, we describe the commitment and distinct efforts of a notable agri-business firm to maintain resilient businesses and communities in the face of climate change.

25.4.4   Climate Change Adaptation

Many of the carbon emissions affecting the climate are the result of business-driven economic activities. Nevertheless, business activities can also contribute to innovation and solutions to prevent, mitigate and adapt to climate change. Businesses therefore have a crucial role to play in supporting social, ecological and economic resilience to climate change impacts. At the same time, businesses have a responsibility to protect their value chain and serve their customers. To better understand the private sector's complex role in adaptation in developing countries, lessons can be learned from Olam International.

Olam International is a leading agri-business operating in sixty-five countries, including Côte d'Ivoire, Ghana, Nigeria, Uganda, Ecuador, Peru, Indonesia and Tanzania. Olam is renowned for its agricultural activities in cocoa, coffee, cashew, rice and cotton. The company has about 23,000 employees, and supplies food and industrial raw materials to over 13,800 customers worldwide (Olam, 2020a).

Between 2011 and 2014, Olam partnered with the Rainforest Alliance to develop and implement the 'Climate Cocoa Partnership for REDD+ Preparation' project in Ghana. The aim of this project was to tackle Ghana's cocoa industry challenges, especially those concerning cocoa production and deforestation. Agricultural forecasts in previous years had identified that cocoa trees in Ghana were highly susceptible to changes in the seasonal distribution and total volume of rainfall. Using these predictions as a guide, Olam undertook a further risk assessment. The company identified that a shortfall in cocoa yield and quality in Ghana would not only affect its own business operations, but also the communities on which they relied for supply. The assessment also revealed that many Ghanaian cocoa producers were likely to shift to other forms of agriculture. This change could exacerbate deforestation, and ultimately lead to an increase in pests, diseases and forest fires.

Realising that the company's usual producer support programme could not address the identified climate change problems and other resource risks, Olam sought a partnership with Rainforest Alliance (Olam, 2020b). Olam's partnership with Rainforest Alliance is seen as strategic because the objective of Rainforest Alliance mostly seeks to 'ensure the long-term economic health of forest communities through protecting ecosystems, safeguarding the well-being of local communities and improving productivity' (Rainforest Alliance, n.d.). Accordingly, Olam and Rainforest Alliance developed a project centred on sustainable cocoa-growing practices that conserves biodiversity, increases productivity, provides greater long-

Table 25.1 Key insights from case studies on business impact on development outcomes

Development goal	Country	Business contribution
Poverty Reduction	Vietnam	Supporting poverty reduction through FDI
Gender	Mexico	Upholding gender inequality by downgrading the place and valuation of women workers
Democracy Promotion	South Africa	Supporting the transition to a democratic state
Climate Change Adaptation	Ghana	Supporting local farmers with the world's first climate-smart cocoa

term stability to all value chain participants and increases the income of smallholder farmers. The project involved training around 2,000 farmers from thirty-four communities in sustainable cocoa production following the Sustainable Agriculture Network (SAN) standards. The trainings were to help the farmers understand how to build more resilient farming systems and be better prepared to adapt to the impacts of climate change. As part of the project, both farmers and students were also educated on climate change and REDD+ (Reducing Emissions from Deforestation and Forest Degradation, a UN advisory and knowledge partnership). Additionally, the project restored forest areas through the provision of native tree seedlings and protected and restored forests in the target communities.

The case of Olam presented here demonstrates how companies are addressing real-world adaptation challenges in ways that support sustainable development. It also emphasises the private sector's strength in recognising and managing risk, promoting education on sustainable development and creating new employment opportunities – all of which are necessary to maintain resilient businesses and communities in the face of climate change. For businesses in particular, the discovery of marketable solutions and the development of business models to help deal with global challenges such as climate change, water scarcity and unemployment is a huge opportunity for business growth and building new markets. Table 25.1 lists some key insights from case studies discussing business impact on development outcomes.

25.4.5 Aligning Business and Societal Interests for Development

A key lesson from the MDGs was the importance of national and local contexts. Evaluations done on the MDGs highlighted that adapting development approaches to local contexts (especially its socio-cultural aspects) is critical to the success of the development programmes. And so, to best align core business and societal interests for development, the following must be considered:

1. Firms must acknowledge the fact that their presence, decisions and activities can have a long-term influence on people and societies. To support development, therefore, firms must make it a high obligation to act sustainably in all their operations. Being able to recognise and take ownership of the mark they directly and indirectly leave on society is the foremost and important role businesses can play in the development process.

2. Firms must be careful and knowledgeable about the socio-cultural context in which they decide to operate. Culture plays an important role in poverty reduction and all other sustainable development efforts. When firms are well informed about the cultural values of communities, they can undertake development interventions using culturally sensitive approaches.

3. Businesses must be guided by their values and be strategic about which countries to set up in. When companies are guided by a core set of values, it becomes easier for them to make decisions about the kind of development initiatives to support and promote.

4. Corporations must embed community participation as a principle in their corporate sustainability agenda. This will ensure that corporate sustainability policies and strategies become aligned with human rights approaches. In addition, including communities in the conception and implementation of corporate sustainability efforts will go to improve the quality of these initiatives. For example, substantive change can only come about with the inclusion of women workers in the decision-making processes related to corporate sustainability policies and strategies.

25.5 Chapter Summary

The key take-away from this chapter is: The market functions of corporations create both intended and unintended development impacts on society. The case studies we discuss in this chapter highlight that while governments may be responsible for meeting the needs of poor and vulnerable populations, businesses can also help to address these problems.

The emerging development agendas such as the SDGs Agenda 2030 encompass a set of goals that are more complex, transformative, interdependent and universally applicable. All stakeholders including businesses must therefore be involved. In this regard, business and management students should learn how to prepare, manage and evaluate development projects. It is also requisite that students develop insights about how to measure efficiency and increase the impact of development projects that are business driven. Development studies still attracts, perhaps remarkably so, many students. The reasons for development studies have not changed over the years. Students continue to have a genuine concern for the plight of the poor in developing countries, indignation about the unequal distribution of resources on a global scale and the urge to do something about this. Nonetheless, the discussions in this chapter are key reflections on the distinctive features of the *private sector for development agenda*. The aim is to trigger discussion rather than attempt closure.

CHAPTER QUESTIONS

1. What motivates businesses to become involved in development work?
2. What are the key factors that businesses should take into account when getting involved in development work?
3. What are the differences between multinational corporations and small and medium-sized enterprises with regard to their role and contribution in development work?
4. Apart from foreign direct investment, in what other ways can business contribute to poverty reduction?

FURTHER RESOURCES

- Business for 2030 website, www.businessfor2030.org/.

  This website provides examples of real-life cases of different businesses that are involved in advancing the UN 2030 development agenda. It also embeds how corporations are responding to the COVID-19 pandemic.

- Desai, V. and Potter, R. B. (2008). *The Companion to Development Studies* (2nd ed.). London: Routledge.

  This book offers a comprehensive overview of the key theoretical and practical issues dominating contemporary development studies.

- Dotsey, S. and Kumi, E. (2020). Does Religious Faith Matter in Development Practice? Perspectives from the Savelugu-Nanton District in Northern Ghana. *Forum for Development Studies*, 47(2), 351–381.

  This article provides an example of how socio-cultural values can shape development practice, to increase students' understanding of the importance of firms' knowledgeability of a context.

- Gleick, P. H. (2009). Three Gorges Dam Project, Yangtze River, China. In *The World's Water 2008–2009: The Biennial Report on Freshwater Resources* (pp. 139–150), Washington, DC: Island Press. Online version: http://worldwater.org/water-data/.

This book chapter provides a good overview of the challenges and consequences of promoting economic growth over sustainable and long-term development goals.

- Amini, M. and Bienstock, C. C. (2014). Corporate Sustainability: An Integrative Definition and Framework to Evaluate Corporate Practice and Guide Academic Research. *Journal of Cleaner Production*, 76, 12–19.

This article discusses more on corporate sustainability frameworks, mostly highlighting the elements that academics and businesses can look out for when evaluating tangible corporate sustainability activities and actions.

- Oldekop, J. A., Horner, R., Hulme, D., Adhikari, R., Agarwal, B., Alford, M., et al. (2020). COVID-19 and the Case for Global Development. *World Development*, 134, 105044.

This article provides an insight into how COVID-19 accentuates the case for a global, rather than an international, development paradigm.

26 | Corporate Sustainability: Where Are We Going?

ARNO KOURULA, ANDREAS RASCHE, METTE MORSING AND JEREMY MOON

LEARNING OBJECTIVES

- Reflect on the key lessons of each section of the book.
- Identify key trends and tensions throughout the book.
- Reflect on our individual roles within corporate sustainability.

26.1   Introduction

We started this book by imagining that we are in 2050. It remains to be seen whether we chose the path of 'business as usual' or tackled sustainability challenges head on. Did we continue down the path of prioritising economic growth above other goals? On the one hand, we may have solved extreme poverty and made great advances in combatting hunger. On the other hand, a prospering economy may have come at the cost of equality, climate stability and biodiversity. It may be questioned, however, whether we always have to think in dichotomies, pick sides and remain comfortably in our own trenches or bubbles.

In this concluding chapter, we provide insights into what the future might actually look like. This is a difficult task as the object of analysis (corporations and business in general), the topic at hand (sustainability), the core relationship (between business, society and nature) and the broader context (the institutional environment) are all rapidly changing. This is why forecasting the long-term future can sometimes seem a rather futile and impossible exercise. Nonetheless, anticipating and reflecting on the near-future trends of corporate sustainability can help us understand the role of business alongside other actors in sustainability transformations and help us imagine the future we want to create.

To understand the sustainability transformations that we need to achieve in the near future, Sachs et al. (2019) offer some useful insights. If we take as a starting point that we want to address major social issues such as inequality (i.e., 'leave no one behind') and address environmental challenges (i.e., 'circularity and decoupling'), the authors outline a set of six interdependent transformations: (1) education, gender and inequality; (2) health, well-being and demography; (3) energy decarbonisation and sustainable industry; (4) sustainable food, land, water and oceans; (5) sustainable cities and communities; and (6) digital revolution for sustainable development. Each of these will involve widespread changes in societal structures and our everyday practices.

At the end of this concluding chapter, we provide further resources for you to map out key global sustainability trends. In this conclusion, let's reflect how business fits into these transformations.

26.2   Themes, Developments and Tensions

Our book on corporate sustainability is organised in four sections: (1) Approaches (identifying historical, ethical, stakeholder, strategy, political and ecological lenses); (2) Actors (exploring the different roles played by SMEs, MNCs, social enterprises, new organisational forms, sustainability professionals, employees, investors, governmental organisations, civil society, social movements and consumers); (3) Processes (analysing how governing corporations, communicating, reporting, partnering, innovating and standardising takes place); and (4) Issues (exploring how human rights, labour rights, climate change, corruption and development relate to business activities). The twenty-six chapters bring in different perspectives and tools that are useful to understand and act in corporate sustainability.

Let's first reflect on the key topics from each section. Table 26.1 provides a list of keywords for the chapters of each part.

Four things become clear after reviewing this summary of keywords. First, we can adopt different approaches to corporate sustainability and each of these brings something new to the table in the sense of being a new perspective. Second, the number of actors involved in corporate sustainability is large. Third, corporate sustainability involves the entire organisation and formalised processes exist in terms of implementing sustainability inside businesses and within stakeholder relationships. Fourth, corporate sustainability encompasses a broad range of issues that need to be addressed.

Now that we have summarised the key topics of the book, let's reflect on some key developments for each of the four sections. We focus on developments of the recent past and trends in the near future. These are listed in Table 26.2.

While broader developments within corporate sustainability become clear from the chapters of the book, core tensions to be resolved still remain. These are listed in Table 26.3.

Based on the key tensions identified in Table 26.3, the contested nature of corporate sustainability becomes clear. While we do not want to approach the key

Table 26.1 Keywords from each section of the book

SECTION 1: APPROACHES

Chapters 2–7:
- Issues, modes, rationales; actors; industrialisation, modern corporation, internationalisation.
- Business ethics, ethics management, ethical decision-making, compliance, integrity.
- Stakeholder approach, sustainability, Nordic, corporate social responsibility.
- Corporate strategy, corporate sustainability, creating shared value, materiality, value chain.
- Corporations, CEO activism, digital technology, multi-stakeholder initiatives, politics.
- Ecology, natural environment, sustainability, systems.

SECTION 2: ACTORS

Chapters 8–14:
- Multinational corporation (MNC), small and medium-sized enterprise (SME), small business, small business social responsibility (SBSR).
- Hybrid organisations, foundation-owned companies, cooperatives, social businesses, B Corps.
- Sustainability professionals, tensions in sustainability work, motivations in sustainability work, sustainability practices.
- Sustainable finance, sustainable investing, ESG integration, active ownership, impact investing.
- Government, regulatory issues, regulatory approaches, corporate responses, public private regulatory interactions, governance spheres.
- Activism, NGO, stakeholders, tactics.
- Pro-company behaviours, consumer psychology, sustainability understanding, sustainability utility, sustainability-based unity, sustainability contingencies, consumer responses to corporate sustainability, consumer psychology, consumer decision-making.

SECTION 3: PROCESSES

Chapters 15–20:
- Corporate governance, corporate sustainability, ownership, ESG, stakeholder.
- Corporate social responsibility, corporate sustainability, image, identity, legitimacy, reputation.
- Sustainability reporting, environmental and social accountability, materiality, assurance, stakeholder engagement, transparency.
- Collaboration, partnerships, Sustainable Development Goal 17 (SDG17), sustainability.
- Corporate sustainability, business model, business model innovation, value creation, stakeholders.
- Sustainability standards, multi-stakeholder initiatives, legitimacy, impact, certification.

SECTION 4: ISSUES

Chapters 21–25:
- Access to remedy for victims, accountability, corporate responsibility to respect human rights, human rights due diligence, state duties to protect human rights.
- Labour rights, labour standards, sweatshops, global supply chains, globalisation.
- Climate change, Anthropocene, business education, market transformation, enterprise integration.
- Corruption, integrity, transparency, compliance, collective action.
- Corporate sustainability, sustainable development goals, business, Global South, gender.

Table 26.2 Key developments within each section of the book

SECTION 1: KEY DEVELOPMENTS IN APPROACHES

- Corporate sustainability has become very prevalent as a term and it can be seen to encompass a range of related concepts. Corporate sustainability is inherently interdisciplinary and this makes it such a rich and contested space for many different expertise areas and opinions to meet and discuss. As it is typical when concepts become very popular and a new paradigm in their own right, some of the origins and meanings become watered down.
- While corporate sustainability is a global trend, there are likely to be regional differences in meaning, policies and practices.
- We see some new links being developed between ethics and sustainability, even if these are typically seen as different units or tasks within an organisation (ethical compliance, environmental management and philanthropy programmes are most often managed by different parts of the organisation).
- More and more firms bring sustainability concerns to the core of their business as they are being challenged by a range of stakeholders calling for more sustainability (such as non-governmental organisations and governments) or showing how sustainability can be implemented differently (e.g., social enterprises).
- Corporate sustainability is inherently political, meaning that it involves a societal debate and decision about what is the appropriate role(s) of business in relation to the public sector and civil society. We see regional trends of increasing regulatory intervention in corporate sustainability in the sense that issues that used to be voluntary are becoming mandatory.
- As societal progress stagnates, environmental impacts increase and resource productivity decreases, societies contemplate whether the pathway of the future should be a business- and innovation-focused green growth, a regulatory-led forced green, a community-driven green growth or some other ideology.
- In our understanding of corporate sustainability, we no longer rely solely on management approaches, but history, applied ethics, political science, sociology, psychology, environmental studies and Earth system sciences join management to offer an interdisciplinarity foundation for our understanding.

SECTION 2: KEY DEVELOPMENTS IN ACTORS

- Internal motivations for firms to adopt corporate sustainability are on the rise, but with a wide variance in levels of adoption, especially in small and medium-sized enterprises. As organisations grow larger, sustainability and its management become more systematic and formal.
- We are likely to see continued experimentation in organisational forms and approaches as the discussion has moved beyond the multinational firm. Although an old organisational form as such, social enterprises are currently a very popular market-based way of advancing sustainability and are likely to continue being a way for organisations to frame themselves as responsible.
- Sustainability as a professional field can be considered to be fully established and institutionalised with a wide variety of dedicated jobs available.
- Sustainability has rapidly become integrated into finance as in some regions a majority of professionally managed funds use ESG criteria. The sustainable finance industry has recently seen significant integration which is likely to lead to further standardisation on the definition and measurement of sustainability in finance.
- The theme of sustainability is likely to face a continued battle for attention in corporate board rooms as it becomes less and less of a differentiating factor for firms. The link between sustainability and competitive advantage needs to be clear for top management to pay attention.
- Sustainable consumption and products can no longer be considered a fringe, but they are squarely in the mainstream.

Table 26.2 (*cont.*)

SECTION 3: KEY DEVELOPMENTS IN PROCESSES

- We are likely to see continuingly increasing interest in corporate sustainability and integration into the operations of businesses. Sustainability can be considered to be a global megatrend. In many geographical regions, sustainability has become a so-called 'hygiene factor', which means that companies need to adopt sustainability practices as all other firms are doing it.
- In terms of being on the agenda of top management and receiving larger budgets within companies, there will be a lot of variance across firms and depending on prevailing conditions.
- Sustainability reporting is likely to become more sophisticated in targeting the most important stakeholders in stakeholder-specific ways.
- Partnerships across societal sectors will continue to be a popular way of addressing sustainability challenges as each actor seems to struggle in terms of their individual legitimacy.
- We will see a lot of experimentation in innovative business models related to sustainability and, for instance, sharing and circular economies.
- Technology will become more and more intertwined with sustainability choices and practices.
- Corporate sustainability has seen significant levels of standardisation and this trend is likely to continue.

SECTION 4: KEY DEVELOPMENTS IN ISSUES

- Corporate sustainability is more strongly linked to global agendas such as the UN Sustainable Development Goals.
- Corporations have increasingly been perceived as legitimate actors in trying to address societal and developmental challenges.
- Issues such as climate change and energy transitions are likely to continue being the primary focus of corporate (environmental) sustainability initiatives, while other important themes such as biodiversity are likely to receive less attention. Given the spotlight on specific types of sustainability challenges, these will see more development, funding and disruption.
- There is a wide variance in implementation of corporate sustainability at the local level.
- Digital technology becomes an ever-more defining feature of corporate sustainability as economic, social, environmental and technological boundaries are being redefined.

tensions inherent in corporate sustainability in a dichotomous way – of having only two opposing perspectives – portraying tensions in this way can help tease out some key differences in thinking. This is especially helpful in understanding how the corporate sustainability discourse has evolved over the years. Many of these tensions can be considered to be resolved, at least in corporate sustainability circles. For instance, corporate sustainability is typically seen as long-term value creation through stakeholder engagement by putting sustainability to the core of strategy. It is no longer possible for firms to claim that they are not responsible for serious social or environmental violations in their global supply chains. Morality and politics is an inherent part of this endeavour. Some other

Table 26.3 Key tensions within each section of the book

SECTION 1: TENSIONS IN APPROACHES	
Short-term vs. long-term?	What is our time perspective when we speak of sustainability?
Amoral vs. moral	Should we see business as separate from ethical considerations or perceive business actors through a moral lens?
Shareholder vs. stakeholder	Do firms exist for shareholder value maximisation or for the benefit of a broader set of constituents?
Marginal vs. core	How core to strategy are sustainability issues for businesses in achieving their aims of purpose?
Apolitical vs. political	Are firms merely market actors or do they play important political roles in society?
Profit vs. triple bottom line	Should we focus (primarily) on financial profit or on the so-called triple bottom line of economic, environmental and social (or people, planet, profit or economy, ecology, equity)?
Home vs. host country	How should we balance the expectations of the country of the headquarters and the local markets where international firms operate?
SECTION 2: ACTORS	
Talk vs. walk	Does the sustainability communication match the actual sustainability performance of organisations (or are companies practising, for example, greenwashing)?
Large vs. small	Is corporate sustainability about multinational firms (often considered the 'usual suspects' in defining what is corporate sustainability) or about all kinds of other organisations, including SMEs?
Transformation vs. experimentation	Is sustainability a top-down agenda to transform large incumbent organisations or a bottom-up phenomenon of experimentation?
Voluntary vs. mandatory	Is corporate sustainability a voluntary endeavour where business aims to improve its sustainable performance (and work with private regulatory schemes) or a mandatory compliance issue where it is integrated into the institutional structures (especially regulation) of a particular location or country?
Internal (individual) vs. external (institutional) pressure	Is the main driver of sustainability for business internal normative pressure related to managerial agency or external coercive pressure within the institutional context?
Supply vs. demand-driven	Is corporate sustainability primarily driven by firms developing sustainable products and services or by consumers demanding these products and services?
SECTION 3: PROCESSES	
Focused vs. comprehensive	Should corporate communication on sustainability provide focused stories or a comprehensive overview of all activities?
Organisational vs. inter-organisational	Should companies focus on integrating sustainability into their own operations or emphasise inter-organisational collaboration?

Table 26.3 (*cont.*)	
Incremental vs. disruptive	Should corporate sustainability focus on incremental change or disruptive innovation?
Standardised vs. contextualised	Should corporate sustainability follow a standardised format or take a more original and contextualised form of storytelling?
SECTION 4: ISSUES	
Firm vs. supply chain	Is a firm responsible for its own activities or for the entire supply chain?
Limelight vs. shadow	Should companies focus on very topical sustainability issues or on those which do not get enough attention?
Risk vs. opportunity	Should we frame societal challenges as risks to be mitigated or opportunities for business innovation?
Economic development vs. sustainability	Should we focus on economic development or a sustainability-first agenda?
Organisational vs. systemic	Should sustainability be understood as an organisational or system-related feature?
Competitive vs. collaborative	Is the key to sustainability competition or collaboration?
Global vs. local	Should companies focus sustainability efforts in a globally standardised way or in a locally adapted one?

tensions are likely to remain a constant balancing exercise, such as addressing the triple bottom line in the short and the long term and choosing between standardised and contextualised corporate sustainability approaches. Corporate sustainability is not about either enterprise integration or market transformation, but about both.

Tensions are indeed inherent in many facets of our lives and they do not necessarily need to be paralysing. Scholars studying tensions (Hahn et al., 2014; 2015; Van der Byl and Slawinski, 2015) have shown that we can approach them in different ways. We can accept tensions as a part of life and live with them. We can choose one element over another. We can optimise to find the best solution. We can organise a broader discourse to try to find a compromise solution. We can aim to transform tensions into more manageable challenges. We can synthesise by introducing a new element that accommodates both sides. Finally, we can separate the opposites of the tension and address them in different locations or at different times. Ultimately reflecting on these tensions and addressing them through these different strategies can be a very fruitful learning exercise in corporate sustainability.

26.3   A Call for Reflection and Action

Instead of aiming to give definitive answers, we want to provide you with a final set of broad reflection questions:

- What is the purpose of a firm?
- For whom does a business exist?
- What are the roles of business in society and society in business?
- How do you see the relationship between the economic, social and environmental dimensions of business activities?
- What do you see as the biggest challenges for business to engage in sustainable development?
- What do you see as the biggest opportunities for business to act as a force for positive societal development?
- How will corporate sustainability be a part of your future?

In conclusion, we hope that this book brings awareness to sustainability issues as they pertain to corporate responsibility, helps structure thinking and drives your actions to take into consideration sustainability.

FURTHER RESOURCES

- Gapminder Foundation, www.gapminder.org.

  Developed by Ola Rosling, Anna Rosling Rönnlund and Hans Rosling, this foundation uses available statistics to question your worldview and related systemic misconceptions about important global trends. Take the quizzes on the website to test your knowledge!

- United Nations and Sustainable Development

  The United Nations has several initiatives and organisations which are very useful in terms of determining global sustainability agendas and monitoring progress. These include the UN Sustainable Development Goals (https://sdgs.un.org/goals), The World in 2050 global research initiative (www.unsdsn.org/the-world-in-2050) and the UN Statistics Division (https://unstats.un.org/home/). Another initiative is the UN Global Compact and Accenture CEO Survey (www.unglobalcompact.org/library/5976), which provides important insights specifically related to corporate sustainability.

- World Economic Forum, www.weforum.org.

  The World Economic Forum is a non-profit organisation headquartered in Geneva, Switzerland. It aims to be an international organisation for public-private collaboration. The WEF tracks a range of trends, such as the future skills that university graduates will need.

References

Abbott, K. W. and Snidal, D. (2000). Hard and Soft Law in International Governance. *International Organization*, 54(3), 421–456.

Abeselom, K. (2018). The Impact of Foreign Aid in Sustainable Development in Africa: A Case Study of Ethiopia. *Open Journal of Political Science*, 8(4), 365–422.

Accenture. (2019). More than Half of Consumers Would Pay More for Sustainable Products Designed, Accenture Survey Finds. Retrieved on 17 October 2022 from https://newsroom.accenture.com/news/more-than-half-of-consumers-would-pay-more-for-sustainable-products-designed-to-be-reused-or-recycled-accenture-survey-finds.htm.

AccountAbility. (2018). AA1000 AccountAbility Principles 2018.

Acquier, A., Gond, J.-P. and Pasquero, J. (2011). Rediscovering Howard R. Bowen's Legacy: The Unachieved Agenda and Continuous Relevance of *Social Responsibilities of the Businessman. Business and Society*, 50 (4), 607–646.

Adams, C., Cohen, E. and Baraka, D. (2014). *Better Corporate Reporting*. New York, NY: Routledge.

Adams, C. and Narayanan, V. (2007). The Standardization of Sustainability Reporting. In J. Bebbington, J. Unerman and B. O'Dwyer. (Eds.), *Sustainability Accounting and Accountability* (pp. 70–85). New York, NY: Routledge.

Adams, C. A. (2004). The Ethical, Social and Environmental Reporting-Performance Portrayal Gap. *Accounting, Auditing & Accountability Journal*, 17(5), 731–757.

Adams, C. A., Alhamood, A., He, X., Tian, J., Wang, L. and Wang, Y. (2021). *The Double-Materiality Concept: Application and Issues*. Amsterdam: KPMG.

Adams, R., Jeanrenaud, S., Bessant, J., Denyer, D. and Overy, P. (2016). Sustainability-Oriented Innovation: A Systematic Review. *International Journal of Management Reviews*, 18(2), 180–205.

Agbebi, M. and Virtanen, P. (2017). Dependency Theory – A Conceptual Lens to Understand China's Presence in Africa? *Forum for Development Studies*, 44(3), 429–451.

Agrawal, A. K. (2012). Corporate Governance Objectives of Labor Union Shareholders: Evidence from Proxy Voting. *The Review of Financial Studies*, 25(1), 187–226.

Akemu, O., Whiteman, G. and Kennedy, S. (2016). Social Enterprise Emergence from Social Movement Activism: The Fairphone Case. *Journal of Management Studies*, 53(5), 846–877.

Albareda, L., Lozano, J. M., Tencati, A., Midttun, A. and Perrini, F. (2008). The

Changing Role of Governments in Corporate Social Responsibility: Drivers and Responses. *Business Ethics: A European Review*, 17(4), 347–363.

Ali, M. S. B. and Mdhillat, M. (2015). Does Corruption Impede International Trade? New Evidence from the EU and the MENA Countries. *Journal of Economic Cooperation and Development*, 36(4), 107–120.

Anderson, J. (2020). What Can We Learn from Trends in Corruption and Anticorruption? Governance for Development Blog. 23 October. World Bank. Retrieved on 17 October 2022 from https://blogs.worldbank.org/governance/what-can-we-learn-trends-corruption-and-anticorruption.

Anderson, R. C. (2009). *Confessions of a Radical Industrialist: Profits, People, Purpose – Doing Business by Respecting the Earth*. New York, NY: St. Martin's Press.

Anker, P. and Witoszek, N. (1998). The Dream of the Biocentric Community and the Structure of Utopias. *Worldviews*, 2(3), 239–256.

Aretoulakis, E. (2014). Towards a Posthumanist Ecology. *European Journal of English Studies*, 18(2), 172–190.

Argandoña, A. (2017). Petty Corruption – Facilitating Payments and Grease Money. In M. S. AÔländer and S. Hudson. (Eds.), *The Handbook of Business and Corruption: Cross-Sectoral Experiences* (pp. 49–70). Bingley, UK: Emerald Publishing.

(2003). Private-to-Private Corruption. *Journal of Business Ethics*, 47(3), 253–267.

Aristotle. (2000). *Nichomachean Ethics*. Translated by R. Crisp. Cambridge: Cambridge University Press.

Arla Foods. (2021). Annual Report 2020. Retrieved on 17 October 2022 from https://mea.arla.com/.

Arnold, D. (2010). Transnational Corporations and the Duty to Respect Basic Human Rights. *Business Ethics Quarterly*, 20(3), 371–399.

Arnold, D. G. and Bowie, N. E. (2007). Respect for Workers in Global Supply Chains. *Business Ethics Quarterly*, 17 (1), 135–145.

Arnold, D. G. and Hartman, L. P. (2006). Worker Rights and Low Wage Industrialization: How to Avoid Sweatshops. *Human Rights Quarterly*, 28(3), 676–700.

Ashforth, B. E. and Anand, V. (2003). The Normalization of Corruption in Organizations. *Research in Organizational Behavior*, 25(1), 1–52.

Atwood, D. F., Coperine, K. and Hart, M. (2016). Current Trends in Hiring Sustainability Professionals. *Sustainability*, 9(4), 193–199.

Auld, G. (2014). Confronting Trade-Offs and Interactive Effects in the Choice of Policy Focus: Specialized versus Comprehensive Private Governance. *Regulation & Governance*, 8(1), 126–148.

Austin, J. E. and Seitanidi, M. M. (2012). Collaborative Value Creation: A Review of Partnering between Nonprofits and Businesses: Part I. Value Creation Spectrum and Collaboration Stages. *Nonprofit and Voluntary Sector Quarterly*, 41(5), 726–758.

Avetisyan, E. and Hockerts, K. (2017). The Consolidation of the ESG Rating Industry as an Enactment of Institutional Retrogression. *Business Strategy and the Environment*, 26(3), 316–330.

Avi-Yonah, R. (2005). The Cyclical Transformations of the Corporate Form: A Historical Perspective on Corporate Social Responsibility. *Delaware Journal of Corporate Law*, 30 (3), 767–818.

Babri, M., Davidson, B. and Helin, S. (2021). An Updated Inquiry into the Study of Corporate Codes of Ethics: 2005–2016. *Journal of Business Ethics*, 168(1), 71–108.

Baden, D., Harwood, I. and Woodward, D. (2009). The Effect of Buyer Pressure on Suppliers in SMEs to Demonstrate CSR Practices: An Added Incentive or Counter Productive? *European Management Journal*, 27(6), 429–441.

Baghuis, M. (2017). Navigating the Sustainability Manager's Roles. Changeincontext.com. Retrieved on 17 October 2022 from https:// changeincontext.com/sustainability-manager-navigating-roles/.

Bakan, J. (2004). *The Corporation: The Pathological Pursuit of Profit and Power*. London: Constable & Robinson.

Baliga, B. R., Moyer, R. C. and Rao, R. S. (1996). CEO Duality and Firm Performance: What's the Fuss? *Strategic Management Journal*, 17(1), 41–53.

Banerjee, S. B. (2012). A Climate for Change? Critical Reflections on the Durban United Nations Climate Change Conference. *Organization Studies*, 33 (12), 1761–1786.

Banerjee, S. B. and Arjaliès, D.-L. (2021). Celebrating the End of Enlightenment: Organization Theory in the Age of the Anthropocene and Gaia (and Why Neither Is the Solution to Our Ecological Crisis). *Organization Theory*. Retrieved on 17 October 2022 from https://doi.org/10.1177/26317877211036714.

Bansal, P. (2005). Evolving Sustainably: A Longitudinal Study of Corporate Sustainable Development. *Strategic Management Journal*, 26(3), 197–218.

Bansal, P. and Song, H.-C. (2017). Similar But Not the Same: Differentiating Corporate Responsibility from Sustainability. *Academy of Management Annals*, 11(1), 105–149.

Barnett, M., Jermier, J. and Lafferty, B. (2006). Corporate Reputation: The Definitional Landscape. *Corporate Reputation Review*, 9(1), 26–38.

Barrientos, S. and Smith, S. (2007). Do Workers Benefit from Ethical Trade? Assessing Codes of Labour Practice in Global Production Systems. *Third World Quarterly*, 28(4), 713–729.

Barth, F., Hübel, B. and Scholz, H. (2020). ESG and Corporate Credit Spreads. Retrieved on 17 October 2022 from https://papers.ssrn.com/sol3/Papers .cfm?abstract_id=3179468.

Bartley, T. and Child, C. (2011). Movements, Markets and Fields: The Effects of Anti-Sweatshop Campaigns on U.S. firms, 1993–2000. *Social Forces*, 90(2), 425–451.

Bartley, T. and Egels-Zandén, N. (2015). Responsibility and Neglect in Global

Production Networks: The Uneven Significance of Codes of Conduct in Indonesian Factories. *Global Networks*, 15(s1), S21–S44.

Battilana, J. and Lee, M. (2014). Advancing Research on Hybrid Organizing: Insights from the Study of Social Enterprises. *Academy of Management Annals*, 8(1), 397–441.

Baumann-Pauly, D., Scherer, A. G. and Palazzo, G. (2016). Managing Institutional Complexity: A Longitudinal Study of Legitimacy Strategies at a Sportswear Brand Company. *Journal of Business Ethics*, 131(1), 31–51.

Baumann-Pauly, D., Wickert, C., Spence, L. and Scherer, A. (2013). Organizing Corporate Social Responsibility in Small and Large Firms: Size Matters. *Journal of Business Ethics*, 115(4), 693–705.

Baur, D. and Schmitz, H. P. (2012). Corporations and NGOs: When Accountability Leads to Co-optation. *Journal of Business Ethics*, 106(1), 9–21.

Baxter, G. D. and Rarick, C. A. (1987). Education for the Moral Development of Managers: Kohlberg's Stages of Moral Development and Integrative Education. *Journal of Business Ethics*, 6(3), 243–248.

Bazerman, M. H. and Tenbrunsel, A. E. (2011). *Blind Spots*. Princeton, NJ: Princeton University Press.

BBC. (2021a). US Congress Passes Import Ban on Chinese Uyghur Region. 17 December. Retrieved on 17 October 2022 from: www.bbc.com/news/world-us-canada-59692826.

(2021b). Covid: Huge Protests across Europe over New Restrictions. 21 November. Retrieved on 17 October 2022 from www.bbc.com/news/world-europe-59363256.

B Corp. (2022). The B Corp Certification Pathway for Eligible Multinationals and Large Enterprise Businesses. Retrieved on 17 October 2022 from www.bcorporation.net/en-us/certification/large-enterprise-multinational.

Becker-Olsen, K., Cudmore, B. and Hill, R. (2006). The Impact of Perceived Corporate Social Responsibility on Consumer Behaviour. *Journal of Business Research*, 59(1), 46–53.

Beddewela, E. and Herzig, C. (2013). Corporate Social Reporting by MNCs' Subsidiaries in Sri Lanka. *Accounting Forum*, 37(2), 135–149.

Bennett, W. (2003). Communicating Global Activism. *Information, Communication & Society*, 6(2), 143–168.

Berg, F., Kölbel, J. F. and Rigobon, R. (2019). Aggregate Confusion: The Divergence of ESG Ratings (MIT Sloan School Working Paper 5822-19). Cambridge, MA: The MIT Press.

Berger, I.. E., Cunningham, P. H. and Drumwright, M. E. (2004). Social Alliances: Company/Nonprofit Collaboration. *California Management Review*, 47(1), 58–90.

Berkey, B. (2021). Sweatshops, Structural Injustice, and the Wrong of Exploitation: Why Multinational Corporations Have Positive Duties to the Global Poor. *Journal of Business Ethics*, 169(1), 43–56.

Berle, A. and Means, G. (1932). *The Modern Corporate and Private Property.* New York, NY: Macmillan.

Berrier-Lucas, C. (2014). *Emergence de la dimension environnementale de la RSE: une étude historique franco-québécoise d'EDF et d'Hydro-Québec* [Emergence of the environmental dimension of CSR: A Franco-Quebecquer historical study of EDF and hydro-Quebec]. PhD dissertation, University Paris Dauphine.

Better Work. (2019). Workplace Safety. Adding Value to Workplace Safety in Garment Supply Chains. Retrieved on 17 October 2022 from https:// betterwork.org/wp-content/uploads/ 2019/04/Workplace-Safety-Brochure_ BWB_2019.pdf.

Bhattacharya, C. B., Sen, S. and Korschun, D. (2011). *Leveraging Corporate Responsibility: The Stakeholder Route to Maximizing Business and Social Value.* Cambridge: Cambridge University Press.

Bird, F. (2015). Moral Muteness. *Wiley Encyclopedia of Management.* Retrieved on 17 October 2022 from https://doi .org/10.1002/9781118785317 .weom020151.

Black, D. (2010). The Ambiguities of Development: Implications for 'Development through Sport'. *Sport in Society*, 13(1), 121–129.

Blom, E., van Burg, J. C., Verhagen, P. and Hillen, M. (2015). Tony's Chocolonely: How a Social Enterprise is Changing the Chocolate Industry. Retrieved on 17 October 2022 from https://research .vu.nl/en/publications/tonys- chocolonely-how-a-social-enterprise- is-changing-the-chocola.

Bloomberg. (2020). Older ESG Funds Outperform Their Newer Rivals in Market Tumult. Retrieved on 17 October 2022 from www.bloomberg .com/news/articles/2020-03-13/older- esg-funds-outperform-their-newer- rivals-in-market-tumult.

Blowfield, M. (1999). Ethical Trade: A Review of Developments and Issues. *Third World Quarterly*, 20(4), 753–770.

Blythe, I. (2006). From Philanthropy to Essential Business Investment – the Evolution of CSR at Boots UK. Retrieved on 17 October 2022 from www.jpf.org.uk/cms/files/ japan_foundation_csr_presn_- _idb_july_2011_v1.pdf.

Bocken, N., Short, S., Rana, P. and Evans, S. (2013). A Value Mapping Tool for Sustainable Business Modelling. *Corporate Governance: The International Journal of Business in Society*, 13(5), 482–497.

Bodruzic, D. (2015). Promoting International Development through Corporate Social Responsibility: The Canadian Government's Partnership with Canadian Mining Companies. *Canadian Foreign Policy Journal*, 21(2), 129–145.

Boiral, O. (2007). Corporate Greening through ISO 14001: A Rational Myth? *Organization Science*, 18(1), 127–146.

Bonime-Blanc, A. (2020). *Boom to Gloom: How Leaders Transform Risk into Resilience and Value.* London: Routledge.

Borowy, I. and Schmelzer, M. (2017). *History of the Future of Economic Growth: Historical Roots of Current Debates on Sustainable Degrowth.* Routledge

Studies on Ecological Economics. London: Routledge.

Boström, M. (2006). Regulatory Credibility and Authority through Inclusiveness: Standardization Organizations in Cases of Eco-Labelling. *Organization*, 13(3), 345–367.

Boström, M., Micheletti, M. and Oosterveer, P. (Eds.). (2018). *The Oxford Handbook of Political Consumerism*. Oxford: Oxford University Press.

Boswell, J. (1983). The Informal Social Control of Business in Britain: 1880–1939. *Business History Review*, 57(2), 237–257.

Bouzzine, Y. D. and Lueg, R. (2020). The Contagion Effect of Environmental Violations: The Case of Dieselgate in Germany. *Business Strategy and the Environment*, 29(8), 3187–3202.

Bowen, H. R. (1953). *Social Responsibilities of the Businessman*. New York, NY: Harper & Row.

Bower, J. L. and Paine, L. S. (2017). The Error at the Heart of Corporate Leadership. *Harvard Business Review*, 95(3), 50–61.

Bowie, N. E. (1998a). A Kantian Theory of Capitalism. *Business Ethics Quarterly*, 8 (S1), 37–60.

(1998b). A Kantian Theory of Meaningful Work. *Journal of Business Ethics*, 17 (9–10), 1083–1092.

Brammer, S. and Pavelin, S. (2004). Building a Good Reputation. *European Management Journal*, 22(6), 704–713.

Brave New Work. (2021). How Patagonia Became Patagonia – with Vincent Stanley. Retrieved on 17 October 2022 from https://getpodcast.com/at/ podcast/brave-new-work/how-patagonia-became-patagonia-w-vincent-stanley_17e6c770ed.

Breuer, H. (2013). Lean Venturing: Learning to Create New Business through Exploration, Elaboration, Evaluation, Experimentation, and Evolution. *International Journal of Innovation Management*, 17(3), Article 1340013.

Breuer, H., Fichter, K., Lüdeke-Freund, F. and Tiemann, I. (2018). Sustainability-Oriented Business Model Development: Principles, Criteria and Tools. *International Journal of Entrepreneurial Venturing*, 10(2), 256–286.

Breuer, H. and Lüdeke-Freund, F. (2017). Values-Based Network and Business Model Innovation. *International Journal of Innovation Management*, 21 (3), 1–35.

Bromley, P. and Meyer, J. (2017). 'They Are All Organizations': The Cultural Roots of Blurring between the Nonprofit, Business, and Government Sectors. *Administration & Society*, 49(7), 939–966.

Bromley, P. and Sharkey, A. (2017). Accounting, Organizations and Society Casting Call: The Expanding Nature of Actorhood in U.S. Firms, Capital. *Accounting, Organizations and Society*, 59, 3–20.

Brown, E. and Cloke, J. (2004). Neoliberal Reform, Governance and Corruption in the South: Assessing the International Anti-Corruption Crusade. *Antipode*, 36 (2), 272–294.

Brown, J. and Fraser, M. (2006). Approaches and Perspectives in Social and Environmental Accounting: An Overview of the Conceptual Landscape.

Business Strategy and the Environment, 15(2), 103–117.

Browne, J. (2010). *Beyond Business: An Inspirational Memoir from a Visionary Leader*. London: Weindenfeld & Nicolson.

Browne, R. (2020). 'The Enron of Germany': Wirecard Scandal Casts a Shadow on Corporate Governance. Retrieved on 17 October 2022 from www.cnbc.com/2020/06/29/enron-of-germany-wirecard-scandal-casts-a-shadow-on-governance.html.

Brück, M. (2019). Wie „Mr. Froschkönig" sich gegen übermächtige Konkurrenz aus Amerika wehrt. WirtschaftsWoche. Retrieved on 17 October 2022 from www.wiwo.de/unternehmen/mittelstand/frosch-gegen-fairy-wie-mr-froschkoenig-sich-gegen-uebermaechtige-konkurrenz-aus-amerika-wehrt/24232164.html.

Brundtland, G. (1987). *Report of the World Commission on Environment and Development: Our Common Future*. UN General Assembly Doc. A/42/427.

Brunsson, N., Rasche, A. and Seidl, D. (2012). The Dynamics of Standardization: Three Perspectives on Standards in Organization Studies. *Organization Studies*, 33(5–6), 613–632.

B Team. (2018). A New Bar for Responsible Tax: The B Team Responsible Tax Principles. Retrieved on 17 October 2022 from https://bteam.org/our-thinking/reports/responsibletax-2.

Buchholtz, A. K., Brown, J. A. and Shabana, K. M. (2009). Corporate Governance and Corporate Social Responsibility. In A. Crane, A. Williams, D. Matten, J. Moon and D. Siegel. (Eds.), *Oxford Handbook of Corporate Social Responsibility* (pp. 327–345). Oxford and New York, NY: Oxford University Press.

Buhmann, K. (2021). *Human Rights – a Key Idea for Business and Society*. Abingdon, UK and New York, NY: Routledge.

(2018). Analyzing OECD National Contact Point Statements for Guidance on Human Rights Due Diligence: Method, Findings and Outlook, *Nordic Journal of Human Rights*, 36(4), 390–410.

(2017). *Changing Sustainability Norms through Communicative Processes: The Emergence of the Business & Human Rights Regime as Transnational Law*. Cheltenham, UK and Northampton, MA: Edward Elgar.

(2015). Public Regulators and CSR: The 'Social Licence to Operate' in Recent United Nations Instruments on Business and Human Rights and the Juridification of CSR. *Journal of Business Ethics*, 136(4), 699–714.

Buhmann, K., Jonsson, J. and Fisker, M. (2019). Do No Harm and Do More Good Too: Connecting Business & and Human Rights Theory with Political CSR to Help Companies Identify Opportunities for Contributing to the SDGs. *Corporate Governance: The International Journal of Business in Society*, 19(3), 389–403.

Buhr, N., Gray, R. and Milne, M. (2014). Histories, Rationales, Voluntary Standards and Future Prospects for Sustainability Reporting: CSR, GRI,

IIRC and Beyond. In J. Bebbington, J. Unerman and B. O'Dwyer. (Eds.), *Sustainability Accounting and Accountability* (pp. 51–71). New York, NY: Routledge.

Bundesministerium für Arbeit und Soziales. (2021). Gesetzentwurf der Bundesregierung – Entwurf eines Gesetzes über die unternehmerischen Sorgfaltspflichten in Lieferketten (Referentenentwurf). Retrieved on 17 October 2022 from www.bmas.de/SharedDocs/Downloads/DE/Gesetze/Regierungsentwuerfe/reg-sorgfaltspflichtengesetz.pdf?__blob=publicationFile&v=1.

Bundesministerium für wirtschaftliche Zusammenarbeit und Entwicklung. (2021). Fragen und Antworten zum Lieferkettengesetz. Retrieved on 17 October 2022 from www.bmz.de/resource/blob/60000/84f32c49acea03b883e1223c66b3e227/lieferkettengesetz-fragen-und-antworten-data.pdf.

Bundesregierung. (2017). Gesetz zur Stärkung der nichtfinanziellen Berichterstattung der Unternehmen in ihren Lage- und Konzernlageberichten (CSR-Richtlinie-Umsetzungsgesetz). In *Bundesgesetzblatt* (20), pp. 802–814. Retrieved on 17 October 2022 from www.bgbl.de/xaver/bgbl/start.xav?start=%2F%2F*%5B%40attr_id%3D%27bgbl117s0802.pdf%27%5D#__bgbl__%2F%2F*%5B%40attr_id%3D%27bgbl117s0802.pdf%27%5D__1616510776736.

Business and Human Rights Resource Centre. (2020). Mandatory Due Diligence. Retrieved on 17 October 2022 from www.business-humanrights.org/en/big-issues/mandatory-due-diligence/.

Business Roundtable. (2019). Business Roundtable Redefines the Purpose of a Corporation to Promote 'an Economy that Serves All Americans'. Retrieved on 17 October 2022 from www.businessroundtable.org/business-roundtable-redefines-the-purpose-of-a-corporation-to-promote-an-economy-that-serves-all-americans.

Byiers, B. and Rosengren, A. (2012). Common or Conflicting Interests? Reflections on the Private Sector (for) Development Agenda (ECDPM Discussion Paper No. 131). Maastricht: European Centre for Development Policy Management.

Børsting, C. and Thomsen, S. (2017). Foundation Ownership, Reputation, and Labour. *Oxford Review of Economic Policy*, 33(2), 317–338.

Callinicos, A. (1988). *South Africa between Reform and Revolution*. London: Bookmarks.

Capgemini Research Institute. (2020). Consumer Products and Retail – How Sustainability Is Fundamentally Changing Consumer Preferences. Retrieved on 17 October 2022 from www.capgemini.com/wp-content/uploads/2020/07/20-06_9880_Sustainability-in-CPR_Final_Web-1.pdf.

Caradonna, J. L. (2014). *Sustainability: A History*. Oxford: Oxford University Press.

Carmine, S., Andriopoulos, C., Gotsi, M., Härtel, C. E. J., Krzeminska, A., Mafico, N., et al. (2021). A Paradox Approach to

Organizational Tensions During the Pandemic Crisis. *Journal of Management Inquiry*, 30(2), 138–153.

Carollo, L. and Guerci, M. (2018). 'Activists in a Suit': Paradoxes and Metaphors in Sustainability Managers' Identity Work. *Journal of Business Ethics*, 148 (2), 249–268.

Carr, I. (2009). The Public Rules for Private Enterprise: Corporate Anti-Corruption Legislation in Comparative and International Perspective. In D. Zinnbauer, R. Dobson, and K. Despota. (Eds.), *Global Corruption Report 2009*. Cambridge: Cambridge University Press.

Carrington, D. (2019). Most 'Meat' in 2040 Will Not Come from Dead Animals, Says Report. *The Guardian*. Retrieved on 17 October 2022 from www.theguardian.com/environment/ 2019/jun/12/most-meat-in-2040-will-not-come-from-slaughtered-animals-report#:~:text=Most%20of%20the% 20meat%20people,look%20and% 20taste%20like%20meat.

Carroll, A. B., Lipartito, K..J., Post, J. E. and Werhane, P. H. (2012). *Corporate Responsibility: The American Experience*. Cambridge: Cambridge University Press.

Carroll, A. B. (2018). Strategic Philanthropy. *The SAGE Encyclopedia of Business Ethics and Society*. Retrieved on 17 October 2022 from https://sk .sagepub.com/reference/sage-encyclopedia-of-business-ethics-and-society-2e/i39130.xml.

(1991). The Pyramid of Corporate Social Responsibility: Toward the Moral Management of Organizational

Stakeholders. *Business Horizons*, 34(4), 39–48.

(1979). A Three-Dimensional Conceptual Model of Corporate Performance. *Academy of Management Review*, 4(4), 497–505.

Carroll, A. B. and Shabana, K. M. (2010). The Business Case for Corporate Social Responsibility: A Review of Concepts, Research and Practice. *International Journal of Management Reviews*, 12(1), 85–105.

Carson, R. (1962). *Silent Spring*. Boston: Houghton Mifflin.

Cashore, B., Knudsen, J. S., Moon, J. and van der Ven, H. (2021). Private Authority and Public Policy in Global Context: Governance Spheres for Problem Solving. *Regulation and Governance*, 15(4), 1166–1182.

Castelló, I., Etter, M. and Nielsen, F. A. (2016). Strategies of Legitimacy through Social Media: The Networked Strategy. *Journal of Management Studies*, 53(3), 402–432.

Castells, M. (2000). *The Information Age: Economy, Society and Culture* (2nd ed., Vol. I), *The Rise of the Network Society*. Oxford: Blackwell.

Caulfield, P. A. (2013). The Evolution of Strategic Corporate Social Responsibility. *EuroMed Journal of Business*, 8(3), 220–242.

Center for Research on Multinational Corporations (SOMO). (2012). Freedom of Association in the Electronics Industry. Retrieved on 17 October 2022 from www.somo.nl/publications-en/ Publication_3804.

Center for Research on Multinational Corporations (SOMO) and India

Committee of the Netherlands (ICN).
(2014). Flawed Fabrics: The Abuse of
Girls and Women Workers in the South
Indian Textile Industry. Retrieved on
17 October 2022 from www.indianet
.nl/pdf/FlawedFabrics.pdf.

Chakrabortty, A. (2013). How Boots Went
Rogue. *The Guardian*. Retrieved on
17 October 2022 from www.
theguardian.com/news/2016/apr/13/
how-boots-went-rogue.

Chandler, A. D. (1984). The Emergence of
Managerial Capitalism. *Business
History Review*, 58(04), 473–503.
  (1962). *Strategy and Structure: Chapters
in the History of the Industrial
Enterprise*. Cambridge, MA: The MIT
Press.

Chatterji, A. K. and Toffel, M. W. (2018). The
New CEO Activists. *Harvard Business
Review*, January–February. Retrieved
on 17 October 2022 from https://hbr
.org/2018/01/the-new-ceo-activists.

Cheng, J. (2007). Congress Unimpressed by
Yahoo Apology for China Dissident E-
mail Testimony. Retrieved on
17 October 2022 from https://
arstechnica.com/tech-policy/2007/11/
yahoo-calls-withholding-of-info-on-
chinese-arrests-a-misunderstanding/.

Chernev, A. and Blair, S. (2020). When
Sustainability Is Not a Liability: The
Halo Effect of Marketplace Morality.
Journal of Consumer Psychology, 31(3),
551–569.

Chessel, A.-M. (2012). *Consommateurs
engagés à la Belle Époque. La Ligue
sociale des acheteurs* [Engaged
Consumption during the Belle Epoque:
The Social League of Buyers]. Paris: Les
Presses de Sciences Po.

Christensen, L. T., Morsing, M. and Thyssen,
O. (2021). Talk-Action Dynamics:
Modalities of Aspirational Talk.
Organization Studies, 42(3), 407–427.
  (2013). CSR as Aspirational Talk.
Organization, 20(3), 372–393.

Christmann, P. and Taylor, G. (2006). Firm
Self-Regulation through International
Certifiable Standards: Determinants of
Symbolic versus Substantive
Implementation. *Journal of
International Business Studies*, 37(6),
863–878.

Chuan, K., Mitchell, I. and Tomson, L.
(2019). *Another Link in the Chain:
Uncovering the Role of Proxy Advisors
in Investor Voting*. London: Share
Action.

Chun, R. and Davies, G. (2006). The
Influence of Corporate Character on
Customers and Employees: Exploring
Similarities and Differences. *Journal of
the Academy of Marketing Science*, 34
(6), 138–146.

Cifuentes, A. and Espinoza, D. (2016).
Infrastructure Investing and the
Peril of Discounted Cash Flow.
Financial Times. Retrieved on
17 October 2022 from www.ft.com/
content/c9257c6c-a0db-11e6-891e-
abe238dee8e2.

Clark, J. M. (1916). The Changing Basis of
Economic Responsibility. *Journal of
Political Economy*, 24(3), 209–229.

Clarke, A. and Crane, A. (2018). Cross-Sector
Partnerships for Systemic Change:
Systematized Literature Review and
Agenda for Further Research. *Journal
of Business Ethics*, 150(2), 303–313.

Clausewitz, C. (1983). *On War*. London:
Penguin.

Clean Clothes Campaign (CCC). (2019). Tailored Wages 2019: The State of Pay in the Global Garment Industry. Retrieved on 17 October 2022 from https://archive.cleanclothes.org/resources/publications/tailored-wages-2019-the-state-of-pay-in-the-global-garment-industry/view.

Cohen, B. and Winn, M. I. (2007). Market Imperfections, Opportunity and Sustainable Entrepreneurship. *Journal of Business Venturing*, 22(1), 29–49.

Cook, M. L. (1995). The Future of U.S. Agricultural Cooperatives: A Neo-Institutional Approach. *American Journal of Agricultural Economics*, 77 (5), 1153–1159.

Cooper, S. M. and Owen, D. L. (2007). Corporate Social Reporting and Stakeholder Accountability: The Missing Link. *Accounting, Organizations and Society*, 32(7–8), 649–667.

Cornelissen, J. (2021). *Corporate Communications: A Guide to Theory & Practice* (6th ed.). London: Sage.

Cowan, S. and Gadenne, D. (2005). Australian Corporate Environmental Reporting: A Comparative Analysis of Disclosure Practices across voluntary and Mandatory Disclosure Systems. *Journal of Accounting & Organizational Change*, 1(2), 165–179.

Cragg, W. (2012). Ethics, Enlightened Self-Interest, and the Corporate Responsibility to Respect Human Rights: A Critical Look at the Justificatory Foundations of the UN Framework, 22(1), *Business Ethics Quarterly*, 9–36.

Crane, A. (2000). Corporate Greening as Amoralization. *Organization Studies*, 21(4), 673–696.

Crane, A., Matten, D., Glozer, S. and Spence, L. (2019). *Business Ethics: Managing Corporate Citizenship and Sustainability in the Age of Globalization*. Oxford: Oxford University Press.

Crane, A., Matten, D. and Moon, J. (2008). *Corporations and Citizenship*. Cambridge: Cambridge University Press.

Crane, A., Palazzo, G., Spence, L. and Matten, D. (2014). Contesting the Value of 'Creating Shared Value'. *California Management Review*, 56(2), 130–153.

Cremer, A. and Bergin, T. (2015). Fear and Respect: VW's Culture under Winterkorn. Retrieved on 17 October 2022 from www.reuters.com/article/us-volkswagen-emissions-culture-idUSKCN0S40MT20151010.

Crifo, P., Durand, R. and Gond, J. P. (2019). Encouraging Investors to Enable Corporate Sustainability Transitions: The Case of Responsible Investment in France. *Organization & Environment*, 32(2), 125–144.

Crutzen, P. and Stoermer, E. (2000). The 'Anthropocene'. *Global Change Newsletter*, 41(1), 17–18.

CSR Europe. (n.d.). Responsible and Transparent Tax Behaviour Build Trust in Your Business – Our Service Offer to Companies (pp. 1–). Retrieved on 17 October 2022 from https://static1.squarespace.com/static/5df776f6866c14507f2df68a/t/6050aba228382d15adff1a09/1615899556335/Tax+Service_Companies_Digital.pdf5.

Cuervo-Cazurra, A. (2006). Who Cares about Corruption? *Journal of International Business Studies*, 37(6), 807–822.

Cushman, F., Young, L. and Hauser, M. (2006). The Role of Conscious Reasoning and Intuition in Moral Judgment: Testing Three Principles of Harm. *Psychological Science*, 17(12), 1082–1089.

Dal Bó, E. and Rossi, M. A. (2007). Corruption and Inefficiency: Theory and Evidence from Electric Utilities. *Journal of Public Economics*, 91(5–6), 939–962.

Danaher, J. (2016). The Threat of Algocracy: Reality, Resistance and Accommodation. *Philosophy and Technology*, 29(3), 245–268.

Davis, K. (1973). The Case for and against Business Assumption of Social Responsibilities. *Academy of Management Journal*, 16(2), 312–322.

(1960). Can Business Afford to Ignore Social Responsibilities? *California Management Review*, 2(3), 70–76.

de Bakker, F. G. A., Rasche, A. and Ponte, S. (2019). Multi-Stakeholder Initiatives on Sustainability: A Cross-Disciplinary Review and Research Agenda for Business Ethics. *Business Ethics Quarterly*, 29(3), 343–383.

De Bernardi, C. and Pedrini, M. (2019). Senior Managers of Sustainability and corporate social responsibility in Europe. European Association of Sustainability Professional. Retrieved on 17 October 2022 from www.europeanasp.eu/files/news/2019_Report_EASP.pdf.

De Cuyper, L., Clarysse, B. and Phillips, N. (2020). Imprinting beyond the Founding Phase: How Sedimented Imprints Develop over Time. *Organization Science*, 31(6), 1579–1600.

Deegan, C. (2019). Legitimacy Theory: Despite Its Enduring Popularity and Contribution, Time Is Right for a Necessary Makeover. *Accounting, Auditing & Accountability Journal*, 32 (8), 2307–2329.

(2014). An Overview of Legitimacy Theory as Applied within the Social and Environmental Accounting Literature. In J. Unerman, J. Bebbington and B. O'Dwyer. (Eds.), *Sustainability Accounting and Accountability* (pp. 248–272). New York, NY: Routledge.

Defourny, J. (2014). From Third Sector to Social Enterprise: A European Research Trajectory. In J. Defourny, L. Hulgård and V. Pestoff. (Eds.), *Social Enterprise and the Third Sector: Changing European Landscapes in a Comparative Perspective* (pp. 33–57). Abingdon, UK and New York, NY: Routledge.

Delacote, P. (2009). On the Sources of Consumer Boycotts Ineffectiveness. *Journal of Environment & Development*, 18(3), 306–322.

De la O, A. L., Domínguez, J. I., Greene, K. F., Lawson, C. H. and Moreno, A. (2015). How Governmental Corruption Breeds Clientelism. In J. I. Domínguez, K. F. Greene, C. H. Lawson and A. Moreno. (Eds.), *Mexico's Evolving Democracy: A Comparative Study of the 2012 Elections*. Baltimore, MD: Johns Hopkins University Press.

della Porta, D. and Diani, M. (1999). *Social Movements: An Introduction.* Oxford: Blackwell.

den Hond, F. and de Bakker, F. G. A. (2007). Ideologically Motivated Activism: How Activist Groups Influence Corporate Social Change. *Academy of Management Review*, 32(3), 901–924.

den Hond, F., Rehbein, K. A., Bakker, F. G. A. and Lankveld, H. K. (2014). Playing on Two Chessboards: Reputation Effects between Corporate Social Responsibility (CSR) and Corporate Political Activity (CPA). *Journal of Management Studies*, 51(5), 790–813.

de Sardan, J. O. (1999). A Moral Economy of Corruption in Africa?. *Journal of Modern African Studies*, 37(1), 25–52.

Descola, P. (2013). *Beyond Nature and Culture.* Translated by Janet Lloyd with a foreword by Marshall Sahlins. Chicago, IL: University of Chicago Press.

DesJardine, M. R., Marti, E. and Durand, R. (2020). Why Activist Hedge Funds Target Socially Responsible Firms: The Reaction Costs of Signaling Corporate Social Responsibility. *Academy of Management Journal*, 64(3), 851–872.

De Sousa, L. (2010). Anti-Corruption Agencies: Between Empowerment and Irrelevance. *Crime, Law and Social Change*, 53(1), 5–22.

Devall, B. and Sessions, G. (1985). *Deep Ecology: Living as If Nature Mattered.* Layton, UT: Gibbs Smith.

de Villiers, C., Rinaldi, L. and Unerman, J. (2014). Integrated Reporting: Insights, Gaps, and an Agenda for Future Research. *Accounting, Auditing and Accountability Journal*, 27(7), 1042–1067.

Dey, C. (2007). Developing Silent and Shadow Accounts. In J. Unerman, J. Bebbington and B. O'Dwyer. (Eds.), *Sustainability Accounting and Accountability* (pp. 307–327). New York, NY: Routledge.

Dey, C., Russell, S. and Thomson, I. (2011). Exploring the Potential of Shadow Accounts in Problematising Institutional Conduct. In S. Osbourne and A. Ball. (Eds.), *Social Accounting and Public Management: Accountability for the Public Good* (pp. 64–75). New York, NY: Routledge.

Djelic, M.-L. and Etchanchu, H. (2017). Contextualizing Political Responsibilities: Neoliberal CSR in Historical Perspective. *Journal of Business Ethics*, 142(4), 641–661.

Doherty, B., Haugh, H. and Lyon, F. (2014). Social Enterprises as Hybrid Organizations: A Review and Research Agenda. *International Journal of Management Reviews*, 16(4), 417–436.

Doherty, B. and Hayes, G. (2019). Tactics and Strategic Action. In D. A. Snow, S. A. Soule, H. Kriesi and H. J. McCammon. (Eds.). *The Wiley Blackwell Companion to Social Movements* (2nd ed., pp. 271–288). Hoboken, NJ: Wiley.

Donaldson, T. and Preston, L. E. (1995). The Stakeholder Theory of the Corporation: Concepts, Evidence, and Implications. *Academy of Management Review*, 20(1), 65–91.

Dowling, G. and Moran, P. (2012). Corporate Reputations: Built in or Bolted on? *California Management Review*, 54(2), 25–42.

Driscoll, C. and Starik, M. (2004). The Primordial Stakeholder: Advancing the Conceptual Consideration of Stakeholder Status for the Natural Environment. *Journal of Business Ethics*, 49(1), 55–73.

Drucker, P. (1954). *The Practice of Management*. New York, NY: Harper Collins.

Du, S., Bhattacharya, C. B. and Sen, S. (2011). Corporate Social Responsibility and Competitive Advantage: Overcoming the Trust Barrier. *Management Science*, 57(9), 1528–1545.

Dwumfour, R. A. (2020). Poverty in Sub-Saharan Africa: The Role of Business Regulations, Policies and Institutions. *Social Indicators Research*, 149(3), 861–890.

Easterlin, R. A. (1974). Does Economic Growth Improve the Human Lot? Some Empirical Evidence. In P. A. David and M. W. Reder (Eds.), *Nations and Households in Economic Growth: Essays in Honor of Moses Abramovitz* (pp. 89–125). London and New York, NY: Academic Press.

econsense and twentyfifty. (2019). No Way around Due Diligence. Overview of Human Rights Due Diligence Frameworks and Legislation. Retrieved on 6 March 2022 from https://econsense.de/wp-content/uploads/2019/07/190322_Due_Diligence.pdf.

Edelman. (2022). Edelman Trust Barometer 2021. Retrieved on 17 October 2022 from edelman.com/trust/2021-trust-barometer.

Edinger-Schons, L., Sipilä, J., Sen, S. Mende, G. and Wieseke, J. (2018). Are Two Reasons Better than One? The Role of Appeal Type in Consumer Responses to Sustainable Products. *Journal of Consumer Psychology*, 28(4), 644–664.

Edmans, A. (2021). How Brown Stocks Produce Green Patents. Retrieved on 17 October 2022 from www.growthepie.net/how-brown-stocks-produce-green-patents/.

Ehrenfeld, J. (2008). *Sustainability by Design*. New Haven, CT. Yale University Press.

Ehrhardt-Martinez, K. (1998). Social Determinants of Deforestation in Developing Countries: A Cross-National Study. *Social Forces*, 77(2), 567–586.

Eisenegger, M. and Schranz, M. (2011). Reputation Management and Corporate Social Responsibility. In O. Ihlen, J. Bartlett and S. May. (Eds.), *Handbook of Communication and Corporate Social Responsibility*. Oxford: Wiley.

Elhacham, E., Ben-Uri, L., Grozovski, J., Baron, Y. M. and Milo, R. (2020). Global Human-Made Mass Exceeds All Living Biomass. *Nature*, 588(7838), 442–444.

Elkington, J. (1997). *Cannibals with Forks: The Triple Bottom Line of 21st Century Business*. Oxford: Capstone.

  (1994). Towards the Sustainable Corporation: Win-win-win Business Strategies for Sustainable Development. *California Management Review*, 36(2), 90–100.

Ellen MacArthur Foundation. (2019). Completing the Picture: How the Circular Economy Tackles Climate Change. Ellen MacArthur Foundation. https://ellenmacarthurfoundation.org/completing-the-picture.

(2013). Towards the Circular Economy: Economic and Business Rationale for an Accelerated Transition. Ellen MacArthur Foundation. Retrieved on 17 October 2022 from www.werktrends.nl/app/uploads/2015/06/Rapport_McKinsey-Towards_A_Circular_Economy.pdf.

Ellis, K. and Tran, K. T. L. (2016). Sweatshops Persist in U.S. Garment Industry. Retrieved on 17 October 2022 from https://wwd.com/business-news/government-trade/sweatshops-persist-in-u-s-garment-industry-10716742/.

El Madani, A. (2018). SME Policy: Comparative Analysis of SME Definitions. *International Journal of Academic Research in Business and Social Sciences*, 8(8), 100–111.

Endregat, N. and Pennink, B. (2021). Exploring the Coevolution of Traditional and Sustainable Business Models: A Paradox Perspective. *Journal of Business Models*, 9(2), 1–21.

Epley, N. and Kumar, A. (2019). How to Design an Ethical Organization. *Harvard Business Review*, 97(3), 144–150.

Etchanchu, H. and Djelic, M.-L. (2019). Old Wine in New Bottles? Parentalism, Power, and Its Legitimacy in Business–Society Relations. *Journal of Business Ethics*, 160(4), 893–911.

Etzion, D. and Ferraro, F. (2010). The Role of Analogy in the Institutionalization of Sustainability Reporting. *Organization Science*, 21(5), 1092–1107.

European Commission. (2020a). Why Do We Need an EU Taxonomy? Retrieved on 17 October 2022 from https://ec.europa.eu/info/business-economy-euro/banking-and-finance/sustainable-finance/eu-taxonomy-sustainable-activities_en.

(2020b). Inception Impact Assessment – Sustainable Corporate Governance. Retrieved on 17 October 2022 from https://ec.europa.eu/info/law/better-regulation/have-your-say/initiatives/12548-Sustainable-corporate-governance_en.

(2011). Communication from the Commission to the European Parliament, the Council, and European Economic and Social Committee and the Committee of the Regions: A Renewed EU Strategy 2011-14 for Corporate Social Responsibility (COM (2011) 681 final). Retrieved on 18 January 2022 from https://op.europa.eu/en/publication-detail/-/publication/ae5ada03-0dc3-48f8-9a32-0460e65ba7ed/language-en.

(2001). Promoting a European Framework for Corporate Social Responsibility (Green Paper, COM, 2001, 366 final). Retrieved on 17 October 2022 from https://eur-lex.europa.eu/legal-content/EN/TXT/PDF/?uri=CELEX:52001DC0366&from=EN.

European Financial Reporting Advisory Group (EFRAG). (2021). *Proposals for a Relevant and Dynamic EU Sustainability Reporting Standard-Setting*. Brussels, Belgium: EFRAG.

European Parliament. (2021). Report with Recommendations to the Commission on Corporate Due Diligence and Corporate Accountability (A9-0018/

2021). Retrieved on 2 December 2021 from www.europarl.europa.eu/doceo/document/A-9-2021-0018_EN.pdf.

(2013). *Directive 2013/34/EU of the European Parliament and of the Council of 26 June 2013 on the Annual Financial Statements, Consolidated Financial Statements and Related Reports of Certain Types of Undertakings.* Retrieved on 17 October 2022 from https://eur-lex.europa.eu/legal-content/EN/TXT/?uri=celex%3A32013L0034.

and European Council. (2014). *Directive 2014/95/EU of the European Parliament and of the Council as of 22 October 2014.* Brussels, Belgium: European Parliament and European Council.

and European Council. (2004). *Directive 2004/109/EC of the European Parliament and of the European Council as of 15 December 2004.* Brussels, Belgium: European Parliament and European Council.

European Parliamentary Research Service (EPRS). (2020). Towards a Mandatory EU System of Due Diligence for Supply Chains. Retrieved on 17 October 2022 from www.europarl.europa.eu/RegData/etudes/BRIE/2020/659299/EPRS_BRI(2020)659299_EN.pdf.

Evan, W. M. and Freeman, E. (1993). A Stakeholder Theory of the Modern Corporation: Kantian Capitalism. In T. L. Beauchamp and N. E. Bowie. (Eds.), *Ethical Theory and Business* (pp. 75–84). Englewood Cliffs, NJ: Prentice Hall.

Evans, S., Vladimirova, D., Holgado, M., van Fossen, K., Yang, M., Silva, E. and

Barlow, C. (2017). Business Model Innovation for Sustainability: Towards a Unified Perspective for Creation of Sustainable Business Models. *Business Strategy and the Environment,* 26(5), 597–608.

Everett, J. A. C., Pizarro, D. A. and Crockett, M. J. (2016). Inference of Trustworthiness from Intuitive Moral Judgments. *Journal of Experimental Psychology: General,* 145(6), 772–787.

Fagan, M. and Huang, C. (2019). A Look at How People around the World View Climate Change, Pew Research Center. Retrieved on 17 October 2022 from www.pewresearch.org/fact-tank/2019/04/18/a-look-at-how-people-around-the-world-view-climate-change/.

Fairphone. (2022). The Phone that Cares for People and Planet. Retrieved on 16 January 2022 from www.fairphone.com/en/.

Faraci, D. (2019). Wage Exploitation and the Nonworseness Claim: Allowing the Wrong, to Do More Good. *Business Ethics Quarterly,* 29(2), 169–188.

Faust, E. and Steuer, M. (2019). Climate Change Increases Wildfire Risk in California. Munich RE. Retrieved on 21 January 2022 from www.munichre.com/topics-online/en/climate-change-and-natural-disasters/climate-change/climate-change-has-increased-wildfire-risk.html.

Federman, S. (2022). How Companies Can Address Their Historical Transgressions: Lessons from the Slave Trade and the Holocaust. *Harvard Business Review,* January–February.

Fédération Internationale de Football Association (FIFA). (2017). FIFA's

Human Rights Policy. Retrieved on 17 October 2022 from https://img.fifa.com/image/upload/kr05dqyhwr1uhqy2lh6r.pdf.

Fifka, M. S. (2013). Corporate Responsibility Reporting and Its Determinants in Comparative Perspective – A Review of the Empirical Literature and a Meta-Analysis. *Business Strategy and the Environment*, 22(1), 1–35.

Fine, G. A. (2019). Moral Cultures, Reputation Work, and the Politics of Scandal. *Annual Review of Sociology*, 45(1), 247–264.

Fink, L. (2019). Larry Fink's 2019 Letter to CEOS: The Power of Capitalism. Retrieved on 22 October 2022 from www.blackrock.com/corporate/investor-relations/larry-fink-ceo-letter.

Finkelstein, S. and D'aveni, R. A. (1994). CEO Duality as a Double-Edged Sword: How Boards of Directors Balance Entrenchment Avoidance and Unity of Command. *Academy of Management Journal*, 37(5), 1079–1108.

Flammer, C., Hong, B. and Minor, D. (2019). Corporate Governance and the Rise of Integrating Corporate Social Responsibility Criteria in Executive Compensation: Effectiveness and Implications for Firm Outcomes. *Strategic Management Journal*, 40(7), 1097–1122.

Flammer, C. and Luo, J. (2018). Corporate Social Responsibility as an Employee Governance Tool: Evidence from a Quasi-Experiment. *Strategic Management Journal*, 38(2), 163–183.

Flanigan, J. (2018). Sweatshop Regulation and Workers' Choices. *Journal of Business Ethics*, 153(1), 79–94.

Flyverbom, M. and Whelan, G. (2019). Digital Transformation, Informed Realities, and Human Conduct. In R. FrankJørgensen. (Ed.), *Human Rights in the Age of Platforms* (pp. 53–72). Cambridge, MA: The MIT Press.

Forbes. (2017). What Will Car Ownership Look Like in the Future? *Forbes*. Retrieved on 17 October 2022 from www.forbes.com/sites/quora/2017/06/22/what-will-car-ownership-look-like-in-the-future/.

Forno, F. (2013). *Co-operative Movement*. In D. A. Snow, D. Della Porta, B. Klandermans and D. McAdam. (Eds.), *Blackwell Encyclopedia of Social and Political Movements* (pp. 278–280). Oxford: Blackwell.

Fox, J. (2012). Throwing Out Insiders Won't Fix Corporate Boards. *Harvard Business Review* (digital articles). Retrieved on 17 October 2022 from https://hbr.org/2012/10/throwing-out-insiders-corporate-boards.html.

Fox, T., Ward, H. and Howard, B. (2002). *The Public Sector Roles in Strengthening Corporate Social Responsibility: A Baseline Study*. Washington, DC: World Bank.

Fransen, L. W. and Kolk, A. (2007). Global Rule-Setting for Business: A Critical Analysis of Multi-Stakeholder Standards. *Organization*, 14(5), 667–684.

Free, C. W. and Macintosh, N. B. (2006). Management Control Practice and Culture at Enron: The Untold Story. 8 August CAAA 2006 Annual Conference Paper. Retrieved on 17 October 2022 from https://papers.ssrn.com/sol3/papers.cfm?abstract_id=873636.

Freeman, R. E. (2008). *Managing for Stakeholders: Ethical Theory and Business* (8th ed.), edited by T. L. Beauchamp, N. E. Bowie and D. G. Arnold. Englewood Cliffs, NJ: Pearson Prentice Hall.

  (1984a). *Stakeholder Management: Framework and Philosophy.* Mansfield, MA: Pitman Publishing.

  (1984b). *Strategic Management: A Stakeholder Approach.* Boston, MA: Pitman Publishing.

Freeman, R. E. and Dmytriyev, S. (2017). Corporate Social Responsibility and Stakeholder Theory: Learning from Each Other. *Symphonya. Emerging Issues in Management,* 2(1), 7–15.

Freeman, R. E., Harrison, J. S., Wicks, A. C., Parmar, B. L. and De Colle, S. (2010). *Stakeholder Theory: The State of the Art.* Cambridge: Cambridge University Press.

Freudenreich, B., Lüdeke-Freund, F. and Schaltegger, S. (2020). A Stakeholder Theory Perspective on Business Models: Value Creation for Sustainability. *Journal of Business Ethics,* 166(1), 3–18.

Frey, B. S. (1997). *Not Just for the Money: An Economic Theory of Personal Motivation.* Cheltenham, UK.: Edward Elgar.

Friede, G., Busch, T. and Bassen, A. (2015). ESG and Financial Performance: Aggregated Evidence from More than 2000 Empirical Studies. *Journal of Sustainable Finance and Investment,* 5 (4), 210–233.

Friedman, M. (2007). The Social Responsibility of Business Is to Increase Its Profits BT – Corporate Ethics and Corporate Governance. In W. C. Zimmerli, M. Holzinger and K. Richter. (Eds.), *Corporate Ethics and Corporate Governance* (pp. 173–178). Berlin and Heidelberg: Springer. (Originally published in *The New York Times Magazine,* 13 September 1970.)

  (1973). The Playboy Interview. *Playboy,* 1973.

Friedman, M. (1970). The Social Responsibility of Business Is to Increase Its Profits. *The New York Times Magazine.*

Friedman, M. and Friedman, R. D. (1998). *Two Lucky People: Memoirs.* Chicago, IL: University of Chicago Press.

Fritsch, B., Schmidheiny, S. and Seifritz, W. (1994). *Towards an Ecologically Sustainable Growth Society.* Berlin: Springer.

Frynas, J. (2012). Corporate Social Responsibility or Government Regulation? Evidence on Oil Spill Prevention. *Ecology and Society,* 17(4), 1–13.

  (2009). *Beyond Corporate Social Responsibility.* Cambridge: Cambridge University Press.

Fusaro, P. C. and Miller, R. M. (2003). *What Went Wrong at Enron.* Hoboken, NJ: Wiley.

Gallie, W. B. (1956). IX. Essentially Contested Concepts. *Proceedings of the Aristotelian Society,* 56(1), 167–198.

Gassmann, O., Frankenberger, K. and Choudury, M. (2020). *Business Model Navigator: The Strategies behind the Most Successful Companies.* Harlow, UK: Pearson.

Gatti, L., Vishwanath, B., Seele, P. and Cottier, B. (2019). Are We Moving

Beyond Voluntary CSR? Exploring Theoretical and Managerial Implications of Mandatory CSR Resulting from the New Indian Companies Act. *Journal of Business Ethics*, 160(4), 961–972.

George, B. (2004). *Authentic Leadership*. San Francisco, CA: Jossey Bass.

Gerde, V. W. and Wokutch, R. E. (1998). 25 Years and Going Strong: A Content Analysis of the First 25 Years of the Social Issues in Management Division Proceedings. *Business and Society*, 37 (4), 414–446.

Gereffi, G. (2020). What Does the COVID-19 Pandemic Teach Us about Global Value Chains? The Case of Medical Supplies. *Journal of International Business Policy*, 3(3), 287–301.

Germanwatch. (2021). Stellungnahme an das Bundesministerium für Arbeit und Soziales zum Referentenentwurf eines Gesetzes über die unternehmerischen Sorgfaltspflichten in Lieferketten vom 1. März 2021. Retrieved on 17 October 2022 from www.bmas.de/SharedDocs/ Downloads/DE/Gesetze/Stellungnahmen/ sorgfaltspflichtengesetz-germanwatch .pdf;jsessionid=FFD3228472CE97ED C95E771B220189BF.delivery1- replication?__blob=publicationFile&tv=2.

Gert, B. and Gert, J. (2020). The Definition of Morality. *Stanford Encyclopedia of Philosophy*. Retrieved on 17 October 2022 from https://plato.stanford.edu/ entries/morality-definition/.

Giamporcaro, S., Gond, J.-P. and O'Sullivan, N. (2020). Orchestrating Governmental Corporate Social Responsibility Interventions through Financial Markets: The Case of French Socially Responsible Investment. *Business Ethics Quarterly*, 33(3), 288–334.

Gilbert, D. U. and Rasche, A. (2007). Discourse Ethics and Social Accountability: The Ethics of SA 8000. *Business Ethics Quarterly*, 17(2), 187–216.

Gilbert, D. U., Rasche, A. and Waddock, S. (2011). Accountability in a Global Economy: The Emergence of International Accountability Standards. *Business Ethics Quarterly*, 21(1), 23–44.

Gilens, M. and Page, B. (2014). Testing Theories of American Politics: Elites, Interest Groups, and Average Citizens. *Perspectives on Politics*, 12(3), 564–581.

Girschik, V., Hotho, J. and Rasche, A. (2021). Partnering for Change: Novo Nordisk's Partnership with the International Committee of the Red Cross and the Danish Red Cross (Teaching Case). Retrieved on 17 October 2022 from www.thecasecentre.org/products/view? id=178840.

Girschik, V., Svystunova, L. and Lysova, E. (2022). Transforming Corporate Social Responsibilities: Toward an Intellectual Activist Research Agenda for Micro-CSR Research. *Human Relations*, 75(1), 3–32.

Gleick, P. H. (2009). Three Gorges Dam Project, Yangtze River, China. In the World's Water 2008–2009, pp. 139–150, Washington, DC: Island Press. Retrieved on 17 October 2022 from http://worldwater.org/water-data/.

Glendon, M.-A. (2001). *A World Made New: Eleanor Roosevelt and the Universal*

Declaration of Human Rights. New York, NY: Random House.

Global Impact Investing Network (GIIN). (2019). Annual Impact Investor Survey 2018. Retrieved on 17 October 2022 from https://thegiin.org/assets/GIIN_2019 Annual Impact Investor Survey_webfile.pdf.

Global Reporting Initiative (GRI). (2017). Mapping G4 to the GRI Standards – Disclosures. Retrieved on 22 October 2022 from www.globalreporting.org/ standards/media/1098/mapping-g4-to-the-gri-standards-disclosures-full-overview.pdf.

Global Reporting Initiative (GRI), University of Stellenbosch Business School and UN Environmental Programme (UNEP). (2020). Carrots and Sticks. Sustainability Reporting Policy: Global Trends in Disclosure as the ESG Agenda Goes Mainstream. Retrieved on 17 October 2022 from www. carrotsandsticks.net/media/zirbzabv/ carrots-and-sticks-2020-june2020.pdf.

Global Sustainable Investment Alliance (GSIA). (2021). Global Sustainable Investment Review 2020. Retrieved on 17 October 2022 from www.gsi-alliance.org/wp-content/uploads/2021/ 08/GSIR-20201.pdf.

(2018). Global Sustainable Investment Review 2018. Retrieved on 17 October 2022 from www.gsi-alliance.org/wp-content/uploads/2019/06/GSIR_ Review2018F.pdf.

Goglio, S. and Kalmi, P. (2017). Credit Unions and Co-operative Banks across the World. In J. Michie, J. R. Blasi and C. Borzaga. (Eds.), *The Oxford Handbook of Mutual, Co-operative, and Co-owned Business* (pp. 145–157). Oxford: Oxford University Press.

Gomez-Carrasco, P. and Michelon, G. (2017). The Power of Stakeholders' Voice: The Effects of Social Media Activism on Stock Markets. *Business Strategy and the Environment*, 26(6), 855–872.

Gond, J. and Brès, L. (2020). Designing the Tools of the Trade: How Corporate Social Responsibility Consultants and Their Tool-Based Practices Created Market Shifts. *Organization Studies*, 41 (5), 703–726.

Gond, J., Igalens, J., Swaen, V. and El Akremi, A. (2011a). The Human Resources Contribution to Responsible Leadership: An Exploration of the CSR-HR Interface. *Journal of Business Ethics*, 98(1), 115–132.

Gond, J.-P., Kang, N. and Moon, J. (2011b). The Government of Self-Regulation: On the Comparative Dynamics of Corporate Social Responsibility. *Economy & Society*, 40(4), 640–671.

Gond, J. and Moser, C. (2021). Critical Essay: The Reconciliation of Fraternal Twins: Integrating the Psychological and Sociological Approaches to 'Micro' Corporate Social Responsibility. *Human Relations*, 74(1), 5–40.

Gond, J.-P. and Moon, J. (2011). Corporate Social Responsibility in Retrospect and Prospect: Exploring the Life-cycle of an Essentially Contested Concept. In J.-P. Gond and J. Moon. (Eds.), *Corporate Social Responsibility: A Reader. Critical Perspectives in Business and Management* (Vol. 1, pp. 1–28). New York, NY: Routledge.

Gond, J.-P., O'Sullivan, N., Slager, R., Hormanen, M., Viehs, M. and Mosony, S. (2018). How Engagement Creates Value for Investors and Companies. Retrieved on 17 October 2022 from www.unpri.org/download?ac=4637.

Goodpaster, K. E. and Mathews J. B. (1982). Can a Corporation Have a Conscience? *Harvard Business Review*, 60(1), 132–141.

Google. (2021). About Google, Our Culture & Company News. Retrieved on 17 October 2022 from https://about.google/.

Goranova, M. and Ryan, L. V. (2014). Shareholder Activism: A Multidisciplinary Review. *Journal of Management*, 40(5), 1230–1268.

Graafland, J. and van de Ven, B. (2014). Strategic and Moral Motivation for Corporate Social Responsibility. *Journal of Corporate Citizenship*, 2006 (22), 111–123.

Grabosch, R. (2019). *Unternehmen und Menschenrechte. Gesetzliche Verpflichtungen zur Sorgfalt im weltweiten Vergleich*. Berlin: Friedrich-Ebert-Stiftung, Global Policy and Development (Studie).

Grabs, J. (2020). Assessing the Institutionalization of Private Sustainability Governance in a Changing Coffee Sector. *Regulation and Governance*, 14(2), 362–387.

Graves, S. B., Rehbein, K. and Waddock, S. (2001). Fad and Fashion in Shareholder Activism: The Landscape of Shareholder Resolutions, 1988–1998. *Business and Society Review*, 106(4), 293–314.

Gray, B. (1989). *Collaborating: Finding Common Ground for Multiparty Problems*. San Francisco, CA: Jossey-Bass.

Gray, R. (2006). Does Sustainability Reporting Improve Corporate Behaviour? Wrong Question? Right Time? *Accounting and Business Research*, 36(Sup1), 65–88.

Gray, R. H., Adams, C. and Owen, D. (Eds.) (2014). *Accountability, Social Responsibility and Sustainability: Accounting for Society and the Environment*. Harlow, UK: Pearson Education.

Grayson, D. and Kakabadse, A. (2013). Sustainable Business Leadership: Take It from the Top. *Ethical Corporation*, February, pp. 36–39.

Grayson, D. and Nelson, J. (2013). *Corporate Responsibility Coalitions: The Past, Present, and Future of Alliances for Sustainable Capitalism*. Stanford, CA: Stanford University Press.

Grennan, J. A. (2013). A Corporate Culture Channel: How Increased Shareholder Governance Reduces Firm Value. *SSRN*. Retrieved on 17 October 2022 from https://doi.org/10.2139/ssrn .2345384

Grimes, M. G., Williams, T. A. and Zhao, E. Y. (2019). Anchors Aweigh: The Sources, Variety, and Challenges of Mission Drift. *Academy of Management Review*, 44(4), 819–845.

Grimstad, S. M. F., Glavee-Geo, R. and Fjørtoft, B. E. (2020). SMEs Motivations for CSR: An Exploratory Study. *European Business Review*, 32(4), 553–572.

Grin, J., Rotmans, J. and Schot, J. (2010). *Transitions to Sustainable Development: New Directions in the*

Study of Long-Term Transformative Change. London and New York, NY: Routledge.

Guay, T., Doh, J. P. and Sinclair, G. (2004). Non-Governmental Organizations, Shareholder Activism, and Socially Responsible Investments: Ethical, Strategic, and Governance Implications. *Journal of Business Ethics*, 52(1), 125–139.

Guerrera, F. (2009). Welch Condemns Share Price Focus, *Financial Times*. Retrieved on 17 October 2022 from www.ft.com/content/294ff1f2-0f27-11de-ba10-0000779fd2ac.

Guillén, L., Sergio, A. and Manuel, C. (2021). Research on Social Responsibility of Small and Medium Enterprises: A Bibliometric Analysis. *Management Review Quarterly*, 1–53. Retrieved on 17 October 2022 from https://link.springer.com/article/10.1007/s11301-021-00217-w#citeas.

Gulbrandsen, L. H. (2012). *Transnational Environmental Governance: The Emergence and Effects of the Certification of Forests and Fisheries*. Cheltenham, UK: Edward Elgar.

Gunningham, N., Kagan, R. A. and Thornton, D. (2017). Social License and Environmental Protection: Why Businesses Go beyond Compliance. *Law & Social Inquiry*, 29(2), 307–341.

Haack, P., Martignoni, D. and Schoeneborn, D. (2021). A Bait-and-Switch Model of Corporate Social Responsibility. *Academy of Management Review*, 46(3), 440–464.

Haack, P. and Rasche, A. (2022). The Legitimacy of Sustainability Standards: A Paradox Perspective. *Organization Theory*, 2(4), Article 26317877.

Haack, P., Schoeneborn, D. and Wickert, C. (2012). Talking the Talk, Moral Entrapment, Creeping Commitment? Exploring Narrative Dynamics in Corporate Responsibility Standardization. *Organization Studies*, 33(5–63), 815–845.

Hadani, M., Doh, J. P. and Schneider, M. (2019). Social Movements and Corporate Political Activity: Managerial Responses to Socially Oriented Shareholder Activism. *Journal of Business Research*, 95(C), 156–170.

Haffar, M. and Searcy, C. (2020). Legitimizing Potential 'Bad News': How Companies Disclose on Their Tension Experiences in Their Sustainability Reports. *Organization & Environment*, 33(4), 534–553.

Hahn, T., Figge, F., Pinkse, J. and Preuss, L. (2018). A Paradox Perspective on Corporate Sustainability: Descriptive, Instrumental, and Normative Aspects. *Journal of Business Ethics*, 148(2), 235–248.

Hahn, T., Pinkse, J., Preuss, L. and Figge, F. (2015). Tensions in Corporate Sustainability: Towards an Integrative Framework. *Journal of Business Ethics*, 127(2), 297–316.

Hahn, T., Preuss, L., Pinkse, J. and Figge, F. (2014). Cognitive Frames in Corporate Sustainability: Managerial Sensemaking with Paradoxical and Business Case Frames. *Academy of Management Review*, 39(4), 463–487.

Haidt, J. (2012). *The Righteous Mind: Why Good People Are Divided by Politics and Religion*. New York, NY: Vintage.

Haines, H. (1984). Black Radicalization and the Funding of Civil Rights: 1957–1970. *Social Problems*, 32(1), 31–43.

Hale, T. N. (2008). Transparency, Accountability, and Global Governance. *Global Governance*, 14(1), 73–94.

Haller, K., Lee, J. and Cheung, J. (2020). Meet the 2020 Consumers Driving Change. Retrieved on 17 October 2022 from www.ibm.com/downloads/cas/EXK4XKX8.

Handley, A. (2005). Business, Government and Economic Policymaking in the New South Africa, 1990–2000. *Journal of Modern African Studies*, 43(2), 211–239.

Hansen, E. G. and Schmitt, J. C. (2021). Orchestrating Cradle-to-Cradle Innovation across the Value Chain: Overcoming Barriers through Innovation Communities, Collaboration Mechanisms, and Intermediation. *Journal of Industrial Ecology*, 25(3), 627–647.

Hansen, H. K. (2011). Managing Corruption Risks. *Review of International Political Economy*, 18(2), 251–275.

Harjoto, M., Laksmana, I. and Lee, R. (2015). Board Diversity and Corporate Social Responsibility. *Journal of Business Ethics*, 132(4), 641–660.

Harrison, A. and Scorse, J. (2006). Improving the Conditions of Workers? Minimum Wage Legislation and Anti-Sweatshop Activism. *California Management Review*, 48(2), 144–160.

Hatch, M. J. (1997). Jazzing up the Theory of Organizational Improvisation. *Advances in Strategic Management*, 14 (2), 181–191.

Haufler, V. (2015). Shaming the Shameless? Campaigning against Corporations. In H. Friman. (Ed.), *The Politics of Leverage in International Relations* (pp. 185–200). London: Palgrave Macmillan.

Havas Group. (2021). Havas' Meaningful Brands Report 2021 Finds We Are Entering the Age of Cynicism. Retrieved on 17 October 2022 from www.havasgroup.com/press_release/havas-meaningful-brands-report-2021-finds-we-are-entering-the-age-of-cynicism/.

Haws, K. L., Winterich, K. P. and Naylor, R. W. (2014). Seeing the World through GREEN-Tinted Glasses: Green Consumption Values and Responses to Environmentally Friendly Products. *Journal of Consumer Psychology*, 24(3), 336–354.

Haxhi, I. and Aguilera, R. V. (2014). Corporate Governance through Codes. In C. Cooper. (Ed.), *Wiley Encyclopedia of Management* (3rd ed.). Oxford: Wiley-Blackwell.

Heald, M. (1970). *The Social Responsibilities of Business: Company and Community, 1900–1960*. Cleveland, OH: Case Western Reserve University Press.

Hechler, H. (2010). UNCAC in a Nutshell. A Quick Guide to the United Nations Convention against Corruption for Embassy and Donor Agency Staff. U4 Brief, 2010(6).

Heidenheimer, A. J. and Moroff, H. (2017). Controlling Business Payoffs to Foreign Officials: The 1998 OECD Anti-bribery Convention. In M. Johnston. (Ed.), *Political Corruption: Readings in Comparative Analysis* (pp. 943–959). London and New York, NY: Routledge.

Heisler, R. (2018). Strategic Philanthropy. Retrieved on 17 October 2022 from https://growthmastery.net/strategic-philanthropy/.

Hellman, J. S., Jones, G. and Kaufmann, D. (2000). *Seize the State, Seize the Day: State Capture, Corruption, and Influence in Transition* (Policy Research Working Paper 2444). The World Bank.

Helper, S. and Henderson, R. (2014). *Management Practices, Relational Contracts and the Decline of General Motors* (Working paper, Harvard Business School, 14-062), 28 January. Retrieved on 17 October 2022 from www.hbs.edu/faculty/Publication%20Files/14-062_29ad7901-c306-44fa-88df-31e97a17cbbf.pdf.

Hemingway, C. A. and Maclagan, P. W. (2004). Managers' Personal Values as Drivers of Corporate Social Responsibility. *Journal of Business Ethics*, 50(1), 33–44.

Hemmer, H. R. and Hoa, N. T. (2002). *Contribution of Foreign Direct Investment to Poverty Reduction: The Case of Vietnam in the 1990s* (Discussion Paper in Development Economics 30). Justus Liebig University Giessen: Institute for Development Economics. Retrieved on 17 October 2022 from https://core.ac.uk/download/pdf/56347911.pdf.

Hendry, J. R. (2006). Taking Aim at Business: What Factors Lead Environmental Non-Governmental Organizations to Target Particular Firms? *Business & Society*, 45(1), 47–86.

Hengst, I.-A., Jarzabkowski, P., Hoegl, M. and Muethel, M. (2019). Toward a Process Theory of Making Sustainability Strategies Legitimate in Action. *Academy of Management Journal*, 63(1), 246–271.

Herzig, C. and Ghosh, B. (2017). Sustainability Reporting. In P. Moltan-Hill. (Ed.), *The Business Student's Guide to Sustainable Management: Principles and Practice* (2nd ed., pp. 160–195). Sheffield: Greenleaf.

Herzig, C. and Godemann, J. (2010). Internet-Supported Sustainability Reporting: Developments in Germany. *Management Research Review*, 33(11), 1064–1082.

Herzig, C. and Kühn, A.-L. (2017). Corporate Responsibility Reporting. In J. Moon, M. Morsing and A. Rasche. (Eds.), *Corporate Social Responsibility: Strategy, Communication and Governance* (pp. 340–392). Cambridge: Cambridge University Press.

Herzig, C. and Schaltegger, S. (2011). Corporate Sustainability Reporting. In J. Godemann and G. Michelsen (Eds.), *Sustainability Communication - Interdisciplinary Perspectives and Theoretical Foundations* (pp. 151–169). Heidelberg, Berlin: Springer.

Heyen, D., Hermwille, L. and Wehnert, T. (2017). Out of the Comfort Zone! Governing the Exnovation of Unsustainable Technologies and Practices. *GAIA – Ecological Perspectives for Science and Society*, 26 (4), 326–331.

Heywood, P. (1997). Political Corruption: Problems and Perspectives. *Political Studies*, 45(3), 417–435.

Higgins, C. and Larrinaga, C. (2014). Sustainability Reporting: Insights from

Institutional Theory. In J. Bebbington, J. Unerman and B. O'Dwyer. (Eds.), *Sustainability Accounting and Accountability* (pp. 273–285). New York, NY: Routledge.

Hileman, J., Kallstenius, I., Häyhä, T., Palm, C. and Cornell, S. (2020). Keystone Actors Do Not Act Alone: A Business Ecosystem Perspective on Sustainability in the Global Clothing Industry. *PLoS ONE*, 15(10), 1–17.

Hilling, A. and Ostas, D. T. (2017). *Corporate Taxation and Social Responsibility*. Stockholm: Wolters Kluwer.

Hockerts, K. and Wüstenhagen, R. (2010). Greening Goliaths versus Emerging Davids – Theorizing about the Role of Incumbents and New Entrants in Sustainable Entrepreneurship. *Journal of Business Venturing*, 25(5), 481–492.

Hoffman, A. (2021). *Management as a Calling: Leading Business, Serving Society*. Palo Alto, CA: Stanford University Press.

  (2019a). Business Sustainability as Systems Change: Market Transformation, Conceptual Note #5-720-388 (William Davidson Institute).

  (2019b). Climate Change and Our Emerging Cultural Shift. *Behavioral Scientist*, 30 September.

  (2018). Communicating about Climate Change with Corporate Leaders and Stakeholders. In M. Nisbet, S. Ho, E. Markowitz, S. O'Neill, M. S. Schafer and J. Thaker. (Eds.), *The Oxford Encyclopedia of Climate Change Communication* (Vol. 2, pp. 1–23). Oxford: Oxford University Press.

  (1999). Institutional Evolution and Change: Environmentalism and the U.S. Chemical Industry. *Academy of Management Journal*, 42(4), 351–371.

Hofman, P. S. and Moon, J. with Wu, B. (2017). Corporate Social Responsibility under Authoritarian Capitalism: Dynamics and Prospects of State-Led and Society-Driven CSR, *Business and Society*, 56(5), 651–671.

Howard, L. (2018). Natural Catastrophe Claims in 2017 Reached a Record $135B, Munich RE. *Insurance Journal*. Retrieved on 22 October 2022 from www.insurancejournal.com/news/national/2018/01/04/476093.htm.

Hursthouse, R. and Pettigrove, G. (2016). Virtue Ethics. *Stanford Encyclopedia of Philosophy*. Retrieved on 17 October 2022 from https://plato.stanford.edu/entries/ethics-virtue/.

Husted, B. W. (2015). Corporate Social Responsibility Practice from 1800–1914: Past Initiatives and Current Debates. *Business Ethics Quarterly*, 25(1), 125–141.

Huxham, C. and Vangen, S. (2004). Doing Things Collaboratively: Realizing the Advantage or Succumbing to Inertia? *Organizational Dynamics*, 33(2), 190–201.

InfluenceMap. (2020). Influence Map. Retrieved on 17 October 2022 from https://influencemap.org/.

Initiative Lieferkettengesetz. (2021). Stellungnahme zum Gesetzentwurf für ein Lieferkettengesetz. Retrieved on 17 October 2022 from www.bmas.de/SharedDocs/Downloads/DE/Gesetze/Stellungnahmen/sorgfaltspflichtengesetz-initiative-lieferkettengesetz.pdf;jsessionid=FFD3228472CE97EDC95E77

1B220189BF.delivery1-replication?__
blob=publicationFile&tv=2.

Interface. (2022). The Net-Works
Program. Retrieved on 16 January
2022 from www.interface.com.cn/
page/thenet-worksprogram.

International Integrated
Reporting Council (IIRC). (2021).
International <IR> Framework.
London: IIRC.

(2018). *Breaking Through – IIRC
Integrated Report 2017.* London: IIRC.

(2013). *The International IR Framework.*
London: IIRC.

International Labor Rights Forum (ILRF).
(2021). Living Wage. Retrieved on
17 October 2022 from https://
laborrights.org/issues/living-wage.

International Labour Organization
(ILO). (2021). Wages. Retrieved on
17 October 2022 from www.ilo.org/
global/topics/wages/lang-en/index
.htm.

(2020). Covid-19 and Child Labour:
A Time of Crisis, a Time to Act.
International Labour Organization.
Geneva: International Labour
Organization. Retrieved on 17 October
2022 from www.ilo.org/wcmsp5/
groups/public/−ed_norm/−ipec/
documents/publication/wcms_747421
.pdf.

(2019). Securing the Competitiveness of
Asia's Garment Sector: A Framework
for Enhancing Factory-Level
Productivity. Geneva: International
Labour Organization. Retrieved on
17 October 2022 from www.ilo.org/
wcmsp5/groups/public/−asia/−ro-
bangkok/documents/publication/
wcms_732907.pdf.

(2018). Ending Child Labour by 2025.
A Review of Policies and Programmes.
Geneva: International Labour
Organization.

(2017a). Global Estimates of Child Labour:
Results and Trends, 2012-2016.
Geneva: International Labour
Organization. Retrieved on 17 October
2022 from www.ilo.org/global/
publications/books/WCMS_575499/
lang−en/index.htm.

(2017b). Global Estimates of Modern
Slavery. Forced Labour and Forced
Marriage. Geneva: International
Labour Organization. Retrieved on
17 October 2022 from www.ilo.org/
wcmsp5/groups/public/@dgreports/
@dcomm/documents/publication/
wcms_575479.pdf.

(2015). International Labour
Organization. Retrieved on 17 October
2022 from www.ilo.org/global/lang-
en/index.htm.

(1989). Indigenous and Tribal Peoples
Convention (Convention No. 169).

International Monetary Fund (IMF). (2020).
Conquering the Great Divide: The
Pandemic Has Laid Bare Deep
Divisions, But It Is Not Too Late to
Change Course. Retrieved on
3 December 2021 from www.imf.org/
external/pubs/ft/fandd/2020/09/
COVID19-and-global-inequality-
joseph-stiglitz.htm.

(2019). *Global Financial Stability Report:
Lower for Longer.* Washington, DC:
IMF.

Intergovernmental Panel on Climate Change
(IPCC). (2021). *Climate Change 2021:
The Physical Science Basis.
Contribution of Working Group I to the*

Sixth Assessment Report of the Intergovernmental Panel on Climate Change. Cambridge: Cambridge University Press.

International Resource Panel (IRP). (2019). Global Resources Outlook 2019: Natural Resources for the Future We Want. A Report of the International Resource Panel (Implications for Business Leaders). Retrieved on 17 October 2022 from www .resourcepanel.org/reports/global-resources-outlook.

International Society of Sustainability Professionals (ISSP). (2016). Annual report of the International Society of Sustainability Professionals (ISSP). Retrieved on 6 March 2022 from https://cdn.ymaws.com/ sustainabilityprofessionals.site-ym .com/resource/collection/1D79407B-EE07-4900-A6A7-B7E7C6426682/ 2015-2016_ISSP_ANNUAL_REPORT_ WEB.pdf.

International Trade Union Confederation (ITUC). (2020). 2020 ITUC Global Rights Index: The World's Worst Countries for Workers. Retrieved on 17 October 2022 from www.ituc-csi .org/IMG/pdf/ituc_globalrightsindex_ 2020_en.pdf.

Ioannou, I. and Serafeim, G. (2011). The Consequences of Mandatory Corporate Sustainability Reporting: Evidence from Four Countries (Working paper no. 11-100), *Harvard Business Review.* Retrieved on 17 October 2022 from https://hbswk.hbs.edu/item/the-consequences-of-mandatory-corporate-sustainability-reporting.

Ipsos Global Advisor. (2020). EARTH DAY 2020. How Does the World View Climate Change and Covid-19? Retrieved on 17 October 2022 from www.ipsos.com/sites/default/files/ct/ news/documents/2020-04/earth-day-2020-ipsos.pdf.

Irwin, J. R. and Naylor, R. W. (2009). Ethical Decisions and Response Mode Compatibility: Weighting of Ethical Attributes in Consideration Sets Formed by Excluding versus Including Product Alternatives. *Journal of Marketing Research*, 46(2), 234–246.

Jackson, D. (2014). Cheney Again Defends Interrogation Techniques. Retrieved on 17 October 2022 from https://eu .usatoday.com/story/theoval/2014/12/ 14/obama-dick-cheney-meet-the-press-senate-torture-report-interrogation-techniques/20394435/.

Jackson, G., Bartosch, J., Avetisyan, E., Kinderman, D. and Knudsen, J. S. (2020). Mandatory Non-Financial Disclosure and Its Influence on CSR: An International Comparison. *Journal of Business Ethics*, 162(2), 323–342.

Jamali, D., Zanhour, M. and Keshishian, T. (2009). Peculiar Strengths and Relational Attributes of SMEs in the Context of CSR. *Journal of Business Ethics*, 87(3), 355–377.

Jellema, S., Werner, M., Rasche, A. and Cornelissen, J. (2022). Questioning Impact: A Cross-Disciplinary Review of Certification Standards for Sustainability. *Business & Society*, 61 (5). Retrieved on 17 October 2022 from https://doi.org/10.1177/ 00076503211056332.

Jensen, M. C. and Meckling, W. H. (1976). Theory of the Firm: Managerial Behavior, Agency Costs and Onwership Structure. *Journal of Financial Economics*, 3(4), 305–360.

Jensen, Steven L. B. (2016). *The Making of International Human Rights.* Cambridge: Cambridge University Press.

Johnson, G. and Scholes, K. (1999). *Exploring Corporate Strategy* (5th ed.). London: Prentice Hall.

Johnson, M. and Schaltegger, S. (2020). Entrepreneurship for Sustainable Development: A Review and Multilevel Causal Mechanism Framework. *Entrepreneurship Theory and Practice*, 44(6), 1141–1173.

Johnston, M. (2005). *Syndromes of Corruption: Wealth, Power, and Democracy.* New York, NY: Cambridge University Press.

Jones, P. and Comfort, D. (2019). Business Contributions to Sustainable Development: A Study of Leading US Retailers. *Advances in Environmental Studies*, 3(1), 132–140.

Joyce, A. and Paquin, R. L. (2016). The Triple Layered Business Model Canvas: A Tool to Design More Sustainable Business Models. *Journal of Cleaner Production*, 135, 1474–1486.

Jugov, T. and Ypi, L. (2019). Structural Injustice, Epistemic Opacity, and the Responsibilities of the Oppressed. *Journal of Social Philosophy*, 50(1), 7–27.

Kano, L. and Oh, C. H. (2020). Global Value Chains in the Post-COVID World: Governance for Reliability. *Journal of Management Studies*, 57(8), 1773–1777.

Kant, I. (1785/1964). *Groundwork of the Metaphysics of Morals.* Translated by H. J. Paton. New York, NY: Harper & Row. (First published in 1785.)

Kaplan, R. (2015). Who Has Been Regulating Whom, Business or Society? The Mid-20th-Century Institutionalization of 'Corporate Responsibility' in the USA. *Socio-Economic Review*, 13(1), 125–155.

Kaptein, M. (2011a). Toward Effective Codes: Testing the Relationship with Unethical Behavior. *Journal of Business Ethics*, 99(2), 233–251.

(2011b). Understanding Unethical Behavior by Unraveling Ethical Culture. *Human Relations*, 64(6), 843–869.

(2004). Business Codes of Multinational Firms: What Do They Say? *Journal of Business Ethics*, 50(1), 13–31.

Kates, M. (2015). The Ethics of Sweatshops and the Limits of Choice. *Business Ethics Quarterly*, 25(02), 191–212.

Kennedy, D. (2003). The Climate Divide. *Science*, 299(5614), 1813.

Kesner, I. F. and Johnson, R. B. (1990). An Investigation of the Relationship between Board Composition and Stockholder Suits. *Strategic Management Journal*, 11(4), 327–336.

Kiliç, M., Kuzey, C. and Uyar, A. (2015). The Impact of Ownership and Board Structure on Corporate Social Responsibility (CSR) Reporting in the

Turkish Banking Industry. *Corporate Governance*, 15(3), 357–374.

Kim, E. (2021). Bitcoin Mining Consumes 0.5% of All Electricity Used Globally and 7 Times Google's Total Usage, New Report Says. Retrieved on 17 October 2022 from www.businessinsider.com/bitcoin-mining-electricity-usage-more-than-google-2021-9?r=US&IR=T.

Kim, J. and Park, T. (2020). How Corporate Social Responsibility (CSR) Saves a Company: The Role of Gratitude in Buffering Vindictive Consumer Behavior from Product Failures. *Journal of Business Research*, 117, 461–472.

Kim, R. C. and Moon, J. (2015). Dynamics of Corporate Social Responsibility in Asia: Knowledge and Norms. *Asian Business and Management*, 14(5), 349–382.

King, A. A. and Pucker, K. P. (2021). The Dangerous Allure of Win-Win Strategies. *Stanford Social Innovation Review*, 19(1), 34–39.

King, B., Felin, T. and Whetten, D. (2010). Finding the Organization in Organizational Theory: A Meta-Theory of the Organization as a Social Actor. *Organization Science*, 21(1), 290–305.

King, B. G. and Soule, S. A. (2007). Social Movements as Extra-Institutional Entrepreneurs: The Effect of Protests on Stock Price Returns. *Administrative Science Quarterly*, 52(3), 413–442.

Kirkpatrick, G. (2009). Corporate Governance: Lessons from the Financial Crisis. *OECD Journal Financial Market Trends*, 1(3), 61–87.

Kiron, D., Kruschwitz, N., Haanaes, K., Reeves, M., Fuisz-Kehrbach, S. K. and Kell, G. (2015). Joining Forces: Collaboration and Leadership for Sustainability. MIT Sloan Management Review (Online Edition). Retrieved on 17 October 2022 from https://sloanreview.mit.edu/projects/joining-forces/.

Kiron, D., Unruh, G., Kruschwitz, N., Reeves, M., Rubel, H. and zum Felde, A. M. (2017). Corporate Sustainability at a Crossroads: Progress toward Our Common Future in Uncertain Times. MIT Sloan Management Review. Retrieved on 17 October 2022 from https://sloanreview.mit.edu/projects/corporate-sustainability-at-a-crossroads/.

Kleine, A. and von Hauff, M. (2009). Sustainability-Driven Implementation of Corporate Social Responsibility: Application of the Integrative Sustainability Triangle. *Journal of Business Ethics*, 85(S3), 517–533.

KnowTheChain. (2018). Eradicating Forced Labor in Electronics. What Do Company Statements under the UK Modern Slavery Act Tell Us? Retrieved on 17 October 2022 from https://knowthechain.org/wp-content/uploads/KTC-ICT-MSA-Report_Final_Web.pdf.

Knudsen, J. S. (2018). Government Regulation of International Corporate Social Responsibility in the US and the UK: How Domestic Institutions Shape Mandatory and Supportive Initiatives – Government Regulation of International Corporate Social Responsibility. *British Journal of Industrial Relations*, 56(1), 164–188.

Knudsen, J. S. and Brown, D. (2015). Why Governments Intervene: Exploring

Mixed Motives for Public Policies on CSR. *Public Policy and Administration*, 30(1), 51–72.

Knudsen, J. S. and Moon, J. (2022). Corporate Social Responsibility and Government: The Role of Discretion for Engagement with Public Policy. *Business Ethics Quarterly*, 32(2), 243–271.

(2017). *Visible Hands: Government Regulation of Corporate Social Responsibility in Global Business.* Cambridge: Cambridge University Press.

Knudsen, J. S., Moon, J. and Slager, R. (2015). Government Policies for Corporate Social Responsibility in Europe: Support and Institutionalization. *Policy and Politics*, 43(1), 81–99.

Koehler, M. (2012). The Story of the Foreign Corrupt Practices Act. *Ohio State Law Journal*, 73(5), 929–1014.

Koehn, D. (1995). A Role for Virtue Ethics in the Analysis of Business Practice. *Business Ethics Quarterly*, 5(3), 533–540.

Kohlberg, L. (1973). The Claim to Moral Adequacy of a Highest Stage of Moral Judgment. *Journal of Philosophy*, 70 (18), 630–646.

Köhler, J., Geels, F. W., Kern, F., Markard, J., Onsongo, E., Wieczorek, A., et al. (2019). An Agenda for Sustainability Transitions Research: State of the Art and Future Directions. *Environmental Innovation and Societal Transitions*, 31 (1), 1–32.

Kölbel, J. F., Heeb, F., Paetzold, F. and Busch, T. (2020). Can Sustainable Investing Save the World? Reviewing the Mechanisms of Investor Impact. *Organization and Environment*, 33(4), 554–574.

Kolk, A. (2004). A Decade of Sustainability Reporting: Developments and Significance. *International Journal for Environmental and Sustainable Development*, 3(1), 51–64.

Kolk, A., van Tulder, R. and Kostwinder, E. (2008). Business and Partnerships for Development. *European Management Journal*, 26(4), 262–273.

Kolstad, I. (2012). Human Rights and Positive Corporate Duties: The Importance of Corporate–State Interaction. *Business Ethics: A European Review*, 21(3), 276–285.

Kong, H. M., Witmaier, A. and Ko, E. (2021). Sustainability and Social Media Communication: How Consumers Respond to Marketing Efforts of Luxury and Non-Luxury Fashion Brands. *Journal of Business Research*, 131(1), 640–651.

Kotchen, M. and Moon, J. J. (2012). Corporate Social Responsibility for Irresponsibility. *The B.E. Journal of Economic Analysis & Policy*, 12(1), Article 55.

Kourula, A., Moon, J., Salles-Djelic, M. L. and Wickert, C. (2019). New Roles of Government in the Governance of Business Conduct: Implications for Management and Organizational Research. *Organization Studies*, 40(8), 1101–1123.

KPMG. (1993–2020). Various international surveys of corporate responsibility reporting. Retrieved on 17 October 2022 from www.kpmg.com/.

KPMG, Global Reporting Initiative (GRI), UN Environmental Programme (UNEP) and Centre for Corporate Governance in Africa. (2016). Carrots and Sticks. Global Trends in Sustainability Reporting Regulation and Policy. Retrieved on 17 October 2022 from https://assets.kpmg/content/dam/kpmg/pdf/2016/05/carrots-and-sticks-may-2016.pdf.

KPMG Impact. (2020). The Time Has Come. The KPMG Survey of Sustainability Reporting 2020. Retrieved on 17 October 2022 from https://home.kpmg/xx/en/home/insights/2020/11/the-time-has-come-survey-of-sustainability-reporting.html.

Kraaijenbrink, J. (2019). How to Bring Sustainability to the Masses: Tony's Chocolonely's Impact Strategy. Retrieved on 17 October 2022 from www.forbes.com/sites/jeroenkraaijenbrink/2019/11/08/how-to-bring-sustainability-to-the-masses-tonys-chocolonely-impact-strategy/?sh=50f1db1c712a.

Kraus, P., Stokes, P., Cooper, C., Liu, Y., Moore, N., Britzelmaier, B. and Tarba, S. (2020). Cultural Antecedents of Sustainability and Regional Economic Development: A Study of SME 'Mittelstand' Firms in Baden-Würtemberg (Germany). *Entrepreneurship and Regional Development.* 32(7–8), 629–653.

Krause, R. and Semadeni, M. (2013). Apprentice, Departure, and Demotion: An Examination of the Three Types of CEO-Board Chair Separation. *Academy of Management Journal*, 56(3), 805–826.

Krausmann, F., Gingrich, S., Eisenmenger, N., Erb, K., Haberl, H. and Fischer-Kowalski, M.. (2009). Growth in Global Materials Use, GDP and Population During the 20th Century. *Ecological Economics*, 68(10), 2696–2705.

Krugman, P. (1997). In Praise of Cheap Labor: Bad Jobs at Bad Wages Are Better than No Jobs at All. Retrieved on 17 October 2022 from https://slate.com/business/1997/03/in-praise-of-cheap-labor.html.

Kuruvilla, S., Liu, M., Li, C. and Chen, W. (2020). Field Opacity and Practice-Outcome Decoupling: Private Regulation of Labor Standards in Global Supply Chains. *ILR Review*, 73 (4), 841–872.

Kuyumcuoglu, H. S. (2021). Sweatshops, Harm, and Interference: A Contractualist Approach. *Journal of Business Ethics*, 169(1), 1–11.

Laamanen, M., Moser, C., Bor, S. and den Hond, F. (2020). A Partial Organization Approach to the Dynamics of Social Order in Social Movement Organizing. *Current Sociology*, 68(4), 520–545.

Lafakis, C., Ratz, L., Fazio, E. and Cosma, M. (2019). The Economic Implications of Climate Change. *Moody's Analytics*.

Lähdesmäki, M., Siltaoja, M. and Spence, L. J. (2019). Stakeholder Salience for Small Businesses: A Social Proximity Perspective. *Journal of Business Ethics*, 158(2), 373–385.

Lambin, E. F. and Thorlakson, T. (2018). Sustainability Standards: Interactions between Private Actors, Civil Society, and Governments. *Annual Review of Environmental Resources*, 43(3), 369–393.

Lange, D., Lee, P. and Dai, Y. (2011). Organizational Reputation: A Review. *Journal of Management*, 37(1), 153–184.

Larrinaga, C., Carrasco, F., Correa, C., Llena, F. and Moneva, J. M. (2002). Accountability and Accounting Regulation: The Case of the Spanish Environmental Disclosure Standard. *European Accounting Review*, 11(4), 723–740.

Laville, S. (2019). Top Oil Firms Spending Millions Lobbying to Block Climate Change Policies, Says Report. *The Guardian*, 21 March.

Lawrence, J., Rasche, A. and Kenny, K. (2019). Sustainability as Opportunity: Unilever's Sustainable Living Plan. In C. N. Smith and G. Lenssen. (Eds.), *Building the Responsible Corporation* (pp. 439–459). New York, NY: Springer.

(2015). *Sustainability as Opportunity: Unilever's Sustainable Living Plan.* Hult International Business School Case (HLT 327-13-1001 rev 2015).

Lawton, T., McGuire, S. and Rajwani, T. (2012). Corporate Political Activity: A Literature Review and Research Agenda. *International Journal of Management Reviews*, 15(1), 86–105.

Lear, D. (2018). Eliminating Ocean Plastic Pollution Must Be a Commercial and Global Priority. *The National*, 14 November.

Lebaron, G. (2021). Wages: An Overlooked Dimension of Business and Human Rights in Global Supply Chains. *Business and Human Rights Journal*, 6 (1), 1–20.

Leitheiser, E. (2021). How Domestic Contexts Shape International Private Governance: The Case of the European Accord and American Alliance in Bangladesh. *Regulation & Governance*, 15(4), 1286–1303.

Leopold, A. (1949). *A Sand County Almanac: With Other Essays on Conservation from Round River.* Oxford: Oxford University Press.

Levillain, K. and Segrestin, B. (2019). From Primacy to Purpose Commitment: How Emerging Profit-with-Purpose Corporations Open New Corporate Governance Avenues. *European Management Journal*, 37(5), 637–647.

Levin, K., Cashore, B. and Koppell, J. (2009). Can Non-state Certification Systems Bolster State-Centered Efforts to Promote Sustainable Development through the Clean Development Mechanism? *Wake Forest Law Review*, 44(3), 777–798.

Levitt, T. (1958). The Dangers of Social Responsibility. *Harvard Business Review*, 36(5), 41–50.

Levy, D. L. (2008). Political Contestation in Global Production Networks. *Academy of Management Review*, 33(4), 943–963.

Levy, D. L. and Egan, D. (1998). Capital Contests: National and Transnational Channels of Corporate Influence on the Climate Change Negotiations. *Politics & Society*, 26(3), 337–361.

Lewis, S. (2003). Reputation and Corporate Responsibility. *Journal of Communication Management*, 7(4), 356–366.

Leys, C. (1996). *The Rise and Fall of Development Theory.* Nairobi: East African Educational Publishers.

Li, Y., Johnson, E. J. and Zaval, L. (2011). Local warming: Daily Temperature Change Influences Belief in Global Warming. *Psychological Science*, 22(4), 454–459.

Lipton, M. (2016). The New Paradigm: A Roadmap for an Implicit Corporate Governance Partnership between Corporations and Investors to Achieve Sustainable Long-Term Investment and Growth. Retrieved on 17 October 2022 from www.wlrk.com/webdocs/wlrknew/AttorneyPubs/WLRK.25960.16.pdf.

Locke, R. M. (2013). *The Promise and Limits of Private Power: Promoting Labor Standards in a Global Economy.* Cambridge: Cambridge University Press.

Logistics Cluster. (2020). LET Annual Report 2019. Retrieved on 17 October 2022 from https://logcluster.org/document/let-annual-report-2019.

(n.d.). Logistics Emergency Team. Retrieved on 17 October 2022 from https://logcluster.org/logistics-emergency-team.

Longstreth, A. (2012). How Gray Area of Bribery Law Could Play Out in Wal-Mart. Retrieved on 17 October 2022 from www.reuters.com/article/us-walmart-grease-idUSBRE8301GJ20120425.

Loureiro, M. L. and Lotade, J. (2005). Do Fair Trade and Eco-Labels in Coffee Wake Up the Consumer Conscience? *Ecological Economics*, 53(1), 129–138.

Lowery, C. and Ramachandran, V. (2015). Unintended Consequences of Anti-Money Laundering Policies for Poor Countries. Center for Global Development. Retrieved on 17 October 2022 from www.cgdev.org/sites/default/files/CGD-WG-Report-Unintended-Consequences-AML-Policies-2015.pdf.

Loxley, J. (2004). What Is Distinctive about International Development Studies? *Canadian Journal of Development Studies*, 25(1), 25–38.

Lüdeke-Freund, F. (2020). Sustainable Entrepreneurship, Innovation, and Business Models: Integrative Framework and Propositions for Future Research. *Business Strategy and the Environment*, 29(2), 665–681.

Lüdeke-Freund, F., Bohnsack, R., Breuer, H. and Massa, L. (2019a). Research on Sustainable Business Model Patterns – Status Quo, Methodological Issues, and a Research Agenda. In A. Aagaard. (Ed.), *Sustainable Business Models* (pp. 25–60). Houndmills, UK: Palgrave.

Lüdeke-Freund, F., Breuer, H. and Massa, L. (2022). *Sustainable Business Model Design – 45 Patterns.* Berlin: Self-published. Retrieved on 17 October 2022 from www.sustainablebusiness.design.

Lüdeke-Freund, F., Carroux, S., Joyce, A., Massa, L. and Breuer, H. (2018). The Sustainable Business Model Pattern Taxonomy – 45 Patterns to Support Sustainability-Oriented Business Model Innovation. *Sustainable Production and Consumption*, 15, 145–162.

Lüdeke-Freund, F., Froese, T. and Schaltegger, S. (2019b). The Role of Business Models for Sustainable Consumption: A Pattern Approach. In O. Mont. (Ed.), *A Research Agenda for Sustainable Consumption Governance* (pp. 86–104). Cheltenham, UK: Edward Elgar.

Lüdeke-Freund, F., Gold, S. and Bocken, N. (2019c). A Review and Typology of Circular Economy Business Model Patterns. *Journal of Industrial Ecology*, 23(1), 36–61.

Lüdeke-Freund, F., Rauter, R., Pedersen, E. and Nielsen, C. (2020). Sustainable Value Creation through Business Models: The What, the Who and the How. *Journal of Business Models*, 8(3), 62–90.

Lüdeke-Freund, F., Schaltegger, S. and Dembek, K. (2019d). Strategies and Drivers of Sustainable Business Model Innovation. In F. Boons and A. McMeekin. (Eds.), *Handbook of Sustainability Innovation* (pp. 101–123). Cheltenham, UK: Edward Elgar.

Luke, B. and Chu, V. (2013). Social Enterprise versus Social Entrepreneurship: An Examination of the 'Why' and 'How' in Pursuing Social Change. *International Small Business Journal*, 31(7), 764–784.

Lund-Yates, S. (2021). FTSE 100 – The 5 Highest ESG Rated Companies. Retrieved on 17 October 2022 from www.hl.co.uk/news/articles/archive/ ftse-100-the-5-highest-esg-rated-companies.

Luyckx, J., Schneider, A. and Kourula, A. (Eds.). (2022). *The Corporation: Rethinking the Iconic Form of Business Organization*. Bingley, UK: Emerald Publishing.

Lyon, T. and Delmas, M. (2018). When Corporations Take Credit for Green Deeds Their Lobbying May Tell Another Story. *The Conversation (US)*. Retrieved on 17 October 2022 from https:// theconversation.com/when-corporations-take-credit-for-green-deeds-their-lobbying-may-tell-another-story-98988.

Lyon, T. P., Delmas, M. A., Maxwell, J. W., Tima Bansal, P., Chiroleu-Assouline, M., Crifo, P., et al. (2018). CSR Needs CPR: Corporate Sustainability and Politics. *California Management Review*, 60(4), 5–24.

Lyons, T. S. and Kickul, J. R. (2013). The Social Enterprise Financing Landscape: The Lay of the Land and New Research on the Horizon. *Entrepreneurship Research Journal*, 3 (2), 147–159.

Lysova, E. I. and Khapova, S. N. (2019). Enacting Creative Calling When Established Career Structures Are Not in Place: The Case of the Dutch Video Game Industry. *Journal of Vocational Behavior*, 114, 31–43.

MacDonald, A., Clarke, A., Ordonez-Ponce, E., Chai, Z. and Andreasen, J. (2020). Sustainability Managers: The Job Roles and Competencies of Building Sustainable Cities and Communities. *Public Performance and Management Review*, 43(6), 1413–1444.

MacDonald, A. and Stadtler, L. (2017). It's More than the Reading Assignment: Skillsets and Competencies for Effective Cross-Sector Collaboration. *Annual Review of Social Partnerships*, 12, 45–49.

Maersk. (2019). Responsible Tax. Retrieved on 17 October 2022 from www.maersk .com/news/articles/2019/02/21/ responsible-tax-practices.

Maier, F., Meyer, M. and Steinbereithner, M. (2016). Nonprofit Organizations Becoming Business-Like. *Nonprofit and Voluntary Sector Quarterly*, 45(1), 64–86.

Maignan, I. and Ralston, D. A. (2002). Corporate Social Responsibility in Europe and the US: Insights from Businesses' Self-Presentations. *Journal of International Business Studies*, 33(3), 497–514.

Mair, J. (2020). Social Entrepreneurship: Research as Disciplined Exploration.In W. W. Powell and P. Bromley. (Eds.), *The Nonprofit Sector: A Research Handbook* (3rd ed., pp. 333–357). Redwood City, CA: Stanford University Press.

(Eds.). (2022). *The Corporation: Rethinking the Iconic Form of Business Organization*. Bingley, UK: Emerald Publishing.

Makower, J. (2020). State of Green Business. *GreenBiz*, 13 January. Retrieved from www.greenbiz.com/article/state-green-business-2020.

Maloney, T. and Almeida, R. (2018). Lengthening the Investment Time Horizon. Retrieved on 17 October 2022 from https://globalfundsearch.com/wp-content/uploads/2019/12/Lengthening-the-Investment-Time-Horizon.pdf.

Managi, S. and Kumar, P. (2018). *Inclusive Wealth Report 2018: Measuring Progress towards Sustainability*. London: Routledge.

Manila Bulletin. (2021). Coca-Cola and Eco Rangers Improving Communities with Blastik Project. Retrieved on 17 October 2022 from https://mb.com.ph/2021/11/15/coca-cola-and-eco-rangers-improving-communities-with-blastik-project.

Marens, R. (2012). Generous in Victory? American Managerial Autonomy, Labour Relations and the Invention of Corporate Social Responsibility. *Socio-Economic Review*, 10(1), 59–84.

(2008). Getting Past the 'Government Sucks' Story: How Government Really Matters. *Journal of Management Inquiry*, 17(2), 84–94.

Margolis, J. D. and Walsh, J. P. (2003). Misery Loves Companies: Rethinking Social Initiatives by Business. *Administrative Science Quarterly*, 48(2), 268–305.

Massa, L. and Tucci, C. (2014). Business Model Innovation. In M. Dodgson, D. Gann and N. Phillips. (Eds.), *The Oxford Handbook of Innovation Management* (pp. 420–441). Oxford: Oxford University Press.

Massa, L., Tucci, C. and Afuah, A. (2017). A Critical Assessment of Business Model Research. *Academy of Management Annals*, 11(1), 73–104.

Massa, L., Viscusi, G. and Tucci, C. (2018). Business Models and Complexity. *Journal of Business Models*, 6(1), 59–71.

Matten, D. and Crane, A. (2005). Corporate Citizenship: Toward an Extended Theoretical Conceptualization. *Academy of Management Review*, 30(1), 166–179.

Matten, D. and Moon, J. (2020). Reflections on the 2018 Decade Award: The Meaning and Dynamics of Corporate Social Responsibility. *Academy of Management Review*, 45(1), 7–28.

(2008). 'Implicit' and 'Explicit' CSR: A Conceptual Framework for a Comparative Understanding of Corporate Social Responsibility. *Academy of Management Review*, 33(2), 404–424.

Mawani, A. and Trivedi, V. U. (2021). Collusive vs. Coercively Corrupt Tax Auditors and Their Impact on Tax Compliance. *Journal of Behavioral and Experimental Finance*, 30, Article 100470.

Mayer, R. (2007). What's Wrong with Exploitation? *Journal of Applied Philosophy*, 24(2), 137–150.

Mayer-Schönberger, V. and Cukier, K. (2013). *Big Data: A Revolution that Will Transform How We Live, Work and Think*. London: John Murray.

Mayntz, R. (2010). Legitimacy and Compliance in Transnational Governance (Max-Planck-Institut für Gesellschaftsforschung Working Paper 10/5). Cologne: Max Planck Institute for the Study of Societies.

Mazzarol, T., Clark, D., Reboud, S. and Mamouni Limnios, E. (2018). Developing a Conceptual Framework for the Co-operative and Mutual Enterprise Business Model. *Journal of Management & Organization*, 24(4), 551–581.

McBarnet, D. (2007). Corporate Social Responsibility beyond Law, through Law, for Law: The New Corporate Accountability. In D. McBarnet, A. Voiculescu and T. Campbell. (Eds.), *The New Corporate Accountability: Corporate Social Responsibility and the Law* (pp. 9–58). Cambridge: Cambridge University Press.

McCorquedale, R., Smith, L., Neely, S. and Brooks, R. (2017). Human Rights Due Diligence in Law and Practice: Good Practices and Challenges for Business Enterprises. *Business and Human Rights Journal*, 2(2), 195–224.

McCrum, D. and Storbeck, O. (2019). Wirecard Says €1.9bn of Cash Is Missing. Retrieved on 17 October 2022 from www.ft.com/content/1e753e2b-f576-4f32-aa19-d240be26e773.

McDonnell, M. H. (2016). Radical Repertoires: The Incidence and Impact of Corporate-Sponsored Social Activism. *Organization Science*, 27(1), 53–71.

McKay, S., Moro, D., Teasdale, S. and Clifford, D. (2014). The Marketisation of Charities in England and Wales. *VOLUNTAS: International Journal of Voluntary and Nonprofit Organizations*, 26(1), 336–354.

McWilliams, A. and Siegel, D. (2001). Corporate Social Responsibility: A Theory of the Firm Perspective. *Academy of Management Review*, 26(1), 117–127.

Meadows, D. H., Meadows, D. L., Randers, J. and Behrens, W. W. (1972). *The Limits to Growth*. New York, NY: Universe Books.

Media and Climate Change Observatory. (2021). Nothing Cool about It. Retrieved on 17 October 2022 from https://sciencepolicy.colorado.edu/icecaps/research/media_coverage/summaries/issue56.html.

Mena, S. and Palazzo, G. (2012). Input and Output Legitimacy of Multi-Stakeholder Initiatives. *Business Ethics Quarterly*, 22(3), 527–556.

Mensah, J. (2019). Sustainable Development: Meaning, History, Principles, Pillars, and Implications for Human Action: Literature Review. *Cogent Social Sciences*, 5(1), 1653531.

Merchant, C. (1992). *Radical Ecology: The Search for a Livable World*. New York, NY: Routledge.

Messner, M. (2009). The Limits of Accountability. *Accounting, Organizations & Society*, 34(8), 918–938.

Micheletti, M. (2003). *Political Virtue and Shopping: Individuals, Consumerism, and Collective Action*. New York, NY: Palgrave Macmillan.

Michie, J. and Padayachee, V. (2019). South African Business in the Transition to Democracy. *International Review of Applied Economics*, 33(1), 1–10.

Midttun, A., Gjølberg, M., Kourula, A., Sweet, S. and Vallentin, S. (2015). Public Policies for Corporate Social Responsibility in Four Nordic Countries Harmony of Goals and Conflict of Means. *Business and Society*, 54(4), 464–500.

Miller, J. (2003). Why Economists Are Wrong about Sweatshops and the Antisweatshop Movement. *Challenge*, 46(1), 93–122.

Minor, D. and Morgan, J. (2011). CSR as Reputation Insurance: Primum Non Nocere. *California Management Review*, 53(3), 40–59.

Minton, E. A. and Cornwell, T. B. (2015). The Cause Cue Effect: Cause-Related Marketing and Consumer Health Perceptions. *Journal of Consumer Affairs*, 50(2), 372–402.

Mintzberg, H. (2015). *Rebalancing Society: Radical Renewal beyond Left, Right, and Center*. Oakland, CA: Berrett-Koehler.

Mirvis, P. and Googins, B. (2006). Stages of Corporate Citizenship. *California Management Review*, 48(2), 104–126.

Mishel, L. and Kandra, J. (2020). CEO Compensation Surged 15% in 2019 to $21.3 Million. Retrieved on 17 October 2020 from www.epi.org/publication/ceo-compensation-surged-14-in-2019-to-21-3-million-ceos-now-earn-320-times-as-much-as-a-typical-worker/.

Mitchell, R. K., Agle, B. R. and Wood, D. J. (1997). Toward a Theory of Stakeholder Identification and Salience: Defining the Principle of Who and What Really Counts. *Academy of Management Review*, 22(4), 853–886.

Mitra, R. and Buzzanell, P. M. (2017). Communicative Tensions of Meaningful Work: The Case of Sustainability Practitioners. *Human Relations*, 70(5), 594–616.

Montiel, I. (2008). Corporate Social Responsibility and Corporate Sustainability Separate Pasts, Common Futures. *Organization & Environment*, 21(3), 245–269.

Moog, S., Spicer, A. and Bohm, S. (2014). The Politics of Multi-stakeholder Initiatives: The Crisis of the Forest Stewardship Council. *Journal of Business Ethics*, 128(3), 469–493.

Moon, J. (2014). *Corporate Social Responsibility: A Very Short Introduction*. Oxford: Oxford University Press.

(2007). The Contribution of Corporate Social Responsibility to Sustainable

Development. *Sustainable Development*, 15(5), 275–327.

(2002). Business Social Responsibility and New Governance. *Government and Opposition*, 37(3), 385–408.

Moon, J., Crane, A. and Matten, D. (2005). Can Corporations Be Citizens? Corporate Citizenship as a Metaphor for Business Participation in Society. *Business Ethics Quarterly*, 15(3), 429–453.

Moon, J., Kang, N. and Gond, J. P. (2010). Corporate Social Responsibility and Government. In D. Coen, W. Grant and G. Wilson. (Eds.), *Oxford Handbook of Business and Government* (pp. 512–543). Oxford: Oxford University Press.

Moon, J. and Sochacki, R. (1996). The Social Responsibility of Business in Job and Enterprise Creation: Motives, Means and Implications. *Australian Quarterly*, 68(1), 21–30.

Moon, J. and Vallentin, S. (2020). Tax Avoidance and Corporate Irresponsibility – CSR as Problem or Solution? In K. K. Egholm Elgaard, R. K. Feldthusen, A. Hilling and M. Kukkonen. (Eds.), *Fair Taxation and Corporate Sustainability Responsibility* (pp. 19–52). Copenhagen, Denmark: Ex Tuto.

Moon, J. and Vogel, D. (2008). Corporate Social Responsibility, Government, and Civil Society. In A. Crane, A. McWilliams, D. Matten, J. Moon and D. Siegel. (Eds.), *The Oxford Handbook of Corporate Social Responsibility* (pp. 303–323). Oxford: Oxford University Press.

Moore, C., Richardson, J. J. and Moon, J. (1989). *Local Partnership and the Unemployment Crisis in Britain*. London: Allen & Unwin.

Morgans, C. L., Meijaard, E., Santika, T., Law, E., Budiharta, S., Ancrenaz, M. and Wilson, K. A. (2018). Evaluating the Effectiveness of Palm Oil Certification in Delivering Multiple Sustainability Objectives. *Environmental Research Letters*, 13(6), Article 064032.

Morningstar. (2019). Proxy Season Shows ESG Concerns on Shareholders' Minds. Retrieved on 17 October 2022 from www.morningstar.com/articles/943448/proxy-season-shows-esg-concerns-on-shareholders-minds.

Morsing, M. and Schultz, M. (2006). Corporate Social Responsibility Communication: Stakeholder Information, Response and Involvement Strategies. *Business Ethics: A European Review*, 15(4), 323–338.

Morsing, M. and Spence, L. J. (2021). Unpublished Research on SMEs and Social Responsibility in Denmark. with the United Nations Global Compact Danish Chapter.

(2019). Corporate Social Responsibility (CSR) Communication and Small and Medium Sized Enterprises: The Governmentality Dilemma of Explicit and Implicit CSR Communication. *Human Relations*, 72 (12), 1920–1947.

Moser, C. (2020). Managerial Practices of Reducing Food Waste in Supermarkets. In E. Närvänen, N. Mesiranta, M. Mattila and A. Heikkinen. (Eds.), *Food*

Waste Management: Solving the Wicked Problem (pp. 89–112). Dordrecht: Springer.

Moses, C. (2021). Netherlands Is Maxing Out Its Covid Testing Capacity. *The New York Times*, 17 November. Retrieved on 17 October 2022 from www.nytimes.com/2021/11/17/world/europe/covid-testing-netherlands.html.

Moyo, D. (2009). *Dead Aid: Why Aid Is Not Working and How There Is a Better Way for Africa*. London: Allen Lane.

Mukherji, A. (2013). Evidence on Community-Driven Development from an Indian Village. *Journal of Development Studies*, 49(11), 1548–1563.

Muthuri, J. N., Chapple, W. and Moon, J. 2008. An Integrated Approach to Implementing 'Community Participation' in Corporate Community Involvement Programmes: Lessons from Magadi Soda Company. *Journal of Business Ethics*, 85(2), 431–444.

National Commission on the BP Deepwater Horizon Oil Spill and Offshore Drilling. (2011). Deep Water: The Gulf Oil Disaster and the Future of Offshore Drilling. Retrieved on 17 October 2022 from www.govinfo.gov/content/pkg/GPO-OILCOMMISSION/pdf/GPO-OILCOMMISSION.pdf.

National Law Review. (2021). ESG in Mergers and Acquisitions. Retrieved on 5 February 2022 from www.natlawreview.com/article/what-to-watch-esg-mergers-and-acquisitions.

Neubaum, D. O. and Zahra, S. A. (2006). Institutional Ownership and Corporate Social Performance: The Moderating Effects of Investment Horizon, Activism, and Coordination. *Journal of Management*, 32(1), 108–131.

Newsweek. (2019). America's Most Responsible Companies 2020. Retrieved on 17 November from https://d.newsweek.com/en/file/459820/methodology-americas-most-responsible-companies.pdf.

Nielsen, K. S., Nicholas, K. A., Creutzig, F., Dietz, T. and Stern, P. C. (2021). The Role of High-Socioeconomic-Status People in Locking in or Rapidly Reducing Energy-Driven Greenhouse Gas Emissions. *Nature Energy*, 6(11), 1011–1016.

Nike. (2021). Human Rights and Labor Compliance Standards. Retrieved on 17 November 2022 from https://purpose.nike.com/human-rights.

Nike Circular Design. (2022). Circularity. Retrieved on 17 November 2022 from www.nikecirculardesign.com/.

Novak, P., Amicis, L. and Mozetic, I. (2018). Impact Investing Market on Twitter: Influential Users and Communities. *Applied Network Science*, 3(1), 40.

Novo Nordisk Fonden. (2020). Who Are We? Articles of Association. Retrieved on 17 October 2022 from https://novonordiskfonden.dk/en/about-the-foundation/articles-of-association/.

O'Callaghan 1, T. (2007). Disciplining Multinational Enterprises: The Regulatory Power of Reputation Risk. *Global Society*, 21(1), 95–117.

Okoye, A. (2009). Theorising Corporate Social Responsibility as an Essentially Contested Concept: Is a Definition Necessary? *Journal of Business Ethics*, 89(4), 613–627.

Olam. (2020a). Remaining Olam Group. Retrieved on 17 October 2022 from www.olamgroup.com/about-olam/group-overview/olam-group.html.

(2020b). Olam and Rainforest Alliance Announce World's First Climate-friendly Cocoa. Retrieved on 17 October 2022 from www.olamgroup.com/news/all-news/press-release/olam-and-rainforest-alliance-announces.html.

Oldekop, J. A., Horner, R., Hulme, D., Adhikari, R., Agarwal, B., Alford, et al. (2020). COVID-19 and the Case for Global Development. *World Development*, 134, Article 105044. Retrieved on 17 October 2022 from https://doi.org/10.1016/j.worlddev.2020.105044.

Oldham, S. (2021). *A Pragmatist Stance on the Practice and Maintenance of Organisational Values in the Small Firm Context*. PhD dissertation, Royal Holloway, University of London.

Oldham, S. and Spence, L. J. (2021). A Typology of Small- and Medium-sized Supplier Approaches to Social Responsibility. *Business Ethics, the Environment, and Responsibility*. Retrieved on 17 October 2022 from https://doi.org/10.1111/beer.12391.

Oliver, C. (1991). Strategic Responses to Institutional Processes. *Academy of Management Review*, 16(1), 145–179.

O'Regan, M. (2019). B Corp Certification Won't Guarantee Companies Really Care for People, Planet, and Profit. *The Conversation*. Retrieved on 17 October 2022 from https://theconversation.com/b-corp-certification-wont-guarantee-companies-really-care-for-people-planet-and-profit-124459.

O'Reilly, C. and Chatman, J. (1996). Culture as Social Control: Corporations, Cults, and Commitment. In B. M. Staw and L. L. Cummings. (Eds.), *Research in Organizational Behavior* (pp. 157–200). Greenwich, CT: JAI Press.

Organisation for Economic Co-operation and Development (OECD). (2018). *OECD Due Diligence Guidance for Responsible Business Conduct*. Paris: OECD.

(2017). *OECD Due Diligence Guidance for Meaningful Stakeholder Engagement in the Extractive Sector*. Paris: OECD.

(2016). *Implementing the OECD Guidelines for Multinational Enterprises: the National Contact Points from 2000–2015*. Paris: OECD.

(2011). *Guidelines for Multinational Enterprises, 2011 Revision*. Paris: OECD.

Orlitzky, M., Siegel, D. S. and Waldman, D. A. (2011). Strategic Corporate Social Responsibility and Environmental Sustainability. *Business & Society*, 50 (1), 6–27.

Osagie, E. R., Wesselink, R., Blok, V., Lans, T. and Mulder, M. (2016). Individual Competencies for Corporate Social Responsibility: A Literature and Practice Perspective. *Journal of Business Ethics*, 135(2), 233–252.

Österblom, H., Jouffray, J. B., Folke, C., Crona, B., Troell, M., Merrie, A. and Rockström, J. (2015). Transnational Corporations as Keystone Actors in Marine Ecosystems. *PLoS ONE*, 10(5), 1–15.

Osterwalder, A. and Pigneur, Y. (2009). *Business Model Generation: A Handbook for Visionaries, Game*

Changers, and Challengers. Amsterdam: self-published.

Owen, D. L. and O'Dwyer, B. (2008). Corporate Social Responsibility: The Reporting and Assurance Dimension. In J. Crane, A. McWilliams, D. Matten, J. Moon and D. Siegel. (Eds.), *The Oxford Handbook of Corporate Social Responsibility* (pp. 384–412). Oxford: Oxford University Press.

Oxfam. (2015). Extreme Carbon Inequality. 2 December. Retrieved on 17 October 2022 from www-cdn.oxfam .org/s3fs-public/file_attachments/mb-extreme-carbon-inequality-021215-en .pdf.

Ozkazanc-Pan, B. (2019). CSR as Gendered Neocoloniality in the Global South. *Journal of Business Ethics*, 160(4), 851–864.

Pache, A.-C. and Santos, F. (2013). Inside the Hybrid Organization: Selective Coupling as a Response to Competing Institutional Logics. *Academy of Management Journal*, 56(4), 972–1001.

Paine, L. S. (2014). Sustainability in the Boardroom. *Harvard Business Review*, 92(7/8), 86–94.

(1994). Managing for Organizational Integrity. *Harvard Business Review*, 72 (2), 106–117.

Palazzo, G. (2007). Organizational Integrity: Understanding the Dimensions of Ethical and Unethical Behavior. In W. C. Zimmerli, M. Holzinger and K. Richter. (Eds.), *Corporate Ethics and Corporate Governance* (pp. 113–128). Berlin and Heidelberg: Springer.

Palazzo, G., Krings, F. and Hoffrage, U. (2012). Ethical Blindness. *Journal of Business Ethics*, 109(3), 323–338.

Parker, C. and Ruschena, D. A. (2012). The Pressures of Billable Hours: Lessons from a Survey of Billing Practices Inside Law Firms. *University of St. Thomas Law Journal*, 9(2), 619–664.

Parrique, T., Barth, J., Briens F., Kerschner, C., Kraus-Polk, A., Kuokkanen, A. and Spangenberg, J. H. (2019). *Decoupling Debunked: Evidence and Arguments against Green Growth as a Sole Strategy for Sustainability*. Brussels, Belgium: European Environmental Bureau.

Patagonia. (2022). Patagonia – Company History. Retrieved on 17 October 2022 from www.patagonia.com/company-history/.

Pattberg, P. and Widerberg, O. (2014). Multi-Stakeholder Partnerships: Building-Blocs for Success. International Civil Society Centre. Retrieved on 17 October 2022 from www.researchgate.net/ publication/281268765_ Multistakeholder_Partnerships_ Building-Blocs_for_Success.

Pauw, W. P. (2015). Not a Panacea: Private-Sector Engagement in Adaptation and Adaptation Finance in Developing and Adaptation Finance in Developing Countries. *Climate Policy*, 15(5), 583–603.

Pearl Meyer. (2017). Environmental and Social Governance and Its Potential Link to Incentives. Retrieved on 17 October 2022 from www.pearlmeyer .com/pearl-meyer-quick-poll-environmental-and-social-governance-esg-and-its-potential-link-incentives.pdf.

Pearson, R. (2007). Beyond Women Workers: Gendering CSR. *Third World Quarterly*, 28(4), 731–749.

Pedersen, E., Lüdeke-Freund, F., Henriques, I. and Seitanidi, M. (2021). Toward Collaborative Cross-Sector Business Models for Sustainability. *Business & Society*, 60(5), 1039–1058.

Pedersen, E. R. G., Neergaard, P., Pedersen, J. T. and Gwozdz, W. (2013). Conformance and Deviance: Company Responses to Institutional Pressures for Corporate Social Responsibility Reporting. *Business Strategy and the Environment*, 22(6), 357–373.

Peloza, J., Ye, C. and Montford, W. J. (2015). When Companies Do Good, Are Their Products Good for You? How Corporate Social Responsibility Creates a Health Halo. *Journal of Public Policy & Marketing*, 34(1), 19–31.

Persson, L., Carney Almroth, B. M., Collins, C. D., Cornell, S., de Wit, C. A., Diamond, M. L., et al. (2022). Outside the Safe Operating Space of the Planetary Boundary for Novel Entities. *Environmental Science & Technology*, 56(3), 1510–1521.

Peter, J. P. and Olsen, J. (2009). *Consumer Behavior and Marketing Strategy* (9th ed.). New York, NY: McGraw-Hill Education.

Phillips, R. and Caldwell, C. B. (2005). Value Chain Responsibility: A Farewell to Arm's Length. *Business & Society Review*, 110(4), 345–370.

Phillips, R., Freeman, R. E. and Wicks, A. C. (2003). What Stakeholder Theory Is Not. *Business Ethics Quarterly*, 13(4), 479–502.

Phillips, R., Schrempf-Stirling, J. and Stutz, C. (2020). The Past, History and Corporate Social Responsibility. *Journal of Business Ethics*, 166(2), 203–213.

Pichai, S. (2020). Our Third Decade of Climate Action: Realizing a Carbon-Free Future. *Google: The Key Word*. 14 September. Retrieved on 17 October 2022 from https://blog.google/outreach-initiatives/sustainability/our-third-decade-climate-action-realizing-carbon-free-future/.

Plumptre, A. J., Baisero, D., Travis Belote, R., Vázquez-Domínguez, E., Faurby, S., Jędrzejewski, et al. (2021). Where Might We Find Ecologically Intact Communities? *Frontiers in Forests and Global Change*, 4, Article 626635.

Polanyi, K. (1944). *The Great Transformation*. Boston, MA: Beacon Press.

Pollack, J. M., Garcia, R., Michaelis, T. L., Hanson, S., Carr, J. C. and Sheats, L. (2021). Pursuing B Corp Certification: Exploring Firms' Entrepreneurial Orientation and Prosocial Motivation. *Academy of Management Discoveries*, 7(2), 294–316.

Ponte, S. (2019). *Business, Power and Sustainability in a World of Global Value Chains*. London: ZED.

Porter, M. E. (1998). *The Competitive Advantage of Nations*. London and New York, NY: The Free Press.

(1985). *Competitive Advantage: Creating and Sustaining Superior Performance.* London and New York, NY: The Free Press.

Porter, M. E. and Kramer, M. R. (2011). Creating Shared Value. *Harvard Business Review*, 89(1/2), 62–77.

(2006). Strategy & Society: The Link between Competitive Advantage and Corporate Social Responsibility. *Harvard Business Review*, 84(12), 78–92.

(2002). The Competitive Advantage of Corporate Philanthropy. *Harvard Business Review*, 80(12), 56–69.

Powell, B. (2014). *Out of Poverty: Sweatshops in the Global Economy* (1. publ). Cambridge Studies in Economics, Choice, and Society. Cambridge: Cambridge University Press.

Powell, B. and Skarbek, D. (2006). Sweatshops and Third World Living Standards: Are the Jobs Worth the Sweat? *Journal of Labor Research*, 27 (2), 263–274.

Powell, B. and Zwolinski, M. (2012). The Ethical and Economic Case against Sweatshop Labor: A Critical Assessment. *Journal of Business Ethics*, 107(4), 449–472.

Power, M. (2008). *Organized Uncertainty: Designing a World of Risk Management.* Oxford: Oxford University Press.

Prahalad, C. K. and Hart, S. L. (2002). The Fortune at the Bottom of the Pyramid. *Strategy and Business*, 26(1), 54–67.

Prakash, A. and Potoski, M. (2007). Investing Up: FDI and the Cross-Country Diffusion of ISO 14001 Management systems. *International Studies Quarterly*, 51(3), 723–744.

Preiss, J. (2019). Freedom, Autonomy, and Harm in Global Supply Chains. *Journal of Business Ethics*, 160(4), 881–891.

Preston, L. and Post, J. E. (1975). *Private Management and Public Policy: The Principle of Public Responsibility.* Englewood Cliffs, NJ: Prentice Hall.

Principles for Responsible Investment (PRI). (2020). What Is Responsible Investment? Retrieved on 17 October 2022 from www.unpri.org/an-introduction-to-responsible-investment/what-is-responsible-investment/4780.article.

(2016). A Practical Guide to ESG Integration for Equity Investing. Retrieved on 17 October 2022 from www.unpri.org/listed-equity/a-practical-guide-to-esg-integration-for-equity-investing/10.article.

(2013). Getting Started with Collaborative Engagement: How Institutional Investors Can Effectively Collaborate in Dialogue with Companies. Retrieved on 17 October 2022 from www.unpri.org/download? ac=4156.

PR Newswire. (2014). 2014 Annual Automotive OEM-Supplier Relations Study Shows Toyota and Honda on Top; Nissan displacing Ford in the Middle; Chrysler and GM Falling Behind. *The Business Journals.* Retrieved on 17 October 2022 from www.prnewswire.com/news-releases/2014-annual-automotive-oem-supplier-relations-study-shows-toyota-and-honda-on-top-nissan-displacing-ford-in-the-middle-chrysler-and-gm-falling-behind-258885661.html.

Provan, K. G. and Kenis, P. (2008). Modes of Network Governance: Structure, Management, and Effectiveness. *Journal of Public Administration Research and Theory*, 18(2), 229–252.

Pucker, K. (2021). Overselling Sustainability Reporting. *Harvard Business Review*, May–June. Retrieved on 17 October 2022 from https://hbr.org/2021/05/overselling-sustainability-reporting.

Putnam, L. L., Fairhurst, G. T. and Banghart, S. (2016). Contradictions, Dialectics, and Paradoxes in Organizations: A Constitutive Approach. *Academy of Management Annals*, 10(1), 65–171.

PwC. (2021). Taking on Change: The Director's New Playbook (PwC's 2021 Annual Corporate Directors Survey). Retrieved on 17 October 2022 from www.pwc.com/us/en/services/governance-insights-center/assets/pwc-2021-annual-corporate-directors-survey.pdf.

PwC Global Consumer Insights Pulse Survey. (2021). Four Fault Lines Show a Fracturing among Global Consumers. Retrieved on 17 October 2022 from www.pwc.dk/da/publikationer/2021/pwc-global-consumer-insights-pulse%20-survey-2021.pdf.

Rainforest Alliance. (n.d.). Our Alliance. Retrieved on 21 October 2021 from www.rainforest-alliance.org/.

Randers, J., Rockström, J., Stoknes, P. E., Golüke, U., Collste, D. and Cornell, S. (2018). Transformation Is Feasible: How to Achieve the Sustainable Development Goals within Planetary Boundaries. Retrieved on 17 October 2022 from www.stockholmresilience.org/download/18.51d83659166367a9a16353/1539675518425/Report_Achieving%20the%20Sustainable%20Development%20Goals_WEB.pdf.

Randerson, K. (2022). Conceptualizing Family Business Social Responsibility. *Technological Forecasting and Social Change*, 174, Article 121225.

Rappaport, A. (1999). *Creating Shareholder Value: A Guide for Managers and Investors* (revised and updated). New York, NY: The Free Press.

Rasche, A. (2020): The United Nations Global Compact and the Sustainable Development Goals. In O. Laasch, D. Jamali, R. E. Freeman and R. Suddaby. (Eds.), *Research Handbook of Responsbile Management* (pp. 228–241). Cheltenham, UK: Edward Elgar.

Rasche, A. (2014). The Corporation as a Political Actor – European and North American Perspectives. *European Management Journal*, 33(1), 4–8.

(2012). Global Policies and Local Practice: Loose and Tight Couplings in Multi-Stakeholder Initiatives. *Business Ethics Quarterly*, 22(4), 679–708.

(2009). 'A Necessary Supplement': What the United Nations Global Compact Is and Is Not. *Business & Society*, 48(4), 511–537.

(2008). *The Paradoxical Foundation of Strategic Management*. Heidelberg and New York, NY: Springer.

Rasche, A., de Bakker, F. G. A. and Moon, J. (2013). Complete and Partial

Organizing for Corporate Social Responsibility. *Journal of Business Ethics*, 115(4), 651–663.

Rasche, A. and Esser, D. E. (2006). From Stakeholder Management to Stakeholder Accountability. *Journal of Business Ethics*, 65(3), 251–267.

Rasche, A., Gwozdz, W., Lund Larsen, M. and Moon, J. (2021). Which Firms Leave Multi-stakeholder Initiatives? An Analysis of Delistings from the United Nations Global Compact. *Regulation and Governance*, 16(1), 309–326.

Rasche, A. and Lawrence, J. (2016). *How Boards Organize Oversight for Corporate Sustainability. Background Note*. Boston. MA: Hult International Business Publishing (HLT 327-14-1003BN).

Rasche, A., Morsing, M. and Moon, J. (2017). The Changing Role of Business in Global Society: CSR and beyond. In A. Rasche, M. Morsing and J. Moon. (Eds.), *Corporate Social Responsibility: Strategy, Communication, Governance* (pp. 1–30). Cambridge: Cambridge University Press.

Rawhouser, H., Cummings, M. and Crane, A., (2015). Benefit Corporation Legislation and the Emergence of a Social Hybrid Category. *California Management Review*, 57(3), 13–35.

Raworth, K. (2017). *Doughnut Economics: Seven Ways to Think Like a 21st Century Economist*. London: Penguin Random House.

Ray, D. E., Berman, S. L., Johnson-Cramer, M. E. and Van Buren III, H. J. (2014). Refining Normative Stakeholder Theory: Insights from Judaism, Christianity, and Islam. *Journal of*

Management, Spirituality and Religion, 11(4), 331–356.

Rein, M. (1982). The Social Policy of the Firm. *Policy Sciences*, 14(2), 117–135.

Reinecke, J. and Ansari, S. (2016). Taming Wicked Problems: The Role of Framing in the Construction of Corporate Social Responsibility. *Journal of Management Studies*, 53(3), 299–329.

Reinecke, J., Manning, S. and von Hagen, O. (2012). The Emergence of a Standards Market: Multiplicity of Sustainability Standards in the Global Coffee Industry. *Organization Studies*, 33(5/6), 791–814.

Reisman, S. M. (2019). Charitable Organizations in the United States (New York): Overview. *Thomsons Reuters Practical Law*. Retrieved on 17 October 2022 from https://uk.practicallaw .thomsonreuters.com/w-007-0252.

Renneboog, L., Jenke Ter, H. and Chendi, Z. (2008). The Price of Ethics and Stakeholder Governance: The Performance of Socially Responsible Mutual Funds. *Journal of Corporate Finance*, 14(3), 302–322.

Reputation Institute. (2015). Global CSR RepTrak Ranking. Retrieved on 15 February 2015 from www .reputationinstitute.com/thought-leadership/csr-reptrak-100.

Revkin, A. (2019). Most Americans Now Worry about Climate Change – and Want to Fix It. Retrieved on 17 October 2022 from www.nationalgeographic. com/environment/article/climate-change-awareness-polls-show-rising-concern-for-global-warming.

Reyes, G. (2001). Four Main Theories of Development: Modernization, Dependency, World-Systems, and

Globalization. *Nómadas. Revista Crítica de Ciencias Sociales y Jurídicas*, 4(2), 109–124.

Rhenman, E. (1968). *Industrial Democracy and Industrial Management*. London: Tavistock.

Right to Play. (2021). Saio Mané Is Empowering Girls through Sport and Play in Senegal. Retrieved on 24 November 2021 from https://righttoplay.com/en/news/empowering-girls-through-sport-and-play-in-senegal/.

Rinaldi, L., Unerman, J. and de Villiers, C. (2018). Evaluating the Integrated Reporting journey: Insights, Gaps and Agendas for Future Research. *Accounting Auditing & Accountability Journal*, 31(5), 1294–1318.

Rinaldi, L., Unerman, J. and Tilt, C. (2014). The Role of Stakeholder Engagement and Dialogue within the Sustainability Accounting and Reporting Process. In J. Bebbington, J. Unerman and B. O'Dwyer. (Eds.), *Sustainability Accounting and Accountability* (pp. 86–107). New York, NY: Routledge.

Ripple, W. J., Wolf, C., Newsome, T. M., Galetti, M., Alamgir, M., Crist, E., et al. (2017). World's Scientists' Warning to Humanity: A Second Notice. *Bioscience*, 67(12), 1026–1028.

Risi, D. and Wickert, C. (2017). Reconsidering the 'Symmetry' between Institutionalization and Professionalization: The Case of Corporate Social Responsibility Managers. *Journal of Management Studies*, 54(5), 613–646.

Robé, J.-P. (2011). The Legal Structure of the Firm. *Accounting, Economics, and Law*, 1(1), Article 5.

RobecoSAM. (2015). Measuring Country Intangibles: RobecoSAM's Country Sustainability Ranking. Retrieved on 18 May 2020 from www.robecosam.com/media/1/a/5/1a51002e61285110bc976df72cdb5dd5_country-sustainability-paper-en_tcm1011-15827.pdf.

Robinson, S. R., Irmak, C. and Jayachandran, S. (2012). Choice of Cause in Cause-Related Marketing. *Journal of Marketing*, 76(4), 126–139.

Rockström, J., Steffen, W., Noone, K., Persson, Å., Chapin III, F. S., Lambin, E. F., et al. (2009). A Safe Operating Space for Humanity. *Nature*, 461(7263), 472–475.

Rodrik, D., Subramanian, A. and Trebbi, F. (2004). Institutions Rule: The Primacy of Institutions over Geography and Integration in Economic Development. *Journal of Economic Growth*, 9(2), 131–165.

Rosenau, J. (1990). *Turbulence in World Politics: A Theory of Change and Continuity*. Princeton, NJ: Princeton University Press.

Rowley, T. J. (1997). Moving beyond Dyadic Ties: A Network Theory of Stakeholder Influences. *Academy of Management Review*, 22(4), 887–910.

Rowley, T. J. and Moldoveanu, M. (2003). When Will Stakeholder Groups Act? An Interest- and Identity-Based Model of Stakeholder Group Mobilization. *Academy of Management Review*, 28(2), 204–219.

Rowlinson, M., Hassard, J. and Decker, S. (2014). Research Strategies for Organizational History: A Dialogue between Historical Theory and

Organization Theory. *Academy of Management Review*, 39(3), 250–274.

Ruddick, G. and Stewart, H. (2016). Tata Steel to Sell Off Entire British Business. *The Guardian*. Retrieved on 17 October 2022 from www.theguardian.com/business/2016/mar/29/tata-set-to-announce-sale-of-uk-steel-business-port-talbot.

Ruggie, J. G. (2013). *Just Business*. Boston, MA: Norton Publishers.

   (2008). Protect, Respect and Remedy: A Framework for Business and Human Rights. Report of the Special Representative of the Secretary-General on the Issue of Human Rights and Transnational Corporations and Other Business Enterprises. UN Doc. A/HRC/8/5 (7 April).

   (1982). International Regimes, Transactions, and Change: Embedded Liberalism in the Postwar Economic Order. *International Organization*, 36 (2), 379–415.

Ruggie, J. G. and Sherman, J. F. III. (2017). The Concept of 'Due Diligence' in the UN Guiding Principles on Business and Human Rights: Reply to Professors Bonnitcha and McCorquedale. *European Journal of International Law*. Retrieved on 17 October 2022 from www.ejil.org/article.php?article=2799&issue=137.

Ryan, M. R. (2021). Business Ethics as a Form of Practical Reasoning: What Philosophers Can Learn from Patagonia. *Humanistic Management Journal*, 6(1), 103–116.

Sachs, J. D., Schmidt-Traub, G., Mazzucato, M., Messner, D., Nakicenovic, N. and Rockström, J. (2019). Six Transformations to Achieve the Sustainable Development Goals, *Nature Sustainability*, 2(9), 805–814.

Saebi, T., Foss, N. J. and Linder, S. (2019). Social Entrepreneurship Research: Past Achievements and Future Promises. *Journal of Management*, 45(1), 70–95.

Safian, R. (2018). Ford CEO Jim Hackett on the Future of Car Ownership and Driving. *Fast Company*, 9 January.

Salovaara, J. J. and Soini, K. (2021). Educated Professionals of Sustainability and the Dimensions of Practices. *International Journal of Sustainability in Higher Education*, 22 (8), 69–87.

Sampson, S. (2010). The Anti-Corruption Industry: From Movement to Institution. *Global Crime*, 11(2), 261–278.

Sandel, M. J. (2010). *Justice: What's the Right Thing to Do?* London: Penguin.

Sanga, N., Benson, O. G. and Josyula, L. (2021). Top-Down Processes Derail Bottom-Up Objectives: A Study in Community Engagement and 'Slum-Free City Planning'. *Community Development Journal*, 57(4), 615–634.

Santayana, G. (1905). *Reason in Common Sense: Volume One of 'The Life of Reason'*. New York, NY: Dover Publications.

Schaltegger, S. and Burritt, R. (2005). Corporate Sustainability. In H. Folmer and T. Tietenberg. (Eds.), *International Yearbook of Environmental and Resource Economics 2005/2006: A Survey of Current Issues* (pp. 185–222). Cheltenham, UK: Edward Elgar.

Schaltegger, S., Hansen, E. and Lüdeke-Freund, F. (2016a). Business Models for

Sustainability: Origins, Present Research, and Future Avenues. *Organization & Environment*, 29(1), 3–10.

Schaltegger, S., Lüdeke-Freund, F. and Hansen, E. (2016b). Business Models for Sustainability: A Co-Evolutionary Analysis of Sustainable Entrepreneurship, Innovation, and Transformation. *Organization & Environment*, 29(3), 264–289.

Schaltegger, S. and Wagner, M. (2011). Sustainable Entrepreneurship and Sustainability Innovation: Categories and Interactions. *Business Strategy and the Environment*, 20(4), 222–237.

Scharpf, F. W. (2009). Legitimacy in the Multilevel European Polity. *European Political Science Review*, 1(2), 173–204.

Schembera, S. (2018). Implementing Corporate Social Responsibility: Empirical Insights on the Impact of the UN Global Compact on Its Business Participants. *Business & Society*, 57(5), 783–825.

Scherer, A. G. and Palazzo, G. (2011). The New Political Role of Business in a Globalized world: A Review of a New perspective on CSR and Its Implications for the Firm, Governance, and Democracy. *Journal of Management Studies*, 48(4), 899–931.

(2008). Globalization and Corporate Social Responsibility. In A. Crane, A. McWilliams, D. Matten, D. J. Moon and D. Siegel. (Eds.), *The Oxford Handbook of Corporate Social Responsibility* (pp. 413–431). Oxford: Oxford University Press.

(2007). Toward a Political Conception of Corporate Responsibility: Business and Society Seen from a Habermasian Perspective. *Academy of Management Review*, 32(4), 1096–1120.

Scherer, A. G., Rasche, A., Palazzo, G. and Spicer, A. (2016). Managing for Political Corporate Social Responsibility: New Challenges and Directions for PCSR 2.0. *Journal of Management Studies*, 53(3), 273–298.

Schoenmaker, D. and Schramade, W. (2019). *Principles of Sustainable Finance*. Oxford and New York, NY: Oxford University Press.

Schouten, G., Leroy, P. and Glasbergen, P. (2012). On the Deliberative Capacity of Private Multi-Stakeholder Governance: The Roundtables on Responsible Soy and Sustainable Palm Oil. *Ecological Economics*, 83, 42–50.

Schrempf-Stirling, J. (2018). State Power: Rethinking the Role of the State in Political Corporate Social Responsibility. *Journal of Business Ethics*, 150(1), 1–14.

Schrempf-Stirling, J. and Wettstein, F. (2017). Beyond Guilty Verdicts: Human Rights Litigation and Its Impact on Corporations' Human Rights Policies. *Journal of Business Ethics*, 145(3), 545–562.

Schroders. (2017). *Demystifying Negative Screens: The Full Implications of ESG Exclusions*. London: Schroders.

Schuler, D., Rasche, A., Etzion, D. and Newton, L. (2017). Corporate Sustainability Management and Environmental Ethics. *Business Ethics Quarterly*, 27(02), 213–237.

Schwab, K. (2019). *Davos Manifesto 2020: The Universal Purpose of a Company in the Fourth Industrial Revolution.* Davos, Switzerland: World Economic Forum.

Scott, J. C. (1969). Corruption, Machine Politics, and Political Change. *American Political Science Review*, 63 (4), 1142–1158.

Seelos, C. (2014). Theorizing and Strategizing with Models: Generative Models of Social Enterprises. *International Journal of Entrepreneurial Venturing*, 6(1), 6–21.

Seitanidi, M. and Crane, A. (Eds.). (2014). *Social Partnerships and Responsible Business: A Research Handbook.* New York, NY: Routledge.

Seitanidi, M. M. and Crane, A. (2009). Implementing CSR through Partnerships: Understanding the Selection, Design and Institutionalization of Nonprofit-Business Partnerships. *Journal of Business Ethics*, 85(Sup2), 413–429.

Selim, O. (2021). ESG and AI. In H. Bril, G. Kell and A. Rasche. (Eds.), *Sustainable Investing: A Path to a New Horizon* (pp. 227–243). Abingdon, UK and New York, NY: Routledge.

Sen, A. (2004). Elements of a Theory of Human Rights. *Philosophy and Public Affairs*, 32(4), 315–356.

(1999). *Development as Freedom.* New York, NY: Alfred A. Knopf.

Sepinwall, A. J. (2017). Blame, Emotion, and the Corporation. In E. W. Orts and N. C. Smith. (Eds.), *The Moral Responsibility of Firms* (pp. 143–166). Oxford: Oxford University Press.

Serrano-Cinca, C., Fuertes-Callén, Y. and Cuellar-Fernández, B. (2021). Managing for Stakeholders Using Multiple-Criteria Decision-Making Techniques. *Social Indicators Research*, 157, 587–601.

Shah, A. (2014). Consumption and Consumerism. *Global Issues*, 5 January. Retrieved on 17 October 2022 from www.globalissues.org/issue/235/consumption-and-consumerism.

Shanker, D., Mulvany, L. and Hytha, M. (2019). Beyond Meat Just Had the Best IPO of 2019 as Value Soars to $3.8 Billion. *Bloomberg.* Retrieved on 17 October 2022 from https://finance.yahoo.com/news/beyond-meat-inc-may-just-201250023.html.

Sharma, D. (2021). Human Rights and Environmental Due Diligence Legislation in Europe – Implications for Global Supply Chains. DLA Piper. Retrieved on 17 October 2022 from www.dlapiper.com/fr/france/insights/publications/2021/05/human-rights-and-environmental-due-diligence-legislation-in-europe/.

Shelton, D. L. (2014). *Advanced Introduction to International Human Rights Law.* Cheltenham, UK and Northampton, MA: Edward Elgar.

Shepherd, D. A., Williams, T. A. and Zhao, E. Y. (2019). A Framework for Exploring the Degree of Hybridity in Entrepreneurship. *Academy of Management Perspectives*, 33(4), 491–512.

Shift. (2019). Fulfilling the State Duty to Protect: A Statement on the Role of Mandatory Measures in a 'Smart Mix'. Retrieved on 17 October 2022 from https://shiftproject.org/fulfilling-the-state-duty-to-protect-a-statement-on-the-role-of-mandatory-measures-in-a-smart-mix/.

Shleifer, A. and Vishny, R. W. (1997). A Survey of Corporate Governance. *Journal Of Finance*, 52(2), 737–783.

Short, J. L., Toffel, M. W. and Hugill, A. R. (2020). Improving Working Conditions in Global Supply Chains: The Role of Institutional Environments and Monitoring Program Design. *ILR Review*, 73(4), 873–912.

Shrivastava, P. (1995). Ecocentric Management for a Risk Society. *Academy of Manageement Review*, 20 (1), 118–137.

Sikavica, K. and Pozner, J.-E. (2013). Paradise Sold: Resource Partitioning and the Organic Movement in the US Farming Industry. *Organization Studies*, 34(5–6), 623–651.

Sillars, P. (2021). Boohoo Cuts Hundreds of Suppliers to Fashion a New Future after Factory Scandal. *Sky News*. Retrieved on 17 October 2022 from https://news.sky.com/story/boohoo-cuts-hundreds-of-suppliers-to-fashion-new-future-after-factory-scandal-12256064.

Sims, R. R. (1992). Linking Groupthink to Unethical Behavior in Organizations. *Journal of Business Ethics*, 11(9), 651–662.

Sims, R. R. and Brinkmann, J. (2003). Enron Ethics (Or: Culture Matters More than Codes). *Journal of Business Ethics*, 45 (3), 243–256.

Sinclair, U. (1927). *Oil!* Boston, MA: Albert & Charles Boni.

Skapinker, M. and Daneshkhu, S. (2016). Can Unilever's Paul Polman Change the Way We Do business? Why the Chief Executive Is Determined to Make His Company Environmentally Sustainable. *Financial Times*. Retrieved on 17 October 2022 from www.ft.com/content/e6696b4a-8505-11e6-8897-2359a58ac7a5.

Skeel, D. A. (2001). Shaming in Corporate Law. *University of Pennsylvania Law Review*, 149(6), 1811–1868.

Smit, D. (1992). Urban Foundations: Transformation Possibilities. *Transformation*, 18–19, 35–42.

Smith, A. (1776/1982). *An Inquiry into the Nature and Causes of the Wealth of Nations*. London: Penguin.

Smith, J. (2013). The Companies with the Best CSR Reputations. *Forbes*. Retrieved on 17 October 2022 from www.forbes.com/sites/jacquelynsmith/2013/10/02/the-companies-with-the-best-csr-reputations-2/?sh=67d6e5a034ff.

Smith, W. K., Gonin, M. and Besharov, M. L. (2013). Managing Social-Business Tensions: A Review and Research Agenda for Social Enterprise. *Business Ethics Quarterly*, 23(3), 407–442.

Social Enterprise Law Tracker. (2022). Status Tool. Retrieved on 17 October 2022 from https://socentlawtracker.org/#/bcorps.

Soundararajan, V., Jamali, D. and Spence, L. J. (2018). Small Business Social Responsibility: A Critical Multi-Level Review, Synthesis and Research Agenda. *International Journal of Management Reviews*, 57(7), 1301–1336.

Sovacool, B. K. and Hess, D. J. (2017). Ordering Theories: Typologies and Conceptual Frameworks for

Sociotechnical Change. *Social Studies of Science*, 47(5), 703–750.

Spaiser, V., Ranganathan, S., Swain, R. B. and Sumpter, D. J. T. (2017). The Sustainable Development Oxymoron: Quantifying and Modelling the Incompatibility of Sustainable Development Goals. *International Journal of Sustainable Development and World Ecology*, 24(6), 457–470.

Spence, L. J. (2016). Small Business Social Responsibility: Redrawing Core CSR Theory. *Business & Society*, 55(1), 23–55.

Spence, L. and Rutherford, R. (2003). Small Business and Empirical Perspectives in Business Ethics: Editoral. *Journal of Business Ethics*, 47(1), 1–5.

Spiro, L. N. (2002). Business; More Scorn, Fewer Giggles at This Year's Meetings. The New York Times, 17 February.

Spraul, K., Hufnagel, J., Friedrich, C. and Brill, N. (2019). Talents for Key Positions in Organizations: Sustainability Management as a Profession. In Y. Liu. (Ed.), *Research Handbook of International Talent Management* (pp. 274–317). Cheltenham, UK and Northampton, MA: Edward Elgar.

Stanford Law School. (n.d.). Foreign Corrupt Practices Act Clearing House. Retrieved on 17 October 2022 from https://fcpa .stanford.edu/statistics-top-ten.html.

Starbucks. (2017). Starbucks Strategy in relation to Taxation. Retrieved on 17 October 2022 from http:// globalassets.starbucks.com/assets/ 77CB10D4E6DD403A92D568DE90 148166.pdf.

State Street Global Advisors. (2019). Into the Mainstream: ESG at the Tipping Point. Retrieved on 17 October 2022 from www.ssga.com/library-content/pdfs/ insights/into-the-mainstream.pdf.

Statista. (2017). Retail Sales for Fairtrade Products in Selected Countries in Europe in 2017. Retrieved on 17 October 2022 from www.statista. com/statistics/859892/retail-sales-of-fairtrade-products-by-country-europe/.

Steering Committee of the State-of-Knowledge Assessment of Standards and Certification. (2012). *Towards Sustainability: The Roles and Limitations of Certification.* Washington, DC: Resolve, Inc.

Steffen, A. (2009). Bright Green, Light Green, Dark Green, Gray: The New Environmental Spectrum. *Worldchanging.* Retrieved on 17 October 2022 from https://web .archive.org/web/20160112194947/ http:/www.worldchanging.com/ archives/009499.html.

Steffen, W., Broadgate, W., Deutsch, L., Gaffney, O. and Ludwig, C. (2015a). "The Trajectory of the Anthropocene: The Great Acceleration." *The Anthropocene Review*, 2(1), 81–98.

Steffen, W., Richardson, K., Rockström, J., Cornell, S. E., Fetzer, I., Bennett, E. M., et al. (2015b). Planetary Boundaries: Guiding Human Development on a Changing Planet. *Science*, 347(6223), Article 1259855.

Stenfeldt, N. (2019). The Impact of Foundational Ownership on the Socially Responsible Organization. Retrieved on 17 October 2022 from www.linkedin.com/pulse/impact-foundational-ownership-socially-responsible-niels-stenfeldt/.

Stern, N. (2007). *The Economics of Climate Change: The Stern Review*. Cambridge: Cambridge University Press.

Stern, N., Peters, S., Bakhshi, V., Bowen, A., Cameron, C., Catovsky, S. et al. (2006). *Stern Review: The Economics of Climate Change*. London: HM Treasury.

Steurer, R. (2010). The Role of Governments in Corporate Social Responsibility: Characterising Public Policies on CSR in Europe. *Policy Sciences*, 43(1), 49–72.

Stevens, B. (2008). Corporate Ethical Codes: Effective Instruments for Influencing Behavior. *Journal of Business Ethics*, 78(4), 601–609.

Stiglitz, J., Sen, A. and Fitoussi, J. (2010). *Mismeasuring Our Lives: Why GDP Doesn't Add Up*. New York, NY: The New Press.

Stockholm Resilience Centre. (2015). The SDGs Wedding Cake. Retrieved on 17 October 2022 from www.stockholmresilience.org/research/research-news/2016-06-14-the-sdgs-wedding-cake.html.

Stoll, S. (2008). Fear of Fallowing: The Specter of a No-Growth World. *Harper's Magazine*. Retrieved on 17 October 2022 from https://harpers.org/archive/2008/03/fear-of-fallowing/.

Stout, L. (2012a). *The Shareholder Value Myth: How Putting Shareholders First Harms Investors, Corporations, and the Public*. San Francisco, CA: Berrett-Koehler.

(2012b). The Problem with Corporate Purpose. *Brookings*

Institution Issues in Governance Studies, 48(1), 1–14.

Strand, R. and Freeman, E. (2015). Scandinavian Cooperative Advantage: The Theory and Practice of Stakeholder Engagement in Scandinavia. *Journal of Business Ethics*, 127(1), 65–85.

Strand, R., Freeman, R. E. and Hockerts, K. (2015). Corporate Social Responsibility and Sustainability in Scandinavia: An Overview. *Journal of Business Ethics*, 127(1), 1–15.

Strategyzer. (2022). Business Canvas – Business Models & Value Propositions. Retrieved on 17 October 2022 from www.strategyzer.com/canvas.

Strike, V. M., Gao, J. and Bansal, P. (2006). Being Good While Being Bad: Social Responsibility and the International Diversification of US Firms. *Journal of International Business Studies*, 37(6), 850–862.

Strong, C., Ansons, T. and Long, J. (2021). *Addressing the Sustainability Say-Do Gap: Leading the Way to Activate Consumer Behavior Change*. Paris: Ipsos MORI.

Suchman, M. C. (1995). Managing Legitimacy: Strategic and Institutional Approaches. *Academy of Management Review*, 20(3), 571–610.

Sulkowski, A. J., Edwards, M. and Freeman, R. E. (2018). Shake Your Stakeholder: Firms Leading Engagement to Cocreate Sustainable Value. *Organization & Environment*, 31(3), 223–241.

Sumner, A. (2006). What Is Development Studies? *Development in Practice*, 16 (6), 644–650.

Sumner, A. and Tribe, M. (2008). *International Development Studies:*

Theories and Methods in Research and Practice. London: Sage.

Sustainability Accounting Standards Board (SASB). (2022). Materiality Finder. Retrieved on 17 October 2022 from www.sasb.org/standards/materiality-finder/.

Sustainable Brand Index. (2020). Sustainable Brand Index 2020. Retrieved on 17 October 2022 from www.sb-index.nl/2021#close.

Sustainable Stock Exchanges Initiative (SSE). (2020). ESG Disclosure Guidance Database. Retrieved on 17 October 2022 from https://sseinitiative.org/esg-guidance-database/.

(2018). 2018 Report on Progress: A Paper Prepared for the Sustainable Stock Exchanges 2018 Global Dialogue. New York, NY.

(2014). Sustainable Stock Exchanges: Report on Progress 2014. New York, NY.

Swiss Re. (2021). The Economics of Climate Change, 22 April. Retrieved on 21 January 2022 from www.swissre.com/institute/research/topics-and-risk-dialogues/climate-and-natural-catastrophe-risk/expertise-publication-economics-of-climate-change.html.

(2018). Natural Catastrophes and Man-Made Disasters in 2017: A Year of Record-breaking Losses. *Sigma*, 1/2018.

Sylvester, C. (1999). Development Studies and Postcolonial Studies: Disparate Tales of the Third World. *Third World Quarterly*, 20(4), 703–721.

Szakály, Z., Popp, J., Kontor, E., Kovács, S., Pető, K. and Jasák, H. (2017). Attitudes of the Lifestyle of Health and Sustainability Segment in Hungary. *Sustainability*, 9(10), 1763–1779.

Søreide, T. (2002). Corruption in Public Procurement: Causes, Consequences and Cures. Chr. Michelsen Institute.

Taebi, B. and Safari, A. (2017). On Effectiveness and Legitimacy of 'Shaming' as a Strategy for Combatting Climate Change. *Science and Engineering Ethics*, 23(5), 1289–1306.

Tams, S. and Marshall, J. (2011). Responsible Careers: Systemic Reflexivity in Shifting Landscapes. *Human Relations*, 64(1), 109–131.

Tata, R. N. and Matten, D. (2016). Corporate Community Involvement in the 21st Century. In D. Barton, D. Horvath and M. Kipping. (Eds.), *Re-imagining Capitalism* (pp. 68–83). Oxford: Oxford University Press.

Tata Sons Ltd. (2022). An Ode to Independence, Retrieved on 17 October 2022 from www.tata.com/about-us/tata-group-our-heritage.

(2016). Tata Releases Report on Contribution to Sustainable Development Goals. Retrieved on 17 October 2022 from www.tata.com/newsroom/tata-group-report-sustainable-development-goals.

Taylor, A. (2019). Exploring Employee Activism: Why This Stakeholder Group Can No Longer Be Ignored. *GreenBiz*, 27 May. Retrieved on 6 February 2022 from www.greenbiz.com/article/exploring-employee-activism-why-stakeholder-group-can-no-longer-be-ignored.

Taylor, A. (2017). We Shouldn't Always Need a 'Business Case' to Do the Right

Thing. *Harvard Business Review Digital Articles*. Retrieved on 17 October 2022 from https://hbr.org/2017/09/we-shouldnt-always-need-a-business-case-to-do-the-right-thing.

TCI Fund Management. (2020). Open Letter to Thomas Eichelmann – Chairperson of the Supervisory Board of Wirecard AG. Retrieved on 11 November 2020 from www.tcifund.com/files/corporateengageement/wirecard/TCI%20-%20Letter%20to%20Wirecard%2028%20April%202020.pdf.

Tefera, D. A., Bijman, J. and Slingerland, M. A. (2017). Agricultural Co-operatives in Ethiopia: Evolution, Functions and Impact. *Journal of International Development*, 29(4), 431–453.

Teisl, M. E., Peavey, S., Newman, F., Buono, J. and Hermann, M. (2002). Consumer Reactions to Environmental Labels for Forest Products: A Preliminary Look. *Forest Products Journal*, 52(1), 44–50.

Tenbrunsel, A. E. and Smith-Crowe, K. (2008). Ethical Decision Making: Where We've Been and Where We're Going. *Academy of Management Annals*, 2(1), 545–607.

Tennyson, R. (2011). The Partnering Toolbook. The International Business Leaders Forum (IBLF) and the Global Alliance for Improved Nutrition (GAIN). Retrieved on 17 October 2022 from https://thepartneringinitiative.org/publications/toolbook-series/the-partnering-toolbook/.

Teviño, L. K. (1986). Ethical Decision Making in Organizations. *Academy of Management Review*, 11(3), 601–617.

Tezer, A. and Bodur, H. O. (2020). The Green Consumption Effect: How Using Green Products Improves Consumption Experience. *Journal of Consumer Research*, 47(1), 25–39.

The Boots Company PLC. (2016). Corporate Social Responsibility. Retrieved on 19 April 2016 from www.boots-uk.com/corporate_social_responsibility/.

(2015a). Boots Heritage. Retrieved on 19 April 2016 from www.boots-uk.com/about-boots-uk/company-information/boots-heritage/.

(2015b). Our Approach. Retrieved on 19 April 2016 from www.boots-uk.com/corporate-social-responsibility/our-approach/.

The Committee on the Financial Aspects of Corporate Governance. (1992). *The Report of the Cadbury Committee on The Financial Aspects of Corporate Governance: The Code of Best Practice*. London: Professional Publishing.

The Economist. (2021). The War against Money-Laundering Is Being Lost. Retrieved on 17 October 2022 from www.economist.com/finance-and-economics/2021/04/12/the-war-against-money-laundering-is-being-lost.

The Fund for Peace. (2021). Fragile States Index. Retrieved on 17 October 2022 from https://fragilestatesindex.org/data/.

The Guardian. (2021). 'A Great Deception': Oil Giants Taken to Task over Greenwash Ads. Retrieved on 17 October 2022 from www.theguardian.com/business/2021/apr/19/a-great-deception-oil-giants-taken-to-task-over-greenwash-ads.

(2016). The Panama Papers. Retrieved on 6 March 2022 from www.theguardian.com/news/series/panama-papers.

The Hauser Institute for Civil Society. (2014). *Corporate Social Responsibility Disclosure Efforts by National Governments and Stock Exchanges.* Cambridge, MA: The Hauser Institute for Civil Society – Harvard Kennedy School.

The Hofstede Centre. (2016). Compare Countries. The Hofstede Centre website. Retrieved on 17 October 2022 from www.hofstede-insights.com/fi/product/compare-countries/.

Thelen, K. (2014). *Varieties of Liberalization and the New Politics of Social Solidarity.* New York, NY: Cambridge University Press.

Thomassen, J. P., Leliveld, M. C., Ahaus, K. and Van de Walle, S. (2020). Prosocial Compensation Following a Service Failure: Fulfilling an Organization's Ethical and Philanthropic Responsibilities. *Journal of Business Ethics*, 162(1), 123–147.

Thomsen, S., Poulsen, T., Børsting, C. and Kuhn, J. (2018). Industrial Foundations as Long-Term Owners. *Corporate Governance: An International Review*, 26(3), 180–196.

Thomson, J. J. (1985). The Trolley Problem. *Yale Law Journal*, 94(6), 1395–1415.

Tjernström, E. and Tietenberg, T. (2008). Do Differences in Attitudes Explain Differences in National Climate Change Policies? *Ecological Economics*, 65(2), 315–324.

Todaro, M. P. and Smith, S. C. (2003). *Economic Development* (8th ed.). Reading, MA: Addison-Wesley.

Transparency International. (2022). Exporting Corruption 2022: Assessing Enforcement of the OECD Anti-Bribery Convention. Retrieved on 17 October 2022 from www.transparency.org/en/publications/exporting-corruption-2022.

(2021a). Corruption Perceptions Index 2020. Retrieved on 12 November 2021 from www.transparency.org/en/cpi/2020.

(2021b). Global Corruption Barometer. European Union. Retrieved on 17 October 2022 from www.transparency.org/en/gcb/eu/european-union-2021.

(n.d.). What Is Corruption? Retrieved on 17 October 2022 from www.transparency.org/en/what-is-corruption.

Treviño, L. K. (1986). Ethical Decision Making in Organizations. *Academy of Management Review*, 11(3), 601–617.

Treviño, L. K., Weaver, G. R., Gibson, D. G. and Toffler, B. L. (1999). Managing Ethics and Legal Compliance: What Works and What Hurts. *California Management Review*, 41(2), 131–151.

Trudel, R. and Cotte, J. (2009). Does It Pay to Be Good? *MIT Sloan Management Review*, 50(2), 61–68.

Truth in Advertising. (2022). Earth Day 2021: Companies Accused of Greenwashing. 22 April. Retrieved on 17 October 2022 from www.truthinadvertising.org/six-companies-accused-greenwashing/.

Turban, D. B. and Greening, D. W. (1997). Corporate Social Performance and Organizational Attractiveness to Prospective Employees. *Academy of Management Journal*, 40(3), 658–672.

Turpin, A., Shier, M. and Scowen, K. (2021). Assessing the Social Impact of Mental Health Service Accessibility by a Nonprofit Social Enterprise: A Mixed-methods Case Study. *Canadian Journal of Nonprofit and Social Economy Research*, 12(1), 82–106.

US Department of Labor. (2013). Cote d'Ivoire. Retrieved on 17 October 2022 from www.dol.gov/agencies/ilab/resources/reports/child-labor/cote-divoire.

US General Accounting Office. (1988). *'SWEATSHOPS'. IN THE U.S. Opinions on Their Sweatshops in the U.S.: Opinions on Their Extent and Possible Enforcement Options*. Washington, DC: US General Accounting Office.

United Nations (UN). (2022a). Sustainable Development Goals. Retrieved on 17 October 2022 from https://sdgs.un.org/goals.

(2022b). The Lazy Person's Guide to Saving the World. Retrieved on 17 October 2022 from www.un.org/sustainabledevelopment/takeaction/.

(2015). Transforming Our World: The 2030 Agenda for Sustainable Development. Retrieved on 17 October 2022 from https://sustainabledevelopment.un.org/post2015/transformingourworld/publication.

(2011). Guiding Principles on Business and Human Rights: Implementing the United Nations 'Protect, Respect, Remedy' Framework. Report of the Special Representative of the Secretary-General on the Issue of Human Rights and Transnational Corporations and Other Business Enterprises. UN Doc. A/HRC/17/31.

(2008). Protect, Respect and Remedy: A Framework for Business and Human Rights. Report of the Special Representative of the Secretary-General on the Issue of Human Rights and Transnational Corporations and Other Business Enterprises, John Ruggie. UN Doc. A/HRC/8/5.

(2007). UN Declaration on the Rights of Indigenous Peoples. Retrieved on 17 October 2022 from www.un.org/development/desa/indigenouspeoples/declaration-on-the-rights-of-indigenous-peoples.html.

(1966a). International Covenant on Economic, Social and Cultural Rights. Retrieved on 17 October 2022 from www.ohchr.org/EN/ProfessionalInterest/Pages/CESCR.aspx.

(1966b). International Covenant on Civil and Political Rights. Retrieved on 17 October 2022 from www.ohchr.org/en/professionalinterest/pages/ccpr.aspx.

(1948). Universal Declaration of Human Rights. Retrieved on 17 October 2022 from www.un.org/en/documents/udhr/.

UN Conference on Trade and Development (UNCTAD). (2013). *Capital Flows to Developing Countries: When Are They Good for Development?* Geneva, Switzerland: United Nations.

UN Development Programme (UNDP). (2015). Putting Resilience at the Heart of Development: Investing in Prevention and Resilient Recovery. Retrieved on 17 October 2022 from www.undp.org/publications/putting-resilience-heart-development.

UN Global Compact. (2014). Guide to Corporate Sustainability. Retrieved on

17 October 2022 from https://d306pr3pise04h.cloudfront.net/docs/publications%2FUN_Global_Compact_Guide_to_Corporate_Sustainability.pdf.

(n.d.a). Making Global Goals Local Business. Retrieved on 17 October 2022 from www.unglobalcompact.org/sdgs.

(n.d.b). Principle Ten. Anti-Corruption. Retrieved on 17 October 2022 from www.unglobalcompact.org/what-is-gc/mission/principles/principle-10.

UN Global Compact and Principles for Responsible Investment. (2013). *A Tool for Communicating the Business Value of Sustainability*. New York, NY: UN Global Compact Office.

Unilever. (2021). Unilever Statement on Ben & Jerry's Decision. Retrieved on 17 October 2022 from www.unilever.com/news/press-and-media/press-releases/2021/unilever-statement-on-ben-and-jerrys-decision/.

(2020). Statement on the Implementation of Unilever's Remuneration Policy. Retrieved on 17 October 2022 from www.unilever.com/files/origin/d34ce4e388c62b26e721107ea3494f16806db321.pdf/statement-on-the-renewal-of-unilevers-remuneration-policy-in-2021.pdf.

Union of Concerned Scientists. (1992). World Scientists' Warning to Humanity. Retrieved on 17 October 2022 from www.ucsusa.org.

Unruh, B. G., Kiron, D., Kruschwitz, N. and Reeves, M. (2016). Investing for a Sustainable Future. In Sloan Management Review Research Report (No. 57480).

Unterberg, M., Richter, D., Jahnke, T., Spiess-Knafl, W., Sänger, R. and Förster, N. (2015). Herausforderungen bei der Gründung und Skalierung von Sozialunternehmen. Welche Rahmenbedingungen benötigen Social Entrepreneurs? Retrieved on 17 October 2022 from www.bmwk.de/Redaktion/DE/Publikationen/Studien/herausforderungen-bei-der-gruendung-und-skalierung-von-sozialunternehmen.html.

Upward, A. and Jones, P. (2016). An Ontology for Strongly Sustainable Business Models: Defining an Enterprise Framework Compatible with Natural and Social Science. *Organization & Environment*, 29(1), 97–123.

US Department of Energy (US DOE). (2020). Vision of the Future Grid. Retrieved on 17 October 2022 from www.energy.gov/doe-grid-tech-team/vision-future-grid.

US District Court for DC. (2020). Deferred Prosecution Agreement USA v. Airbus. Retrieved on 17 October 2022 from www.justice.gov/opa/press-release/file/1241466/download.

Utting, P. (2008). The Struggle for Corporate Accountability. *Development & Change*, 39(6), 959–975.

Valente, M. (2017). Corporate Responsibility Strategies for Sustainability. In A. Rasche, M. Morsing and J. Moon. (Eds.), *Corporate Social Responsibility: Strategy, Communication, Governance* (pp. 86–109). Cambridge: Cambridge University Press.

Vallentin, S. (2015a). Governmentalities of CSR: Danish Government Policy as a

Reflection of Political Difference. *Journal of Business Ethics*, 127(1), 33–47.

(2015b). Instrumental and Political Currents in the CSR Debate: On the Demise and (Possible) Resurgence of 'Ethics'. In A. Pullen and C. Rhodes. (Eds.), *The Routledge Companion to Ethics, Politics and Organizations* (pp. 13–31). London: Routledge.

Vallentin, S. and Spence, L. (2017). Strategic CSR: Ambitions and Critique. In A. Rasche, M. Morsing and J. Moon. (Eds.), *Corporate Social Responsibility: Strategy, Communication, Governance* (pp. 63–85). Cambridge: Cambridge University Press.

Van der Byl, C. A. and Slawinski, N. (2015). Embracing Tensions in Corporate Sustainability: A Review of Research from Win-Wins and Trade-Offs to Paradoxes and Beyond. *Organization & Environment*, 28(1), 54–79.

Vangen, S. and Huxham, C. (2003). Nurturing Collaborative Relations: Building Trust in Interorganizational Collaboration. *Journal of Applied Behavioral Science*, 39(1), 5–31.

Vedula, S., Doblinger, C., Pacheco, D., York, J. G., Bacq, S., Russo, M. and Dean, T. J. (2021). Entrepreneurship for the Public Good: A Review, Critique, and Path Forward for Social and Environmental Entrepreneurship Research. *Academy of Management Annals*, 16(1), 391–425.

Venturely. (2022). Award-Winning Business Modeling & Venture Creation Platform. Retrieved on 16 January 2022 from https://venturely.io/.

Verbeke, A. (2020). Will the COVID-19 Pandemic Really Change the Governance of Global Value Chains? *British Journal of Management*, 31(3), 444–446.

Vérité. (2014). Forced Labour in the Production of Electronic Goods in Malaysia. A Comprehensive Study of Scope and Characteristics. Retrieved on 17 October 2022 from www.verite.org/sites/default/files/images/Verite ForcedLaborMalaysianElectronics2014 .pdf.

Vigneau, L., Humphreys, M. and Moon, J. (2015). How Do Firms Comply with International Sustainability Standards? Processes and Consequences of Adopting the Global Reporting Initiative. *Journal of Business Ethics*, 131(2), 469–486.

Villela, M., Bulgacov, S. and Morgan, G. (2021). B Corp Certification and Its Impact on Organizations over Time. *Journal of Business Ethics*, 170(2), 343–357.

Visser, W. and Crane, A. (2012). Corporate Sustainability and the Individual: Understanding What Drives Sustainability Professionals as Change Agents (Working paper). Retrieved on 17 October 2022 from https://doi.org/10.2139/ssrn .1559087.

Vladimirova, D. (2019). Building Sustainable Value Propositions for Multiple Stakeholders: A Practical Tool. *Journal of Business Models*, 7(1), 1–8.

Vogel, D. (2005). *The Market for Virtue: The Potential and Limits of Corporate Social Responsibility*. Washington, DC: Brookings Institution Press.

Vogel, D. J. (1996). The Study of Business and Politics. *California Management Review*, 38(3), 146–165.

Waddock, S. A. (1991). A Typology of Social Partnership Organizations. *Administration & Society*, 22(4), 480–515.

(1988). Building Successful Social Partnerships. *Sloan Management Review*, 29(4), 17–23.

Waddock, S. A. and Rasche, A. (2012). *Building the Responsible Enterprise: Where Vision and Values Add Value*. Stanford, CA: Stanford University Press.

Waldner, C. J. (2020). In the Centre of Attention: How Social Entrepreneurs Influence Organisational Reputation. *Journal of Social Entrepreneurship*, 1–23. Retrieved on 17 October 2022 from https://doi.org/10.1080/19420676 .2020.1823456.

Waldron, T. L., Navis, C. and Fisher, G. (2013). Explaining Differences in Firms' Responses to Activism. *Academy of Management Review*, 38(3), 397–417.

Warren, D. E., Gaspar, J. P. and Laufer, W. S. (2014). Is Formal Ethics Training Merely Cosmetic? A Study of Ethics Training and Ethical Organizational Culture. *Business Ethics Quarterly*, 24 (1), 85–117.

Weaver, G. R., Treviño, L. K. and Cochran, P. L. (1999). Corporate Ethics Programs as Control Systems: Influences of Executive Commitment and Environmental Factors. *Academy of Management Journal*, 42(1), 41–57.

Webb, T. and Cheney, G. (2014). Worker-Owned-and-Governed Co-operatives and the Wider Co-operative Movement: Challenges and Opportunities Within and Beyond the Global Economic Crisis. In M. Parker, G. Cheney, V. Fournier and C. Land. (Eds.), *The Routledge Companion to Alternative Organization* (pp. 88–112). Abingdon, UK and New York, NY: Routledge.

Weber, M. (1968). *Economy and Society: An Outline of Interpretative Sociology* (Vol. 1). New York, NY: Bedminster Press.

Wedel, J. R. (2012). Rethinking Corruption in an Age of Ambiguity. *Annual Review of Law and Social Science*, 8(1), 453–498.

Welford, R. (1999). *Corporate Environmental Management 1: Systems and Strategies*. London and New York, NY: Routledge.

Wertheimer, A. (1996). *Exploitation*. Princeton, NJ: Princeton University Press.

Wettstein, F. (2015). Normativity, Ethics and the UN Guiding Principles on Business and Human Rights: A Critical Assessment. *Journal of Human Rights*, 14(2), 162–182.

(2012). CSR and the Debate on Business and Human Rights: Bridging the Great Divide. *Business Ethics Quarterly*, 22 (4), 739–770.

Whelan, G. (2021). *Megacorporation: The Infinite Times of Alphabet*. Cambridge: Cambridge University Press.

(2012). The Political Perspective of Corporate Social Responsibility: A Critical Research Agenda. *Business Ethics Quarterly*, 22(4), 709–737.

Whelan, G., de Bakker, F. G. A., den Hond, F. and Muthuri, J. N. (2019). Talking the Walk: The Deflation Response to Legitimacy Challenges. *Management*, 22(4), 636–663.

Whelan, G., Moon, J. and Grant, B. (2013). Corporations and Citizenship Arenas in the Age of Social Media. *Journal of Business Ethics*, 118(4), 777–790.

White, K., Habib, R. and Hardisty, D. J. (2019). How to SHIFT Consumer Behaviors to Be More Sustainable: A Literature Review and Guiding Framework. *Journal of Marketing*, 83 (3), 22–49.

Whiteman, G., Walker, B. and Perego, P. (2013). Planetary Boundaries: Ecological Foundations for Corporate Sustainability. *Journal of Management Studies*, 50(2), 307–336.

Wickert, C. (2016). 'Political' Corporate Social Responsibility in Small- and Medium-Sized Enterprises: A Conceptual Framework. *Business & Society*, 55(6), 792–824.

Wickert, C. and de Bakker, F. (2019). How CSR Managers Can Inspire Other Leaders to Act on Sustainability. *Harvard Business Review Digital Articles*, January. Retrieved on 17 October 2022 from https://hbr.org/2019/01/how-csr-managers-can-inspire-other-leaders-to-act-on-sustainability.

(2018). Pitching for Social Change: Towards a Relational Approach to Selling and Buying Social Issues. *Academy of Management Discoveries*, 4 (1), 50–73.

Wickert, C. and Risi, D. (2019). *Corporate Social Responsibility*. Cambridge: Cambridge University Press.

Wickert, C., Scherer, A. G. and Spence, L. (2016). Walking and Talking Corporate Social Responsibility: Implications of Firm Size and Organizational Cost.

Journal of Management Studies, 53(7), 1169–1196.

Widlitz, S. (2020). Retailers Get Serious about Sustainability into 2020. *Forbes*. Retrieved on 17 October 2022 from www.forbes.com/sites/staceywidlitz/2020/02/03/retailers-get-serious-about-sustainability-into-2020/#3c7bbdff5e09.

Wielenga, C., Sooliman, Q. and Gouvelis, H. (2021). The Role of Business in South Africa's Transition to Democracy. Retrieved on 17 October 2022 from www.ilo.org/africa/countries-covered/south-africa/WCMS_775667/lang-en/index.htm.

Wieneke, A. and Gries, T. (2011). SME Performance in Transition Economies: The Financial Regulation and Firm-level Corruption Nexus. *Journal of Comparative Economics*, 39(2), 221–229.

Wilmsen, B., Webber, M. and Yuefang, D. (2011). Development for Whom? Rural to Urban Resettlement at the Three Gorges Dam, China. *Asian Studies Review*, 35(1), 21–42.

Wood, Z. (2019). Unilever Warns that It Will Sell Off Brands that Hurt the Planet or Society. *The Guardian*, 25 July. Retrieved on 17 October 2022 from www.theguardian.com/business/2019/jul/25/unilever-warns-it-will-sell-off-brands-that-hurt-the-planet-or-society.

World Business Council for Sustainable Development (WBCSD). (2011). *A Vision for Sustainable Consumption*. Geneva, Switzerland: World Business Council for Sustainable Development.

World Commission on Environment and Development. (1987). *Report of the World Commission on Environment and Development (UN General Assembly A/42/427, 4 August 1987)*. New York, NY: United Nations.

World Economic Forum. (2020). These Are the Top 10 Job Skills of Tomorrow – and How Long It Takes to Learn Them. Retrieved on 17 October 2022 from www.weforum.org/agenda/2020/10/top-10-work-skills-of-tomorrow-how-long-it-takes-to-learn-them/.

Wright, C. and Nyberg, D. (2012). Working with Passion: Emotionology, Corporate Environmentalism and Climate Change. *Human Relations*, 65(12), 1561–1587.

Wu, Y., Zhang, K. and Xie, J. (2020). Bad Greenwashing, Good Greenwashing: Corporate Social Responsibility and Information Transparency. *Management Science*, 66(7), 3095–3112.

Wunderman Thompson. (2021). Regeneration Rising: Sustainability Futures. Retrieved on 17 October 2022 from www.wundermanthompson.com/insight/regeneration-rising.

Xie, C., Bagozzi, R. P. and Grønhaug, K. (2019). The Impact of Corporate Social Responsibility on Consumer Brand Advocacy: The Role of Moral Emotions, Attitudes, and Individual Differences. *Journal of Business Research*, 95, 514–530.

Yaffe-Bellany, D. (2019). Shareholder Value Is No Longer Everything, Top CEOs Say. *The New York Times*, 19 August.

Yoon, Y., Gürhan-Canli, Z. and Schwarz, N. (2006). The Effect of Corporate Social Responsibility (CSR) Activities on Companies with Bad Reputations. *Journal of Consumer Psychology*, 16(4), 377–390.

Zadek, S. (2004). The Path to Corporate Responsibility. *Harvard Business Review*, 82(12), 125–132.

Zahra, S. A., Gedajlovic, E., Neubaum, D. O. and Shulman, J. M. (2009). A Typology of Social Entrepreneurs: Motives, Search Processes and Ethical Challenges. *Journal of Business Venturing*, 24(5), 519–532.

Zald, M. N. and McCarthy, J. D. (1980). Social Movement Industries: Cooperation and Conflict amongst Social Movement Organizations. In L. Kriesberg. (Ed.), *Research in Social Movements, Conflicts and Change* (pp. 1–20). Greenwich, CT: JAI Press.

Zaman, I. (2014). Corruption Rampant a Year after Bangladesh Factory Collapse. *Financial Times*. Retrieved on 17 October 2022 from http://blogs.ft.com/beyond-brics/2014/04/24/guest-post-corruption-rampant-a-year-after-bangladesh-factory-fire/.

Zerk, J. A. (2010). Extraterritorial Jurisdiction: Lessons for the Business and Human Rights Sphere from Six Regulatory Areas (Corporate Social Responsibility Initiative Working Paper No. 59). Cambridge, MA: Harvard Kennedy School of Government.

Zhou, M. Y. (2011). Synergy, Coordination Costs and Diversification Choices. *Strategic Management Journal*, 32(6), 624–639.

Zinnbauer, D. (2020). Urbanisation, Informality, and Corruption: Designing

Policies for Integrity in the City. U4 Issue 2020:6, Chr. Michelsen Institute.

Zinnbauer, D., Dobson, R. and Despota, K. (Eds.). (2009). *Global Corruption Report 2009*. Cambridge: Cambridge University Press.

Zuboff, S. (2015). Big Other: Surveillance Capitalism and the Prospects of an Information Civilization. *Journal of Information Technology*, 30(1), 75–89.

Zwolinski, M. (2012). Structural Exploitation. *Social Philosophy and Policy*, 29(1), 154–179.

(2007). Sweatshops, Choice, and Exploitation. *Business Ethics Quarterly*, 17(4), 689–727.

Name Index

Subject Index

Printed in the United States
by Baker & Taylor Publisher Services